The Big Outside

Also by Dave Foreman

Ecodefense
Confessions of an Eco-Warrior

revised edition

The Big Outside

A Descriptive Inventory of the Big Wilderness Areas of the United States

Dave Foreman and
Howie Wolke

Harmony Books/New York

The Big Outside

is dedicated to three men who are the visionary, uncompromising leaders of the wilderness generation after Marshall and Leopold's generation. After campaigning for passage of the 1964 Wilderness Act, they led grass-roots activists in the crusade to establish new Wilderness Areas under the Wilderness Act. They are still active, still leading, still visionary, and still uncompromising. We thank them for teaching us what we know, for inspiring us to carry on, and for saving the Big Outside for which we still fight.

CLIFTON R. MERRITT STEWART BRANDBORG ERNIE DICKERMAN

Published by Harmony Books, a division of Crown Publishers, Inc., 201 East 50th Street, New York, New York 10022.
Member of the Crown Publishing Group.

Originally published in different form by Ned Ludd Books in 1989.
HARMONY and colophon are trademarks of Crown Publishers, Inc.

Manufactured in the United States of America

Maps by Helen Wilson, Kelly Cranston, and Dave Foreman

Chapter Titles by Charles Withuhn and Cathy Seymoure of Signs & Graphic Designs, Chico, California

Library of Congress Cataloging-in-Publication Data
Foreman, Dave, 1946–
The big outside: a descriptive inventory of the big wilderness areas of the United States / Dave Foreman & Howie Wolke. —Rev. Ed.
p. cm.
Includes bibliographical references and index.
1. Wilderness areas—United States. I. Wolke, Howie. II. Title.
QH76.F67 1992
333.78′2′0973—dc20
92-2272 CIP

ISBN 0-517-58737-8

10 9 8 7 6 5 4 3 2 1

First Harmony Edition

Contents

In Appreciation

Obviously a project as complex as *The Big Outside* would not have been possible without the help and support of many individuals. We acknowledge the assistance we received from grass-roots wilderness experts around the United States in Appendix G ("A Note on the Research"). Here, we would like to thank those other folks whose help and support made *The Big Outside* possible.

Our wives, Nancy Morton and Marilyn Olsen, encouraged us in this seemingly unending task and put up with bushels of maps and government documents cluttering our homes. We appreciate their support and patience. Dave's sister and business manager for Books of the Big Outside, Roxanne Pacheco, gave continual assistance, including the last-minute checking of acreage figures in the manuscript. Thank you, Roxanne, we couldn't have done it without you. Kris Sommerville and Nancy Zierenberg made it possible for Dave to finish the first edition. John Davis, editor of *Wild Earth,* copyedited the manuscript before we sent it to Harmony. His many suggestions made it a far more readable and usable document.

Helen Wilson applied her fine cartographic talent to prepare the final maps from base maps produced by the authors. Helen, a professional biological illustrator, also illustrated the maps with critters appropriate to each state or region. Kelly Cranston, Helen's husband, helped in the final preparation of maps.

Charles Withuhn and Cathy Seymoure of Signs & Graphic Designs in Chico, California, created the distinctive chapter headings.

Our agent, Tim Schaffner, did a fine job of representing *The Big Outside.* Michael Pietsch and Peter Guzzardi at Harmony Books had the foresight to believe that *The Big Outside* deserved the larger and wider audience a major publishing house like Harmony could reach. We appreciate the faith Tim, Michael, and Peter had in this project. Our editor at Harmony Books, John Michel, was a pleasure to work with, and cheerfully encouraged us as we struggled with last-minute hassles (of our own making) in finishing the manuscript. The copy editor and designers at Harmony/Crown did a superb job in turning the manuscript into a book. Every author should be so fortunate.

Our thanks to all of these friends for their support, and for their belief in the value of this project.

Foreword

In the beginning, when the planet was new and fresh, all of it was wilderness. It was Earth National Park. God in His wisdom, or Her wisdom, or in the wisdom of the Dolphin-God, or of many many gods in sky, rocks, trees, and water, did not call it an ecosystem, and didn't even know the word. There was no need to. All of that came later. God, as mother of life, simply set evolution in motion and watched the emergence and development of different kinds of creatures and loved them all.

The point is that the Wilderness Act of 1964 did not "create" wilderness, any more than the Yellowstone Act of 1872, or the National Park Organic Act of 1916, "created" parks. Those laws are mere human contrivances, definitions establishing boundaries—political boundaries influenced by the goals of an economic system—where Earth itself knows no such boundaries because it operates on a different and much older system.

Thus, congressional action to include this area or that one in the National Wilderness Preservation System doesn't really add to our storehouse of wild nature preserved. To the contrary, it *subtracts* from it. I learned this particular lesson during the four years I spent in Idaho, a state with more wilderness, classified and unclassified, than any other state outside of Alaska. The Idaho national forests in the late 1980s, the time of this writing, embrace more than 9 million acres of roadless land—that is, *de facto* wilderness, protected as such until Congress or the forest planning process determines otherwise. If the proposal of Senator James McClure and Governor Cecil Andrus for about 1.6 million acres of wilderness were accepted, the remaining 7.4 million acres would then be open to road construction, logging, and other forms of development and disturbance. If conservation groups united behind a proposal of 4 million acres of wilderness and were successful, another 5 million would still be lost.

Humankind plainly has been chip-chip-chipping away at Earth National Park, devouring the goodies. "Places of scenic beauty do not increase," observed Lord Bryce many years ago while serving as the Ambassador of Great Britain to the United States, "but on the contrary are in danger of being reduced in number and diminished in quantity." God, alas, isn't making any more of it.

This wonderful and important book by Dave Foreman and Howie Wolke challenges human conscience and courage to rescue the few remaining fragments of original America while there is still a chance to do so. Every word between its covers counts toward that end. Dave and Howie tell where wilderness is located, and where and how to rescue each and every bit of it. If I were to choose a single sentence to summarize the spirit of the book, it would be this one near the opening: "There is not enough wilderness left to compromise any further."

Let us not compromise any further, not out on the land, nor in our own hearts and minds. Yes, national parks and wilderness in the national forests appear to be extensive, but all the units have been very carefully selected, not to insure protection of the choicest, most inspiring, but to be sure that anything with commercial potential is *not* set aside. Rock and ice are abundant, but very little of great forests, and even less of our wildlife heritage. Let us not settle for any less, but rather set our sights on higher goals. I think of the redwoods to make the point. Of 2 million acres of these ancients that clothed the California north coast only one century ago, a small fraction has been saved, and that only after struggle, sacrifice, and bitter tears. The national park is a meager representation: 106,000 acres, including the 1978 expansion area of 48,000 acres, mostly cutover lands—with 200 miles of logging roads, 3,000 miles of skid trails, and thousands upon thousands of burnt stumps of what once were magnificent redwood trees.

In ten centuries, another forest of giants may grace the north coast of California. I pray that civilization will endure that long. But none of us will be around the see the rebirth and bloom. For our own time, let us vow that no more standing redwoods be cut, not on public or private land. No more big trees anywhere. Leave them be. They are more meaningful as trees than as paper, pulp, or plywood. Let us learn to live within our means, rediscovering the essentials of life, so that trees and other life-forms may live, too.

Dave Foreman and Howie Wolke are blessed with the clear vision. I respect and admire Dave and Howie as models of individual empowerment. Accepting self-responsibility, as they have done, brings power and clarity of purpose. In the most modest but determined of ways, they call for missionaries like themselves to go forth among the people with glad tidings: We can have a better world, and each of us can make the difference.

I see wilderness, the Big Outside, as sanctuary of the spirit, the heart of a moral world governed by peace and love. Thank you, Dave and Howie, for the valuable descriptive inventory that points the way.

MICHAEL FROME
BELLINGHAM, WA
NOVEMBER 1988

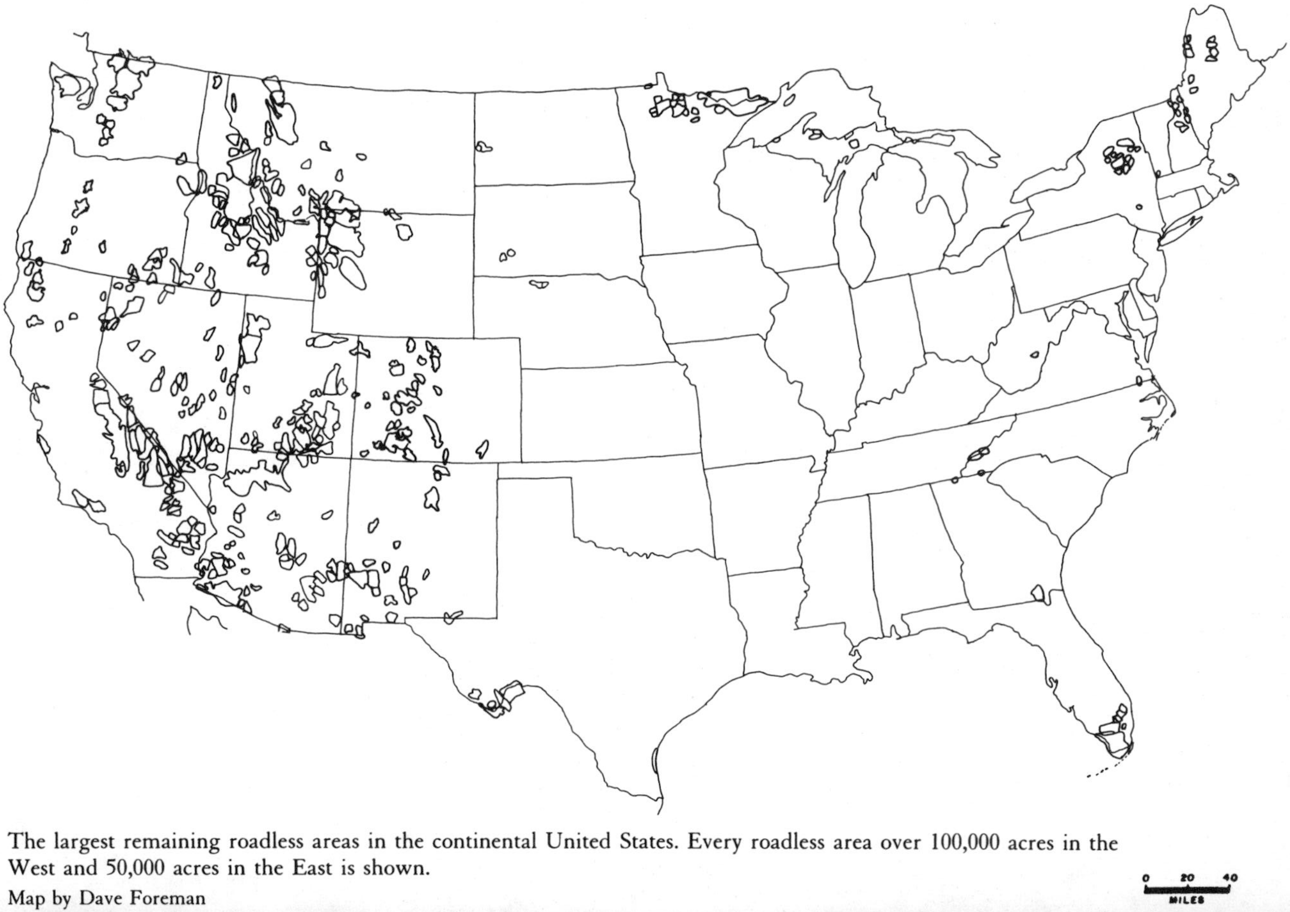

The largest remaining roadless areas in the continental United States. Every roadless area over 100,000 acres in the West and 50,000 acres in the East is shown.

Map by Dave Foreman

The Big Outside

The universe of the wilderness is disappearing

like a snowbank on a south-facing

slope on a warm June day.

—Robert Marshall

This book is a descriptive inventory of the remaining large roadless areas in the United States outside of Alaska and Hawaii: Every roadless area of 100,000 acres or larger in the Western states and 50,000 acres or larger in the Eastern states is listed and described, regardless of land ownership or administrative agency. It is as objective an inventory of the "Big Outside" as we, the authors, are capable of compiling.

It is also an argument for the idea of "Big Wilderness," for the notion that size is an important criterion for nature preserves. In other words, while protecting all remaining wildlands is important, protecting all remaining *large* tracts of wild country is absolutely crucial. We hope that by identifying the big areas that remain in an essentially roadless and undeveloped condition, we will be able to focus the attention of preservationists on them. The areas listed in this book are the most important wild areas in the United

States.[1] Conservation groups, individual activists, and conservation biologists should place a priority on these areas and defend them to the best of their abilities. In that sense, this book is a call to arms and a guidebook for action. Our research shows that there is a surprising number of large roadless areas left in many parts of the country, but a closer look reveals that these areas compose only a tiny fraction of the total acreage of the United States. (See page xii.) They represent the remaining natural heritage of temperate North America and are the paramount reservoirs of native diversity and ecological integrity in the United States.

This book is also a sad, lingering look at the vanishing American Wilderness. Many of these areas are under imminent threat of destruction from roading, logging, mining, grazing, and other abuses. In "The Destruction of Wilderness," we discuss the threats to wilderness in general, and in the remainder of the book, we tally the specific threats to each of the big roadless areas.

In the 1920s, Will Dilg, founder of the Izaak Walton League, wrote:

> *I am weary of civilization's madness and I yearn for the harmonious gladness of the woods and of the streams. I am tired of your piles of buildings and I ache from your iron streets. I feel jailed in your greatest cities and I long for the unharnessed freedom of the big outside.*

The Big Outside is most especially an expression of our agreement with Dilg and of our absolute, fervid love for wilderness. We hope it will serve as a box of ammunition in the age-old struggle to defend the wild against those who "know the price of everything and the value of nothing."

It is important, however, to understand that *this book is not a proposal.* The areas and acreages listed do not constitute Wilderness proposals from us or from any conservation group. We discuss proposals for preservation, yes, but the roadless areas inventoried herein make up just that—an inventory. This is a methodically researched account of what, by our definition, is roadless. In nearly every case, we would argue for the preservation of larger areas than those listed here. Roads should be closed, vehicles banned, clearcuts rehabilitated, rivers freed of dams, cattle and sheep removed, extirpated wildlife reintroduced, and *ecological wilderness* restored to larger areas. This inven-

[1] The United States outside of Alaska and Hawaii. For reasons discussed later, Alaska and Hawaii are not included in *The Big Outside.* When we refer to the United States in this book, we generally mean only the lower forty-eight states.

tory of existing large roadless areas forms the basis for visionary wilderness rehabilitation proposals that will be the subject of a future book. But before we can preserve what remains and restore what has been lost, we need a basic inventory of the large areas that retain a fundamental wildness.

During the mid-1930s, Robert Marshall, legendary hiker, Alaska explorer, and founder of The Wilderness Society, conducted a personal inventory of the largest remaining roadless areas in the United States. He found forty-eight forested areas of over 300,000 acres and twenty-nine desert areas larger than 500,000 acres. (He felt the larger size was necessary in nonforested areas to give one a similar sense of solitude.) His purpose was to draw attention to the vanishing universe of the wilderness and to encourage efforts toward the preservation of the largest and most important remnants of the American heritage.

Marshall hoped *The New York Times* would publish an article about his inventory. It did not, nor did any major periodical. Marshall eventually presented his study, with an accompanying map by Althea Dobbins, in the November 1936 issue of *The Living Wilderness,* the magazine of The Wilderness Society. There it was printed, and there it was forgotten. The *Earth First! Journal* reprinted it in September 1982, and it is included as Appendix C of this book.

Marshall's inventory was unprecedented, and it has not been updated until now—half a century later. To be sure, Marshall had done a preliminary inventory of National Forest roadless areas over 1 million acres in size in 1927. I found a handwritten card with this inventory in the Robert Marshall Papers at the University of California's Bancroft Library (Berkeley) in 1982. Even George Marshall, Bob's surviving brother, was unaware of the 1927 inventory when I wrote him about it. The information from it is presented in Appendix D.

Marshall, as head of Recreation for the U.S. Forest Service in the late 1930s, was responsible for setting up a system for protecting the "Primitive Areas" administratively established by the Forest Service. Under Marshall's regulations, these areas would, after study, be designated "Wilderness Areas" if covering 100,000 acres or more and as "Wild Areas" if under 100,000 acres. Marshall died suddenly in 1939, and without him to watchdog the process, the Forest Service began to pare back protection.

By the 1950s, conservation groups, led by Howard Zahniser of The Wilderness Society and David Brower of the Sierra Club, became alarmed at the Forest Service's continuing dismemberment of Marshall's system and began calling for congressional protection of Wilderness Areas. Hubert Humphrey and John Saylor introduced the first Wilderness bills into the Senate and House, respectively, in 1956. The national campaign for the Wilderness Act required eight years to overcome entrenched opposition from loggers, miners, ranchers (their champion was Representative Wayne Aspinall of Colorado, Chairman of the House Interior Committee), and federal agencies (the Forest Service and Park Service stridently opposed the bill). President Lyndon Johnson signed the Wilderness Act on September 3, 1964.

By the early 1960s, conservation groups lobbying for passage of the Wilderness Act had compiled rough figures of what they thought might qualify for Wilderness designation on the federal lands. Roadlessness was one of the characteristics they used. But their list was by no means comprehensive.

In 1961, the University of California Wildland Research Center conducted an independent study for the Outdoor Recreation Resources Review Commission. This survey found sixty-four roadless areas of 100,000 acres or larger in the National Forests and National Parks. Michael Frome points out in *Battle for the Wilderness* that the largest area found was about 2 million acres, whereas a Forest Service study in 1926 had found the largest roadless area to be 7 million acres. Moreover, the 1961 study found only nineteen areas over 230,400 acres, totaling 17 million acres, where there had been seventy-four areas of that size or larger, totaling 55 million acres, in 1926.

The Wilderness Act instructed the National Park Service and the United States Fish and Wildlife Service[2] to review the lands they managed for

[2] Land ownership and management in the United States is complicated, unplanned, and often irrational. For example, there may be private and state school trust land inholdings in National Parks. Some Bureau of Land Management or Forest Service lands are "checkerboarded" with intermixed sections (a section is one square mile—640 acres) of state school trust, railroad, or other private lands. Although this is not the place for a detailed explanation of land managing agencies in the United States, some understanding is necessary to follow any intelligent discussion of Wilderness Areas.

Land owned by the federal government accounts for approximately one third of all land in the country and falls under one of five government agencies, each part of a cabinet-level department (the following abbreviations are used throughout the book):

(1) **U.S. Forest Service (USFS or FS)—Department of Agriculture:** National Forests (NFs), National Grasslands, and some National Recreation Areas (NRAs). These are "multiple-use" lands generally open to commercial timber harvesting, livestock grazing, mining, energy extraction, off-road vehicles (ORVs), fuelwood collecting, hunting, and other extractive activities.

(2) **National Park Service (NPS)—Department of the Interior:** National Parks (NPs), National Monuments (NMs), National Seashores and Lakeshores, National Recreation Areas (NRAs), and National Preserves. NPS-managed lands are generally

possible Wilderness recommendation (they were to consider every roadless area of over 5,000 acres). The agencies did so, often in a rather desultory fashion, and looking only at the specific lands they managed. No effort was made to look at all federal lands in a coordinated way. (Under the Act, only Congress can designate or declassify an area as Wilderness; the agencies only make recommendations.)

The Wilderness and Wild Areas on the National Forests were immediately placed under protection of the Wilderness Act in 1964 (fifty-four areas, totaling 9.1 million acres out of the 191-million-acre National Forest system). The Forest Service was instructed to present Wilderness recommendations to Congress by 1974 for the thirty-four remaining Primitive Areas, totaling 5.5 million acres (those areas not yet designated as Wilderness or Wild by the Forest Service). Conservationists in several Western states encouraged the Forest Service to appraise additional roadless areas for Wilderness recommendation, but the agency refused. When Congress in 1968 considered a bill that would add the Lincoln-Scapegoat area (not a Primitive Area) in Montana to the Wilderness System over FS objection, conservation groups throughout the West began to end-run the agency and make proposals directly to Congress.

The Forest Service undertook a "Roadless Area Review and Evaluation" (RARE) in 1971–72 to head off the citizen initiatives by supposedly considering all roadless areas on the National Forests for Wilderness Area potential. Although RARE was meant to be an objective and comprehensive inventory of what was still roadless on the National Forests (in areas of 5,000 acres or larger), it was fraught with sloppiness, inaccuracy, inconsistency, and

---

not open to hunting, ORVs, livestock grazing, logging, mining, or energy extraction, but there are notable exceptions.

(3) **U.S. Fish and Wildlife Service (FWS)—Department of the Interior:** National Wildlife Refuges (NWRs). Although ostensibly dedicated to wildlife production (unfortunately, not to habitat protection), some NWRs are open to logging, mining, energy extraction, grazing, ORVs, and hunting.

(4) **Bureau of Land Management (BLM)—Department of the Interior:** National Conservation Areas and other public lands. These are multiple-use lands, like the National Forests, but with even less supervision from the agency.

(5) **Air Force, Army, Navy, and Marine Corps—Department of Defense:** reservations, ranges, test sites, bases, and forts.

Other large land managers include various other federal agencies, the states (including state parks, state wildlife refuges, conservation lands, school trust lands), Indian Tribes (Indian Reservations—IRs), The Nature Conservancy, and timber companies.

insouciance. Conservationists sued the Forest Service (*Sierra Club* v. *Butz*), but after an out-of-court settlement proved inadequate, conservation groups once again went to Congress (with the Endangered American Wilderness Act in 1976) to protest the botched job and ask Congress to directly designate a select group of areas as Wilderness without FS study. The Forest Service responded with RARE II—a far more detailed review, but nearly as disappointing as its predecessor.

Following the dismal RARE II recommendations in 1979 (only 15 million acres out of a total of 80 million roadless acres on the National Forests were proposed for Wilderness designation[3]), conservation groups again approached Congress. But by this time, the timber industry and other Wilderness opponents were bending Congress with more muscle than that flexed by conservationists. The informal solution was for each state's congressional delegation to develop a National Forest Wilderness bill for that particular state. This approach was an unfortunate strategic error by conservationists, because it made Wilderness designation more of a local issue than a national decision. Powerful pressure groups with economic interests in the National Forests—mining, grazing, and logging industries—and user groups—like ORV owners—are more influential on the state level, particularly in states with large National Forest acreages. Two bills passed in 1980; bills for the bulk of states in 1984; and bills for Montana, Michigan, and Oklahoma in 1988. President Reagan pocket-vetoed the Montana bill in what fittingly served as the conservation finale to his administration. A Nevada RARE II bill passed in 1989. Idaho, North Dakota, Puerto Rico, and, because of Reagan's veto, Montana still did not have RARE II Wilderness bills passed through Congress at the close of 1990.

The Wilderness Society and the Sierra Club realized in 1979 that the RARE II Final Environmental Impact Statement (EIS) was inadequate and thereby open to a court challenge, but they feared the political repercussions of such a suit. Huey Johnson, the scrappy Secretary of Resources for the State of California, did not fear political repercussions and sued the Forest Service to prevent development in a select list of roadless areas in California (*Cali-*

[3] The Forest Service inventoried and considered 62 million acres of roadless areas in RARE II. An additional 18 million acres or so that were largely roadless and undeveloped were not included in RARE II because (1) the FS had completed "unit plans" covering these areas and had determined against Wilderness recommendation; or (2) the RARE II inventory was shabby in certain National Forests. Therefore, there were a total of 80 million acres of NF land meeting the Forest Service's criteria as roadless in 1978.

fornia v. *Block*). The Federal District Court agreed with Johnson and prohibited the Forest Service from destroying the wilderness values of the cited roadless areas without an adequate environmental impact statement. Earth First! and the Oregon Natural Resources Council successfully sued the Forest Service on identical grounds in 1983, seeking to halt the Bald Mountain timber access road in Oregon's North Kalmiopsis roadless area. This suit effectively extended the *California* v. *Block* decision to all RARE II areas.

The timber industry also realized in 1979 that RARE II was vulnerable in court. As a result of industry pressure on members of Congress, a central feature of the proposed RARE II bills became "release language." Most FS roadless areas not designated as Wilderness in a state bill (the overwhelming majority of the roadless acreage) are "released" by Congress, which means that they are available for logging, roading, and other multiple-use ("multiple-abuse," according to many conservationists), and that such activity is not subject to judicial review on the grounds of inadequate consideration of Wilderness by the agency (in other words, *California* v. *Block* is nullified, and conservation groups cannot further sue to stop development in such roadless areas on the basis of the inadequacy of the FS's RARE II Final Environmental Impact Statement). Furthermore, this release language directs the Forest Service not to consider released roadless areas for possible Wilderness recommendation until the next round of Forest Plans in the late 1990s. This is the standard "soft" release language that was developed by the Sierra Club as a compromise. The timber industry proposed more draconian language—"hard" release—that would *mandate* development of released roadless areas and prohibit the Forest Service from *ever* considering such areas for Wilderness recommendation. In essence, then, it would be fair to label the RARE II bills passed so far as "Wilderness release bills" rather than "Wilderness bills," because these bills have opened more de facto wilderness acreage to development than they have protected as Wilderness. The RARE II process constitutes a net loss of wild country, not a means to protect it.

The 1964 Wilderness Act left the BLM, the largest land manager in the United States, out of the Wilderness System. In 1976, this was rectified when Congress passed the "Organic Act" (Federal Lands Policy and Management Act—FLPMA) for BLM. In it, BLM was mandated to perform a roadless area review, select Wilderness Study Areas (WSAs), study them, and make Wilderness recommendations to Congress by 1991. That review, completed on schedule, has been at best a mixed bag in terms of accuracy and fairness—much like the RAREs of its sibling agency. Of the 175 million acres managed by BLM in the lower forty-eight states, only 25 million were studied for possible Wilderness recommendation. In late 1991, BLM recommended 328 units, totaling 9,720,490 acres, for Wilderness designation by Congress.[4]

With few exceptions, there has been no effort to inventory roadless areas on Indian Reservations, military reservations, other federal lands, state lands, or private lands. There have, though, been several efforts to safeguard wilderness values on such lands. Bob Marshall, as Director of Forestry for the Bureau of Indian Affairs, was instrumental in establishing a roadless area system on reservations in 1937, but most of those areas had been declassified by the 1960s. Some reservations do, however, have Tribal Wilderness Areas. California, New York, and Michigan have Wilderness Systems for their state parks. Pennsylvania has a Wild Areas System for its state forests.

Despite all this, Bob Marshall's 1936 inventory stands alone as an effort to document the large wild areas of our country, irrespective of ownership or management.

Until now.

Since 1982, Howie Wolke and I have been compiling an inventory of the big roadless areas left in the United States. The first edition of this book, in 1989, was the initial comprehensive account of that ongoing study. This revised edition updates the first edition with new information, corrections, and changes since 1989.

It is instructive to compare Marshall's half-century-old inventory with ours to document what has been lost. In doing so, it is important to recognize that Marshall had less-accurate information to use in assembling his inventory than we have had for ours. As he pointed out in *The Living Wilderness,*

[4] This is in addition to BLM Wilderness already designated by Congress: about 470,000 acres in Arizona, Utah, California, Idaho, Montana, New Mexico, Oregon, and Washington before 1990, and 1,098,000 acres in the 1990 Arizona Desert Wilderness Act. So, there are 1,668,000 acres of designated BLM Wilderness as of the fall of 1991. Those, added to the 9,720,000 acres further recommended for Wilderness by BLM, bring the total to 11,388,000 acres.

[5] For example, let's consider an imaginary square roadless area 20 miles on the side. It is 256,000 acres. By excluding half a mile into the roadless area because of the encircling roads, Marshall would have deleted 25,600 acres and arrived at an acreage of 230,400.

[6] Analyzing Marshall's inventory is difficult because none of his maps or other documentation still exist, to the best of our knowledge. The Robert Marshall Papers in the University of California's Bancroft Library in Berkeley do not have this material, and his brothers, George and James Marshall, when asked, did not know where it might be. All that is available is reprinted in Appendix C.

his "is only a preliminary study," and "there will be a number of mistakes. This is especially true of the desert areas." Moreover, Marshall was conservative in determining what was roadless, and in calculating his acreages, he excluded a half-mile-wide buffer zone along boundary roads and on either side of cherrystem (intruding) roads. We calculate our acreages right down to the boundary roads.[5]

Marshall also overlooked a number of areas: Cabeza Prieta in Arizona, Saline Range in California, Black Rock Desert in Nevada, Black Range in New Mexico, and Everglades in Florida. He artificially divided two very large areas: Central Idaho (the Selway-Bitterroot from the Idaho Primitive Area—now the River of No Return Wilderness—along the Salmon River) and California's High Sierra (southern Yosemite National Park from the main body of the range to the south). And he calculated a number of acreages as smaller than what they certainly must have been in 1936: Gila (New Mexico), High Uintas (Utah), Salmon–Trinity Alps (California), Gros Ventre (Wyoming), and Eagle Cap (Oregon).[6]

In a very few cases, roadless areas may actually be larger today than they were in 1936 because of homesteaders' or others' giving up their efforts to make a buck on a hardscrabble piece of country—many rural areas today are less populated than they were in the early part of the century. Additionally, wildlife protection laws and scientific game management have increased populations of some species after wildlife populations bottomed out at the turn of the century because of market hunting and other unrestrained forms of exploitation. While, overall, native diversity and wildness have suffered immeasurably in these fifty years, lovers of the wild can be encouraged by the recovery of wilderness in specific locations.

Nonetheless, in looking at Marshall's 1936 study, one is struck by what we have lost. Fifty years ago, the largest roadless area in the United States was the Escalante–Glen Canyon region along the Colorado River in southern Utah—nearly 9 million acres (14,000 square miles) in one piece! The Owyhee Canyonlands where Idaho, Oregon, and Nevada come together had over 4 million acres unbroken by a road; the Grand Canyon, 4 million; Desolation Canyon on the Green River in Utah, 2.5 million; the North Cascades, as yet undivided by the "North Cascades Scenic Highway," nearly 3 million. Even more illustrative of what we have lost in two generations is Marshall's 1927 inventory—Central Idaho had over 7.5 million acres in one roadless area; the North Cascades, nearly 3.5 million; Mt. Rainier, 1.3 million; the Gila, 1.3 million; the mountains above Santa Barbara, California, 1 million. Keep these figures in mind as you read our inventory, which is correct to 1991.[7]

In conducting our inventory, we have looked simply at the land. The Forest Service in RARE and RARE II stopped at National Forest boundaries, always ignoring the continuation of biological roadless areas after they left FS jurisdiction. In some cases, the Forest Service even artificially subdivided intact roadless areas when they overlapped two or more National Forests. The Park Service, in conducting its mandated Wilderness review, looked only at roadless areas within the National Parks, and not at contiguous roadless areas outside the Park boundary. No one has looked at military lands, Indian Reservations, state lands, or private lands in a comprehensive fashion. In other words, no one has looked at the land, at the biological wilderness, in a way unfettered by artificial boundaries. Other roadless inventories have looked at administrative designations, not at the true roadless area.

A telling example is the High Sierra roadless area in California. At 2.8 million acres, it is the second-largest roadless area in the forty-eight contiguous states. But no one heretofore knew it was the second-largest roadless area because no one had ever calculated its size. Why? Because it embraces three National Parks; seven National Forest Wilderness Areas; undesignated roadless areas in three National Forests; a dozen Bureau of Land Management roadless areas; and scattered tracts of Forest Service, BLM, NPS, and private land. Similarly, many large roadless areas in the West include state, private, military, or Indian land, as well as land administered by one or more federal agencies.

The inventory in this book outlines intact areas that are essentially roadless and undeveloped, irrespective of land ownership or administrative agency. To identify the large primitive areas remaining in the United States, we have used roadlessness as our major criterion. Although the presence or absence of roads is not the only factor determining whether an area is wilderness or possesses a significant degree of ecological integrity and native diversity, it is a key one.

Napoleon's army may have marched on its stomach, but the army of

[7] In certain cases, we will cross-reference our roadless areas with Marshall's 1927 and 1936 inventories in italics. For example, *RM27: 1,327,360* under New Mexico's Gila indicates Marshall found that roadless acreage there in his 1927 inventory. *RM36* refers to his 1936 inventory. An asterisk on the acreage means that other roadless areas inventoried in this book were part of Marshall's single roadless area at that time.

wilderness destruction travels by road and motorized vehicle. Roads are used for logging; dam building; oil and gas exploration; grazing management; power-line construction and maintenance; mineral exploration and extraction; and ski area, recreational, and subdivision development. Trappers, poachers, slob hunters, prospectors, seismographic crews, archaeological site vandals, and other vanguards of the industrial spoliation of the wild use roads. Roads provide freebooters with access to key areas of wildlife habitat and to the core of wild areas. Roads cause erosion, damage roots of nearby trees, disrupt wildlife migration, and create an "edge effect" that allows common weedy species of plants and animals to invade pristine areas that otherwise provide refuge to sensitive and rare native species. Many creatures are killed by vehicles on roads.

Without roads, without mechanized access, native species are more secure from harassment and habitat destruction, and fewer people with fewer tools are able to abuse the land.[8]

Yet, some roads rest relatively lightly on the terrain. If they were closed to motorized vehicles, they would be irrelevant. When one looks at a large wild area from the air, a dirt road cutting across it can be very small indeed. These roads impact the wild insofar as they provide access for the commercial and recreational destruction of natural values. The presence of roads should not disqualify an area from Wilderness designation. Closing a road and prohibiting motorized vehicles can remove or radically lessen the road's impact in most cases.

Nevertheless, we have chosen "roadlessness" as the key characteristic for easily identifying the most pristine large areas in the United States. We have done so because the presence of roads nearly always indicates the presence of other impacts on the natural integrity of an area. Also, roadlessness has traditionally been, since Aldo Leopold's 1921 Gila Wilderness proposal, the primary factor for Wilderness consideration.[9]

The first step in identifying a roadless area is to define a "road." Roads, of

[8] The best summary of the impact of roads on native ecosystems and wildlife is the *Impact of Roads* tabloid, available free from Wild Earth, POB 492, Canton, NY 13617.

[9] However, just because an area is roadless does not mean that it is entirely "wild" in an ecological sense. For example, many roadless areas included in this inventory have been severely overgrazed for many decades, resulting in drastic declines in native diversity. In addition, barbed wire fences, small impoundments, acid rain, poaching, and other problems abound in many of our remaining wild areas. In essence, the American wilderness of the 1990s, grand though it is, is wilderness with an asterisk. The acreage in this inventory overstates the true wilderness of modern America.

course, cover a broad spectrum, from the onetime passage of four tires to a four-lane, divided interstate highway. In 1972, the Southwest Region of the Forest Service (New Mexico and Arizona) defined "road" for the first RARE process as a parallel set of tire tracks that remained visible into the next season. In other words, if an irresponsible hunter drove a Jeep across a wet meadow during the fall Elk season and the tracks were visible the next summer, that was a "road" and the area was disqualified from Wilderness consideration. It is instructive to note that in 1977, using a more realistic definition of "road" in RARE II, the Forest Service found three times the roadless acreage on Southwestern National Forests.

While acknowledging that the determination of what is and is not a "road" is a somewhat arbitrary process, for the purposes of this inventory, we have essentially followed the general criteria used by the Forest Service in RARE II and by BLM in its Wilderness review. (It would be more accurate to say the criteria the Forest Service and BLM were *supposed to objectively use.*) This definition of a "road" is succinctly spelled out in the 1976 BLM "Organic Act" House Report:

> *The word "roadless" refers to the absence of roads which have been improved and maintained by mechanical means to insure relatively regular and continuous use. A way maintained solely by the passage of vehicles does not constitute a road.*

In many cases, a road penetrates, but does not cross, an otherwise roadless area. Such roads are referred to as "cherrystem" roads in the wilderness business. We draw the boundaries of the roadless areas in this book along the edges of both cherrystem and boundary roads. Where it is feasible to do so, such cherrystems are indicated on the location maps or mentioned in the text.

We have generally used major pipelines and power lines to disqualify lands from this inventory. (In the few exceptions, their presence is noted.) Reservoirs, recent clearcuts, large vegetative manipulation projects (chainings and seedings), and dense networks of Jeep trails have similarly served to eliminate areas from this inventory. Solitary Jeep trails, "ways" and other unconstructed routes, or constructed roads that have not been maintained or that have been closed to vehicle use have not been considered as "roads" in this inventory.

Our determination in each case is unavoidably arbitrary, since it is based on personal judgment and, in some cases, scanty information and a lack of direct observation (we have obviously not been able to inspect every one of these areas, although we can't think of anything we'd rather do with the rest of our lives). In some cases, specific roadless areas discussed in this book could be considerably expanded if marginal dirt roads were not considered to be real roads; in other cases, what we have called a single roadless area is crossed by a vehicle route that is on the borderline of being a "road." Such cases are noted in the descriptions for each area. (Future editions of this book will have more accurate information, including our further personal inspection, on which to base judgments for such areas.) As Marshall did, we must leave the reader with the caveat that this inventory is not exact, that there are undoubtedly mistakes in it. The maps included are not precise; they merely indicate the general location of individual roadless areas and the relationship of groups of roadless areas. Our acreage figures are rounded off to indicate this lack of absolute certainty in our figures; in some cases, acreage figures are estimates.

Another question to be asked is, "Why is size important for wilderness?" Howie Wolke discusses this in the next chapter. Size is obviously not the only standard to determine the importance of a wilderness. Some areas—like the Huachuca Mountains in Arizona, Salmo-Priest in Washington and Idaho, Big Thicket in Texas, Joyce Kilmer–Slickrock in North Carolina, and Middle Santiam in Oregon—are internationally significant for the native biological diversity they contain, but all are too small to be included in this inventory.

Our minimum acreage is not entirely arbitrary. In 1937, Bob Marshall used 100,000 acres as the dividing line between Wilderness Areas and Wild Areas. We simply had to select some least common denominator on which to base our inventory. This is an inventory of *large roadless areas.* We think that identifying roadless areas of 100,000 or more acres in the West and 50,000 acres or more in the East is the best general starting point from which to identify areas in the lower forty-eight states that retain significant degrees of ecological integrity and wildness, and that hold the possibility of serving as the cores for wilderness restoration.[10]

[10] Also important are clusters of large roadless areas. There are sundry locations in the United States where minor dirt roads or other developments separate two or more large roadless areas. Because groups of wild areas function as a single habitat for populations of species, and offer greater diversity, such clusters are generally more important than a single large roadless area (unless, of course, it is very large—a solitary 500,000-acre roadless area is obviously more important than a complex of five 100,000-acre roadless areas, but the complex of five is more

Because so few areas in the East met our 100,000-acre floor, we decided to also include areas between 50,000 and 100,000 acres east of the Rocky Mountains. Furthermore, areas in the more humid East generally have greater ecological resiliency than do areas in the West.

As I previously stated, only the forty-eight coterminous states are included in this inventory. Alaska is excluded because roadless areas there are on a different scale, and because motorboats, snowmobiles, airplanes, and all-terrain vehicles (ATVs) provide access to permanently inhabited communities far from a constructed road. Hawaii is excluded because we were unable to compile information on roadless areas there. We hope to include Hawaii in future editions of this book and would welcome information on roadless areas of 50,000 acres or larger in the island state. Thus, when we refer to the United States in this book, we usually mean only the forty-eight coterminous states.

Since this is an inventory of large, ecologically important areas, we considered listing areas by Ecoregion (Northern Rocky Mountains, Great Basin, for example) instead of by state. We finally decided to organize the inventory by state because the protection or destruction of these areas is fundamentally through the political process, which is based on states. Moreover, we decided that most readers would be better able to grasp the location of inventoried roadless areas if they were oriented by state. In a future edition of this book, though, we hope to do an analysis of the Big Outside by Ecoregion or even by the 106 Kuchler Potential Natural Vegetation types.[11]

Within each state, we have further divided the inventory by region to aid the reader in locating individual areas and in comprehending their relationship to one another. This regional breakdown within states is arbitrary and somewhat inconsistent—for some states, we have used bioregional divisions;

---

important than five widely separated 100,000-acre areas in similar habitat). We have indicated the relationship between roadless areas in our discussion. The maps also graphically portray such roadless area complexes. We especially call the attention of conservationists to these clusters, since they are generally more valuable as cores for wilderness restoration than are isolated single roadless areas.

[11] Let it be pointed out here, however, that of the twenty-four Ecoregions defined by R. G. Bailey, seven do not have any large roadless areas remaining and six others are very weakly represented in our inventory. Furthermore, twenty-one states out of forty-eight (Kansas, Oklahoma, Louisiana, Arkansas, Missouri, Iowa, Wisconsin, Illinois, Indiana, Ohio, Kentucky, Mississippi, Alabama, South Carolina, Maryland, Delaware, New Jersey, Pennsylvania, Connecticut, Rhode Island, and Massachusetts) do not have any roadless areas of 50,000 acres or larger left within their boundaries. Three—Vermont, Virginia, and West Virginia—are questionably represented.

for others, we have simply used geographic divisions (e.g., northwest, southwest).

The format for the inventory portion of this book is as follows:

- An introductory discussion for each state or region, including the history of the state's Big Outside, an ecological description, specific and general threats, recent preservation efforts, and the conservation groups involved there
- The name and acreage for each roadless area with a breakdown of the roadless acreage by ownership or administrative agency
- A description of the terrain, flora, and fauna of the area, with historical tidbits thrown in
- A status report on the area—what is protected, what is proposed for preservation, what threatens it

A listing of all 385 roadless areas in order of acreage is in Appendix A. A listing in order of acreage within each state is in Appendix B.

In the inventory, we mention conservation groups involved in protecting these areas. Addresses for these groups and others are given in Appendix E. In certain cases, we may criticize some organizations in this book. That is because conservation groups have sometimes been timid and compromising. It is the task of conservationists to advocate protection of wilderness and native diversity. Period. It is not our job to devise pragmatic, compromised solutions. *There is not enough wilderness left to compromise any further.* We must fight for every acre. We should not give up one inch. Where we are critical of conservation groups in this book, it is to encourage them to see the integrity of these larger areas. It is an extraordinary responsibility to acquiesce in the destruction of a wilderness. It is not a decision to be made lightly. Nonetheless, we applaud the efforts of all conservation groups and active individuals—whatever approach they take, from lobbying to monkeywrenching—to protect these areas. We encourage the readers of this book to contact those groups covering the areas in which they are interested and offer their support.

Finally, a word about style. Throughout this book we have capitalized the proper names of species. Therefore, "Gray Wolf" and "Big Sagebrush," being distinct species, are capitalized; "wolf" and "sagebrush," being generic terms, are not. We capitalize "Wilderness" when it refers to formal, congressionally designated Wilderness; we leave "wilderness" uncapitalized when it refers to de facto or undesignated wilderness. We capitalize "National Park," "National Forest," and "National Wildlife Refuge" whether they refer to a specific unit (e.g., Grand Canyon National Park) or simply to a generalized area or concept. Capitalization denotes a form of respect, and formal species' names and preservation systems deserve, we believe, that respect. It goes without saying that we therefore capitalize "Earth."

Note: Howie Wolke wrote the next chapter and generally compiled and wrote the inventory for Idaho, Montana, and Wyoming. Dave Foreman generally wrote and compiled the rest of the book. Each of us reviewed and edited the other's work and contributed supplemental information. When "we" is used, it refers to both authors; when "I" is used, it refers to the individual author responsible for that section.

Big Wilderness Is Ecological Wilderness

Merely a few centuries ago, the land we now call the United States of America was a wilderness paradise, vibrant and diverse, cyclical yet stable, pure and unpolluted. Within its mountains, deserts, prairies, tundras, and forests lived a diversity and abundance of life that staggers the imagination. It was home to an estimated 60 million Bison; billions of Passenger Pigeons; 100,000 or so Grizzlies ranging from the Pacific Coast nearly to the Mississippi; and Gray Wolves, Mountain Lions, Elk, Bighorn, Prairie Chicken, Eskimo Curlew, anadromous salmon, and other wild animals in nearly unbelievable profusion.

So great was the pre-Columbian American wilderness that the fragmented remnants that we today call "wild" pale in comparison. The most diverse temperate forest on Earth blanketed the eastern third of the country, gradually becoming interspersed with the lush Tallgrass Prairies of the Mississippi Valley. To the west, the Mid- and Shortgrass Prairies supported a post-Pleistocene megafauna second only to that of Africa's Serengeti. And the rugged front of the high Rockies rising above the grassland sea was the fortress of a rich wilderness of soaring peaks; towering conifers; glacial lakes; deep canyons; broad river valleys; and thriving populations of Elk, Bison, Bighorn, Mountain Goat, Mule Deer, White-tailed Deer, Black Bear, Grizzly Bear, Mountain Lion, Gray Wolf, Lynx, Bobcat, Wolverine, Beaver, River Otter, Fisher, Bald Eagle, Golden Eagle, Peregrine Falcon, Pileated Woodpecker, Whooping Crane, Trumpeter Swan, and many more species.

The Great Basin was an unblemished world of bunchgrass, sagebrush, and Pronghorn, broken by conifer-clad island mountain ranges. The mighty Colorado River formed a 2,000-mile-long oasis, gouging precipitous canyons through some of the world's most spectacular and colorful sedimentary rocks. And in the Northwest, an unbroken forest of coniferous giants—unlike any other on Earth—guarded the rugged peaks of the Coast Range, the Olympics, and the Cascades.

In pre-Columbian America, those humans whom we now call Indians hunted Bison, Elk, deer, and bear; foraged for roots and berries; set fire to forests and prairies to improve the hunting; and, in some places, grew crops. But the wilderness was huge and diverse, and all life—including human—was subservient to the overwhelming forces of nature.

Today, the American wilderness is under attack and vanishing rapidly. Most of America's wild places are on public lands managed by various federal and state agencies. But rather than protecting these sacred bastions of natural diversity, public agencies most often promote their destruction. For example, with unguarded arrogance, the U.S. Forest Service brags that it has been eliminating 1–2 million acres of wild, unroaded country each year, and that the devastation will continue well into the next century. That agency plans to construct a minimum of 100,000 miles of new roads in inventoried roadless areas alone! There are already about 375,000 miles of constructed roads in our National Forests, not including state, county, and federal rights of way. Road construction in the National Forests proceeds at the rate of about 10,000 miles per year.

Similarly, the Bureau of Land Management is allowing exploiters to destroy wilderness at nearly the same rate; the National Park Service is too often wedded to industrial tourism at the expense of preservation; and the U.S. Fish and Wildlife Service (and most state wildlife agencies) frequently can't differentiate between a game farm and a natural ecosystem. (For example, in order to provide motorized access for hunters to herds of Desert Bighorn Sheep, the agency recently bladed roads into the heart of its wildest unit, the Cabeza Prieta National Wildlife Refuge in Arizona's Sonoran Desert.) On the public lands as a whole, wilderness is disappearing at the rate of *at least* 2 million acres a year. That is an area roughly equivalent in size to Yellowstone National Park!

Today, perhaps 700–800 Grizzlies survive south of Canada. Only thirty or so Florida Panthers remain in the wild, and the few scattered reports of Cougar elsewhere in the East suggest that no viable populations remain. The Tallgrass Prairie no longer exists except as tiny relict museum patches surrounded by crops and suburbs, or as heavily grazed and fenced cow pastures. The Passenger Pigeon is extinct. So are the Carolina Parakeet, Heath Hen, Great Auk, Eastern Elk, and Sea Mink. Ivory-billed Woodpeckers are probably extinct on the North American Continent, though ornithologists think that several survive in Cuba. The Red Wolf was extinct from the wild; a small population has been reintroduced to Alligator National Wildlife Refuge in coastal North Carolina. The Black-footed Ferret and California Condor survive only in captivity. (With several of these extirpated species, occasional reported sightings do lend a small degree of hope that a few last individuals survive in the wild, but even if the sightings are valid, the remaining individuals do not constitute viable breeding populations.)

Only a few remnants of the Eastern Deciduous Forest survive relatively intact. The Great Plains are barren of Elk, Gray Wolves, Grizzlies, Bison, and wildness. The Rockies are laced with roads, clearcuts, ski resorts, condominiums, and mines. The Great Basin is a huge overgrazed cow pasture of sagebrush, dirt, and exotic plants—Cheatgrass, Crested Wheatgrass, Halogeton, and Russian Thistle (tumbleweed). Except for a few scattered stands, the great Pacific conifers have been milled into two-by-fours for condominiums, hot tubs, homes, offices, and picnic tables. Real wilderness in chunks big enough to support all native species, all native predator-prey relationships, all natural perturbations (such as fire, insect outbreaks, drought, flood)—no longer exist in the United States outside of Alaska. That's the sad truth of the 1990s.

In the American West, several areas are perhaps large enough and natural enough in and of themselves to *almost* be considered real wilderness. They are few and far between, and include the River of No Return and Selway-Bitterroot Wildernesses of central Idaho and extreme western Montana, the Bob Marshall complex of northwestern Montana, the South Absaroka complex of northwestern Wyoming, and the Cabeza Prieta and Organ Pipe

Cactus country of southern Arizona. But on the whole, wilderness in America survives only as small scattered remnants, biologically impoverished to varying extents, geographically isolated, frequently polluted by exotic species—yet still sublime, diverse, eminently salvageable. The surviving wildlands provide our last hope in a world of ecological despair, our only chance to balance humanity's insane destruction of the natural world with sane ecological policy.

Today, approximately 9 percent of the land area of the contiguous forty-eight states is still "wild"—that is, in a wilderness condition as defined by America's only federal Wilderness law. Section 2(c) of the 1964 Wilderness Act defines wilderness as an area "untrammeled by man . . . retaining its primeval character and influence . . . which generally appears to have been affected primarily by the forces of nature, with the imprint of man's work substantially unnoticeable . . . [and which] has at least 5,000 acres of land. . . ."

To put this in perspective, 5,000 acres equals about 8 square miles. That's not very large. At an average walking pace in gentle terrain, one could cross a 5,000-acre square in about an hour. Today, most of America's remnant wildlands are wild only relative to the industrial wasteland surrounding them. Even most of today's ostensible big wildernesses—areas of 100,000 acres or more (50,000 acres or more in the East)—are far too small to be considered wilderness in the real, biological sense of the term. One hundred thousand acres is about 156 square miles, or the equivalent of a 12-by-13-mile rectangular block of country. That is not nearly large enough—unless adjacent to other wildlands—to harbor a complete representation of native flora and fauna, including top-trophic-level carnivores, such as wolves, Mountain Lions, and Grizzlies. To illustrate the smallness of even our biggest wildernesses, there is no place in the contiguous forty-eight states farther than 21 air miles from a constructed road. The farthest point from a road, outside Alaska, is along the Thorofare River in Wyoming's Teton Wilderness, part of the 2-million-acre South Absaroka wilderness complex. Even in the huge Bob Marshall and River of No Return Wildernesses, there is no place more than 18 air miles from a road.

Nonetheless, all remaining wildlands, however small and incomplete, are important and should be protected. Despite their indigence, they still provide habitat for a multitude of species that cannot tolerate logging, mining, roads, agriculture, and other forms of industrial development. They still provide reservoirs of genetic diversity, and they still provide the opportunity for species to evolve under a wide range of ecological conditions. In addition, they still provide opportunities for human creativity and enlightenment.

From a biological standpoint, big means diverse. Not only is it likely that a big chunk of wilderness will include more kinds of habitats—and thus more species—than will a small wilderness, but we're learning, too, that even in comparable habitats, bigger is better with regard to native diversity. Scientists studying the new discipline of Island Biogeography are learning that, not surprisingly, in most any given biological region, large blocks of habitat can support more species than can smaller blocks. Small blocks of natural habitat that are isolated from other parcels of wild country are particularly vulnerable to species extinctions, while big wildernesses, particularly if adjacent to or connected via corridors with other wild areas, are best able to support the full array of indigenous species in a given region. Protecting *natural,* or *native, diversity,* then, must be the major goal of the wilderness movement. In the highest sense of the term, native diversity means that all indigenous species must be free to evolve under natural conditions, in as many natural habitats as possible. It also means that land managers and citizen activists must pay particular attention to wilderness-dependent species—such as Grizzly, Mountain Goat, and Wolverine—and species of late seral stages—such as Marten, Fisher, Spotted Owl, Prairie Chicken, and Red-cockaded Woodpecker. These species, nowadays, are rare, especially when compared with early successional species and those that readily adapt to civilization, such as White-tailed Deer and Song Sparrow.

Maintaining native diversity means that Grizzlies and Gray Wolves should be allowed to thrive and evolve in the Southern Rockies and on the Shortgrass Prairie, that Elk should be allowed to thrive and evolve on the prairies and in the eastern hardwoods, that Bison should no longer be restricted to Yellowstone Park and a few other tiny enclaves, and that kangaroo rats should be allowed to evolve free from human assault and harassment in big chunks of wild country where cows and sheep haven't devoured the native bunchgrasses.

Managing for native diversity in a holistic sense is the biocentric antithesis of anthropocentric overmanipulation. Managing in accordance with the concept of native diversity means all native species of a particular bioregion (and on a larger scale, of the biosphere), including top-trophic-level predators and omnivores, must be allowed and encouraged to thrive under natural conditions. Thus, all management—passive or active—should be designed to promote the goal of maximum *native* diversity. This does not necessarily mean that each acre—or even each square mile—should be managed to maximize the number of species within it. Nor does it mean that it is sound policy for bureaucrats to create artificial mosaics of different communities, as the Forest Service now does by interspersing clearcuts with standing forest. Such manipulations tend to benefit "weed species" that are adapted to disturbed areas and that are abundant elsewhere. Exotics also benefit from such misguided manipulations. Again, it is wilderness-dependent and late-successional species that usually are in short supply. They benefit from wilderness and suffer from artificial manipulation and habitat fragmentation.

To promote maximum *native* diversity for the biosphere, humans must protect big wilderness wherever it survives. As I've mentioned, large wild areas naturally include more kinds of habitats and more species than do smaller ones. Thus, large wildernesses are inherently more valuable than are small ones. Furthermore, big wilderness offers a buffer not only against the effects of industrial civilization, but against periodic natural catastrophes as well. Forest fires, insect infestations, volcanoes, floods, earthquakes, and even ice ages fuel the fires of evolution, but only if ample undisturbed areas exist to serve as refugia, and only if there remain corridors of natural habitat to provide for migration, recolonization, and gene flow. It is sad to note that in the coterminous United States, there is no individual wild area nearly large enough to incorporate a shifting mosaic of habitats controlled by natural disturbances.

Nonetheless, the preservation of big wilderness provides us with at least a measure of insurance against the continued biological and genetic impoverishment of this magnificent planet, and these last vestiges of natural diversity can become the building blocks for a wilderness system that resembles the primordial wonderland that once spanned the continent.

Big wilderness also provides refuge for those of us desperate to periodically escape the industrial juggernaut; the preservation of all big wilderness can thus ameliorate the deterioration, due to human overcrowding, of National Parks and other popular wild areas. Furthermore, big wilderness is self-protecting. Its core is buffered against the ill effects of civilization by its outskirts. It is important that we protect all remaining wild country, but it is *absolutely critical* that we protect all remaining big wilderness.

It is important to note that protecting big wilderness is but one aspect, albeit a crucial one, of an overall wildland conservation strategy geared toward protecting and restoring native diversity. Habitat destruction has already proceeded so far that even if all remaining wildernesses were protected, without related actions, native diversity will remain depleted, even on America's public lands. I've mentioned that there must be wildland or semiwild habitat corridors linking big wilderness units. Or several wildlands must be proximate to one another, and not fragmented by major barriers to migration and dispersal.

Unfortunately, many potential migration and dispersal corridors have already been (or are being) degraded. Many of our smaller, lesser known wildernesses are in this category; so are semiwild, lightly developed pieces of habitat. Also, heavy development commonly fragments relatively proximate wildlands. Therefore, any effective wildland conservation strategy will have to include an extensive program of wildland recovery areas. Moreover, many of our richest habitats, such as cottonwood floodplains, marshes, and low-elevation grasslands and old-growth forest, are either entirely developed or greatly diminished. Wildland habitat restoration is also essential for these areas; the recovering habitats can then be incorporated into an overall wildland conservation plan.

Unfortunately, timber companies, mining companies, real estate and ski area developers, some cattlemen, and at least four huge federal bureaucracies (especially the Forest Service and the BLM) are working diligently to make certain that wilderness in America—big or small—is not protected. Thus far, they are winning. In their favor, the developers have powerful allies in Congress, unfair laws and regulations that are inherently biased against the preservation of natural diversity, and the deadweight momentum of intransigent bureaucracy. Moreover, as Dave points out in the next chapter, humans have been destroying wilderness since well before modern agriculture, industry, and bureaucracy. Today's destruction, then, can also be viewed as an illogical but predictable extension of a very old trend. And until now, the modern wilderness despoilers have had another important advantage—the political demarcation of American lands.

As noted in the previous chapter, the history of America's public lands is complex and sordid. Today's resulting ownership patterns and administrative boundaries make little biological, ecological, or economic sense. For example, in many Western mountains, the Forest Service administers the high forests, meadows, and peaks. These habitats are primary summer ranges for various migratory or wide-ranging mammals—such as Elk, Bighorn, and Grizzly—and various migratory birds—such as Mountain Chickadee and Townsend's Solitaire. But the low-elevation habitats that are critical winter ranges for Elk, Bighorn, Mule Deer, and other species—including Mountain Chickadee and Townsend's Solitaire—often fall under BLM, state, or private jurisdiction, or a mixture of all three. Furthermore, National Forest boundaries often follow hydrographic divides along the crests of rugged mountain ranges. Such administrative divisions as these often effectively subdivide coherent wildland units so that the organic whole—the cohesive undivided wilderness—loses its true identity and appears to be much smaller than it really is. There are scores of examples of this throughout America's public lands. In addition, National Park boundaries frequently bisect ecological systems by artificially following lines of latitude and longitude. Scattered sections (a section is a square mile: 640 acres) of state land, or of private or corporate lands so resulting from nineteenth-century railroad grants, lie embedded within the boundaries of National Forests and other public lands. Privately owned wildlands, controlled by developers, timber companies, miners, ranchers, and others, contain enormous ecological wealth, but are being severely degraded. This also impoverishes adjacent public wildlands. Generally speaking, land ownership patterns in the United States make development easy, preservation difficult.

Too often, wilderness advocates allow themselves to be constrained by artificial bureaucratic and administrative boundaries. They accept agency boundaries as the limits of what might be protected rather than defining and defending an entire unroaded wildland entity, regardless of the artificial political boundaries lying within. As the last big wildernesses edge toward oblivion, it is imperative that eco-activists develop and advance proposals for wildland ecosystem protection that utterly disregard political and bureaucratic boundaries and jurisdictions. The biological whole is the overriding entity to which politics must become subservient.

Let us advocate wilderness as if wilderness mattered. Aldo Leopold once said that "the first rule for intelligent tinkering is to save all the parts." On a micro scale, that's true for genes. On a macro scale, it's true for wilderness. But first we must begin to *recognize* all the parts. This inventory is an attempt to do just that. We hope it will be a step toward the recognition of wilderness as an organic whole—not as a political subdivision—and toward the preservation of *all* that remains wild. The destruction of wild country must stop. Period. No qualifier. Already there is too little wilderness remaining, and even our remaining big wilderness is too small.

The Destruction of Wilderness

To ask the question "Why do we destroy wilderness?" is to grapple with the fundamental problem of our species. The profound questions with which philosophers have danced since the Athenian Academy—"What is Beauty?" "What is Truth?" "Who are we?" "Where are we going?" "What is the purpose of life?" "What is the Nature of Man?"—are subsumed by that of human destruction of the wild. It is the keystone to understanding our alienation from Nature, which is the central problem of Civilization.

Analyzing why we destroy wilderness requires us to step back 10,000 years to the nascency of agriculture, which brought with it the city, bureaucracy, patriarchy, war, and empire. It was agriculture that severed our kind from the natural world and prompted our devastation of native diversity. (Some, like Paul Martin of the University of Arizona, argue persuasively that this devastation began earlier, at the close of the last glaciation, as small bands of skilled hunters first entered Australia, Oceania, Siberia, Madagascar, and North and South America and caused the extinction of dozens of genera of large mammals and birds that were not experienced in evading so skilled a predator.)

Before agriculture was midwifed in the Middle East, humans were in the wilderness. We had no concept of "wilderness" because everything was wilderness and we were *a part of* it. But with irrigation ditches, crop surpluses, and permanent villages, we became *apart from* the natural world and substituted our fields, habitations, temples, and storehouses. Between the wilderness that created us and the civilization created by us grew an ever widening rift.

Fortunately, we do not need to delve further into this complex question here. The topic of this chapter is far simpler: *How* are we destroying wilderness in the United States of America in the late twentieth century? As we discuss this, we will also uncover *who* is destroying wilderness.[1]

The ways in which we are destroying the last American wilderness are synergistic in their effects, but can be broken down into the following categories:

- Road building
- Logging
- Grazing
- Mining
- Energy extraction
- Dams and other water developments
- Pipeline and power-line corridors
- Slob hunting
- Wildlife "management"
- Eradication of species
- Introduction of exotics
- Wildfire suppression
- Use of off-road vehicles
- Industrial tourism
- Wilderness recreation

[1] In fairness, however, we must recognize that all of us are destroying wilderness, because of the alienation of our society from nature; because of human arrogance; and because of the gross overpopulation of our species combined with the wasteful life-style of modern humans, which converts 30 percent of Earth's photosynthetic production to human purposes.

We will briefly discuss each of these in this chapter. The inventory section of the book will relate each to threats toward specific large roadless areas. Since space limits us to only touching the surface of the factors threatening the Big Outside, references for further reading are given in Appendix F.

Road Building

The army of wilderness destruction travels by road. With few exceptions, each of the items on the above laundry list requires roads or motorized vehicles to exploit the wild. The previous chapter demonstrated just how pervasive the road network is in the United States—that there are few areas 10 miles or more from a road.

The National Forest System contains a large share of the Big Outside in the lower forty-eight states, but it also boasts 375,000 miles of road—the largest road network managed by any single entity in the world. The U.S. Forest Service employs the second-highest number of road engineers of any agency in the world (over 1,000). During the next half century, the FS plans to build an additional 350,000–580,000 miles of road—mostly for logging. At least 100,000 miles of that will be in currently roadless areas. This road construction costs the American taxpayer half a billion dollars a year. Reducing—better yet, eliminating—the bloated FS road-building budget in the congressional appropriations process is one of the best ways to defend wilderness. Simply writing one's members of Congress and demanding that the FS road budget be cut or eliminated is one of the more effective acts any of us can perform.

The Bureau of Land Management is also beefing up its road network—for the benefit of graziers, energy companies, and motorized recreationists. Many regions of BLM land could be classified and protected as vast wilderness preserves if a handful of dirt roads were closed.

The wilderness of our best-known National Parks has been rent by "scenic motorways." The Going-to-the-Sun road in Glacier, Tioga Pass road in Yosemite, Skyline Drive in Shenandoah, Newfound Gap road in Great Smoky Mountains, Trail Ridge road in Rocky Mountain, and Island in the Sky road in Canyonlands are prime examples. A battle is now raging in Capitol Reef National Park in Utah as local boosters persevere in their effort to pave the Burr Trail.

The impacts of roads on wilderness were summarized in the chapter "The Big Outside."

Logging

As the pioneers encountered the frontier in their march from the Atlantic seaboard to the Mississippi River, their first step in civilizing the land was to "open it up": The oppressive forest, harboring savages, wild beasts, and godlessness, and shutting out sunlight and progress, had to be cleared. While much of this ancient forest was simply burned, some of it fed the growing timber industry, which quickly became dominated by larger and larger companies as the timber frontier moved from New England to the Upper Midwest to the Pacific Northwest. In the view of the timbermen, the forests were endless and it was perfectly justifiable to ransack an area, leave it raw and bleeding, and move farther west. In the late 1880s and 1890s, public outcry over this rapaciousness led to the protection of Adirondack State Park in New York and the establishment of forest reserves in the West to protect watersheds.

John Muir hoped the forest reserves would be off-limits to logging, but under the leadership of Gifford Pinchot, they became the National Forests and were dedicated to "wise use." Pinchot established his prescripts quickly: (1) The first principle of conservation is development. (2) There are only two things in the world—people and natural resources.

The early-day Forest Service hoped to sell its timber to private companies, but these companies still had plenty of old growth on their millions of acres of private lands and were not interested. Not until after World War II did the marketing of NF timber attract interest as the stocks on corporate lands became depleted. In the last forty years, the annual cut on the National Forests has steadily increased, until today the Forest Service brags that it is logging (i.e., destroying) a million acres of wilderness a year.

It is important to keep in mind not only that "harvesting" 10–12 billion board feet of timber a year from the National Forests (less than 15 percent of the nation's total timber production) exceeds sustained yield (the amount of timber harvested is more than that grown), but that most timber sales in remaining roadless areas on the National Forests are *below-cost sales*. It costs the Forest Service (thus the taxpayer) more to offer and prepare these sales for cutting than timber companies pay for them. The Office of Management and Budget reported that, in 1985, Forest Service below-cost sales cost the taxpayer $600 million. Moreover, this figure does not include the associated costs of destroyed watersheds, devastated wildlife habitat, loss of recreation, herbicide pollution of air and water, decreased native diversity, concentration of wealth in fewer hands, and bureaucratic growth in the FS to administer the program.

The situation is getting even worse. According to a recent study by The Wilderness Society, proposed Forest Plans nationwide call for a 25 percent increase in logging over the next decade. Virtually every unprotected large, forested roadless area on the National Forests is threatened with logging and associated road building. Except for the small amounts of old-growth forest in designated Wilderness Areas, the Forest Service plans to convert the remaining old growth to intensively managed tree farms during the next fifty years. (Unfortunately, the FS is not always successful in this: Many clearcuts have not regenerated, even with expensive replanting, fertilizing, and herbiciding. Hundreds of Forest Service clearcuts remain butchered, bleeding wastelands decades after clearcutting.)

Grazing

The livestock industry has probably done more basic ecological damage to the Western United States than has any other single agent. The Gray Wolf and Grizzly Bear have been exterminated throughout most of the West for stockmen (Grizzlies are still being killed around Yellowstone National Park and the Rocky Mountain Front for sheep ranchers; the new Gray Wolf pack in Glacier National Park has been largely wiped out to protect cattle; and ranchers are the leading opponents of wolf reintroduction in Yellowstone and the Southwest). The Mountain Lion, Bobcat, Black Bear, Coyote, Golden Eagle, and Raven have been relentlessly shot, trapped, and poisoned by and for ranchers until lion and Bobcat populations are fractions of their former numbers. Elk, Bighorn, Pronghorn, and Bison populations have been tragically reduced through the impacts of livestock grazing. Streams and riparian vegetation have been degraded almost to the point of no return throughout much of the West. The grazing of cattle and sheep has dramatically altered native vegetation communities and has led to the introduction of non-native grasses palatable only to domestic livestock. Sheet and gully erosion from overgrazing have swept away most of the topsoil in the West. In nontimbered areas, most "developments" on public lands—roads, fences, juniper chainings, windmills, pipelines, stock tanks, and the like—benefit only a few ranchers.

Immense areas of the Great Basin and Southwest could be designated as Wilderness were it not for the motorized operations of the livestock industry.

Throughout the rural West, public lands ranchers are the most vocal and militant lobby against environmental protection or Wilderness designation. Sadly, even designation of an area as Wilderness or National Wildlife Refuge does not necessarily eliminate commercial livestock grazing. Even some National Parks are legally grazed. Of course, nearly all National Forest, BLM, and state lands in the West are grazed by domestic livestock.

To make this situation more outrageous, all this is done to produce only 2 percent of the nation's red meat; 98 percent of U.S. beef production is on private lands, mostly in the Eastern states. The ranchers using the public lands are *welfare ranchers*. In 1990, they paid only $1.81 per AUM (Animal Unit Month—the average amount of forage a cow and her calf eat during a month), which is less than one fourth of the cost of grazing leases on private lands. Additionally, BLM and Forest Service range specialists perform many services for their welfare charges, and fences, roads, stock ponds, and other improvements for increased grazing are often built at taxpayer expense. All in all, the Forest Service and BLM lose about $100 million a year with their grazing programs—and this does not count the costs of environmental degradation, which run into the hundreds of millions of dollars annually. The 30,000 ranchers with BLM or FS grazing leases are among the most accomplished welfare chiselers in the nation (perhaps only military contractors are more facile at living on the public dole). And of those 30,000 federal land permittees, few are the crusty ol' mom-and-pop ranchers celebrated by the cowboy myth; many permits are held by large corporations or by wealthy physicians, lawyers, and other urban professionals.

Mining

Although mining, where it has occurred, has affected a smaller acreage than has logging or grazing, its impact has been momentous, as a glance at the Morenci open-pit copper mine in Arizona or uranium tailings around Moab, Utah, will attest. Besides the scarification of the land and attendant air, water, and soil pollution, mining requires a network of roads, power lines, pipelines, and other infrastructure, which drives away wildlife and dispels wildness. Geologic processes are such that minerals tend to be most concentrated in rugged terrain, which not only is more vulnerable to damage but is also more likely to be wild and roadless than is gentler country.

Mining on the National Forests and BLM lands is sanctioned by the 1872

Mining Law, an antique from the days of the early gold rushes in the Wild West. This law allows any individual or corporation to claim minerals on federal lands. Such claims are staked by only a small filing fee and maintained by only $100 worth of work a year, and can be taken to patent (passed into private ownership) if a reasonable mineral production is made. Like logging and grazing, mining on the public lands is a gigantic rip-off. Most National Parks and Wildlife Refuges are closed to new claims, as were Wilderness Areas after 1984 (previous claims—those filed prior to 1984 for Wilderness Areas and prior to designation for Parks and Refuges—can be mined in all of these areas, however). The FS and BLM are limited in restricting or regulating mining on their lands, although they have more authority than they exercise.

There are essentially two types of miners operating today: the so-called small miner and the mining corporation. Small miners are typically ne'er-do-wells with a bulldozer and a fanatical conviction that they're going to make a big strike that they can sell to a large corporation for millions. These colorful characters live in backwater towns near their diggings, or commute on weekends from Phoenix, Los Angeles, and other cities to the backcountry. Although these little guys have made virtually no large strikes, they seem to be everywhere in the West and can be enormously destructive to wild country as they prospect. They are also likely to poach, trap, and pursue other unsavory habits. In spite of their quaintness, they are vocal and potentially violent opponents of Wilderness designation and other "lockups."

Medium-to-large corporations do the real mining. They employ professional geologists, use sophisticated methods to locate potential ore bodies, and carry large exploration budgets. Although financially and institutionally better able to practice mining and reclamation in a less environmentally destructive manner than small miners, they are not inclined to do so unless forced. Mining companies have considerable political clout in the Western states, and they and their lobbying association, the American Mining Congress, are powerful opponents of Wilderness and National Park designations, arguing that all the public lands must remain available for more sophisticated prospecting techniques that will be developed in the future so they can patriotically produce the strategic minerals America needs to hold the worldwide godless communist conspiracy at bay.

A national effort to replace the 1872 Mining Law with a lease and royalty system, having environmental safeguards, failed in the late 1970s because of pressure from both types of miners. National conservation groups are again launching such a campaign. It is long overdue. Even more overdue is a ban on mining in all remaining wild (roadless) areas.

Energy Extraction

Unlike hard-rock mining, energy extraction (oil and gas, coal, tar sands, geothermal) on the public lands by private companies is governed by leasing. Leasing, in contrast to claiming, returns fees to the federal treasury and does not transfer ownership of the land from the federal government. It is based on several laws more recent than the 1872 Mining Law. Although the Secretary of the Interior has considerable discretion in leasing, the federal government (especially under the Reagan and Bush administrations) has been enthusiastic to lease as much of its land as possible to the few giant corporations (Exxon, Mobile, Shell, Chevron, Union, Getty, etc.) that dominate all facets of the industry.

Exploration for oil and gas begins with seismographic crews, who use explosives or "thumper trucks" to produce vibrations in the ground. Subterranean echoes are then read on monitors to determine where potentially favorable geologic formations exist. Because each of several competing companies carefully guards its information, sometimes a dozen seismo crews go over the same terrain. Their blasting disturbs wildlife, and thousands of miles of road have been bladed through Western wildlands for thumper trucks.

After a favorable formation is found and an exploration lease obtained, exploratory drilling begins. Roads are built into wild areas, drilling pads are cleared, and outsize drilling rigs are set up for several weeks or months. The roughnecks who work on such crews are often ORVers, poachers, pot hunters, and other rough-and-tumble users of the wild. Even if a strike is not made (a dry hole), exploration roads frequently become part of the permanent road system of the National Forest or BLM District and provide access to wild country for the motorbound public.

If a strike is made, more wells are drilled, roads built, pipelines constructed, and pumping stations installed until dozens of square miles of public land become an industrial complex, and Elk, bear, and other critters are displaced. Such is the scenario for hundreds of thousands of acres of roadless country in the so-called Overthrust Belt of the Central and Northern Rockies.

Geothermal leasing, exploration, and extraction generally follow the same pattern as that for oil and gas. Coal (usually strip-mined) is a leasable mineral on the public lands. It is a threat to wilderness primarily in Utah (as are tar sands).

Dams and Other Water Developments

Some of the most remarkable wildlands and rivers in the United States have been flooded by dams and their reservoirs. Glen Canyon, Hetch Hetchy, and much of Hells Canyon have been drowned beneath stagnant reservoir water. Only all-out national campaigns by conservationists have prevented dams in the Grand Canyon, Dinosaur National Monument, the Gila Wilderness, and the remainder of Hells Canyon. Dams on the Columbia River and its tributaries have annihilated salmon runs in the wildernesses of the Northwest and Central Idaho. Upstream dams on the Colorado River, Green River, and Rio Grande have severely affected wildlands downstream.

These dams have been built by the Army Corps of Engineers, Bureau of Reclamation, and Bonneville Power Administration for electric power generation, flood control, irrigation, and "recreation."

The era of giant dam building in the United States is coming to a close, and only a few large roadless areas are threatened by future construction. A new threat, however, is that of "small hydro"—the construction of small dams and power plants to produce electricity from thousands of small rivers and streams that are often in the wilder corners of the National Forests. As encouraged by the Public Utilities Regulatory Power Act (PURPA), the Federal Energy Regulatory Commission (FERC) can issue permits to private individuals for such projects. Applications threaten dozens of areas inventoried in this book—mostly on the West Coast.

The best tool for protecting free-flowing rivers and streams is designation as part of the National Wild and Scenic Rivers System or a state river protection system. The national system was established by the 1968 National Wild and Scenic Rivers Act; many state systems have since been established as well. Although Wild and Scenic River designation has been inadequately utilized during the past twenty years, conservationists are gearing up a major new national campaign and are developing substantial and comprehensive proposals in states like California and Oregon. Inclusion in the system generally places only a quarter-mile-wide zone on each side of the river under protection, but it does protect a river from dams and other development that would modify its free-flowing character.

Pipeline and Power-line Corridors

Associated with the extraction of energy sources is the construction of pipelines, power lines, coal-fired power plants, and so forth. Power lines and pipelines slice across the backcountry and divide many units of the Big Outside from one another. Irrigation canals, aqueducts, and power lines from hydropower and water storage dams cut across many remote sections of the country, dividing large roadless areas from one another. More lines are projected, and new transmission corridors are continually proposed through large roadless areas.

Slob Hunting

Both authors of this book are hunters. We are proud to be hunters, and we recognize that hunters have been among the most effective wilderness and wildlife conservationists. This does not negate, however, the impact of the slob hunter (and of poor public policy catering to slob hunters) on wildlife and wildlands. The popular conception of the hunter as a fat, drunken bumpkin or an urban good ol' boy cruising the backwoods in a Jeep, armed with little natural history or appreciation for nature but with plenty of ammunition, is all too true. Slob hunters fall into several categories:

The market hunter. A booming black market exists for body parts of Black Bears (gallbladders, paws), Elk antlers and teeth, Grizzly claws and skins, and so on for practitioners of oriental medicine, collectors, and sexually deficient oddballs who believe these items possess aphrodisiacal or restorative properties. Big bucks can be made by both individuals and well-organized rings. Overworked game wardens catch only a handful of these dangerous criminals.

Apologists for hunting claim that no species has become extinct because of hunting. In reality, market hunting and "game hogging" for American Alligator, Bison, Gray Wolf, Elk, Bighorn, Walrus, Passenger Pigeon, Wild Turkey, and numerous species of waterfowl and shorebirds played as major a role as did habitat destruction in extirpating or drastically reducing these species.

The road hunter. This is the stereotypical hunter. He wants to drive his

Jeep, trail bike, or ATV to where he'll shoot his freezer meat or anything else that moves. He opposes Wilderness because he can't drive in it. He doesn't like predators because they're eating *his* deer, Elk, or Moose. The Arizona Wildlife Federation, for example, generally opposes Wilderness designations because it largely represents this type of hunter. On the other hand, the Oregon Wildlife Federation supports more Wilderness than does the Sierra Club because it's made up of *real* hunters—men and women who know that wilderness provides hunting at its best.

The "gut hunter." These fellows shoot at any game they see, regardless of the distance. Firing countless rounds at an Elk or deer several hundred yards away, gut hunters miss more often than not. Too often, however, they succeed in gut-shooting a critter that then wanders off to die in agony.

The poacher. These people also need roads. They shoot without respect, and outside the law. Many poachers "spotlight"—freezing deer or Elk with a spotlight along a back road at night and then blasting it. Often, the animal is wounded and there is no chance of tracking it at night and finishing it off.

The trophy hunter. Some trophy hunters are conservationists and support protection of the land. Others, such as many in the Foundation for North American Wild Sheep, want to eliminate predators and have road access everywhere. Trophy Bighorn Sheep hunters are usually wealthy, and are leading opponents of Wilderness designation for areas in the California Desert. Other hairy-chested trophy hunters concentrate on Mountain Lion, Grizzly, and other top-level predators. Often, dogs are used to tree a cat or corner a bear until the hunter on horseback is able to reach the trapped animal and shoot it at leisure—a fine display of sportsmanship.

The trapper. Trapping is legal and encouraged by fish and game departments in most states. Not only is it cruel, but it is usually done from road vehicles or ATVs. Trapping targets Bobcat, Lynx, Marten, Mink, Fisher, River Otter, and other predators with low reproductive rates. Trapping upsets the normal predator-prey balance. Trapping caused the near-extermination of Beaver from much of the United States, and trapping today continues to keep Beaver populations at an unnatural low. (Trapping by Native Americans in Canada and Alaska is arguably another matter.)

The "put-and-take" fisher. While flyfishing for native, naturally reproducing fish is one of life's higher callings, many fishers just want to catch their limit (or exceed it if no game warden is about). They are a powerful lobby that has created a fish farming orientation among state wildlife agencies. Non-native, hatchery-reared fish that compete with natives have been introduced throughout the United States. Put-and-take fishers have caused the introduction of trout to many high country lakes and tarns in Wilderness Areas that did not naturally contain fish. This has upset delicate aquatic ecosystems. Lake and riverine fauna has been more transformed than any other in the United States. Put-and-take fishers have been as much to blame for this as have polluters and dam builders.

Slob hunters of all flavors oppose Wilderness designations; they create roads, kill excessive numbers of wildlife, and help turn the backcountry into a game farm.

Wildlife "Management"

The U.S. Fish and Wildlife Service and state game and fish departments are partially composed of outstanding professionals who love wildlife and wilderness. They are disciples of Aldo Leopold, who founded the science of wildlife management and argued for the "land ethic." Unfortunately, many wildlife agencies are controlled by political appointees who represent slob hunters or welfare ranchers, and are staffed by arrogant bureaucrats who believe in running game farms on the public lands for their constituency—road hunters and put-and-take fishermen. This kind of wildlife manager supports clearcutting, vegetative manipulation, predator control, and roads because these often favor weedy species like deer or provide hunter access. This kind of wildlife manager stocks lakes and rivers with exotic fish or hatchery-reared fish because such stocking sells licenses and brings more money to the department. This kind of manager promotes hunting of top-level carnivores such as Mountain Lion and Grizzly because politically powerful ranchers and trophy hunters demand it. This kind of wildlife manager releases non-native birds like pheasant and Chukar because quail and grouse don't provide enough hunting. In bizarre cases, such as occurred with the New Mexico Game and Fish Department in the early 1970s, exotic species such as Oryx, Barbary Sheep, and Iranian Ibex have been released on the public lands to create huntable populations for which high license fees are charged.

Of course, we must understand that any bureaucracy promotes programs that create work for the bureaucracy itself. Not until wildlife managers realize that their job is not to maximize the production of deer, pheasant, trout, or other "desirable" game species, but to maintain wildness and native diversity, will the profession live up to the standards Aldo Leopold established for it.

Eradication of Species

With rare exceptions, every ecosystem in temperate North America has lost key species. The Passenger Pigeon and Carolina Parakeet—once the two most abundant birds on Earth—are totally extinct. In the East, Cougar, Gray Wolf, and Elk have virtually disappeared. In the heartland, Bison, once 60 million strong, are gone. In the West, Grizzly and Gray Wolf have been largely extirpated. Along the northern border, Wolverine, Woodland Caribou, Lynx, and Fisher are ghosts, lingering only in the wildest places. In the Southwest, the tropical cats (Jaguar, Ocelot, Jaguarundi) are shadows seldom seen. Bighorn Sheep, Black Bear, and Wild Turkey have been severely reduced in number wherever they once ranged. Riparian systems have had their native fish and invertebrate faunas so altered that exotics now dominate. Without the sensitive, wilderness-dependent species, wilderness is a hollow shell. Without the top carnivores, the dynamic balance no longer exists. What will become of the deer without the wolf to whittle its swift legs? Is the mountain still alive without the bear?

Extirpation of native species is perhaps the most insidious tool of wilderness destruction. For conservationists, it is not enough to merely protect the land from the bulldozer and chain saw. We must return the rightful inhabitants to their homes. As Lois Crisler wrote, "Wilderness without wildlife is just scenery."

Introduction of Exotics

As native species have disappeared, as the balance has been upset, exotic, weedy species have invaded, thereby changing whole ecosystems. Fragmented ecosystems, with smaller cores and greater area in "edge" conditions, are highly vulnerable to invasion by such species. Many of these exotics were deliberately introduced by unthinking people. Most of the grasses in California are exotics. The salt cedar (tamarisk), from the Middle East, crowds out cottonwood and willow in the Colorado and Rio Grande drainages. House Sparrows, Rock Doves, Starlings, and Chukars have taken over the air and fields in many places. Spotted Knapweed chokes out native grasses in the Northern Rockies of Idaho and Montana. Alfred Crosby, in his brilliant and ground-breaking *Ecological Imperialism,* argues that we have created "Neo-Europes" in temperate areas around the world. The deliberate and unconscionable introduction of Crested Wheatgrass by the BLM in the Great Basin is probably the major current attack on the Big Outside from this angle.

Wildfire Suppression

Naturally occurring wildfire (generally started by lightning) is an important component of most ecosystems in the lower forty-eight states. Periodic fire is necessary to cause certain seeds to sprout, recycle nutrients, maintain prairies, thin out vegetation, and accomplish other ecosystem services. The suppression of wildfire (the "Smokey the Bear Syndrome") has degraded wildernesses throughout the country. The fires that raged through the Pacific Coast forests in 1987 and across Yellowstone in 1988 were simply inevitable natural events to which the ecosystem has adapted over many thousands of years. The Forest Service and Park Service have begun to acknowledge the valuable role of fire in wilderness ecosystems and have, in some cases, established "let-burn" policies for natural fire in Wilderness Areas. Unfortunately, when commercial timberland or private property outside the Wilderness is threatened, full-scale fire control, including bulldozers and slurry bombers, is unleashed. Fighting a forest or grass fire is nearly always more destructive than letting it burn.

Use of Off-Road Vehicles

Twenty-five years ago, the problem of ORVs scarcely existed. Jeeps, four-wheel-drive pickups, dirt bikes, and snowmobiles were rare. Motorized tricycles and other all-terrain vehicles had not been invented. Today, however, millions of these infernal machines are piloted by boys trying to exorcise the demons of their puberty, or by soft people who want to "get into the back-country" to hunt, fish, trap, poach, treasure-hunt, prospect, or camp. ORVs destroy vegetation, disrupt wildlife, erode the land, foul streams and air, and provide access to pristine areas for people who do not respect such places. Barry Goldwater may be correct in calling ORVs "the Japanese revenge."

The disturbing question is, "Why do land managers allow ORVs?" Both the BLM and the Forest Service have full power to restrict or prohibit off-road travel. Presidents Nixon and Carter each issued Executive Orders giving federal agencies explicit authority to control ORVs. The vast majority of the over 300 million acres of National Forest and BLM land in the lower forty-eight, however, is open to ORVs—not just on Jeep routes or dirt bike trails, but *cross-country*. ORVs carve thousands of miles of new low-standard roads into roadless areas of the public lands every year. At the very least, vehicles should be restricted to designated roads with all cross-country travel absolutely banned.

Why is this not done? Two reasons come to mind. First, many FS and BLM employees and managers use ORVs in the backcountry themselves, and therefore identify with other recreational ORVers. Second, ORVers are well organized and vocal. They scream like scalded hogs when they are restricted in any way from exercising their "constitutional rights" to drive wherever they wish. Although the public dislikes ORVs and their use on the public lands, this rude minority gets its way.

Four-wheelers, dirt bikers, and other motorized recreationists present the strongest opposition to protection of the California Desert. They represent a large anti-Wilderness constituency in other areas as well. Snowmobilers are a similar stumbling block to protection of wildlands in the northern states and Rockies.

Industrial Tourism

Outdoor recreation has become a big business. Large corporations, land developers, and small businesses operating in National Parks (concessionaires) and "gateway" towns (including local chambers of commerce) have exploitive attitudes toward wildlands that rival those of loggers or miners. National Park administrators rank their "success" by the number of visitors they host (as indicated by the Yellowstone National Park administrators' declaration that they planned heavy advertising to get visitation up again after the adverse publicity of the 1988 fires). A large number of outdoor recreationists loathe "roughing it" and demand full hookups (electricity, water, sewage) for their travel trailers or motor homes—recreation vehicles (RVs).

RV campgrounds, condominiums, second-home subdivisions, resorts, golf courses, ski areas, tennis clubs, recreational reservoirs, marinas, scenic highways, visitor centers, motels, and access roads serve these industrial tourists. In doing so, they usurp prime winter habitat for Elk and Bighorn, cause (indirectly) the death of Grizzly (in Yellowstone and Glacier), create air pollution and traffic jams in remote areas, replace native vegetation with exotics, destroy wild rivers and streams, overfish and overhunt (thereby encouraging the game-farming mentality), and bring far too many inexperienced and careless people into delicate ecosystems.

Large roadless areas are threatened by ski area development in California and Colorado; ambitious wilderness recovery plans are being torpedoed by condos and recreation subdivisions in New England and the Adirondacks; the survival of the Grizzly in Yellowstone is jeopardized by RV campgrounds; and water-skiers zip over the drowned Glen Canyon. In every section of the country, wilderness and wildlife are trampled underfoot by various manifestations of industrial tourism.

The National Park Service has many fine employees (as do the Forest Service and BLM), people who value the wild and answer a calling to protect it. Unfortunately, some of the top administrators have lost touch with the wild nature their Parks were established to preserve, and have become, in many cases, leading threats to the Parks. Developments such as Fishing Bridge and Grant Village and the arrogant mismanagement of Grizzlies have disrupted the ecological integrity of Yellowstone National Park. The tacky urban center of Yosemite Valley is a national disgrace. Commercial outfitters dictate policies on river running in Grand Canyon and other Parks and lock out private boaters. Corporations offering "scenic overflights" are given free access to skies over Parks by Park Superintendents who enjoy buzzing around in helicopters, too. Concentrating on scenic views and visitor services, Park Superintendents have allowed development in sensitive ecosystems. The primary constituency of the Parks is not the residents—wildlife—but local chambers of commerce, concessionaires, and the motorized tourist. Indeed, concessionaires (often subsidiaries of multinational corporations) have largely usurped management of popular Parks from the Park Service, and run them to maximize their profits.

Unless the National Park Service can get back on track with a philosophy of ecosystem management, and kick out the concessionaires, the National Park ideal that the United States gave the world will become a cruel hoax.

Wilderness Recreation

One would think that those who take the time to hike, float, or horsepack into Wilderness Areas would seek to protect the pristine quality of the land.

Most do, although a minority—often locals on horseback, but sometimes urban backpackers—show no respect for the Wilderness. Fire rings without number, semiburned aluminum foil, toilet paper "flowers," hacked green trees, empty beer cans, discarded fishing line, soap in streams and lakes, horse tethering in campsites or hobbling around lakes—all are the calling cards of wilderness slobs. In extreme cases, commercial hunting guides and packers establish semipermanent Wilderness camps that resemble small towns. Some outfitters have even packed in prostitutes to service hunters in places like Wyoming's Teton Wilderness Area.

Proper backcountry practices amount to little more than good outdoor manners. Neglecting these manners can hurt a lot more than feelings, however, so enforcing them must be a priority. Wilderness recreationists who fail to practice sensitive backcountry ethics should be fined and banned for specific periods from entering Wilderness Areas. Commercial outfitters should be carefully supervised and have their permits yanked for trashing Wildernesses. The FS, BLM, FWS, and NPS need to hire more and better-qualified Wilderness Rangers to enforce proper backcountry use.

In case anyone has forgotten—or was never properly instructed in the first place—I've included a brief refresher on good manners in the Big Outside.

Good Manners in the Big Outside

Twenty-five years ago, I took a college Outward Bound course. On a midwinter backpacking trip into the high country of New Mexico's Pecos Wilderness, we were up to our rears in snow. Temperatures dropped below zero at night. But being an adolescent male mammal and thus willing to try virtually anything, I slept out without tent or sleeping bag. Surprisingly, I spent a comfortable night.

All I needed were pioneer skills and the resources of the forest—fir boughs for a bed and lean-to, and lots of wood for a fire. Whenever the fire burned to coals, I'd awaken from the cold and throw on more wood. It was one of the best nights I have spent, a night that stirred primal feelings of kinship with my ancestors who (according to family legend) trailed Dan'l Boone over the Wilderness Road into the dark and bloody ground of Kaintuck in the days preceding the American Revolution. Ever since northern Europeans became Americans, Americans have traveled comfortably in wild country by using the resources of the wilderness. But today, there are so many of us out tramping around the last tiny islands of wildness that we can't play mountain man anymore; we have to walk more softly.

Some argue that being gentle in the wilderness destroys the fantasy of reliving the pioneer experience, that tiptoeing around in the back of beyond conflicts with the freedom of the wild. Here, we confuse the value of our wilderness *experience* with the value of the wilderness *reality.* With wild country increasingly isolated, fragmented, and injured, and with more and more of *us,* we will walk softly, or we will repeat the historic curse of America: killing that which we love.

No responsible outdoorsperson still follows the old Boy Scout traditions we learned decades ago—"First, take a green bough, and then with your ax . . ." But good manners in the Big Outside go beyond such obvious restrictions. And while this isn't the place for a detailed course in low-impact camping, here are a few ground rules that will help ensure that your camping experience is as pleasing for the land as it is for you. (Many books today offer detailed instructions on how to minimize your impact on the wilderness, and I strongly encourage anyone who plans to hike, backpack, or run rivers to learn and practice those techniques.)

Don't cut across switchbacks. When you're a young pup with immortal knees, you can run downhill at breakneck speed or climb straight up any slope. Who needs those long, slow switchbacks? Well, the mountain does. Cutting switchbacks on a trail causes erosion just as surely, though not as awesomely, as a cable yarder snaking logs upslope.

Think before you void. Bears do shit in the woods. People do, too. And while I enjoy sitting down by a nice, steaming pile of bear plop and poking through it with a stick to try to figure out what ol' bruin's been eating, I've never had the slightest desire to do that with human offal. Nor do toilet paper "flowers" carry the same beauty that columbines bear.

More important than scenic considerations, though, human feces are a pollutant if not properly dumped. Dig a little cat hole well away from any water; from temporarily dry watercourses; and from campsites, trails, and other places where hikers may tarry. All you need to do is get down into the first few inches of soil with enough dirt piled up to entirely cover your creation. The living soil will gobble up your dung almost as quick as a six-year-old will gobble up a quart of chocolate ice cream. In the wrong place, a human turd is a tiny toxic waste dump; in the right place, it is a banquet for all the little bugs and worms that live in the topsoil.

As for toilet paper, carefully burn it. (Carefully! Some yahoo burned down the priceless Spanish Bottom riparian grove in Canyonlands National Park by carelessly burning toilet paper.) If you can't burn the TP because of high fire danger or other reasons, pack it out in an airtight plastic bag for later burning in a campfire or for disposal out of the wilderness.

On raft trips, use the portable potty method described in agency river permits.

Don't build new fire rings. I like campfires and with good reason. Our kind has been sitting around fires for the last one hundred and ten million nights. This long history with the campfire is the reason for the popularity of TV. We've been staring into the flickering blue flame for so long that it is deeply ingrained in the way we socialize. The flickering blue light from the TV reaches back behind our frontal lobes into our skull boxes and triggers a memory of long Paleolithic nights around the campfire warding off the Ice Age chill and marauding Dire Wolves.

However, by now there are more than enough venerable and entirely serviceable campfire rings in the backcountry. No wilderness needs another. Unless you can completely remove all signs of your fire (the how-to books tell you how, but it requires a serious commitment to do so properly), build a fire only in a previous hearth. Moreover, never break limbs or twigs off dead or living trees—use only down and dead wood. Never build a fire in overused or fragile areas like timberline lakeshores or above the tree line. Use a fire pan on raft and canoe trips, and follow the specific instructions for ash and charcoal disposal for that particular river (pack them out or deposit them in the main current). Better yet, forgo the fire entirely and rely on a backpacker's camp stove.

Pack it all out. Unbelievably, some backpackers, hikers, horsepackers, and boaters still leave their trash in the wilderness. You have my permission to knee-cap anyone you catch doing this. But if you can't catch the slobs, clean up after them.

Follow the rules on float trips. One area where the BLM, Park Service, and Forest Service have done a good job for wilderness in the last decade is in the development of invisible camping techniques for popular wild rivers. These techniques involve the use of fire pans, portable toilets, proper disposal of dishwashing water, and the like. The best testimony for these sometimes lengthy instructions is that river campsites, while much more heavily used today, are far less trampled than they were twenty years ago. Any river permit you receive will have clear instructions on minimum-impact techniques. Practice them until they become habit.

Be dull. If you're in rut and find yourself in a singles bar or the big ol' shopping mall, you don't want to be dull. Judging from what I have seen in such places (and I try to avoid them), people there want to outshine birds of paradise. But the wilderness is no place for fluorescent colors on your tent, backpack, or clothes. Blend in. Let fellow campers, and the bears and the birds, see the natural scene, not you and your fashionable gear.

Don't camp by water in deserts. Desert water sources are few and far between. That lovely little spring or elfin tinaja may be the only source of water for miles around. If you plop down and set up housekeeping next to a water hole, the White-winged Doves, Desert Bighorns, and Yuma Pumas that are counting on a drink there will be repelled and may even die from losing that drink. Camp at least a quarter of a mile (farther is better) from isolated water sources.

Don't pollute the water. Don't wash your dishes, clean your fish, take your bath, or introduce soap, grease, or other pollutants (biodegradable or not) into backcountry streams, lakes, potholes, or springs. Someone else is depending on that water, and whoever the critter is, he doesn't want to find your stink in his cool water. Swimming (not soaping up!) in well-watered areas is usually harmless.

Don't remove native wildlife or natural objects. Many plants and animals are now imperiled in part because of collecting by aficionados and purveyors of such creatures. Leave the Furbish Lousewort or Twin-spotted Rattlesnake in its home. Similarly, leave fossils, potsherds, crystals, petroglyphs, and other treasures in place.

Wilderness is, admittedly, a place where many of us go to escape rules, regimentation, and government agents. Constantly comparing your behavior against a checklist of "invisible camping guidelines" can take the sense of freedom out of your wilderness wandering. However, the "escape" from such an onerous burden is all in your attitude—you simply must decide not to consider the techniques of soft wilderness travel to be rules imposed from outside. Don't step lightly in the wildwood because a government agency or a book tells you to do so. Tread gently out of affection, out of respect, out of a generosity of spirit toward the land and its wild inhabitants. Simply develop good, old-fashioned manners and consideration for others. You are visiting the Big Outside because you are one of those who loves wild things and sunsets with Aldo Leopold. Develop that affection toward the land. Treat the wilderness with respect, with good will to all life, and with consideration. The burdensome rules will slough off your back, and your good manners will become second—no, *first* nature to you.

Good manners and affection for Earth are your passport into the Big Outside.

Getting to Know the Big Outside

The principles of Island Biogeography and the need for large ecological preserves were discussed in "Big Wilderness Is Ecological Wilderness." Let us simply state here that when large ecosystems are chopped into smaller pieces, not only do these pieces become extremely vulnerable to disruption, they can no longer support the full array of native animals and vegetation that they once supported as larger areas. None of the remaining roadless areas in the United States is large enough to stand alone. None is large enough to maintain the minimum viable populations of top-trophic-level, wide-ranging carnivores. Identifying the remnants of the Big Outside in the lower forty-eight states is the first step toward restoring healthy wilderness ecosystems.

In 1956, conservationists accepted a compromise on the Colorado River Storage Act that canceled a huge dam on the Green and Yampa Rivers in Dinosaur National Monument in favor of one on the Colorado River at Glen Canyon. Except for a few pioneer river runners like Ken Sleight and Katie Lee, no one objected. The conservationists who made that compromise knew the canyons of Dinosaur, but they didn't know Glen Canyon. David Brower has said that that compromise was the greatest mistake he ever made. It was the tragedy of "the place no one knew." The damming of Glen Canyon cut the heart out of the largest roadless area in the United States.

Other great roadless areas have similarly been destroyed because they were unknown. The southern Nevada desert, described by Bob Marshall as the finest desert wilderness he ever visited, also was neglected. It became an atomic bomb testing range. In too many other cases, conservationists have not fought for areas, large and small, because they were known merely as blank spots on maps.

It is the purpose of this book to prevent that from happening again. With its publication, the largest roadless areas left in the United States have been delineated and described. May we never again lose the place no one knew.

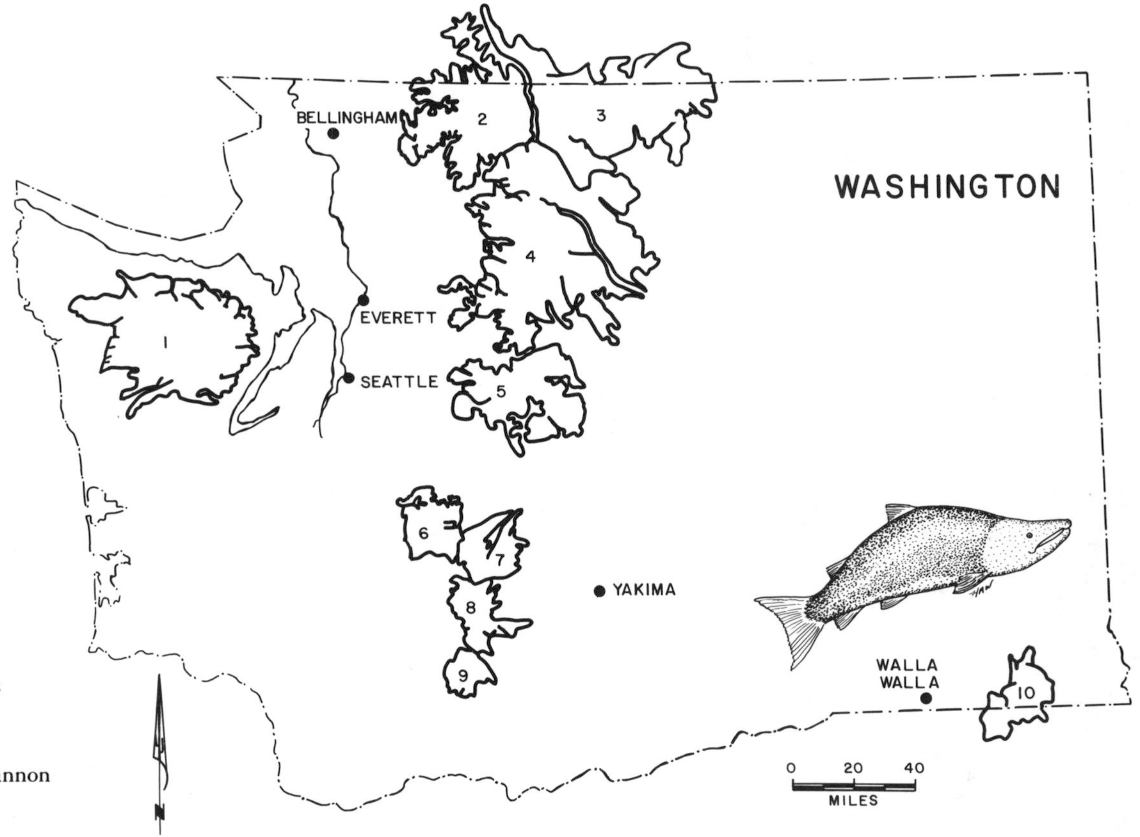

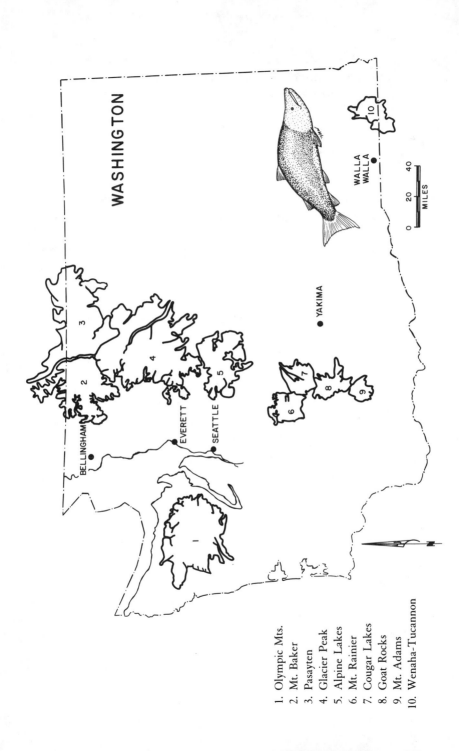

1. Olympic Mts.
2. Mt. Baker
3. Pasayten
4. Glacier Peak
5. Alpine Lakes
6. Mt. Rainier
7. Cougar Lakes
8. Goat Rocks
9. Mt. Adams
10. Wenaha-Tucannon

Washington

Upon first glance at any map showing Wilderness Areas and National Parks, the state of Washington appears to be particularly favored. Of the forty-eight coterminous states, it has the largest percentage of its land area in such protective classifications. Moreover, Washington is the only state with three roadless areas of a million acres or more primarily within its borders.

Unfortunately, an ecological appraisal of Washington's Parks and Wildernesses shatters this pleasant illusion. Olympic, North Cascades, and Mt. Rainier National Parks are mostly higher-elevation rocks and ice, as are Mt. Baker, Pasayten, Glacier Peak, Alpine Lakes, William O. Douglas, and other Wilderness Areas. The alpine areas of Washington above timberline are well protected. The ecologically productive, diverse, and fragile old-growth forests at lower elevations are not.

On the Olympic Peninsula and the west slope of the Cascades, coniferous forest achieves a magnificence unsurpassed elsewhere in the world. East of the Cascade crest, the forests are more arid and less diverse and have smaller trees, but are ecologically notable nonetheless. These forests—the western rain forest and the drier east slope Ponderosa Pine, Lodgepole Pine, and Douglas-fir forests—are where the battle for Washington's Big Outside is joined.

There are ancient forests protected in the National Parks and designated Wilderness Areas. But they are isolated island patches of what was once continuous temperate rain forest for nearly 2,000 miles along the Pacific Coast. Each of the remaining large roadless areas in Washington represents a core of alpine wilderness fringed with disjunct old-growth fingers in the valleys. These fingers are isolated from the ancient forests edging the next core highland. In most cases, the protected natural forest fragments around individual alpine cores are not even well connected—the lower ends of the valleys and lower mountain slopes where the forests would connect with each other have been clearcut and intensively roaded.

Before settlement, there were at least 1.5 million acres of low-elevation (below 2,000-foot elevation) old-growth forest in western Washington, not including the Olympic Peninsula. Nearly all the low-elevation old growth that remains in 1992 is on the Mt. Baker–Snoqualmie NF—where there are a mere 38,400 acres. Virtually none of this is in Wilderness Areas. And The Wilderness Society, in its publication *Ancient Forests of the Mt. Baker–Snoqualmie National Forest,*[1] reports that while there are 298,300 acres of all types of old growth on the Forest, only 102,700 acres are protected in Wilderness or Research Natural Areas.

Because of widespread support for environmental protection in Washington, members of Congress from the state generally try to portray themselves as conservationists. But they reveal their true timber-industry colors in the ancient forest battle. With one happy exception, members of Washington's congressional delegation are supporting timber-industry bills that would mandate the liquidation of old growth, hamstring the Endangered Species Act, and prevent conservationists from challenging timber sales. The exception is Senator Brock Adams, who has introduced a surprisingly good bill—the Pacific Northwest Forest Community Recovery and Ecosystem Conservation Act of 1991.

Until the last decade, Washington's wildlands on the Canadian border were joined to a chain of wilderness stretching to the arctic sea. With timber

[1] Available from The Wilderness Society, 900 Seventeenth St., NW, Washington, DC 20006-2596.

practices and overhunting even worse in British Columbia today than in the United States, that connection has also been severed.

This isolation and fragmentation of old-growth habitats is devastating to sensitive species, from Grizzly Bear to Red-backed Vole. Unless conservation groups covering the spectrum from the National Wildlife Federation to Earth First!, using every tool at their disposal, can halt the destruction of the unprotected forests linking the preserved units, the fabric of native diversity will unravel in Washington, and that state will have a scenic but ecologically gelded system of National Parks and Wilderness Areas.

Politically, Washington is more liberal than other Western states. Although the timber industry is powerful, conservationists are also influential. In the past, however, preservation of Wilderness has focused on prime recreational areas—the scenic lakes and peaks of timberline regions—at the expense of the most ecologically significant areas—ancient forests. Hiking, backpacking, kayaking, mountain climbing, and cross-country skiing are compatible uses of National Parks and Wilderness Areas, but they are not—or should not be—the purpose for such areas. The fundamental reason for designating National Parks and Wilderness Areas is to preserve reservoirs of native diversity, reserves for continuing evolution. Such areas are not mere scenery or outdoor exercise yards. They are the repository of 4 billion years of organic evolution on Earth. Within a few decades, we will destroy that continuum of life, unless we act now.

Washington is one of the places where we have the best chance to save the shards of wildness that remain.

To the east of the Cascades, a rain shadow falls, creating what once was a fascinating semidesert region—the Palouse Grasslands—in southeastern Washington. That area of rolling hills has been transformed into wheat fields. North of the Palouse, the richly forested mountains of the Kettle Range and Selkirks combine Cascade and Northern Rocky Mountain characteristics. A few Grizzly Bear and possibly Woodland Caribou remain, but there are no roadless areas of more than 100,000 acres. Clearcut logging and road building have fractured the wild. Visionary wilderness restoration is essential here in Washington's northeast quadrant, but the immediate task at hand is saving the smaller pieces of old-growth habitat that still exist. South of the Palouse, the Blue Mountains ride the Washington-Oregon border. This area of interior forest has one big roadless area.

The 1984 Washington Wilderness Act designated 1,021,933 out of

2,128,464 RARE II inventoried acres (Washington conservation groups proposed 2,655,355 National Forest acres for Wilderness). A total of 1,723,189 acres in Olympic (885,656), Mt. Rainier (228,480), and North Cascades (609,053) National Parks were designated as Wilderness by a bill passed by Congress and signed by President Reagan late in 1988, giving the state a total of 4,315,007 acres in the Wilderness System.

In the last couple of years, a new conservation group—the Greater Ecosystem Alliance (GEA)—has stepped into the forefront of conservation leadership in Washington. This farsighted group, combining the best of conservation biology and citizen activism, is one of the trailblazers in the world today for the preservation of biological diversity. The Alliance has developed a comprehensive and visionary plan to restore the North Cascades Ecosystem in Washington and British Columbia. Its other priorities include ancient forest protection; restoration of wild trout and salmon; restoration of viable Gray Wolf populations in the Cascades, Selkirks, Okanogan Highlands, and Olympics; and protection of the Grizzly Bear and Lynx in the North Cascades.

OLYMPIC MOUNTAINS 1,060,000 acres	
Olympic National Park Wilderness Area	860,000
Designated Buckhorn Wilderness Area (Olympic NF)	45,257
Designated The Brothers Wilderness Area (Olympic NF)	17,226
Designated Mt. Skokamish Wilderness Area (Olympic NF)	15,700
Designated Colonel Bob Wilderness Area (Olympic NF)	12,200
Designated Wonder Mountain Wilderness Area (Olympic NF)	2,320
Additional Olympic National Forest roadless	87,000
Clearwater River state roadless	20,000

Description: Olympic National Park and surrounding National Forest and state lands on the Olympic Peninsula in western Washington. The deeply carved glacial mountains of the Olympics (Mt. Olympus is 7,965 feet) drop down to 400-foot elevations in the big, gentle valleys of the Hoh, Queets, and Quinault Rivers. These lower-elevation valleys are filled with the crowning temperate rain forest on Earth: Douglas-fir, Western Red Cedar, Sitka Spruce, and Western Hemlock reach nearly 300 feet in height and over 8 feet in diameter. Grand Fir, Pacific Silver Fir, and Big-leaf Maple are also widespread. Up to 140 inches of precipitation a year fall here, allowing many epiphytic mosses, lichens, and ferns to grow. Olympic Rockmat is an imperiled plant in the area; there are ten endemic plants, including Flett's Violet and Piper's Bellflower. Mountain Lion (possibly the densest population in the United States), Roosevelt Elk (14,000 in several herds), Olympic Marmot, Black-tailed Deer, Black Bear, Marbled Murrelet, and Olympic Giant Salamander are native. The Mountain Goat was introduced in the 1920s, and the herd has grown to over 1,000 individuals. Many small lakes, sixty glaciers (three are more than 2 miles long), and large areas of alpine tundra make this one of the most glacially influenced areas in the country.

The peerless old-growth forest of the Olympics was nearly lost in the 1930s, when the entire area was under Forest Service management and slated for "truck trails" and logging, and again during World War II, after the National Park was established, when large timber companies, seeking profit under the guise of patriotism, demanded entry to convert its perfect spruce into airplanes for the war effort against fascism. Each time, conservation groups, led by The Wilderness Society, rallied to protect the wilderness forests.

Status: The area surrounding the roadless area has been devastated by industrial logging. The roadless but unprotected NF areas are scheduled to be roaded and clearcut (both old-growth and roadless acreage on the Olympic NF will be halved in the next decade). The Northern Spotted Owl is particularly imperiled here, since clearcutting and metropolitan development have severed the Olympic population from those in the Cascades. Because of the isolation of the Olympic wilderness from other wildlands due to logging, some biologists predict the Park will lose 50 percent of its large carnivores over the next century. Restoration of surrounding lower-elevation areas should be a high priority in order to develop habitat for such sensitive species.

In its 1990 report *Ancient Forests of the Olympic National Forest,*[2] The Wilderness Society found that while 390,000 acres of old growth existed on the Olympic National Forest in the 1940s, only 94,400 acres remained by 1988, and a mere 11,500 acres of that were protected as Wilderness or Research Natural Areas. Most of the 87,800 acres in Olympic National Forest Wilderness Areas is high-elevation land without ancient forest. Even more

[2] Available from The Wilderness Society, 900 Seventeenth St., NW, Washington, DC 20006-2596. This report and others on ancient forests from the Society are filled with maps, photos, and graphs, and are the best analyses of the ancient-forest situation.

important than the small total acreage of old-growth forest is its fragmentation: In the 1940s, 87 percent of the old growth was in patches greater than 10,000 acres in size; in 1988, 60 percent was in patches smaller than 100 acres. The only bright spot in the report was that 224,000 acres of old growth was mapped within Olympic National Park. This is the largest concentration of protected ancient forest west of the Cascades.

In the first edition of *The Big Outside,* we included 57,450 acres of roadless land in the Clearwater State Forest to the west of Olympic National Park. We have sadly learned that most of that once-splendid ancient forest was devastated by industrial logging during the 1980s. The loss of the prime Spotted Owl habitat in the Hoh and Clearwater valleys adjacent to the Park is one of the little-known ecological disasters of the last decade. And the mopping-up operations continue: Late in 1988, the Washington Department of Natural Resources (DNR) began clearcutting some of the largest cedars remaining on Earth. Trees up to 16 feet in diameter were felled. An observer of the carnage reported, "This tree was thousands of years old. When it hit the ground it shattered, sending a swarm of bats into the sky." As a result of public outrage, the Washington State DNR is considering the deferral of logging on 15,000 acres of mature, natural forest in order to maintain Spotted Owl habitat. Most of this acreage is adjacent to Olympic National Park, but all of the roadless or old-growth acreage in Clearwater State Forest is by no means protected. We estimate that 20,000 acres of roadless state land still exist adjacent to the western boundary of Olympic National Park, but that only half—10,000 acres—is included in the proposed deferred areas. The remaining unlogged areas in Clearwater State Forest should be immediately added to the National Park, and the rest of the area established as an old-growth forest recovery area.

Olympic National Park is a prime site for reintroduction of the Gray Wolf, but local stockmen around the Park defeated a reintroduction proposal several years ago. Widespread support for wolf reintroduction is needed to prod the Park Service into acting with courage. GEA is working with local activists on a comprehensive wolf recovery plan. The introduced Mountain Goats (not historically present) are damaging the delicate alpine areas. They are slated to be removed from the core of the Park but allowed to remain in the adjacent Olympic NF (presumably to mollify trophy hunters). This is no solution, since they will repopulate the Park from their FS refuge.

The Elwha River historically boasted excellent salmon runs. Now-unneeded hydroelectric dams (one is in the Park) destroyed those runs.

Washington conservationists are campaigning to remove the dams and restore the Elwha River and its salmon—there is a good chance that the dam in the Park will be removed.

Nearly all of the roadless area in the Park was designated as Wilderness late in 1988.

RM36: 1,200,000 RM27: 1,440,640

MT. BAKER 742,000 acres (also in Canada)	
Designated Mt. Baker Wilderness Area (Mt. Baker–Snoqualmie NF)	116,100
North Cascades National Park Wilderness Area and roadless	271,400
Ross Lake National Recreation Area roadless	29,100
Designated Noisy-Diobsud Wilderness Area (Mt. Baker–Snoqualmie NF)	14,300
Additional Mt. Baker–Snoqualmie NF roadless	144,800
British Columbia roadless	166,000

Description: Northwestern Washington east of Bellingham, centered on the 10,750-foot-high volcanic cone of Mt. Baker in the North Cascades, divided from the Glacier Peak area by the North Cascades Highway, and from the Pasayten area by Ross "Lake," a reservoir behind Ross Dam. This spectacular landscape of ice and fire, including Mt. Shuksan at 9,127 feet, drops to 1,600 feet along Ross "Lake." These archetypal alpine mountains have over 300 glaciers, large rushing streams, hanging valleys, lakes in cirques, pinnacles, massifs, ridges, and cols. The area's heavy precipitation—over 100 inches on the west side, including 500 inches of snow—has produced commanding old-growth forests of Douglas-fir, cedar, fir, spruce, Western White Pine, and Mountain Hemlock below the alpine zone. Mountain Goat (native in the Cascades, although not in the Olympics), Wolverine, Fisher, Black Bear, Cougar, salmon, Peregrine Falcon, Bald Eagle, and Spotted Owl are key wilderness-dependent species. A small Grizzly Bear population remains, and Gray Wolves have recently returned to the Cascades from Canada. Three to five packs of wolves are now present in the North Cascades, and several litters of pups have been produced. (This information on Grizzly Bear and Gray Wolf applies to the entire complex of large roadless areas in the North Cascades and not just to the Mt. Baker area.) There are more than fifty sensitive, Threatened, or Endangered plants in the North Cascades Ecosystem.

Status: Clearcutting and roads are planned for the unprotected NF areas. There has already been severe erosion from clearcuts along the Nooksack River, the main timber harvest drainage in the Mt. Baker area outside roadless areas. The west slope is especially sensitive to acid rain, which is beginning to damage lakes and forests here.

Most of the roadless area in North Cascades NP was designated as Wilderness late in 1988.

Mt. Baker was part of a 3-million-acre roadless area in the United States until Ross Dam and the North Cascades "Scenic Highway" cut it off from the Pasayten and Glacier Peak areas in the early 1960s. These intrusions should be removed and a single 3-million-acre Wilderness established. The creation of North Cascades National Park was a campaign fought over several decades. The Greater Ecosystem Alliance has developed a detailed, carefully researched proposal for an 8.5-million-acre North Cascades Ecological Preserve in Washington and British Columbia. GEA may sue the Fish and Wildlife Service over the agency's inexplicable refusal to designate the Cascades Grizzly population as federally Endangered.

The portion of the roadless area in British Columbia is also under assault. The timber beasts are in control of BC, and the clearcutting is even worse than in the United States. The BC portion is cut into four small areas and one large irregular unit penetrated by many roaded and logged cherrystems, all connected by roadless corridors to the roadless area in Washington. Except for the Skagit Valley Recreation Area, most of this adjacent roadless country in BC will not last long (indeed, the northern half is connected to the rest by a narrow roadless "wasp waist"). The ongoing destruction of wild country in southern Canada is cutting wildlands in Washington, Idaho, and Montana off from the great wilderness stretching north to the Arctic and will make it difficult for Grizzly, Wolverine, Caribou, Gray Wolf, Lynx, and other wildlife to travel down into the States. In effect, the North Cascades in Washington are being transformed into a habitat island and will suffer losses of wilderness-dependent species as a result.

RM36: 2,800,000 RM27: 3,435,520**

PASAYTEN 1,191,000 acres (also in Canada)	
Designated Pasayten Wilderness Area (Mt. Baker–Snoqualmie and Okanogan NFs)	529,607
Additional Okanogan National Forest roadless	215,000
North Cascades Scenic Highway corridor roadless	39,730
Ross Lake National Recreation Area Wilderness Area and roadless	26,350
State and private roadless to east	25,000
British Columbia roadless	355,000

Description: North-central Washington west of Oroville; the North Cascades along the border with British Columbia. Jack Mountain, at 8,928 feet, is the high point; elevations drop to 1,600 feet on the shore of Ross "Lake" on the west side and 1,200 feet near Chopaka Lake on the east side. An ecological west-east transect from lower-elevation wet forest (Douglas-fir, cedar, spruce, fir, hemlock) to jagged mountains of rock and ice down into dry Lodgepole Pine forest and sagebrush makes this an extremely diverse area. Subalpine Larch and Whitebark Pine are trees of the higher elevations. White-tailed Ptarmigan, Wolverine, Mountain Lion, Fisher, Mountain Goat, Lynx, Moose (one of the few populations in Washington), Gray Wolf, and a few Grizzly Bear inhabit the area.

Status: As elsewhere in the Northwest, the Forest Service is eager to log the unprotected portions of this area. The agency especially wants to connect the Touts-Coulee road on the southeast border of the Pasayten Wilderness with other roads and cut the Lodgepole Pine in the Long Swamp area—the best Lynx habitat in Washington. This would cut off 84,000 acres from the roadless area in one fell swoop. As of this writing, however, the Forest Service says it has no plans to complete the road across the roadless neck, so the southeastern leg of this area remains attached. Pressure from conservationists is working. GEA has petitioned the Fish and Wildlife Service to declare this Lynx population—the largest in the lower forty-eight states, but down to only 30 individuals or fewer—as federally Endangered.

The Pasayten country should be reconnected with the Glacier Peak Wilderness by closing the North Cascades "Scenic Highway." Grizzly Bear populations should be augmented, and the naturally repatriated Gray Wolf population stringently protected.

The western portion of the British Columbia area includes part of Manning Provincial Park, and a long unprotected finger to the northwest (up to Hope) that is being steadily chewed away by chain saws and bulldozers. The eastern portion, less cut up by corridors but also under attack, includes Cathedral Park. See Mt. Baker for a discussion of the Canadian situation.

The portion of this roadless area in the Ross Lake NRA was designated as Wilderness late in 1988.

RM36: 2,800,000 RM27: 3,435,520**

GLACIER PEAK 1,607,000 acres	
Designated Glacier Peak Wilderness Area (Mt. Baker–Snoqualmie and Wenatchee NFs)	576,600
Designated Lake Chelan–Sawtooth Wilderness Area (Okanogan and Wenatchee NFs)	152,835
Designated Henry M. Jackson Wilderness Area (Mt. Baker–Snoqualmie and Wenatchee NFs)	102,024
North Cascades National Park Wilderness Area and roadless	222,500
North Cascades Scenic Highway corridor roadless	38,780
Lake Chelan National Recreation Area Wilderness Area and roadless	59,000
Additional Mt. Baker–Snoqualmie, Wenatchee, and Okanogan NFs roadless	455,000

Description: Northwestern Washington east of Everett. This internationally significant alpine wilderness is centered on Glacier Peak, a 10,541-foot glacier-clad volcanic cone, and includes rushing rivers and streams (the headwaters of the Entiat, Suiattle, and Sauk Rivers), many lakes, well over a hundred glaciers, deep old-growth forests, and rolling alpine country. Western White Pine, Douglas-fir, Grand and Silver Firs, Mountain and Western Hemlocks, Engelmann and Sitka Spruces, Alaska and Western Red Cedars constitute a temperate forest with few peers. Wildlife includes Mountain Goat, Black-tailed Deer, Wolverine, Marten, Fisher, Hoary Marmot, Gray Wolf, a few Grizzly Bear, grouse (Ruffed, Spruce, and Blue), White-tailed Ptarmigan, Cutthroat Trout, Steelhead, and Chinook Salmon. Elevations drop to 1,100 feet on Lake Chelan. The Lake Chelan–Sawtooth Wilderness is on the east side of Lake Chelan, while the bulk of the roadless complex is west of the lake. Rattlesnakes are common on dry slopes in the eastern portion.

Status: The nearly half million acres of unprotected National Forests of the

Glacier Peak roadless area are among the most threatened wildlands in America. The Wenatchee National Forest is mounting a full-scale assault of logging and roading on the hundreds of thousands of acres of Lodgepole Pine/Ponderosa Pine/Douglas-fir forests on the east slope of the Cascades. All other NF roadless areas around the protected units are under similar attack.

The National Park Service is not fighting expanded development in the Park-surrounded town of Stehekin at the upper end of Lake Chelan. Ongoing development in this private enclave will adversely affect adjacent roadless areas, even though virtually all of the NPS-managed portion of this roadless area was designated as Wilderness late in 1988.

The Glacier Peak roadless area is penetrated by numerous cherrystem roads, as are most of the large roadless areas in Washington. Indeed, the Lake Chelan–Stehekin exclusion almost cuts the roadless area in half. Only 4 miles of roadless high country in North Cascades NP separates the terminus of the Stehekin road from the Mineral Park road on the western side of the divide. These intrusions reduce the effective size of the roadless area, since the core is closer to roads than would be the case in an equally large area that was not burdened with such cherrystems. These penetrating roads considerably increase the amount of developed "edge" around the roadless area and cause greater stress for wildlife. Conservationists should fight not only to protect all of the currently roadless land here, but also to close or push back as far as possible these penetrating roads in order to restore the integrity of the greater wilderness ecosystem.

Until the early 1960s, Glacier Peak was connected with the Pasayten and Mt. Baker regions in a huge North Cascades roadless area of over 3 million acres, but the ill-conceived North Cascades "Scenic Highway" and Ross Dam and reservoir split this wildland into thirds. The highway should be closed, the reservoir drained, and the areas reunited in an unbroken Wilderness of 3 million acres—the highway is closed because of snow half the year as it is.

RM36: 2,800,000 RM27: 3,435,520**

ALPINE LAKES 464,000 acres	
Designated Alpine Lakes Wilderness Area (Mt. Baker–Snoqualmie and Wenatchee NFs)	391,558
Additional Mt. Baker–Snoqualmie and Wenatchee NFs roadless	72,000

Description: Western Washington east of Seattle; in the central Cascades south of Stevens Pass from the Glacier Peak roadless area. This popular region of lakes, tarns, and stunning alpine scenery is home to Marten, Pika, and Spotted Owl. Exotic Rainbow Trout are stocked. Old-growth cedar and Douglas-fir fill the deep, glacial valleys. Lovely alpine meadows, Mountain Hemlock forests, and rock scree dominate the high country. Ecologically, it is similar to other North Cascades areas.

Status: The FS proposes building a major bridge across the Middle Fork Snoqualmie River to gain access for road building and clearcutting in the old growth and regenerated second growth of the Pratt River valley, which was left out of the Wilderness. This drainage was railroad logged sixty years ago, but is roadless and in relatively good shape today. Conservationists should rally to defend this entire roadless area. The Alpine Lakes are the most sensitive area in Washington to acid rain and are already suffering.

South of the roadless area, the state Department of Natural Resources, Weyerhaeuser, and Burlington Northern are massacring their lands, thereby cutting off Spotted Owl and other old-growth–dependent populations from their counterparts to the south. The Wenatchee NF is chipping away at the Teanaway area with logging and gold mining. ORVs from the town of Wenatchee are also a threat.

RM36: 550,000

MT. RAINIER 221,000 acres	
Designated Mt. Rainier National Park Wilderness Area	185,650
Designated Clearwater Wilderness Area (Mt. Baker–Snoqualmie NF)	14,300
Additional Mt. Baker–Snoqualmie and Gifford Pinchot NFs roadless	20,680

Description: Southwestern Washington southeast of Seattle. The ice fields and glaciers of 14,410-foot-high Mt. Rainier drop down into thousand-year-old forests of huge Western Hemlock and Western Red Cedar. Snow accumulation is extremely heavy (Emmons Glacier is the largest in the nation outside of Alaska). Deer, Black Bear, Elk, Mountain Goat, and Bobcat are noteworthy inhabitants. Ice caves, steaming fumaroles, twenty-seven species of trees, over one hundred species of moss, and many beautiful waterfalls distinguish this area.

Status: The Greater Mt. Rainier Ecosystem exists in name only. The core of this once-great area, Mt. Rainier National Park, is largely cut off from lower elevation wildlands in the Cascades by habitat fragmentation and clearcut logging (the Mt. Baker–Snoqualmie NF is currently trashing the northern border of the area). Nonetheless, Mt. Rainier, Cougar Lakes, Goat Rocks, Mt. Adams, and several smaller roadless areas form a complex that is severed only by single roads. These areas are, of course, largely rock and ice.

Excessive tourism is a problem in the Park, as is acid rain. An overabundance of climbers has created a human waste problem on Mt. Rainier's glaciers, where a fall into a crevasse can be a vile experience.

Most of the roadless area in the Park was designated as Wilderness in 1988.

*RM27: 1,356,800**

COUGAR LAKES 219,000 acres	
Designated William O. Douglas Wilderness Area (Gifford Pinchot and Wenatchee NFs)	164,969
Designated Mt. Rainier National Park Wilderness Area	19,370
Additional Mt. Rainier NP roadless	430
Additional Wenatchee and Gifford Pinchot NFs roadless	34,000

Description: Southwestern Washington northwest of Yakima and east of Mt. Rainier in the central Cascades. The Cougar Lakes country is the old stomping grounds of William O. Douglas. Elevations range from 3,200 feet in the valley bottoms to 7,779 feet on Mt. Aix. Mule and Black-tailed Deer, Elk, Black Bear, Lynx, Mountain Goat, Wolverine, Fisher, Cougar, Cascade Red Fox, and grouse dwell here. Scattered peaks, sharp ridges, the large, flat Tumac Plateau, and hundreds of small lakes adorn this area, which is along the divide of the Cascades. Forests are similar to those of other Cascades areas, although there are relatively few trees.

Status: Clearcutting and roads are currently chewing up the unprotected area. The Mt. Rainier NP portion was largely designated Wilderness in 1988.

*RM27: 1,356,800**

GOAT ROCKS 196,000 acres	
Designated Goat Rocks Wilderness Area (Gifford Pinchot and Wenatchee NFs)	109,235
Yakima Indian Reservation roadless	75,000
Additional Wenatchee and Gifford Pinchot NFs roadless	11,400

Description: Southwestern Washington southwest of Yakima. The Goat Rocks are an "alpine wonderland," according to the U.S. Forest Service. Visitors may find mist-shrouded rocky crags and a glacier; Mountain Goats and Elk; good trout fishing in the lakes and streams; Blue, Ruffed, and Spruce Grouse; and excellent views of Mt. Rainier, Mt. Adams, and Mt. St. Helens. Elevation drops from 8,201 feet to 3,000 feet. The 1981 eruption of Mt. St. Helens gave this area a good dusting of ash. Western Larch, White-bark Pine, and Noble Fir complement the more prevalent Douglas-fir, cedar, and spruce.

Status: The Forest Service has chain saws and bulldozers poised to deforest and road the unprotected portion. The status of the Yakima reservation is uncertain.

RM36: 370,000

MT. ADAMS 103,000 acres	
Designated Mt. Adams Wilderness Area (Gifford Pinchot NF)	36,721
Designated Mt. Adams Wilderness Area (Yakima Indian Reservation)	10,055
Additional Yakima Indian Reservation roadless	28,000
Additional Gifford Pinchot NF roadless	28,120

Description: Southwestern Washington southwest of Yakima. This roadless area encompasses the volcanic cone and slopes of 12,307-foot Mt. Adams, second-highest in Washington. Glaciers, rushing streams, gentle terrain, large meadows and marshes, Black Bear, grouse, Elk, and Black-tailed Deer grace this varied area. The lower elevations support a rich variety of trees combining both west slope old-growth and drier interior forests.

Status: Roads and clearcuts are the future for the unprotected NF areas. The status of the Yakima lands is uncertain, except for the 10,000 acres of the Mt. Adams Wilderness Area on the reservation (to the best of our knowledge, this is the only unit of the National Wilderness Preservation System on Indian Reservation lands).

WENAHA-TUCANNON 200,000 acres (also in Oregon)	
Designated Wenaha-Tucannon Wilderness Area (Umatilla NF, WA)	111,048
Designated Wenaha-Tucannon Wilderness Area (Umatilla NF, OR)	66,375
Additional Umatilla NF roadless (WA and OR)	22,100

Description: Extreme southeastern Washington and northeastern Oregon, east of Walla Walla in the Blue Mountains. Extremely steep canyons bisect this glacially carved plateau of deep basalts. Oregon Butte is 6,401 feet; the low point along the Wenaha River is under 2,000 feet. Interior dry forest of Ponderosa Pine covers much of the area. Other lower-elevation trees include Douglas-fir, Western Larch, Grand Fir, and Engelmann Spruce; trees above 4,000 feet include Lodgepole Pine, Subalpine Fir, Grand Fir, spruce, and larch. Lush grasslands are made up of Bluebunch Wheatgrass and Idaho Fescue. Wildlife includes Elk, Mule Deer, White-tailed Deer, Mountain Lion, Marten, Black Bear, Goshawk, Bald and Golden Eagles, and Barred Owl (the Barred Owl is extending its range west and is a direct competitor with the declining, old-growth–dependent Spotted Owl). Spawning runs of Chinook Salmon and Steelhead are still good but have declined as a result of dams on the Columbia River. Native Rainbow Trout thrive in the watercourses; there is no hatchery stocking in the area.

Status: Logging threatens the undesignated portion.

1. Kalmiopsis
2. Red Buttes
3. Sky Lakes
4. Mount Thielsen
5. Three Sisters
6. Mt. Jefferson
7. Hells Canyon
8. Eagle Cap
9. Wenaha-Tucannon
10. Owyhee Canyons
11. Myotis (Saddle Butte)
12. Sheepshead Mts.
13. Alvord Desert
14. Trout Creek Mts.
15. Basque Hills
16. Catlow Rim (Rincon)
17. Hawksie-Walksie
18. Diablo Mt.

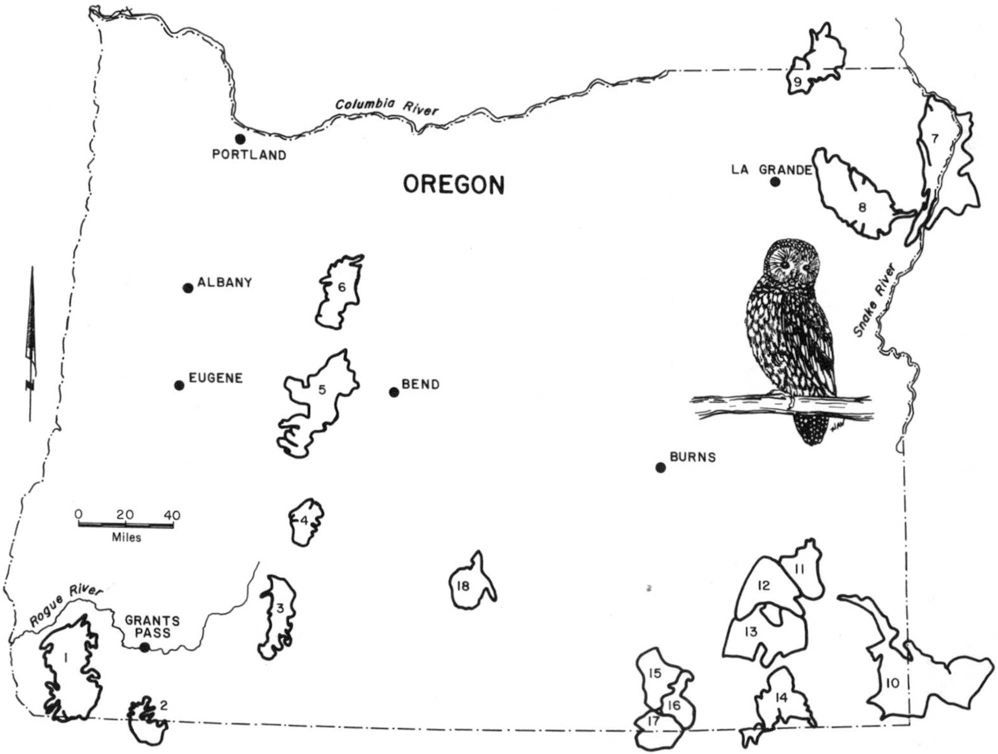

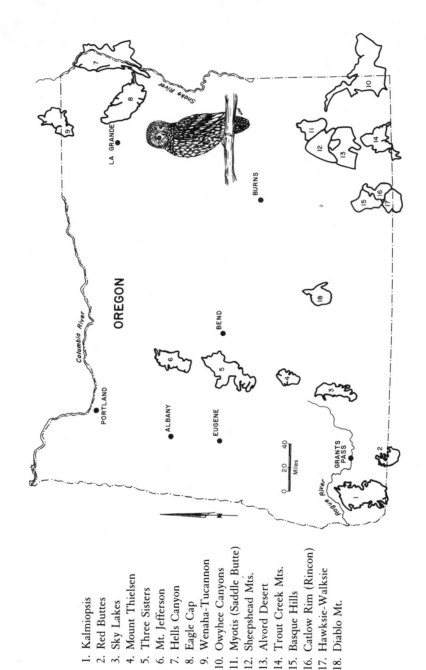

Oregon

Some 140 years ago, when their wagons came to a welcome halt after traversing half the continent on the Oregon Trail, the pioneers were greeted by the grandest coniferous forest on Earth. From California's Big Sur coast south of Monterey Bay to Glacier Bay in Alaska, over two dozen species of pine, cedar, spruce, fir, hemlock, and other conifers grew—some to heights of 300 feet and ages of 1,000 or more years. These were not just large individual trees, however. They were bound together as a *forest,* were a single, interlocked entity—a community. The web of mycorrhizal fungi in the Pacific Northwest forest floor, aided by Red-backed Voles, Northern Flying Squirrels, and Northern Spotted Owls, tied the trees together into a whole far greater than the sum of individual trees. This old-growth forest, this *ancient forest,* watered by the fog and plentiful rain of the Pacific Ocean, created—with the sodden reservoir of water trapped in fallen trees, thick duff, and moss—its own climate beneath the overstory. The coastal forest was a graceful interpenetration of land and sea, with salmon and Steelhead as much members of the community as Black Bear and Pacific Salamander; with the Marbled Murrelet, an ocean bird, nesting in the crowns of the tallest trees; with seals and sea lions hauling themselves out where the big woods came down to the sea.

This forest flowed east to the crest of the Cascades, which split Oregon on a north-south line. Douglas-fir, hemlock, spruce, cedar, and fir exchanged dominance in the forest with distance from the sea, proximity to watercourses, elevation, and elapsed time since previous catastrophic events such as forest fires. Nevertheless, it was a forest from the Pacific Ocean to the heights of the Cascades such as we shall never see again for a thousand years.

The wealth of this forest, its awesome grandeur and silence, its powerful, constant recycling of life, should have been a humbling experience, drawing the Oregonians into a new relationship with the land. Instead, it was merely an inducement to greed.

During the next half century, the best of these forests passed into the ownership of large logging companies, as the timber frontier moved from the North Woods to the Pacific Northwest. By the end of World War II, most of the old-growth forests on corporate land had been sacked, and the timber industry turned its eyes toward the remaining giants—on the National Forests. The Forest Service, long eager to open its holdings to the timber industry, readily complied with industry wishes. Tens of thousands of miles of road were bulldozed on the National Forests, clearcuts appeared like mange through the Coast Range and the lower elevations of the Cascades, streams turned thick with silt, and profits from the dismemberment of the titans flowed into the pockets of timber company stockholders.

The ancient forests of Oregon and Washington, west of the Cascade crest, contained 19 million acres of pure old growth before logging on an industrial scale began in the 1860–65 era. This figure allows for the fact that all forests here were not old growth—as a result of fire and disease outbreaks. Of that original 19 million acres in the two states, The Wilderness Society has inventoried only 950,000 acres of remaining old growth that is protected in Wilderness Areas or National Parks, and a mere 1.3 million acres of quality old growth left that is unprotected on National Forest lands. Ancient-forest experts in Oregon estimate that only 2 percent of Oregon's original old growth is "saved," while another 3 percent remains. Even these minuscule figures are misleading, because many of the ancient-forest tracts are surrounded by seas of clearcuts and naked, eroding land. Such remnants have already lost their integrity as forests: They are isolated island habitats open to windthrow, catastrophic fire, and invasion by alien species along their edges; and they are unable to sustain their natural fauna of Wolverine, Fisher, River Otter, Pileated Woodpecker, Spotted Owl. . . .

Only a precious few ancient-forest areas in western Oregon are of such a size that they can be preserved as real old growth, can be secure as forests and not simply as collections of large trees in open-air museums. But even as the Forest Service's own researchers tell the agency that an ancient forest isn't a farm of big trees that can be cut down and regrown, that an ancient forest is an interdependent, functioning *cycle* that maintains its own climate and life-support system, the Forest Service is destroying the last large ancient-forest ecosystems in Oregon, California, Washington, and Alaska. (British Columbia, sadly, is doing the same.)

We have not simply turned trees into lumber. We have destroyed a complex, stable, ancient community. In the space of a century, we have wrought a holocaust in the wilderness. And we continue.

On the east slope of the Cascades, the forest becomes drier, emphasizing Ponderosa Pine. Farther east, Oregon becomes a world apart as the Cascade rain shadow falls for hundreds of miles. The forests of northeastern Oregon in the Blue and Wallowa Mountains are more akin to those of the Northern Rocky Mountains than to the coastal rain forests. In southeastern Oregon, the Great Basin lays claim to the land with sagebrush steppe, creating a cold desert resistant to being "civilized."

Logging and road building assault the large roadless areas of northeastern Oregon, as they do the coastal and Cascade forests. On the 2.2-million-acre Wallowa-Whitman NF, FS engineers have built 10,000 miles of road, and clearcutting has encroached even to timberline. The Forest Service is even swiftly destroying the scattered forests that exist in Hells Canyon National Recreation Area. Furthermore, disruption of the natural fire cycle that created the open, parklike stands of age-old Ponderosa Pine has led to further degradation. Here, additionally, sheep and cattle damage the National Forests. Forest Service policies have destroyed much habitat for Elk, Pine Marten, Spotted Frog, Goshawk, and Great Gray Owl.

The high desert of southeastern Oregon, managed by the Bureau of Land Management, is cow country. The blading of roads, digging of stock tanks, stringing of barbed wire, extermination of Gray Wolf, control of Mountain

Lion and Coyote, and transformation of sagebrush steppe into artificial pastures of exotic Crested Wheatgrass—all has been done for the benefit of a few big ranches. And more is yet to come.

The BLM has proposed 1,128,850 acres of Wilderness out of 2,648,749 acres of Wilderness Study Areas.

Oregon conservation groups, led by the Oregon Natural Resources Council (ONRC), in a remarkably farsighted initiative, have developed the Oregon High Desert Protection Act (OHDPA), which would establish 5,064,086 acres of Wilderness in forty-seven units. In several cases, ONRC recommends closing minor dirt roads and combining roadless areas to create large Wilderness Areas. The OHDPA would also establish a 1,023,000-acre Steens National Park and Preserve (hunting is allowed in National Preserves), three new National Monuments, fifty-four National Wild and Scenic Rivers (a total of 835 river miles), a new Abert Rim National Wildlife Refuge, and additions to the Hart Mountain National Wildlife Refuge. Commercial livestock grazing would be phased out in the above protected areas over a ten-year period, and 356,700 acres of undeveloped private lands would be acquired by the federal government. The Oregon affiliate of the National Wildlife Federation and many chapters of the National Audubon Society have endorsed the proposal; as yet, no member of Congress has introduced it. Conservationists around the nation should write their members of Congress in support of the Oregon High Desert Protection Act. It is the most visionary and ecologically sensible Wilderness bill developed to date by any mainstream conservation group.

In no other state can one man take the credit for destroying wilderness as single-handedly as can Senator Mark Hatfield in Oregon. Hatfield, with his brick-wall arrogance; Hatfield, handmaiden to the timber industry; Hatfield, the dovish, liberal Republican—it is he who has ensured that the Forest Service will not be constrained from its chosen task of liquidating the last Oregon old growth. At every step of the political process, Mark Hatfield has used his legislative mastery and power of seniority to block protection of Wilderness with trees in it, to thwart restrictions on Forest Service roading and logging, to deny consideration of old growth as anything more than a collection of dying trees that must be harvested.

Hatfield crushed Oregon Congressman Jim Weaver in 1978 as Weaver tried to gain Wilderness designation for the North Kalmiopsis roadless area, the largest, most intact, most diverse, and healthiest tract of ancient forest left in Oregon. Hatfield encouraged the Forest Service in RARE II to make forested roadless areas available for clearcutting. Hatfield designed the 1984 Oregon Wilderness bill to protect only 853,062 out of 4 million roadless acres on the Oregon National Forests—and nearly all of that rock and ice, except for a few museum pieces of ancient forest. It is Mark Hatfield who has defended the bloated road-building budget of the Forest Service as conservationists have tried to pare it back. And Mark Hatfield is the manipulator of the legislative process who has inserted rider after rider in appropriations bills to prevent legal challenges by conservationists to Forest Service timber sales.[1]

Protecting ancient-forest ecosystems and reforming Forest Service logging practices has become the most volatile conservation issue in the United States. Several forest reform bills, running the gamut from very good to dreadful, were before Congress at this writing. Because this issue is moving so quickly and is so complex, we will not try to summarize the various bills here or detail the recent history of the ancient-forest battle. Readers interested in the issue should contact the forest reform groups listed in Appendix E.

If Oregon didn't have a gutsy statewide wilderness group like ONRC, if hundreds of Earth First!ers hadn't blockaded bulldozers and chain saws with their own bodies, Hatfield and the Forest Service would be even more effective in their service to the timber industry. But as 1991 becomes 1992, efforts to save the North Kalmiopsis by tree-sitters, legislation, and lawsuits appear to have failed. Like the Nazis after Kristallnacht, the Forest Service stands before a helpless community. Without swift enactment of comprehensive legislation to protect all remaining natural forests, without meat-ax cuts to the Forest Service road-building budget, without prohibition of below-cost timber sales, without strengthening the Endangered Species Act—without all of this, the Holocaust of the Forests will consume the remaining viable native forest ecosystems before the third millennium of the current era begins.

When the time comes for Oregon to remember Mark Hatfield, a stump, a giant, bronzed stump, will suffice.

[1] This is not to pretend that Hatfield has done his dirty work without assistance. Much of it has been done with the eager support of a supposedly conservation-oriented Democratic congressman from Oregon—Les AuCoin. AuCoin, regularly supported for reelection by the Sierra Club (but not by the Oregon League of Conservation Voters), has led the fight for an increased Forest Service road-building budget in the House, and in 1984, he knifed Weaver in the back during negotiations between the larger House-passed Oregon Wilderness bill and Hatfield's inadequate measure.

Western Oregon

The Coast Range and Cascades parallel each other through Oregon and Northern California with the Willamette and Sacramento Valleys, respectively, dividing them. Along the state border, the Siskiyou Mountains bridge the gap between the two ranges and create an area of astonishing diversity. Some areas in western Oregon receive more than 100 inches of precipitation a year. Several National Forests share these ranges.

KALMIOPSIS 408,000 acres (also in California)	
Designated Kalmiopsis Wilderness Area (Siskiyou NF, OR)	168,900
Additional Siskiyou NF roadless (OR)	235,000
Six Rivers NF roadless (CA)	4,000

Description: Extreme southwestern Oregon west of Grants Pass and extreme northeastern California north of Crescent City. Elevations drop from 4,903 feet to 240 feet in this rugged area of ridges divided by deep river canyons. The many streams form the headwaters of the Chetco and Smith Rivers and of tributaries to the Rogue. The Illinois Wild and Scenic River flows through the area and offers an extremely challenging float trip.

The Kalmiopsis holds the most diverse coniferous forest on Earth (twenty-eight conifer species) and may be the center of conifer evolution. The Coast Redwood reaches its northern limit, and Alaska Cedar and Pacific Silver Fir are at their southern extremes here. The Forest Service calls this the most interesting botanical area in the Northwest (but that doesn't stop the agency from using chain saws to make it less interesting). Only the Southern Appalachians surpass the Kalmiopsis for botanical diversity in the United States. There are ninety-two distinct plant communities and over one hundred rare and sensitive plants here. Most of the area under Wilderness protection has serpentine soils that cause stunted tree growth (*Kalmiopsis leachiana*—a rare heath—grows here). The area north of Bald Mountain (outside the Wilderness Area boundary) has dense old-growth forests in Silver, Indigo, Lawson, and Shasta Costa Creeks, harboring possibly the largest Spotted Owl population in the Northwest and the largest area of virgin forest on the Oregon coast. Brewer Spruce, Port-Orford Cedar, and Sadler Oak are rare plants that are common in this area. Black Bear, Cougar, Pine Marten, Wolverine, Mountain Beaver (a rare rodent not closely related to the Beaver), Vaux's

Swift, and Pacific Salamander are among the forest denizens. Some folks swear that Bigfoot lives here, too. The area is also noted for vicious yellow jackets, rattlesnakes, ticks, and Poison Oak. See David Rains Wallace's *The Klamath Knot* (Sierra Club Books, 1983) for details on this fascinating region.

Status: One of the most important and threatened roadless areas in America, the 130,000-acre North Kalmiopsis is slated for clearcutting and roading by the Forest Service over the next several years. Senator Mark Hatfield, pit bull of the timber industry, kept the North Kalmiopsis from being designated as part of the Kalmiopsis Wilderness in the late 1970s. A famous Earth First! blockade (forty-four arrests) and lawsuit (*EF!, ONRC, et al.* v. *Block*) stopped Forest Service destruction in 1983, but the battle has been renewed, with several dozen Earth First!ers arrested in 1987–88. The Forest Service is using the 1987 Silver Fire, which burned through the North Kalmiopsis, as an excuse to road and log the area (supposedly to rehabilitate it). In reality, the fire did relatively little damage and was beneficial overall. Less than 10 percent burned, like in Smokey the Bear posters, and that was recovering nicely by 1988. Logging after a forest fire is like raping a burn victim. The Siskiyou NF proposes its Shasta-Costa plan as a showpiece of the "New Forestry"—a kinder, gentler, more ecological forest management scheme—but when we look under its skirts, we discover it is nothing more than Klaus Barbie dressed up as Mother Teresa.

The Forest Service is also launching an attack on the 104,000-acre South Kalmiopsis roadless area with its Canyon Project, which also is nothing more than old-fashioned clearcut logging and road building disguised as "New Forestry."

The Kalmiopsis is the centerpiece of a 750,000-acre Siskiyou National Park proposal (including the Wild Rogue Wilderness) advocated by the Oregon Natural Resources Council; this Park proposal should be expanded to the south to include the Smith River–Siskiyou country in California for a 2-million-acre National Park protecting matchless old-growth forest and wild rivers. The prime area in Oregon for reintroduction of Grizzly Bear and Gray Wolf is the Kalmiopsis.

RM36: 830,000

RED BUTTES 104,000 acres (also in California)

See California for description and status.

SKY LAKES 166,000 acres	
Designated Sky Lakes Wilderness Area (Rogue River and Winema NFs)	116,300
Crater Lake National Park roadless	23,100
Additional Rogue River and Winema NFs roadless	26,800

Description: Southwestern Oregon northwest of Klamath Falls; south of Crater Lake National Park along the southern Cascade crest to Mt. McLoughlin—at 9,495 feet, the high point. Elevations drop to 3,800 feet on the Middle Fork of the Rogue River. Over two hundred pools of water, from ponds to 40-acre lakes, display the lushness of the area. Common trees include Shasta Red Fir, Pacific Yew, White Fir, Mountain Hemlock, and Subalpine Fir. Elk, deer, and Pronghorn live here.

Status: The NPS and conservationists propose the Crater Lake National Park roadless area for Wilderness. Unprotected FS areas will eventually fall to the chain saw. Pelican Butte, on the southeastern portion of the roadless area and at the western edge of Upper Klamath Lake, is particularly threatened by FS roading and logging. It has the highest concentration of Spotted Owls on the east side of Oregon's Cascades, and is also important habitat for Bald Eagles. Chamber of commerce boosters and other fast-buck artists in Klamath Falls have long proposed a downhill ski area on Pelican Butte, too.

MOUNT THIELSEN 105,000 acres	
Designated Mount Thielsen Wilderness Area (Umpqua, Deschutes, and Winema NFs)	55,100
Additional Umpqua, Deschutes, and Winema NFs roadless	50,000

Description: Southwestern Oregon east of Roseburg and north of Crater Lake National Park along the Cascade crest. Mount Thielsen reaches 9,182 feet; the low point is 4,300 feet. The Pacific Crest National Scenic Trail traverses the length of the area, attaining the high point of the Oregon portion of the trail: 7,650 feet. The area offers spectacular vistas west to the Oregon Coast Range, and east all the way to Steens Mountain. Mount Thielsen is a stately landmark of rugged basalt with a distinctively pointed cap, or volcanic plug. The east side is characterized by U-shaped glacial valleys punctuated by flats with large marshes, while the west side is heavily forested with a young, fire-shaped ecosystem.

Status: Threats include snowmobiles and logging outside the Wilderness. The non-Wilderness portions are under a federal "recreation area" designation; that designation was applied mainly to allow snowmobile use, which is prohibited in Wilderness.

RM36: 640,000

THREE SISTERS 424,000 acres	
Designated Three Sisters Wilderness Area (Deschutes and Willamette NFs)	285,202
Waldo Lake Wilderness Area (Willamette NF)	39,200
Additional Deschutes and Willamette NF roadless	100,000

Description: Western Oregon along the Cascade crest east of Eugene. The snowcapped Three Sisters and other volcanic cones above the timberline drop down to lower elevation old-growth forest of Douglas-fir in French Pete Creek on the west side and to Ponderosa Pine forests on the drier east side of the Cascades. The Three Sisters are stratovolcanos—individual conically shaped, very young volcanos. South Sister is the third-highest point in Oregon at 10,358 feet; the low elevation in this roadless area is 2,000 feet in French Pete Creek. Trees also include Silver Fir, Subalpine Fir, Mountain Hemlock, Western Hemlock, and Lodgepole Pine. The largest contiguous block of ancient forest (and ecologically more valuable lower-elevation ancient forest) in Oregon is protected in the western half of the Three Sisters Wilderness. The area includes a large area above tree line, many lakes (Mink Lake covers 360 acres), waterfalls, lava fields, obsidian cliffs, and the north and west shores of Waldo Lake. Collier Glacier, between North and Middle Sisters, is the largest in Oregon. Roosevelt Elk, Mule Deer, Black-tailed Deer, Black Bear, Marten, Mink, Wolverine, and grouse are natives. Snow depths reach 20 feet. This is the only truly representative area of the western Cascade forest-and-volcano ecosystem.

Status: In the 1960s and 1970s, Three Sisters was the site of a major conservation battle to protect the ancient forests of French Pete Creek. Unprotected roadless areas, including old-growth lower-elevation forests, are under severe threat of clearcutting and roading by the Forest Service. A major campaign is needed to protect the undesignated 100,000 acres of the Three Sisters. Fisher, Grizzly, Gray Wolf, and Lynx should be reintroduced.

Waldo Lake, the purest large body of water in the world (purer than lab-grade distilled water), is threatened by ski areas, logging, human waste, motor oil waste, and other human impacts. Waldo Lake is generally surrounded by Wilderness and adjacent roadless lands, but has motorized access at two spots and associated development. Only complete and total protection will save this exceptional lake.

MT. JEFFERSON 191,000 acres	
Designated Mt. Jefferson Wilderness Area (Willamette and Deschutes NFs)	107,008
Warm Springs Indian Reservation Whitewater River Roadless Area	65,300
Additional Willamette and Deschutes NFs roadless	18,400

Description: Western Oregon east of Corvallis and Albany along the Cascade crest. Mt. Jefferson, at 10,497 feet, is the second-highest peak in Oregon and is flanked with glaciers. Three Fingered Jack is another prominent peak. Both are popular climbs. The low point is 2,400 feet. Rock outcrops, talus slopes, alpine meadows, spectacular wildflowers, and over 150 lakes add to the beauty of the area. Total precipitation is 75 inches annually. Roosevelt Elk, Black Bear, Mountain Lion, and deer are present. Douglas-fir, cedar, fir, spruce, and Ponderosa Pine are the most common trees; 62 percent of the area is timbered.

Status: Unprotected NF portions are under threat of clearcutting and roading. Status of the Indian Reservation area is uncertain.

Northeastern Oregon

Northeastern Oregon, with Hells Canyon and the Blue and Wallowa Mountains, is ecologically more like Idaho than it is like western Oregon. The large roadless areas left are in Hells Canyon National Recreation Area (managed by the FS) and the Wallowa-Whitman and Umatilla NFs.

HELLS CANYON 563,000 acres (also in Idaho)	
Designated Hells Canyon Wilderness Area (FS, OR)	109,850
Designated Hells Canyon Wilderness Area (FS, ID)	83,800
Additional Hells Canyon NRA, BLM, and private roadless (OR)	153,500
Additional Hells Canyon NRA, FS, and private roadless (ID)	204,000
Snake Wild and Scenic River roadless (OR)	6,000
Snake Wild and Scenic River roadless (ID)	6,000

Description: Extreme northeastern Oregon east of Enterprise, and west-central Idaho west of Riggins. Hells Canyon on the Snake River is the deepest canyon in North America (over 8,000 feet deep in places), according to folks in Idaho and Oregon. (Californians claim the title for Kings Canyon, but the Northwesterners argue persuasively that Hells Canyon was formed by erosion—water flow—instead of faulting, and that it is a distinct, two-sided abyss cut in a wide plateau, not a mountain "gorge.") The Idaho portion consists of high peaks with lakes (Seven Devils Mountains); the Oregon portion is made up of grassy benches and timbered ridges; the Snake River roars between. Very large and powerful rapids on the Snake River make it one of the "big water" runs of North America. Elevations drop from 9,393 feet (He Devil Mountain in Idaho) to 800 feet along the Snake. Black Bear, Mountain Lion, Elk, Mountain Goat, Bighorn Sheep, White Sturgeon, and Peregrine Falcon populate the area. The last authenticated Grizzly in Oregon was killed here in 1937, although the number of possible Grizzly sightings has been increasing. Moose have recently been spotted. They are evidently extending their range, as they have not been historically reported in Hells Canyon. Vegetation ranges from mixed conifer forest (Douglas-fir, Ponderosa Pine, Western Larch, Engelmann Spruce, and Subalpine Fir) down to sagebrush-grassland.

In the 1960s and 1970s, Hells Canyon was the site of major conservation battles over additional dams on the Snake River. Today, 67 miles of the Snake is a National Wild and Scenic River, and Hells Canyon is a National Recreation Area, which is supposedly better protected than run-of-the-mill National Forest land. It's nice to win one now and then.

Status: A major battle is raging over protection of the undesignated wildlands in Hells Canyon NRA (it seems we didn't entirely win back in the

1970s). The Forest Service proposes major clearcutting and roading in the area, and loggers have threatened violence against "obstructionist" conservationists (eco-terrorism?). Oregon Senator Bob Packwood proposed additional Wilderness in the 1980s, but backed off after such threats. The FS has logged well over 150 million board feet in the NRA since it was established in 1975. Conservationists, led by the tough Hells Canyon Preservation Council, are now proposing a 1.6-million-acre National Park and Preserve, inspired by the FS's destructive and illegal management practices in the Hells Canyon NRA and the Eagle Cap Wilderness Area. (Hunting would continue to be allowed in the Preserve.) Litigation filed in 1988 by the ONRC and Hells Canyon Preservation Council was successful, as the Ninth Circuit Court of Appeals found that the FS violated the 1975 law that established the Hells Canyon NRA. National conservation groups need to make this campaign a priority.

Motors on boats on the Snake River should be prohibited. A major RV park is proposed in the Scenic River corridor at Pittsburg Landing in one of the most archaeologically sensitive areas in the West. It should be stopped dead in its tracks. An additional 34 miles of the Snake was studied and recommended for Scenic River protection, but this designation has not been forthcoming. Upriver dams on the Snake are causing erosion of beaches in Hells Canyon even faster than in the Grand Canyon.

Minor roads should be closed and past logging abuses rehabilitated to join Hells Canyon with the Eagle Cap Wilderness to the west in order to establish a 1.5-million-acre Wilderness; Grizzlies and Gray Wolves should be reintroduced. Cattle and sheep grazing is permitted in the Wilderness; it should be eliminated.

In this edition, we drop from the Hells Canyon Roadless Area 27,850 acres of designated Wilderness and roadless land on the southern Oregon side because a power line from Hells Canyon Dam divides it from the rest of the roadless area.

RM27: 1,203,840

EAGLE CAP 452,000 acres	
Designated Eagle Cap Wilderness Area (Wallowa-Whitman NF)	359,976
Additional Wallowa-Whitman NF roadless	92,000

Description: East of La Grande and west of Hells Canyon in northeastern Oregon. The craggy Wallowa Mountain Range features exposed granite, limestone, and marble; four major rivers (Minam, Imnaha, Wallowa, and Lostine); and over fifty lakes (including Legore Lake at 8,800 feet—the highest in Oregon). The high point is Sacajawea, at 9,839 feet; thirty-one other peaks exceed 8,000 feet; the low point is 2,800 feet. Mixed conifer forests (Douglas-fir, Engelmann Spruce, Subalpine and Grand Firs, Whitebark and Limber Pines) drop into Ponderosa Pine. The contiguous roadless lands are lower-elevation, more biologically productive forests than the "rocks and ice" in the designated Wilderness. The Bighorn has been reintroduced. Mountain Lion, Black Bear, Elk, Fisher (reintroduced in 1961), Beaver, Mule Deer, and the very rare Wolverine are among the native mammals. The entire population of the Wallowa Gray-crowned Rosy Finch (a subspecies) nests here. Other birds include the Great Gray Owl, Goshawk, and Pileated Woodpecker. Now a popular backpacking and rock-climbing area, it is the former range of Chief Joseph and the Nez Percé. Eagle Cap is the largest protected Wilderness in Oregon, and the Minam River is the only fully protected major or intermediate drainage in the state.

Status: Logging and roading threaten the portion outside of the Wilderness. The FS plans logging all the way to timberline along the southern boundary. The Eagle Cap should be combined with Hells Canyon for a 1.5-million-acre Wilderness. Of the formerly large herd of Bighorn Sheep (including "Spot"—the largest recorded ram in the United States), 75 percent have died of a disease transmitted from domestic sheep. Grazing has been suspended by the FS, but there is great pressure to put the "hoofed locusts" (as John Muir called them) back in. The recent FS attempt to put domestics back into the Standley Allotment (where Bighorns were infected) was stopped by a successful Hells Canyon Preservation Council appeal.

WENAHA-TUCANNON 200,000 acres (also in Washington)
See Washington for description and status.

Southeastern Oregon

In surprising contrast to the deep forests of western Oregon, southeastern Oregon is part of the Great Basin Desert that covers most of Nevada. Some of the least-visited areas in the United States are tucked away in this high lonesome. The western three quarters of the Oregon High Desert, including Steens Mountain and the Alvord Desert, is part of the geographic Great Basin with no outlet to the sea.

The eastern quarter takes in the Owyhee Canyons, which are part of the Snake River basin. Except for several large National Wildlife Refuges, the public lands here are under the control of the Bureau of Land Management. Some salute the Oregon High Desert as the last bastion of the "real" cowboy. Others kick the cow shit.

The Oregon Natural Resources Council and other conservation groups have developed a visionary Wilderness plan for the Oregon High Desert, called the Oregon High Desert Protection Act, which would designate over 5 million acres of Wilderness. See the Oregon introduction for details. Acreages for the OHDPA Wilderness proposals are given for the following areas.

OWYHEE CANYONS 619,000 acres (also in Idaho)

See Idaho for description and status.

MYOTIS (SADDLE BUTTE) 210,000 acres	
BLM WSA 3-111 (Saddle Butte)	86,300
Additional BLM, private, and state roadless to south	87,000
State and private roadless to northwest	37,000

Description: Southeastern Oregon north of Burns Junction. This apparently flat but diverse area of lava flow, sagebrush steppe, salt desert scrub, spring-fed sinks, and dry lake beds is on the divide between the Owyhee drainage and the Great Basin. Tub Spring is the only natural perennial source of water in the area. Bluebunch Wheatgrass, Big Sagebrush, and the exotic invader Cheatgrass are the dominant plants, although Shadscale and Indian Ricegrass are present in the southeast. The Salt Desert Scrub community here is one of the northernmost examples of that ecosystem. The bunchgrass communities are in relatively healthy condition—most bunchgrass throughout the West has been severely damaged by livestock grazing. *Padiocactus simpson robustar,* a rare and sensitive species for Oregon, is present. Lava tubes and caves in the Saddle Butte Lava Field provide important habitat for several species of bats, including the rare Long-eared Myotis and Townsend's Big-eared Bat (proposed for listing under the Endangered Species Act), and for mosses and ferns—unusual in this arid landscape. Myotis is the northern limit for the Kit Fox (Threatened in Oregon) and has some of Oregon's best winter range for Pronghorn. Other inhabitants include Mule Deer, Bobcat, Yellow-bellied Marmot, Swainson's Hawk, and Sage Grouse (both birds are being considered for Endangered Species Act listing). Feral horses roam the area.

Status: Threats include construction of additional developments for livestock grazing and the doubling of Animal Unit Months, which would cause severe damage to the generally healthy range here. Jeep trails and a few grazing developments are the main blemishes in the roadless area. BLM subdivided this roadless area into five units because of the presence of rough Jeep trails. Conservationists have inspected all these routes and have determined they are not "roads." A 476-acre ranch inholding near the western boundary is scheduled for acquisition by BLM, and the buildings and three-mile-long access road and power line are to be dismantled.

BLM proposes a 500-kilovolt power line through the area, along with an access road. Wilderness designation would prevent this. Although there were no mining claims in this area as of the summer of 1990, there is some interest in cyanide heap leach mining for possible gold in the Saddle Butte area. There are also oil and gas leases in the Saddle Butte area.

The Oregon Natural Resources Council proposes a 173,890-acre Wilderness on BLM land here through the Oregon High Desert Protection Act. This would be one of the finest examples of sagebrush steppe in the Wilderness System. BLM opposes Wilderness designation for this area. A dirt county road separates Myotis from the scenic Lower Owyhee Canyons—this road should be closed, and a single 400,000-acre Wilderness established. As a result of a land exchange, 37,000 acres to the northeast, including Saddle Butte in this roadless area, were transferred from BLM to the state. The state should be encouraged to protect its portion as Wilderness.

SHEEPSHEAD MOUNTAINS 232,000 acres	
BLM WSAs 2-72 and 3-114	231,467
Private roadless	500

Description: Southeastern Oregon northwest of Burns Junction and north of the Alvord Desert. Rolling sagebrush- and grass-covered hills are cut by a lava flow, steep draws and canyons, ridgelines, and escarpments to form this complex area. Ephemeral lakes create good waterfowl habitat in moist years. Elevations generally range from 4,000 feet to over 5,000 feet, with Mickey Butte reaching 6,294 feet and nearby Mickey Basin dropping to 3,912 feet. Intermittent creeks include Heath, Wildcat, Mickey, Bone, Palomino, and Antelope. Vegetative communities are Big Sagebrush and Bluebunch Wheatgrass, Shadscale and Indian Ricegrass, Low Sagebrush and Bunchgrass, Silver Sage, Great Basin Wildrye, playa margin, saline meadows, and Winter-fat, with numerous grass, forb, and shrub species represented. Three potential Endangered or Threatened plants—Weak Milk-vetch, Davis's Pepper Cress, and Lemmon's Onion—are present. Pronghorn, Sage Grouse, Mule Deer, Bobcat, Kit Fox, Black-tailed Jackrabbit, Sage Sparrow, and Long-eared Owl reside in the area. Raptors, including American Kestrel, Golden Eagle, and Prairie Falcon, nest on the cliffs. There is potential for reintroduction of Bighorn Sheep. The Sheepsheads afford excellent views of Steens Mountain and the Alvord Desert.

Status: BLM divided this area into several Wilderness Study Areas on the basis of a network of Jeep trails and range developments. ONRC proposes a 260,282-acre Wilderness; although BLM considered designating the entire area as Wilderness and closing the intervening vehicle routes, it is proposing only 105,720 acres in three of the WSAs for Wilderness and closure of the routes between them. Minor dirt roads separate the Sheepshead complex from the Alvord Desert complex to the south; at the very least, the Sheepsheads and Alvord Desert should be combined for a single Wilderness of 750,000 acres. Preferably, however, this area should be part of a 3-million-acre Oregon Desert National Wilderness Park (see Alvord Desert for details).

The main threats are welfare ranching (several range "improvement" projects are planned—including ripping out native plant communities and replacing them with exotic Crested Wheatgrass) and ORVs.

ALVORD DESERT 361,000 acres	
BLM WSAs 2-74 and 2-73A and H	294,110
Additional BLM roadless	22,000
Mixed private, state, and BLM roadless	45,000

Description: Southeastern Oregon southwest of Burns Junction. The huge Alvord Playa (dry lake bed) is one of the few places where the curvature of Earth can be easily perceived; it is also one of the starkest desert areas in the nation (portions receive only 5 inches of precipitation a year). Hot springs (up to 210 degrees Fahrenheit), sand dunes, canyons, and cliffs vary the landscape. Massive Steens Mountain abruptly rises west of this unit. The most extensive plant community is a combination of Big Sagebrush–Bunchgrass and Shadscale-Budsage. Greasewood-Saltgrass and Great Basin Wildrye are other important communities. Solitary Milk-vetch and Davis's Pepper Cress are candidates for federal Endangered status. The area provides important winter range for Pronghorn and Bighorn Sheep. Other noteworthy denizens include Snowy Plover (Threatened in Oregon), American Avocet, Sage Thrasher, Prairie Falcon, Golden Eagle, and Bobcat. Ord Kangaroo Rat, Dark Kangaroo Mouse, Merriam Shrew, Collared Lizard, Great Basin Spadefoot Toad, and several other species reach the northern limits of their ranges here.

Status: Some vehicle ways cut through this area, although a 160,000-acre core is pristine. BLM divided the area into three WSAs on the basis of Jeep trails. A few range developments are on the periphery. Threats include geothermal development, ORVs, a 500-kilovolt power line, and continued overgrazing.

BLM proposes a scant 69,165 acres for Wilderness; the Oregon Natural Resources Council, in the OHDPA, proposes a 350,000-acre Alvord Desert Wilderness.

The Alvord Desert is the center of a huge, essentially uninhabited northern Great Basin Desert wilderness crossed only by minor dirt roads. A 3-million-acre Oregon Desert National Wilderness Park (including some land in Nevada) should be established here, consisting of the Alvord Desert, the Sheepshead Mountains to the north, Trout Creek Mountains to the south, Steens Mountain to the west, and the Pueblo Mountains/Beatys Butte/Basque Hills/Catlow Rim/Hawksie-Walksie/Sheldon country to the southwest. Gray Wolf should be reintroduced, and livestock grazing eliminated.

TROUT CREEK MOUNTAINS 212,000 acres (also in Nevada)	
BLM WSAs 3-156 et al. (OR)	173,515
Additional BLM and private roadless (OR)	16,000
BLM WSA 2-859 (NV)	13,200
Additional BLM roadless (NV)	9,000

Description: Southeastern Oregon and northwestern Nevada west of McDermitt, Nevada. The Trout Creek Mountains are an uplifted, tilted block with a steep southeastern escarpment. South of the escarpment is a collapsed volcanic dome, McDermitt Caldera. Many semiparallel canyons flow from the south to the northwest. Elevations rise from 6,500 feet to 8,500 feet. Vegetation consists primarily of grass and sagebrush, with several other shrubs common, including snowbrush, wild rose, Squaw Currant, and snowberry. Mountain mahogany and Aspen grow along the streams and form extensive stands in the higher elevations; willow is also common in riparian zones. Five plants are on the Oregon state rare or endangered list, and one, Bristle-flowered Collomia, is a candidate for federal Endangered listing. This is one of the most diverse and productive wildlife habitats in southeastern Oregon. Species include Beaver, Pronghorn, Mule Deer, Bobcat, Mountain Lion, Sage Grouse, Whitehorse Cutthroat Trout, Lahontan Redside Shiner, and possibly the Endangered Lahontan Cutthroat Trout. The Oregon Fish and Game Department considers the Trout Creeks to be the best area for reintroduction of California Bighorn Sheep in Oregon, but competition from livestock severely compromises this area for wild sheep.

Status: Continued overgrazing and related developments are the major threats. The BLM is proposing to spend more than $500,000 on major range developments in the roadless area to accommodate one welfare rancher and to mitigate the impacts from his cattle. The BLM refused to consider cancellation of the grazing leases, and also refused to do a cost-benefit analysis of its proposed alternatives. ORVs use the Jeep trails in the area.

BLM divided the Trout Creeks into five WSAs on the basis of Jeep trails between them. ONRC proposes a single 320,120-acre Wilderness by closing Jeep trails and minor dirt roads, and BLM recommends closing some Jeep trails to form a single Wilderness of 176,720 acres. This area is separated from the Alvord Desert country, to the north, by a gravel road. It should be part of a 3-million-acre Oregon Desert National Wilderness Park.

BASQUE HILLS 159,000 acres	
BLM WSA 2-84	141,730
Checkerboard BLM and private roadless	17,000

Description: Southeastern Oregon south of Blitzen. The Basque Hills are in the middle of nowhere. Nowhere, by the way, is a virtually uninhabited area, far from paved roads in the Oregon High Desert, consisting of several large roadless areas broken only by minor dirt roads. The Basque Hills are a range of gently rolling hills, rims, and buttes; the roadless area also includes a large flat area to the west. A wide diversity of native grasses remains because of a lack of water for domestic livestock. Vegetative communities in this austere landscape are Big Sagebrush and Bluebunch Wheatgrass, Big Sagebrush and Greasewood, Indian Ricegrass and Needlegrass, and Winterfat, contrasting with bare playa and playa margin. A newly discovered plant, Crosby's Buckwheat, is a candidate for federal Endangered listing. Raptors nesting along Coyote Rim and other rims include Golden Eagle, Prairie Falcon, Red-tailed Hawk, American Kestrel, Raven, and Great Horned Owl. The Basque Hills are a major wintering area for Pronghorn; other critters include Brewer's Sparrow, Horned Lark, Western Rattlesnake, Canyon Mouse, and Bushy-tailed Woodrat.

Status: A 500-kilovolt power line may be constructed through the area. Phony wildlife improvement projects ("brush removal") and livestock developments, including Crested Wheatgrass seedings, also threaten it. Ranchers and pickup truck hunters use a few Jeep trails and cherrystem dirt roads in the area.

The Basque Hills are part of an important complex of roadless areas that includes Catlow Rim, Hawksie-Walksie, Beatys Butte, and the Pueblo Mountains and that are separated only by poor dirt roads; all should be part of a 3-million-acre Oregon Desert National Wilderness Park (see Alvord Desert). ONRC proposes a 524,300-acre Oregon Grasslands Wilderness incorporating Basque Hills and some of the adjacent areas. BLM opposes Wilderness for Basque Hills.

*RM36: 980,000**

CATLOW RIM (RINCON) 104,000 acres	
BLM WSA 2-82	104,085

Description: Southeastern Oregon west of Fields. Catlow Rim rises nearly 2,000 feet above the valley floor and hosts one of the highest raptor concentrations in Oregon on its west-facing cliffs. The rim, reaching 6,350 feet on Square Mountain in the north, is broken by canyons and springs. In the southern portion of the unit, Lone Mountain rises to 6,903 feet in elevation and has rock outcroppings of rhyodacitic rock forming pinnacles, columns, and natural bridges. The tables are ringed with rimrock. The lowest elevation is 4,450 feet, in Catlow Valley. Vegetation is primarily the Big Sagebrush–Bunchgrass community with numerous grass species. Low Sagebrush and Black Sagebrush communities also occur. A small area of Western Juniper and mountain mahogany is found on Lone Mountain. Over two thousand Pronghorn sometimes winter in the southeastern portion of the area. Sage Grouse and other birds and mammals typical of the sagebrush steppe are present. Bighorn Sheep may be reintroduced. There are a couple of important archaeological sites—Catlow Cave (a well-known Paleo-Indian site) and an area with a concentration of rock art.

Status: The primary threat is the construction of "improvements" for the welfare ranchers in the area, including pipelines, fences, stock tanks, and Crested Wheatgrass seedings—all at taxpayer expense, all so more cattle can destroy the vegetation and wildlife of the area. It should be part of a 3-million-acre Oregon Desert National Wilderness Park (see Alvord Desert). ONRC includes this area in its 524,300-acre Oregon Grasslands Wilderness proposal. BLM opposes Wilderness here.

*RM36: 980,000**

HAWKSIE-WALKSIE 144,000 acres (also in Nevada)	
Sheldon National Wildlife Refuge roadless (Big Table, NV)	71,000
BLM WSA 1-146 (Hawk Mountain, OR)	73,340

Description: Extreme northwestern Nevada and southeastern Oregon west of Denio, Nevada. This high sagebrush steppe on the basaltic mesa of Big Spring Table includes a major wintering area for the Oregon-Nevada Interstate Pronghorn herd. Other wildlife includes Coyote, Mountain Lion, Mule Deer, Bobcat, Peregrine Falcon, and nesting Prairie Falcon. Numerous Sage Grouse strutting grounds are present. Feral horses roam the area as well. Bunchgrasses and other grasses are in fairly good condition, making this an important area for preservation. There are scattered Western Juniper and one stand of mountain mahogany. Big Spring Butte is the high point on the Refuge, at 6,547 feet, while Hawk Mountain in Oregon reaches 7,234 feet. Hawksie-Walksie itself is a dry lake basin that fills with water in the spring, attracting waterfowl. It is the low point, at 5,600 feet. This is a cold desert with a very short frost-free period, wide summer temperature swings of 50 degrees between night and day, and precipitation varying from 5 inches to 15 inches annually, mostly in snow and winter rain.

Status: Threats include Crested Wheatgrass seedings, increased livestock use, and "improvements" to allow the "slow elk" to "more effectively utilize the resource."

Conservationists propose 92,000 acres of Wilderness on the Refuge by closing minor dirt roads. The FWS proposes 65,500 acres for Wilderness, and BLM proposes 69,640, for a total agency proposal of 135,000 acres. This area is separated from the Catlow Rim and Basque Hills roadless areas by minor dirt roads, and should be part of a 3-million-acre Oregon Desert National Wilderness Park. ONRC includes the Oregon BLM lands in its 524,300-acre Oregon Grasslands Wilderness.

*RM36: 980,000**

DIABLO MOUNTAIN 142,000 acres	
BLM WSA 1-58	114,930
Summer Lake State Wildlife Management Area roadless	8,000
Private roadless (Summer Dry Lake)	19,000

Description: South-central Oregon north of Lakeview. Encompassing Summer Lake playa (4,146 feet) and adjacent salt flats and sand dunes, this area rises 1,800 feet above the desert to the east. Rimrock sets off Diablo Mountain. A vegetative transition from salt desert shrub (Black Greasewood, Spiny Hopsage, Shadscale, Budsage, Horsebrush, Desert Saltgrass, and many wildflowers) to sagebrush communities occurs here. Bighorn Sheep may be reintroduced. Wildlife also includes Pronghorn, Mule Deer, and other species typical of the Great Basin. The Snowy Plover, a candidate for federal Endangered or Threatened species listing, is present.

Status: Threats include geothermal development, ORVs, and continued overgrazing. ONRC proposes a 484,500-acre Wilderness by closing dirt roads that currently divide this roadless area from adjacent roadless country. BLM proposes 85,150 acres as Wilderness.

RM36: 540,000

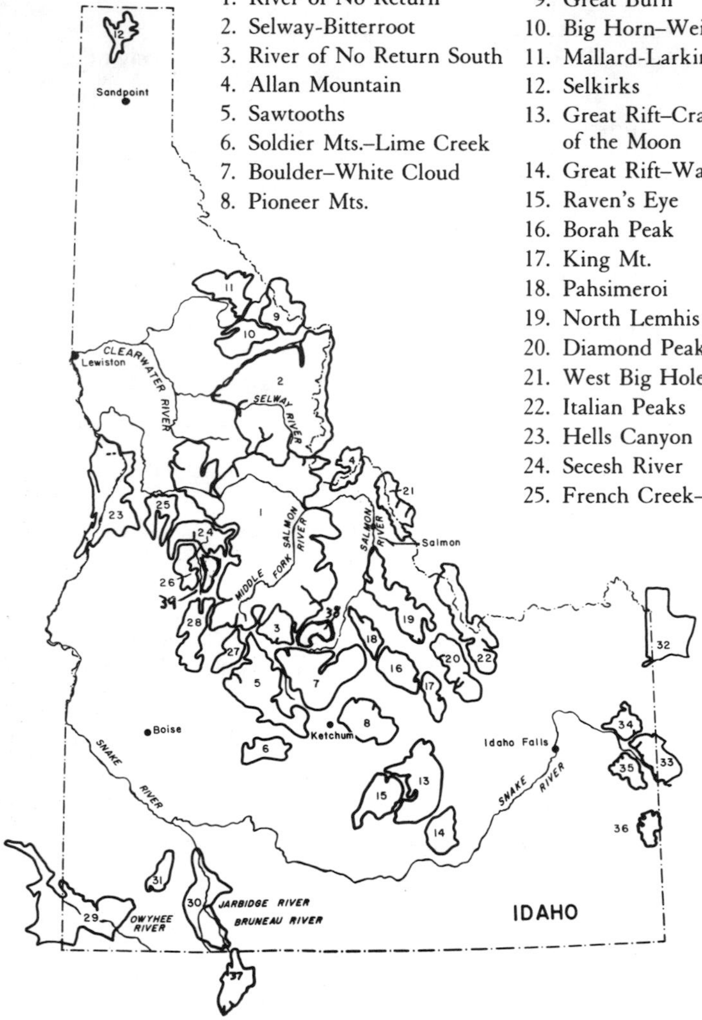

1. River of No Return
2. Selway-Bitterroot
3. River of No Return South
4. Allan Mountain
5. Sawtooths
6. Soldier Mts.–Lime Creek
7. Boulder–White Cloud
8. Pioneer Mts.
9. Great Burn
10. Big Horn–Weitas
11. Mallard-Larkins
12. Selkirks
13. Great Rift–Craters of the Moon
14. Great Rift–Wapi
15. Raven's Eye
16. Borah Peak
17. King Mt.
18. Pahsimeroi
19. North Lemhis
20. Diamond Peak (South Lemhis)
21. West Big Hole
22. Italian Peaks
23. Hells Canyon
24. Secesh River
25. French Creek–Patrick Butte
26. Needles
27. Red Mt.
28. Peace Rock
29. Owyhee Canyons
30. Bruneau-Jarbidge Rivers
31. Jacks Creek
32. Bechler-Pitchstone
33. Palisades
34. Garns Mt.
35. Bear Creek
36. Stump Creek
37. Jarbidge
38. Squaw Creek
39. Caton Lake

Idaho

Idaho is the Wilderness State, not the Potato State. True, Idaho spud growers dominate parts of southern and southeastern Idaho, but north, east, and west of the spuds is a diverse wilderness that can be described only in superlatives. For example, as a percentage of its land base, Idaho has more wilderness (designated and de facto) than any other of the contiguous states. Outside of Alaska, the nation's largest designated Wilderness Area (or wildland unit of any kind) is almost wholly within Idaho—the Frank Church–River of No Return Wilderness. The two longest true wilderness rivers in the contiguous states, the Salmon and Selway, are also in Idaho. Idaho has the largest expanse of virgin forest in the lower forty-eight states, in addition to its splendid wild deserts. And Idaho's National Forests include more unprotected de facto wilderness than any other state: over 9 million vulnerable acres. Despite the spuds, Idaho is above all else a land of untamed mountains, forests, rivers, canyons, and deserts.

The natural bioregions of Idaho are defined by three major areas: (1) the arid and semiarid plains and deserts of the south, including the Snake River Plain; (2) the eastern fringe mountains, part of the Greater Yellowstone Wildland complex; and (3) wild central and northern Idaho—an unbelievable expanse of mountains, forests, rivers, and canyons.

Within the arid south are the volcanic wilds of the Great Rift–Craters of the Moon country; in the far southwest, the remote Owyhee canyons, deserts, and mountains. Within these areas are huge chunks of desert wilderness, equal in rugged wild grandeur to any of the nation's better-known desert wildlands to the south. Nonetheless, it is the mountainous wilds of central and northern Idaho that really define this state. Particularly in this region, Idaho still presents the opportunity to protect big, ecologically complete wilderness representing all or most of its native ecosystems.

The native ecosystems of much of the Snake River Plain and the upper Snake River Valley, though, have been obliterated and replaced with agriculture. Much of this part of southern Idaho was once a fertile intermountain grassland, rich in Bison, Elk, Pronghorn, Sandhill Crane, Long-billed Curlew, Bald Eagle, Trumpeter Swan, and numerous other species now either regionally extinct or reduced to fragmented remnant populations.

In the mountains of central and northern Idaho, however, viable populations of most of the native species survive. Even Gray Wolves and Grizzlies are hanging on in parts of this region (not as viable populations, but as scattered individuals), and the mountains of central Idaho are one of the great strongholds of the Mountain Lion. A remnant population of Woodland Caribou has recently been augmented with reintroductions in the far north. This Endangered subspecies of Caribou once ranged south nearly to the Salmon River, and they, like Grizzlies and Gray Wolves, should be reintroduced to the Selway-Bitterroot Wilderness and adjacent wildlands of the Clearwater and Panhandle National Forests. Concurrently, various roads should be closed: The closure of one dirt road—the Magruder Corridor—would unite the River of No Return (RNR) and Selway-Bitterroot Wildernesses into a single 5-million-acre unit; to the north, the closure of a few lightly used dirt logging roads on the Clearwater and Panhandle National Forests would mean a Wilderness unit of roughly a million acres. With these road closures, the core of Idaho would consist of million-acre or nearly million-acre Wildernesses all the way from the desert lava flows near Craters of the Moon National Monument to the wet northern panhandle. Indeed, although today's Idaho wilderness is immense by modern standards, the potential for ecologically whole multimillion-acre future Wildernesses is staggering!

The standard things threaten Idaho wilderness. Forest Service–sponsored logging and road building top the list, but hard-rock mining runs a close second, especially in various areas around and within the fringes of the RNR. ORVs, subdivisions, hobby trapping, and other threats can't be ignored either. In the Great Rift and Owyhee country, entrenched welfare ranching is the primary threat, as well as the main roadblock to eventual Wilderness designation.

Thus far, Congress has failed to enact post–RARE II Wilderness legislation for Idaho and Montana. Although Idaho's two House members, Richard Stallings and Larry LaRocco, are both Democrats with little apparent interest in the wilderness issue, its two senators, Steve Symms (soon to retire) and Larry Craig, are both right-wing Republican anti-Wilderness zealots of the Simpson and Wallop mode (see Wyoming introduction). Fortunately, both senators are fairly inept and neither is taken very seriously by his colleagues. Unfortunately, though, Idaho's governor, Democrat Cecil Andrus, has joined the anti-Wilderness brigade. In 1988, he teamed with now-retired Senator Jim McClure to promote a Wilderness release bill that would have sanctioned the development of over 7 million acres of Idaho's unprotected National Forest wildlands. Only a few scattered areas of high-altitude rock and ice would have been protected. The bill was so bad that it was opposed by moderates in Congress as well as by conservation groups, and it was stopped cold. Nonetheless, the assault on wild Idaho by bulldozers and chain saws continues, justified by BLM and Forest Service land management plans, and opposed by few conservationists. In fact, with the notable exception of the Alliance for the Wild Rockies (see Montana) and a couple of sportsmen's groups, Idaho conservation groups continue to propose only about half of the state's unprotected wildlands for Wilderness. Unless the Forest Service, the BLM, and their industry and congressional cohorts of calamity can be stopped, Idaho will indeed become the Potato State.

Central Idaho

Central Idaho is, quite simply, the wild heart of the largest complex of temperate-zone wildlands remaining in North America and perhaps anywhere on Earth. Lacking the name recognition of the Greater Yellowstone, although dwarf-

ing it in sheer size, the Central Idaho Wildland Complex includes both designated and de facto wildernesses in the Big Hole and Bitterroot drainages of far western Montana, and in the Hells Canyon and Wallowa Mountains region of eastern Oregon. The complex extends from the Great Rift in the south through the Mallard-Larkins roadless area in the northern Panhandle of Idaho. Nowhere in the temperate world is there a more stupendous and diverse concentration of wildlands than here: from desert to tundra; from open, parklike stands of Ponderosa Pine to moist conifer forests rife with disjunct Pacific rain forest species; from mile-deep (and deeper) river canyons to rolling plateaus of forest and meadow.

At the core of the Central Idaho Wildland Complex is a geologic formation known as the Idaho Batholith. A huge granitic intrusion, 70–80 million years old and roughly 60 miles wide by over 200 miles long along a north-south axis, the batholith constitutes a gigantic, often mountainous upland, dissected by the Salmon, Selway, Clearwater, and St. Joe river systems, and partially smoothed, gouged, and accentuated by Pleistocene glaciers. To the geologist, central Idaho is the batholith. To the ecologist and the Wilderness activist, the batholith defines the true Central Idaho Wildland Ecosystem, the core of the sprawling wildland complex.

RIVER OF NO RETURN 3,253,000 acres (also in Montana)	
Designated River of No Return Wilderness Area (Bitterroot, Boise, Challis, Nezperce, Payette, and Salmon NFs)	2,316,000
Designated Gospel Hump Wilderness Area (Nezperce NF)	207,000
Additional Bitterroot, Boise, Challis, Nezperce, Payette, and Salmon NFs roadless to RNR	660,000
Additional Nezperce NF roadless contiguous to Gospel Hump	70,000

Description: Central Idaho and extreme western Montana between Salmon and McCall. This is the largest designated Wilderness and the largest roadless area in the lower forty-eight states. It is extremely diverse, ranging from semiarid grass and brushlands at 2,000 feet along the lower Main Salmon River to alpine summits over 10,000 feet in the Bighorn Crags. In general, the Wilderness is distinguished by extensive coniferous forest, scattered meadows, and open, grassy slopes breaking into steep, rugged canyons. The RNR is probably the largest temperate-climate wilderness in the world, and it forms the core of what is probably the largest complex of temperate-zone wildlands on Earth. Along with adjacent parts of the neighboring Selway-Bitterroot Wilderness, the RNR—especially its northern half—includes the largest tract of unlogged virgin forest remaining in temperate America.

Known for its large population of Mountain Lions, the RNR's wildlife also includes Marten, Fisher, Lynx, Bobcat, Coyote, Red Fox, Mule and White-tailed Deer, Elk, Moose, Mountain Goat, Bighorn Sheep, Black Bear, Wolverine, and numerous raptors. In 1984, a population of Boreal Owls was found deep in the RNR, well south of what had been thought their exclusively Canadian geographic range. A small number of individual Gray Wolves may move through the area. Expansive areas of big game winter range are entirely within the Wilderness. The major forest type is Douglas-fir. Other important tree species are Ponderosa Pine, Lodgepole Pine, Engelmann Spruce, and Subalpine Fir, with some Western Larch, Grand Fir, and Alpine Larch in the wetter northern and western parts of the Wilderness. *Penstemon lemhiensis* (Scrophulariaceae), which is now vulnerable to extinction, probably survives in the proposed Bluejoint (Montana) addition.

The rugged canyons of the Middle Fork and main Salmon are very popular for float trips, and are among the deepest and most spectacular canyons on Earth. They are renowned for their endangered Chinook Salmon and Steelhead fisheries.

Status: Timbering threatens the contiguous roadless areas, particularly on the Salmon, Payette, and Nezperce NFs. The imminent Cove timber sale (Nezperce NF) would demolish 20,000 acres of contiguous roadless land above the Salmon River, just outside the RNR Wilderness boundary, near the Gospel Hump. Hard-rock mining is occurring in cherrystem exclusions in the RNR Wilderness and is proposed with road construction inside the actual Wilderness near Big Creek. Gold mining threatens the proposed 66,000-acre Bluejoint addition in Montana. Mining threats are extensive around the entire periphery of the RNR and in the "Special Mining Management Zone" in the designated Wilderness on the Salmon NF. A young but rapidly spreading infestation of Spotted Knapweed (native to Eurasia) threatens to choke out natural grasslands in the Salmon River canyon. Grandfathered use of numerous airstrips and of jetboats on the Main Salmon River should be phased out. ("Grandfathered use" refers to legislation—grandfather clauses—that allows previously existing but otherwise incompatible use to continue in an area after it is designated as Wilderness.) Illegal outfitter "camps" include cabins and lodges. Some have been recently constructed in the designated Wilderness! The Wilderness Area is poorly administered by the FS, which divides management responsibility between different National Forest and Ranger Districts.

Closure of the mostly dirt Magruder Corridor road (northern boundary) and addition of adjacent roadless lands would unite the RNR and the Selway-Bitterroot Wilderness into a single Wilderness of nearly 5 million acres. Except for the Salmon River Breaks link between the RNR and Gospel Hump, the Idaho Wildlands Defense Coalition has proposed zero additions to the RNR in its statewide Wilderness proposal. The Coalition should be encouraged to propose the addition of all contiguous roadless lands to the Wilderness, and to defend those lands. Reintroduction of Grizzly Bear and Gray Wolf would create a more biologically complete central Idaho Wilderness ecosystem.

The increase of acreage for this roadless area is due to the upward revision of the FS figure for designated Wilderness acreage. There has, however, been a decline in roadless acreage in surrounding unprotected NF lands.

RM36: 4,800,000 RM27: 7,668,480**

SELWAY-BITTERROOT 1,858,000 acres (also in Montana)	
Designated Selway-Bitterroot Wilderness Area (Bitterroot, Clearwater, Nezperce, and Lolo NFs)	1,338,000
Additional Nezperce and Clearwater NFs (ID) roadless	400,000
Bitterroot NF roadless (MT)	115,000
Contiguous state and private roadless	5,000

Description: Central Idaho and western Montana southwest of Missoula, Montana. Except along the classically rugged and glacially carved crest of the Bitterroots, most of the Wilderness is characterized by high ridges dropping off to deep canyons clothed in a dense mantle of coniferous forest. This tremendously diverse area also includes low valleys with old-growth stands of Western Red Cedar, Grand Fir, Douglas-fir, Western Larch; forested ridges and rugged granite peaks; extensive subalpine spruce-fir forests; and a plethora of subalpine lakes, bogs, and marshes. Rattlesnakes sun themselves on warm slopes at lower elevations. A few stray Grizzlies and Gray Wolves may occasionally roam the Selway-Bitterroot, but there are no viable populations remaining. Elk, Moose, Mountain Goat, Black Bear, Wolverine, Pine

Marten, Pileated Woodpecker, Vaux's Swift, Great Gray Owl, and other species characteristic of the Northern Rockies thrive in healthy numbers. One of the biggest Elk herds in the United States is here. The proposed Sheephead-Watchtower addition, along with the nearby proposed Bluejoint addition to the RNR, is habitat for a genetically pure population of Rocky Mountain Bighorn Sheep. This population has never been augmented with genetic material from elsewhere, which makes this population rare for the species.

Status: Much of the area outside the Wilderness is severely threatened by timber sales, including the potential Elk Summit addition, which has the densest Moose population in Idaho. This huge area is separated from the more than 3-million-acre River of No Return Wilderness only by the Magruder Corridor road to the south. Shutting down this road would unite the Selway-Bitterroot and RNR into a single 5-million-acre Wilderness.

As in the RNR, Gray Wolf and Grizzly Bear should be reintroduced (or augmented) in order to assure viable populations. This is former habitat for the Woodland Caribou, which should also be reintroduced. High in the Bitterroots, a number of small dams on the outlets of numerous natural lakes should be removed.

It is interesting to note that in 1963, prior to the enactment of the 1964 Wilderness Act, the Forest Service declassified nearly 500,000 acres from the Selway-Bitterroot Primitive Area in order to open wild forestlands to loggers. Although the Central Idaho Wilderness bill of 1980 reinstated about 100,000 acres to the Wilderness, the "protected" Selway-Bitterroot Wilderness is still smaller than it was when Bob Marshall secured administrative protection for it in 1936. (Marshall's protection came in the nick of time—a competing plan within the Forest Service during the mid-1930s for "truck trail" construction would have chopped up the entire Selway-Bitterroot to the extent that the largest remaining roadless area would have been less than 100,000 acres!)

RM36: 4,800,000 RM27: 7,668,480**

RIVER OF NO RETURN SOUTH 158,000 acres	
Designated River of No Return Wilderness Area (Challis NF)	45,000
Additional Challis NF roadless	113,000

Description: Central Idaho north of Stanley. The southern lobe of the RNR is separated from the main RNR by a dirt road loop. Alpine peaks here reach

10,000 feet, and clear subalpine lakes adorn the upper Loon Creek drainage. Roaring streams, deep canyons, and lakes pervade the area. This is an important link between the main RNR and the Sawtooth complex to the south. It is not widely known that this area is separated from the main RNR.

Status: The area outside the Wilderness is threatened by timbering and hard-rock mining. It was proposed for "Reserved Status" by the Idaho Wildlife Federation, but not proposed for protection by the Idaho Conservation League. Only Earth First! and the Alliance for the Wild Rockies are supporting additional Wilderness here.

*RM27: 7,668,480**

ALLAN MOUNTAIN 164,000 acres (also in Montana)

See Montana for description and status.

SAWTOOTHS 800,000 acres

Designated Sawtooth Wilderness Area (Boise, Sawtooth, and Challis NFs)	217,088
Additional Boise, Sawtooth, and Challis NFs roadless	583,000

Description: Central Idaho northwest of Ketchum. This rich area is nationally known for rugged peaks, alpine lakes, and stunning scenery. Extensive conifer forests of spruce, fir, Douglas-fir, Ponderosa Pine, and Lodgepole Pine sprawl across lower elevations. The designated Wilderness is heavily used by recreationists, but the use of adjacent roadless areas is light. Mountain Goat, Puma, Black Bear, Lynx, Marten, Elk, and deer inhabit the area. The Smokey Mountains are a major stronghold for Wolverine. The headwaters of the South Fork Payette and the South and Middle Forks of the Boise Rivers have important fisheries. Elevations rise from about 4,000 feet to nearly 11,000 feet; the area includes most of two major mountain ranges—the Sawtooths and the lower, less-rugged, and more heavily vegetated Smokey Mountains (which contain numerous geothermal features). The striking eastern escarpment of the Sawtooths rises above Stanley Basin, one of the coldest places in the lower forty-eight states. Winter temperatures often break 50 degrees below zero.

Status: The existing Wilderness is a textbook "Wilderness on the Rocks." Nearly all of the important wildlife habitat is in the adjacent but unprotected roadless country that includes the Smokey Mountains. The FS recommended only 150,000 acres for Wilderness in RARE II, and parts of the area are threatened by timber sales. State conservation groups are recommending only 320,000 acres of Wilderness additions. In a classic demonstration of "sensitive" Forest Service management, ORV use is being permitted in areas where studies of the rare and elusive Wolverine are ongoing.

RM36: 820,000 RM27: 1,130,240

SOLDIER MOUNTAINS–LIME CREEK 135,000 acres	
Sawtooth NF roadless	100,000
BLM and private roadless	10,000
Boise NF roadless	25,000

Description: South-central Idaho northwest of Fairfield. The Soldiers are a subrange of the Boise Mountains and separated from them by the South Fork of the Boise River. This roadless area is immediately south of the greater Sawtooth–Smokey Mountains roadless area. Elevations range from 4,400 feet along the South Fork of the Boise River to 10,095 feet atop Smokey Dome. This part of the Idaho Batholith rises above the "Camas Prairie" to the south. The steep drainages, high ridges, and peaks of this area provide winter and summer habitat for deer and Elk. Sagebrush-grassland dominates with scattered stands of Aspen, Douglas-fir, Lodgepole Pine, and other conifers. Lime Creek is a superb trout fishery.

Status: The FS inventoried only 14,000 acres of this area in RARE II and recommended it for non-Wilderness. Idaho conservationists recommend 90,000 acres for Wilderness. A few cherrystem roads intrude from the east and should be closed. Threats to this overlooked area include logging, mining, and ORVs.

SQUAW CREEK 116,000 acres	
Challis NF roadless	108,000
BLM and private roadless	8,000

Description: Central Idaho just west of Challis. This is an amoeba-shaped roadless area separated from the southeast lobe of the vast RNR by just one dirt road. Elevations range from 5,500 feet along the Salmon River to 10,314 feet atop Bald Mountain. This is arid and semiarid country with sagebrush-grasslands and slow-growing Douglas-fir as the predominant vegetation, with some pockets of spruce-fir and Lodgepole Pine. Large areas of winter range for Elk, Bighorn, and Mule Deer are within the area.

Status: Mining, livestock, and ORV abuse are the major threats. There isn't much timber. A number of low-grade dirt roads should be closed to make this a more cohesive area.

BOULDER–WHITE CLOUD 545,000 acres	
Sawtooth and Challis NFs roadless (some private)	475,000
BLM roadless	70,000

Description: Central Idaho north of Ketchum. This is the largest unprotected National Forest roadless area in the contiguous United States. Castle Peak in the White Clouds is 11,820 feet. This area is extremely diverse: Mountain Goat, Pika, and marmot thrive on the craggy peaks and in the numerous glacial lake basins; Black Bear, Elk, Fisher, and Wolverine grace its conifer forests and meadows; "wild" horses, Pronghorn, Sage Grouse, and White-tailed Jackrabbit abound on the dry sagebrush-grasslands (BLM-administered) of the east slope, which drops to 6,000 feet. Quaking Aspen groves are common in moist pockets in the foothills. Oceangoing Chinook Salmon and Steelhead spawn in east side streams. The spectacular Boulder and White Cloud Mountains are very popular for recreationists, but the drier east slope is the best wildlife habitat.

Status: Much of the Forest Service land is in the Sawtooth National Recreation Area, and the Forest Service is studying only 283,750 acres for possible Wilderness designation. Nearly all of that acreage is—you guessed it—alpine and subalpine terrain. An ASARCO proposal to mine Castle Peak in the early 1970s instigated the big brouhaha that resulted in the National Recreation Area. There are numerous ORV conflicts throughout the area. Overgrazing is a major problem, especially on the BLM lands. A few unnecessary low-grade dirt roads could be closed and rehabilitated to increase the roadless acreage to nearly 700,000 acres.

PIONEER MOUNTAINS 255,000 acres	
Challis and Sawtooth NFs roadless	230,000
BLM roadless	25,000

Description: South-central Idaho east of Ketchum. Idaho's second-highest mountain range has rugged glacial canyons, tarns, dense coniferous forests, meadows, and abundant wildlife, including Mule Deer, Elk, Mountain Goat, and Black Bear. Elevations range from 6,000 feet to 12,078 feet atop Hyndman Peak. With picture-perfect glaciated mountain terrain, this is a popular area for hiking, fishing, and hunting. Only one dirt road separates the Pioneers from the Boulder–White Cloud roadless area.

Status: The FS recommended only 106,000 acres in the western half of the range for Wilderness in RARE II. Local wilderness support is strong. Some marginal timber sales and ORV use threaten the area.

Northern Idaho

For our purposes, northern Idaho includes the wet "Panhandle" (bordering Canada)—represented here by the Selkirks—and the northern end of the Idaho Batholith—represented by the Great Burn, Mallard-Larkins, and Bighorn-Weitas areas. These three areas constitute the northernmost extension of the great Central Idaho Wildlands Complex.

GREAT BURN 275,000 acres (also in Montana)	
Lolo and Clearwater NFs roadless	275,000

Description: Northern Idaho and northwestern Montana west of Missoula, Montana. This northern portion of the Bitterroot Mountains was burned in the Great Fire of August 20–22, 1910. Deep valley pockets of old-growth cedar and hemlock escaped the fire. High subalpine cirques, meadows, impressive stands of Mountain Hemlock, and crystal-clear lakes are along the crest. Precipitation is heavy. Forested ridges are in various stages of ecological succession. One of the largest Elk herds in the Northern Rockies lives here, there is a good population of Mountain Goat, and Grizzly Bear and Gray Wolf have been sighted. Over 5,000 Elk winter in the Great Burn and adjacent Bighorn-Weitas area. Kelly and Cayuse are river-size creeks on the Idaho side and are blue-ribbon trout streams. These streams and their tributaries also provide good habitat for Harlequin Duck. This is one of the largest and wildest unprotected roadless areas in the country.

Status: The FS recommended only 178,000 acres for Wilderness in RARE II and now has extensive plans for logging, including along tributaries of

Kelly Creek. The Montana slope of the area has become a major focus of anti-Wilderness welfare loggers. Popular support for Wilderness is high. Any Wilderness bill that releases parts of the Great Burn should be vigorously resisted!

*RM27: 7,668,480**

BIGHORN-WEITAS 240,000 acres	
Clearwater NF roadless	240,000

Description: Northern Idaho east of Moscow. High ridges, steep canyons, pellucid streams, montane and subalpine forests characterize the area. Elevations generally are 3,000–6,000 feet. Cayuse Creek is a blue-ribbon trout stream. Sightings of Gray Wolf have been reported. Along with the Mallard-Larkins, Meadow Creek, and the Great Burn, this area is a major component of the northernmost wild areas of the Central Idaho–Western Montana Wilderness Complex.

Status: The FS recommended this area for non-Wilderness in RARE II, and the entire area is threatened by timber sales. A number of cherrystem dirt roads intrude into the area. They should be closed and rehabilitated. The closure of a few additional dirt logging roads would allow the combination of the Bighorn-Weitas with the Mallard-Larkins, Great Burn, and Meadow Creek areas for a roadless area of 900,000 acres!

*RM27: 7,668,480**

MALLARD-LARKINS 285,000 acres	
Clearwater and Idaho Panhandle NFs roadless	268,000
Private roadless	17,000

Description: Northern Idaho east of Moscow. On the west slope of the northern Bitterroot Range (sometimes known as the St. Joe Mountains), this area of subalpine and montane forest straddles the high divide between the Clearwater and St. Joe river drainages. The upper St. Joe River is designated Wild and Scenic. Features of this area include glacial cirques, U-shaped canyons, three subalpine lake basins, extensive Lodgepole Pine and Mountain Hemlock forests, and pockets of old-growth Western Red Cedar, Western Hemlock, and Western White Pine in the valleys. Cutthroat and Rainbow

Trout are abundant. Elk, Mule and White-tailed Deer, Black Bear, and Moose are common. Prime Gray Wolf habitat makes this an ideal reintroduction site. The Mountain Goat herd is very productive and is used for transplants to other areas. Pileated Woodpeckers thrive in the old growth. Northern Bog Lemming (*Synaptomys borealis*) may inhabit the area. The Idaho Fish and Game Department rates the Mallard-Larkins and Great Burn areas as *the* most important unprotected roadless areas in the state for wildlife. The areas are popular for hunting, fishing, and backpacking.

Status: The FS recommended 156,000 acres for Wilderness in RARE II. Below-cost (welfare) timber sales threaten much of the area. Burlington Northern "owns" 17,000 acres of "checkerboarded" land here, largely in the Canyon Creek area. This critical Elk habitat is the focus of a land exchange proposed by Idaho Fish and Game. All Idaho conservation groups, plus Fish and Game, support Wilderness for all or most of the area. This may be the most controversial roadless area in Idaho, pitting local logging interests and the FS against conservationists in a classic logging vs. Wilderness battle. On the east, the Meadow Creek roadless area, under 100,000 acres, along the northern Bitterroot Divide is a vital link between the Mallard-Larkins and Great Burn roadless areas. The FS wants to log this area, too.

*RM27: 7,668,480**

SELKIRKS 155,000 acres	
Idaho Panhandle NF roadless	115,000
Priest State Forest and private roadless	40,000

Description: Extreme northern Idaho west of Bonners Ferry. This rugged, glaciated mountain range receives high precipitation. The crest consists of subalpine cirques, lakes, and rugged alpine peaks draped in perennial snowfields. Long Canyon, an 18-mile-long glacial valley and the last remaining unlogged wild canyon emanating from the Selkirk Crest, is filled with outstanding intermediate and old-growth disjunct Pacific rain forest of Western Red Cedar, Western Hemlock, Western Larch, Douglas-fir, Grand Fir, and Western White Pine. Long Canyon is extremely important habitat for old-growth–dependent species. Spruce-fir forest is at the higher elevations. The only remnant bands of Woodland Caribou in the lower forty-eight states are in the Selkirks; they are being supplemented with Caribou from British Columbia as part of the National Woodland Caribou Recovery effort. The

Selkirks also contain rich Grizzly Bear habitat that has supported a small population of Grizzly up to the present day. Other species include Moose, White-tailed Deer, Mountain Goat, Northern Bog Lemming, Northern Goshawk, and Harlequin Duck. Along with the Mallard-Larkins, this is the easternmost extension of habitat for the Pacific Giant Salamander (*Dicamptodon ensatus*).

Status: The FS inventoried 105,000 acres in RARE II and recommended only the crest for Wilderness (22,875 acres). Logging is proposed for Long Canyon. The west slope of the range is the Priest State Forest, and a narrow area along the western crest is managed as a roadless area by the state to complement the FS high-altitude rock-and-ice Wilderness proposal. Much of the lower slope of the state forest has been logged. Long Canyon is *the* critical component of the area.

South-central Idaho

Here is a superb group of volcanic high desert wildlands, lying just south of the mountainous Idaho Batholith. This is the southern extension of the vast central Idaho Wilderness Complex.

GREAT RIFT—CRATERS OF THE MOON 463,000 acres	
Designated Craters of the Moon National Monument Wilderness Area	43,243
BLM Great Rift Wilderness Study Area	290,000
Additional BLM and state roadless	130,000

Description: South-central Idaho southwest of Arco. Geologically recent basaltic lava flows constitute the core of this area and are flanked by high desert sagebrush steppe and desert grassland. Isolated "kipukas"—areas within the lava flow but not covered by lava—have received little or no domestic grazing and are rare examples of virgin northern desert scrub grassland. Some plant communities here are unique. Mule Deer, Pronghorn (mostly around the lava flow fringes), Bobcat, Coyote, White-tailed Jackrabbit, Prairie Falcon, and rattlesnakes make this their home. This area, in the shadow of the Pioneer and Lost River Mountains directly to the north and northeast, is an outstanding example of recent geologic activity (between 2,000 and 15,000 years old). Elevations are generally 5,000–6,000 feet.

Status: BLM has recommended 268,000 acres for Wilderness, but the proposal excludes virtually all of the roadless desert rangelands around the lava flow. Major additions on the east and west sides of the flow would protect important wildlife habitat, especially for Pronghorn. There is growing support for a Craters of the Moon National Park, which would encompass both the Monument and adjacent roadless lands. The Park should include the sagebrush-grasslands around the lava flow, and it should exclude cattle.

GREAT RIFT–WAPI 164,000 acres	
BLM Wilderness Study Area	84,000
Additional BLM, state, and private roadless	80,000

Description: Southern Idaho west of American Falls. Like the Craters of the Moon Flow to the north, the Wapi Lava Flow is a huge area of recent volcanism slowly developing plant and animal communities via primary succession in the basaltic substrate. The Crystal Ice Caves are along the north edge of the unit. The area remains extremely wild, and has isolated kipukas.

Status: BLM has recommended just 73,000 acres for Wilderness. The proposal includes only the lava flow proper and excludes virtually all the high-quality wildlife habitat around the fringes, particularly on the west side. Thus, like the Forest Service, the BLM shows little interest in protecting biological diversity; once again, the bureaucrats propose "Wilderness on the Rocks."

RAVEN'S EYE 263,000 acres	
BLM roadless	263,000

Description: Southern Idaho southeast of Carey. A diverse area of young basaltic lava flows and expansive high desert grasslands and shrub-steppe. Excellent Pronghorn habitat, this little-known area provides substantially better wildlife habitat than the two Great Rift units to the east and southeast. It is an excellent example of the Columbia Plateau geologic province, with flora and fauna characteristic of the northern Great Basin.

Status: BLM proposes new cattle and sheep allotments with intensive grazing systems that would allocate very little forage to wildlife. The Bureau has subdivided the area along a series of primitive Jeep trails into six roadless areas, three of which are Wilderness Study Areas totaling 121,433 acres. This area is virtually unknown and needs a constituency. The Jeep trails should be closed and rehabilitated.

East-central Idaho

This is the eastern portion of the Central Idaho Wildland Complex, extending across the border into southwestern Montana. This is a high and dry land of big open valleys and rugged, narrow mountain ranges.

BORAH PEAK 179,000 acres	
Challis NF roadless	141,000
BLM roadless	38,000

Description: Central Idaho northeast of Ketchum. The central Lost River Range has nine summits over 12,000 feet, including Idaho's highest, 12,665-foot Borah Peak. Stark peaks rise above desert basins on the east and west, making the topography and general character of the land very similar to that of the Great Basin, with some elements of the Northern Rockies. Features of this area include twenty lakes, the only real glacier in Idaho (on the northeast face of Borah Peak); and Pronghorn, Mule Deer, Bighorn Sheep, and Elk. Sagebrush steppe and semidesert grassland rise to alpine tundra, rock and ice, and snowfields through a narrow and discontinuous band of conifers.

Status: The FS currently recommends 116,000 acres for Wilderness; 25,000 acres of adjacent BLM land are a Wilderness Study Area. There is virtually no timber in the area. Mining and ORVs are the major threats. Cattle grazing has severely degraded many riparian areas throughout the Lost River Range.

KING MOUNTAIN 109,000 acres	
Challis NF roadless	95,000
BLM roadless	14,000

Description: Central Idaho north of Arco. The southern Lost River Range. This unusual semidesert range includes excellent Bighorn Sheep habitat and, on the east slope, unique plant communities. Caves, natural bridges, and archaeological sites including pictographs abound.

Status: The FS recommended the entire NF area for further planning in RARE II, but now proposes at least one timber sale within this high, arid area. ORVs are also a threat.

PAHSIMEROI 130,000 acres	
Challis NF roadless	100,000
BLM roadless	30,000

Description: Central Idaho east of Challis. This is the northern part of Idaho's highest mountain range, the Lost Rivers. Flanked by arid desert valleys, the area ranges from desert sagebrush-grasslands at 5,000 feet to alpine zones reaching 11,085 feet on Grouse Creek Mountain. Gigantic cliffs and rugged valleys distinguish this extremely pristine, little-known and little-used area. Deer, Elk, Bighorn Sheep, and Pronghorn inhabit the area.

Status: The FS recommended 55,000 acres for study in RARE II. Although it is a high, arid area, planned timber sales in small pockets of slow-growing timber threaten it. Such proposed sales lend credence to charges that, as an agency, the Forest Service is collectively insane. The BLM portion is completely unprotected. ORVs and cattle are creating damage.

NORTH LEMHIS 410,000 acres	
Salmon and Challis NFs roadless	360,000
BLM and state roadless	50,000

Description: East-central Idaho south of Salmon. Rugged peaks, glacial canyons, lush meadows, coniferous forests, subalpine lakes, alpine tundra plateaus, and steep, rocky slopes rise above the arid Pahsimeroi and Lemhi valleys. A relatively thin band of conifers (Douglas-fir, Lodgepole Pine, Whitebark Pine, Englemann Spruce, and Subalpine Fir) separates the high desert grassland from the alpine zone. Thickets of mountain mahogany are in the lower canyons. It is important habitat for Black Bear, Mountain Lion, Mountain Goat, Elk, Mule Deer, Bighorn Sheep, Golden Eagle, Red-tailed and Swainson's Hawks, and other Northern Rockies species. Sightings of

Rocky Mountain Gray Wolf have been reported. Hiking, hunting, and fishing are growing in popularity here. The Lemhis, like the Lost Rivers, are biologically and geologically a combination of the Great Basin desert ranges and the Northern Rockies, with an emphasis on the latter.

Status: The FS recommended 280,000 acres for Wilderness in RARE II, but is now opposing *any* Wilderness in the Lemhis. Timber sales threaten some of the lower canyons. An old dirt road for mining exploration could easily be closed, thus uniting the entire Lemhi Range into a single roadless unit of nearly 650,000 acres.

DIAMOND PEAK (SOUTH LEMHIS) 230,000 acres	
Challis and Targhee NFs roadless	185,000
BLM, state, and private roadless	45,000

Description: East-central Idaho northeast of Idaho Falls. The South Lemhi Mountains rise abruptly from the arid Birch Creek and Little Lost River valleys as a striking escarpment roughly 40 miles in length. This area is not as well watered as the northern part of the range, and there are few perennial streams. Components include open grassland with pockets and stringers of Douglas-fir and Lodgepole Pine, steep slopes, rugged peaks, giant limestone cliffs, and glacial cirques at the crest. Diamond Peak is the third-highest in Idaho, at 12,197 feet. Some mountain grasslands have never been grazed by livestock. Archaeological sites are scattered throughout the area. Wildlife is diverse: Pronghorn, Black Bear, Cougar, Mountain Goat, Mule Deer, Bighorn Sheep (recently reintroduced), Elk, and nesting raptors. This area receives very little use.

Status: A RARE II further planning area, the entire area is threatened by oil and gas exploration and development. Much of it is already under lease or lease application. It is also threatened by FS plans to open up virgin grasslands to domestic livestock grazing. The Idaho congressional delegation opposes Wilderness in the Lemhis. Radiation from the adjacent Idaho National Engineering Laboratory (INEL) is a constant threat.

WEST BIG HOLE 215,000 acres (also in Montana)
See Montana for description and status.

ITALIAN PEAKS 360,000 acres (also in Montana)	
Salmon, Targhee, and Beaverhead NFs roadless	300,000
BLM roadless	45,000
State and private roadless	15,000

Description: Idaho-Montana border southwest of Dillon, Montana. This large area runs along the Continental Divide and includes arid to semiarid sagebrush-grassland, pockets of coniferous forest, alpine peaks, a very high and rugged crest (with the highest point in the Beaverhead Range, Eighteen Mile Peak, at 11,141 feet), and large areas of Quaking Aspen. It is excellent habitat for Pronghorn, Elk, Mule Deer, Black Bear, and Golden Eagle.

Status: Except for the Alliance for the Wild Rockies and Earth First! (which propose complete protection), conservation groups have recommended only part of the southern half of this large area for Wilderness (95,000 acres); the FS recommended only 56,000 acres in RARE II. The area should be treated as a single unit, not piecemeal because of state and agency boundaries. The Idaho BLM portion particularly needs to be treated as a coherent part of this larger area. Threats include mining, oil and gas, ORVs, and radiation from INEL. Overgrazing is degrading parts of the area. The area is an important "biological connector," allowing wildlife to migrate and disperse between the Greater Yellowstone and Central Idaho Wilderness Ecosystems.

West-central Idaho

This is the western and southwestern edge of the Idaho Batholith, and includes the rugged Hells Canyon of the Snake River country.

HELLS CANYON 563,000 acres (also in Oregon)
See Oregon for description and status.

SECESH RIVER 273,000 acres	
Payette NF roadless	266,000
Private roadless	7,000

Description: Western Idaho northeast of McCall. Adjacent to the western boundary of the River of No Return Wilderness and part of the Payette Crest complex, the Secesh River and a major portion of the lower South Fork of the Salmon River are within this area of high ridges, cirques, lakes, large subalpine meadows, and extensive stands of Ponderosa Pine and other conifers. It is valuable habitat for Bighorn Sheep, Mountain Goat, Cougar, Black Bear, Elk, Mule Deer, and perhaps a few Gray Wolves. Soils are extremely erosive, as they are throughout the South Fork of the Salmon. The Secesh River is a prime salmon and Steelhead fishery.

Status: This area was only partially inventoried and then subdivided into two widely separated areas by the FS in RARE II. The FS now supports Wilderness for less than half of the area. Timbering plans would destroy the Secesh River watershed.

FRENCH CREEK–PATRICK BUTTE 175,000 acres	
Payette NF roadless	172,000
Private roadless	3,000

Description: Western Idaho northeast of McCall. Biological diversity is high, as volcanic mountains meet the Idaho Batholith. Features include steep river breaks, high ridges, glacial cirques, over fifty lakes, subalpine meadows, unusual rock formations, and dense coniferous forests. French Creek is a major tributary of the Salmon River. The area provides important habitat for Elk, Bighorn Sheep, and other species. This area and the Secesh and Needles roadless areas constitute the Payette Crest, a large complex of completely unprotected wild country along the western edge of the fragile Idaho Batholith.

Status: The FS subdivided this area into two units in RARE II and recommended both for non-Wilderness. Timber sales threaten important Elk calving areas.

NEEDLES 160,000 acres	
Payette NF roadless	157,000
Private roadless	3,000

Description: Western Idaho northeast of McCall, part of the Payette Crest complex. The South Fork of the Salmon River, for which it is a critical watershed, forms the eastern boundary. Steep river breaks, high ridges, lakes, and coniferous forests offer habitat for Bighorn Sheep, Mountain Goat, Cougar, and Black Bear. High, glacially carved terrain includes the pinnacles of the Needles on the roadless area's southern boundary.

Status: The FS plans to log the southern part of the area. Logging on the highly erosive soils of the Idaho Batholith in the 1960s caused extensive damage to the South Fork of the Salmon River salmon and Steelhead fishery. The watershed is slowly recovering, but is threatened anew by FS logging plans.

CATON LAKE 105,000 acres	
Boise NF roadless	55,000
Payette NF roadless	50,000

Description: Western Idaho, northeast of McCall. This little-known area lies between the Needles roadless area and the vast River of No Return country. The South Fork of the Salmon runs along the western boundary. Steep granite ridges and canyons rise to glacial-cut craggy peaks, lakes, and U-shaped canyons. Elk, Mule Deer, Black Bear, Puma, and Bobcat abound. Ponderosa Pine, Douglas-fir, Lodgepole Pine, and some spruce-fir forest cover most of the area. There have been Gray Wolf sightings. Much of the area is a critical watershed for the South Fork of the Salmon River.

Status: This area has been basically ignored by most conservation groups. Despite fragile Idaho Batholith soils and past logging-induced watershed disasters in the South Fork (see Needles above), the FS, like a bull in a china shop, plans extensive logging in this area and elsewhere in the South Fork's watershed. ORVs and mining are also threats. This area was not included in the first edition of *The Big Outside* because of oversight.

RED MOUNTAIN 110,000 acres	
Boise and Challis NFs roadless	110,000

Description: Central Idaho northeast of Boise. Located between the greater Sawtooth Wilderness complex and the RNR Wilderness, the Red Mountain area forms an important watershed for the South Fork of the Payette River, replete with high granite ridges, cirque lakes, deep stream valleys, coniferous forests, and large meadows. Red Mountain reaches 8,733 feet, and the area drops to about 4,400 feet on the South Fork of the Payette. As in other areas in the Idaho Batholith, soils are very unstable. Good habitat for Elk, Mountain Goat, Wolverine, and Black Bear is provided here.

Status: Not included in RARE II because of a completed land use plan, major parts of the area are now threatened by timber sales. Much of the roadless area originally identified in RARE I has already been destroyed by timber sales and road building. ORVs are creating erosion and harassing Mountain Goats.

PEACE ROCK 196,000 acres	
Boise NF roadless	196,000

Description: West-central Idaho northeast of Boise, in the western part of the Idaho Batholith, just southwest of the River of No Return Wilderness. Rugged granite ridges, streams, V-shaped canyons, hot springs, winter range for Elk and Mule Deer, extensive stands of Ponderosa Pine, Douglas-fir, Subalpine Fir, Lodgepole Pine, and other conifers characterize this area. Elevation varies from just over 3,000 feet to nearly 9,000 feet. The largest unprotected roadless area on the Boise NF, it forms an important watershed for the South Fork of the Payette River, South Fork of the Salmon, and the Deadwood. All are being studied for Wild and Scenic River designation.

Status: This area wasn't in RARE II because of a completed land use plan. Its proximity to Boise makes it an increasingly popular recreation area—for ORVs as well as for hikers, hunters, and fishers. Major timber sales are planned, and some logging may have already reduced the size of this area. The Idaho Conservation League proposes only 121,000 acres for Wilderness.

Southwestern Idaho

Southwestern Idaho is part of a high-desert bioregion that includes extreme southeastern Oregon and northern Nevada. The biota represents both the volcanic Columbia Plateau and the Basin and Range Province, most of which lies to the south in arid Nevada.

OWYHEE CANYONS 619,000 acres (also in Oregon)	
BLM roadless with intermixed state and private (ID)	333,000
BLM roadless with intermixed state and private (OR)	286,000

Description: Extreme southwestern Idaho south of Boise and extreme southeastern Oregon. Rising from its headwaters in the high desert of Nevada, Idaho, and Oregon, the Owyhee River and its tributaries cut a stunning complex of deep, steep walled canyons through the basaltic plateaus of the area, making this one of the finest wilderness and wild river complexes in the nation, and offering challenging white-water boating, solitary hiking, and hot springs. Mule Deer, Mountain Lion, River Otter, Beaver, Pronghorn, Redband Trout, Golden Eagle, Bald Eagle, Prairie Falcon, Sage Grouse, Mountain Quail, and many other mammals, birds, and fish find homes here. This is important habitat for the California Bighorn (*Ovis canadensis californiana*), an increasingly rare subspecies listed as "sensitive" by Idaho wildlife officials. The upper Owyhee River system is a rich reproductive area for waterfowl, and eighteen species of ducks and four of geese occur as residents or migrants. Salmon spawned in the Owyhee until downstream dams were built. The plateaus are a mosaic of low sagebrush species, Big Sagebrush, bunchgrasses, and Antelope Bitterbrush. Eight species of sensitive, Threatened, or Endangered plants occur in the area. Scattered stands of juniper dot the northern portion of the area.

Status: Unfortunately, vehicle "ways" penetrate this area on the flat sagebrush steppe mesas above the canyons, and there are numerous "range improvements"—all for the benefit of a few welfare ranchers. Moreover, cattle have caused the deterioration of the native bunchgrasses and allowed them to be replaced by exotic and noxious Cheatgrass, and have decimated riparian habitats, nearly eliminating willow, cottonwood, and Aspen, except in tributary canyons.

Determining what is actually a "road" in this area is not easy, but the 619,000-acre figure represents our best judgment. Surrounding this canyon and mesa wilderness are hundreds of thousands of acres of the same kind of landscape in several additional roadless areas separated by minor dirt roads.

Threats to the Owyhee come from the welfare ranchers in the area, whose political clout is grossly out of proportion to their number. They are opposed to any wilderness designation and want more roads and government-funded developments (including the seeding of areas with exotic Crested Wheatgrass after scraping away the sagebrush) for their overgrazing. Small hydro projects are also a possibility, as are mining and power-line construction. A major gas pipeline with pumping stations forms the southeastern boundary of the roadless area.

BLM is proposing a 172,100-acre Wilderness. The Committee for Idaho's High Desert (CIHD) and other conservation groups have recommended a far more visionary Wilderness of 1,189,337 acres in Idaho, Oregon, and Nevada by closing several minor dirt roads. The Oregon Natural Resources Council proposes a 480,020-acre Owyhee Canyonlands Wilderness as part of the Oregon High Desert Protection Act for the Oregon portion of this roadless area. The Owyhee country should be on the top of the agenda for national conservation groups. Areas with minor intrusions for the promotion of ranching in this dry country should be rehabilitated, and livestock grazing prohibited. Much of southwestern Idaho, including the Owyhee, Jacks Creek, and Bruneau-Jarbidge areas, is threatened by proposed Air Force National Guard bombing range expansions. A Wilderness National Park of 8–10 million acres should be established, including the Bruneau-Jarbidge and Jacks Creek river systems, as well as the Owyhee River.

RM36: 4,130,000

BRUNEAU-JARBIDGE RIVERS 350,000 acres	
BLM with intermixed state and private roadless	350,000

Description: Southwestern Idaho south of Mountain Home. The Bruneau and Jarbidge Rivers rise in the high country of Nevada's Humboldt National Forest and Jarbidge Wilderness, and flow north into Idaho, cutting 800-foot-deep canyons for 100 miles through the basaltic plateaus of Idaho's high desert. The free-flowing Bruneau River is a blue-ribbon trout stream; before the downstream dams on the Columbia and Snake were built, it had sturgeon and salmon. It is also a nationally recognized technical white-water run. Wildlife includes deer, Bighorn, Mountain Lion, Bobcat, River Otter, Golden Eagle, Red-tailed Hawk, Great Blue Heron, and rattlesnake. See Owyhee Canyons for general description.

Status: See Owyhee Canyons for general status. Grazing and mining are the primary threats, although geothermal development could dry up the delightful hot springs along the rivers. BLM has proposed three tiny Wildernesses totaling 43,100 acres (canyons only, no benchland included); CIHD and its allies recommend 450,000 acres by closing minor dirt roads.

RM36: 650,000

JACKS CREEK 100,000 acres	
BLM and intermixed state and private roadless	100,000

Description: Southwestern Idaho south of Boise, west of the Bruneau-Jarbidge canyons and northeast of the Owyhee canyons. Similar country to the Owyhee and Bruneau-Jarbidge, this roadless area encompasses an awe-inspiring canyon along Big Jacks Creek. Virgin high-desert grassland on the mesas makes this area extraordinarily important ecologically, in particular for California Bighorn Sheep. It is separated from several hundred thousand acres of similar wild canyon and mesa country by minor dirt roads used for ranching. See Owyhee for general description.

Status: A major battle is brewing here over conservationists' efforts to protect the never-cowed grasslands of this area and the adjacent Little Jacks country. BLM and welfare ranchers in the area propose to exploit the relict grassland communities by building a water pipeline along a dirt road separating the roadless areas so that cattle can have water and graze the area. This must be stopped.

BLM proposes 49,900 acres as Wilderness; CIHD calls for a 265,000-acre Wilderness by closing several minor dirt roads and joining Little Jacks with Big Jacks. This should be part of a large Owyhee Canyons National Park.

JARBIDGE 189,000 acres (also in Nevada)
See Nevada for description and status.

Eastern Idaho

These areas along the Wyoming border are part of the Greater Yellowstone Wildlands Complex; they lie adjacent to a number of other Big Outside units in Yellowstone and Grand Teton National Parks, and the Bridger-Teton National Forest.

BECHLER-PITCHSTONE 468,000 acres (also in Wyoming)
See Wyoming for description and status.

PALISADES 245,000 acres (also in Wyoming)	
See Wyoming for description and status.	

GARNS MOUNTAIN 110,000 acres	
Targhee NF roadless	110,000

Description: Eastern Idaho east of Idaho Falls. This sedimentary range lies across the Pierre's Hole valley from the Teton Range in Wyoming, and is actually a northwestern extension of the Snake River Range (a narrow highway separates it from the Palisades roadless area). Characteristics are stream canyons; coniferous forests interspersed with lush meadows and Quaking Aspen; steep-to-rolling terrain; 5,100–9,000-foot elevations; and Mule Deer, Elk, Moose, and Black Bear. It is known locally as the "Big Hole" Mountains.

Status: Recommended for non-Wilderness by the FS in RARE II, it is threatened by oil and gas development (entire area) and timber sales (northern end). ORVers have recently begun to use the area; the FS should bar them, but instead views them as an "established" use, adding to the Forest Service's anti-Wilderness arguments.

BEAR CREEK 113,000 acres	
Caribou and Targhee NFs roadless	113,000

Description: Southeastern Idaho southeast of Idaho Falls along the Wyoming border adjacent to the Snake River. Rugged ridges and steep stream valleys provide excellent wildlife habitat as a result of a vegetative mosaic of coniferous forest interspersed with big meadows. Douglas-fir, Lodgepole Pine, Engelmann Spruce, Subalpine Fir, and Aspen are common tree species. Excellent winter range, calving, and fawning areas for Moose, Elk, and deer are within the roadless area. Bald Eagle are common along the Snake.

Status: The entire area is part of the "Overthrust Belt" and is severely threatened by oil and gas development. Timber sales are a lesser but real threat. It was recommended for non-Wilderness in RARE II.

STUMP CREEK 103,000 acres	
Caribou NF roadless	103,000

Description: Southeastern Idaho. This area consists of ridges, open valleys, meadows, stands of Quaking Aspen, and scattered patches of coniferous forest. It includes excellent summer range and calving areas for Elk. Moose, Mule Deer, and Black Bear also inhabit the area. The Fine-spotted Snake River Cutthroat Trout, listed as a subspecies of special concern by Idaho Fish and Game, occurs in Stump Creek and in the South Fork of Tincup Creek. Soils are particularly erodible. It is interesting to note that, historically, Caribou never occurred in the Caribou National Forest.

Status: The entire area is severely threatened by oil and gas development. There is little commercial timber. The Caribou City roadless area just to the north comprised over 100,000 acres prior to RARE II, but oil and gas exploration and logging have reduced its size. Like nearly all roadless lands in the "Overthrust Belt," Stump Creek was recommended for non-Wilderness in RARE II. Phosphate mining is also a threat.

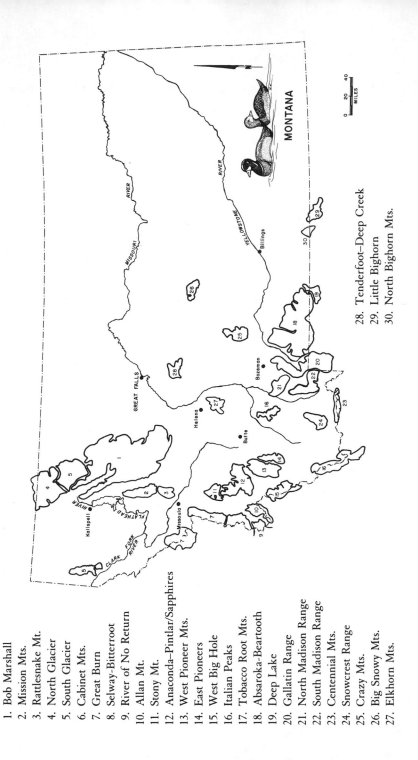

1. Bob Marshall
2. Mission Mts.
3. Rattlesnake Mt.
4. North Glacier
5. South Glacier
6. Cabinet Mts.
7. Great Burn
8. Selway-Bitterroot
9. River of No Return
10. Allan Mt.
11. Stony Mt.
12. Anaconda–Pintlar/Sapphires
13. West Pioneer Mts.
14. East Pioneers
15. West Big Hole
16. Italian Peaks
17. Tobacco Root Mts.
18. Absaroka-Beartooth
19. Deep Lake
20. Gallatin Range
21. North Madison Range
22. South Madison Range
23. Centennial Mts.
24. Snowcrest Range
25. Crazy Mts.
26. Big Snowy Mts.
27. Elkhorn Mts.

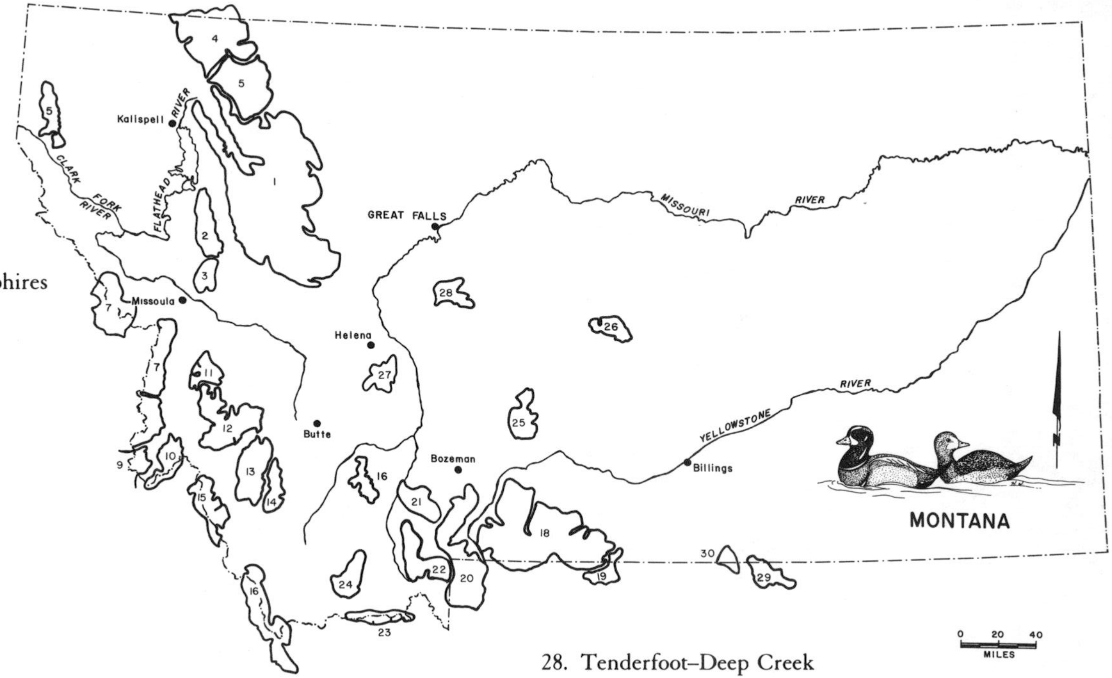

28. Tenderfoot–Deep Creek
29. Little Bighorn
30. North Bighorn Mts.

Montana

Montana is a land of soaring mountains and rolling prairies. Here, the Rocky Mountains rise abruptly above the western edge of the Great Plains in a seemingly endless series of individual ranges. Montana is big, wild, and diverse, and within the perimeter of our fourth-largest state lie major portions of three of the nation's great wildland complexes: the Central Idaho–Western Montana (which includes the River of No Return and Selway-Bitterroot Wildernesses); Greater Yellowstone; and the Northern Continental Divide (which includes Glacier National Park and the Bob Marshall Wilderness region).

Montana can easily be divided into two major bioregions, the Great Plains and the Rocky Mountains. The ironic nature of this state, though, is the duality of landforms within the two bioregions. Rising above the high plains of central and eastern Montana are a number of isolated "island ranges," such as the Big Snowies and the Crazies. And separating many of the major mountain ranges of the state's western third are a series of north-south trending valleys dominated by sagebrush, grass, or both. This diversity of intermingled habitats and climates adds immeasurably to the natural diversity of this awesome and beautiful land.

As with most of the West, big wilderness survives almost exclusively in the high, rugged, spectacular, and cold mountain ranges, which characterize the state's western third. Once again, humanity's penchant for populating the protected valleys and humanity's prejudice against preserving valleys and plains have resulted in an alarming lack of representation of these gentler habitats among the state's protected public lands. True, Montanans can boast about the wild beauty of Glacier National Park, the Bob Marshall and Selway-Bitterroot Wilderness Areas, and the unmatched trout fishing of the Big Hole River. But until restoration efforts reclaim the big wilderness on the plains and in the valleys, Montana Wilderness will remain half a loaf, at best.

Montana's plains and valleys once harbored wildlife in unbelievable abundance. Central and eastern Montana was arguably the richest and most productive prairie ecosystem in North America. Of course, today, the Grizzly, Elk, Gray Wolf, and Black-footed Ferret are gone; the grasses are overgrazed and fenced in; and although much of eastern Montana still is an open and powerful land of big sky and waving grass, it's a tame land.

The Grizzly and wolf are gone even from most of the state's western mountains; so is the Woodland Caribou, once an important inhabitant of the state's heavily forested northwest. The Trumpeter Swan survives only in the vicinity of Red Rocks Lake. Many other species, even in the state's mountain ranges, are endangered and severely depleted. The Northern Bog Lemming and Harlequin Duck are two such imperiled creatures. Even while there is growing sentiment for some kind of large prairie nature reserve in eastern Montana (possibly in the Missouri River Breaks country), habitat destruction on the state's National Forests in western and central Montana continues at a shocking rate. Once again, Forest Service logging and roading are the chief culprits. Which brings us to Montana politics.

Unlike politics in most states in the Rockies, prior to the 1988 elections, Montana politics had generally been dominated by Democrats, particularly in the state's mountainous western third. Its former senior senator, Democrat John Melcher, opposed nearly all sizable Wilderness proposals. Montana's other senator, Max Baucus, and western district Congressman Pat Williams—both of whom purport to be sympathetic to environmental protection—never had the courage to cross Melcher and his deranged views. But now, Melcher is gone. In 1988, his bid for reelection was thwarted by right-wing anti-Wilderness Republican Conrad Burns. Eastern district Representative Ron Marlenee, once the delegation's lone Republican, is an anti-Wilderness extremist of the Wallop-McClure-Hatfield mold. It is already obvious that he and Burns share an anti-Wilderness idiot-ology.

Along with Idaho, Montana continues to lack a post–RARE II Wilderness bill, and like most Western states, it has precious little Wilderness designated in National Parks, or National Wildlife Refuges, or on BLM lands. In 1988, Melcher, Baucus, and Williams agreed on a bad bill that would have protected only 1.4 million out of 6.2 million roadless National Forest acres in the state. The bill would have formally released over 4 million acres of wild country to multiple abuse—although many of those lands are already being logged and roaded with little effective opposition from environmental groups. Ironically, Marlenee may have done Wilderness lovers a favor by helping to convince President Reagan to pocket-veto the awful bill (too much Wilderness for the two Rons). This was the first time a Wilderness bill had been vetoed because it contained too much Wilderness. (Reagan vetoed a Florida Wilderness bill early in his administration because of a spending provision. That provision was removed during the next session of Congress, and Reagan signed the bill.)

In 1990, the Montana Wilderness Association and others negotiated with local loggers the fate of all remaining unprotected wildlands on the Kootenai and Lolo National Forests. The historic "Kootenai and Lolo Accords" would release 400,000 roadless acres on the Lolo, and 94,490 on the Kootenai to logging and road building. Most of these lands are low- and mid-elevation forest, including much old growth, precisely the kind of habitat most in need of protection.

Needless to say, the accords have kindled a bitter debate among conservationists. The Lolo agreement, in particular, would invite biological disaster to the northern Rockies. Increased habitat fragmentation, loss of migratory corridors, loss of old growth, increased erosion and stream sedimentation, and an overall reduction in biological diversity would inevitably result from the enacting of the Lolo Accord.

Other groups, led by the Alliance for the Wild Rockies, are promoting a more visionary approach. Their Northern Rockies Ecosystem Protection Act would protect nearly all remaining roadless lands in Montana, Idaho, northwestern Wyoming, northeastern Oregon, and northeastern Washington. That bill is based upon conservation biology, not politics. Biological corridors for genetic exchange, old-growth protection, and a pilot system of Wilderness

Recovery Areas (implemented by a federal "Wildland Recovery Corps") are included in the bill.

As we go to press, Burns and Baucus have agreed on a bill that would designate 1.1 million acres of steep, high-altitude, rock and ice Wilderness; it would release to loggers over 4 million acres of the best unprotected roadless habitat in Montana's National Forests—in fact, some of the best unprotected roadless habitat in the United States. The past support by conservation groups for a Wilderness alternative of only 2.4 million acres has proved to be ill-advised. Simply put, Montana's remaining National Forest wildlands will continue to be destroyed by the Forest Service and the loggers unless Wilderness advocates can develop stronger support for the protection of all remaining wildlands in the state. All conservation groups should support the Northern Rockies Ecosystem Protection Act. Although isolated pockets of pro-logging, anti-Wilderness greed and ignorance exist, pro-Wilderness hotbeds such as Missoula, as well as Wilderness support elsewhere in the state, make Montana ripe for escalated ecodefense efforts. The politicians and the Forest Service will, no doubt, meet increased resistance to the destruction of wildlands under the Big Sky.

Northern Continental Divide

The Northern Continental Divide Ecosystem (NCDE), although smaller than its two big-sister wildland complexes in the Rockies, the Central Idaho and Greater Yellowstone, is the healthiest big mountain ecosystem in America south of Canada. (See the description below of the Bob Marshall area.) The Bob Marshall Wilderness and Glacier National Park highlight the NCDE, but also included are lands along the Rocky Mountain Front where the Great Plains meet the Rockies, the rugged Mission Mountains, and the Whitefish Range. Although Forest Service–sponsored logging and roading have liquidated big wilderness in the Whitefish Range, this well-watered, Grizzly-rich area (adjacent to the western edge of Glacier Park's north unit) should be a top priority for conservationist efforts to restore at least one unit of big wilderness.

BOB MARSHALL 2,536,000 acres	
Designated Bob Marshall Wilderness Area (Flathead, Lewis and Clark NFs)	1,009,356
Designated Great Bear Wilderness Area (Flathead NF)	286,700
Designated Scapegoat Wilderness Area (Helena, Lewis and Clark, and Lolo NFs)	239,296
Additional Helena, Flathead, Lolo, and Lewis and Clark NFs roadless	940,976
State, private, and BLM roadless	60,000

Description: Northwestern Montana northeast of Missoula. The "Bob" is the most ecologically complete mountain Wilderness in the country and is a key component of the Northern Continental Divide Ecosystem. Rugged peaks, big river valleys (North and South Forks of the Sun, and Middle and South Forks of the Flathead), lakes, large meadows, and extensive coniferous forests characterize this area. The Chinese Wall along the Continental Divide is a well-known landmark. The Rocky Mountain Front Range on the east is relatively dry and open, while the Continental Divide, Flathead, and Swan Ranges receive more precipitation and have dense timber. A healthy Grizzly population ranges down onto the Great Plains from the Rocky Mountain Front (the only place this still occurs). The Bob is our last true stronghold south of Canada for Griz. Every species of mammal indigenous to the Northern Rockies (including a few Gray Wolves) still lives in the Bob Marshall–Glacier National Park bioregion, except for Plains Bison, which formerly roamed the adjacent high plains and lower slopes of the Rocky Mountain Front, and Woodland Caribou, which historically roamed the western side of Glacier National Park and the Whitefish Range along the U.S.-Canadian border. The Bob is noted for huge herds of Elk, Bighorn, and Mountain Goat. Glacier National Park, an International Biosphere Reserve, is adjacent on the north.

Status: The Rocky Mountain Front (outside the small portion with Wilderness protection) is severely threatened by oil and gas exploration. Conservationists are engaged in a major battle as they try to add this area to the Wilderness. The Front is more critical for wildlife than the areas already protected as Wilderness. Ironically, the Front's Deep Creek roadless area received a perfect Wilderness Attribute Rating from the FS in RARE II, despite agency opposition to Wilderness for that area. There's a major ongoing battle to protect the 115,000-acre proposed Badger–Two Medicine addition from oil and gas exploration. Other potential additions on the south and west of the designated Wildernesses are threatened by timbering. The Flathead National Forest allows ORV use in Grizzly habitat; subdivision of adjacent private lands also threatens Grizzly, and ranchers on the plains adjacent to the Front want carte blanche to blow away Grizzlies and Gray Wolves to protect their sheep and cattle. Public support for adding large acreages to the Wilderness is high.

MISSION MOUNTAINS 176,000 acres	
Designated Mission Mountain Wilderness Area (Flathead NF)	73,877
Mission Mountains Tribal Wilderness Area (Flathead Reservation)	89,500
Flathead NF and state roadless	11,000
Private roadless	2,000

Description: Northwestern Montana north of Missoula. The Missions rise abruptly 7,000 feet above the Mission Valley, to the west. Elevations range from 3,500 feet to 9,820 feet atop McDonald Peak. A few miles west of the Bob, the Missions have over two hundred high lakes; jagged peaks; active glaciers; and dense, Pacific Northwest forests of larch, Douglas-fir, Western Red Cedar, spruce, fir, Lodgepole and Ponderosa Pines. Mission and Elizabeth Falls plunge 1,000 feet. A dense but dwindling Grizzly population inhabits the Missions, along with Mountain Goat, Black Bear, deer, Wolverine, Lynx, and other species of the Northern Rockies.

Status: The lower east slope of the Missions has been unbelievably denuded by the Forest Service and private companies, including Champion International and Plum Creek, that "own" thousands of acres of checkerboarded lands within the Flathead and Lolo NFs. The tribal Wilderness extends all the way down the steep west slope to the valley floor and was designated in 1979. Logging and roading on the Swan Valley (east) side are severing the Missions from the rest of the Northern Continental Divide Ecosystem, creating a classic habitat island situation. Unless the destruction is reversed, the Missions will suffer the dramatic loss of biodiversity that the discipline of Insular Ecology (Island Biogeography) has documented for other areas.

RM36: 310,000

RATTLESNAKE MOUNTAINS 101,000 acres	
Designated Rattlesnake Wilderness Area (Lolo NF)	32,844
Rattlesnake National Recreation Area roadless (Lolo NF)	22,000
Additional Lolo NF roadless	10,156
South Fork Tribal Primitive Area (Flathead Reservation)	36,000

Description: Only 4 miles north of Missoula. High north-south ridges have steep east-facing cirques and gentler western slopes. There are over thirty high mountain lakes. Twisted krummholz timberline conifers drop into subalpine spruce-fir forest, then down to open, parklike Douglas-fir and Ponderosa Pine. Western Larch and Lodgepole Pine are also abundant. The outskirts of Missoula are under 4,000 feet, and McLeod Peak is 8,620 feet. To the north, the Rattlesnakes are separated from the Missions only by a dirt road, and Griz and wolves occasionally grace this wilderness.

Status: The remote tribal Primitive Area is the northern portion of the wilderness and is a sacred area, off-limits to nontribal members. The Rattlesnake is a tribute to grass-roots activists in Missoula, who prevailed over the anti-Wilderness Forest Service. As we've learned from other FS-administered NRAs, though, NRA lands not formally designated Wilderness are never secure from FS road-building and logging schemes. The designated Rattlesnake Wilderness includes some formerly logged-over lands that are regaining their wilderness character. Air pollution degrades the lower slopes near Missoula during frequent winter temperature inversions.

NORTH GLACIER 660,000 acres (also in Canada)	
Glacier National Park roadless	545,000
Blackfoot Indian Reservation roadless (MT)	30,000
British Columbia roadless	25,000
Waterton Lakes National Park roadless (Alberta)	60,000

Description: Northwestern Montana northeast of Kalispell. This is unparalleled rugged glaciated mountain country along the Continental Divide. The spectacular scenery of glacial lakes, glaciers, cirques, peaks, waterfalls, flower-strewn meadows, and thick diverse coniferous forest is world-renowned. The west slope is very moist, with over 100 inches of annual precipitation in places and lush old-growth forests of Douglas-fir, Western

Larch, Englemann Spruce, and Subalpine Fir. Cedar, hemlock, and White Pine thrive in the McDonald Valley. On the much drier east slope, shortgrass prairie grades into Aspen, Lodgepole Pine, and spruce-fir forest. Along the west-slope lower valleys draining into the North Fork of the Flathead are a number of large, spectacular, fjordlike glacial lakes. Wildlife includes Grizzly and Black Bears, Gray Wolf (the only active wolf pack in the West is here), Moose, Elk, Mule and White-tailed Deer, Bighorn Sheep, Mountain Goat, Lynx, Marten, Wolverine, Bald Eagle, and over two hundred other bird species. Mt. Cleveland, the highest point in the Park, is 10,466 feet.

Status: The Park Service has recommended most of this area for Wilderness designation, but improvements are needed in the proposal. The Cabin Creek Coal Mine in Canada is a threat to the North Fork of the Flathead, and pollution from the Columbia Falls smelter reaches the Park. Trapping and hunting in adjacent Canada also threaten the newly established wolf pack. Moreover, at the insistence of local welfare ranchers, the U.S. Department of Agriculture has set up a $40,000 program to kill the wolves, as the U.S. Fish and Wildlife Service tries to protect them. Oil and gas drilling and subdivisions threaten the North Fork of the Flathead.

To the north of Glacier Park, only one road crosses Canada's Great Divide between the U.S. border and Canadian Route 3. That logging road, still considered by us as this area's northern boundary, has recently been closed. North to Route 3, roads and clearcuts have penetrated every major drainage beneath the divide, up to about 5,000 feet (although the crest itself and a few spur ridges remain roadless to Route 3). With additional closures and rehabilitation, another 200,000 acres could easily be added to this unit (over 100,000 acres of mostly rocks and ice are roadless along this stretch of the Continental Divide today).

SOUTH GLACIER 430,000 acres	
Glacier National Park roadless	415,000
Blackfoot Indian Reservation roadless	15,000

Description: Just south of the Going to the Sun Road from North Glacier (see above for description) and north of U.S. 2 from the huge Bob Marshall complex. Like the north unit of the Park, here is more unparalleled glaciated mountain terrain along the Continental Divide. The high basins along the divide are only slightly less well-watered than those to the north, and old-growth Pacific Northwest–type forests thrive in scattered lowland pockets here, too. There is nice high prairie Aspen parkland in the eastern foothills. Triple Divide Peak (8,011 feet) divides the headwaters of river systems draining three of the continent's major watersheds: Hudson Bay, Pacific Ocean, and Gulf of Mexico. Mt. Stimson, at 10,142 feet, is the highest point.

Status: Similar to North Glacier. Subdivisions outside the Park threaten wildlife. In autumn, a regional haze often blights the air in Glacier and all of northwest Montana. The haze is created by timber industry and Forest Service slash burning in new clearcuts. Hello, Amazon.

Northwestern Montana

Northwestern Montana is an inland extension of the wet Pacific Northwest. Aside from the Cabinets and the Great Burn, extensive logging has wiped out the Big Outside here. This lush region is primary potential Wilderness Recovery Area land.

CABINET MOUNTAINS 187,000 acres	
Designated Cabinet Mountains Wilderness (Kootenai and Kaniksu NFs)	94,272
Additional Kootenai and Kaniksu NFs roadless	92,600

Description: Extreme northwestern Montana southwest of Libby. A narrow, north-south range, parts of the Cabinets receive over 100 inches of precipitation annually, resulting in thick lowland forests of Western Red Cedar, Douglas-fir, Western White Pine, Western Hemlock, and other conifers. Rugged peaks and glacial cirques rise above the forests, lakes, and subalpine meadows. The high point is 8,712-foot Snowshoe Peak. Wildlife is abundant and typical of the Northern Rockies. There may be as few as a dozen Grizzlies left here; the Great Bear is in serious trouble in northwest Montana. The Rough-skinned Newt (*Taricha granulosa*) may occur here.

Status: Most of the designated Wilderness is "rock and ice" and high subalpine basins. In RARE II, the FS recommended 15,600 acres, including a few remnant unlogged valleys of old-growth timber, but the remaining roadless lands, including old growth, are slated to be clearcut. *Much of the designated Wilderness is under imminent threat of large-scale hard-rock mining for silver.* Conservation groups have not been able to thwart this major mining assault on the National Wilderness Preservation System. The FS and some locals are opposing a plan to augment the tiny Grizzly population.

GREAT BURN 275,000 acres (also in Idaho)	
See Idaho for description and status.	

Western and Southwestern Montana

Most of these wildlands, excluding the Tobacco Roots, are adjacent to the big wilds of central Idaho, which lie to the west. Thus, most of these areas can be considered part of the vast Central Idaho–Western Montana Wildlands Complex.

SELWAY-BITTERROOT 1,858,000 acres (also in Idaho)	
See Idaho for description and status.	

RIVER OF NO RETURN 3,253,000 acres (also in Idaho)	
See Idaho for description and status.	

ALLAN MOUNTAIN 164,000 acres (also in Idaho)	
Bitterroot and Salmon NFs roadless	164,000

Description: Idaho-Montana border northwest of Salmon, Idaho. In contrast to the high and rocky main Bitterroot Range to the north, this section of the Bitterroot Mountains is characterized by high forested ridges, meadows, and steep stream canyons. The area is an important watershed for the Bitterroot and Salmon Rivers, and is the closest major roadless area east of the Selway-Bitterroot and River of No Return Wildernesses. As such, it's a critical "Biological Corridor," linking the central Idaho wilderness with a string of wildlands that extend along the Continental Divide all the way to the Greater Yellowstone Ecosystem. The loss of such areas would preclude the migration of many species between the major ecosystems of the Wild Rockies. Wildlife includes Elk, Black Bear, Mountain Goat, Pine Marten, and Pileated Woodpecker. Old-growth Ponderosa Pine and Douglas-fir, coveted by loggers, still survives in some drainages. The roadless area is now defined by a sea of clearcuts around the perimeter. Allan Mountain is 9,154 feet; the area drops to 4,800 feet near the West Fork of the Bitterroot.

Spectacular Overwhich Falls is a major attraction. *Mimulus primuloides* (Primrose Monkeyflower) and *Gentianopsis simplex* (Hiker's Gentian) are sensitive species occurring in wet meadows.

Status: The entire area was recommended for non-Wilderness in RARE II and is under siege by loggers. A modest roadless core would survive the next decade under the Bitterroot and Salmon Forest Plans. For the first time, some conservation groups (Alliance for the Wild Rockies, Friends of the Bitterroot) are proposing Allan Mountain for Wilderness. Friends of the Bitterroot and Wild Allan Mountain are defending the area via timber sale appeals.

STONY MOUNTAIN 103,000 acres	
Bitterroot and Deerlodge NFs roadless	103,000

Description: West-central Montana between Hamilton and Anaconda. This central part of the Sapphire Range (see Anaconda-Pintlar/Sapphires below) is an important watershed for the Bitterroot River to the west and for Rock Creek—a blue-ribbon trout fishery—to the east. Rockpiles and Whitebark Pine along the Sapphire crest drop to mixed Rocky Mountain conifers, including extensive forests of Douglas-fir and Lodgepole Pine. The 25,000-acre Skalkaho Game Preserve is within the area. Fuse Lake has Arctic Grayling. There is no "Stony Mountain"; Dome Shaped Mountain, at 8,656 feet, is the high point.

Status: Recommended by the FS for non-Wilderness, the entire area is severely threatened by logging. A cherrystem road and logging operation invading the wilderness from the Bitterroot Valley should be closed, and the area included in a 115,000-acre Stony Mountain Wilderness. Like the Sapphires roadless area, the lower-elevation slopes here have been heavily logged and are not included in this roadless area. In the first edition of *The Big Outside,* we listed the acreage at 110,000; 7,000 acres have since been lost because of logging.

ANACONDA-PINTLAR/SAPPHIRES 368,000 acres	
Designated Anaconda-Pintlar Wilderness Area (Beaverhead, Bitterroot, and Deerlodge NFs)	157,874
Sapphires Roadless Area (Bitterroot and Deerlodge NFs)	117,500
Additional Beaverhead, Bitterroot, and Deerlodge NFs roadless to Anaconda-Pintlar	93,000

Description: Western Montana between Anaconda and Darby, just south of the Stony Mountain roadless area. A 4-mile-wide corridor in the Moose Creek drainage unites these two mountain ranges. The Anaconda-Pintlar country has old-growth forest and rugged alpine peaks along the Continental Divide. The East Fork of the Bitterroot River is 5,400 feet; West Goat Peak is 10,793 feet. A dozen species of conifers thrive on the north slope; the south slope, drained by the Big Hole River, is mostly Lodgepole Pine with spruce-fir on the "wet" canyon bottoms. Lakes and U-shaped canyons reveal past glaciation; a few remnant glaciers hang on along the divide. The Sapphires are lower rolling mountains, mostly under 9,000 feet and heavily forested, except for parts of the rocky crest. The lower elevations of the Sapphires, draining into the Bitterroot River (west) and Rock Creek (east), have been heavily logged. This big, diverse area supports over one thousand Elk and includes some of Montana's best Moose habitat. Other species are Black Bear, Mountain Goat, Bighorn, Puma, Wolverine, Lynx, Pileated Woodpecker, and Arctic Grayling. Native cutthroats still abound.

Status: Forest Service logging and road building continues to nibble at this wildland. Recent clearcuts now literally abut parts of the Anaconda-Pintlar Wilderness boundary. Thanks to the late Senator Lee Metcalf, 98,000 acres of the Sapphires are a Congressional Wilderness Study Area. The FS recommended only 18,000 acres of additions to the Anaconda-Pintlar Wilderness in RARE II. Conservationist proposals range from only 45,000 acres of additions to complete ecosystem protection, as promoted by the Alliance for the Wild Rockies. Since the first edition of *The Big Outside,* logging has reduced this area from 391,000 acres to 368,000 acres.

WEST PIONEER MOUNTAINS 239,000 acres	
Congressional Wilderness Study Area (Beaverhead NF)	148,000
Additional Beaverhead NF roadless	91,000

Description: Southwestern Montana southwest of Butte. These rolling, wooded hills rise above the high sagebrush of the Big Hole River Valley to 9,497 feet atop Stine Mountain. One of Montana's healthiest Elk herds is here. Lakes include a pure strain population of Arctic Grayling, perhaps the last south of Canada. Big, old Whitebark Pines grace the high ridges and slopes; the oldest known stand of Lodgepole Pine anywhere (over 500 years old) is the Effie Creek drainage. Spruce-fir stands cover valley bottoms. The peaks aren't classically spectacular, but what an ecological treasure this area is! Other wildlife includes Black Bear, Moose, Pine Marten, Wolverine, and Northern Goshawk.

Status: The 148,000-acre core is a Congressional Wilderness Study Area, thanks again to Lee Metcalf. The rest was released by the Forest Service prior to RARE II via a unit plan and is already being logged in places, including at least three 1987 clearcuts that can be seen from the Big Hole Valley. The FS hopes to cut the entire area, but local opposition is strong. The FS is proceeding here with illegal timber sales in a display of arrogance that is unusually blatant—even for the FS. The first edition of *The Big Outside* listed this area at 243,000 acres; 4,000 acres have been lost to logging since then. One congressional proposal would open the entire area to ORVs.

EAST PIONEERS 150,000 acres	
Beaverhead NF roadless	145,000
State, private, and BLM roadless	5,000

Description: Southwestern Montana southwest of Butte. Separated from the West Pioneers by the Wise River road, the East Pioneers are, by contrast, a striking glacially carved escarpment of classic peaks, glacial canyons, and trout-filled lakes. It's a narrow north-south range with a number of dirt-road cherrystem intrusions. Tweedy Peak rises to 11,154 feet. Pronghorn speed across the open foothills, and Mountain Goats cling to high crags. Grayling Lake is named for its inhabitants.

Status: The FS recommended 94,000 acres for Wilderness in RARE II; the rest was released by the Beaverhead Unit Plan and is now open to development under the Forest Plan. Hard-rock mining exploits the shrinking fringes of the area, and the Montana Wilderness Association supports only the old FS proposal for Wilderness. The recently "improved" Wise River road should be closed, and the East and West Pioneers united into a 400,000-acre Wilderness. A number of Jeep trails should be closed. We have increased the acreage of this area by 40,000 acres since the first edition of *The Big Outside* because a couple of "roads" turned out to be merely Jeep trails.

WEST BIG HOLE 215,000 acres (also in Idaho)	
Beaverhead NF roadless (MT)	130,000
Salmon NF roadless (ID)	70,000
BLM roadless (ID)	15,000

Description: Idaho-Montana border east of Salmon, Idaho. The Beaverheads, a subrange of the Bitterroots, rise abruptly nearly 7,000 feet above the Salmon River. Rugged peaks, semiarid foothills (Idaho side), glacial valleys and lakes, and thick forests (Montana side) are prevalent. Elevation ranges from 4,500 feet to 10,620 feet, at Homer Youngs Peak. The east slope drains into a world-famous blue-ribbon trout fishery, the Big Hole River. Wildlife includes Black Bear, Mountain Goat, Bighorn Sheep, deer, Lynx, and Marten. A large Elk herd migrates from its summer range on the Montana side to its winter range on the Idaho side. Marshy glacial valleys on the east slope constitute some of the best Moose habitat in Montana.

Status: In RARE II, the FS recommended it for non-Wilderness, but there is much support for protection in Montana. The area would be greatly enhanced by closing four cherrystem roads on the Montana side. Threats include ORVs on the Idaho side. Logging is an *immediate* threat on the Montana side, despite local opposition to logging in the Big Hole drainage.

ITALIAN PEAKS 360,000 acres (also in Idaho)
See Idaho for description and status.

TOBACCO ROOT MOUNTAINS 104,000 acres	
Beaverhead NF roadless	98,000
Private roadless	6,000

Description: Southwestern Montana west of Bozeman. This isolated alpine range—with a dense concentration of 10,000-foot peaks, glacial lakes, and cirques—forms a prominent southwestern Montana landmark and the watershed for the Madison and Jefferson Rivers. Wildlife is typical of the Northern Rockies.

Status: This range is highly mineralized, and there has been much small-scale mining in the past. Mining roads form numerous cherrystems into the roadless core of the range. Wilderness recovery is needed along the periphery, and private land within the roadless area should be acquired. The FS recommended 40,000 acres for Further Planning in RARE II. The Church Universal Triumphant (CUT) has recently bought land along the lower slopes, which it plans to log.

Yellowstone Region

These rich wildlands of south-central and southwestern Montana are a major component of the Greater Yellowstone Ecosystem (see Wyoming for description).

ABSAROKA-BEARTOOTH 1,249,000 acres (also in Wyoming)	
Designated Absaroka-Beartooth Wilderness Area (Custer and Gallatin NFs, MT)	920,310
Designated Absaroka-Beartooth Wilderness Area (Shoshone NF, WY)	23,750
Yellowstone National Park roadless (WY and MT)	90,000
Additional Gallatin, Custer, and Shoshone NFs roadless (MT and WY)	215,000

Description: South-central Montana south of Big Timber and northwestern Wyoming. This very large area consists of two major mountain ranges: on the east, the Beartooths are rugged, glaciated, granitic, and predominantly above tree line with huge alpine plateaus; the Absarokas on the west are more heavily forested, with rugged peaks along the crest. The Black Canyon of the Yellowstone River (in the Park) is in the southwest portion, and the Wyoming High Lakes define the southeast. This diverse area has semiarid grasslands at 5,000 feet, with elevations up to the highest point in Montana, 12,799-foot Granite Peak. It is a key part of the Greater Yellowstone Ecosystem with habitat for Grizzly and Black Bears, Bighorn Sheep, Elk, Moose, Mountain Lion, Pronghorn, Bison, Lynx, and Marten.

Status: The Grizzly is in trouble here, as it is throughout the Yellowstone area. Hard-rock mining is the major threat to this area, especially along the northeast face of the Beartooths outside the designated Wilderness. Major additions are needed in both Montana (west slope of the Absarokas and northeast face of the Beartooths) and Wyoming (remaining part of the High Lakes). The acreage summary for this very large area includes 95,000 acres of NF roadless country that has been identified and added since the first edition.

DEEP LAKE 135,000 acres (also in Wyoming)	
See Wyoming for description and status.	

GALLATIN RANGE 525,000 acres (also in Wyoming)	
See Wyoming for description and status.	

NORTH MADISON RANGE 140,000 acres	
Designated Lee Metcalf Wilderness Area (Spanish Peaks unit—Beaverhead and Gallatin NFs)	76,406
Designated BLM Lee Metcalf Wilderness (Beartrap Canyon unit)	6,000
Beaverhead and Gallatin NFs roadless (Cowboy's Heaven)	28,000
Turner Ranch roadless	25,000
Additional BLM and private roadless	5,000

Description: Southwestern Montana southwest of Bozeman. This jumbled region of alpine peaks drops into semiarid Beartrap Canyon on the northwest along the Madison River and into Gallatin Canyon on the east. This important component of the Greater Yellowstone Ecosystem is crucial Grizzly habitat. Extensive stands of Lodgepole Pine grow beneath craggy peaks and subalpine lakes. Elevations range from 4,500 feet along the Madison to 11,015 feet atop Gallatin Peak. This is an extremely popular recreation area and is the former home of imprisoned Mountain Man Don Nichols and his recently released son, Dan. A roadless chunk of Ted Turner's ranch abuts the northern boundary of the Wilderness.

Status: The Lee Metcalf Wilderness Act (a Montana Wilderness bill), one of the worst Wilderness bills to be passed, severed Beartrap Canyon from the main Spanish Peaks area by excluding the rich Cowboy's Heaven country from the Wilderness, even though the entire area was and still is one contiguous roadless unit. The same bill allowed this North Madison area to be cut from the South Madisons by roading and logging in the Jacks Creek drainage west of the Big Sky Resort (the area was a 575,000-acre roadless area before this). Logging, especially on Burlington Northern lands, threatens the northern part of the North Madisons. Senator Lee Metcalf was arguably the greatest champion of Wilderness ever to serve in the Senate.

After Metcalf's untimely death, Montana Senator John Melcher ramrodded a dreadful Wilderness bill through Congress. Naming the area to be designated Wilderness after the highly respected Lee Metcalf was a calculated Melcher ploy to pass the bill—whose main purpose was to release wildlands in the Madison Range for development. He succeeded.

The acreage summary for this area has been refigured from the acreage given in the first edition of *The Big Outside.*

SOUTH MADISON RANGE 242,000 acres	
Designated Lee Metcalf Wilderness (Taylor-Hilgard unit—Gallatin and Beaverhead NFs)	141,000
Designated Lee Metcalf Wilderness (Monument unit—Gallatin and Beaverhead NFs)	32,891
Cabin Creek Wildlife Management Area roadless	37,000
Yellowstone National Park roadless	16,000
Private and BLM roadless	15,000

Description: Southwestern Montana south of Bozeman at the northwest corner of Yellowstone Park. This area encompasses glaciated peaks, high lakes, deep canyons, meadows, Lodgepole Pine and spruce-fir forests, and exceptional habitat for Elk, Moose, Bighorn, and Grizzly. Hilgard Peak is 11,316 feet. It is a major recreation area and borders the western edge of Yellowstone National Park.

Status: The South Madison was recently part of a larger roadless area (575,000 acres!), but has been severed from the North Madison by roading and logging in the Jacks Creek drainage. Logging has also decimated virtually all of the Burlington Northern checkerboarded lands on the east slope. Therefore, 134,000 acres of checkerboarded NF and Burlington Northern lands that were included in this roadless area in the first edition of *The Big Outside* are deleted from this edition. John Melcher's Lee Metcalf Wilderness bill guaranteed ORV abuse in the Cabin Creek Wildlife Management area, a roadless corridor that separates the Monument and Taylor-Hilgard units of the Lee Metcalf Wilderness. On the bright side, the proposed Ski Yellowstone resort appears dead. Although conservationists once recognized the roadless and ecological unity of the Madisons, here is an example of political fragmentation of a wild area into various depleted political subunits. Biodiversity was knocked down and out here, and now-retired Senator John

Melcher has on his hands the blood of a severely wounded Yellowstone Ecosystem. The name of the Wilderness is an insult to the memory of Lee Metcalf.

CENTENNIAL MOUNTAINS 104,000 acres (also in Idaho)	
BLM Centennial Mountains Primitive Area (MT)	27,691
USDA Agricultural Research Station Sheep Station roadless	16,650
Red Rock Lakes National Wildlife Refuge roadless	2,400
State roadless	1,200
Mt. Jefferson roadless area—Targhee NF (ID) and Beaverhead NF (MT)	46,500
Private roadless	10,000

Description: Extreme southwestern Montana and eastern Idaho west of Yellowstone National Park. The Centennials constitute a rare east-west stretch of the Continental Divide. Some 326 vascular plant species have been identified here—an unusual botanical diversity for the Yellowstone Rockies. Sagebrush-grasslands rise to Aspen, Douglas-fir, Englemann Spruce, and Subalpine Fir forests, then to alpine tundra, rock, and permanent snow at nearly 10,000 feet atop Mt. Jefferson. Nearly all species indigenous to the Yellowstone Ecosystem are found here, including Grizzlies. A gravel road separates this wildland from the 32,350-acre Red Rocks Lakes NWR Wilderness Area. The north slope is a spectacular escarpment, abruptly rising over 3,000 feet from the lofty wetlands, grasslands, and lakes of the Centennial Valley. The Centennials are a critical biological corridor, linking the core Yellowstone Ecosystem with the massive Central Idaho Wilderness Ecosystem via a string of wildlands along the Continental Divide (the Montana-Idaho border).

Status: The usual threats are here: ORVs, mining, and logging. Oil and gas exploration is also a threat. Some cherrystem Jeep trails and dirt roads should be closed on the Idaho side. The Sheep Research Station should be closed. Livestock grazing is a major conflict with Grizzlies and other large predators, which too often suffer acute lead poisoning at the hands of public-land welfare ranchers. This area was not included in the first edition of *The Big Outside* because of our lack of knowledge.

CASCADE MOUNTAIN 66,000 acres

We inventoried this roadless area at 127,000 acres in the first edition of *The Big Outside.* A recent timber sale in the West Fork of the Madison (Beaverhead NF) has severed this former big roadless area into two areas, the largest of which is only 66,000 acres. In the Forest Service, business as usual continues to destroy, fragment, and diminish wilderness.

SNOWCREST RANGE 166,000 acres	
Beaverhead NF roadless	97,000
State big-game winter range roadless	17,000
BLM roadless	20,000
Private roadless	32,000

Description: Southwestern Montana southeast of Dillon. This is a little-known but extremely wild block of country with few cherrystem intrusions. It's a north-south mountain range with substantial BLM, state, and private roadless lands along the south and west flanks, adjacent to the National Forest. Spectacular grassland foothills and slopes rise through a thin band of Limber Pine, Douglas-fir, Aspen, spruce, and fir to alpine summits. Sunset Peak is 10,573 feet. This is high, dry, east-slope country, and the rich habitat mosaic is superb for Elk, Bighorn, Moose, Mule Deer, Red-tailed Hawk, Swainson's Hawk, and Golden Eagle. Grizzlies occasionally utilize the area. Excellent big-game winter range is included. The area receives little use, except in hunting season.

Status: Finally, conservation groups led by the Alliance for the Wild Rockies are proposing the Snowcrest for Wilderness. As the Gravellies, to the east, are increasingly fragmented, this westernmost extension of the Yellowstone Ecosystem assumes increasing importance. Because of a prior Beaverhead NF Unit Plan, the Snowcrest was excluded from RARE II. The FS—behaving like a drug addict unable to just say no to destructive activities, no matter how frivolous—allows unrestricted ORV abuse on the east slope. A number of primitive two-track Jeep trails should be closed. Also, overzealous fire control is allowing conifers (mostly Douglas-fir and Limber Pine) to invade fire-maintained grasslands and Aspen groves, degrading the ecosystem. The Snowcrest is part of the Upper Ruby grazing allotment, in which, according to the FS, 70 percent of the riparian habitat has been severely degraded by livestock. In an uncharacteristic display of sanity, the FS is proposing grazing reductions. The state has recently acquired big-game winter range on the west slope. Nearby ranchers should be encouraged to sell or donate roadless wildlife habitat easements along the west slope, where the roadless area extends well down onto private land, despite a few small water developments, fences, Jeep trails, and cattle.

Central Montana

At least a dozen mountain ranges rise above the surrounding prairies and farmlands of Montana's high plains, forming an inland archipelago of spectacular montane habitat islands. Only three, however, are still wild enough to be part of the Big Outside.

CRAZY MOUNTAINS 140,000 acres	
Gallatin, Lewis and Clark NFs roadless	88,000
Intermingled private roadless	52,000

Description: South-central Montana north of Livingston. The Crazies are a spectacular escarpment, abruptly rising over 7,000 feet from the Great Plains to 11,214-foot Crazy Peak. There's a dense concentration of glacier-cut, knife-edged crags, snowfields, alpine lakes, flower-strewn basins, and serpentine drainages emanating from the convoluted heights. Alpine tundra has been damaged by the initial population "boom" of introduced Mountain Goats. Spruce-fir, Lodgepole Pine, Limber Pine, Douglas-fir, and Aspen drop to shortgrass prairie. Elk, Pronghorn, Mule Deer, White-tailed Deer, Black Bear, and Golden Eagle are natives. The entire range is drained by the Yellowstone River, and the last free-roaming Crow chief, Plenty Coups, had his famous vision here.

Status: The FS opposes Wilderness. Ho hum. Much of the area is checkerboard private and FS ownership as a result of nineteenth-century railroad grants. Congress has approved $4 million to buy 22,000 private acres presently owned by the Galt family, in the northern Crazies. Similar purchases are needed for the heart of the range. A major FS timber sale would degrade spectacular Cottonwood Canyon in the southeast corner of the Crazies. Mining and oil and gas exploration are also threats.

BIG SNOWY MOUNTAINS 112,000 acres	
Big Snowies Congressional WSA (Lewis and Clark NF)	98,000
Additional Lewis and Clark NF roadless	7,000
BLM Twin Coulees WSA	6,870

Description: Central Montana, south of Lewistown. A high, east-west summit ridge of limestone rises above the prairie. Giant subalpine meadows top the range, and from 8,681-foot Greathouse Peak, one can see from Canada to Yellowstone. Various limestone caverns are on the west slope. The north slope is forested with Ponderosa Pine, Douglas-fir, Subalpine Fir, and spruce. The south slope is drier. Rattlesnakes and Pronghorn are at the grassy lower elevation. Deer and Black Bear are abundant.

Status: Virtually the entire FS portion is a congressionally designated Wilderness Study Area, but is now proposed for non-Wilderness by Montana politicos and the FS. Logging has therefore become a major threat. The Big Snowies are a very popular area for recreationists. The entire area is grazed by cows (moo) and sheep (baa).

ELKHORN MOUNTAINS 103,000 acres	
Helena and Deerlodge NFs roadless	85,000
BLM roadless	5,000
State roadless	1,000
Private roadless	12,000

Description: Western Montana just southeast of Helena. Though one range east of the Continental Divide, the Elkhorns rise higher than the divide and therefore catch more Pacific moisture than do most east-slope ranges. High ridges and steep canyons are clothed with lush forests and meadows. Crow Peak is 9,414 feet. The Elkhorns are unusually diverse, with 148 documented resident vertebrate species. One of Montana's most productive (and heavily hunted) Elk herds is here.

Status: The NF portion is part of a 175,700-acre "Elkhorns Wildlife Management Area," designated by Congress. Nonetheless, the FS proposes timber sales, and miners continue to hack away at this great chunk of habitat. A number of Jeep trails and mining claims (some patented) intrude into the southern and central parts of the roadless area, and should be closed and rehabilitated. Most of the private lands are owned by ranchers along the western foothills. This is a new area; it was overlooked for the first edition of *The Big Outside.*

TENDERFOOT–DEEP CREEK 108,000 acres	
Lewis and Clark NF roadless	98,000
Private roadless	10,000

Description: Central Montana southeast of Great Falls, the Little Belt Mountains rise from the rolling prairies of central Montana. Forested ridges under 9,000 feet and spectacular limestone river canyons characterize this westernmost roadless area in the Little Belts. Ponderosa Pine and Douglas-fir are common tree species. The Smith River Canyon along the western fringe of the area is a popular float trip. Private, mostly roadless lands abut the river on the west. Mule and White-tailed Deer, Black Bear, and Elk inhabit this bit of Montana canyon country.

Status: Recommended for non-Wilderness by the Forest Service, but proposed for protection by conservationists, threats to Tenderfoot–Deep Creek include logging and mining. To the east, the 92,000-acre Middle Fork–Judith Wilderness Study Area (again, thanks to Lee Metcalf) is the other major wildland in the Little Belts. The rest of this gentle mountain range has been severely fragmented by roads and logging. A few other small roadless areas persist.

Bighorn Mountains

The Bighorns are an expansive mountain range, mostly in Wyoming, but extending north into Montana. Two Big Outside units lie astride the state border.

LITTLE BIGHORN 155,000 acres (also in Wyoming)
See Wyoming for description and status.

NORTH BIGHORN MOUNTAINS 144,000 acres (also in Wyoming)	
Devil's Canyon roadless area (Bighorn NF, WY)	34,000
BLM with some private roadless (WY)	6,000
Bighorn Canyon NRA roadless (MT)	4,000
Crow Indian Reservation Tribal Reserve roadless (MT)	100,000

Description: Northwest flank of Bighorn Mountains astride the Montana-Wyoming border northeast of Lovell, Wyoming. Sheer canyon walls rise out of Yellowtail Reservoir in the National Recreation Area. Most of this area is semidesert prairie foothills and plateaus cut by steep drainages. Rocky Mountain Juniper and Limber Pine are scattered across the hills. Colorful rock formations and canyons rise to timbered (mostly Douglas-fir) ridges. Elevations vary from approximately 3,500 feet to over 9,000 feet on the National Forest. The Crow manage a wild Bison herd on the reservation. Other wildlife includes Pronghorn, Mule Deer, rattlesnake, Golden Eagle, and Ferruginous Hawk. There are Elk and Black Bear at the higher elevations. Because of different ownerships and political subdivisions, this was never before recognized as a distinct wildland.

Status: There are a number of Jeep trails throughout the area. The Tribal Reserve appears fairly well protected, and because it is sacred land to the Crow, it's closed to the nontribal public. The Devil's Canyon roadless area was recommended for non-Wilderness in RARE II and has been ignored by conservationists. This area was overlooked for the first edition of *The Big Outside.*

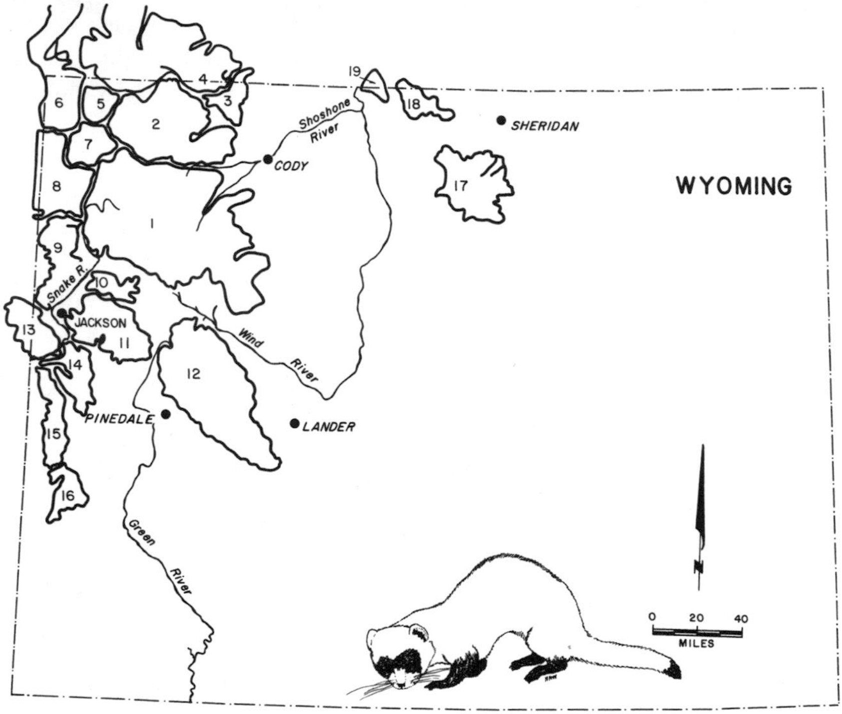

1. South Absaroka
2. North Absaroka
3. Deep Lake
4. Absaroka-Beartooth
5. Washburn Range
6. Gallatin Range
7. Central Plateau
8. Bechler-Pitchstone
9. Teton Range
10. Mt. Leidy
11. Gros Ventre
12. Wind River Range
13. Palisades
14. Grayback Ridge
15. Salt River Range
16. Commissary Ridge
17. Cloud Peak
18. Little Bighorn
19. North Bighorn Mts.

Wyoming

Wyoming is a high-altitude land where sky-scraping snowy mountains meet high plains and wind-ripped desert basins. This is a land of open space, wild mountains, and a grandeur unmatched anywhere else in the contiguous forty-eight states. Indeed, former Wyoming Congressman Teno Roncalio once referred to Wyoming as "the Alaska of the lower forty-eight states."

The state encompasses six bioregions: (1) the northern extension of the Southern Rocky Mountains (most of which lie to the south in Colorado), including the Laramie, Medicine Bow, and Sierra Madre ranges of southeastern Wyoming; (2) the Great Plains of eastern and central Wyoming; (3) the Red Desert and adjacent arid lands of west-central and southwestern Wyoming; (4) the Bighorn Basin (Desert) of north-central Wyoming; (5) the Bighorn Mountains and adjacent foothills that lie just east of the Bighorn Basin; and (6) the Greater Yellowstone Highlands of the Middle Rocky

Mountains Province with the ranges of western and northwestern Wyoming, overlapping into the adjacent states of Idaho and Montana. The last region includes Yellowstone and Grand Teton National Parks, and the Bridger-Teton, Targhee, and Shoshone National Forests, which hold some of the largest wild tracts in the contiguous forty-eight states.

Unfortunately, much of Wyoming's former richness and grandeur has already been lost. Big wilderness survives only in the high mountains of regions five and six (see above). Wyoming's prairies and deserts have been laced with roads, gouged for metals and uranium, ripped apart for fossil fuels, and overgrazed by livestock. Here, vigorous wilderness restoration efforts are essential. Bison, Gray Wolf, Elk, Black-footed Ferret, Swift Fox, Wyoming Toad, and multitudes of other creatures large and small are either extinct or nearly extinct from Wyoming rangelands.

It is important to note that southwestern Wyoming's Red Desert offers an impressive opportunity to restore ecologically viable big wilderness where today there remain no roadless tracts exceeding 100,000 acres. The closure of some dirt roads, coupled with reintroductions (including Bison) and protective management, could easily result in a million-acre high-desert grassland Wilderness in this vast, open, uninhabited region.

Even in the wild mountains of the west, wolves no longer roam and the Grizzly survives only precariously in diminished numbers. New Forest Service roads and clearcuts continue to penetrate formerly wild country. Periodic "energy booms" lure seismic crews, oil riggers, road bladers, and ultimately more loggers, ORVers, and other yahoos into the high country, diminishing Wyoming's wilderness further, and pushing more species closer to the brink of extinction.

Wyoming's congressional delegation consists of three "conservative" Republicans: Senators Alan Simpson and Malcolm Wallop, and Representative Craig Thomas, who replaced Dick Cheney when Cheney became U.S. Secretary of Defense. Though no conservationist, Thomas is relatively quiet on wildland issues. Simpson and Wallop, though, are vocal anti-Wilderness zealots. Both are generally on the wrong side of every issue, from wolf reintroduction in Yellowstone (opposed) to federal subsidies for below-cost timber sales (for). Wallop, Simpson, and Cheney dictated the dismal 1984 Wyoming "Wilderness" Act, which protected only 883,359 acres out of 4,162,878 acres that were inventoried in RARE II. Even worse than the acreage figure, much of the "protected" acreage consisted primarily of high-altitude rock and ice. The Popo Agie (Wind River Range) and Cloud Peak (Bighorn Mountains) Wildernesses are classic examples of "Wilderness on the Rocks." The bill released about two and a half million acres—mostly of high-quality low- or mid-elevation habitat—to the abusive practices of the Forest Service. Moreover, were it not for now-retired Congressman John Seiberling of Ohio, the bill would have been even worse. For the most part, the bill's boundaries closely followed the Forest Service's horrible RARE II recommendations. As a result, throughout Wyoming's high and dry forests, Forest Service–sponsored habitat destruction continues, nearly unabated.

Furthermore, the Wyoming delegation has thwarted efforts to designate the Yellowstone and Grand Teton National Park backcountry as Wilderness (the Park Service made its Wilderness recommendations in 1972). Wallop and Simpson are responsible for keeping most of Wyoming's "Overthrust Belt," which includes the Grayback Ridge and Salt River Range roadless areas, open to oil and gas development. The Senate's duo of doom is also to blame for allowing the notorious Fishing Bridge development to remain in prime Grizzly habitat in Yellowstone. Proposals to protect the state's extremely threatened BLM wildlands have never been seriously considered by Congress. Ironically, most public opinion polls indicate that Wyoming's population is far more sympathetic to Wilderness and environmental protection in general than is the congressional delegation. Therefore, it's up to Wilderness activists to resist the onslaught of Forest Service and BLM-sponsored development, to continue to educate and organize, and to expose these Three Stooges of environmental folly for the corporate-bureaucratic dupes that they are.

Yellowstone Region

This is the core of the Greater Yellowstone Ecosystem (GYE), including Yellowstone National Park and immediately adjacent wildlands in northwestern Wyoming, southern Montana, and extreme eastern Idaho. Yellowstone is an International Biosphere Reserve, and the Greater Yellowstone Ecosystem is, in many ways, the epitome of wildness and natural diversity. The GYE is arguably the most significant—and threatened—wildland complex in the temperate world.

SOUTH ABSAROKA 2,190,000 acres	
Yellowstone National Park roadless	483,000
Designated Washakie Wilderness Area (Shoshone NF)	703,981
Designated Teton Wilderness Area (Bridger-Teton NF)	585,468
Additional Shoshone and Bridger-Teton NFs roadless	347,000
Wind River Indian Reservation roadless	60,000
State and private roadless	10,000

Description: Northwestern Wyoming between Moran Junction and Cody. One of the largest and wildest areas in the lower forty-eight states, the South Absaroka includes the farthest point from a road in the United States outside of Alaska (21 miles, near the Thorofare River in the Teton Wilderness Area). This diverse area has giant Elk herds, Grizzly and Black Bears, Bison (occasionally), Moose, Mule and White-tailed Deer, Bighorn Sheep, Pronghorn, Cougar, Lynx, Marten, Bald and Golden Eagles, Trumpeter Swan, Common Loon, Sandhill Crane; huge meadows; extensive spruce-fir and Lodgepole Pine forests; and Douglas-fir, Aspen, and sagebrush at lower elevations. Yellowstone Lake is the northwestern corner of this vast area and is included in the roadless acreage. The Absarokas consist primarily of layered volcanic rock and include rugged glacial canyons, extensive plateaus with well-developed alpine tundra, craggy peaks, small glaciers, petrified wood, geysers, and hot springs. White-tailed Ptarmigan are locally common on the Absaroka tundra. West of the main Absaroka range is an extensive area of low mountains, rolling hills, and gentle plateaus clothed in a rich mosaic of forest, meadow, and riparian habitats. Big river valleys, rare in the Wilderness System, include the Upper Yellowstone, Snake, and Thorofare. The upper Snake and Yellowstone drainages are the major stronghold in Wyoming for River Otter and Osprey. In many ways, the South Absaroka is the wild heart of Greater Yellowstone. Elevations range from 5,500 feet to 13,140 feet, atop Franc's Peak.

Status: Hard-rock mining is a threat in the Kirwin (upper Wood River) area on the east side outside the designated Wilderness. NF lands outside of Wilderness are threatened by logging, particularly the 30,000-acre DuNoir Special Management Area, which is temporarily protected by Congress. Here, FS clearcutting plans would devastate a major Elk calving and migration route, occupied Grizzly habitat, and important habitat for Trumpeter Swan and Moose. The DuNoir would be a splendid addition to the Washakie Wilderness. Oil and gas development threatens the east slope of the Absarokas. The 1984 Wyoming Wilderness Act released about 300,000 acres of roadless country here. The new Grant Village Resort in Yellowstone and poor bear management policies in general threaten the Grizzly. There are only about 200 Grizzlies remaining in the entire Yellowstone Ecosystem! The NPS recommends 367,200 acres of Yellowstone NP (excluding most of Yellowstone Lake) in this area for Wilderness.

NORTH ABSAROKA 950,000 acres	
Designated North Absaroka Wilderness Area (Shoshone NF)	350,488
Yellowstone National Park roadless	430,000
Additional Shoshone NF roadless	170,000

Description: Northwestern Wyoming west of Cody. The most densely populated Grizzly habitat in the Greater Yellowstone Ecosystem is here. This area ranges from semidesert sagebrush foothills on the east slope of the Absarokas to moist subalpine forest and alpine tundra. The Absaroka crest has volcanic plateaus and rugged peaks, while there are broad alluvial valleys along Pelican Creek and the Lamar River in Yellowstone Park. Extensive Lodgepole Pine forests, spruce-fir along the east slope of the Absarokas, and Douglas-fir at lower elevations adorn the land. Lakes and thermal features, the Grand Canyon of the Yellowstone, the Mirror Plateau, and a superb petrified forest on Specimen Ridge are among the area's spectacles. The little-known Preble's Shrew (*Sorex preblei*) has been identified at the Lamar Ranger Station in Yellowstone. The North Absaroka area may be the southernmost habitat in the Rockies for Fisher, and is certainly the major wilderness stronghold for native Bison in the United States. Other wildlife includes Grizzly and Black Bears, Moose, Elk, Mule and White-tailed Deer, Bighorn Sheep, Lynx, Marten, and Cougar. Much of the Lamar drainage burned during the dry summer of 1988. This will provide a superb opportunity to study the natural process of secondary ecological succession in an extensive area of Rocky Mountain forest habitat.

Status: All the NF roadless lands outside the Wilderness have been released by Congress. Threats to these areas include oil and gas development along the east slope of the Absarokas, timbering in Grizzly habitat, snowmobiles, and hard-rock mining in Sunlight and Sulfur Creek drainages. Timber sales may already have decreased the size of unprotected wilderness on the Shoshone NF. Despite substantial big-game winter range along the North Fork of the Shoshone and Lamar Rivers, much of the Yellowstone Ecosystem's best winter habitat is outside the Park. Bison have discovered this, and they meet their demise when they migrate to grassy low elevation winter habitat in the Yellowstone River valley near Gardiner, Montana. The Park Service proposes 418,600 acres of its land in this roadless area for Wilderness.

DEEP LAKE 135,000 acres (also in Montana)	
Shoshone and Custer NFs roadless	132,000
BLM and private roadless	3,000

Description: Northwestern Wyoming and southern Montana northwest of Cody. The southern end of the Beartooth Plateau has spectacular geologic features, including Deep Lake and Clarks Fork River Canyon. Peat beds on the plateau are underlain by permafrost—a unique feature in the forty-eight coterminous states. The plateau is mostly alpine and subalpine, but drops steeply down to semiarid benches above the Clarks Fork and the Bighorn Basin Desert to the east. Elevation varies from 4,500 feet to 11,000 feet. Wildlife includes Grizzly, Moose, Elk, and Mule Deer. Mountain Goat have been introduced. The rare Pallid Bat (*Antrozous pallidus*) may occur at the lowest elevations. The 21,000-acre Montana portion is known as the Line Creek Plateau. Owing to a unique fibrous organic soil that lies upon limestone bedrock, the Line Creek Plateau's dry tundra harbors more than twenty rare plant species.

Status: ORV use has caused localized erosion damage. The Forest Service has recently "improved" Jeep trails; this threatens to sever the area into two parcels. Chief opposition to Wilderness designation is from a small number of snowmobilers and four-wheel-drive yahoos in Cody, Wyoming. The entire area is released, although Congress recently designated the Clarks Fork a National Wild and Scenic River, thus protecting this superb canyon from proposed dam-building schemes. A proposal to drill for oil and gas on the fragile tundra of the Line Creek Plateau should be defeated.

ABSAROKA-BEARTOOTH 1,249,000 acres (also in Montana)	
See Montana for description and status.	

WASHBURN RANGE 125,000 acres	
Yellowstone National Park roadless	125,000

Description: Northwestern Wyoming inside the Mammoth, Tower, Norris, and Canyon road loop in Yellowstone NP. The area consists of rolling hills to steep mountains, volcanic plateaus, coniferous forests of Lodgepole Pine and Douglas-fir, and expansive grassy meadows. Elevations vary from 6,000 feet to 9,900 feet, atop Dunraven Peak. Tower Creek and Lava Creek are the main drainages, forming deep and rugged canyons. Elk find important summer range here. Bison, Moose, Bighorn Sheep, Mule Deer, and Grizzly and Black Bears also inhabit the area.

Status: The Park Service recommends 122,000 acres of this area for Wilderness. The Norris to Mammoth or Canyon to Tower road should be closed in order to give the Grizzly more unbroken habitat. Yellowstone National Park, the world's first, was established in 1872. In the early 1900s, the government intentionally extirpated most of the Park's larger predators. Today, Pumas are still rare in the GYE, and although efforts to reintroduce the Gray Wolf have immense popular support, Senators Simpson and Wallop continue to oppose reintroduction. Many biologists think the northern Yellowstone Elk herd has overpopulated its range, and a dearth of large predators is the reason.

GALLATIN RANGE 525,000 acres (also in Montana)	
Yellowstone National Park roadless (WY and MT)	325,000
Gallatin National Forest roadless (MT)	150,000
Intermingled state and private roadless in Gallatin NF (MT)	50,000

Description: Extreme northwestern Wyoming and southwestern Montana west of Gardiner, Montana. An integral part of the Greater Yellowstone Ecosystem, the Gallatin Range is important habitat for Grizzly, Elk, Bighorn Sheep, Wolverine, and other wilderness-dependent species. The area is characterized by 10,000-foot-high peaks, large subalpine basins, and long stream valleys. In the Park, the Gardiner River valley, with grass, sagebrush, Aspen, and conifers, is crucial wildlife habitat. Northward, the peaks constitute the rugged backdrop for the Yellowstone and Gallatin River valleys. Big-game hunting, backpacking, and horsepacking are becoming more popular.

Status: The Park Service has recommended 304,800 acres for Wilderness, but has failed to recommend that a telephone line corridor along the eastern fringe be relocated along the road so that the entire area can be protected. Because of checkerboard land ownership—a legacy of nineteenth-century railroad land grants—logging by Burlington Northern threatens much of the northern half of the area. However, 150,000 acres, including intermixed private and state land, are a congressional Wilderness Study Area, thanks to the late Senator Lee Metcalf. Off-road vehicles continue to degrade the Gallatin NF portion of the area.

CENTRAL PLATEAU 185,000 acres	
Yellowstone National Park roadless	185,000

Description: Northwestern Wyoming, the central core of Yellowstone surrounded by the Fishing Bridge, Old Faithful, Madison, Canyon, West Thumb, and Norris developments. A high, cold plateau of broad grassy valleys, vast Lodgepole Pine forests, clear streams, thermal features, and small lakes distinguishes this area. This is an especially important Grizzly and Bison area. Other wildlife includes Moose, Elk, Mule Deer, Lynx, Marten, and Bald Eagle. Few trails invade this very primitive area. The well-known Hayden Valley is in this area. John and Frank Craighead did much of their landmark Grizzly Bear study during the late 1950s and early 1960s here.

Status: The Park Service recommends 181,500 acres for Wilderness.

BECHLER-PITCHSTONE 468,000 acres (also in Idaho)	
Yellowstone National Park roadless (WY and ID)	440,300
John D. Rockefeller Parkway NRA roadless (WY)	11,000
Designated Winegar Hole Wilderness Area (Targhee NF, WY)	14,000
Additional Targhee NF roadless (WY and ID)	3,000

Description: Northwestern Wyoming and extreme eastern Idaho west of Old Faithful. This area includes the remote and unusual Pitchstone Plateau in the southwestern corner of Yellowstone NP. It also includes the Bechler River, big waterfalls, roaring streams, glacial canyons, and extensive Lodgepole Pine forests. This area averages 40–50 inches of annual precipitation, which is very high for the Central Rockies. Shoshone Lake is the largest entirely wilderness lake in the lower forty-eight states. Geyser basins, hot springs, and mud pots are among the area's thermal features. The Pitchstone Plateau's waters are naturally radioactive. Elevation is generally between 6,000 feet and 8,500 feet. Wildlife includes Grizzly and Black Bears, Elk, Moose, Mule Deer, Lynx, Common Loon, Trumpeter Swan, Great Gray Owl, and Bald Eagle. The extensive marshy habitat in Winegar Hole is unusual in the Rockies.

Status: The NPS proposes 415,900 acres in Yellowstone for Wilderness. Closure of a portion of the narrow, dirt Grassy Lake Road would unite this part of Yellowstone with the roadless Tetons to the south, forming a Wilderness unit of about 700,000 acres. South of the town of West Yellowstone, the Forest Service has so extensively clearcut "its" land that from the air, one can see a shocking linear demarcation of National Park versus bare, eroding National "Forest." The Alliance for the Wild Rockies proposes a 100,000-acre Yellowstone West Wilderness Recovery Area abutting the Park, in the now-denuded Targhee NF.

TETON RANGE 334,000 acres	
Grand Teton National Park roadless	145,000
Designated Jedediah Smith Wilderness Area (Targhee NF)	116,535
Additional Targhee and Bridger-Teton NFs roadless	60,000
John D. Rockefeller Parkway NRA roadless	12,000

Description: Northwestern Wyoming north of Jackson and south of Yellowstone NP. The stunning fault block escarpment of the Grand Tetons rises an abrupt 7,000 feet above Jackson Hole. These peaks, cirques, glaciers, rugged U-shaped canyons, streams, and lakes are world-famous scenery. The steep east face consists of Precambrian granitic rocks; the more gentle west slope (the Jedediah Smith Wilderness and other FS lands) consists predominantly of overlying sediments above the granitic core. Low-elevation coniferous forests and lush subalpine meadows are the main vegetation types, with scattered Aspen groves on the west slope. The Tetons are an internationally popular climbing area. Grand Teton Peak is 13,770 feet. Grizzly Bears utilize the north half of the range; other wildlife includes Moose, Elk, Black Bear, Pika, and Yellow-bellied Marmot.

Status: The Jedediah Smith Wilderness is being severely degraded by excessive sheep grazing and by poaching. A few timber sales threaten the lower west slope. The NPS has recommended 115,807 acres in Grand Teton NP for Wilderness. Jackson Lake is not included in the roadless acreage here because its level has been artificially raised by Jackson Lake Dam. The dam should be removed, and the lake returned to its natural level.

MT. LEIDY 112,000 acres	
Bridger-Teton NF roadless	110,000
Grand Teton National Park roadless	2,000

Description: Northwestern Wyoming northeast of Jackson. The Mt. Leidy highlands are a major unprotected part of the Greater Yellowstone Ecosystem, linking the Gros Ventre Wilderness to the south with the Teton Wilderness of the vast South Absaroka complex to the north. Mt. Leidy provides excellent habitat for Elk, Mule Deer, Moose, Black Bear, Mountain Lion, and many smaller creatures. There are important wintering areas along the southern boundary for Bighorn Sheep. Grizzlies occasionally wander into the area from the north. Extensive coniferous forests, Aspen groves, open meadows, steep ridges, and a few prominent peaks make up a varied landscape. Elevations range from 7,000 feet, along the Gros Ventre River, to 10,337 feet, on Grouse Mountain.

Status: This area is critical for reestablishing the traditional north-south Jackson Hole Elk herd migration and for expanding Grizzly habitat to help ensure the survival of the Grizzly in the Greater Yellowstone Ecosystem. There is good local support for protecting the area. On much of the east and north, the roadless area is defined by the adjacent sea of logging roads and clearcuts. FS plans for additional extensive logging and road building have been postponed but not canceled. Oil and gas exploration is a serious threat as well. Much of the Mt. Leidy highlands adjacent to this roadless area that have been heavily logged and roaded should be managed as a wilderness recovery area. This would establish an important link for wildlife between the Gros Venture and Teton Wildernesses.

GROS VENTRE 455,000 acres	
Designated Gros Ventre Wilderness Area (Bridger-Teton NF)	287,000
Shoal Creek Wilderness Study Area (Bridger-Teton NF)	30,000
Additional Bridger-Teton NF roadless	133,000
Jackson Hole National Elk Refuge roadless	5,000

Description: Western Wyoming east of Jackson. The Gros Ventre is an imposing mountain range rising from sagebrush-grassland foothills at 6,000 feet to alpine tundra and rocky peaks. Doubletop Peak is 11,682 feet. Long stream valleys, lakes, cirques, limestone peaks, coniferous forests of Engelmann Spruce, Subalpine Fir, and Lodgepole Pine characterize the area. There are lots of rich subalpine meadows, too. Douglas-fir and Aspen are at lower elevations. The gigantic Gros Ventre Rock Slide (of June 23, 1925) dammed the Gros Ventre River; the population of nearby Kelly thinned out when the dam broke two years later. The extremely abundant wildlife includes Elk, Moose, Mule Deer, Bighorn Sheep, Black Bear, Cougar, and Golden and Bald Eagles. This is an important summer range, calving, and migratory area for a major portion of the Jackson Hole Elk herd. The area is used for big-game hunting, fishing, hiking, and trail riding. Some of the best wildlife habitat in the Gros Ventre is on the eastern flank of the range, draining into the Green River. Much of the Gros Ventre's Green River slope was excluded from the Wilderness by Congress. The Green River drainage of the Gros Ventre includes populations of Colorado Cutthroat Trout (*Salmo clarki pleuriticus*), a rare subspecies that is becoming Endangered as a result of clearcutting, livestock grazing, and hybridization.

Status: Unprotected areas are extremely threatened by logging, especially on the east slope, draining into the Green River. Oil and gas development is a threat in some areas, including Little Granite Creek, where Texaco has proposed a well inside the designated Wilderness. Major big-game wintering areas were excluded from the Wilderness; they should be added.

Western Wyoming

The southern extension of the Greater Yellowstone Ecosystem includes the rugged Wind Rivers and the rapidly diminishing wilds of the so-called Overthrust Belt along Wyoming's western border south of Jackson Hole.

WIND RIVER RANGE 1,171,000 acres	
Designated Bridger Wilderness Area (Bridger-Teton NF)	428,169
Designated Fitzpatrick Wilderness Area (Shoshone NF)	198,525
Designated Popo Agie Wilderness Area (Shoshone NF)	101,991
Wind River Indian Reservation roadless	190,000
BLM Scab Creek Primitive Area	7,000
Additional Shoshone and Bridger-Teton NFs roadless	230,000
Additional BLM roadless	10,000
Private roadless	5,000

Description: Western Wyoming west of Lander. This nationally famous glaciated mountain range features granite peaks, cirques, turquoise streams filled with "glacial flour," vast alpine rock and tundra fields, and the biggest glaciers in the Rockies south of Canada. There are sixty-three glaciers and over 1,300 lakes, most of which are alpine and subalpine tarns. This is a major destination for climbing, fishing, hiking, and trail riding. Sagebrush foothills at 6,000 feet rise through a band of Aspen, Douglas-fir, Lodgepole Pine, and spruce-fir forest to Wyoming's highest point, 13,804-foot Gannett Peak, atop the Continental Divide, which forms the crest of the Winds. The headwaters of the Green River form west of the divide; east of the divide, the Wind River is an important tributary of the Yellowstone-Missouri river system. Wildlife includes Elk, Mule Deer, Black Bear, Moose, Pronghorn, Pika, Yellow-bellied Marmot, and Rosy Finch. The productive Whiskey Mountain Bighorn Sheep herd is the largest single herd of Rocky Mountain Bighorn in the world.

Status: The addition of low- and mid-elevation FS and BLM lands mainly to the Bridger and Popo Agie Wildernesses would help complete the protected area ecologically. Timber sales threaten potential additions to the Bridger Wilderness, and ORV abuse has already degraded the Seven Lakes area on the northwestern end of the Bridger. Overgrazing by sheep and cattle, and overuse by recreationists (especially horsepackers and rock climbers) are localized problems. The BLM has recommended the Scab Creek

Primitive Area (7,600 acres) for Wilderness, and most of the Indian roadless lands are managed as a Tribal Roadless Area.

PALISADES 245,000 acres (also in Idaho)	
Targhee and Bridger-Teton NFs roadless	240,000
Private roadless	5,000

Description: Wyoming-Idaho border west of Jackson, the Snake River Range. Features include steep, heavily vegetated sedimentary mountains with deep stream canyons; scattered coniferous forests; extensive lush meadows and mountain shrublands; and habitat for Black Bear, Moose, Mule Deer, and Bighorn Sheep. Mountain Goat have been introduced. Elevations range from 5,500 feet to 10,000 feet. Excellent big-game hunting and cross-country skiing attract visitors. Although not as "scenic" in the popular sense as the adjacent Grand Tetons, the Palisades are a vital chunk of productive habitat crucial to the survival of the Greater Yellowstone Ecosystem.

Status: The Wyoming side (135,840 acres) is a Congressional Wilderness Study Area; the Idaho portion is a FS Further Planning Area, but oil and gas leases have already been given for extensive areas. ORV use on the Idaho side, logging on the Wyoming side, and domestic sheep grazing are additional threats to this area. Also, a helicopter skiing company opposes Wilderness designation. Popular support for Wilderness is high in Jackson Hole.

GRAYBACK RIDGE 225,000 acres	
Bridger-Teton NF roadless	225,000

Description: Western Wyoming south of Jackson. This northern end of the Wyoming Range, locally known as the "Hoback Mountains," includes superb U-shaped valleys, waterfalls, high ridges, peaks, cirques; and a diverse vegetative mosaic of coniferous forests interspersed with Aspen, lush montane and subalpine meadows, and sagebrush on lower-elevation southerly exposures. Some of the best Aspen stands in any Wyoming roadless area are here, but fire suppression and livestock grazing threaten their survival. Wildlife includes "trophy-size" Mule Deer, as well as Elk, Moose, Black Bear, Lynx, Badger, Sandhill Crane, Bald Eagle, and native Cutthroat Trout. Elevations range from 6,000 feet to 10,862-foot Hoback Peak. Grayback

Ridge is a prominent 18-mile-long escarpment rising to 9,700 feet along the west side of the Willow Creek drainage. Major uses are trail riding and big-game hunting.

Status: The entire area has been released by Congress. The Forest Service is proposing roadless management for the Willow Creek core, but has extensive logging plans for most of the rest of the area. Part of the so-called Overthrust Belt, nearly the entire area is under oil and gas lease and is extremely threatened by associated roading and development. The FS often uses oil and gas exploration roads to gain access to slow-growing high-altitude stands of timber. One of the authors, Howie Wolke, spent six months in jail in 1986 for pulling up survey stakes for a new oil exploration road that the Forest Service planned to maintain for below-cost logging. Grayback Ridge and the nearby Salt River Range (see below) are the "forgotten gems" of western Wyoming, and need an active constituency very badly.

RM36: 560,000

SALT RIVER RANGE 245,000 acres	
Bridger-Teton NF roadless	240,000
Private roadless	5,000

Description: Western Wyoming east of Afton. An extremely rugged north-south range of folded and faulted sedimentary rocks, glacial cirques, lakes, U-shaped canyons, waterfalls, lush subalpine meadows, coniferous forests, and scattered Aspen groves, the Salt River Range has very steep, unstable slopes, and is part of the Overthrust Belt. Elevations rise from 6,000 feet to nearly 11,000 feet. The area offers excellent habitat for Mule Deer and Elk; also extant are Moose, Black Bear, Mountain Lion, and Lynx. The steep western slope drains to the Salt River (Star Valley); the east slope, to the Greys River, which is characterized by long drainages, forested benches, and lush meadows. The major recreation use is hunting.

Status: This is a little-known area, except locally in the Star Valley, where there appears to be scant support for its preservation. On the Greys River side, most of the lower slope adjacent to the roadless area has recently been logged. Timber sales and oil and gas exploration threaten the entire area, except for parts of the crest and the west slope where steep terrain will limit development. The entire area was released by the so-called Wyoming Wilderness Act. We have deleted 5,000 acres from this roadless area since the first edition of *The Big Outside* because of logging—however, considerably more acreage may have been lost since then.

COMMISSARY RIDGE 175,000 acres	
Bridger-Teton NF roadless	155,000
BLM roadless	20,000

Description: Western Wyoming north of Kemmerer. This southernmost extension of the Bridger-Teton NF rises above the arid Green River basin. It is a mostly montane and subalpine wilderness of steep, folded sedimentary ridges, extensive spruce-fir and Lodgepole Pine forests, numerous meadows, streams, a few lakes (including Lake Alice—a major recreational attraction), and large populations of Elk and Mule Deer. Other wildlife includes Moose, Black Bear, Pronghorn, and Cougar. Major uses are hunting and fishing. An unhybridized population of Utah Cutthroat Trout (*Salmo clarki utah*), an increasingly rare subspecies, can be found in Lake Alice and nearby streams within this area.

Status: This is one of the most immediately and completely threatened roadless areas in the country. The entire area is covered with oil and gas leases and is a focal point of energy company interest. Timber sales are a major threat and are already reducing the size of the area—we have deleted 15,000 acres from this roadless area since the first edition of *The Big Outside* because of logging—however, considerably more acreage may have been lost since then. ORV abuse has also degraded the area. Comissary Ridge is near the huge La Barge oil and gas field where Exxon operates a sour gas plant.

North-central Wyoming

The rugged Bighorn Mountains rise above the high plains to the east and the arid Bighorn Basin to the west.

CLOUD PEAK 443,000 acres	
Designated Cloud Peak Wilderness Area (Bighorn NF)	195,500
Additional Bighorn NF roadless	224,000
BLM roadless	13,000
State roadless	5,000
Private roadless	5,000

Description: North-central Wyoming west of Buffalo. The central core of the Bighorn Mountains is a land of precipitous peaks, lakes, cirques, U-shaped canyons, extensive high alpine terrain, and coniferous forests at lower elevations. The typical wildlife of the Central Rockies lives here, including Mule Deer, Elk, Black Bear, and Mountain Lion. Elevations range from 5,000 feet to 13,175 feet, atop Cloud Peak. It is a popular recreation area. The Bighorns are traditional sacred mountains for the Sioux, Crow, and Cheyenne.

Status: Most of the Cloud Peak Wilderness Area is above tree line. Nearly all of the lower-elevation lands are threatened by FS timber and road-building plans, even though these timberlands are some of the most unproductive in the nation. The Bighorn Forest Plan allows development on most of the unprotected roadless lands adjacent to the Wilderness. Other threats include mining, ORVs, and overuse by recreationists in the Wilderness. The entire 224,000 acres of roadless NF lands were released by Congress, thanks to Wyoming anti-Wilderness Senator Malcolm Wallop. Retired Congressman John Seiberling attempted to add the Rock Creek drainage (on the east slope) to the Wilderness. This would have protected a continuum of habitats from alpine rock and tundra down to Great Plains prairie, but Wallop made sure that Cloud Peak became a classic "Wilderness on the Rocks."

LITTLE BIGHORN 155,000 acres (also in Montana)	
Bighorn NF roadless (WY)	135,000
Crow Indian Reservation roadless (MT)	15,000
State and private roadless	5,000

Description: Northern Wyoming and southern Montana west of Sheridan, Wyoming. The northern end of the Bighorn Range is a little-known area of subalpine basins, meadows, and forests, with steep canyons and river breaks dropping to the Great Plains on the east. Wildlife includes Mountain Lion,

Black Bear, Pronghorn, Mule Deer, and Elk. The primary human use is by hunters and fishermen.

Status: The entire area was released by Congress and is threatened by water development schemes, timber sales, and road construction. By the time this book is in print, much of this area may already be developed.

NORTH BIGHORN MOUNTAINS 144,000 acres (also in Montana)

See Montana for description and status.

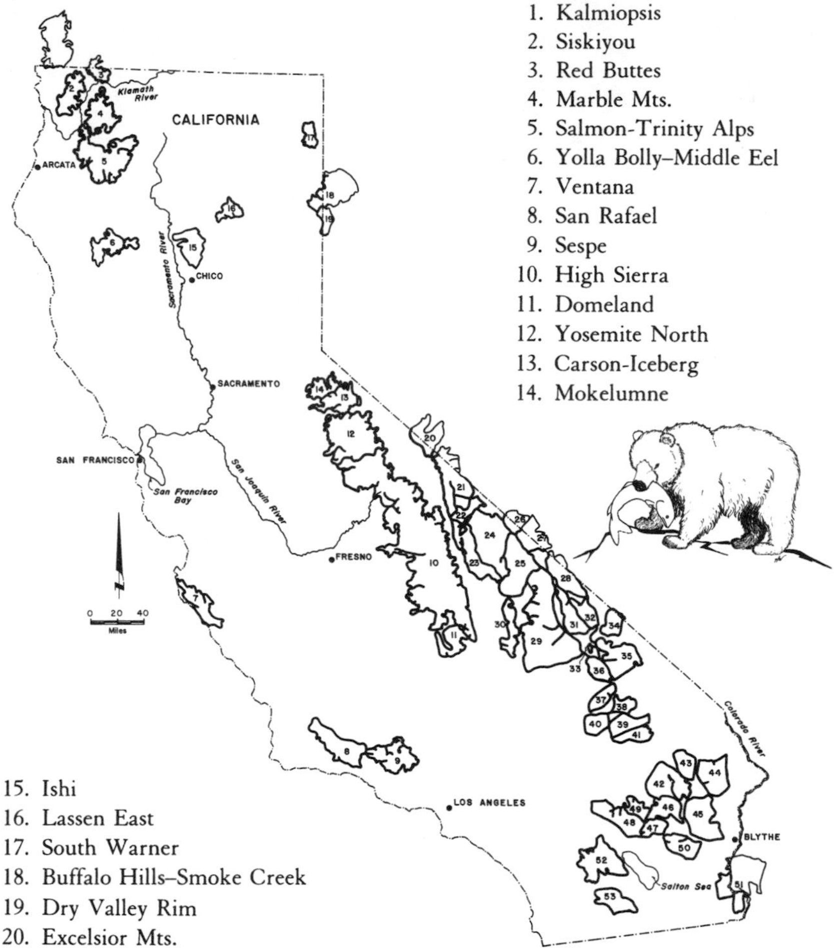

1. Kalmiopsis
2. Siskiyou
3. Red Buttes
4. Marble Mts.
5. Salmon-Trinity Alps
6. Yolla Bolly–Middle Eel
7. Ventana
8. San Rafael
9. Sespe
10. High Sierra
11. Domeland
12. Yosemite North
13. Carson-Iceberg
14. Mokelumne
15. Ishi
16. Lassen East
17. South Warner
18. Buffalo Hills–Smoke Creek
19. Dry Valley Rim
20. Excelsior Mts.
21. White Mts.
22. Piper Mt.-Soldier Canyon
23. Inyo Mts.
24. Saline–Last Chance
25. Cottonwood Mts.
26. Queer Mt.
27. Grapevine Mts.
28. Funeral Mts.
29. Panamint Mts.
30. Argus Range
31. Amargosa Range
32. Greenwater Range
33. Ibex Hills
34. Nopah Range
35. Kingston Range
36. Avawatz
37. Soda Mt.
38. Old Dad Mt.
39. Kelso Dunes
40. Cady Mts.
41. Granite Mts.
42. Sheep Hole
43. Old Woman Mts.
44. Turtle Mts.
45. Palen-McCoy
46. Coxcomb
47. Eagle Mt.
48. Hexie–Li'l San Berdo Mts.
49. Pinto Mts.
50. Chuckwalla Mts.
51. Lower Colorado River
52. Santa Rosa Mts.
53. Vallecito Mts.

California

What a land of contrasts is California! It has the highest mountain in the forty-eight contiguous states and the lowest point; the largest trees on Earth and the driest, hottest, most barren desert in the United States. Perhaps the most surprising contrast, however, is that while California has the largest human population of any state, it also has the most land in the National Wilderness Preservation System (nearly 6 million acres) and the greatest number of roadless areas over 100,000 acres (not counting Alaska).

Natural California begins with the Coast Range, flanking the Pacific Ocean. A misty forest of giant, ancient trees (over twenty species of conifers) envelops the Coast Range in the north, San Francisco Bay punches its way through the mountains in their center, and vegetation reflecting steadily drier habitats grows south into Mexico. Inside the Coast Range is the great Central Valley, formed by the Sacramento and San Joaquin Rivers. Once it was a haven for Tule Elk, Pronghorn, Grizzly, and waterfowl in mosquitolike profusion; now it is an agricultural factory. East of the Central Valley, the

Cascades in northern California and the Sierra Nevada in central California rear up in a stupendous mountain wall, with dark forests on the west slope, an expanse of rock and ice on the crest, and sagebrush dropping down the arid east side into the Great Basin. South and east of the Sierra, east of Los Angeles and the Coast Range, the California Desert combines three ecological deserts—the Great Basin, Mojave, and Colorado (Sonoran).

Except for the Central Valley, all of these regions still have big wilderness.

This is not to say all is well with California's wilderness. Its wildlife populations have been more devastated than those of any other Western state—the Golden Bear exists only on the state flag (once California had the largest population of Grizzlies, as well as the biggest bears outside of coastal Alaska); Tule Elk and Pronghorn are virtually gone; Bighorn Sheep are but a reminder of their former populations. Moreover, no state in the West has been more thoroughly invaded by exotics, from grasses to eucalyptus. No state has sucked more from its rivers. The peerless Redwood Forest, once stretching from the Big Sur to the Oregon border, remains only in tiny museum pieces (96 percent has been cut in the last hundred years, and another 2 percent faces the chain saw today). The distraught denizens of Los Angeles, San Bernardino, and San Diego relieve their frustrations from living and working in such impossible cities by ripping up the desert with knobby tires, and pity the poor creature—Desert Tortoise or Creosote Bush—that gets in their way.

But because of the population and urbanity of California, the traditional land barons of the West—ranchers, timbermen, miners—are relatively less powerful here. California is also the home of the Sierra Club and has more members of conservation groups than do all of the other Western states combined. As a result, a greater percentage of California has been preserved. In RARE II, the Forest Service identified 6.5 million acres as roadless; conservationists asked for 6 million; and in 1984, Congress established 1,779,432 acres of new National Forest Wilderness and postponed a decision on another 1.7 million acres. The same bill designated as Wilderness much of Yosemite, Kings Canyon, and Sequoia National Parks. Wilderness Areas had been previously established in Joshua Tree, Lava Beds, and Pinnacles National Monuments; Pt. Reyes National Seashore; and Lassen Volcanic NP. Death Valley NM is the only California unit of the NPS still awaiting Wilderness designation.

The BLM Organic Act (FLPMA) in 1976 singled out most of the Bureau of Land Management's acreage in California (12 million acres) as a special unit: the California Desert Conservation Area (CDCA). BLM was instructed to prepare a management plan and accelerate the Wilderness review. That review, mediocre under the Carter administration, was corrupted further by the Reaganauts. In 1987, conservationists turned to Senator Alan Cranston, who introduced the largest, and arguably the strongest, Wilderness bill ever in the lower forty-eight states—the California Desert Protection Act (CDPA). (Certainly far stronger Wilderness proposals have been developed in legislative form by conservationists—notably the Oregon High Desert Protection Act and the Wild Rockies Act—but they have not as yet been introduced by any member of Congress.)

The CDPA would establish a new National Park, the 1.5-million-acre Mojave NP; enlarge Death Valley National Monument by 1.3 million acres to a total of 3.4 million acres and redesignate it as a National Park; enlarge Joshua Tree National Monument by 245,000 acres to 795,000 acres and redesignate it as a National Park; designate 4.3 million acres in the three Parks as Wilderness; and designate 81 BLM Wilderness Areas with an acreage of 4.5 million acres. In all, 8.8 million acres of Wilderness would be established. (BLM lands outside the CDCA are not involved in the Cranston bill.)

Make no mistake, though: This bill is not visionary. It leaves unnecessary Jeep trails and dirt roads open in the Parks and on BLM land; gives dirt bikers and Jeepers millions of acres to pulverize; and continues grazing and mining, even in the Parks. Far better is the 16-million-acre California Desert National Wilderness Park proposal developed by Earth First! in 1986.

Moderate though it is, the Cranston bill is under heavy fire from the whole panoply of desert abusers. It stalled in Congress during the 1989–90 session because Senator Pete Wilson waffled, and because Senator Cranston lost influence because of his cuddly relationship with financial swashbuckler Charles Keating. Cranston reintroduced the bill early in 1991. Wilson left the Senate to successfully run for the California governorship in 1990, and there were hopes that his replacement, Republican John Seymour, would be more sympathetic to desert Wilderness.

However, in the summer of 1991, conservationists began the downhill slide of compromise when the Sierra Club and other groups praised a watered-down version of Cranston's bill introduced in the House of Representatives by Representatives Mel Levine, Richard Lehman, and George Miller. Their bill, which will replace Cranston's already compromised bill as the ceiling for new Wilderness and Park designation in the California Desert, chops a quarter of a million acres from Wilderness status to accommodate dirt bikers and small miners, downgrades the proposed Mojave Desert National Park to a National Monument, and allows continued cattle grazing in the Monument for twenty-five years. It's only fair to point out that conservation groups have said they will try to strengthen the Levine bill as it moves through the House. And as the bill overwhelmingly passed the House of Representatives in November 1991, it appeared that conservationists had held the line on additional cuts. On the other side of the fence, Representative Jerry Lewis introduced the Bush administration proposal—sixty-two BLM Wilderness Areas covering 2.1 million acres, no Mojave National Park or Monument, and minimal transfers of 108,600 acres from BLM to Death Valley and Joshua Tree. It was decisively voted down by the House in November 1991. But Senator Seymour, dashing conservationists' hopes with cold vinegar, announced that he believed the Levine bill was "a long way from what most people would consider an acceptable compromise." No, he was not expressing support for a visionary biodiversity approach for the California Desert, but signaling to dirt bikers, two-bit miners, developers, and others that it was open season on legislation for the Desert, and inviting them to swing their meat axes when the bill moved to the Senate.

Conservationists across the country need to voice their support for protecting the California Desert—that is, at a bare minimum support for the original Cranston proposal. Although the figures for the original Cranston bill will quickly become outdated, we have included them in our discussion for individual areas because they offer some kind of baseline.

At the other end of the state, conservationists, from Earth First! to the California Wilderness Coalition, are valiantly fighting big timber companies and the Forest Service to protect the remaining ancient forests. Small hydro projects are proposed for streams in many of the big roadless areas, and Friends of the River is working against those projects.

Of course, California's wilderness is sometimes crowded with backpackers, as hacked green trees at timberline lakes and wide, eroding trails attest. Sprawling cities encroach more and more on wildlife habitat, and the air turns brown.

California may no longer be paradise, but it ain't all a parking lot either.

Northern Coast Range

Northwestern California is a land of richly forested mountains, where fog strokes the earth like a lover, where pellucid rivers carry snow to the sea. Over 100 inches of precipitation fall in places. The eastern side of the northern Coast Range drops into the Sacramento Valley. Because the cloud-catching crest of the range forms a rain shadow, the forest to the east is transformed into Digger Pine and chaparral. The Big Outside here is managed largely by the U.S. Forest Service.

KALMIOPSIS 408,000 acres (also in Oregon)

See Oregon for description and status.

SISKIYOU 249,000 acres

Designated Siskiyou Wilderness Area (Klamath, Six Rivers, and Siskiyou NFs)	153,000
Additional Six Rivers, Klamath, and Siskiyou NF roadless	96,000

Description: Extreme northwestern California east of Crescent City between the Smith and Klamath Rivers in the Siskiyou Mountains. High precipitation and steep terrain with narrow ridges and sheer granite faces make the Siskiyous highly vulnerable to damage from road building and logging. Elevations drop from 7,309 feet, on Preston Peak, to 600 feet. There are some open valleys and a few lakes. Because much of the area escaped Pleistocene glaciation, vegetation is extremely diverse, with over twenty species of conifers, including Grand Fir, Port-Orford-Cedar, Knobcone Pine, Whitebark Pine, Yew, Noble Fir, and the rare Weeping Spruce; and the world's largest concentration of lily species. Perhaps the finest National Forest Wilderness–protected old-growth Pacific forest is located in the Siskiyou Wilderness Area. Wildlife includes Black Bear, Black-tailed Deer, River Otter, Fisher, Wolverine, Mountain Beaver, Pacific Salamander, Pileated Woodpecker, Spotted Owl, Goshawk, Osprey, and, some swear, Bigfoot. Portions of the headwaters for the Klamath, Smith, and Illinois Rivers are located here. The Upper South Fork of the Smith is a National Wild River. Summer runs of Steelhead and salmon are unhindered by human-caused obstructions. Sacred sites for the Yurok and Karok tribes are protected in the Wilderness, but some are located in adjacent unprotected roadless areas.

Status: The 1984 California Wilderness Act left a corridor for the controversial Gasquet-Orleans (G-O) Road and excluded significant old-growth forest in Blue Creek and Dillon Creek from the designated Wilderness Area. This remains an important battleground for ancient forests. Construction of the G-O Road was halted in 1983 by a landmark federal court decision based on First Amendment protection for the religious rights of Native American groups that use the high country. In 1988, the Supreme Court overturned the decision protecting Native American religious rights in the Siskiyous and remanded the case to a lower court. In a surprising move, local Congressman Doug Bosco (who was not considered a friend of Wilderness) quietly added the G-O Road corridor to the Siskiyou Wilderness late in 1990 as part of a bill establishing the Smith River National Recreation Area. The G-O Road is finally stopped. The acreage of the Wilderness Area addition is less than one thousand acres; because the FS has not calculated an exact figure, we leave the acreage summary for the Siskiyous unchanged. Ironically, Bosco was defeated in the 1990 election by a Republican who ran as something of an environmentalist.

The ancient forests of Blue and Dillon Creeks are still unprotected, however. California conservationists need to take advantage of the changed political situation to mount a major push to add these vital areas to the Siskiyou Wilderness now. Dillon Creek is especially valuable as a biological corridor linking the Siskiyous to the Marble Mountain Wilderness. Although logging is planned in Dillon Creek, it is not currently approved.

RED BUTTES 104,000 acres (also in Oregon)	
Designated Red Buttes Wilderness Area (Rogue River NF, CA)	16,150
Designated Red Buttes Wilderness Area (Rogue River and Siskiyou NFs, OR)	3,750
Additional Klamath, Siskiyou, and Rogue River NFs roadless (CA)	49,000
Additional Rogue River NF roadless (OR)	31,800
Oregon Caves NM and BLM roadless (OR)	3,500

Description: Southwestern Oregon and northwestern California south of Medford on the Siskiyou Mountains divide between the Klamath and Rogue River watersheds. This diverse Siskiyous ancient forest includes giant cedar groves, while landforms feature glacially sculptured peaks, lakes, marshes, and permanent snowfields. Elevations drop from 6,739 feet (Red Buttes) to 2,500 feet. Uncommon plants include Siskiyou Bitterroot, Weeping Spruce, Huckleberry Oak, and Sadler's Oak, making this area important botanically.

Black Bear, Bobcat, deer, and other wildlife abound. The headwaters of the Applegate River and part of the Illinois River drainage lie in this area.

Status: The undesignated area is under imminent threat of logging and roading.

MARBLE MOUNTAIN 320,000 acres	
Designated Marble Mountain Wilderness Area (Klamath NF)	241,744
Additional Klamath NF, BLM, and private roadless	78,000

Description: Northwestern California west of Yreka and east of the Klamath River. This alpine region in the Klamath Mountains has deep, timber-choked canyons and nearly one hundred lakes. The old-growth forest contains twenty-one coniferous species (Douglas-fir; Incense Cedar; Silver, Noble, Grand, Shasta Red, White, Red Firs; Knobcone, Digger, Sugar, Foxtail, Jeffrey, Ponderosa, Whitebark, Western White, Lodgepole Pines; Western Juniper; Weeping Spruce; Yew; and Mountain Hemlock). Red and White Firs predominate above 5,000 feet. The Weeping (Brewer) Spruce attains its greatest abundance here. A total of 535 plant species have been identified, seventeen of them being endemic to the Marbles and Siskiyous. Marble Mountain is crystallized limestone—marble. Because of this marble, alpine flora occurs at unusually low elevations, leading to greater endemism. Some lush meadows produce wildflowers reaching six feet in height. Elevations drop from 8,299 feet, on Boulder Peak, to 800 feet, where Wooley Creek meets the Salmon River. Wooley Creek supports Steelhead and King Salmon runs. Wildlife includes Wolverine (very rare), Black-tailed Deer, and, some believe, Bigfoot; and Marble Mountain is a potential Grizzly reintroduction site. The northern part of the Wilderness has some of the highest Black Bear densities in California. Elk have recently been reintroduced from Oregon. A large expanse of the southwestern part of the Wilderness is trailless except along Wooley Creek (part of which is a primitive route), making it arguably the wildest place in northern California.

Status: The Klamath Forest Alliance has stepped into national conservation leadership with its scientifically grounded proposal for biological corridors to link the Wilderness Areas of northwestern California to one another. Such linkages are the best tool to combat the fragmentation of wild habitat and old-growth forests, and to allow sensitive species more extensive ranges. Corridors linking core Wilderness Areas represent the cutting edge of conservation today and the marriage of conservation biology to grass-roots activism.

As in the rest of the northern coast region of California, the unprotected parts of this area, including portions along the Pacific Crest Trail, are under full-scale assault from logging and road building.

The 1984 California Wilderness Act made some minor additions to the Marbles, but not the vital Crapo Creek area to the southwest, which almost links the Marble Mountain Wilderness to the Salmon–Trinity Alps Wilderness, or the equally critical Grider Creek wildlife corridor adjacent to the Marbles on the north, providing a link to the Red Buttes Wilderness. Using the extensive 1987 forest fires in the area as an excuse, the FS wanted to salvage-log much of the Grider Creek ancient forest (most of the forest was unharmed by the fires). The Natural Resources Defense Council successfully appealed the logging in 1990 on biological corridor grounds. This may be the first instance of corridors' being defended in court.

Unfortunately, the FS recently logged right up to the western Wilderness boundary in the Ukonom Creek corridor, proposed for linking the Marbles to the Siskiyou Wilderness and Dillon Creek, and did heavy salvage-logging in the Crapo Creek corridor during 1988–89.

The Wilderness Area is plagued with excessive cattle, which not only ruin the experience of hikers, but trample and overgraze meadows, eliminate rare wildflowers, compete directly with bears favoring subalpine meadows, and infest watercourses with giardia. The overgrazing in the Marbles is also a major stumbling block to reintroduction of Grizzly. It is time to get the cows out of the Marbles.

RM36: 440,000

SALMON–TRINITY ALPS 620,000 acres	
Designated Trinity Alps Wilderness Area (Klamath, Shasta-Trinity, and Six Rivers NFs; BLM)	500,000
Additional Klamath, Shasta-Trinity, and Six Rivers NFs; BLM; and Hoopa Valley Indian Reservation roadless	120,000

Description: Northwestern California east of Arcata and north of the Trinity River. This large, high area in the southern Klamath Mountains features ice-sculpted peaks, small glaciers, glacial lakes, waterfalls, fine wildflower displays, large subalpine meadows, deep U-shaped valleys, and old-growth forests of Red Fir. Elevations range from below 1,500 feet to 9,002 feet, on Thompson Peak. Big Leaf Maple, Vine Maple, oak, and Dogwood show bright fall colors. This large Wilderness consists of three regions: the "White Trinities" high country in the center, named for its light-color granite; the "Red Trinities" to the east, with red, gray, and brown peaks; and the "Green Trinities" to the west, with lower-elevation forest. During some winters, 12 feet of snow accumulates in places. Salmon and Steelhead swim the many streams, including the South Fork of the Salmon River, Stuart Fork River, North Fork Trinity River, and New River. Wolverine, many Black Bear, and perhaps a remnant population of Bigfoot live here.

Status: Protection of most of this fine Wilderness was the major victory in the 1984 California Wilderness Act, but vital lower-elevation areas remain outside of protection and under threat of logging. A particularly important part denied protection was Orleans Mountain. This northwestern extension links the Alps to the Marble Mountain area via Crapo Creek. Conservationists should make a priority of protecting this linkage so that these two large northern California Wildernesses will not be further isolated and fragmented. Sadly, much of this corridor was salvage-logged by the FS in 1988–89. The Ladder Rock–Tish Tang Ridge area west of the Wilderness has an unusual parklike old-growth Douglas-fir forest; the FS plans to log it, of course, although no sales have yet been offered. Two dirt roads were cherrystemmed deep into the eastern part of the Wilderness Area; they should be closed and rehabilitated.

YOLLA BOLLY–MIDDLE EEL 260,000 acres	
Designated Yolla Bolly–Middle Eel Wilderness Area (Mendocino and Shasta-Trinity NFs, BLM)	153,404
Additional Mendocino, Six Rivers, and Shasta-Trinity NFs; BLM; Round Valley Indian Reservation; and private roadless	107,000

Description: Central part of the Coast Range in northwestern California, west of Red Bluff. The headwaters of the Middle Eel River (still partly covered by old-growth coniferous forest) lie between the North and South Yolla Bolly Mountains. Elevations drop from 8,000 feet to 800 feet. The lush forests include Douglas-fir, White and Red Firs, Ponderosa and Sugar Pines, Incense Cedar, Western Juniper, Western Hemlock, and Black Cottonwood.

Chamise and manzanita cover the lower elevations. This is one of the best wildlife strongholds in California, according to the California Wilderness Coalition, with 13 wilderness-associated species, including Wolverine, Mountain Beaver, Mink, River Otter, Mountain Lion, Ringtail, Golden Eagle, Marten, and Fisher; 150 bird species, including Bald Eagle, Golden Eagle, Peregrine Falcon, Goshawk, Spotted Owl, Pygmy Owl, and Short-eared Owl; and 80 percent of California's summer Steelhead. Black Bear and Black-tailed Deer are abundant. Much of the area is lower in elevation than other mountain wildernesses in California, so it is especially important ecologically. The Middle Fork of the Eel River and its tributaries are spectacular streams, with waterfalls, deep pools, and rock formations.

Status: Unprotected areas are under threat of logging and roading; they should be added to the Wilderness Area. BLM has recommended against Wilderness for its 640-acre WSA (30-501) contiguous to the eastern border of the designated Wilderness Area, and the 2,391-acre Big Butte WSA (50-211) contiguous to the west—BLM plans to road and log this western WSA (but conservationists are resisting).

The eastern WSA is part of a 35,000-acre roadless area of checkerboard BLM, FS, and private land that encompasses lower-elevation oak foothill country. The western WSA is part of a 30,000-acre roadless area of BLM, private, FS, and Round Valley Indian land. Both areas should be major priorities for federal acquisition and addition to the Wilderness. There is no other roadless area in northern California that covers such a complete transition from semiarid Central Valley foothills over the Coast Range and down into the coastal rain forest. Logging on the west and grazing on the east could sunder this totality unless conservationists can successfully act.

A band of visionary local conservationists (Mendocino Forest Watch) has proposed a very strong system of ancient-forest reserves linked by corridors to each other and to the Yolla Bolly. Their proposal includes a 57,000-acre Middle Fork Eel Wilderness Recovery Area addition to the existing Wilderness.

Southern Coast Range

Where San Francisco Bay breaks through the Coast Range, the Central Valley finds an outlet to the Pacific Ocean. South of the Bay, the Coast Range again forms the western wall of the continent. Mists and Coast Redwood predominate at first. But as the mountains tramp south, their vegetation becomes drier and less forested until it becomes dominated by coast chaparral. The Los Padres NF manages most of the Big Outside of the South Coast Range.

VENTANA 217,000 acres	
Designated Ventana Wilderness Area (Los Padres NF)	151,000
Additional Los Padres NF and Hunter-Liggett Military Reservation roadless	20,000
Private and state roadless	46,000

Description: West-central California south of Monterey. In the coastal Santa Lucia Mountains east of Highway 1 along the Big Sur, topography is characterized by sharp-crested ridges dividing V-shaped valleys. Elevations range from 400 feet to 5,000 feet. Waterfalls, hot springs, and deep pools are common along the plunging streams. Precipitation varies from over 100 inches to under 30 inches; summer fog fills the coastal valleys. Frequent fire has shaped this chaparral and oak woodland. Virgin stands of Coast Redwood line Big and Little Sur Rivers. Bristlecone (Santa Lucia) Fir is an endemic conifer. Other trees include California Madrone (up to 125 feet tall), Tanoak, Coast Live Oak, Coulter Pine, Ponderosa Pine, Douglas-fir, and California Bay Laurel. Wildlife includes Mountain Lion (one of the densest populations on the continent), Mule Deer, Gray Fox, Ringtail, Red-shouldered Hawk, Prairie Falcon, Mountain Plover, Spotted Owl, Golden Eagle, Peregrine Falcon, native Rainbow Trout, and Steelhead. Feral boar compete with some of these natives, to the detriment of the natives. This is the landscape that inspired poet Robinson Jeffers.

Status: Largely protected; contiguous roadless lands should be added to the Wilderness. The dirt Arroyo Seco–Indians Road cuts this larger roadless area off from a second unit of the Ventana Wilderness that has a significant amount of roadless NF land around it (about 80,000 acres total). The road should be closed, adjacent wild private and state land added, and a unified Wilderness of at least 300,000 acres protected. The entire two-unit Ventana Wilderness totals 167,440 acres; in the first edition of *The Big Outside,* we failed to delete the approximately 16,000 acres in the detached smaller unit, but we have corrected the acreage for the large Ventana roadless area accordingly in this edition. In 1990, Congress deleted 23 acres from the northern border of the Wilderness to allow for the expansion of the Los Padres Reservoir and added 140 acres as compensation. This acreage adjustment is also reflected.

Legislation was introduced in 1991 in the Senate and House to designate additional Wilderness and Wild Rivers in the Los Padres National Forest (the Los Padres Condor Range and River Protection Act). Unfortunately, the bill is very weak and would release 726,650 acres of RARE II areas throughout the Los Padres NF, while designating a mere 398,750 acres in five new Wilderness Areas and in additions to the existing Ventana and San Rafael Wilderness Areas. This bill should be unacceptable to conservationists until it is considerably enlarged. Although Senator Cranston originally proposed 66,300 acres of additions to the Ventana Wilderness, that was chopped in the 1991 bills to a mere 38,000 acres. Most of this addition is to the detached second unit of the Ventana Wilderness, which is not included as part of this roadless area because of the Arroyo Seco–Indians Road. About 19 miles of the Big Sur River would be protected as Wild and Scenic, and 23 miles of the Little Sur River would be studied under the act.

SAN RAFAEL 381,000 acres	
Designated San Rafael Wilderness Area (Los Padres NF)	151,040
Designated Dick Smith Wilderness Area (Los Padres NF)	64,700
Additional Los Padres NF roadless	159,000
Private roadless	6,000

Description: The mountainous backdrop to coastal Santa Barbara in southern California. Elevations decrease from 6,800 feet, on Big Pine Mountain, to under 1,000 feet. These rugged mountains, cut by sheer canyons, were a crucial part of the California Condor's habitat. The two Wilderness Areas are separated by a fire road, which is closed to all non–Forest Service vehicles but is used illegally by ORVs. Other roadless areas are separated only by Jeep trails and dirt bike routes. In this area of frequent fire, vegetation is mostly chaparral, with riparian zones along the streams, and pines (Knobcone, Jeffrey, Ponderosa, and Coulter) and Big Cone Douglas-fir at higher elevations. Of particular interest are the southernmost stand of Sargent Cypress and exquisite Chumash Indian cave paintings. Wildlife includes Black Bear, Mountain Lion, and Peregrine Falcon. The San Rafael was the first Forest Service Primitive Area to be designated Wilderness under the Wilderness Act (1968).

Status: Unprotected areas are under pressure from ORVs, illegal wood cutting, and oil and gas leasing. This is a potential Grizzly reintroduction site.

The 1991 Los Padres Condor Range and River Protection Act proposes 43,000 acres of additions to the San Rafael Wilderness thereby sentencing over 100,000 acres of roadless land to ORV play and other destruction. Only 33 miles of the Sisquoc River would be protected as Wild and Scenic.

*RM27: 1,097,600**

SESPE 335,000 acres	
Sespe-Frazier roadless area (Los Padres NF)	320,700
Private roadless	14,000

Description: Southern California north of Ventura. This rugged area of mountains and canyons rises up from the Santa Clara River Valley at under 1,000 feet to nearly 7,500 feet on Pine Mountain. Coastal chaparral grades into conifer forest (Knobcone, Jeffrey, Ponderosa, Coulter Pines, and Big Cone Douglas-fir). The many permanent streams cut sheer canyons, including the almost impassable Sespe Gorge. Wildlife includes Black Bear, Mountain Lion, Bobcat, Mt. Pinos Chipmunk, Mt. Pinos Blue Grouse, Spotted Owl, Peregrine Falcon, and Rubber Boa. This was the last refuge for the highly Endangered California Condor (all of the condors are now behind bars for a captive breeding program). Hot springs and Chumash Indian cave paintings attract hikers. The Sespe is the second-largest completely unprotected National Forest roadless area (only Idaho's Boulder–White Clouds is larger).

Status: This is one of the more threatened wild areas in California. ORVs are assaulting it on all sides. Demands for oil and gas leasing are pressing. Two dams are currently proposed—Oat Mountain and Cold Spring.

The last free California Condor was captured in 1987 for a controversial captive breeding program. Chicks from that program are scheduled for experimental release in the Sespe during 1992. Conservationist Joe Bernhard makes a strong case that poisoning of rodents with 1080 led to secondary poisoning of condors and was a key factor in their rapid decline. A complete prohibition on the use of 1080 and other predator poisons in the condor's range is a prerequisite for successful reintroduction. Sespe should also be one of the priority sites for reintroduction of the Grizzly into California.

The FS, in its final Los Padres Forest Plan, recommended 197,047 acres for Wilderness; the 1991 Los Padres Condor Range and River Protection Act would designate a piddling 220,500-acre Sespe Wilderness Area, which would leave 100,000 acres of the area open to oil and gas extraction, ORVs, illegal wood cutting, and mining. Part of the Sespe River would be protected as a Wild River, but other parts of it would remain unprotected and vulnerable to damming. Conservationists are pushing hard, however, for protection of the entire river and have gotten support from the Ventura Board of Supervisors and three local city governments.

*RM27: 1,097,600**

Sierra Nevada

Perhaps no other mountain range in the United States has been so glorified, loved, and fought for as the Sierra Nevada. With good reason. Bare granite domes, crystal lakes, rushing streams, waterfalls, Giant Sequoias, dark old-growth forests, glacier-carved valleys, friendly Black Bears. . . . For nearly four hundred miles, the Sierra Nevada forms the backbone of California. "Climb the mountains and get their good tidings," wrote John Muir. He was writing of the Sierra Nevada.

HIGH SIERRA 2,800,000 acres	
Designated Yosemite National Park Wilderness Area (southern portion)	304,000
Designated Ansel Adams Wilderness Area (Sierra and Inyo NFs)	228,669
Designated John Muir Wilderness Area (Sierra and Inyo NFs)	580,675
Designated Dinkey Lakes Wilderness Area (Sierra NF)	30,000
Designated Sequoia–Kings Canyon National Park Wilderness Area	736,980
Designated Monarch Wilderness Area (Sequoia and Sierra NFs)	45,000
Designated Jennie Lakes Wilderness Area (Sequoia NF)	10,500
Designated Golden Trout Wilderness Area (Inyo and Sequoia NFs)	303,287
Designated South Sierra Wilderness Area (Inyo and Sequoia NFs)	63,000
Additional National Forest roadless	406,000
Additional National Park roadless	14,000
BLM roadless	78,000

Description: East-central California east of Fresno. Say "wilderness," and most people will think of John Muir's "Range of Light"—the High Sierra. Although within an easy day's drive of the metastasizing population centers of California, the Sierra contains the second-largest roadless area remaining in the United States outside of Alaska. From Mt. Whitney, at 14,495 feet the highest point in the lower forty-eight states, to the Giant Sequoias (several groves occur in this roadless area), this is a wilderness writ in superlatives. Vegetation ranges from the oak and chaparral of the west slope foothills (lowest elevations of 2,300 feet); through forests of Red Fir, Lodgepole, Jeffrey, and Ponderosa Pines; to great expanses of tundra, granite domes, and small glaciers; down the east slope into piñon-juniper woodland and finally to the sagebrush desert of the Great Basin. Deep canyons of the San Joaquin, Kings, Kern, and other rivers cut down through the mountains. Awesome (in its proper meaning) Kings Canyon is the deepest gorge in North America, Californians aver (although Idaho and Oregon chauvinists claim this distinction for Hells Canyon). Countless lakes, waterfalls, and lush meadows spice the scene. Some basins are trailless. Snow is possible during any month in the high country. Wolverine (very rare), Bighorn Sheep, Black Bear, and Mountain Lion still roam this backcountry of the most populous state. Nowhere else in the United States is there a straight line of 150 miles that is roadless—from Bald Mountain north to Tioga Pass, no road crosses the Sierra.

Status: While most of this area is protected, parts of it suffer from extreme overuse by wilderness recreationists. Portions of the roadless area outside of the protected Wildernesses and Parks are under siege from timber harvest and ORVs. ORVs are a particular threat to the Monache Meadow area next to the South Sierra Wilderness—the FS is planning new roads and trails for vehicles there. A major dam project on Dinkey Creek has been dropped by its promoters, but other dams are still being discussed. More ski area destruction is proposed on the east side near Mammoth Mountain in the San Joaquin roadless area, which is adjacent to the Ansel Adams Wilderness; habitat for sensitive species such as the Yosemite Toad and Aplodontia (the Mountain Beaver, presumed to be the world's most primitive living rodent) would be damaged.

A significant victory in the 1984 California Wilderness Bill was protection for the "missing link" San Joaquin headwaters between Yosemite and the John Muir Wilderness, thereby preventing another trans-Sierra highway. The Dinkey Lakes Wilderness is separated from the John Muir Wilderness by a Jeep trail, which should be closed to vehicles. Despite the length of the Wilderness backbone, numerous cherrystem intrusions penetrate from both east and west. They should be closed and restored to Wilderness.

Yosemite Valley, which is surrounded by the northern part of this roadless area, is an appalling indictment of National Park Service mismanagement. Monumental traffic jams (twenty thousand cars one Memorial Day Weekend), trashy tourist developments, lowing herds of visitors, and the resultant air pollution have transformed what was once America's most glorious mountain valley into a slum. To the south, the Central Valley gathers the airborne waste of millions of acres of factory farms and the exhaust of valley cities and drives the whole noxious, roiling mass into Sequoia and Kings Canyon, creating some of the most turbid air in the world, and choking the great trees. Even Muir's High Sierra is not immune to the by-products of the world's greatest standard of living.

RM27: 2,906,240

DOMELAND 212,000 acres	
Designated Domeland Wilderness Area (Sequoia NF)	94,695
Additional Sequoia NF roadless	64,000
BLM WSAs 10-29/32	37,004
Private and additional BLM roadless	16,000

Description: East-central California east of Kernville. This southern extension of the Sierra crest includes many granite domes; elevations rise from 2,800 feet to 9,977 feet, on Sirretta Peak. The northern part is a large basin surrounded by rock formations with scattered forests of Jeffrey Pine, mixed conifer, rolling sagebrush country, and wet meadows. The southern part is semiarid with rock outcrops and domes. The South Fork of the Kern River runs through the entire area north to south. A minor dirt road separates this little-used area from the South Sierra Wilderness in the High Sierra roadless area.

Status: The Sirretta Peak–Little Trout Creek area outside the Wilderness is threatened by logging. BLM has recommended against Wilderness for its contiguous lands, but the California Desert Protection Act would designate 36,300 BLM acres as Wilderness.

YOSEMITE NORTH 744,000 acres	
Yosemite National Park Wilderness Area and additional NP roadless (northern portion)	402,000
Designated Emigrant Wilderness Area (Stanislaus NF)	112,191
Designated Hoover Wilderness Area (Inyo and Toiyabe NFs)	48,601
Hall Natural Area (Inyo NF)	5,209
Additional Inyo, Stanislaus, and Toiyabe NFs, and BLM roadless	176,000

Description: East-central California east of Sonora. The Sierra Nevada in the northern half of Yosemite National Park includes the unparalleled Grand Canyon of the Tuolumne. Mt. Conness, at 12,590 feet, is the high point; the low point is about 3,800 feet, along Hetch Hetchy Reservoir. The Tioga Pass road separates Yosemite North from the main High Sierra roadless area to the south. Numerous Black Bear are infamous for their ability to fetch "bear-bagged" packs. Largely a high plateau of exposed granite and innumerable lakes, the land varies from lava-capped alpine peaks down to broiling oak savannah in the western foothills. Many deep, granite-walled canyons drain the high country. This roadless area surrounds Hetch Hetchy, where John Muir battled the City of San Francisco to prevent construction of a dam in Yosemite National Park early this century. Probably not coincidentally, Muir died shortly after Congress approved the dam. This battle was one of the seminal events of the American conservation movement. See High Sierra roadless area for general ecological description.

Status: While largely protected, the undesignated National Forest areas are under the typical threats of logging and ORVs that most NF areas in California face. The Toiyabe NF is recommending for Wilderness designation all of the Hoover Additions Congressional Study Area (West Walker area) and about half of the Hoover Further Planning Area.

CARSON-ICEBERG 279,000 acres	
Designated Carson-Iceberg Wilderness Area (Toiyabe NF)	160,000
Additional Stanislaus and Toiyabe NFs roadless	99,000
BLM, California Fish and Game, and private roadless	20,000

Description: East-central California east of Jackson. In the High Sierra between Sonora and Ebbetts Passes, just north of the Yosemite North area, geology combines black basaltic rock with white and gray granite to form a dozen peaks over 10,000 feet. The high point is 11,462-foot Sonora Peak. Scattered forests consist of Sugar, Jeffrey, Lodgepole, and Western White Pines; and Red and White Firs. Several long valleys with meadows are filled each summer with stunning wildflowers. The headwaters of the East Fork Carson, Stanislaus, and Mokelumne Rivers are given birth here. The Endangered Pauite Cutthroat and Threatened Lahontan Cutthroat are present in isolated creeks. Other trout species and Rocky Mountain Whitefish inhabit additional streams. River Otter and Mink fish the streams. Wolverine have been sighted in the area.

Status: A 10,000-acre area outside the protected area in Pacific Valley is being studied for a downhill ski resort. The rest of the unprotected area is under threat by logging, dam construction, and ORVs. BLM is proposing 550 contiguous acres for Wilderness designation; conservationists should propose 10,000 acres of BLM land for addition to the Carson-Iceberg Wilderness Area. Some private roadless land in the Slinkard Valley adjacent to the BLM land has been purchased by the California Department of Fish and Game.

MOKELUMNE 164,000 acres	
Designated Mokelumne Wilderness Area (Eldorado, Stanislaus, and Toiyabe National Forests)	104,461
Additional NF roadless	60,000

Description: East-central California east of Sacramento in the High Sierra, south of Lake Tahoe between Ebbetts and Carson Passes and north of the Carson-Iceberg area. Elevations drop from 10,830 feet, on Round Top, to 4,000 feet, at Salt Springs Reservoir. Popular for cross-country skiing in winter, Mokelumne's spectacular wildflower displays attract recreationists in summer. Headwaters of the Mokelumne and West Fork Carson Rivers spring here. The Mokelumne River Canyon is extremely rugged. Shallow valleys with many small lakes and scattered timber characterize the area.

Status: A Jeep trail divides part of the designated Wilderness from the rest. It should be closed. Standard threats of logging and ORVs apply to undesignated portions.

ISHI 225,000 acres	
Designated Ishi Wilderness Area (Lassen NF and BLM)	41,840
Tehama State Wildlife Area, private, and additional Lassen NF roadless	183,000

Description: Northeastern California between Chico and Lassen National Park. The largest wild remnant of the California valley and foothills survives here. The high point is 4,488 feet, and the low point is under 400 feet. Fine oak (and Poison Oak!) and Digger Pine forest cover the ridges; oak savannah and chaparral cloak the slopes; oaks and annual grasses clothe the foothills. Deer, Mill, and Antelope Creeks have cut deep canyons lined with California Sycamore riparian forest. Scattered Ponderosa Pine and Douglas-fir grow at higher elevations. Some of the best Blue Oak woodlands left in California are present in the lower foothills. Federally Endangered Orcutt Grass is present. Black Bear, the Tehama Mule Deer herd, Mountain Lion, Bobcat, Peregrine Falcon, Prairie Falcon, Golden Eagle, and a "wild" horse herd are among Ishi's animals. Mill Creek has Steelhead and Chinook Salmon runs. Lava rimrock and many shallow caves make Ishi geologically fascinating. This was the home of Ishi, the last wild Indian in the United States. About 80 percent of the designated Wilderness burned in 1990.

Status: The unprotected area is threatened by small hydroelectric projects, continued welfare ranching, excessive "game management," and ORVs. Deer, Mill, and Antelope Creeks are being recommended for Wild and Scenic River protection. There is a minor threat of logging on the unprotected NF lands. The State Game Refuge has Jeep trails cutting through it. The lower part of the foothills and upper valley are private lands used for ranching. A power line (but no road) crosses the west end. Protection of the roadless private lands should be a high priority for California conservationists. The Nature Conservancy manages the Dye Creek Ranch, southwest of the Tehama State Wildlife Area, in this roadless area. Perhaps the Conservancy could explore ways of maintaining the wild character of other private lands in the Ishi.

LASSEN EAST 100,000 acres	
Designated Lassen Volcanic National Park Wilderness Area (eastern portion) and roadless	68,000
Designated Caribou Wilderness Area (Lassen NF)	20,625
Additional Lassen NF roadless	12,000

Description: Northeastern California east of Redding and west of Susanville in the southern Cascades. This high, gentle plateau east of Lassen Peak is dotted with lakes and volcanic cones. Bumpass Mountain, at 8,763 feet, is the high point. The fascinating recent volcanic landscape includes Snag Lake (formed by a lava flow in the 1880s), the Cinder Cones, hot springs, geysers, mud pots, and other thermal features. Aspen and old-growth Red Fir, White Fir, and Lodgepole Pine grow throughout this high country. Black Bear, Black-tailed Deer, Wolverine, Marten, Fisher, Osprey, and mosquitoes live here. Bufflehead Ducks breed on the lakes.

Status: The unprotected Lassen NF area is threatened by timber sales.

Great Basin

The eastern border of California slips into what should properly be Nevada. East from the crest of the Sierra and the Cascades, a rain shadow falls, creating a high, cool desert of sagebrush steppe in the north that southward gradually warms, culminating in the blistering hot Mojave Desert around Death Valley. The Modoc, Inyo, and Toiyabe NFs, BLM, and Death Valley National Monument manage these areas.

SOUTH WARNER 100,000 acres	
Designated South Warner Wilderness Area (Modoc NF)	70,385
Additional Modoc NF roadless	16,500
BLM WSA 20-708	4,500
Private roadless	8,500

Description: Extreme northeastern California east of Alturas. The Cascades meet the Great Basin in the Warners. To the west of the undulating crest of this classic fault-block range, the snow-capped cone of Shasta rises, while dry lakes, sagebrush steppe, and basin and range stretch into Nevada to the east. Elevations climb from 4,600 feet to 9,892 feet, on Eagle Peak. The vegetation is an unusual blend: Big Sagebrush climbs from the foothills (with Idaho Fescue, Bluebunch Wheatgrass, and Squirrel-tail) to the highest peaks, while extensive Aspen forests and isolated groves deck the basins and slopes, and line the streams. Piñon and juniper are common at lower elevations; as the elevation increases, they are replaced by Jeffrey and Ponderosa Pines (including some very large individuals), Lodgepole Pine, White Fir, and thick forests of Whitebark Pine along the crest. Mules Ear and lupine join sagebrush in the meadows. Several glacial lakes, cirques, rushing streams, wet meadows, and colorful rock formations are features of this relatively well-watered Great Basin range. Wildlife includes Mule Deer, Pronghorn, Beaver, Mountain Lion, Badger, Mink, Osprey, Pileated Woodpecker, California Quail, Goshawk, Golden Eagle, and Peregrine Falcon. California Bighorn Sheep were reintroduced in 1980, but the herd was wiped out in early 1988 by a disease spread by domestic sheep, which graze much of the Modoc NF.

Status: Overgrazing by cattle and sheep is occurring in the Wilderness and adjacent lands. The Modoc NF refuses to restrict grazing by woollies, despite the incompatibility of wild and domestic sheep and despite the presence of prime Bighorn habitat in the Warners. Although the Wilderness is generally lightly used, slob campers (particularly horsepackers) are damaging the Patterson Lake area. ORVs are an increasing problem outside the Wilderness, and logging is a potential threat. The closure of minor dirt roads (scarcely more than Jeep trails) on the NF could add around 20,000 acres to what is currently roadless. BLM is recommending only 1,187 acres of its WSA for addition to the Wilderness.

BUFFALO HILLS–SMOKE CREEK 387,000 acres (also in Nevada)
See Nevada for description and status.

EAGLE HEAD (DRY VALLEY RIM) 100,000 acres (also in Nevada)
See Nevada for description and status.

EXCELSIOR MOUNTAINS 232,000 acres (also in Nevada)
See Nevada for description and status.

WHITE MOUNTAINS 379,000 acres (also in Nevada)	
Inyo National Forest roadless (California)	281,600
Designated Boundary Peak Wilderness Area (Inyo NF, NV)	10,000
Additional Inyo NF roadless (NV)	30,000
BLM WSAs CDCA 102 and 103	20,369
Additional BLM roadless (CA)	17,000
Additional BLM and private roadless (NV)	20,000

Description: Central California-Nevada border northeast of Bishop. Across the Owens Valley from the Sierra Nevada, the White Mountains, the highest range in the Great Basin, leap up 10,000 feet from the valley floor (White Mountain Peak, at 14,246 feet, is the second-highest point in California; Boundary Peak, at 13,140 feet, is the highest point in Nevada). The lower slopes support a sagebrush community that merges into a piñon-juniper forest. One of the best examples of Bristlecone Pine forest grows in the high country, and alpine vegetation occurs along the rarefied crest. Additional trees include Aspen, Limber Pine, Jeffrey Pine, and Water Birch. A relict stand of Lodgepole Pine grows in one eastside canyon. There are four sensitive plant species in the area. Wildlife includes Inyo Shrew, Pika, Nuttall Cottontail, Yellow-bellied Marmot, Gray Fox, Ringtail, Pine Marten, Wolverine (very rare), Mountain Lion, Pronghorn, and Bighorn Sheep. Tule Elk, native to the Sacramento Valley but extirpated there, were transplanted to the Owens Valley, and some range into the White Mountains. No fish are native to the Whites, but several trout species have been introduced, including the Endangered Paiute Cutthroat. There have been sightings of Black Bear.

Status: Several Jeep trails intrude into this wild area, and ORVs are the major threat to it (the FS divided the roadless area into three separate RARE II areas based on Jeep trails). Cattle grazing continues to degrade the fragile meadows, riparian areas, and other habitats in the area. Mining is a minor threat on the periphery.

This is perhaps the most important area, after the Sespe-Frazier, left out of the 1984 California Wilderness Act. The FS proposes 120,000 acres for Wilderness, the Sierra Club and Friends of the Inyo recommend about 300,000 acres (California only) and call for closing several Jeep trails and rough cherrystem roads. Their proposal also closes the Wyman Canyon Road to add the 32,705-acre Birch Creek RARE II area to a unified White Mountains Wilderness.

The 1989 Nevada Wilderness Act designated a 10,000-acre Boundary Peak Wilderness in the Nevada portion of the Whites. The 1988 Nevada Enhancement Act transferred a net total of 14,000 acres from BLM to the FS in this roadless area; the acreage summary reflects this change, as well as the correction of minor errors in calculating the roadless acreage in the first edition.

PIPER MOUNTAIN–SOLDIER CANYON 130,500 acres	
BLM WSA CDCA 115 (Piper Mountain)	69,282
Additional BLM roadless	13,000
Inyo NF roadless (Soldier Canyon RARE II)	44,774
Additional BLM roadless to west (non-CDCA)	3,500

Description: East-central California east of Big Pine, between the Westgard Pass and Devils Gate roads. This is a complicated roadless area, consisting of the northern end of the Eureka Valley on the east, rising to the eastern ridge of the Inyo Mountains (7,730-foot Piper Peak), dropping into Deep Springs Valley, rising again over the main ridge of the Inyos to 9,000 feet, and dropping into the Owens Valley on the west. The low point is 3,400 feet, in the Eureka Valley, where a Shadscale community, including the Pale Kangaroo Mouse, exists. The northernmost Joshua Tree forest in California is in the Inyos, and higher are Singleleaf Piñon. Desert Bighorn, Tule Elk, and a large Mule Deer herd are present. The rare Black Toad lives in Deep Springs Valley, and the Western Snowy Plover (a candidate for federal Endangered Species listing) nests at Deep Springs Lake. Other sensitive wildlife species include Golden Eagle and Prairie Falcon (with at least one aerie). Rock art is found throughout the area.

Status: Opposition to Wilderness designation comes from miners, ranchers, and, unfortunately, local Indians who want to gather piñon nuts with pickup trucks. This last is not a real issue, since areas accessible by truck are not included in the Wilderness proposal. The primary threat is a proposed Los Angeles Department of Water and Power power line through the released Soldier Canyon RARE II area.

The FS and BLM oppose any Wilderness in the area. The Cranston bill would designate 81,880 acres of Wilderness (7,040 acres would be added to

Death Valley National Park). None of the Inyo NF land would be included. Conservation groups should encourage Cranston to add the NF lands for a 125,000-acre Wilderness Area.

INYO MOUNTAINS 333,000 acres	
Inyo National Forest roadless	144,182
BLM WSAs 10-56/55/60 and CDCA 120/122 and additional roadless	189,000

Description: East-central California east of Independence. This high (up to 11,123 feet) but very dry mountain range east of the Owens Valley and Sierra Nevada drops down to 1,000 feet above sea level on the Saline Valley salt lake. A rough dirt road in Saline Valley separates it from the even bigger Saline and Cottonwood roadless areas. The crest affords views of the Owens Valley and Sierra Crest to the west and the Saline country to the east. Vegetation is Bristlecone Pine down through piñon and juniper to Great Basin desert scrub. Golden Eagle, Prairie Falcon, Mule Deer, and Bighorn Sheep find refuge here. The very rare Inyo Slender Salamander lives in the running water of deep canyons coming off the Inyo crest. Some canyons have waterfalls and hanging gardens of Maidenhair Fern. Rare endemic plants grow on the limestone formations.

Status: Dirt roads on the crest nearly divide the FS portion of the roadless area into western and eastern halves, although there is a roadless connection of a few miles between road ends. South of the Inyo NF, the BLM portion of the roadless area has a network of rough Jeep trails and small-scale mines on its periphery. Several dirt roads penetrate to the eastern base of the mountains.

In 1990, the Inyo NF denied a permit for a large organized motorcycle event through the roadless area; in protest, some ninety outlaw dirt bikers roared through the area, damaging archaeological sites. The crotch rocket jockeys threaten more illegal events. An additional threat is the diversion of water from eastside canyons for various reasons. Such diversions would be devastating to the Inyo Mountains Slender Salamander, under consideration for federal Endangered Species listing.

The Cranston bill would designate 55,440 acres of current BLM land as Wilderness in an expanded Death Valley NP, and 210,660 acres as BLM and FS Wilderness. Conservationists and Senator Cranston have bent over backward to appease two-bit miners and the Inyo County Supervisors by excluding possible mining areas and leaving Jeep trails open. The Forest Service supports a small Wilderness on its lands, and BLM is recommending part of its WSA. Possible mineralization is the major conflict.

The Saline Valley road should be closed, and a two-million-acre Wilderness established in this region. While mainstream conservationists may feel politically unable to propose this, they should feel comfortable proposing that at least half a million acres be designated as Wilderness in the Inyos through the closure of Jeep trails and dirt roads.

SALINE–LAST CHANCE 631,000 acres	
Saline–Eureka–Last Chance BLM WSA CDCA 117	486,300
Last Chance Range roadless area, Death Valley National Monument area	106,500
Additional BLM roadless	36,600
Inyo NF roadless	1,500

Description: East-central California east of Independence. This exquisite area, containing the northern part of Death Valley National Monument, comprises the Eureka Dunes (the highest in North America—800 feet), the untracked Saline Range, and the Last Chance Range. It is one of the largest and most diverse desert roadless areas left in the nation. The high elevation is 8,674 feet, on Dry Mountain. Oddities include the Racetrack, a playa where the wind pushes rocks across slick mud, thereby leaving their tracks. The volcanic, blocky Saline Range is one of the most remote and pristine areas in the United States (its highest peak was not climbed until 1973). Saline Valley has warm springs, a dry lake, and a heavily vegetated salt marsh. The Last Chance Range is spectacular with its abrupt, multicolor rocky face rising from the stunning Eureka Dunes. Desert Bighorn Sheep, Mule Deer, Desert Tortoise, Panamint Alligator Lizard, and raptors dwell here. Numerous rock art sites remain intact. See Panamint Mountains for a brief overview of plant communities (piñon-juniper to salt flat) in the Death Valley region.

Status: Most of this area is included in Senator Alan Cranston's Desert Wilderness bill as an addition to Death Valley National Park (upgraded from Monument) and as Wilderness within the Park (including most of the BLM lands).

The poor dirt road to the Racetrack and its even rougher continuation to Saline Valley should be closed. This lightly used road is all that separates this large roadless area from the nearly equally large Cottonwood roadless area to the south. Simply closing this road would create a 1,150,000-acre desert Wilderness. Closing the Saline Valley road could establish a 2-million-acre Wilderness including the Inyos.

The main opposition to protection is from ORVers, small miners, and carbound nudists who fear having to walk a mile to the Saline Valley Hot Springs. A Known Geothermal Resource Area (KGRA) is around the warm springs, and the U.S. Geological Survey (USGS) has offered leases, but there have been no takers. There are threats from mining, as well as irregular trespass occupancy by various weirdos around the warm springs (the Manson Family hung out here). ORVers are increasing their use in the roadless area, particularly on the Steel Pass Jeep trail separating the Saline Range from the Last Chance Range, around the Saline Valley hot springs, and in a sand dune area near the hot springs. BLM currently allows vehicles on the Steel Pass corridor, evidently hoping that continued use will cause the corridor to be excised from Wilderness designation. ORVers are using the Jeep trail as a jump-off to try to punch new ORV routes into currently untracked areas. It is imperative that the Steel Pass Jeep trail be effectively closed to all vehicles—including those of government agencies.

COTTONWOOD MOUNTAINS–PANAMINT DUNES 524,000 acres	
Cottonwood Mountains roadless area, Death Valley National Monument	410,300
Panamint Dunes BLM WSA CDCA 127	113,440

Description: East-central California east of Lone Pine. This superb desert expanse encompasses sand dunes in Mesquite Flat, the mile-and-a-half-high Cottonwood Mountains, the Darwin Plateau, and, on BLM land, the Panamint Dunes. Elevations range from below sea level in Mesquite Flat to 8,953 feet on Cottonwood Mountain. The 250-foot-tall Panamint Dunes are "star" dunes, which are unusual in California. The dunes support a rare plant and two rare arthropods. Joshua Trees fill the higher country. Desert Bighorn Sheep, Mule Deer, Desert Tortoise, Panamint Alligator Lizard, Prairie Falcon, and Golden Eagle are other denizens of this desert fastness. See Panamint Mountains for a brief overview of plant communities (piñon and juniper to salt flat and sand dunes).

Status: Most of this area is included in Senator Cranston's Desert Wilderness bill. The BLM roadless area would be added to the new Death Valley National Park, and most of the area would be designated as Wilderness. However, several Jeep routes would remain open. These should be closed, as should the poor dirt road to the Devil's Racetrack that splits this area from the Saline–Last Chance area to the north.

Feral burros are a particular problem to many of the roadless areas in Death Valley NM, competing with Bighorn herds, and destroying vital springs. The BLM area has some mining claims, and ORVers want to trash the dunes.

QUEER MOUNTAIN 155,000 acres (also in Nevada)	
Death Valley National Monument roadless (CA)	23,200
BLM WSA CDCA 119 (CA)	50,200
BLM WSA 5-354 (NV)	81,550

Description: Southern California-Nevada border in the northern end of Death Valley NM northwest of Beatty, Nevada. Queer Mountain is separated from the large Saline and Cottonwood roadless areas by a little-used gravel road, and from the Grapevine Mountain roadless area by the narrow paved Scottys Castle road. This low mountain range has many canyons, small valleys, peaks, and bajadas. The high point is 7,925 feet. The northern part of Death Valley itself is on BLM land. BLM has established an Area of Critical Environmental Concern (ACEC) at Sand Spring to protect rare plants. The fine lower Mojave Desert vegetation here consists of the Saltbush-Greasewood community, with a dense stand of Joshua Trees in the northern tip, and piñon and juniper higher. Mule Deer, raptors, and feral horses are among the larger animals.

Status: There are a few decaying mining camps on the periphery. Although no historic production has occurred, 129 mining claims were filed in the California BLM area between October 1983 and February 1984. Livestock grazing is present on the BLM land.

The Cranston bill would add 49,560 acres (California only) to Death Valley NP as Wilderness. The California BLM recommended 32,900 acres for Wilderness. BLM has recommended no Wilderness for the Nevada WSA, where there are threats from gold mining and ORVs.

GRAPEVINE MOUNTAINS 246,000 acres (also in Nevada)	
Death Valley NM roadless (CA and NV)	177,000
BLM roadless (NV)	69,000

Description: Southern California-Nevada border south of Scottys Castle in Death Valley NM and adjacent BLM land in Nevada west of Beatty. These impressive mountains have steep-walled canyons and colorful rock. The low point is below sea level in Death Valley; the high point is 8,740 feet, and then elevation drops 4,500 feet to the east on sweeping bajadas. Numerous peaks in the Nevada portion exceed 7,000 feet. The Saltbush-Greasewood plant community with some Joshua Trees phases into piñon-juniper forest. A few hundred Limber Pines encircle the upper slopes of Grapevine Peak. One Endangered plant (Rocklady—*Maurandya petrophilia*) is present, as are six other rare or endemic plants. Desert Tortoise, Mule Deer, Bighorn Sheep, Mountain Lion, Bobcat, and feral burros are present.

Status: The NPS has proposed the Death Valley NM portion for Wilderness. BLM has recommended no Wilderness for the Nevada WSA. The Titus Canyon road in Death Valley NM should be closed to vehicles, and 75,000 acres added for a combined Wilderness of 325,000 acres.

FUNERAL MOUNTAINS 287,000 acres (also in Nevada)	
Death Valley National Monument roadless (CA)	199,000
BLM WSA CDCA 143 (CA)	65,000
BLM roadless (NV)	23,000

Description: The range east of Furnace Creek in Death Valley NM on the southern California-Nevada border. Pyramid Peak, at 6,703 feet, is the high point; the low point is below sea level. The Funerals are thrust fault blocks of ancient limestone with abundant fossils. The limestone supports many rare and endemic species, and thick populations of several cactus species. There is a good population of Bighorn. The pinkish Panamint Rattlesnake is present. Raptors breed on the higher ridges. The Amargosa River flows through part of this area, supporting an important riparian habitat zone. The Chloride City ghost town is on the northern border of the roadless area. Archaeological sites include stone hunting blinds.

Status: NPS proposes two Wilderness Areas, divided by the brutal Echo

Canyon Jeep trail: 99,200 acres and 51,500 acres. The route should be closed to vehicles. Under the Cranston bill (applies to California only), 34,510 acres would be BLM Wilderness and 25,800 acres of the BLM land would be added to Death Valley NP as Wilderness. California BLM has proposed a 13,709-acre Wilderness. Nevada BLM proposes zip.

PANAMINT MOUNTAINS 1,166,000 acres	
Death Valley National Monument roadless	600,000
Owlshead Mountains BLM WSA CDCA 156	136,100
Additional BLM WSAs and roadless (CDCA)	212,000
Fort Irwin and China Lake Naval Weapons Center (military) roadless	218,000

Description: East-central California northeast of Ridgecrest, at the southern end of Death Valley National Monument. The Panamints, ranging in elevation from 11,049 feet, atop Telescope Peak, to below sea level on the floor of Death Valley, have the second-greatest vertical relief for any roadless area in the lower forty-eight (the High Sierra roadless area has the greatest). Vegetation ranges from Bristlecone Pine and Limber Pine above 10,000 feet; down through piñon, juniper, mountain mahogany, and Cliffrose; to Big Sagebrush and Blackbrush; to Shadscale; to Creosote Bush and Burro Bush; to the Alkali Sink Community of willow, salt bush, mesquite, and Pickleweed; to salt crystals. Some of the canyons support riparian vegetation, and three of the canyons on BLM land have perennial streams. The Endangered Panamint Daisy grows here. The Death Valley floor is one of the driest places in the world, averaging only 2 inches of precipitation per year, while the high country receives up to 15 inches. The highest temperatures in the United States are recorded here (134 degrees is the record). Portions of this immense area receive very little visitation. Desert Bighorn Sheep (the largest herd in California), Mule Deer, Desert Tortoise, Panamint Alligator Lizard, and Cottonball Marsh Pupfish inhabit this roadless area. Other species found throughout the Death Valley region include Ringtail, Bobcat, Kit Fox, Badger, Chuckwalla, Panamint Rattlesnake, Mojave Desert Sidewinder, and California Lyre Snake. The Death Valley area has a remarkable abundance of reptiles and birds (one hundred avian species are permanent or seasonal residents). The Owlshead Mountains to the south of Death Valley NM, with two large, dry lake beds, deep canyons, and rough mountains, are one of the more remote and pristine areas in the country. The Manson Family hung out at Meyers Ranch in the BLM area—Charlie was captured there.

Status: A number of Jeep trails intrude into this area, and one in Butte Valley crosses it. Old mines also scar the area—particularly in the Warm Springs Canyon area. A toxic waste dump, being considered for the southern Panamint Valley, would, of course, impact the nearby Wilderness.

The Cranston bill would transfer the 129,060-acre Owlsheads Wilderness to Death Valley NP, transfer 58,480 acres of other adjacent BLM land to the Park as Wilderness, establish 117,980 acres as BLM Wilderness, and designate most of the present Monument as Wilderness. But, alas, the bill would divide this huge roadless area into several units and leave most Jeep trails open. Mineralized areas have been excluded from Cranston's bill as a sop to rabidly anti-Wilderness prospectors. This is an unnecessary but far too typical compromise. The Park Service should close all Jeep trails in the area and protect this million-acre wilderness as one unit. Conservation groups should also encourage the military to protect the wilderness values of their lands in this area.

ARGUS RANGE 199,000 acres	
BLM WSA CDCA 132B (Argus Range)	80,000
BLM WSA CDCA 132 (Great Falls Basin)	14,000
China Lake Naval Weapons Center roadless	105,000

Description: East-central California north of Trona. The California Desert Protection League says that this roadless area "contains a great diversity of terrain, land forms and geologic features: alluvial fans, broad canyons and washes, and narrow twisting canyons with steep walled sides." The Argus Range rears up west of the Panamint Valley, climbing from 1,600 feet to 8,839 feet on Maturango Peak. Even though it is in the rain shadow of the Sierra Nevada, the range receives enough rainfall, because of its height, to boast perennial springs, streams, and waterfalls with dense riparian vegetation. Darwin Falls is the highest in the California Desert; it is currently threatened by tamarisk invasion and an illegal water diversion. Vegetation ranges from Mojave Desert scrub to piñon and juniper in the high country. Perhaps the lushest and most diverse Joshua Tree forest in California grows on the west slope of the Argus Range. A relative of Creosote, Fagonia, reaches the northern limit of its range here. *Mimulus rupicola,* listed by the

California Native Plant Society as rare and endangered, grows in two canyons, and the Inyo Brown Towhee, a candidate for Endangered species listing, inhabits the riparian areas. There are reports of salamanders in the area, which could be a new species. Desert Bighorn Sheep were reintroduced in 1986.

Status: Small-scale mining and ORVs are the principal threats to this area. BLM and local politicians oppose Wilderness designation, but the Cranston bill would establish two Wilderness Areas, divided by Homewood Canyon, of 79,300 acres (1,920 acres would be in the new Death Valley NP) and 8,800 acres (Great Falls Basin). BLM and the Navy are cooperating to control feral burros in the area. Feral horses are also overgrazing the area.

AMARGOSA RANGE 221,000 acres	
Death Valley National Monument roadless	166,000
BLM WSA CDCA 148	54,600

Description: East-central California, southern part of Death Valley. This area includes the Black Mountains, the southern end of the beautiful Greenwater Valley, and part of the Amargosa Range. The Black Mountains are so rugged that there are only two routes across them that do not require technical climbing. The California Desert Protection League says that in spring, the Greenwater Valley "is a riot of wildflowers with even an occasional desert tortoise grazing amongst them." Golden Eagle, Prairie Falcon, and Desert Bighorn Sheep are among the sensitive species. Rare plants include Death Valley Sandpaper Plant, Sticky Ring, Golden Carpet, and Death Valley Sage. Elevations drop from 6,384 feet to sea level. The area offers extreme solitude. *Timbasha,* a sacred site of the Panamint Shoshone, is in the far south of the Greenwater Valley.

Status: Under the Cranston bill, 52,680 acres of BLM land would be declared Wilderness and added to Death Valley NP. The NPS proposes a 138,900-acre Wilderness. Active mining occurs around Ryan adjacent to the northern end of this area.

GREENWATER RANGE 165,000 acres	
BLM WSA CDCA 147	164,000
Death Valley National Monument roadless	1,000

Description: East-central California just east of Death Valley NM and separated from the Amargosa Range roadless area by a dirt road. The Greenwaters are volcanic and virtually waterless; nonetheless, with good winter rains, they offer one of the best spring wildflower displays in the desert. The green Creosote growing on black basalt is striking. Wildlife includes Golden Eagle, Prairie Falcon, and Chuckwalla. The Greenwaters are an important travel corridor from the Funeral Mountains to the Black Mountains for Desert Bighorn. This area receives very little human use. The highest elevation is 5,148 feet.

Status: The Cranston bill would add 156,220 acres to Death Valley NP as Wilderness. BLM opposes Wilderness for this untracked area. Grandiose claims have been made about mineral wealth in the range, but no commercial extraction has occurred.

IBEX HILLS 143,000 acres	
Death Valley National Monument roadless	72,000
BLM WSAs CDCA 149 and 149A	53,500
BLM WSAs CDCA 219 and 220	17,800

Description: East-central California in the southeastern corner of Death Valley NM southwest of Shoshone. The dirt Saratoga Springs road separates this area from the huge Panamint roadless area; paved Highway 178 over Jubilee Pass separates it from the Amargosa Range roadless area. At 4,749 feet, Ibex Peak is the high point. The southern end of the Black Mountains, Ibex Hills, and Saddle Peak Hills constitute the area. The Amargosa River flows through the southern end. The Saratoga Springs Pupfish is in Saratoga Springs, which is accessible by cherrystem road in this area. Vegetation and wildlife are typical of the Death Valley area. The rare Field Primrose grows south of Jubilee Pass.

Status: The access road to Saratoga Springs and surrounding mine-damaged country is excluded from the roadless area. ORVers from the Dumont Dunes regularly invade the Saddle Peak Hills.

The Cranston bill would add 43,060 BLM acres to Death Valley NP as Wilderness. BLM opposes Wilderness.

NOPAH RANGE 134,000 acres (also in Nevada)	
BLM WSA CDCA 150	116,000
BLM roadless (NV)	18,000

Description: East-central California east of Death Valley NM next to the Nevada border. This area encompasses most of the Nopah Range, part of the Resting Spring Range, and the Chicago Valley between them. Two peaks in the area are popular with hikers for their exceptional views. The west face of the Nopahs, with bands of rusty red, brown, and cream, is termed "unforgettable" by conservationists. Vegetation is diverse, with Desert Willow, mesquite, cactus, Creosote, and three rare plants—two buckwheats and an agave. Chicago Valley has riparian vegetation. Wildlife includes a small Bighorn herd, Prairie Falcon, Golden Eagle, Desert Tortoise, a wide variety of snakes, and some unusual lizards.

Status: The Cranston bill would designate 110,880 acres as Wilderness; BLM originally proposed 78,880 acres for Wilderness, but under pressure from grazing, mining, and development interests, the Bureau dropped the Resting Springs Range and the western Chicago Valley portion from its recommendation in 1982.

Mojave Desert

The central part of the California Desert is part of the Mojave Desert. It is higher and slightly cooler than the torrid Colorado Desert to the south and is characterized by the unlikeliest-looking tree in the United States—the Joshua Tree, a lily that took steroids and LSD. It is hot enough for Creosote Bush and cholla cactus in the lowlands, cool enough for piñon and juniper in the highlands.

KINGSTON RANGE 270,000 acres	
BLM WSA CDCA 222	270,000

Description: Southeastern California north of Baker. This is a varied area southeast of Death Valley National Monument. Kingston Peak, at 7,323 feet, is the high point; the elevation drops to 600 feet. The Amargosa River, one of three perennial streams in the California Desert, provides habitat for the Amargosa Pupfish, Speckled Dace, and Amargosa Toad. Terrain includes high peaks with White Fir (rare in the desert), and piñon and juniper lower down; the limestone Valjean Hills; desert bajadas and washes with cactus, Creosote, and Joshua Tree; and sand dunes. The riparian areas along the Amargosa, Horsethief Springs, and Salt Creek are particularly important. This area has a high concentration of Endangered species and unusual plant communities. Wildlife includes Vermillion Flycatcher, Desert Tortoise, Yellow-billed Cuckoo, Prairie Falcon, Desert Bighorn Sheep, Amargosa Vole (endemic), Kit Fox, Ringtail, and Panamint Chipmunk.

Status: The Cranston bill includes 255,290 acres of Wilderness, but the Dumont Dunes are excluded because of the bleating of ORVers. Overgrazing occurs in parts of the area.

RM36: 650,000

AVAWATZ 101,000 acres	
BLM WSA CDCA 221	69,000
Camp Irwin Military Reservation roadless	32,000

Description: Southern California northwest of Baker, and immediately north of the Soda Mountain roadless area and southeast of Death Valley National Monument. This roadless area contains most of the Avawatz Mountains, with their rugged ridges, precipitous narrow canyons, and colorful slopes, as well as a steep bajada clothed in Creosote and ending in a dry lake. Elevations range from under 800 feet on the playa to 6,154 feet on Avawatz Peak. White talc deposits add to the colorfulness of the area. Numerous springs provide good Bighorn habitat.

Status: The Cranston bill would designate 61,320 acres as BLM Wilderness and add 5,120 acres to Death Valley National Park. BLM, broken to heel in California by small miners and ORVers, opposes any Wilderness.

SODA MOUNTAIN 102,500 acres	
BLM WSA CDCA 242	102,500

Description: Southern California west of Baker and north of Interstate 15. The Soda Mountains have both gentle slopes and highly eroded, rugged ridges. Washes cutting into the mountains have steep, rocky, variegated walls. Several large dry lake beds (playas) are in this roadless area, including Silver Dry Lake, which is a perfect example of a playa, and East Cronese Lake, which often contains water and provides habitat for wintering and migrating shorebirds and waterfowl, including the Endangered Yuma Clapper Rail. This smorgasbord of birds attracts many raptors. The mountains provide good Desert Bighorn habitat. Creosote Bush is the dominant plant; barrel cactus, cholla, and yucca also are present. An old-growth, very tall Crucifixion Thorn stand inhabits the west end. At least one sensitive plant species is present, as are many archaeological sites.

Status: The Cranston bill would designate 92,690 acres as Wilderness; BLM is opposed to Wilderness here. The notorious Barstow-Vegas dirt bike race went through this area in 1983, and ORVers are slobbering mad in their opposition to Wilderness. The Blue Bell Mine area is cherrystemmed.

OLD DAD MOUNTAIN 101,000 acres	
BLM WSA CDCA 243 and additional roadless	101,000

Description: Southern California south of Baker and Interstate 15. This is one of the most topographically varied areas in the California desert, with the crescent dunes of the Devil's Playground, Soda Lake (a Pleistocene lake that fills every twenty years or so), the terminus of the Mojave River, and precipitous Old Dad Mountain (4,250 feet). The largest Bighorn herd in the East Mojave (three hundred animals) is here. Soda Lake is the largest wilderness playa in California. There is a rich mesquite growth in the sand hummocks of the Devil's Playground.

Status: The Cranston bill would designate a 95,760-acre Wilderness. The BLM and its ORV, mining, and grazing overseers strongly oppose Wilderness. The Barstow-Vegas dirt bike race passes through the northern end of the area; the Cranston bill excises the course from the Wilderness. Soda Lake has obligingly swallowed several vehicles whole.

*RM36: 1,970,000**

KELSO DUNES 215,000 acres	
BLM WSA CDCA 250	165,820
Intermixed and adjacent private and state roadless	49,000

Description: Southern California in the East Mojave Desert south of Baker. The Kelso Dunes are the second-highest in California and third-highest in North America. This extensive dune field has a high species diversity, with several endemics and many wildflowers, including Desert Lily, Desert Sunflower, and evening primrose. The dunes have been closed to ORVs since 1972, but ORVers don't obey closures unless the closures are enforced. The Bristol Mountains to the west are essentially untouched. Broadwell Mesa, also in the western end of this roadless area, has a distinctive flat top and sheer sides. Just west of the mesa is one of the few natural arches found in the California Desert. This roadless area is separated from the Granite Mountains by only a pipeline corridor.

Status: Senator Cranston's bill would designate as Wilderness 36,000 acres in Mojave National Park and 129,820 acres of BLM land.

Possible mining of Kelso Dunes for magnitite and rare earth minerals is a serious threat. ORVers are fighting Cranston's bill and hope to "open up" the dunes for their "fun" again. (Claiming that ORVing off established roads in the desert is a legitimate form of recreation is akin to claiming the same for rape or mugging.) Even now, ORVers trespass on the dunes, their long-lasting tracks representing swaths of destruction. Livestock invasion of the dunes is also evident. The ranch at the base of the dunes allows its cattle to graze the dunes' sparse grasses and leave their ubiquitous pies in all but the most inaccessible reaches of these sand hills. The large acreage of private and state land should be a priority for acquisition.

*RM36: 1,970,000**

CADY MOUNTAINS 122,000 acres	
BLM WSA CDCA 251	85,970
Intermixed private and state roadless	36,000

Description: Southern California east of Barstow. The California Desert Protection League describes this as an area of "vast, windblown, sandy valleys and highly eroded volcanic ridges." Two springs make Cady important for Desert Bighorn Sheep. Other wildlife includes Prairie Falcon, Golden Eagle, and abundant Mojave Fringe-toed Lizards. The area is separated from the Kelso Dunes roadless area by a power-line corridor.

Status: The wildlife and wildness of the Cady Mountains are threatened by the growing population of Barstow, ORVs, mining, and overgrazing. A macabre specific threat to this pristine area comes from the private firm of Patrick and Henderson, which wants to locate a commercial toxic waste dump on private land it owns in the center of the WSA.

The Cranston bill would designate 85,970 acres of BLM lands as Wilderness. The checkerboard private lands should also be included in the Wilderness and acquired by the federal government. BLM opposes Wilderness for the Cadys.

*RM36: 1,970,000**

GRANITE MOUNTAINS 135,000 acres	
BLM WSA CDCA 256	99,804
Intermixed state and private roadless	35,000

Description: Southern California north of Interstate 40 midway between Needles and Barstow. This roadless area encompasses the Granite Mountains and portions of the Old Dad Mountains and Bristol Mountains. Elevations reach 6,738 feet, with piñon-pine-juniper forest in the upper elevations, Creosote and yucca lower down. Famed for its granite boulders, similar to those in Joshua Tree NM, Granite's considerable wildlife includes Bighorn, Golden Eagle, Prairie Falcon, Ringtail, and Mule Deer. Numerous archaeological sites from the Chemehuevi and Serrano have been found. A gas pipeline separates the Granite Mountains from the Kelso Dunes roadless area.

Status: The Cranston bill would designate 29,650 acres as Wilderness within the new Mojave National Park and 70,240 acres as BLM Wilderness. BLM has proposed a paltry 29,646 acres for Wilderness because of opposition from the local rancher and ORVers. Much of the area is checkerboard land owned by the state or Southern Pacific. It is likely that a land exchange can be arranged.

*RM36: 1,970,000**

Southern Mojave and Colorado Deserts

The Colorado Desert in the southeastern corner of California is a western extension of Arizona's Sonoran Desert. Although many plants are shared, such as

Creosote, palo verde, Ironwood, and various cacti, the Saguaro and other typically Sonoran species are absent. The pattern of precipitation is the reason. Arizona's Sonoran Desert receives gentle winter rains from the Gulf of California and summer thunderstorms from the Gulf of Mexico. The Colorado Desert shares only the winter rains.

SHEEP HOLE 390,000 acres	
BLM WSA CDCA 305	135,827
Additional BLM and intermixed private and state roadless	254,000

Description: North of Joshua Tree National Monument and east of Twenty-nine Palms Marine Corps Base in southern California. This remote, essentially untouched area consists of the huge Sheep Hole Valley; Cadiz Valley; Calumet Mountains; the steep, granitic Sheep Hole Mountains; Kilbeck Hills; part of the Iron Mountains; and part of Cadiz Playa. The high point is 4,613 feet. A special feature of this large, desert wildland is the Cadiz Dunes, a low, unstable dune system that holds pockets of water and vegetation in its troughs. Galleta Grass, Creosote, and desert shrub are common plant types in the area. Wildlife includes Bighorn Sheep, Desert Tortoise, and Prairie Falcon. Much of this area was part of Joshua Tree National Monument from 1936 until 1950, when it was removed from protection because of potential minerals.

Status: An access road from the south and salt evaporators on Cadiz Playa are cherrystemmed into the center of this area.

The Cranston bill would designate 177,000 acres of Wilderness for the Sheep Hole, with a 42,640-acre Cadiz Dunes Wilderness separated by a vehicle way. BLM, for unfathomed reasons, opposes Wilderness even though this magnificent area has few conflicts (the Bureau originally supported Wilderness in the Desert Plan, but changed its mind in an amendment). The entire area should be designated as a single Wilderness unit.

RM36: 1,100,000

OLD WOMAN MOUNTAINS 150,000 acres	
BLM WSA CDCA 299	100,826
Additional BLM and intermixed private and state roadless	49,000

Description: Southeastern California southwest of Needles, south of Interstate 40 and north of the Colorado River Aqueduct; separated from the Turtle Mountains by a power-line corridor and from the Sheep Hole area by a railroad and dirt road. The California Desert Protection League writes, "The massive, fault-lifted Old Woman Mountains . . . are a wonderland of rockwalls, deep canyons, sandy washes, enclosed valleys and steep spires." The high point is 5,326 feet. Vegetation includes piñon-juniper forest, yucca, nolina, and barrel cactus. Abundant water (sixteen springs) supports a large Mule Deer population and Desert Bighorn Sheep. Other wildlife includes one of the most important populations of Desert Tortoises in California. The numerous Indian sites include burial areas.

Status: The Cranston bill would designate 146,110 acres as BLM Wilderness, but would exclude minor vehicle routes and an area with inconsequential mining impacts. BLM opposes any Wilderness in the Old Womans. Parts of the area have checkerboarded railroad lands. Unexploded military ordnance from World War II lies strewn about in a couple of areas.

*RM36: 950,000**

TURTLE MOUNTAINS 276,000 acres	
BLM WSA CDCA 307	144,500
Additional BLM, state, and private roadless	131,000

Description: Southeastern California south of Needles, west of U.S. 95, north of the Colorado River Aqueduct. The Turtles are a fabulous volcanic range with spires, cliffs, and crags in the northeast and rounded hills in the southwest. A large interior valley (Vidal Valley) with numerous washes is a special attraction. The surrounding bajadas are particularly lush. Mopah Springs has the northernmost occurrence of native Fan Palms. Wildlife includes Desert Bighorn, Desert Tortoise, Mountain Lion, Golden Eagle (two aeries), Prairie Falcon (two aeries), Bendire's Thrasher, and Western Pipistrelle Bat (several roosts). Eleven springs normally provide water, though they may dry up in drought years. The high point is 4,313 feet.

Status: The Cranston bill would designate 144,500 acres as Wilderness. BLM proposes only 105,201 acres for Wilderness, leaving out the northern Turtles and the Lower Vidal Valley. Mining is a minor threat, as is grazing.

The Parker 400 dirt bike race course is on some of the boundary roads. Vidal Valley is receiving some ORV abuse. A proposed ORV play route, the Mojave Road, would desecrate Gary Wash, critical Desert Tortoise habitat.

*RM36: 950,000**

PALEN-MCCOY 380,000 acres	
BLM WSA CDCA 325	225,000
Additional BLM, private, and state roadless	155,000

Description: Northwest of Blythe in southeastern California. The floor of this extensive interior valley in the hot, dry, lower-elevation Colorado Desert is desert pavement and Creosote Bush. It is cut by desert washes with Ironwood, palo verde, and Smoke Tree, and is surrounded by four mountain ranges: Palen, with striated metasedimentary and metavolcanic rock; McCoy, a ridge of striated metasedimentary rock; Granite, a steep granitic range rising north of the Palen Range with scarcely any break between them; and Little Maria, a small but complex limestone range. Other desert valleys, washes, and bajadas enhance this diverse, spacious area. Crucifixion Thorn, Bighorn Sheep, Mojave Fringe-toed Lizard, and Prairie Falcon are among the interesting resident species. The Midland Ironwood Forest in this area is the thickest such thicket in the state. The high point is 4,353 feet, in the Granite Mountains. Numerous Indian sites have been found. The valley between the Palen and McCoy ranges was used for General Patton's maneuvers during World War II. The fifty-year-old scars are healing, as this valley has rarely been visited since then.

Status: The Cranston bill would designate 214,420 acres as Wilderness. Hobby mining and ORVs present minor threats.

*RM36: 1,500,000**

COXCOMB 188,000 acres	
Joshua Tree National Monument Wilderness Area and additional roadless	120,500
BLM WSA CDCA 328	58,700
BLM WSA CDCA 334A	4,000
Additional BLM roadless	5,000

Description: Southern California east of Twenty-nine Palms; the eastern end of Joshua Tree NM and surrounding BLM lands, including the Coxcomb Mountains and Pinto Basin. The granitic Coxcombs are a complex range with steep walls, finlike ridges, and canyons. The valley between the Coxcomb and Pinto ranges is strewn with piles of granite boulders. This is an area of transition from Mojave Desert with Joshua Trees to Colorado Desert with Creosote, cholla cactus, and Ocotillo. Bighorn are declining in the area. A small Desert Tortoise population remains, as does at least one Prairie Falcon nest.

Status: Formerly part of Joshua Tree NM, the BLM land (55,500 acres) would be added to the new Joshua Tree National Park as Wilderness by the Cranston bill.

*RM36: 1,500,000**

EAGLE MOUNTAINS 110,000 acres	
Joshua Tree National Monument Wilderness Area	55,600
BLM WSA CDCA 334	54,700

Description: Southern California northwest of Desert Center and north of Interstate 10; the southeastern corner of Joshua Tree NM. The BLM area was excised from the Monument in the 1940s for iron mining. The BLM part has an interior plateau of broad, flat valleys drained by Big Wash. The massive, rounded mountains are colored gold, brown, and tan. In the south are large exfoliated boulders of quartz monzonite. This lower-elevation country represents the Colorado Desert, as contrasted with the Mojave Desert preserved in the higher reaches of Joshua Tree NM. Washes support dense stands of Ironwood, Smoke Tree, palo verde; slopes have Ocotillo, Bigelow Cholla, Mojave Yucca, Pencil Cholla, and Silver Cholla. Scenic attractions include a palm oasis with flowing water. Bighorn are declining and need further protection on the BLM lands. Desert Tortoise densities of 20–50 per square mile occur in 5 square miles of the BLM portion. The area also features Prairie Falcon aeries and several springs.

Status: The portion currently in the Monument is designated Wilderness; 52,780 acres of the BLM land would receive Wilderness status and be added to an expanded Joshua Tree National Park under Senator Cranston's bill. BLM has proposed 42,700 acres for Wilderness. ORVs and mineral exploration are threats.

*RM36: 1,500,000**

HEXIE–LITTLE SAN BERNARDINO MOUNTAINS 328,000 acres	
Joshua Tree National Monument Wilderness Areas and additional roadless	260,000
BLM and private roadless to south	68,000

Description: Southern California north of Indio. The Hexie Mountains climb almost a mile above the below-sea-level Salton Sea basin to a high point of 4,834 feet (Monument Mountain) on the southern rim of Joshua Tree National Monument. Farther west, Quail Mountain in the Little San Bernardinos attains 5,814 feet. Here is an excellent example of Mojave Desert vegetation (Joshua Tree, California Juniper, Singleleaf Piñon), with Colorado Desert vegetation (cactus, Creosote) in the lower elevations.

Status: The land south of the Monument and north of the Colorado River Aqueduct is checkerboard private and BLM. The Cranston bill would add much of it to the proposed Joshua Tree National Park as Wilderness. There are currently four separate Wilderness units in Joshua Tree NM in this roadless area. The corridors are unnecessary (there are no through roads); a single Wilderness Area of over 300,000 acres should be established with the addition of the southern checkerboard lands.

*RM36: 1,500,000**

PINTO MOUNTAINS 105,000 acres	
Joshua Tree NM Wilderness Area and additional roadless	53,800
BLM WSA CDCA 335	51,300

Description: Southern California southeast of Twenty-nine Palms. Twenty-nine Palms Mountain is 4,562 feet. Mojave Desert vegetation with excellent stands of Joshua Tree.

Status: The Cranston bill would add 51,300 acres (all of BLM WSA CDCA 335) to Joshua Tree National Park as Wilderness. Contiguous BLM lands are being trashed by ORVs.

CHUCKWALLA MOUNTAINS 197,000 acres	
BLM WSA CDCA 348 and additional roadless	197,000

Description: Southern California south of Desert Center on Interstate 10. The high point is 4,604 feet, on Black Butte. These craggy mountains encircle a remote Fan Palm oasis, Corn Springs. Bajadas around the mountain support a rich growth of Ironwood. The Chuckwalla Bench, to the south, is an exemplary transition zone between the Mojave and Colorado Deserts, with exceptional cactus gardens that have not been looted by cactus poachers. *Opuntia munzii,* the largest cholla cactus in California, grows only in this area. The numerous springs support a high diversity and large number of animals, including Bighorn, Chuckwalla, Mule Deer, quail, Prairie Falcon, and a core population of Desert Tortoise. The last Pronghorn in the California Desert were here until World War II, and the area is a prime site for reintroduction. Intaglios (large figures formed in the desert pavement by prehistoric natives) and petroglyphs in the northwestern portion are sacred to the Cahuilla Indians. The California Desert Protection League says this area is "unequalled as an example of a Sonoran desert community in California."

Status: The Cranston bill would designate 165,200 acres as Wilderness (in two units, including an area outside this roadless area to the southwest). BLM has proposed only 57,312 acres for protection. Several dirt roads, including one to Corn Springs, are cherrystemmed.

RM36: 610,000

LOWER COLORADO RIVER 462,000 acres (also in Arizona)

See Arizona for description and status.

SANTA ROSA MOUNTAINS 363,000 acres

Designated Santa Rosa Wilderness Area (San Bernardino NF)	20,160
Designated Santa Rosa Mountains State Wilderness Area (Anza-Borrego State Park)	87,000
Additional San Bernardino NF, state, BLM, private, and Indian Reservation roadless	256,000

Description: Southern California south of Palm Springs. This desert-and-mountain region has a complicated land ownership pattern, rendering its protection difficult. It is an area of steep cliffs, highly eroded canyons, strewn boulders, a desert sink, and sculpted desert hills. Vegetation makes a transition from Ocotillo, agave, Barrel Cactus, and Creosote to piñon pine and mountain mahogany. The Travertine Fan Palm grove is in the area. High-quality desert riparian areas provide habitat for Least Bell's Vireo, a candidate federal Endangered species. Elevations range from below sea level near the Salton Sea to 8,700 feet on the slopes of Toro Peak. The largest herd of rare Peninsular Bighorn Sheep in the United States finds a home here.

Status: Wilderness designation is crucial for the BLM portion to link the FS and state areas together. ORVs are the major threat here, as they are on most public lands in southern California. The State Park recently closed them out of the Lower Willows area, the richest riparian zone in Anza-Borrego. More recently, the California State Parks System banned ORVs from roadless areas in all its Parks, except for the few with prior ORV management plans.

Only 53,240 acres of BLM Wilderness would be designated by the Cranston bill, but conservationists are calling for 136,100 acres. Although many of the private land owners are willing sellers and much of the area is owned by the California Department of Fish and Game for Bighorn management, the checkerboard land ownership complicates protection. Some subdivisions on the edge pose a threat. A primitive cherrystem road for access to private land nearly divides the state Wilderness Area in half.

VALLECITO MOUNTAINS 207,000 acres	
Designated Vallecito Mountains State Wilderness Area (Anza-Borrego Desert State Park)	82,000
Designated Whale Peak State Wilderness Area (Anza-Borrego Desert State Park)	34,000
Designated Carrizo Badlands State Wilderness Area (Anza-Borrego State Park)	19,200
Additional Anza-Borrego State Park roadless	17,000
Carrizo Impact Area (military) roadless	28,000
BLM WSA CDCA 372	27,100

Description: Southern California northeast of San Diego. This central part of Anza-Borrego State Park, just south of State Highway 78 in Lower Borrego Valley, is an area of rugged topography with remote ridges and canyons. Elevations rise from sea level to 5,300 feet, on Whale Peak. The only water in the area consists of intermittent tinajas. Wildlife present includes Mule Deer, Peninsular Bighorn Sheep, Badger, Kit Fox, Pallid Bat, Ringtail, Sora Rail, Golden Eagle, Prairie Falcon, Long-eared Owl, Red-legged Frog,

Switak's Gecko, Desert Blind Snake, Lyre Snake, Red Diamond Rattlesnake, Desert Night Lizard, and Desert Shrimp. A recent Sonoran Pronghorn skull was found in 1957. Pupfish were last found in Split Mountain in 1916 (their pools were silted in by a flood that year). Over a dozen uncommon plant species are present, including the Elephant Tree, the Sand Plant, and the federally Endangered Borrego Bedstraw. Vegetation varies from Creosote and cactus to Singleleaf Piñon Pine and California Juniper. Desert Thorn is common in Lycium Wash. Paleo-Indian sites of national significance are fairly common at the mouth of Harper Canyon. Sedimentary deposits in the south contain Pliocene mammal fossils, with petrified forests near Loop Wash. The west wall of Split Mountain is a nationally known geologic study site.

Status: Much of this area is protected as State Wilderness Areas, but the rest suffers from ORV abuse. A half dozen ORV corridors are cherry-stemmed between and into the Wilderness units. The Cranston bill would designate 27,100 acres as BLM Wilderness. The small Bighorn herd is infested with Parainfluenza 3, transmitted from domestic livestock and responsible for a high lamb mortality.

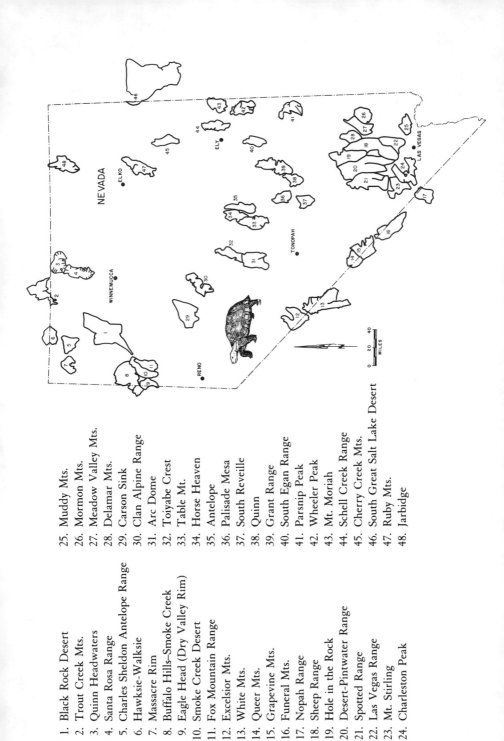

1. Black Rock Desert
2. Trout Creek Mts.
3. Quinn Headwaters
4. Santa Rosa Range
5. Charles Sheldon Antelope Range
6. Hawksie-Walksie
7. Massacre Rim
8. Buffalo Hills–Smoke Creek
9. Eagle Head (Dry Valley Rim)
10. Smoke Creek Desert
11. Fox Mountain Range
12. Excelsior Mts.
13. White Mts.
14. Queer Mts.
15. Grapevine Mts.
16. Funeral Mts.
17. Nopah Range
18. Sheep Range
19. Hole in the Rock
20. Desert-Pintwater Range
21. Spotted Range
22. Las Vegas Range
23. Mt. Stirling
24. Charleston Peak
25. Muddy Mts.
26. Mormon Mts.
27. Meadow Valley Mts.
28. Delamar Mts.
29. Carson Sink
30. Clan Alpine Range
31. Arc Dome
32. Toiyabe Crest
33. Table Mt.
34. Horse Heaven
35. Antelope
36. Palisade Mesa
37. South Reveille
38. Quinn
39. Grant Range
40. South Egan Range
41. Parsnip Peak
42. Wheeler Peak
43. Mt. Moriah
44. Schell Creek Range
45. Cherry Creek Mts.
46. South Great Salt Lake Desert
47. Ruby Mts.
48. Jarbidge

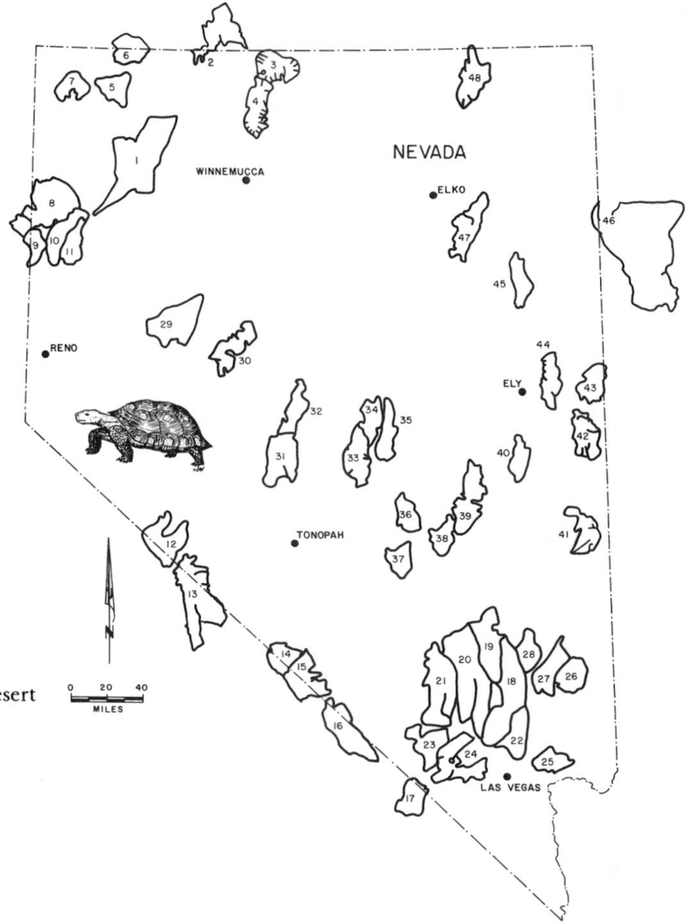

Nevada

Nevada. To most, the name conjures glittering casinos, topless showgirls in elaborate headdresses, and stars like Wayne Newton. There's another Nevada, however. This is the Nevada scorned by the high-speed traveler on Interstate 80: the desolate waste of sagebrush steppe and seemingly barren mountain ranges in the distance.

These images have affected federal land management agencies and even the conservation movement. While the U.S. Forest Service was establishing Wilderness Areas in other Western states in the 1930s, 1940s, and 1950s, it saw fit to designate only one such area in Nevada (and that was not until 1958)—the 64,667-acre Jarbidge Wilderness in far northeastern Nevada. I also recall a meeting in 1975 with the BLM's top staff in Washington, DC, to discuss Wilderness (this was before passage of the BLM "Organic Act," which mandated the Wilderness review). The head of resources, Roman Koenings, finally exploded in exasperation, "How many millions of acres of sagebrush flats do you want in the Wilderness System!"

No national conservation group has ever treated Nevada as more than an afterthought; none has ever committed a portion of the resources to save the Nevada wilderness that has been allocated to other, more "scenic" states. Charles S. Watson, Jr., founder and spark plug of the Nevada Outdoor Recreation Association (NORA), tells how the top brass of the Sierra Club shut him up in the early 1960s when he began agitating for inclusion of the BLM in the Wilderness Act. They were afraid such talk could torpedo chances for passage of the bill.

Small wonder, then, that Nevada's homegrown wilderness preservationists are a timid lot, not given to ambitious proposals or to playing political hardball. Neglected by national conservation groups, lambasted by ranchers and miners who think they own the public lands of the state (Nevada was the birthplace of the so-called Sagebrush Rebellion), played for suckers by the "liberal" Democrats in their congressional delegation, the Toiyabe Chapter of the Sierra Club and Friends of Nevada Wilderness (FNW) have operated cautiously. Even during RARE II, when the Humboldt and Toiyabe NFs identified 2.1 million acres of roadless areas (there were actually 3.9 million acres of roadless areas on NFs in Nevada, but FS land use plans had already removed 1.8 million acres from consideration), conservationists asked only for a little more than 1 million acres as Wilderness. In response to this initial compromise, the FS recommended a mere eleven areas with slightly more than 500,000 acres for Wilderness.

In addition to the diffidence of Nevada conservationists, their other weakness has been a failure to organize the grass roots outside of the population centers of Reno and Las Vegas. Assumed too often to be a wasteland of know-nothings, John Birchers, and wilderness despoilers, the small towns and rural areas of Nevada do have Wilderness supporters. They have shown up at Wilderness hearings, they have written letters. Too little effort, though, has been made to organize them or plug them into the conservation activism of the two big cities. The Nevada conservationists can't be blamed for this; they're volunteers, they work regular jobs and do their conservation work at night, on weekends, and generally at their own expense. They have fought the good fight and deserve praise.

The Wilderness Society and Sierra Club need to hire a regional representative for Nevada, whose primary duty would be grass-roots organizing, in both the urban areas and the hinterlands. Nevada conservationists would then be better prepared to go toe-to-toe with the cowboys and small miners.

(It should be noted that the Sierra Club Regional Representative for Northern California and Nevada devoted a considerable share of her energy to Nevada during the campaign for the 1989 Nevada Wilderness Protection Act.)

But what good is Nevada? What really is there to preserve? Isn't it merely a desolate wasteland, miles on miles of sagebrush steppe?

Beyond the bright lights of Las Vegas and Reno, off the four lanes of the interstate, away from the cat house and the slot machine emporium lies the real Nevada. The Great Basin. A land of basin and range after basin and range running generally on a north-south axis, caught between the Sierra Nevada and Cascades and the Rocky Mountains. Empty valleys carpeted in sage with herds of Pronghorn flashing the bright white of their rumps; valleys that stretch your eyes farther than you thought you could see. Valleys flowing like seas, breaking against the far mountains. Mountains rising up a mile or more to hidden glacier-gouged basins with tiny lakes glistening like turquoise in the dry air of this cold desert. Forests of Aspen, mountain mahogany, or White Fir cloaking the high basins, the rolling summits. And above all, the patriarchs, gnarled, weathered, and deeply wise from their millennial lives—Bristlecone Pines.

There are two Great Basins: one, a geographic region distinguished by internal drainage with no outlet to the sea through the surrounding river systems of the Colorado, Sacramento, or Snake; and the other, an ecological region of high desert, a cold, arid fastness characterized by Big Sagebrush. These Great Basins are both centered on Nevada but do not entirely coincide.

The geographic Great Basin is true basin and range country. Often the low point of a basin is a meandering stream, a marsh, a lake in various degrees of salinity, or a salt flat (playa). The entire state of Nevada, except for its southern tip, draining into the Colorado River, and its northeastern corner, where the Owyhee and Jarbidge Rivers herd the snowmelt into the Snake River, is part of this Great Basin. Much of the California Desert, as well as that part of northern California east of the crest of the Sierra Nevada and Cascades, is included. Western Utah is classic Great Basin topography, as is much of southeastern Oregon outside of the Owyhee drainage.

The ecological Great Basin roughly overlies the central and northern portions of the geographic Great Basin (the southern part of the geographic Great Basin is ecologically part of the much hotter Mojave Desert, characterized by Creosote Bush and Joshua Tree). The Great Basin Desert is a cold, dry highland, dominated by sagebrush steppe and, higher, by piñon-juniper woodland and Aspen. It is a desert because the Sierra Nevada and Cascade mountain ranges capture the moist Pacific air and cast a rain shadow hundreds of miles east. This sagebrush desert laps over the divides into the Snake River drainage (the Owyhee country of Idaho and Oregon) and the Colorado Plateau of Utah, Arizona, and New Mexico.

This vast, empty quarter, lost between the great dividing ranges, is one of the wildest and least-populated regions in the temperate Northern Hemisphere. And with good reason. This is a lean, hungry land, with little fat to make men rich. Tiny Vermont produces more pounds of beef than does huge Nevada. Assignment to Nevada for a Forest Ranger is exile to Siberia—there is no industrial forestry to practice. So, even without priority status from conservation groups, Nevada boasts more roadless areas of 100,000 acres or more than does any other state except California (although it is important to note that Nevada has few truly large roadless areas).

Nevada's Big Outside is nonetheless threatened. Oil companies have begun tentative exploration for oil and gas. Urban ORVers probe deeper into the backcountry. Yellow-toothed trappers run their lines in the piñon-juniper "pygmy forest" from the backs of motorized tricycles. But the gravest threats to the wild places of Nevada come from livestockmen and small miners, and from the federal agencies effectively in thrall to this rustic gentry. Destruction of wilderness is not as spectacular in Nevada as it is in the ancient forests of Oregon or the Grizzly habitat of Montana, but it is a slow, steady gnawing at the fabric of natural integrity, like the grazing of sheep at a mountain meadow in July.

Because of the weakness of state conservationists, Nevada did not pass a comprehensive National Forest Wilderness Act until 1989, when the three Democrats on the Nevada congressional delegation steamrollered Representative Barbara Vucanovich, a far-right Republican who looks like a madam but votes like a Mormon miner (she opposed Wilderness except for four small token areas). Friends of Nevada Wilderness and its allies campaigned for 21 new NF Wilderness Areas with a total acreage of 1.5 million acres. Although this was an improvement over their RARE II proposal, they failed to include many important NF wildlands in their proposal and generally recommended thoroughly inadequate boundaries. Ultimately, only fourteen areas, totaling 733,400 acres, were designated as

Wilderness Areas in the 1989 Nevada Wilderness Protection Act. Those new Wildernesses and their acreages are indicated in the acreage summaries for individual roadless areas.

Late in 1988, Congress passed legislation, the Nevada Enhancement Act, transferring almost a million acres of BLM land in Nevada to the Toiyabe National Forest and some NF land to the BLM. Several BLM WSAs were included. What this means for possible Wilderness designation is anybody's guess. Three general areas were included in the transfer: the White Mountains–Excelsior Mountains region, along the California border; the Spring Mountains, west of Las Vegas; and the Hot Creek Range–Antelope Range area, in central Nevada. The acreage summaries in this second edition reflect the transfers between agencies.

The Bureau of Land Management has been somewhat better than the Forest Service on Wilderness in Nevada (although, of course, it has not been good). Out of 408 units, totaling over 14 million acres, considered for Wilderness Study Area status, 71 areas, totaling 3,388,516 acres, were selected as WSAs. BLM studies and recommendations for or against Wilderness have been completed for these areas (and are tallied with the individual area write-ups that follow). However, a Nevada BLM Wilderness bill lies in the distant future.

So . . . Is Nevada empty? Barren? Desolate? Is all the action in the casinos? All the beauty in the haughty showgirls? Are the sage-filled valleys and blue mountains yonder on the horizon good only for the sheepherder, the cowman, the trapper, the two-bit miner with a bulldozer?

Ask the Mountain Lion in the Grant Range. Ask the Bighorn in the Sheep Range. The Elk in the Schell Creek Range. The Lahontan Cutthroat in a stream cutting down from Toiyabe Crest. The Sage Sparrow lost in the immensity of the Black Rock Desert. The Golden Eagle riding the thermals over the Clan Alpine Range.

Listen to the answer whispered by the ancient limbs of the Bristlecone.

They know.

Northwestern Nevada

Northwestern Nevada is a land of shimmering salt flats—the remnants of Pleistocene lakes—and sloping tablelands carpeted with Big Sagebrush and its companions. The Pronghorn is king beneath this unfenced sky, where roadless areas spill over into California and Oregon. BLM controls most of this acreage, although the Fish and Wildlife Service has one of its largest refuges—Sheldon Antelope Range—here. There are also three Indian Reservations with sections of big wilderness in northwestern Nevada.

BLACK ROCK DESERT 640,000 acres	
BLM WSA 2-62	319,594
Additional BLM roadless	320,000

Description: Northwestern Nevada west of Winnemucca. The bed of prehistoric Lake Lahontan is an immense basin surrounded by rough desert mountains where distance loses meaning. Sometimes, the Black Rock is a perfectly flat and dry salt flat; at other times, it is a shallow lake with abundant waterfowl. The Quinn River meanders from the north for 90 miles into the Black Rock before it disappears in a myriad of channels (an unusual float trip is possible in spring). Willow, Beaver, and Muskrat live along the Quinn. Elevations range from 3,900 feet to 8,594 feet, atop Pahute Peak. Scattered desert playas and expansive flats are lightly vegetated with saltbush, greasewood, and sagebrush: isolated stands of mountain mahogany and Aspen inhabit the Black Rock Range (Big Mountain or Pahute Peak). Two rare plants live here: Winged Milk-vetch and Barneby Wild Cabbage. Pronghorn, Mule Deer, Mountain Lion, Kit Fox, Sage Grouse, Chukar (exotic), and "wild" horses are residents. Important paleontological (Woolly Mammoth, camel, and prehistoric bison remains) and archaeological sites, as well as remnants of emigrant trails, tell stories of the past. Natural arches in the Pahute Peak Range, badlands, and hot springs also distinguish this area.

Status: Conservation groups are proposing only 214,300 acres for Wilderness in two units: Black Rock Desert (174,300) and Pahute Peak (40,000). BLM supports the small conservationist proposal on the Black Rock, but recommends only 25,200 acres for Pahute Peak. At the very least, this entire roadless area should be designated as Wilderness. With even a modicum of vision, a superlative 3-million-acre Wilderness representative of the Great Basin could be designated here merely by closing minor and unnecessary dirt roads. This would include the Calico and Jackson Mountains, the High Rock Canyon region, and the southern part of Sheldon Antelope Range.

ORVs threaten the area. Prospecting and overgrazing occur on the edges. Some oil and gas and geothermal leases are within the roadless area.

TROUT CREEK MOUNTAINS 212,000 (also in Oregon)	
See Oregon for description and status.	

QUINN HEADWATERS 146,000 acres	
Humboldt National Forest roadless	99,000
BLM roadless	37,000
Private roadless	8,000
Fort McDermitt Indian Reservation roadless	2,000

Description: North-central Nevada southeast of McDermitt in the northern part of the Santa Rosa Range. This little-known, remote area has many springs giving rise to the South and East Forks of the Quinn River, which later flows into the Black Rock Desert. The Little Humboldt River also heads here. The high point of 8,700 feet is on the slope of Buckskin Mountain on the southwestern edge of the area (Buckskin reaches 8,743 feet, but a road goes to the top). Capitol Peak in the Calico Mountains hits 8,255 feet. The low elevation is around 4,500 feet, at the confluence of the Forks of the Quinn River. Wildlife includes Mule Deer, Mountain Lion, Golden Eagle, and the Threatened Lahontan Cutthroat Trout. Vegetation includes Big Sagebrush, Limber Pine, and Quaking Aspen.

Status: A Jeep trail along the Santa Rosa crest cuts the area in half. This well-watered area appears to have been virtually ignored by conservationists and never proposed for Wilderness. Threats are unknown, but probably include the standards for Nevada: prospecting, ORVs, overgrazing, firewood cutting. Some old mining zones are on the periphery. This area was not included in the first edition of *The Big Outside.*

SANTA ROSA RANGE 157,000 acres	
Designated Santa Rosa–Paradise Peak Wilderness Area (Humboldt National Forest)	31,000
Additional Humboldt NF roadless	78,000
Private roadless	9,000
BLM and intermixed private roadless	39,000

Description: North-central Nevada north of Winnemucca in the southern half of the Santa Rosa Range. The Santa Rosas spring up 4,000 feet above the high desert floors of the Quinn River Valley to the west and Paradise Valley to the east. The crest tops 9,000 feet on several peaks. Santa Rosa Peak, at 9,701 feet, is the high point in the Wilderness Area, but Granite Peak in the northern section of the roadless area is higher, at 9,732 feet. The high crest catches much snow and rain, giving rise to many streams, which support the Threatened Lahontan Cutthroat Trout. Mule Deer populations are high, and there is what Congress calls "a unique concentration" of Golden Eagles. Big Sagebrush, Aspen, and Limber Pine are dominant plants.

Status: In one of their better proposals, Friends of Nevada Wilderness campaigned for an 80,000-acre Wilderness, but only 31,000 acres were protected in the 1989 Nevada Wilderness Protection Act. The BLM land surrounding the high country is crossed by numerous cherrystem roads and Jeep trails. Overgrazing and ORVs are probably the leading threats to this area. This area was not included in the first edition of *The Big Outside;* a longtime activist with the Nevada Sierra Club brought this oversight to our attention.

CHARLES SHELDON ANTELOPE RANGE 124,000 acres	
Charles Sheldon Antelope Range roadless (FWS)	120,000
BLM and Summit Lake Indian Reservation roadless	4,000

Description: Extreme northwestern Nevada, north of Summit Lake Indian Reservation in the southern part of Charles Sheldon Antelope Range. Features of this high, wild basaltic tableland, cloaked with sagebrush steppe and cut by dramatic canyons, include Rock Spring Table, Hell Creek, Blowout Mountain, Virgin Creek, and Fish Creek Mountain. Pronghorn, reintroduced California Bighorn Sheep, Mountain Lion, Coyote, Bobcat, Mule Deer, and Sage Grouse thrive here. The cirquelike south face of Blowout Mountain probably formed from an ancient volcanic explosion. Virgin Creek cuts a narrow-walled canyon. Elevations vary from under 5,000 feet to over 7,100 feet. Mountain mahogany adorns the highlands; Aspen, cottonwood, and willow line the streams.

Status: Old ranching Jeep trails and intermixed private lands present potential conflicts. The FWS recommends a 93,000-acre Wilderness. Conservation groups forthrightly propose a 234,000-acre Wilderness by closing unimportant dirt roads. Livestock should be removed and dirt roads closed throughout the Sheldon Refuge.

HAWKSIE-WALKSIE 144,000 acres (also in Oregon)	
See Oregon for description and status.	

MASSACRE RIM 112,000 acres	
BLM WSA CA20-1013	110,000
Sheldon National Wildlife Refuge roadless	2,000

Description: Extreme northwestern Nevada northeast of Vya. This juniper-dotted sagebrush steppe plateau, broken by rimbound drainages, slopes up from Massacre Lake. Elevations range from 5,500 feet to 6,800 feet. The western edge of the bench suddenly drops 1,000 feet in a volcanic talus slope. The southern boundary has smaller steep rims above Massacre Lakes Basin. Large flats have scattered dry lake beds. Features include over a dozen flowing springs with wet meadows; Pronghorn, Mule Deer, Sage Grouse, Prairie Falcon, Red-tailed Hawk, and Brewer's Sparrow; "wild" horses; 4-foot-diameter Utah Junipers; and many archaeological sites. Reintroduction of Bighorn Sheep is planned.

Status: Although the area is threatened by continued overgrazing, additional range "improvements," ORVs, archaeological site vandals, and illegal firewood cutters, BLM proposes only a 23,260-acre Wilderness.

BUFFALO HILLS–SMOKE CREEK 387,000 acres (also in California)	
BLM WSA 2-621/618 (Poodle Mountain)	142,050
BLM WSA 2-619 (Buffalo Hills)	47,315
BLM WSA 2-619A (Twin Peaks)	91,405
BLM WSA 2-609 (Five Springs)	48,460
Additional BLM, state, and private roadless	58,000

Description: Northwestern Nevada west of Gerlach and northeastern California east of Susanville. Buffalo Hills, Buffalo Creek, Twin Peaks, Smoke Creek, and Five Springs Mountain form a large wilderness in the remote Smoke Creek Desert north and west of its terminal playa. The Buffalo Hills are a circular basaltic plateau with large canyons radiating from the center.

Some of the country outside the uplands is flat, while some is rolling. Buffalo Creek Canyon has steep 1,000-foot-high talus slopes. The West Fork of Buffalo Creek, a year-round stream, drains Hole-in-the-Ground, a 200-foot-deep, mile-wide volcanic caldera. Rush, Stony, and Smoke Creeks are other perennial streams. Several seasonal lakes are up to 100 acres in size. Poodle Mountain is a recent volcanic vent. The Twin Peaks WSA is the most rugged part of this large roadless area. Elevations range from 3,850 feet to 6,911 feet. Wildlife includes Mule Deer, Pronghorn, Kit Fox, Mountain Lion, Sage Grouse, Valley Quail, Golden Eagle, and Prairie Falcon, as well as Chukar (exotic) and "wild" horses. There is potential for Bighorn Sheep reintroduction. Vegetative zones are sagebrush steppe to juniper woodland. Willows form important riparian areas along the creeks.

Status: Conservationists should develop a million-acre Wilderness proposal for this part of the Smoke Creek Desert that would close Jeep trails and minor dirt roads (only county dirt roads separate Buffalo Hills–Smoke Creek from Eagle Head and the Skedaddle Mountains roadless areas). But conservation groups are calling for only an 87,900-acre Wilderness for Poodle Mountain. BLM opposes Wilderness for this outstanding area (except for a 54,970-acre piece in the Twin Peaks), and during its inventory, the Bureau sliced the area into several roadless units determined by Jeep trails and scattered range improvements. Although several dirt cherrystem roads (including one to the small Smoke Creek Reservoir) and Jeep trails have tracked parts of this area, it remains very wild. The military conducts low-level flights over the area. A few mining claims exist. Ranchers using public land in the area oppose protection. (What else is new?) The name, Buffalo Hills, reminds us that this area of Nevada, California, and Oregon was home to the Oregon race of Bison. Reintroduction of Bison and Gray Wolf should be studied.

EAGLE HEAD (DRY VALLEY RIM) 100,000 acres (also in California)	
BLM WSA 2-615	95,025
Additional BLM, state, and private roadless	5,000

Description: The northern Nevada-California border east of Susanville, California. The Dry Valley Rim is a 17-mile-long, east-facing fault block that rears 1,500 feet above the Smoke Creek Desert to the east (with a sheer

400–600-foot rimrock wall). Flat-topped summits characterize this area, and elevations vary from 3,800 feet to 6,200 feet. The east slope is cut by short, highly dissected drainages; the west slope is more gentle, and includes Skedaddle Creek (a perennial stream). Smoke Creek is on the north side. Grass and sagebrush, Prairie Falcon, Golden Eagle, Sage Grouse (important strutting grounds), Pronghorn, "wild" horses, and large wintering herds of Mule Deer inhabit this area.

Status: BLM has recommended a 52,845-acre Wilderness. Eagle Head is separated from the Buffalo Hills–Smoke Creek area to the north by a dirt road and from the Skedaddle roadless area to the west by a very poor dirt road. It should be part of a single million-acre Wilderness.

SMOKE CREEK DESERT 148,000 acres	
BLM roadless	122,000
Pyramid Lake Indian Reservation roadless	26,000

Description: Northwestern Nevada southwest of Gerlach and north of Pyramid Lake. The Smoke Creek Desert is a large dry lake bed, bordered by desert piedmont and scrub, serving as the basin for Smoke Creek, Buffalo Creek, Squaw Creek, and numerous intermittent drainages flowing from the Fox Range and Buffalo Hills.

Status: BLM, in keeping with its assumption that Wilderness can't be flat or open, refused to even study this reservoir of tranquillity for possible Wilderness recommendation. Conservation groups have obligingly neglected it as well. Those with a more highly developed sense of natural aesthetics know that wilderness isn't limited to regions of "spectacular grandeur" and that true wildness is often found in the most godforsaken zones of the planet. Flat is beautiful.

FOX MOUNTAIN RANGE 105,000 acres	
BLM WSA 2-14	75,404
Pyramid Lake Indian Reservation roadless	30,000

Description: Northwestern Nevada north of Pyramid Lake. The Fox Range is between the Smoke Creek and San Emido Deserts. Elevations are from

3,900 feet to 7,608 feet, on Pah Rum Peak. Vegetation includes Great Basin shrub steppe up to juniper with some riparian vegetation along Rodeo Creek. Steep canyons, rolling hills, bowl-shaped basins, granite outcrops, boulders, and several small sand dune areas in the desert piedmont around the mountains constitute a varied landscape. Pronghorn, Mule Deer, Mountain Lion, "wild" horses, and Sage Grouse occupy the landscape. The proposed National Desert Trail (hiking) would pass through the eastern edge.

Status: A few mining claims, and oil and gas and geothermal leases are the main threats. Low-level military flights occasionally shatter the peace. Conservation groups are asking for only a 23,600-acre BLM Wilderness, and BLM opposes any Wilderness.

Western Nevada

South of Lake Tahoe, Nevada shares several large roadless areas with California. These areas represent a gradient from the cool Great Basin Desert to the hot Mojave Desert. The Toiyabe and Inyo NFs, BLM, and Death Valley National Monument are the land managers.

EXCELSIOR MOUNTAINS 232,000 acres (also in California)	
Inyo National Forest roadless (NV)	118,000
BLM roadless (NV)	57,000
Inyo National Forest roadless (CA)	47,300
BLM roadless (CA)	10,000

Description: The central California-Nevada border east of Mono Lake. This is an enticing low mountain range of volcanic cinder soils with a high point of 8,651 feet. It has no surface water (except in Teels Marsh), and is remote, harsh, and seldom visited. The climate tends toward cool summers and cold winters with very little precipitation, most of that being snow. Vegetative types consist of Big Sagebrush and piñon and juniper, with salt scrub around the alkali flat at Teels Marsh. The BLM portion in Nevada is lower and made up of long, narrow basalt bluffs and flat valleys draining into Teels Marsh on the far east end. There are no trails. Archaeological sites are common. Wildlife populations are characteristically low, although there is a sizable herd of feral horses.

Status: There are no significant conflicts, although ORVs and fuelwood cutting represent possible threats. Friends of Nevada Wilderness proposes a 122,000-acre Wilderness Area. The 1988 Nevada Enhancement Act transferred approximately 13,500 acres of BLM land to the Toiyabe NF and a bit over 12,000 acres of NF land to the BLM in this roadless area. This total change of less than 1,500 acres is reflected in the acreage summary.

WHITE MOUNTAINS 379,000 acres (also in California)
See California for description and status.

QUEER MOUNTAIN 155,000 acres (also in California)
See California for description and status.

GRAPEVINE MOUNTAINS 246,000 acres (also in California)
See California for description and status.

FUNERAL MOUNTAINS 287,000 acres (also in California)
See California for description and status.

NOPAH RANGE 134,000 acres (also in California)
See California for description and status.

Southern Nevada

The southern tip of Nevada is a stronghold of the Mojave Desert, with sparse vegetation and extremely hot temperatures. Nonetheless, several ranges rise out of this geographic oven to create some of the finest forests and wildlife habitats in the state. Las Vegas may be the antithesis of natural beauty and serenity, but surrounding the glitzy strip is incomparable wilderness. The sprawling Desert National Wildlife Refuge, largest in the system (outside of Alaska) at over one and a half million acres, is the centerpiece of big wilderness here, but BLM and the Toiyabe NF have important areas, too.

SHEEP RANGE 468,000 acres	
Desert National Wildlife Refuge roadless	440,000
BLM WSAs 5-201/165/16 and additional BLM roadless	28,000

Description: Southern Nevada north of Las Vegas. This superb desert mountain range rises out of the Mojave Desert at 2,500 feet to reach 9,750 feet on Sheep Peak. Joshua Tree, saltbush, Creosote, and cactus populate the Mojave Desert lowlands, with piñon and juniper, Ponderosa Pine, and White Fir higher up, and a Bristlecone and Limber Pine forest on top. The world's largest population of Desert Bighorn Sheep (over a thousand individuals) is found in the roadless areas on the Desert National Wildlife Refuge, as is the greatest diversity of animal life in Nevada. Other species include Desert Tortoise, Gila Monster, Gambel's Quail, Golden Eagle, Mountain Lion, Bobcat, Mule Deer, Badger, and the rare Kit Fox. Water is limited to a few springs. Only dirt roads separate the Sheep Range from the other large roadless areas on the Desert NWR. In 1936, Bob Marshall called what is now the Desert NWR and Nellis Air Force Range the finest desert wilderness in America. Temperatures range from 117 degrees to below zero, and precipitation from 2 inches to 15 inches a year.

Status: The FWS proposes 440,000 acres for wilderness. BLM recommends none. The U.S. Air Force continues to try to take over the Desert National Wildlife Refuge as a Military Operations Area (a military air zone). Conservationists have so far prevented the military from gaining exclusive control. Some of the BLM land was exchanged to the Aerojet Corporation in a shady land exchange. Of course, the Desert NWR has been downwind of the Nevada Test Site for over forty years. Radiation kills.

*RM36: 2,670,000**

HOLE IN THE ROCK 277,000 acres	
Desert National Wildlife Refuge roadless	115,700
BLM roadless	140,058
Nellis Air Force Range roadless	21,000

Description: Southern Nevada north of Las Vegas. This area consists largely of a broad desert valley between the Sheep and Desert mountain ranges. The southern end includes the large, dry Desert Lake. Elevations range from about 3,200 feet to over 6,200 feet. See Sheep Range for general description.

Status: The FWS proposes 115,700 acres for Wilderness. BLM proposes none.

*RM36: 2,670,000**

DESERT-PINTWATER RANGE 467,000 acres	
Desert National Wildlife Refuge roadless	372,000
Nellis Air Force Range roadless	65,000
BLM roadless	30,000

Description: Southern Nevada north of Las Vegas. The Desert and Pintwater Ranges, with the Three Lakes Valley between them, lie west of the Sheep Range. The high point is 6,400 feet, on Quartz Peak in the Pintwaters. Lower elevations are about 3,200 feet. See Sheep Range for general description.

Status: The FWS proposes 339,500 acres for Wilderness. BLM proposes none. The Three Lakes Valley is used by the military for air-to-ground target practice. Although mostly roadless, the valley does show definite impacts from this use.

*RM36: 2,670,000**

SPOTTED RANGE 354,000 acres	
Desert National Wildlife Refuge roadless	318,000
Nellis Air Force Range roadless	27,000
BLM roadless	9,000

Description: Southern Nevada northwest of Las Vegas and west of the Pintwater Range. This area includes the Papoose Range, Ranger Mountains, Papoose Dry Lake, and parts of the Spotted Range and Emigrant Valley. The high point is 6,300 feet, on Aysees Peak in the Buried Hills. The low point is below 3,200 feet. See Sheep Range for general description.

Status: The FWS proposes 300,700 acres for Wilderness. BLM proposes none.

*RM36: 2,670,000**

LAS VEGAS RANGE 207,000 acres	
Desert National Wildlife Refuge roadless	164,600
BLM WSAs 5-216/217	39,224
Nellis AFB roadless	3,000

Description: Southern Nevada immediately north of Las Vegas. See Sheep Range for general description.

Status: FWS proposes 164,600 acres for Wilderness. BLM recommends none.

*RM36: 2,670,000**

MT. STIRLING 180,000 acres	
Toiyabe National Forest roadless	90,000
BLM and private roadless	90,000

Description: Southern Nevada west of Las Vegas in the Spring Mountains. A dirt road separates this area from the Mt. Charleston roadless area. Elevations in this rugged complex of canyons and ridges, which stretches from U.S. 95 on the north to the Pahrump Valley on the south, vary from about 2,800 feet to 9,618 feet. This is a heavily vegetated range for Nevada with piñon and juniper, Ponderosa Pine, White Fir, and Bristlecone Pine. The fauna includes quail, Elk, Mule Deer, Mountain Lion, Bobcat, and "wild" horses and burros. Potential for Bighorn Sheep reintroduction is high. See Charleston Peak for additional description.

Status: Approximately 90,000 acres of BLM land in this roadless area, including virtually all of BLM WSA 5-401 (BLM had proposed 40,275 acres of this WSA for Wilderness), was transferred to the Toiyabe NF by the 1988 Nevada Enhancement Act. It is uncertain what status the BLM WSA has under Forest Service management and what will become of the Wilderness recommendation. The exchange between agencies is updated in the acreage summary.

CHARLESTON PEAK 200,000 acres	
Designated Mt. Charleston Wilderness Area	43,000
Additional Toiyabe NF and intermixed private roadless	90,000
BLM WSA and additional BLM and private roadless	67,000

Description: The Spring Mountains in southern Nevada west of Las Vegas. Charleston Peak (11,919 feet) is the most prominent peak of the Mojave Desert, and the Spring Mountains are the only range in the southern Great Basin to rise above tree line. Lower elevations are about 3,200 feet. Moving upward, vegetation ranges from southern Mojave Desert scrub to Joshua Tree to scrub oak to piñon and juniper to White Fir and Ponderosa Pine forests, and ultimately to one of the largest forests of Bristlecone Pine in the world. Some 27 species of endemic plants grow in the area. A dirt road separates the Charleston Peak roadless area from the Mt. Stirling roadless area. Some of the BLM portion is in the Red Rock Canyon National Recreation Lands, known for sheer cliffs (up to 1,000 feet high) and canyons of red Aztec sandstone. A large Desert Bighorn Sheep herd and a small herd of Elk use the area. Other wildlife includes Mule Deer, Mountain Lion, the Endangered Spotted Bat, and the endemic Palmer's Chipmunk. Feral burros compete with native wildlife. Brownstone Canyon is included on the National Register of Historical Places as an archaeological district because of its dramatic petroglyphs. This area receives very high precipitation for the Great Basin, up to 28 inches a year, with a snow depth of 6 feet.

Status: This roadless area is rather amoeba-shaped, owing to several cherrystem roads penetrating along canyons. In the 1989 Nevada Wilderness Protection Act, 43,000 acres were designated as Wilderness (FNW proposed 47,000 acres). Approximately 83,000 acres of BLM land in this roadless area were transferred to the Toiyabe NF by the 1988 Nevada Enhancement Act. The acreage summary is updated to show this transfer. The western half of BLM's La Madre Mountain WSA (5-412) was part of the transfer. BLM had proposed 34,010 acres for Wilderness. It remains to be seen what will be done about additional Wilderness designation after the transfer.

Since the remainder of BLM's La Madre Mountain WSA abuts the sprawl of Las Vegas, impacts to the area include, in addition to those from the standard ORV joyriders, the dumping of bodies by beefy guys in tight dark suits and sunglasses. This may be the only BLM area receiving ORV use by Cadillacs. Mining and oil and gas are specific threats.

MUDDY MOUNTAINS 116,000 acres	
BLM WSA 5-229	96,170
Additional BLM roadless	11,000
Lake Mead National Recreation Area roadless	9,000

Description: Southern Nevada east of Las Vegas. Elevations range from 2,000 feet to 5,400 feet. The core of the Muddy Mountains is formed by limestone peaks and canyons with two valleys where orange, red, and cream sandstone are exposed. Lower Mojave Desert plant communities (Creosote, Blackbrush, yucca, Joshua Tree) are complemented by large Desert Willows in the big washes. Gambel's Quail, Desert Bighorn Sheep, Mountain Lion, Bobcat, and "wild" horses live here. Archaeological sites up to four thousand years old, 600-foot-high cliffs, sculpted sandstone formations, and Anniversary Narrows (a 600-foot-deep canyon only 7–15 feet wide) are special attractions.

Status: BLM proposes only 36,850 acres for Wilderness. ORV use is a particular threat because of the area's proximity to Las Vegas (dirt bike racing occurs here). Additional threats include claims for nonmetallic minerals.

MORMON MOUNTAINS 163,000 acres	
BLM WSA 5-161	162,887

Description: Southeastern Nevada southeast of Alamo. The Union Pacific tracks separate this area from the Meadow Valley Mountains roadless area. Mormon Peak is 7,411 feet. The low point is 2,200 feet. The BLM describes the area in this way: "Core is a tortuous collection of rugged limestone peaks, high cliffs, and deep remote canyons. Around core are lesser hills, canyons and dissected bajadas. On the south knife-like Moapa Peak stabs skyward, a beacon to climbers and scramblers. Caves provide spelunking." Vegetation ranges from Blackbrush, Bursage, and Joshua Tree to piñon and juniper with a small relict stand of large Ponderosa Pine near the summit of Mormon Peak. Fauna includes Desert Tortoise, Desert Bighorn Sheep, Mule Deer, and Spotted Bat. The Meadow Valley Range Sandwort is a state protected plant. The many archaeological sites include agave roasting pits and petroglyphs.

Status: BLM recommends a piddling 23,690-acre Wilderness Area; conservation groups have asked for 123,130 acres for Wilderness.

MEADOW VALLEY MOUNTAINS 186,000 acres	
BLM WSA 5-156	185,744

Description: Southeastern Nevada southeast of Alamo. Elevations range from 3,400 feet to 5,700 feet. BLM says, "Landforms include 30 miles of rugged Meadow Valley Mountains along western spine; the Bunker Hills, south; and central bajada stretching from Bunker Hills nearly to Hackberry Canyon. Mountains are jumbled, remote and extremely varied. A natural arch, cliffs, jagged peaks and hidden canyons. Conical Sunflower Mountain focal point. Hackberry Canyon has outstanding wilderness. Vigo Canyon has sculpted cliffs . . . vast desert vistas untrammeled by man." Vegetation includes Creosote Bush, Blackbrush, Joshua Tree, rabbitbrush, and piñon and juniper. Meadow Valley Range Sandwort and Nye Milk-vetch are state protected plants. Large Barrel Cactus grow on the southern end of the roadless area. Desert Tortoise, Golden Eagle, Prairie Falcon, Desert Bighorn Sheep, and Spotted Bat are some of the sensitive species in the area. "Wild" horses are also present.

Status: BLM recommends 97,180 acres for Wilderness; conservation groups, 166,500 acres. Aerojet Corporation has acquired nearby BLM lands in the Coyote Springs Valley in a shady land exchange. This may have some impact on the Meadow Valley Mountains.

DELAMAR MOUNTAINS 127,000 acres	
BLM WSA 5-177	126,700

Description: Southern Nevada southeast of Alamo. This area is separated from the Meadow Valley Mountains by a minor dirt road and from the Sheep Range in the Desert NWR by a narrow paved highway. Elevations rise from 2,600 feet to 6,600 feet. The Delamars are a broad rolling plateau bounded by an abrupt cliff on the west, and with a multicolor caldera in the core. Desert bajadas, badlands, and spectacular, twisting, cliff-lined canyons on the south constitute a varied landscape. Desert scrub dominated by Blackbrush is the most common vegetative community; Big Sagebrush, Joshua

Tree, piñon and juniper, grassland, and salt desert scrub are also present, as is Nye Milkvetch, a state protected plant. Desert Tortoise find habitat here. This area is being considered for Desert Bighorn reintroduction. Paleozoic fossils, and important archaeological sites, including an obsidian quarry, are of scientific interest.

Status: Peace and quiet is disturbed by low-level military flights and ORVs. Conservationists recommend 102,490 acres for Wilderness. Aerojet has acquired nearby BLM lands in the Coyote Springs Valley in a land exchange. This may adversely affect the Delamars.

Central Nevada

There is perhaps no better representation of basin and range than in central Nevada, where a series of long, narrow mountain ranges rise more than a mile above the similarly long, narrow valleys that divide them. This topography differs from the tablelands and sinks of northwestern Nevada, but is ecologically part of the Great Basin Desert, too. The Toiyabe NF generally manages the higher ranges, and BLM has the rest except for Carson Sink, where land management is divided among four agencies.

CARSON SINK 286,000 acres	
BLM, Navy, state, and Fish and Wildlife Service roadless	286,000

Description: West-central Nevada north of Fallon. This little-known alkali flat is the terminus of the Carson River (and one of the remnants of Pleistocene Lake Lahontan). Here, in the midst of the surrounding Great Basin desert, sand dunes meet marshes. Elevations vary only from under 4,000 feet to about 3,870 feet. The roadless portion of the Sink is composed of parts of the Fallon National Wildlife Refuge, the state Stillwater Wildlife Management Area, a Navy bombing range, and, mostly, BLM lands. It is one of the more important areas in Nevada for waterfowl and shorebirds, including White Pelican, Tundra Swan, White-faced Ibis, Bald Eagle, Peregrine Falcon, and several species of more common ducks, geese, and "peeps." Other wildlife includes Coyote, kangaroo rat, and horned lizard. Saltbush, greasewood, sand verbena, and evening primrose are common desert plants in the area. The primary marsh area is roaded and diked on the Wildlife Refuge, and much of the roadless area stretching to the north does not receive water every year.

Status: The U.S. Fish and Wildlife Service has discovered toxic contamination (selenium, arsenic, lead, and boron) at Carson Sink similar to that at Kesterson NWR in California (a case that made national news). There was a large die-off of waterfowl and fish at Stillwater in 1987. Until recently, the area had no water rights and depended entirely on runoff from Newlands Project irrigation; it has been drying up over the last eighty years—from over 170,000 acres of wetlands to less than 38,000 today. The Toiyabe Chapter of the Sierra Club has begun a major campaign to buy water rights from Newlands Project farmers to restore the marshes and dilute the toxins. Support is needed. Some water rights were purchased in 1990.

The Navy wants to expand its Fallon bombing range into this area.

Carson Sink is a prime example of a large, biologically important wild area that has been neglected because it does not fit the classic conception of wilderness. BLM did not consider it for a WSA, and conservationists have not pushed protection.

A particularly gruesome assault on the area is from local good ol' boys who plunder ancient Paiute graves near the marshes. These ghouls rip apart the skeletons of the ancients in order to find artifacts.

CLAN ALPINE RANGE 196,000 acres	
BLM WSA 3-102	196,128

Description: Central Nevada west of Austin. This major north-south trending volcanic range climbs from 3,600 feet in Dixie Valley to 9,966 feet on Mt. Augusta. Several small perennial and intermittent streams lined with riparian vegetation, numerous springs, colorful rock formations, high ridges with groves of mountain mahogany (rare in this part of Nevada), Aspen along the canyons, and piñon-juniper forests are all included in this diverse area. Big Sagebrush and Shadscale predominant in the foothills. Sage Grouse, Golden Eagle, Prairie Falcon, Mule Deer, Mountain Lion, "wild" horses, and introduced Rainbow and Brown Trout dwell here. Desert Bighorn Sheep were reintroduced in 1986. Views extend to the Sierra crest 100 miles to the west. Good cross-country skiing attracts winter enthusiasts.

Status: BLM is recommending only 68,458 acres for Wilderness. ORVs, small-scale mining, continued overgrazing, fuelwood cutting, and geothermal exploration are threats. Some lower-elevation areas are severely cow-trashed (they may be outside this roadless area). Several cherrystem roads penetrate the area, and crude, old Jeep trails scar Mt. Augusta.

ARC DOME 250,000 acres	
Designated Arc Dome Wilderness Area	115,000
Additional Toiyabe National Forest roadless	129,000
BLM and private roadless	6,000

Description: Central Nevada north of Tonopah. Friends of Nevada Wilderness calls the imposing granite domes in the southern end of the Toiyabe Range "the backbone of Central Nevada." Topography varies from gently rolling, piñon-and-juniper-covered lowlands on the south through steep, rocky canyons up to glacial cirques around Arc Dome. The west slope is gentle with deep canyons; the east slope has cliffs and rocky, more rugged canyons. Elevations climb from 6,000 feet on the south to 11,773 feet on Arc Dome. Dense piñon and juniper intermingles with Big Sagebrush and mountain mahogany. It is replaced by pockets of Aspen and Limber Pine higher up. The Reese and the North and South Twin Rivers spring from Arc Dome, with its 25 inches of annual precipitation (very high for the Great Basin). There are eighteen other creeks in the area. Riparian vegetation is mostly cottonwood, willow, maple, and birch. Many small, lush meadows adorn the higher elevations. Desert Bighorn Sheep, Mule Deer, Mountain Lion, Bobcat, Coyote, Beaver, Sage Grouse, Blue Grouse, and raptors prosper here. Fishing is popular. Some Aspens on the lower-elevation west side have classic Basque sheepherder pornographic carvings.

Status: Cherrystem roads penetrate. The mining threat on the periphery is high, as is the potential for commercial cutting of piñon and juniper. Only 115,000 acres of this area (considered one of the "jewels" of Nevada by conservation groups) was designated Wilderness in the 1989 Nevada Wilderness Act. Friends of Nevada Wilderness proposed only 146,000 acres. Miners convinced Senator Harry Reid to drop from the bill a large part of Arc Dome in the North and South Twin River drainages. These small, independent miners are the gravest threat to Arc Dome. They are even causing problems in the designated Wilderness. Reid, who was elected to the

Senate with strong conservationist support, has proved with his Wilderness bill to be a major disappointment.

TOIYABE CREST 126,000 acres	
Toiyabe NF and BLM roadless	126,000

Description: Central Nevada south of Austin. The Toiyabe Range (north of the Arc Dome roadless area) is a high mountain ridge with elevations from 7,500 feet to over 11,000 feet located between two semiarid valleys. The topography is steep and heavily dissected on the east, more gentle on the west. Vegetation rises from sagebrush, to piñon and juniper, to stands of mountain mahogany, Aspen, and occasional Limber Pine in the higher elevations. The Toiyabe Crest Trail runs the length of the area. On the crest is a granite outcrop, the "Wild Granites," which is described by FNW as "a 400-foot wall of granite carved by wind and water into spectacular vertical spikes and columns." A small band of Desert Bighorn Sheep lives here, and several west slope streams contain the Endangered Lahontan Cutthroat Trout. Other wildlife includes Mule Deer, Mountain Lion, Bobcat, Golden Eagle, Blue Grouse, and Sage Grouse.

Status: Cherrystem roads penetrate the area along several canyon bottoms. Mining is a threat throughout the area. Although conservationists asked for only 79,000 acres of Wilderness here, the 1989 Nevada Wilderness Act released the entire area. A minor dirt road is all that separates Toiyabe Crest from Arc Dome. It should be closed, and a single Wilderness of at least 400,000 acres established.

TABLE MOUNTAIN 190,000 acres	
Designated Table Mountain Wilderness Area (Toiyabe NF)	98,000
Additional Toiyabe NF roadless	77,000
BLM roadless	15,000

Description: Central Nevada southeast of Austin in the core of the Monitor Range. Well-watered, rolling mountain uplands with steep, rocky canyons break into foothills and valley floor. Elevations rise from 7,000 feet to over 10,000 feet. One can walk for a dozen miles on a gentle plateau at over 10,000 feet along a precipitous eastern escarpment. Higher-elevation vegetation consists of expansive stands of grass and sagebrush broken by extensive Aspen forests—not simply groves, as exist elsewhere. Lower-elevation vegetation is piñon and juniper, mountain mahogany, and Big Sagebrush. Wildlife includes Mule Deer, Elk (non-native and introduced in 1979), Mountain Lion, Bobcat, Sage Grouse, Blue Grouse, and the Endangered Lahontan Cutthroat Trout in several large creeks. The highest Goshawk nesting density in Nevada occurs here.

Status: Overgrazing is causing erosion. The Forest Service has a burning desire to "manage" the area for wildlife "improvement"—i.e., vegetative manipulation. Jeep trails and old mines scar the area slightly. The 1989 Nevada Wilderness Act established a 98,000-acre Wilderness. About 5,000 acres in this roadless area were transferred from BLM to the FS by the 1988 Nevada Enhancement Act. That change is reflected in the acreage summary.

HORSE HEAVEN 135,000 acres	
Toiyabe NF RARE I	115,000
BLM and private roadless	20,000

Description: Central Nevada in the central Monitor Range southeast of Austin. Rolling mountain uplands with steep, rocky canyons break into foothills and valley floor. Elevations range from 7,000 feet to 9,800 feet. Higher-elevation vegetation consists of grass and sagebrush interspersed with Aspen groves; lower-elevation vegetation is piñon and juniper, mountain mahogany, and Big Sagebrush. Wildlife includes Mule Deer, Elk, Mountain Lion, Bobcat, Sage Grouse, and Blue Grouse.

Status: Jeep trails and overgrazing impact the area. National and state conservation groups are not proposing Wilderness in this worthy but forgotten area. It was dropped from Wilderness consideration by the 1989 Nevada Wilderness Act. A poor dirt road is all that separates Horse Heaven from Table Mountain. It should be closed, and a single 350,000-acre Wilderness established.

ANTELOPE 144,000 acres	
BLM WSA 6-231/241 and additional roadless	94,000
Toiyabe National Forest roadless	50,000

Description: Central Nevada south of Eureka. A north-south ridge 1,000–2,000 feet above the valleys dominates this remote range. Ninemile Peak, on the northern end of the range, is 10,104 feet in elevation. The northern end has several perennial streams with mature riparian forests and extensive Aspen groves on the plateaulike top, while the central part is a barren interior valley. The southern part features flat-topped mountains covered with piñon-juniper forest. Archaeological sites include a group of Shoshone wickiups. Reportedly, this is a very pristine area with the range little damaged by livestock.

Status: BLM has recommended 83,100 acres for Wilderness. Approximately 50,000 acres of BLM land, including some of that recommended for Wilderness, was transferred to the Toiyabe NF by the 1988 Nevada Enhancement Act. What effect this will have on the Wilderness recommendation is uncertain.

PALISADE MESA 116,000 acres	
BLM WSA 6-142/162	115,350

Description: Central Nevada east of Tonopah. This area in the Pancake Range consists of mesas, lava flows, volcanic craters, and cinder cones; it includes Lunar Crater, a maar volcano (low-relief, circular) that is on the National Natural Landmark Register. Large boulders form outcroppings on the mesa tops. Elevations rise from 5,000 feet to 7,394 feet. Vegetation is sagebrush steppe with scattered juniper on the mesas. Wildlife includes Golden Eagle, Prairie Falcon, other raptors, and small populations of Mountain Lion, Pronghorn, Bighorn Sheep, Mule Deer, and exotic Chukar. Archaeological sites include a rock shelter with pictographs. *Astragalus callithrix,* a plant proposed for Threatened or Endangered status, is known in the area.

Status: BLM recommends 66,110 acres for Wilderness.

SOUTH REVEILLE 107,500 acres	
BLM WSA 6-112	107,500

Description: Central Nevada east of Tonopah and north of Nellis Air Force Range. The southern and central parts of the Reveille Range are characterized by large expanses of high-elevation valley bottoms surrounding mesas and mountain peaks, which are cut by narrow canyons. Elevations range from 5,000 feet to 8,910 feet. Sagebrush dominates below 7,000 feet, piñon and juniper above. Abundant wildlife includes Mule Deer, Pronghorn, Mountain Lion, and various raptors.

Status: BLM, in accordance with the name it has earned, "Bureau of Livestock and Mining," proposes only 33,000 acres for Wilderness protection.

Eastern Nevada

The alternating basins and ranges of eastern Nevada are not as symmetrical in their arrangement as are those of central Nevada, but this is still classic Great Basin landscape. The mountain ranges are far enough away from the rain shadow of the Sierra Nevada to be able to support a thicker and more diverse forest than is sustainable elsewhere in Nevada. These forests also show more influence from the Rocky Mountains–type forests than do those in central Nevada. The Humboldt NF generally has the higher ranges, while BLM manages everything else. Several of these limestone ranges hide caves of exceptional size and beauty.

QUINN 120,000 acres	
Designated Quinn Canyon Wilderness Area (Humboldt NF)	27,000
Additional Humboldt NF roadless	74,000
BLM roadless	19,000

Description: East-central Nevada east of Tonopah and southwest of Ely. A poor dirt road separates this area from the Grant Range roadless area. Vegetation is sagebrush steppe through piñon-juniper woodland to Aspen, White Fir, Limber Pine, and Bristlecone Pine. The high crest holds snow into July in many years. Volcanic, as opposed to the limestone Grant Range, Quinn has more water in its canyons. The peaks and ridges, including the high point of 10,229 feet, are unnamed. The low point is about 5,800 feet. Impressive rock cliffs buttress the canyons leading into the high country.

Status: Mining presents a possible threat. Exxon is exploring nearby for oil and gas—the area could be threatened if a strike is made. A 27,000-acre Wilderness was designated by the 1989 Nevada Wilderness Act. The area is heavily overgrazed.

GRANT RANGE 240,000 acres	
Designated Grant Range Wilderness Area (Humboldt NF)	50,000
Additional Humboldt National Forest roadless	55,519
BLM WSAs 4-166/158/199	116,562
Additional BLM roadless	18,000

Description: East-central Nevada east of Tonopah and southwest of Ely. This remote mountain range of limestone cliffs is cut by high-walled canyons. Benchlands and foothills are in the lower elevations. Troy Peak, at 11,298 feet, is the high point. The low point is under 5,000 feet. Vegetation includes sagebrush steppe, piñon-juniper woodland, and, in the high country, large stands of Ponderosa Pine, Aspen, Limber Pine, White Fir, and Bristlecone Pine (one of Nevada's best stands). Cottonwood grow along canyon bottoms. A healthy herd of Desert Bighorn Sheep lives here, and the area is important Mule Deer winter range. Aeries are used by Golden Eagle, Kestrel, Turkey Vulture, Red-tailed Hawk, Ferruginous Hawk, Great Horned Owl, Long-eared Owl, and Prairie Falcon. Other wildlife includes Ringtail, Gray Fox, Bobcat, Mountain Lion, and Elk. Over two hundred species of wildflowers, including a rare Nevada primrose and the state sensitive species One-leaf Torrey Milk-vetch, and over a dozen tree species grow here. A poor dirt road separates it from the Quinn Canyon Range. John Muir wrote about climbing Troy Peak. Other visitors report a superb feeling of solitude.

Status: Threats include small mining operations and so-called livestock improvements. The area is also threatened by Exxon oil and gas exploration. The 1989 Nevada Wilderness Act designated a 50,000-acre Wilderness. BLM proposes an additional 37,542 acres for Wilderness. The dirt road between Quinn and Grant should be closed, and a 400,000-acre Wilderness established.

SOUTH EGAN RANGE 113,000 acres	
BLM WSA 4-168	96,996
Additional BLM and private roadless	16,000

Description: Eastern Nevada south of Ely. This is an unusual mountain range for Nevada in that it is not a single ridgeline, but a more complex series of ridges. Portions of the area are extremely wild and virtually inaccessible, characterized by steep slopes, massive limestone cliffs, and White Fir forests. Long Canyon has an open bowl-like area. Vegetation is sagebrush steppe, piñon and juniper, mixed conifer, scattered stands of Aspen and mountain mahogany, Bristlecone Pine along the ridgelines, and significant stands of Ponderosa Pine (unusual in the Great Basin). Riparian areas are abundant. Angel Cave is a 200-foot-deep pit cave oddly located on the crest at 9,000 feet. Elevations range from 5,600 feet to over 9,600 feet. There are numerous archaeological sites. Red-tailed Hawk, Prairie Falcon, Golden Eagle, Kestrel, Turkey Vulture, Great Horned Owl, and Long-eared Owl have aeries in the limestone cliffs. Gambel's Quail, rare in this part of Nevada, are found in the foothills. Additional species include Sage Grouse, Blue Grouse, Mule Deer, Mountain Lion, Bobcat, and occasional Elk. This is a potential site for reintroduction of Bighorn Sheep.

Status: BLM opposes Wilderness designation for this area.

PARSNIP PEAK 133,000 acres	
BLM WSA 4-206	88,175
Additional BLM roadless	45,000

Description: Eastern Nevada, northeast of Pioche in the southern part of the Wilson Creek Range. BLM describes the area as follows: "Huge stands of aspen turn mountainsides aflame with orange and scarlet in fall. Spectacular rock outcrops. Diverse vegetation ranging from open, grassy areas to ponderosa to dense pinyon and juniper contribute to incredible scenery. Ridgeline which includes Parsnip Peak is open, scoured by the winds at nearly 9,000 feet." Parsnip Peak is 8,942 feet; Mt. Wilson is 9,296 feet (a road goes to the top to service a radio tower, so the high point of the roadless area is about 9,200 feet, on the slope of Mt. Wilson). The low point is about 5,570 feet, on the southwestern edge. BLM reports that livestock and humans have had little impact in the core of the area around Parsnip Peak and that vegetation is in "nearly pristine condition." There is a Ponderosa Pine–Gambel Oak stand, which is rare for Nevada. Wildlife includes Mule Deer, Pronghorn, Mountain Lion, Sage Grouse, and Blue Grouse.

Status: Areas to the north and south of the WSA were excluded by BLM from Wilderness study because of vehicle ways. This area was not included in the first edition of *The Big Outside;* reports from BLM staff alerted us to the additional roadless country around the WSA. The entire area should be protected, and intruding Jeep trails closed. Mining, oil and gas exploration, grazing developments (including extensive juniper chainings and Crested Wheatgrass seedings), fuelwood cutting, and ORV play are threats to the northern and southwestern portions of the area. BLM proposes only 53,560 acres for Wilderness.

WHEELER PEAK 160,000 acres	
Great Basin National Park and Humboldt NF roadless	136,000
BLM roadless	24,000

Description: Eastern Nevada east of Ely. The new 77,100-acre Great Basin National Park encompasses a portion of the South Snake Range, which culminates in 13,063-foot Wheeler Peak and several other peaks over 11,500 feet. Wheeler Peak offers a superb example of glaciation—a small permanent ice field, several small lakes, and U-shaped valleys with rushing streams. The area also has wild caves and the six-story-high Lexington natural arch. Lehman Cave is on the edge of the roadless area. With 8,000 feet of relief, the crest drops down to sagebrush valleys on either side. A well-known ancient Bristlecone Pine forest (4,000 years old) thrives here. In 1964, a fiendish FS District Ranger, Don Cox, chain-sawed down the oldest known Bristlecone Pine (4,900 years old) here. Fauna includes Rocky Mountain Bighorn Sheep, Mule Deer, Cougar, Beaver, Kit Fox, Pygmy Rabbit, and Utah Cutthroat Trout. Vegetation includes a substantial forest (for Nevada) of Douglas-fir, White Fir, Limber Pine, and Engelmann Spruce. Efforts to establish a Great Basin National Park on Wheeler Peak began in 1924. The Park was finally established in 1986, but late compromises cut nearly 100,000 acres from the originally proposed 174,000 acres.

Status: "Great Basin National Park" is a joke—allowing overgrazing and mining (on established claims) to continue, and including only a portion of one mountain range and no valleys—no basin! A true Great Basin National Park is needed that includes several mountain ranges and the intervening valleys—and excludes cows and prospectors. Despite the National Park, the Snake Range is not safe. Conservationists propose 42,000 acres of the South

Snake Range outside of the Park for Wilderness. The Park Service is considering closing a couple of Jeep trails in its management plan and needs to be encouraged to do more. Overgrazing is bad in several areas of the Park, and visitors should complain.

MT. MORIAH 144,000 acres (also in Utah)	
Designated Mt. Moriah Wilderness Area (Humboldt NF)	75,565
Designated Mt. Moriah Wilderness Area (BLM)	6,435
Additional Humboldt NF roadless (NV)	15,000
BLM roadless (partly in UT)	47,000

Description: Eastern Nevada east of Ely in the northern Snake Range. This complex mountain range, well forested for Nevada, is crowned by 12,050-foot Mt. Moriah (Nevada's fifth-highest peak), which sits on a high, geologically unique plateau over 11,000 feet in elevation with steep limestone canyons cutting away in all directions. John Hart, in *Hiking the Great Basin,* writes, "On the rounded peaks, more than on any other Great Basin peak, you have the sensation not just of height but of deep remoteness, of immersion in wilderness." The low point is 5,400 feet. Vegetation includes sagebrush steppe, piñon and juniper, Aspen, mountain mahogany, Douglas-fir, White Fir, Limber Pine, and Bristlecone Pine (including a young, vigorous Bristlecone forest). Rocky Mountain Bighorn Sheep and the rare Utah Cutthroat Trout live here, as do Pronghorn in the lower elevations.

Status: The 1989 Nevada Wilderness Act designated an 82,000-acre Wilderness.

SCHELL CREEK RANGE 145,000 acres	
Humboldt NF roadless	134,000
BLM and private roadless	11,000

Description: Eastern Nevada east of Ely. This long, high ridge above timberline is cut by several deep, rugged canyons with perennial streams. North Schell Peak reaches 11,890 feet, and South Schell Peak 11,765 feet; elevations drop to 6,000 feet in the foothills. Impressive talus slopes flank the range. Wildlife includes Pronghorn, Beaver, Mountain Lion, many Mule Deer, and a small herd of Elk. Wild limestone caves include one where the remains of a Cave Bear were discovered in 1982. Sagebrush steppe and piñon-juniper woodland grade up through Aspen stands and forests of Douglas-fir, Engelmann Spruce (very rare in Nevada), and White Fir to Limber Pine and Bristlecone Pine on top. Several streams have trout.

Status: Threats include continued overgrazing, mining, ORVs, and fuelwood and Christmas tree cutting. Failure to include this splendid Great Basin mountain range was one of the more unfortunate flaws of the 1989 Nevada Wilderness Protection Act. Local road hunters are steadily pushing Jeep trails deeper into this roadless area.

CHERRY CREEK MOUNTAINS 101,000 acres	
BLM WSA 4-015 (Goshute Canyon)	35,594
Additional BLM roadless	65,000

Description: Northeastern Nevada north of Ely. Extensive limestone cliffs and bluffs, a large mountain basin, and a long, high ridge characterize this area, which reaches 10,542 feet in elevation on Exchequer Peak, nearly a mile above the low point. Vegetation ranges from sagebrush steppe to piñon and juniper. Mountain mahogany, cottonwood, and willow are found along the canyons; and Aspen up to forests of White Fir and large stands of Bristlecone Pine are on the summits. Wildlife includes Blue Grouse, Sage Grouse, Mule Deer, Mountain Lion, Bobcat, Yellow-bellied Marmot, Spotted Bat, Elk, and Pronghorn. Nesting sites for raptors are present (both Peregrine Falcon and Bald Eagle are believed to use the area). "Wild" horses roam the area. Many creeks and springs support excellent riparian vegetation and Bonneville Cutthroat Trout. Goshute Cave contains a wide variety of rare speleothelms, including blistered mammalaries and cave pearls.

Status: BLM is proposing a paltry 22,100-acre Wilderness in the Goshute Canyon area. Seismographic crews are encroaching.

SOUTH GREAT SALT LAKE DESERT 1,144,000 acres (also in Utah)

See Utah for description and status.

RUBY MOUNTAINS 190,000 acres	
Designated Ruby Mountains Wilderness Area (Humboldt NF)	90,000
Released Humboldt National Forest RARE II area	74,820
Additional Humboldt NF, BLM, and private roadless	25,000

Description: Northeastern Nevada southeast of Elko. This glorious glacier-carved granite mountain range is the most classically scenic in Nevada. It includes sculpted peaks, U-shaped valleys with snow-fed streams, many lakes, and excellent views of Great Basin valleys and ranges in all directions. Ruby Dome, at 11,400 feet, is the high point. Vegetative types range from sagebrush to Bristlecone Pine. Mountain Goat (non-native) have been introduced. The federally Threatened Lahontan Cutthroat Trout lives in streams draining into the Humboldt River. The other wildlife is characteristic of the Great Basin.

Status: The 1989 Nevada Wilderness Act designated a 90,000-acre Ruby Mountains Wilderness with absurdly distorted boundaries to allow helicopter skiing. Conservationists called for 143,000 acres.

JARBIDGE 189,000 acres (also in Idaho)	
Designated Jarbidge Wilderness Area (Humboldt NF)	113,167
Additional Humboldt NF roadless	46,500
BLM roadless (partly in ID)	29,000

Description: Northeastern Nevada north of Elko. These remote mountains are unusual for Nevada in that they have multiple ridges and are heavily forested. Eight peaks attain 10,000 feet. Other features include a glacial lake and the headwaters of the Jarbidge River, which flows into the Snake River. The west slope drops from 10,800 feet to 7,000 feet in two miles. Sagebrush steppe covers the lower country; mountain mahogany and Aspen, the middle elevations; and Limber Pine and Subalpine Fir, the higher. The precipitation of 30 inches a year is high for Nevada. Winter temperatures are extremely cold. California Bighorn Sheep were reintroduced into the area in 1981 but have been eliminated. The Forest Service blames predators, but they were probably of the pointy-toed, high-heeled, Stetson-wearing kind. The local livestock gentry mounted a successful effort in the mid-1980s to prevent the Nevada Game and Fish Department from reintroducing Elk—the ranchers claimed the Elk would eat too much. Threatened Lahontan Cutthroat Trout inhabit the streams. Within the historical past, Pacific Ocean salmon swam up the Columbia, Snake, Bruneau, and, ultimately, Jarbidge Rivers to spawn in this area.

Status: Before the 1989 Nevada Wilderness Protection Act, a 64,667-acre Jarbidge Wilderness Area was the only Wilderness Area in the state. The 1989 act added 48,500 acres to the Wilderness, despite vociferous opposition from local ranchers and miners.

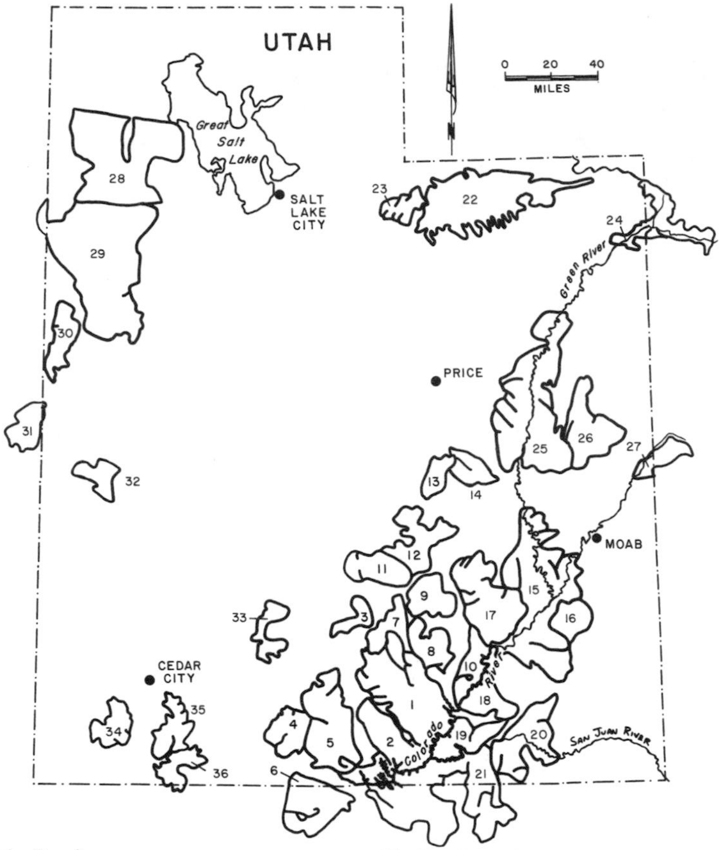

1. Escalante
2. Kaiparowits
3. Boulder Mt.
4. Paria-Hackberry
5. Wahweap-Canaan Peak
6. Paria Canyon
7. Steep Creek–Oak Creek
8. Mt. Pennel
9. Mt. Ellen
10. Little Rockies
11. Wayne Wonderland
12. Muddy Creek
13. Sids Mt.
14. Mexican Mt.
15. Canyonlands
16. Salt Creek
17. Dirty Devil–Fiddler Butte
18. Mancos Mesa
19. Wilson Mesa
20. San Juan River
21. Navajo Mt.
22. High Uintas
23. Lakes
24. Yampa-Green
25. Desolation Canyon
26. Book Cliffs
27. Black Ridge Canyons
28. North Great Salt Lake Desert
29. South Great Salt Lake Desert
30. Deep Creek Mts.
31. Mt. Moriah
32. King Top
33. Casto-Table
34. Pine Valley Mt.
35. Zion
36. Parunuweap

Utah

But for two quirks of history, Utah would today be far wilder and less populated than it is. After Joseph Smith was gunned down in 1844 by a mob in Carthage, Illinois, Brigham Young led the Mormon faithful west to a safer haven—the valley of the Great Salt Lake on the west slope of the Wasatch Mountains in what was then Mexican territory. The Mormons in Utah represented an approach to the frontier different from the rugged individualism that "won" the other lands west of the Alleghenies. The disciplined, centralized communism of the Mormons allowed them to prosper in the arid wilderness of the Great Basin and Colorado Plateau. The atomized, nuclear family approach to the conquest of the frontier would never have worked in Escalante, Blanding, Delta, or, perhaps, even the Wasatch Front. It took the dedicated antlike obedience and single-mindedness of the Mormons to civilize Utah.

Of course, the social and philosophical attributes that enabled the Latter-day Saints to achieve success in a harsh land did not oblige their descendants to preserve the natural world. Verily, the Mormons have outdone the gentiles in waging a holy war against the "howling wilderness."

To make matters worse for wilderness in Utah, the second land rush there featured a group even more hostile toward the Big Outside—the uranium miners, armed with Geiger counters and bulldozers, who swarmed to the canyon country after World War II in the last great grass-roots mining boom.

Whereas the Mormons had settled valleys where they could divert nearby mountain streams for irrigation and had used the back of beyond only for cattle grazing (as was done throughout the West), the uranium frenzy resulted in thousands of miles of rough roads' being ripped across fragile ground by bulldozer jockeys, hundreds of mine shafts' being tunneled, and tons of radioactive tailings' being piled haphazardly about. Today, the old prospecting trails provide Jeep access to wild places that otherwise could never have been reached by vehicle.

Nonetheless, despite the best efforts of the Mormon settlers and the uranium miners, and despite the Bureau of Reclamation ("Wreck-the-Nation"), which drowned Glen Canyon in the early 1960s, Utah has some of the wildest, most remote land in the lower forty-eight states.

The several generally parallel ranges of the Wasatch Mountains run south through the center of Utah from Idaho to the Arizona line. East of the Great Salt Lake, the Uinta Mountains breach the Earth on a west-east course almost to the Colorado border. The Uintas and the northern part of the Wasatch properly belong in the Central Rocky Mountains Ecoregion (centered on Yellowstone), while the southern ranges of the Wasatch are part of the Southern Rockies Ecoregion (centered on Colorado). Because of their elevation (the Uintas exceed 13,000 feet, and several subranges of the Wasatch top 12,000 feet), both are well watered and forested.

The Wasatch Range separates the Great Basin in Utah's western half from the Colorado Plateau in the eastern half of the state. The Great Basin consists of a series of mountain ranges and intervening valleys (basins) that have no outlet to the sea. The best-known of these basins is the Great Salt Lake. Several of the isolated ranges reach over 9,000 feet, and the Deep Creeks hit 12,000 feet.

The Colorado Plateau, or Canyon Country, is like no other place on Earth. There are other deserts with areas of exposed sandstone, yes, but none where great rivers, like the Colorado, Green, and San Juan, cut through with the meltwater of far mountains on their way to the sea.

In RARE II, the Forest Service identified 3,234,759 acres of roadless areas in Utah (most Utah National Forests are in the Wasatch and Uinta ranges). Conservationists, hoping to appear reasonable in a rather unfriendly social climate, asked for only 1.9 million acres as Wilderness. During what became a controversial process, the Utah Wilderness Association (UWA) negotiated a bill with the Utah congressional delegation (all Republican and generally anti-Wilderness at the time). The 1984 Utah Wilderness Act, as passed, established 749,550 acres of Wilderness (including a 460,000-acre High Uintas Wilderness). UWA's critics complained that the Association had compromised too readily and had not included other conservationists in late discussions with the delegation. UWA replied that the bill was the best anyone could have achieved at the time and that it was a starting point for additional Wilderness designations.

In January 1986, the Bureau of Land Management released a massive draft environmental impact statement proposing Wilderness for 1.9 million acres out of 3.2 million acres of Wilderness Study Areas in Utah. Nearly 6 million acres had been considered for WSA status by BLM until 1980, and most observers felt that BLM's selection was marred by insouciant capriciousness at best or downright criminal disregard for the law—FLPMA—at worst.

Previous to the release of the Wilderness EIS, Utah conservation groups had been meeting to develop a single proposal. The UWA argued for a conservative, pragmatic approach, while the Utah Sierra Club, The Wilderness Society, and the newly formed Southern Utah Wilderness Alliance (SUWA) took a bolder stance. Negotiations finally broke down, and the groups agreed to disagree. UWA proposed 3.8 million acres of BLM Wilderness, while the other groups, forming the Utah Wilderness Coalition (UWC), called for 5.2 million. Earth First! offered a visionary proposal for 16 million acres of Wilderness in several very large preserves (this proposal included Park Service and some Forest Service land as well). Local politicians, developers, miners, ranchers, Jeepers, and the rest of the rural establishment opposed the very concept of Wilderness.

BLM was overwhelmed with the responses it received (most favored the UWC proposal). In February 1991, Utah BLM released its final recommendations: 1,975,219 acres for Wilderness. Surprisingly, the Utah Farm Bureau, traditionally the most vocal Wilderness opponent in the state, essentially endorsed the BLM recommendation. Negotiations are now beginning in earnest with the Utah congressional delegation. Fortunately, Democrat Wayne Owens, who is friendly to Wilderness, is a member of Congress from

Utah and has introduced a bill to designate over 5 million acres of Utah BLM land as Wilderness. His bill has over one hundred cosponsors in the House. In 1991, the Utah Wilderness Association essentially endorsed Representative Owens's bill, which encompassed more Wilderness than UWA had initially supported. (Since the split with UWC, UWA seems to have focused more on the High Uintas and other National Forest areas in northern Utah, and on the Desolation Canyon region.) In 1990, the Utah Wilderness Coalition presented its final proposal for 5.7 million acres of BLM land as Wilderness in an exhaustive and very attractive 400-page, large-format book. In addition to descriptions of each of the areas proposed for Wilderness, the book features detailed maps, an introduction by the respected novelist and historian Wallace Stegner, an eloquent and timely discussion of the Wilderness designation issue, and a section of stunning color photographs. It is highly recommended.[1] (Other state wilderness groups should take note of the book and follow suit.) National conservation groups should make the fight to protect Utah's BLM lands a national campaign.

In the area descriptions that follow, we give the BLM and UWC proposals for Wilderness designation. It should be noted that in Utah, state lands are intermixed with BLM lands in a rough ratio of four state sections to thirty-two BLM sections in each township. (A section is a square mile, or 640 acres; there are thirty-six sections in a township.) In the acreage totals for both the BLM and the UWC Wilderness proposals, the state sections—as well as any private land that might be present—are not calculated into the figure. The calculation of total acreage for roadless areas in *The Big Outside,* however, counts all lands. Keep this in mind as you compare the acreage of Wilderness proposals against the roadless acreage we identify.

Utah's National Parks (Canyonlands, Capitol Reef, Arches, Zion, Bryce Canyon), Dinosaur National Monument, and Glen Canyon National Recreation Area have not had Wilderness Areas established, although Congress has proposals for all of them from the NPS and from conservation groups. Various bills to accomplish this continue to be discussed.

The threats to Utah's Big Outside are manifold. The National Forests face logging, road building, and oil and gas exploration. The National Park units confront demands by local boomers for more paved roads and tourist developments. Oil and gas and tar sands development plans are a threat to Glen Canyon NRA. BLM (and FS) areas suffer from continued overgrazing and

[1] *Wilderness at the Edge: A Citizen Proposal to Protect Utah's Canyons and Deserts* is available from Utah Wilderness Coalition, POB 11446, Salt Lake City, UT 84147.

destructive activities like juniper chaining (dragging a ship's anchor chain between two bulldozers to rip out the vegetation to "open" it up for improved cattle grazing), mineral exploration (primarily for uranium, coal, and tar sands), and increasing ORV use. Most distressing, however, is that weak-kneed BLM managers have looked the other way as powerful mining companies and local politicians have illegally invaded wild areas.[2]

Unfortunately, for wild things and those humans who love them, Utah is still the frontier. At the close of World War II, the largest single roadless area in the United States was a 9-million-acre expanse of the Canyon Country centered on the Colorado River. It stretched from the Paria River on the west through Escalante and Capitol Reef to the Needles on the east. The uranium boom began to carve it into smaller pieces, and then Glen Canyon "Damn" flooded its heart in the early 1960s.

Today, the tragedy continues.

Colorado Plateau

The Colorado Plateau is a spectacular but forbidding landscape of exposed sandstone slickrock carved by wind and water into buttes, mesas, arches, natural bridges, goblins, hoodoos, slot canyons, fingers, cliffs, and grottoes. Big rivers—like the Colorado, Green, and San Juan—and smaller watercourses—like the Virgin, Paria, Escalante, San Rafael, and Dirty Devil—cut phenomenal canyons deep into the sandstone. High mountain ranges rise above the red rock. It is little wonder that south-central and southeastern Utah was the last unexplored region in the lower forty-eight states. This is not a land tolerant of human frailty. As one patriarch noted, "It's a hell of a place to lose a cow." The Bureau of Land Management, National Park Service, Forest Service, and Navajo Nation share management responsibility for the Big Outside here.

ESCALANTE 620,000 acres	
Glen Canyon NRA roadless	327,380
Capitol Reef NP roadless	38,560
BLM and intermixed state roadless	254,000

[2] It should be noted that this collusion was no monopoly of the Reaganauts. Gary Wicks, Utah State BLM Director under the Carter administration and one of the more questionable individuals in the history of the agency, drew WSA boundaries to coincide with the edges of mining claims—excluding the claims, even though there was no other difference in the land on either side of the line. Conservationists protested at the highest level, but Secretary of the Interior Cecil Andrus refused to investigate or to overrule Wicks.

Description: South-central Utah north of "Lake" Powell (called "Foul" by true desert rats) and southeast of the town of Escalante. With Glen Canyon drowned beneath dead reservoir water, the Escalante is the heart of the Canyon Country. Sandstone arches, intricate and twisting canyons, slot canyons 100 feet deep and 10 inches wide, slickrock uplands, pygmy forests of piñon and juniper, sagebrush-grassland expanse, and the Escalante River with dense riparian forests of Fremont Cottonwood, willow, and Box Elder make this a wilderness of international significance. This extraordinary landscape reaches from Lake Foul on the south to the Burr Trail on the north, from southern Capitol Reef on the east to the Hole in the Rock road on the west. Elevations reach 6,800 feet on Durffey's Mesa and King Bench in the northern part of the Escalante. The shoreline of the reservoir is at 3,700 feet. Bare rock covers up to 70 percent of large areas. A few Mule Deer, Pronghorn, and Mountain Lion reside in the Escalante, and Elk winter in the Deer Creek area in the northern part. Desert Bighorn Sheep were reintroduced to Glen Canyon NRA in 1981 and 1982. Peregrine Falcon and Bald Eagle pass through, and seven other raptors, including Golden Eagle, nest here. Introduced Brown, Cutthroat, and Rainbow Trout are in Deer and Boulder Creeks. Numerous archaeological sites have been discovered. This is a popular backpacking area.

Status: Portions of the Escalante will be protected by Wilderness designation despite the sulfurous anti-Wilderness stance of locals in such backwater burgs as Escalante and Hanksville. (The good Saints of Escalante town have hung local "environmeddlers" in effigy from light poles on their main street, and vehicles with conservationist bumper stickers are regularly vandalized at trailheads.) However, the area will be broken into small preserves surrounded by lands open to exploitation unless conservation groups see the Escalante roadless area as a single Wilderness to be protected intact. Closure of dirt roads could protect a 3-million-acre Wilderness, stretching from Bullfrog to Bryce Canyon.

The pooh-bahs of the local area and their hand puppets in Washington are screaming to pave the Burr Trail, which forms the northern border of much of this area. SUWA has fought hard against this, but may have lost. A road across the heart of the Escalante was once proposed, but appears to have died a welcome death. Eternal threats to the entire area are oil and gas exploration; ORVs; pot hunting; firewood cutting; and mining for coal, uranium, tar sands, and hard-rock minerals—BLM has left large areas out of its

Wilderness proposal to accommodate such devastation. An additional threat is BLM's penchant for "improving" road access to trailheads.

Cattle grazing is destroying riparian communities and canyon bottom mixed scrub-and-grassland communities throughout the area. Grazing cannot occur in a nondegrading manner in this arid country; the cows gotta go. An additional threat to riparian areas is the invasion by tamarisk (salt cedar), a Middle East exotic that is taking over the Colorado River watershed at lower elevations.

BLM fragments this world-class wilderness with its Wilderness proposal of only 107,296 acres (in three units adjacent to Glen Canyon NRA). UWC has a very good Wilderness proposal of 226,940 acres in six BLM units around Glen Canyon NRA and Capitol Reef National Park. The Park Service proposes 34,000 acres as Wilderness and 4,580 acres as Potential Wilderness Addition for the part of Capitol Reef NP in this roadless area, and 253,105 acres as Wilderness and 48,250 acres as Potential Wilderness Additions for the part of Glen Canyon NRA in this roadless area.

*RM36: 8,890,000**

KAIPAROWITS 360,000 acres	
BLM roadless (Fiftymile Mountain WSA 4-79, etc.)	207,000
Glen Canyon NRA roadless	153,000

Description: South-central Utah south of the town of Escalante and north of Lake Foul. Kaiparowits Plateau (or Fiftymile Mountain) is a high, remote plateau. In the north, it is cloaked in a vast piñon-juniper pygmy forest; in the south, there is much exposed slickrock. The Straight Cliffs above Fiftymile Bench form a remarkable escarpment along the Hole in the Rock road on the east side (which separates this roadless area from the Escalante roadless area). A dirt road divides the area from other large roadless areas on the west. The Rogers Canyon system cuts the plateau to the south. Woolsey Arch and other rock formations dot the area. The high elevation is 7,650 feet, along the Straight Cliffs; the elevation at the reservoir is 3,700 feet. Communities of Aspen, maple, and oak occur in some of the canyons. Big Sagebrush grows throughout. Mule Deer are common. Other wildlife includes Mountain Lion, Desert Bighorn Sheep, and Lewis Woodpecker. Thirteen species of raptors nest in this area. The Utah Wilderness Coalition reports of its Wilderness proposal here: "The unit is virtually unblemished, without a trace of roads or trails except at its boundaries." Numerous Anasazi archaeological sites have been identified.

Status: A great conservation victory of the 1970s was the defeat of coal strip-mining and a huge power plant on Kaiparowits. In a frightening refrain, Andalex Resources company proposes to strip-mine millions of tons of coal from the southern Kaiparowits for export to Japan. This could shape up into a major national conservation battle. Overgrazing, ORVing, looting of archaeological sites, and fuelwood collecting are ongoing problems.

Because the last four miles of the Hole in the Rock Road are nothing more than a Jeep trail over slickrock, it could be argued that the Escalante and Kaiparowits form a single roadless area of one million acres. At the very least, the lower 20 miles of the road should be closed, and a million-acre Wilderness established. Better yet would be to close intervening dirt roads from the Henrys to Paria for a 3-million-acre Preserve.

UWC proposes three Wilderness Areas: Fiftymile Mountain, 173,900 acres; Fiftymile Bench, 11,100 acres; and Cave Point, 4,800 acres (a Jeep trail separates the units). BLM proposes 91,361 acres for Wilderness, dropping the Straight Cliffs; the NPS proposes 58,755 acres as Wilderness and 1,040 acres as Potential Wilderness Addition for the Glen Canyon NRA portion of Kaiparowits.

*RM36: 8,890,000**

BOULDER MOUNTAIN 110,000 acres	
Dixie NF roadless	110,000

Description: South-central Utah south of Torrey. This is the wildest part of the superlative Aquarius Plateau. Largely over 10,000 feet in elevation (with some points at 11,000 feet), this deeply forested area rises north above the Escalante country and west of Capitol Reef with vistas extraordinary even in a state known for scenery. Numerous lakes, streams, and meadows, along with forests of Ponderosa Pine, Aspen, Limber Pine, Blue and Engelmann Spruces, Subalpine and White Firs, Douglas-fir, and some Bristlecone Pine make this the finest high country left in Utah outside of the High Uintas. Wildlife includes Blue Grouse, Golden Eagle, Turkey, Mountain Lion, Bobcat, Mule Deer, and Elk. This roadless area is separated from the Oak Creek–Steep Creek roadless area by a newly paved state highway.

Status: The U.S. Forest Service has pillaged the Aquarius Plateau with logging and road building during the last twenty years. UWC says, "Between 1980 and 1987, loggers swept across its southern and western flanks, blading at least 100 miles of road and transforming 25,000 acres of ponderosa pine forest into a maze of logging roads, tree stumps, and slash." Boulder Mountain is the last significant part of the high country remaining in a natural condition. Unfortunately, the FS now has evil plans for Boulder Mountain (which was not even inventoried in RARE II because it had allegedly been considered in a completed land use plan). According to UWC: "The loggers will move up into the spruce and fir on its summit, where they will cut from rim to rim, slicing an estimated 60 miles of roads across 30,000 acres of lake-dotted forest." A major campaign is needed to save it. SUWA has proposed the entire area (110,000 acres) for Wilderness and has successfully used a lawsuit to pressure the FS to withdraw the Windmill timber sale on Boulder Mountain.

PARIA-HACKBERRY 186,000 acres	
BLM WSA 4-247	135,822
Additional BLM and state roadless	50,000

Description: South-central Utah south of Bryce Canyon National Park. This classic Utah canyon country in the upper reaches of Paria Creek and its tributaries, including Hackberry Canyon, has numerous arches, canyon narrows, natural bridges, and other sandstone erosional features. The 2,000-acre No Man's Mesa, rising isolated 1,000 feet above surrounding lands, has a relict plant community—it has never been grazed by cattle, and wildfires have not been controlled. Elevations run from 4,700 feet up to 7,200 feet. The primary vegetation in this slickrock area is piñon and juniper with some Big Sagebrush, and Ponderosa Pine at higher elevations. The area includes 50 miles of riparian vegetation. Wildlife is sparse, featuring Mule Deer and a few Cougar; Speckled Dace inhabit the streams. Ravens croak overhead.

Status: Grazing is a continuing impact, and BLM wants to chain piñon-juniper woodland in the area excluded from its Wilderness recommendation. Oil and gas exploration threatens. ORVs are allowed up the Paria River and

Hackberry Creek, and Jeep trails and rough dirt roads penetrate the roadless area. A potentially serious threat is the possible location of a uranium mill (to process uranium from the Grand Canyon) within the southern boundary of this roadless area.

Paria-Hackberry is the western end of a wild backcountry area of 3 million acres—including Capitol Reef and the Henrys on the east and Escalante, Wahweap, and Kaiparowits in the center—that is broken only by Jeep trails and a few dirt roads. This entire region should be designated as a single Wilderness Area, and all vehicles prohibited.

BLM proposes only 95,042 acres for Wilderness in two units (excluding the Paria River as an ORV playground!); UWC calls for protecting 158,750 acres. It is vital that the Paria Canyon itself be protected and permanently closed to vehicles.

*RM36: 8,890,000**

WAHWEAP–CANAAN PEAK 367,000 acres	
BLM WSA 4-248 (Wahweap)	144,166
BLM WSA 4-78 (Death Ridge)	66,710
BLM WSA 4-77 (Mud Spring Canyon)	41,116
Dixie NF, state, private, and additional BLM roadless	110,000
Glen Canyon NRA roadless	5,500

Description: South-central Utah north of Glen Canyon City on the western end of the Kaiparowits Plateau and leading up to the high country near the Aquarius Plateau. The Cockscomb, a sharp, double-ribbed, north-south ridge, forms the western part of the area and has the southern high point of 6,742 feet, near The Gut. Coyote, Wahweap, Last Chance, and Warm Creeks cut the plateau to the south; the low point of 4,040 feet is at the confluence of Coyote and Wahweap. The northern part of the area consists of benches and narrow ridges cut by deep canyons. Cretaceous bedrock with fossils, including dinosaur bones, underlies this northern part. Canaan Peak, in the Dixie NF, is the high point of the area, at 9,293 feet. This is a diverse area for the Canyonlands, with vegetation primarily of piñon and juniper, Shadscale, desert shrub, and Big Sagebrush, except near Canaan Peak, where there is Ponderosa Pine, Engelmann Spruce, White Fir, and Douglas-fir. Some of the junipers are 1,400 years old. There are isolated ungrazed mesas and two sensitive plant species. Wildlife includes Mule Deer, Pronghorn,

Mountain Lion, Black Bear, and Blue Grouse (north). Up to thirteen species of raptors nest in the area. An abandoned shack on Four Mile Bench is believed by locals to be haunted.

Status: Threats include coal mining, a possible railroad to haul coal, oil and gas leasing, and ORVs. A few cherrystem dirt roads and Jeep trails penetrate, but this entire area is a unified roadless area. BLM divided it into three WSAs on the basis of these intrusions. A good example is the Four Mile Bench dirt road, which BLM indicates as cutting the area in half from west to east. In actuality, the dirt road penetrates only halfway, and a full 9 miles of wild mesa and canyon landscape connect Wahweap WSA to the Death Ridge and Mud Spring Canyon WSAs to the north. Conservation groups should not be misled by BLM and should propose a unified Wilderness Area here. (We would propose that this entire roadless area be part of a 3-million-acre Escalante Wilderness. See Paria-Hackberry for general discussion.)

BLM opposes Wilderness for any of this outstanding area. UWC originally proposed four Wilderness Areas, but has now at least recognized that Wahweap and Death Ridge are not divided by a road and recommends a 228,000-acre Wahweap–Paradise Canyon Wilderness (incorporating the Death Ridge WSA), and separate 55,100-acre Mud Spring Canyon and 31,600-acre Nipple Bench Wildernesses. The NPS does not propose any Wilderness for the Glen Canyon NRA portion.

*RM36: 8,890,000**

PARIA CANYON 290,000 acres (also in Arizona)

See Arizona for description and status.

STEEP CREEK–OAK CREEK 185,000 acres

Capitol Reef National Park roadless	66,320
BLM WSA 4-61; additional BLM and state roadless	36,500
BLM, state, and private roadless east of Capitol Reef NP	12,000
Dixie NF roadless	70,000

Description: South-central Utah northeast of the town of Boulder. This area consists of the upper Muley Twist Canyon–Oyster Shell Reef portion of the Waterpocket Fold and Oak Creek in Capitol Reef National Park, the upper parts of Deer Creek and The Gulch on BLM and Dixie NF land, and the east slope of Boulder Mountain on the Dixie NF. The high point is 9,670 feet, on the Dixie NF; The Gulch drops to 5,400 feet, at the Burr Trail. The Gulch portion is a northern extension of the Escalante country. Below the slickrock, cottonwood and willows line the creeks; higher, piñon-and-juniper and Big Sagebrush grade into Ponderosa Pine, Aspen, and a bit of mixed conifer. Wildlife is limited and characteristic of the Colorado Plateau, although Elk are present and Mule Deer find critical winter habitat. Reintroduction of Bighorn Sheep is proposed for the Park. Seven raptor species nest within the area.

Status: This area is separated from the huge Escalante roadless area by the Burr Trail, a dirt road currently proposed for paving by the political powers of southern Utah. Not only should this paving be fought (as SUWA and other groups are doing), but the Burr Trail should be closed to vehicles in order to include Steep Creek–Oak Creek in a 3-million-acre Escalante Wilderness. Oil and gas, uranium, overgrazing, ORVs, looting of Anasazi ruins, and poaching threaten this area. The FS wants to log ancient Ponderosa Pine in high portions of the roadless area; conservation groups are appealing.

BLM proposes a 20,806-acre Steep Creek Wilderness; UWC, 34,400 acres. The NPS proposes two units of Wilderness (28,110 acres for Wilderness, plus 4,470 acres for Potential; and 35,010 for Wilderness, plus 320 acres for Potential) in Capitol Reef NP. UWC proposes an 8,400-acre Notom Bench Wilderness and a 3,500-acre Dogwater Creek Wilderness on BLM lands east of Capitol Reef NP on the eastern edge of this roadless area (this 12,000 acres of roadless land was left out of the first edition of *The Big Outside;* it is added to the acreage summary here). SUWA is developing a Wilderness proposal for the NF lands.

*RM36: 8,890,000**

MT. PENNEL 170,000 acres	
BLM WSA 5-248 and state roadless	162,000
Capitol Reef National Park roadless	8,180

Description: South-central Utah north of Bullfrog Marina in the Henry Mountains. The last mountain range in the forty-eight states to be discovered by Anglos, the Henrys are sharp, ragged peaks broken by narrow canyons. They were formed by massive volcanic intrusions pushing up through many sedimentary layers. Mt. Pennel, the second-highest peak in the range and the highest in this roadless area, rises out of badlands and slickrock to 11,371 feet. Ten miles of perennial streams cross the area. Lower-elevation vegetation consists of grass and sagebrush. Above 7,000 feet, oak, pine, spruce, Subalpine Fir, Douglas-fir, and Aspen form a complete vegetation gradient for the region. *Sclerocactus writhiae* is an Endangered cactus in the area. A free-roaming Bison herd makes this mountain range unique in Utah. Other wildlife includes Mule Deer, Coyote, and Mountain Lion.

Status: Mineral and oil and gas exploration, ORVs, overgrazing, and inane opposition to Wilderness from locals threaten the Henrys. An immediate threat is the BLM's plan to chain several thousand acres of piñon and juniper. BLM and the FS commonly employ this "range improvement" technique on pygmy forests in the Southwest and Great Basin. SUWA is appealing. BLM hopes to double grazing use in the Henrys through chaining, fencing, and new water developments.

The Henrys should be added to a 3-million-acre Escalante Wilderness by closing dirt roads.

BLM originally opposed Wilderness, but calls for a tiny 25,800-acre Wilderness in its final recommendation; UWC proposes 141,200 acres. The NPS proposes 6,050 acres for Wilderness and 700 acres as Potential Wilderness Additions for Capitol Reef NP.

*RM36: 8,890,000**

MT. ELLEN 137,000 acres	
BLM WSA 5-238 and additional BLM and state roadless	137,000

Description: The Henry Mountains just north of Mt. Pennel (see above for general description) in south-central Utah. Elevations in this roadless area drop from 11,615 feet to 4,600 feet. Two distinct landforms are present: the 11,000-foot peaks of the northern Henrys and the desolate Blue Hills badlands carved out of Mancos Shale. South Caineville Mesa has not been grazed since 1950 and has thick bunchgrass in a relict community (cattle grazing quickly destroys bunchgrass elsewhere). There is also a relict community of Mat Saltbush in the Gilbert Badlands. The Henrys are in the center of the area with the highest average visibility in the United States; views in all directions are exceptional. Mt. Ellen is the southeastern limit for the Great Basin variety of Bristlecone Pine.

Status: Same as Mt. Pennel. BLM has illegally bulldozed and chained piñon-juniper forest within its WSA. Mainstream conservation groups should at least propose the closure of a few dirt roads to combine Mt. Ellen with Mt. Pennel for a single Wilderness Area. Bolder conservationists should insist that the Henrys be part of a 3-million-acre Escalante Wilderness.

BLM proposes a 65,804-acre Wilderness; UWC calls for 116,900 acres.
*RM36: 8,890,000**

LITTLE ROCKIES 145,000 acres	
Glen Canyon NRA roadless	60,000
BLM WSA 5-247, additional BLM roadless, and intermixed state roadless	85,000

Description: South-central Utah between the Henry Mountains and Lake Foul north of Bullfrog. The Little Rockies are considered to be part of the Henrys. Mt. Holmes and Mt. Ellsworth (8,235 feet) are the high points. (See Mt. Pennel for general description.) *Dalea epica,* a species of indigo brush in the area, is a candidate for Endangered species listing. Blackbrush is the predominant vegetation in the lower elevations of the Henrys, although over half the area is barren rock outcrop. Some stream stretches have perennial flows. Wildlife is not abundant, but includes Desert Bighorn Sheep, reintroduced in 1985.

Status: See Mt. Pennel. BLM proposes a 38,700-acre Wilderness; UWC, 60,000 acres. The NPS proposes 34,795 acres for Wilderness and 640 acres as Potential Wilderness Addition for Glen Canyon NRA.
*RM36: 8,890,000**

WAYNE WONDERLAND 189,000 acres	
Capitol Reef NP roadless	94,000
Fishlake NF roadless	54,000
BLM and state roadless	41,000

Description: South-central Utah north of Torrey. The high point is the 11,306-foot summit of Thousand Lake Mountain; the low point is under 5,000 feet, in the South Desert. The topography of this roadless area varies from the forested slopes of Thousand Lake Mountain down to the slickrock of the Waterpocket Fold in the north end of Capitol Reef National Park and out into the badlands of the South Desert. Several intermittent streams cross the unit, west to east, from the high country into the Fremont River. The Park Service describes this area as "perhaps the most ruggedly beautiful and remote rockscape in America." The streams cut deep, twisting canyons through yellow, orange, buff, red, brown, tan, white, black, gray, and green rocks. The South Desert has volcanic features. Cactus and Fremont Barberry predominate in the desert, with piñon and juniper; then oak, Ponderosa Pine, and Douglas-fir; then Aspen, Engelmann Spruce, and Subalpine Fir growing higher up. A handful of lakes sparkle in the high country. Cottonwood and willows grow along the watercourses. Critters in the NF include Elk, Black Bear, Mountain Lion, Mule Deer, and raptors. Wildlife populations are low in the lower elevations; species are representative of the Colorado Plateau.

Status: Several poor dirt roads are cherrystemmed into the NF portion, and there are some Jeep trails in the Park and BLM parts. Capitol Reef National Park was saddled with commercial livestock grazing at its creation. Fortunately, a dedicated and creative staff at Capitol Reef has developed a plan to buy out more than 90 percent of the commercial Animal Unit Months. This program will remove cattle from all but a small part of the Park.

The FS has proposed a land exchange that would transfer part of its land in the roadless area to a private individual. The Park Service proposes only a 64,290-acre Wilderness (and 4,240 acres of Potential Wilderness Additions); BLM and the FS propose no Wilderness. UWC proposes a 36,800-acre Red Desert Wilderness on BLM land, but excludes a long cherrystem corridor through the middle of the Wilderness for a vehicle way that is not a road. Only minor dirt roads separate this area from the Muddy Creek area in the southern portion of the San Rafael Swell. A million-acre San Rafael Swell Wilderness could be established by closing these unnecessary roads.

*RM36: 1,930,000**

MUDDY CREEK 282,000 acres	
BLM WSA 6-7 and additional BLM and state roadless	280,000
Capitol Reef National Park roadless	1,610

Description: Central Utah in the San Rafael Swell south of Interstate 70, west of Green River. Elevations drop from 7,000 feet to 5,000 feet. Sandstone, limestone, and shale formations produce a highly colorful topography with slickrock and tight, twisting canyons. Vegetation is mainly piñon and juniper and desert shrub, but large areas are rock outcrop. Two plants that inhabit the area are Endangered, and six others are being considered for Endangered status. Hebes Mountain's 650-acre relict plant community is believed never to have been grazed by domestic livestock. Muddy Creek is a perennial stream that has cut a canyon several hundred feet deep. It offers an exciting float trip—"technical inner-tubing"—during spring runoff through the 7-mile-long sheer gorge known as the "Chute of Muddy Creek." Water is otherwise scarce. Low populations of Mule Deer and Desert Bighorn are present. Other wildlife (Bobcat, Coyote, Kit Fox, Gray Fox, Ferruginous Hawk, Rough-legged Hawk, Prairie Falcon, etc.) is characteristic of the Colorado Plateau woodland. Roundtail Chub and Speckled Dace live in the river.

Status: There are potential threats of uranium mining and oil and gas leasing. ORVers have discovered the San Rafael country and are ripping up the canyons. BLM proposes two small Wilderness Areas: 31,400 acres for Muddy Creek and 25,335 for Crack Canyon (separated by a Jeep trail), thereby opening this splendid landscape to roughshod exploitation. UWC recognizes the unity of the area and calls for a single 246,300-acre Wilderness, although corridors cut into the Wilderness to accommodate Jeep trails.

Our estimate of what is actually roadless here is rough—there is an extensive network of rough Jeep trails and minor roads in the half-million-acre expanse of the southern San Rafael Swell. Depending on the definition of "road," there could be 100,000–200,000 more acres "roadless" in this single area, or the area we list could be sliced in half by a low-standard dirt road. Dirt roads and Jeep trails could be easily closed in this area, and a million-acre Wilderness Area established.

*RM36: 1,930,000**

SIDS MOUNTAIN 101,000 acres	
BLM WSA 6-23, and state and private roadless	101,000

Description: Central Utah west of Green River and north of Interstate 70 in the San Rafael Swell. The colorful badlands and mesas of this part of the San Rafael Swell are cut by an intricate complex of canyons with massive sandstone walls, long and twisting routes, and fingered tributary canyons.

Between the canyons and mesa top are flat-to-rolling parklands. Unusual rock formations are scattered throughout the area. Elevations range from 6,800 feet down to 5,100 feet. Piñon and juniper and desert scrub are the primary vegetative communities. Small pockets of Douglas-fir grow high on Sids Mountain. Relict plant communities, little affected by domestic livestock, occur on Pinnacle and Bottleneck Peaks. The perennially flowing San Rafael River has cottonwood and offers an excellent canoeing adventure through its "Little Grand Canyon." Desert Bighorn Sheep were reintroduced to this area in 1978, and it is considered crucial habitat (Utah's second-largest population of Desert Bighorn Sheep live in the San Rafael Swell region). Peregrine Falcon and Bald Eagle are present, as are Mountain Lion.

Status: Oil and gas exploration presents a threat. Conservation groups and Joe Bauman, a popular columnist for the *Desert News,* have proposed a new National Park for the San Rafael that would include this roadless area. ORVs are a major problem—the BLM's Wilderness proposal of 80,084 acres cuts the area into four units with ORV corridors effectively destroying it as a Wilderness. UWC recommends 95,800 acres for Wilderness without the dirt bike corridors. With Jeep trails and minor dirt roads closed, a half-million-acre Wilderness National Park could be established north of the interstate. There has been severe overgrazing in riparian areas.

*RM36: 1,930,000**

MEXICAN MOUNTAIN 130,000 acres	
BLM WSA 6-054 and additional BLM, state, and private roadless	130,000

Description: Central Utah west of Green River, east of Sids Mountain, and north of Interstate 70 in the San Rafael Swell. The Utah Wilderness Coalition rhapsodizes justifiably about this outstanding area: "Geologic wonders typify this unit: the northern reaches of the San Rafael Reef, the mysterious slot canyons of the Upper and Lower Black Boxes, a cliffline north of the river reminiscent of Capitol Reef National Park, Mexican Mountain itself, and countless canyons cutting across the northeast side of the Swell. The most unusual geologic feature in the unit is . . . Windowblind Peak, one of the largest free-standing monoliths in the world." The San Rafael River winds through the area. Vegetation is typical for the Canyonlands. Bighorn

Sheep, Mountain Lion, and Endangered Peregrine Falcon are some of the more interesting critters.

Status: BLM recommends only 46,750 acres for Wilderness, while UWC calls for 102,600 acres, although the Coalition cherrystems the road north of the San Rafael River that almost cuts the roadless area in half. We did not include Mexican Mountain in the first edition of *The Big Outside,* but include it in this edition, having learned that there is a roadless connection of a mile and a half between the northeast and southwest halves. ORVs are the primary threat, and the road north of the river only invites invasion of the roadless country. The road should be closed. With Jeep trails and minor dirt roads closed, a half-million-acre Wilderness National Park could be established north of the interstate.

*RM36: 1,930,000**

CANYONLANDS 875,000 acres	
Designated Dark Canyon Wilderness (Manti–La Sal NF)	45,000
Canyonlands NP and Glen Canyon NRA roadless	410,000
BLM and intermixed state roadless	390,000
Manti–La Sal NF roadless	30,000

Description: Southeastern Utah southwest of Moab. One of the great Wildernesses of North America is formed where the Colorado and Green Rivers cut through sandstone mesas to their confluence. Cataract Canyon, Dark Canyon, the Maze, Fins, Needles, Island in the Sky, Orange Cliffs, Horseshoe Canyon, Labyrinth Canyon, and Stillwater Canyon are some of the renowned features of this wonderland of sandstone slickrock, arches, buttes, cliffs, and canyons. Elevations are from 7,700 feet down to the Lake Foul reservoir line, at 3,700 feet. Dark Canyon is 2,000 feet deep and, according to the UWC, is "arguably the wildest canyon in southern Utah." In addition to the Colorado and Green Rivers, perennial water is found in several canyons, including Dark. Large areas of this vast wildland are very dry with springs far apart. Low precipitation produces a pygmy forest of piñon-juniper with Big Sagebrush and Blackbrush, while barren rock covers much of the landscape. In moist areas in the canyons, riparian "jungles" are formed of dense reed grass, Trailing Virgins Bower, willow, tamarisk (an invading and destructive small tree from the Middle East, also known as salt cedar), and cottonwood. Scattered stands of Douglas-fir and Ponderosa Pine grow in the higher elevations. Wildlife includes Bighorn Sheep, Pronghorn, Mountain Lion, Black Bear, Ringtail, Piñon Mouse, Red-spotted Toad, Midget Faded Rattlesnake, and other species of the Colorado Plateau woodland. The Colorado and Green Rivers support the Endangered Colorado Squawfish and Threatened Razorback Sucker. Anasazi archaeological sites, including some of the finest rock art in North America, abound. The visual range exceeds one hundred miles in the summer. This is a popular backpacking and river running area.

Status: Jeep trails penetrate the area (White Rim, Flint Trail, Elephant Hill); some are significant intrusions, on the borderline of being "roads." They should be closed. Motorboats are currently permitted on the rivers. They should be prohibited. Uranium mining, ORVs, pot hunting, poaching, and overgrazing are continuing threats. Major threats arising in recent years include proposed tar sands mining on the west side and the siting of a nuclear waste repository on the east side (now slated for Nevada, but the vagaries of American politics could still lead to its placement here).

The major obstacle to protection of this area has been its fragmentation into separate pieces based on managing agency. Conservation groups should at least propose an intact million-acre Canyonlands Wilderness. Far better would be a single 2.5-million-acre Wilderness established by closing several dirt roads.

In 1936, Bob Marshall identified a 9-million-acre roadless area stretching from the Canyonlands to Escalante. In 1936, Secretary of the Interior Harold Ickes proposed a 4-million-acre National Monument along the Colorado River including Glen Canyon, the Escalante, and the area up to what is now Canyonlands NP. Glen Canyon Dam, or "Damn," ripped the heart out of that great wilderness, but we can still save the pieces. An 800,000-acre Canyonlands National Park was proposed in the 1960s (after Glen Canyon Damn), but late compromises cut the Park to 337,570 acres. There is a possibility that the Park will be enlarged.

BLM has excluded the Labyrinth Canyon area east of the Green River from Wilderness consideration in order to make it available to potash and uranium mining; fortunately, poor economics have shut down development plans, but Labyrinth will remain vulnerable to destruction unless conservationists' efforts to protect the entire canyon, including the Green River itself, succeed. The UWC Labyrinth proposal allows a corridor for a Jeep trail across the detached Canyonlands NP Horseshoe Canyon unit. This old route is impassable to vehicles, and Upper Horseshoe is included in our roadless area.

Potential BLM Wilderness Areas around Canyonlands NP can be grouped in three general regions: Dark Canyon to the south; Indian Creek–Gooseneck on the northeast; and Labyrinth Canyon to the north. BLM and UWC Wilderness proposals for these regions are as follows: (1) Dark Canyon—BLM, 68,030 acres; UWC, 130,200 acres; (2) Indian Creek–Gooseneck—BLM, 6,870 acres; UWC, 38,300 acres; (3) Labyrinth Canyon—BLM, 56,500 acres; UWC, 171,700 acres. The totals are BLM, 131,400; UWC, 340,200. The Park Service proposes 195,060 acres as Wilderness and 22,740 acres as Potential Wilderness Additions in seven units divided by Jeep trails and the Colorado and Green Rivers in Canyonlands NP, and 72,005 acres as Wilderness and 26,925 as Potential Wilderness Additions in Glen Canyon NRA. Conservationists propose closing many of the Jeep trail corridors for a single 304,320-acre Canyonlands NP Wilderness (which includes the NPS Salt Creek roadless area described below).

Given the size and complicated nature of land ownership and vehicle routes that surround and penetrate the Canyonlands roadless area, our estimate of the roadless acreage in this single unit is not exact.

*RM36: 8,890,000**

SALT CREEK 134,000 acres	
Canyonlands National Park roadless	63,360
BLM WSA 6-169 and additional BLM and state roadless	31,000
BLM WSA 6-167 and additional BLM and state roadless	38,000
Manti–La Sal NF roadless	2,000

Description: Southeastern corner of Canyonlands National Park in southeastern Utah south of Moab. This area is cut off from the main Canyonlands roadless area by a primitive dirt road. It features the Needles, Salt Creek, Six Shooter Peak, Bridger Jack Mesa, slickrock domes, piñon-juniper woodland, open sagebrush parks, and a small Mule Deer population. Salt Creek cuts 600 feet deep into the sandstone. The high point is 7,400 feet. Bridger Jack Mesa has been little grazed and also has a relict Douglas-fir stand. See Canyonlands for full description.

Status: This area should be made part of a larger Canyonlands Wilderness by closing the dirt road. BLM proposes a 5,290-acre Bridger Jack Mesa Wilderness and a 24,350-acre Butler Wash Wilderness; UWC calls for a Wilderness total acreage of 61,000 (32,700 acres and 28,300 acres, respectively). The NPS proposes a 55,640-acre Wilderness with 7,720 acres of Potential Wilderness Additions. Conservation groups would add this area to a single Canyonlands NP Wilderness.

*RM36: 8,890,000**

DIRTY DEVIL—FIDDLER BUTTE 413,000 acres	
BLM Dirty Devil WSA 5-236A	63,560
BLM French Spring–Happy Canyon WSA 5-236B	25,640
BLM Fiddler Butte WSA 5-241	73,100
Glen Canyon NRA roadless	51,000
Additional BLM and state roadless	200,000

Description: Southeastern Utah east of Hanksville and west of Canyonlands National Park. This is a region of slickrock cut by thousand-foot-deep canyons. Mesas, buttes, spires, domes, sand dunes, and benchlands characterize the area. Most of the area is bare rock; Blackbrush, piñon and juniper, and small riparian areas are the vegetative communities. Cliffs are graced by hanging gardens of Eastwood Monkeyflower, Colorado Columbine, Maidenhair Fern, and Giant Helleborine. The Dirty Devil River is perennial, as are a number of springs and seeps. Wildlife includes Desert Bighorn Sheep, Pronghorn, Mule Deer, Beaver, Dwarf Shrew, Golden Eagle, Bell's Vireo, and Chuckwalla (at its northern limit). Raptors find excellent nesting sites on the cliffs. Superb panels of rock art remain. The generally unpolluted air of this region gives it outstanding visibility.

Status: In 1976, as BLM began its Wilderness review, it set aside more than 400,000 acres in the Dirty Devil for consideration. Unfortunately, a sleazy alliance between BLM and the uranium industry allowed the Cotter Corporation into the area. Between 1976 and 1980, more than 50 miles of road were bladed into the WSA and hundreds of exploratory wells were punched in the ground at various sites. The Dirty Devil country is the showcase example of BLM malfeasance in its Wilderness program. The Dirty Devil is also threatened by tar sands and oil and gas development. A very rough Jeep trail, the Poison Spring–North Hatch Canyon "road," divides Fiddler Butte on the south from the rest of the Dirty Devil. We do not consider the trail a road and therefore combine these areas into one roadless area. This Jeep trail should be closed.

The Dirty Devil area should be restored at the expense of Cotter Corporation, and both BLM and Cotter employees should face felony charges and prison sentences. Years of hard labor on a chain gang repairing the damage they have done would be a fitting punishment.

BLM proposes a 61,000-acre Dirty Devil Wilderness, an 11,110-acre French Spring–Happy Canyon Wilderness, and a 32,700-acre Fiddler Butte Wilderness; UWC proposes a single 175,300-acre Dirty Devil–French Spring Wilderness (excluding much flat benchland to the west in the Burr Desert) and a separate 88,200-acre BLM Fiddler Butte Wilderness. The NPS proposes a 21,625-acre Wilderness in Glen Canyon NRA. This is, however, a single roadless area, albeit broken by very poor (and illegal) "roads."

The minor dirt road separating the Dirty Devil region from the Canyonlands complex should be closed, and a 2.5-million-acre Wilderness established.

*RM36: 8,890,000**

MANCOS MESA 204,000 acres	
Glen Canyon NRA roadless	84,000
BLM WSA 6-181 and additional BLM and state roadless	120,000

Description: Southeastern Utah east of Bullfrog Marina across Lake Foul. High point is 6,500 feet; low is 3,700 feet, on the reservoir. This is the largest isolated slickrock mesa in Utah and is bordered on all sides by 1,000–1,500-foot-high cliffs. Several canyons (with depths up to 800 feet) cut Mancos Mesa and drop into the former Colorado River canyon (now Lake Foul). Most of the surface is Navajo sandstone, with some sand dunes. Vegetation is largely Blackbrush with scattered piñon and juniper, and cottonwood, oak, ash, willow, and watercress in the canyons. Because grazing has been limited, vegetation is in near-pristine condition. Wildlife includes Mule Deer, Ringtail, deer mice, cottontail, Common Raven, Canyon Wren, and Side-blotched Lizard. An important herd of Desert Bighorn Sheep here supplies animals for transplant to other areas. Basketmaker and Anasazi ruins are abundant.

Status: BLM allowed 30 miles of uranium exploration road to be bladed into the Mancos Mesa area while it was studying the site for Primitive Area designation in the 1970s. BLM proposes 51,440 acres for Wilderness; UWC proposes a 108,700-acre BLM Wilderness. The NPS proposes a 41,700-acre Wilderness for Glen Canyon NRA.

*RM36: 8,890,000**

WILSON MESA 220,000 acres	
Glen Canyon National Recreation Area roadless	108,000
BLM roadless	112,000

Description: Southeastern Utah in the crotch between the Colorado and San Juan arms of Lake Foul. This is a remote, little-visited area of classic slickrock mesas and canyons, which includes the Hole in the Rock trail. Blackbrush and other desert shrubs are the most common plant community, but there are some piñon and juniper at higher elevations and some fine riparian areas. Wildlife includes Desert Bighorn Sheep, Peregrine Falcon, and Beaver.

Status: BLM did not designate this roadless area a WSA, and opposes Wilderness for it. ORVs, pot hunting, overgrazing, poaching—the standard threats for Utah—continue to encroach on the area. UWC proposes a 93,400-acre Nokai Dome Wilderness on BLM land, but unfortunately leaves corridors for three long Jeep routes. The NPS proposes a 81,910-acre Wilderness with 640 acres of Potential Wilderness Additions. A major threat is the Halls Crossing airport, approved by the Federal Aviation Administration; the airport would intrude on the conservationists' Wilderness proposal and greatly increase use in the area. In the first edition of *The Big Outside,* we miscalculated the BLM roadless acreage; that has been corrected in the acreage summary.

*RM36: 8,890,000**

SAN JUAN RIVER 371,000 acres	
BLM Grand Gulch Instant Study Area	107,920
Glen Canyon NRA roadless	32,000
Navajo Indian Reservation roadless	170,000
Additional BLM and state roadless	61,000

Description: Southeastern Utah west of Mexican Hat. The canyon of the San Juan River includes the famed Goosenecks and wonderful side canyons like Grand Gulch, Slickhorn, and Oljeto. Cedar Mesa rises north of the river. Imposing walls of sheer sandstone, arches, pools, hanging gardens, waterfalls, and views of Monument Valley to the south from high points are some of the features of this area. The San Juan is a fast, red river noted for its "sand waves" and is popular for rafting. Grand Gulch is a renowned backpacking area. Elevations drop from 6,600 feet, on Grand Flat, to the reservoir, at 3,700 feet (the largest rapids on the San Juan were drowned by Lake Foul). Piñon-juniper, sagebrush, and Blackbrush communities adorn the mesas; elsewhere, there is considerable bare rock. Cottonwood and willow populate bottomlands in the canyons. Low populations of Desert Bighorn Sheep, Mule Deer, and Mountain Lion live here. Other wildlife includes Spotted Skunk, Ringtail, Midget Faded Rattlesnake, Bald Eagle, and the Threatened Razorback Sucker. Temperatures range from 110 degrees to below zero. Anasazi sites—some as yet unmolested by Bishop Love and his pot-hunting cronies—abound.

Status: Oil and gas leases, firewood cutting, ORVs, pot hunting, and excessive recreational use (rafting and backpacking) are problems. BLM proposes a 105,520-acre Grand Gulch Wilderness that excludes the upper part of Grand Gulch and the western end of this area around Whirlwind Draw; UWC proposes a 139,800-acre BLM Wilderness, but cherrystems a couple of long vehicle corridors. Grand Gulch was one of the few BLM Primitive Areas established prior to the passage of FLPMA. As such, it was made an Instant Study Area (ISA) by FLPMA. The NPS proposes a 13,010-acre Wilderness with 360 acres of Potential Wilderness Additions. The Navajo Tribe should be encouraged to protect the wilderness qualities of its portion of this area.

*RM36: 8,890,000**

NAVAJO MOUNTAIN 850,000 acres (also in Arizona)
See Arizona for description and status.

Northeastern Utah

Northeastern Utah, north of the Colorado Plateau in the Central and Southern Rocky Mountains Ecoregions, holds superlative high mountains and equally su-

perlative deep canyons. The Wasatch and Ashley NFs, Dinosaur NM, the Uintah and Ouray Indian Reservation, and the BLM are involved here.

HIGH UINTAS 843,000 acres	
Designated High Uintas Wilderness (Ashley and Wasatch NFs)	460,000
Additional Ashley and Wasatch NFs roadless	383,000

Description: East of Salt Lake City in northeastern Utah. The Uintas are the largest east-west mountain range in the forty-eight states and the finest mountain area in Utah. Kings Peak, at 13,528 feet, is the highest point in Utah, and many other peaks exceed 13,000 feet and 12,000 feet (the crest averages 11,000 feet high). The peaks are distinctively red. Elevations drop to 8,000 feet in the river canyons. This landscape, shaped by glaciation, has over 250 lakes and 2,000 tarns, many meadows, rushing streams, a large area above timberline, scenic cirques and basins, and extensive Lodgepole Pine forests on its lower slopes. Other vegetation includes Engelmann Spruce, Douglas-fir, Subalpine Fir, Aspen, and large expanses of alpine tundra. Black Bear, Elk, Moose (southernmost natural population in North America), Rocky Mountain Bighorn Sheep (recently reintroduced), Wolverine (maybe), River Otter, Beaver, Canadian Lynx, Pine Marten, Pika, Mink, Mountain Lion, Osprey, Bald Eagle, Goshawk, Boreal Owl, Great Gray Owl, and Pileated Woodpecker are some of the distinctive mammals and birds; biological (not political) potential for Grizzly Bear and Gray Wolf reintroduction is excellent. Arctic Grayling, Rainbow and Golden Trout (introduced), and native Cutthroat populate the streams. The first rendezvous of the mountain men was held on the north slope of the Uintas in 1825.

Status: The lower-elevation Lodgepole Pine forests (largely left out of the Wilderness) are falling victim to Forest Service timbering and roading. The Forest Service is also promoting oil and gas leasing on the north slope, and oil companies like AMOCO are moving in. Some areas adjacent to the Wilderness boundary have already been leased. These north slope forests are crucial to the overall ecological integrity of the Uintas because they provide necessary wildlife habitat. UWA has made protection of the threatened parts of the Uintas a priority, although a national effort is needed. Acid rain has recently become a problem.

One bit of good news is that the Wasatch NF has closed three domestic sheep allotments because of the reintroduction of Rocky Mountain Bighorn Sheep. Unfortunately, the Ashley NF plans to return domestic sheep to a vacant grazing allotment in Bighorn Sheep range in the far eastern end of the roadless area (but outside the Wilderness Area). Domestic sheep carry diseases that can be fatal to Bighorns.

RM27: 1,109,120

LAKES 112,000 acres	
Wasatch NF roadless	112,000

Description: East of Salt Lake City in northeastern Utah. This lake-dotted high country in the western end of the Uinta Mountains is separated from the High Uintas roadless area by a narrow paved road over a 10,600-foot-high pass. See High Uintas for general description.

Status: The Forest Service has established a 60,000-acre backcountry area with no logging. Oil and gas leasing is a threat here, as it is in the High Uintas. The Utah Wilderness Association is campaigning for the restoration of several alpine lakes that were enlarged with dams for irrigation storage early in the century.

YAMPA-GREEN 250,000 acres (also in Colorado)
See Colorado for description and status.

DESOLATION CANYON 858,000 acres	
BLM WSAs (68A/68B/67) with intermixed state and private	593,000
BLM roadless north of Sand Wash	63,000
State and private roadless to west	12,000
Uintah and Ouray Indian Reservation roadless	164,000
Navy Oil Reserve roadless	26,000

Description: Eastern Utah north of the town of Green River and south of Ouray. This multifaceted and wildlife-rich area centered on Desolation and Gray Canyons of the Green River is beloved by boaters as the "Green River Wilderness." It is far more than simply a marvelous wilderness float trip, however. The UWA points out that only the Grand Canyon forms a more extensive canyon system in the United States. Moreover, the high country of the Tavaputs Plateau is sublime in its own right. Desolation Canyon is a mile deep in places, and elevations vary from 4,000 feet along the river to 9,600 feet on the Roan Cliffs. The thousand-foot-high Book Cliffs are to the south and west. Balanced rocks, arches, waterfalls, caves, and alcoves dot the river canyon. The high country has Douglas-fir, Ponderosa Pine, mountain mahogany, and a few Aspen stands; healthy riparian forests of Fremont Cottonwood, willow, and Box Elder grow along the river; and large areas of piñon and juniper, Big Sagebrush and Shadscale, and Black Greasewood flourish in the mid-elevations. (There are thirteen vegetative types in the area.) Several side canyons to the Green form impressive drainages of their own: Rock Creek, Jacks Creek, Flat Canyon, Range Creek, Price River, and Rattlesnake Canyon. Elk, Black Bear, Mountain Lion, Rocky Mountain Bighorn Sheep, Spotted Owl, Ferruginous Hawk, Goshawk, Peregrine Falcon, Prairie Falcon, Golden Eagle, Bald Eagle, Long-billed Curlew, Yellow-billed Cuckoo, White-faced Ibis, and Midget Faded Rattlesnake are among the sensitive species in this area. Bony-tailed Chub, Humpback Chub, and Colorado Squawfish are Endangered fish species that find some of their best remaining habitat in this part of the Green. Channel Catfish are abundant, and Rock Creek provides a high-quality fishery for Rainbow and Brown Trout (non-native). Other wildlife includes a large herd of Mule Deer (the bottoms provide important winter range), Beaver, Turkey, Ruffed and Blue Grouse, Lazuli Bunting, Lewis Woodpecker, many ducks and geese, Collared Lizard, and Leopard Lizard. The Black-footed Ferret was historically present, and the U.S. Fish and Wildlife Service has identified potential ferret habitat in this roadless area. Archaeological sites of the Fremont culture include major petroglyph panels and ancient granaries.

Status: Conservation groups have justly made this area a priority in the BLM Wilderness Review.

Float trips generally put in at Sand Wash, more than 30 river miles south of the last bridge over the river at Ouray. For this reason, some conservation groups and the BLM have ignored the superb wilderness character of the river and adjacent benchlands and flats north of Sand Wash. This area, while not as spectacular as the deep canyon, is in some respects even wilder and provides finer wildlife habitat, including rookeries for Great Blue Heron and Black-crowned Night Heron, Prairie Falcon aeries, and numerous waterfowl (the Ouray National Wildlife Refuge is just to the north). Indeed, the wildest riverine bottomlands in the West may be along this stretch of the Green. These 30 miles of the Green above Sand Wash are a contiguous part of the Desolation roadless area and should be included in Wilderness recommendations and considered for an expansion of the Ouray NWR. If this area is not protected, roads, oil and gas, livestock grazing, and the other slow but steady destroyers of wilderness will whittle away, and this part of the Green will not long remain wild. It will be another sad chapter in "The Place No One Knew" story.

Additional wildlands are separated from the Desolation Canyon wilderness by dirt roads (such as the Book Cliffs area, discussed below). These primitive roads should be closed, and a 2.2-million-acre Wilderness established.

BLM proposes a 224,850-acre Desolation Canyon Wilderness, a 27,960-acre Turtle Canyon Wilderness, and a 23,140-acre Floy Canyon Wilderness; UWC proposes Wilderness Areas of 527,100 acres for Deso (including some of the river north of Sand Wash) and 36,900 acres for Turtle Canyon. Additionally, the Green has been proposed for National Wild and Scenic River designation. It richly deserves this protection as well as Wilderness, but again, the less-scenic though ecologically richer bottomlands north of Sand Wash and including all of the Ouray NWR should be included. A total of 200,000 acres of land on Uintah and Ouray Indian Reservation, divided between the Desolation and Book Cliffs roadless areas, is managed by the tribe as Wilderness.

Motors are allowed on rafts; these should be prohibited. Additionally, some float trip operators use charter flights to haul their passengers into Sand Wash. These flights go over the roadless area. Oil and gas, coal, and other mining are possible threats to the roadless area and have already impacted considerable acreage around the roadless area. The BLM recently rejected an appeal by UWA, thereby allowing Chevron to begin exploratory drilling near the head of Rabbit Valley in the WSA. Dirt roads cherrystemmed into the roadless area should be closed—particularly the one from Swaseys Rapid upriver to Nefertiti. The Air Force has routed a bomber training run over the roadless area; letters of protest should be sent to the Air Force. BLM hopes to chain piñon and juniper in areas excluded from its Wilderness proposal.

A recalculation of roadless acreage in this area gives nearly 100,000 more acres than was listed in the first edition of *The Big Outside*.

*RM36: 2,420,000**

BOOK CLIFFS 290,000 acres	
BLM WSAs (060-100B/C), additional BLM roadless with intermixed state and private	175,720
Book Cliffs State Roadless Area	48,000
Uintah and Ouray Indian Reservation roadless	50,000
BLM and state roadless to north	16,000

Description: Eastern Utah north of Interstate 70 and immediately east of the Desolation roadless area (a minor dirt road in Sego Canyon separates them) in the Book and Roan Cliffs and East Tavaputs Plateau. Deep canyons slice the area to the north, south, and east. Flat-topped benches and ridges form the uplands. The high point is 8,050 feet, and elevations drop to 5,500 feet. Vegetation varies from desert shrub and piñon and juniper to forests of Douglas-fir and Ponderosa Pine. Willow Creek forms a striking canyon system on the north in the state and Indian land. See Desolation for a more complete description.

Status: In its inventory, BLM hacked this area into several units on the basis of Jeep trails in Cottonwood and other canyons (it claimed they were roads). Oil and gas exploration and development surround the area and threaten it with roads, drilling, and other impacts. The Book Cliffs State Roadless Area was established in 1975 to protect wildlife habitat. The Uintah and Ouray Indian Reservation manages 200,000 acres of reservation land in this and the Desolation roadless areas as wilderness.

The dirt road between the Book Cliffs and Desolation roadless areas should be closed. Other dirt roads should also be closed for a single 2.2-million-acre Wilderness.

BLM originally opposed Wilderness for the eastern Book Cliffs, but in its final Wilderness recommendation in 1991 proposed three small Wilderness Areas: Coal Canyon, 20,774 acres; Spruce Canyon, 14,736 acres; and Flume Canyon, 16,495 acres. UWC proposes a single Eastern Book Cliffs Wilderness Area of 154,600 acres, although it cherrystems several long non-Wilderness Jeep trail corridors.

*RM36: 2,420,000**

BLACK RIDGE CANYONS 115,000 acres (also in Colorado)

See Colorado for description and status.

Western Utah

The western third of Utah lies in the Great Basin and is more akin to Nevada than to the rest of Utah. Desert ranges crowned with Bristlecone Pine rise high above salt flats in the basins below. Little happens here. A few paved highways and dirt roads built for mining or grazing cut through the valleys and penetrate canyons in the mountains. Additional areas in the Utah Great Basin beyond those described could become large roadless areas with minor road closures. In the southwest, the Southern Wasatch Highlands and Colorado Plateau intermingle with the Great Basin around Zion National Park. The military, BLM, Dixie NF, and Zion NP are the primary players here.

NORTH GREAT SALT LAKE DESERT 850,000 acres	
BLM (with scattered state and private) roadless	540,000
Hill Air Force Base roadless	160,000
Wendover Air Force Base roadless	150,000

Description: West of Salt Lake City and north of Interstate 80 in northwestern Utah. This surreal landscape of glistening salt flats became a huge, shallow lake during the wet years of the early 1980s, with waves lapping against sandbags on the interstate, reminding us that this is the bed of Pleistocene Lake Bonneville. Elevations are between 4,000 feet and 5,000 feet. Bonneville Speedway is outside the roadless area on the western edge. The BLM, with uncharacteristic eloquence, describes the area in these words: "Ecologically and geologically the North Salt Desert is unique. To some it is desolate though beautiful; to some a place to be avoided and feared; to others 'A kind of goodness in itself that is worth preserving.' It is in fact a historical narrative, a map and skeletal remains of the land-locked sea that once was Lake Bonneville."

Status: The North Salt Desert is a victim of the "Sierra Club Calendar" syndrome. Although BLM identified a very large WSA here, conservation groups were content to drop it from any proposal for Wilderness because it was "just salt flats." The status of the Air Force bases is uncertain (they are used for air operations).

RM36: 1,700,000

SOUTH GREAT SALT LAKE DESERT 1,144,000 acres (also in Nevada)	
Wendover Air Force Range and Dugway Proving Grounds roadless (UT)	842,000
Wendover U.S. Air Force Auxiliary Field roadless (NV)	12,000
BLM roadless (UT)	275,000
BLM roadless (NV)	12,000
Fish Springs NWR roadless (UT)	3,200

Description: Western Utah south of Interstate 80 and the Western Pacific tracks. The South Great Salt Lake Desert is not a place for a sufferer of agoraphobia. The vastness of empty space and the unrelieved monotony of miles and miles of salt flat in every direction are unparalleled in North America. Most would find this terrain oppressive; nonetheless it is a remarkable reservoir of silence—of wildness. Like its counterpart to the north, this area is largely a flat expanse of clay and sand impregnated with salt. Together, these areas encompass 2 million acres broken only by an interstate highway and railroad corridor.

Status: Although BLM identified all of its lands in this roadless area as "roadless," it did not further consider any of them for Wilderness study; no conservation group protested. The Air Force base is an aerial bombing and gunnery range; no doubt, there is unexploded ordnance on the ground and other signs of use. The Dugway Proving Grounds are used for germ warfare experiments. It is unknown if any activity has occurred in the part of Dugway that is part of this roadless area; if so, human predators may be small in number here.

The Great Salt Lake Desert is an awesome landmark on the planet. Until we as human beings appreciate the beauty and worth of such terrible places, we will be aliens in the natural world despite our appreciation for the Yosemites and Tetons, and will find no more appropriate use for them than testing bombs and anthrax.

RM36: 1,600,000

DEEP CREEK MOUNTAINS 179,000 acres	
BLM WSA with intermixed state and private	72,366
Additional BLM, state, and private roadless	90,000
Goshute Indian Reservation roadless	17,000

Description: West-central Utah between the towns of Callao and Ibapah. The Deep Creeks are one of the more stunning Great Basin ranges, rising 8,000 feet above the Great Salt Lake Desert to an elevation of 12,101 feet on Haystack Peak. BLM says the Deeps are characterized by "sheer granite cliffs and glacial cirques at the higher elevations." The great elevation gradient gives the area five vegetation zones: Montane Conifer (White and Subalpine Firs, Engelmann Spruce, Douglas-fir, Ponderosa and Limber Pines); piñon-juniper (Utah Juniper, Bluebunch Wheatgrass, Singleleaf Piñon, Big Sagebrush); sagebrush-grass and Desert Scrub (Big Sagebrush, Shadscale, Mormon Tea, Snakeweed, Winter-fat, Saltbush); and riparian along eight perennial streams. Bristlecone Pine, including both very large, ancient individuals and significant stands of young, vigorous trees, grow on high ridges. Four potential Endangered or Threatened plants are in the area, and there are a dozen endemic plants. Wildlife includes Mule Deer, Mountain Lion, Pronghorn, Peregrine Falcon, Golden Eagle, Bonneville Cutthroat Trout, and Giant Stonefly. Rocky Mountain Bighorn Sheep were reintroduced in 1984, and Elk, not native, were introduced by the Goshute Indians in 1988.

Status: Wilderness designation for the Deep Creeks is a high priority for Utah conservation groups, with the UWC proposing 90,200 acres. BLM proposes a 57,384-acre Wilderness. BLM currently has an ORV closure on 52,738 acres except for 15 miles of existing ways. Mining, continued grazing, and ORVs are threats to the high country proposed for Wilderness, but even more so for the lower-elevation foothills and valleys ignored in the Wilderness proposals. A major threat is small hydroelectric power projects on Birch, Trout, and Granite Creeks that would dewater sections of the streams. An additional 55,000 acres of Goshute, BLM, and private land (mostly in Nevada) perhaps should be included in this roadless area—the separating vehicle route may be only a Jeep trail.

MT. MORIAH 144,000 acres (also in Nevada)

See Nevada for description and status.

KING TOP 109,000 acres

BLM WSA 5-70 and additional BLM roadless with intermixed state and private	109,000

Description: Western Utah southwest of Delta and immediately south of U.S. 50 in the southern part of the Confusion Range. Elevations in this Great Basin area range from just over 5,000 feet to 8,000 feet, on King Top, a high plateau. Fossil Mountain in the southern portion has Ordovician fossils. Modern-day wildlife includes Mule Deer, Pronghorn, Peregrine Falcon, Golden Eagle, feral horses, and introduced, exotic Chukar. Populations are relatively low because of the harsh climate. Shadscale and other desert shrubs dominate in the lower elevations, and piñon and juniper higher. Some Douglas-fir is present on top.

Status: There are a few Jeep trails on the periphery, but the interior is very wild. BLM opposes Wilderness, although there are few conflicts. UWC recommends that 78,800 acres be designated as Wilderness. King Top was not included in the first edition of *The Big Outside.*

CASTO-TABLE 100,000 acres	
Dixie National Forest RARE II	93,440
Additional Dixie NF and BLM, state, and private roadless	6,500

Description: South-central Utah east of Panguitch on the Sevier Plateau. Mt. Dutton is 11,041 feet. Vegetation ranges from piñon and juniper to Ponderosa Pine and spruce-fir in the higher elevations. Several streams drain the high country. Mule Deer, Elk, Pronghorn, Mountain Lion, Turkey, Blue Grouse, and Golden Eagle populate this high tableland.

Status: A number of dirt roads are cherrystemmed into this amoeba-shaped roadless area. ORVs, logging, and roading will soon reduce its size.

PINE VALLEY MOUNTAIN 125,000 acres	
Designated Pine Valley Mountain Wilderness (Dixie NF)	50,000
Additional Dixie NF, BLM, and private roadless	75,000

Description: Southwestern Utah north of St. George. This laccolithic mountain rises 6,000 feet above the valley. The high point, Signal Peak, is 10,360 feet. Engelmann Spruce, Aspen, Douglas-fir, Limber Pine, and fairly young Bristlecone Pine are in the high country, while oak and mountain mahogany are downslope. Along with a major Mule Deer herd, wildlife includes Mountain Lion, Black Bear, Uinta Chipmunk, Yellow-bellied Marmot, Beaver, Turkey, Golden Eagle, and Peregrine Falcon. Native trout inhabit the streams.

Status: Private developments threaten adjacent lands. Recreational horse use is damaging meadows in the Wilderness.

ZION 148,000 acres	
Zion National Park roadless	88,300
BLM, state, and private roadless	60,000

Description: Southwestern Utah south of Cedar City. Zion is internationally acclaimed as a scenic wonderland for its huge sandstone monoliths and canyons, including the Narrows of the Virgin River—2,000 feet deep and 20 feet wide. Textbook examples of tectonic activity—crossbedding, folding, sheer walls, and block faulting—and of the erosional power of wind and water are visible. Elevations in the Park drop from over 7,000 feet to under 4,000 feet; however, elevations climb to over 9,000 feet on private lands north of the Park in this roadless area. High country forests of Douglas-fir, Aspen, White Fir, and Ponderosa Pine drop to piñon, juniper, and oak woodland and sagebrush. Riparian zones harbor cottonwood and Box Elder. The Northern Black Hawk reaches its northern limit here. Other rare species include Spotted Bat, Ferruginous Hawk, Peregrine Falcon, Prairie Falcon, and the endemic Zion Snail. Mule Deer, Elk, Bobcat, Beaver, and Cougar live here, too. There are numerous archaeological sites, and fossil footprints in the sandstone.

Status: The Park Service proposes 72,600 acres for Wilderness, with 7,900 acres as Potential Wilderness Addition. BLM recommends 6,199 acres for Wilderness; UWC calls for 14,729 acres of Wilderness on BLM lands adjacent to the Park on the north and northeast. There are, however, another 37,000 acres of unroaded private land (with some scattered state and BLM tracts) to the north of the Park—in the canyon complex of Oak Creek, Crystal Creek, and O'Neil Gulch cutting into Cedar Mountain—and 7,500 acres to the northeast. This country forms the headwaters of the North Fork of the Virgin River (which creates Zion Canyon in the Park). Acquisition of private wild lands here should be a high priority for The Nature Conservancy, BLM, NPS, and other conservationists. No doubt there are subdivision threats, given the high population growth in this area of Utah and its growing popularity for retirement and recreation. It is possible that a vehicle route was recently (and illegally) bladed across Deep Creek in the BLM WSA. It should be closed. The first edition of *The Big Outside* did not include these more extensive reaches of private land.

Threats to the Park include a proposed major tourist development in Springdale.

PARUNUWEAP 128,000 acres (also in Arizona)	
Zion National Park roadless (UT)	22,100
BLM Canaan Mountain WSA 4-143 (UT)	46,428
BLM Parunuweap Canyon WSA 4-230 (UT)	32,080
Additional BLM, state, and private roadless (UT)	21,000
Designated Cottonwood Point Wilderness Area (BLM, AZ)	6,500

Description: Southwestern Utah and northwestern Arizona east of St. George. Spectacular Parunuweap Canyon is carved by the East Fork of the Virgin River. Canaan Mountain is a plateau with cliffs of Navajo sandstone that tower 2,000 feet above the surrounding desert. From the top, amid slickrock, balanced rocks, and pinnacles, a panorama of Zion, the Pine Valley Mountains, and the Arizona Strip stretches out. There are four vegetative zones (although slickrock predominates): Ponderosa Pine, Douglas-fir, Aspen, Gambel Oak, manzanita on the plateau; piñon pine, Utah Juniper, Utah Serviceberry, live oak; sagebrush, rabbitbrush; and riparian groves of willow, cottonwood, and Box Elder, along with hanging gardens of Maidenhair Fern, Cliff Columbine, and Scarlet Monkeyflower in the canyons. Wildlife includes Desert Bighorn Sheep, Mule Deer, Cougar, Desert Shrew, Lewis Woodpecker, Bald Eagle, and nesting Peregrine and Prairie Falcons. Speckled Dace is the only fish.

Status: The NPS proposes a 19,800-acre Zion NP Wilderness with 1,040 acres of potential additions. BLM recommends 47,500 acres for Wilderness in Utah; UWC, 90,400 acres. Continued grazing is the major intrusion, with ORVs and firewood cutting secondary problems. The Soil Conservation Service wants to chain piñon and juniper on the absurd assumption that this will reduce salinity in the Colorado River. SUWA is protesting. Growth boosters in St. George want to build a dam on the East Fork of the Virgin within the roadless area.

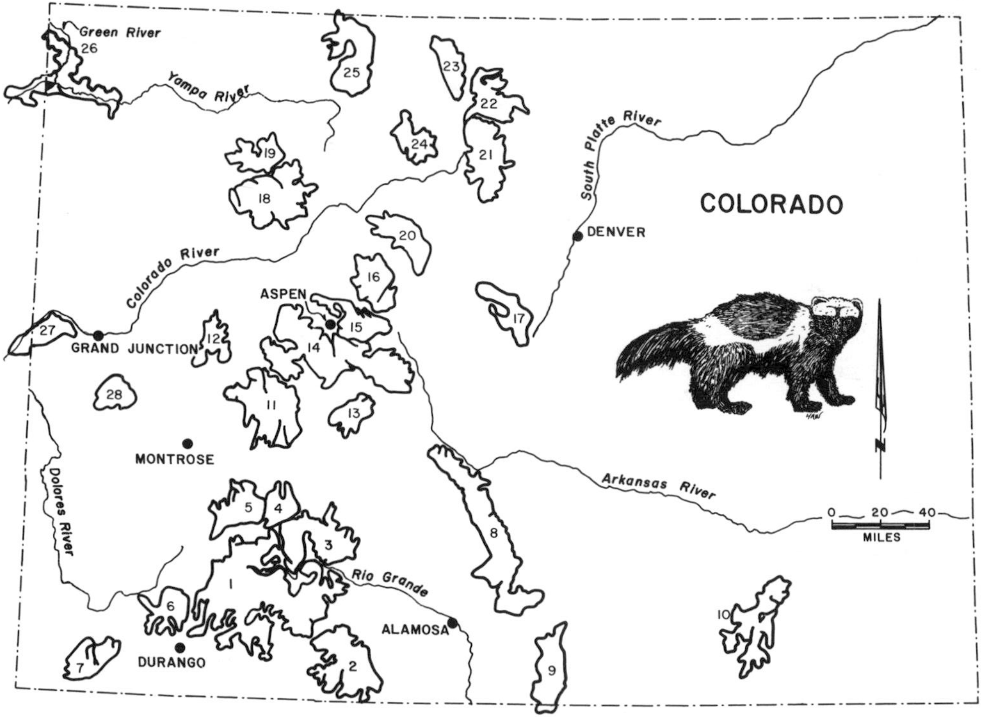

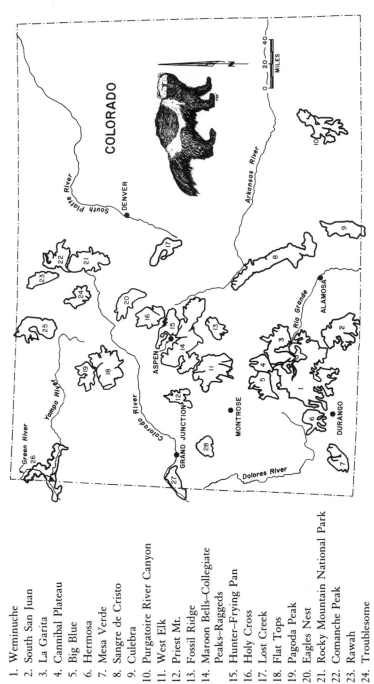

1. Weminuche
2. South San Juan
3. La Garita
4. Cannibal Plateau
5. Big Blue
6. Hermosa
7. Mesa Verde
8. Sangre de Cristo
9. Culebra
10. Purgatoire River Canyon
11. West Elk
12. Priest Mt.
13. Fossil Ridge
14. Maroon Bells–Collegiate Peaks–Raggeds
15. Hunter–Frying Pan
16. Holy Cross
17. Lost Creek
18. Flat Tops
19. Pagoda Peak
20. Eagles Nest
21. Rocky Mountain National Park
22. Comanche Peak
23. Rawah
24. Troublesome
25. Mt. Zirkel
26. Yampa-Green
27. Black Ridge Canyons
28. Dominguez Canyons

Colorado

To most Americans, Colorado is *The* Rocky Mountain State. The Rockies reach their greatest height in Colorado, with fifty-three peaks exceeding 14,000 feet; and perhaps more than mountains in any other state, Colorado's are developed for recreation. Technically, Colorado's mountains are the Southern Rockies, which extend into Utah, northern New Mexico, and southern Wyoming. (The Central Rockies are around Yellowstone, and the Northern Rockies are in Montana, Idaho, and Canada.) Although high and precipitous, the Colorado Rockies provide excellent habitat for Elk, Mule Deer, Mountain Lion, Rocky Mountain Bighorn Sheep, and Black Bear. Wolverine and Lynx reach the southern limits of their ranges in Colorado, and at least one Grizzly Bear survived in southern Colorado until recently. Moose and Mountain Goat, neither native to Colorado, have been transplanted to several parts of the state. The Continental Divide runs through Colorado, and hundreds of streams spill off either side, forming the headwaters of the Rio Grande and the Colorado, Arkansas, South Platte, and other major rivers.

Considering the rugged character of the Colorado Rockies and how much land they cover (two fifths of the state), it is disappointing that Colorado has few very large roadless areas. The most likely explanation for this is that Colorado was one of the principal mining frontiers in the mid-to-late 1800s. Not only do old mining towns and diggings speckle the mountains, but the miners pioneered roads over passes that split the Colorado Big Outside into many smaller pieces.

Mining no longer dominates Colorado, but its ruins are ubiquitous. In addition, current mining plans threaten several important roadless areas and even a few designated Wilderness Areas.

Below the high peaks and ridges rising above timberline, Colorado has lovely forests of Douglas-fir, Colorado Blue and Engelmann Spruces, Ponderosa and Lodgepole Pines, and White and Subalpine Firs, but they are not economical to harvest. Nevertheless, the U.S. Forest Service has encouraged a timber industry in Colorado dependent upon the National Forests. As a result, timber "management," with its attendant clearcuts and roads, is slicing into the wildlands of the Southern Rockies with deadly results for sensitive species and fragile watersheds. Timber sales in Colorado's National Forests, as in most National Forests, are usually below-cost sales—the federal government (and the taxpayer) spends more money offering and preparing the sale than it receives in fees from the logging contractor. Moreover, logging is damaging Colorado's huge Elk herds, which bring in $60 million a year from hunting (more than the annual timber harvest is worth). Despite the bad economics, Colorado has lost more big wilderness than any other state in the three years since the first edition of *The Big Outside*. The descriptions for the individual areas point out the loss of roadless lands.

A slightly lesser threat to wilderness is Colorado's insatiable thirst. Pork-barrel water development has already severely damaged the high country, as Denver and other Front Range cities divert water from the West Slope through tunnels under the Continental Divide to fuel their growth. Although Denver is on the Great Plains and receives the same annual precipitation as does Tucson, Arizona, Denverites refuse to believe they live in a semiarid bioregion and demand bluegrass lawns and trees. Half of all the water Denver consumes is for watering lawns.

Another major threat to Colorado's roadless areas is recreation. Ski areas, condominiums, second-home subdivisions, golf courses, tennis resorts, convention centers, recreation reservoirs, campgrounds, highways, and other facilities to help residents and visitors enjoy a "Rocky Mountain High" are spreading throughout the state. Most of the tourist towns, like Aspen, Vail, Telluride, and Breckenridge, are in valleys that are—or were—prime winter range for wildlife. Ski areas, condos, trendy shops, and gourmet restaurants displace Elk, Bighorn, Lynx, and other species. Such developments also interrupt migration routes for wildlife, fragment habitats, and overtax watersheds with sewage and airsheds with wood smoke and automobile exhaust. Many mountain areas in Colorado are laced with trails for Jeeps, dirt bikes, ATVs, and snowmobiles. Not only do these trails erode, damaging watersheds, but the noise created by the infernal combustion engines disturbs sensitive wildlife. Moreover, these vehicles allow poachers, litterbugs, and other miscreants to reach the backcountry.

Despite these problems, Colorado has a somewhat more sophisticated electorate than have other Rocky Mountain states, and a large and active conservation community. After RARE II, Colorado took the lead in developing a National Forest Wilderness bill, and the Colorado bill, passed in 1980, became the prototype for the state NF Wilderness bills that followed. Among the precedents established were the compromise "standard release" language, which dropped RARE II areas not designated as Wilderness from consideration for Wilderness (for approximately ten years) and nullified their protection from logging, roading, and the like; and grazing management language (in the Committee Report), which allowed ranchers motorized access in Wilderness Areas for livestock management, along with permission for the construction of new fences, stock ponds, and other "improvements." Colorado conservationists endorsed this grazing language in order to get ranchers to support Wilderness designation. Ranchers still oppose Wilderness, but now they have a stronger statutory right to continue to graze in Wilderness Areas.[1]

Out of Colorado's 6,539,201 acres of RARE II areas (second only to Idaho's acreage), conservationists, led by the Wilderness Workshop of the Colorado Open Space Council,[2] proposed over 5 million acres for Wilderness. The 1980 Colorado Wilderness Act designated 1,392,455 acres as Wilderness and left more than 650,000 acres for further study. Colorado conservationists have since pushed a second National Forest Wilderness bill, but that bill has been tied up with questions about "Wilderness water rights." Conservationists propose 1.6 million acres for this bill.

[1] I have to plead guilty to having supported this compromise; I consider the giardiasis I carry to be fitting punishment.

[2] Now renamed the Colorado Environmental Coalition (CEC).

A Sierra Club lawsuit in 1985 established the concept of reserved water rights for Wilderness Areas. This resulted in an anguished howl from traditional water users—ranchers and urban developers. Republican members of Congress, including Senators William Armstrong of Colorado and Jim McClure of Idaho (both now retired, we are pleased to report), tried to pin language onto all Wilderness legislation that would nullify the impact of the court's decision. Attorney General Edwin Meese, just before he was hooted out of office in 1988, issued an opinion against Wilderness water rights, with which Secretary of the Interior Donald Hodel concurred. Of course, conservationists are dissenting.

It was hoped that with Senator Armstrong's retirement, Senator Tim Wirth, a Democrat and self-styled environmentalist, would be able to successfully guide a modest Wilderness bill of about 750,000 acres through Congress in the 1991–92 session. Unfortunately, Wirth's spine seems to be molded out of tofu, and he stunned conservationists in 1991 by introducing a "compromise" Colorado Wilderness bill with new Colorado Senator Hank Brown and Representative Ben Campbell. This bill has been termed "catastrophic" by conservationists: It designates only 641,000 acres of Wilderness (with terrible boundaries for individual areas) and denies federally reserved water rights. Not only would it open much of Colorado's finest wild country to the chain saw, bulldozer, and knobby tire, it would establish an intolerable precedent for Wilderness Areas throughout the nation. Wilderness lovers wherever they live must kill this anti-Wilderness bill.

Not all of Colorado's wilderness is in the Rocky Mountains. Far western Colorado is part of the Colorado Plateau. Dinosaur National Monument and the Bureau of Land Management have several big roadless areas there. Wilderness legislation is a current possibility for Dinosaur, but the BLM areas will probably wait for several years. BLM has recommended Wilderness for only sixteen areas, totaling 430,812 acres, out of thirty-five Wilderness Study Areas with 783,101 acres. Areas with mineral or energy conflicts were dropped; miners and ranchers were so satisfied with BLM's concern for their interests that they have come out in support of the BLM recommendation.

The eastern two fifths of Colorado is part of the Great Plains, where the thundering hooves of 60 million Bison have been replaced by the bucolic lowing of Herefords and the swishing drone of center-pivot irrigation systems. In all of the Great Plains, from Canada to West Texas, from the Mississippi to the Rockies, there are only five roadless areas over 100,000 acres. Two are in the badlands of South Dakota; one straddles the Little

Missouri River in North Dakota; another is in the Sandhills of Nebraska; the other is Purgatoire River Canyon in southeastern Colorado.

Biologically, there are good prospects for the reintroduction of Gray Wolf and Grizzly Bear to Colorado, but Colorado livestockmen have pressured the backward-looking Colorado Wildlife Commission to oppose reintroduction of either dreaded beast. There is growing support, however, among conservationists and the public for restoration of Griz and wolves. One new group, Sinapu, has been formed in Colorado for the sole purpose of campaigning for wolf reintroduction.

Colorado has the potential for significant wilderness preservation and restoration. But conservationists not only must overcome the traditional wilderness destroyers like ranchers, miners, loggers, and ORVers, they must also deal with the explosive growth of the Front Range cities and the impossible demands for water and recreation these urban areas make on the Rocky Mountains.

Southwestern Mountains

The San Juan Mountains of southwestern Colorado hold the largest complex of wild country in the state. The last Grizzly in Colorado was killed here in 1979, and the best habitat for reintroduction of the Grizzly in Colorado remains here—that is, if Forest Service logging and ski area development don't further degrade the San Juans first.

WEMINUCHE 806,000 acres	
Designated Weminuche Wilderness Area (San Juan and Rio Grande NFs)	459,172
Carson Peak roadless area (Rio Grande, San Juan, and Gunnison NFs)	90,000
BLM WSA 030-241 contiguous to Carson Peak	18,860
Piedra roadless area (San Juan NF)	61,000
Additional Rio Grande and San Juan NFs roadless, with adjacent and intermixed private and state	177,000

Description: Along the Continental Divide in the San Juan Mountains northeast of Durango in southwestern Colorado. Several peaks in this vast high-mountain area exceed 14,000 feet. Windom Peak, at 14,091 feet, is the high point; Handies Peak is 14,048 feet. The Weminuche has over fifty lakes

(Emerald Lake is the second-largest natural lake in Colorado) and nearly 200 miles of rushing streams—headwaters of the Rio Grande and San Juan, Animas, Los Pinos, and Piedra Rivers. There are large areas above timberline, as well as old-growth forests (including a very large area of spruce-fir). Predominant tree species are Ponderosa Pine, Douglas-fir, Aspen, Engelmann and Colorado Blue Spruces, Subalpine and White Firs, and Gambel Oak. Lower elevations are 6,800 feet in the Piedra. Significant wildlife populations include Elk, Cougar, Pine Marten, Bighorn Sheep, Mountain Goat (introduced), Black Bear, River Otter (in the Piedra River), native Rio Grande Cutthroat Trout, and raptors. There may be remnant Grizzly Bear and Wolverine populations. The Carson-Handies area on the north has massive volcanic peaks, large glaciated valleys, and volcanic "beehive" cones of ash and lava (some sit astride Pole Creek and form natural bridges). The Piedra area to the south has the finest old-growth forest in Colorado and is absolutely vital wildlife habitat.

Status: The unprotected National Forest lands are under severe attack from road building and logging. The Forest Service is now destroying much of the Piedra roadless area to the south. These unprotected areas are largely lower-elevation forests with more important habitat values than the high country that constitutes most of the protected portion. Along with the South San Juan roadless area (separated only by U.S. 160 over Wolf Creek Pass), the Weminuche is the priority in Colorado for Grizzly Bear reintroduction.

Until 1988, conservationists proposed a separate 49,000-acre Piedra Wilderness against the FS proposal of 41,000. Neither of these proposals connected to the existing Weminuche Wilderness, even though the land between (Slide Mountain) was roadless and undeveloped. This was an outstanding example of fragmented Wilderness proposals designed from a perspective of political compromise instead of from an ecological standpoint incorporating ideas of Island Biogeography. Realizing this, Colorado conservationists developed new boundaries for their Piedra Wilderness proposal that would connect it to the Weminuche and enlarge it to 61,000 acres. But the Forest Service is advocating timber sales in the narrow neck of land that connects the rest of the Piedra to the Weminuche. Conservationists, ranging from mainstream groups like the Sierra Club to direct action protesters like Ancient Forest Rescue, are mounting a major campaign against this Sandbench timber sale, and against the Corral Mountain sale on the southeast—both in the conservationists' Wilderness proposal. The Piedra has the most significant old-growth forests in Colorado, especially Ponderosa Pine. The Stone Container mill in South Fork hopes to devour all of the San Juan forests not protected in Wilderness Areas. The Piedra River is proposed for National Wild and Scenic River designation.

The 1991 Wirth-Brown Colorado anti-Wilderness bill (see introduction for details) would designate a 50,100-acre Piedra Wilderness completely cut off from the Weminuche.

Since the first edition of *The Big Outside,* the 116,000-acre Carson Peak roadless area (FS portion only) has been chain-sawed down to 90,000 acres at the most, owing to a logging and road-building frenzy on the southeast. The conservationists' Wilderness proposal has been reduced from 97,000 acres to 69,000 acres because of this destruction. In this inventory, we consider the Carson Peak area to be part of the Weminuche roadless area, since it is separated from it only by the Stony Pass Jeep trail (which is, unfortunately, a popular one). The agencies propose a token 7,120-acre Wilderness. Extensive logging continues to threaten the east end of Carson Peak, and ORVs are ravaging it. Wirth-Brown drops this area from any Wilderness consideration.

Conservationists also propose 8,650 acres of additions to the Weminuche on the northwest.

We have deleted 150,000 acres of NF land from the Weminuche roadless area since the first edition of *The Big Outside*. Knowledgeable Colorado conservationists believe that much of what we inventoried as roadless in 1989 was roaded, logged, or otherwise developed since the RARE II inventory in 1979. The loss of so much wild habitat graphically illustrates the suicidal destruction of biological diversity that is accelerating all over the world. Calling a halt to taxpayer-funded destruction of the American wilderness has never before been as important as it is today. The timber beasts in charge of the Forest Service must be reined in. The hacking away at contiguous, biologically important roadless areas around the Weminuche is one of the great environmental tragedies of our time.

SOUTH SAN JUAN 292,000 acres	
Designated South San Juan Wilderness Area (Rio Grande and San Juan NFs)	127,594
Additional Rio Grande and San Juan NF roadless	124,000
Private roadless to south	40,000

Description: The southern San Juan Mountains east of Pagosa Springs in southwestern Colorado. The South San Juan has the largest extent of alpine tundra this far south in North America. It is a rolling area of waterfalls, easy peaks (13,300-foot Summit Peak is the highest), numerous lakes, and the headwaters of the San Juan, Conejos, Navajo, and Chama Rivers. The lowest elevation is about 7,500 feet, on the northwest. Wind and water have carved Cenozoic volcanics into spires and cliffs on the west; valleys on the east are glacier-carved. Douglas-fir, Engelmann and Blue Spruces, Limber and Ponderosa Pines, and White and Subalpine Firs are the most common trees. Bristlecone Pine (rare in Colorado) occurs in the East Fork drainage. The last known Grizzly Bear in Colorado was killed in 1979 at the head of the Navajo River. The South San Juan has the southernmost Lynx, Wolverine, and Fisher populations in North America, as well as Turkey, River Otter, Pine Marten, Bighorn Sheep, Mountain Lion, Bobcat, and a large Elk herd. It is separated from the 806,000-acre Weminuche by a narrow paved highway over Wolf Creek Pass and from the Cruces Basin Wilderness Area in New Mexico by a minor paved highway and narrow-gauge railroad over Cumbres Pass.

Status: Mixed conifer forests outside the designated Wilderness Area are being cut and roaded—particularly in the spectacular Chama Basin on the south. It is likely that recent Forest Service roading and logging have chopped tens of thousands of acres off the acreage we list (however, nature is reclaiming some roaded land—a huge mudslide in 1986 destroyed the high-standard Fishhook logging road in the Chama Basin). ORVs invade unprotected areas and sometimes the Wilderness.

The large area of private land to the south along the Navajo River in the Tierra Amarilla Grant is a key part of this roadless area and is important wildlife habitat. The two private ranches on the lower part of the Navajo River are protecting their land, but the upper ranch is logging. Acquisition of this ranch by someone who will protect its important ecological values (The Nature Conservancy?) is needed, since there is good evidence of a small remnant population of Grizzly Bear in the headwaters of the Navajo River. Oil and gas threats in the V-Rock area and possible molybdenum mining in Montezuma Peak have faded.

Major new ski areas—East Fork and Wolf Creek Valley—are proposed adjacent to the north end of the roadless area (around Wolf Creek Pass). They would destroy important habitat for Grizzly, Wolverine, Lynx, and other sensitive species, as well as further sundering the South San Juan from the Weminuche. However, the Wolf Creek Valley ski area proposal has gone belly-up after its proponent was indicted on securities fraud. American Express, the backer of the East Fork ski area, reportedly is reconsidering its involvement because of very strong conservationist opposition. Nonetheless, the Forest Service has approved the East Fork area, even though the bull-wheel for the uppermost lift would sit exactly on the Wilderness Area boundary. There have been two confirmed Lynx sightings in the East Fork recently.

Noted Grizzly Bear expert Doug Peacock is leading an ongoing project to determine whether there is a remnant population of big bears in the South San Juans. He and his associates have strong evidence that a sow Grizzly with cubs lives in the area.

The FS opposes any additional Wilderness here. The Colorado Environmental Coalition supports a 13,000-acre Montezuma Peak addition on the north, a 19,800-acre V-Rock addition on the southwest, and a 23,250-acre Chama Basin addition on the south (including the Fishhook road area). Considerably larger additions should be made—particularly around Montezuma Peak (30,000 acres) and V-Rock (30,000 acres). Wirth-Brown would add 12,000 acres around Montezuma Peak and 7,000 acres for V-Rock.

LA GARITA 253,000 acres	
Designated La Garita Wilderness Area (Gunnison and Rio Grande NFs)	103,986
Additional Gunnison and Rio Grande NFs roadless	149,000

Description: South of Gunnison and north of Creede in southwestern Colorado. San Luis Peak is 14,014 feet, and Stewart Peak is 13,983 feet. Although largely a rugged alpine area, La Garita includes Elk calving grounds and abundant wildlife—Bighorn Sheep, Black Bear, Mountain Lion, Mink, Pine Marten, Bald and Golden Eagles, and native Cutthroat Trout in lakes and streams. Extensive high tablelands have alpine tundra; lower elevations have old-growth spruce-and-fir forest. The Wheeler Geological Area contains rock pinnacles and other formations carved from volcanic tuff. A paved state highway over Slumgullion Pass separates this area from the Carson Peak portion of the Weminuche roadless area.

Status: The standard logging threats affect La Garita. ORV travel to the Wheeler Geological Area, an area of mysterious rock spires, is a continuing problem, as is overgrazing by livestock. The FS opposes any additional Wilderness here, while conservationists propose two additions: 25,000 acres including the Wheeler Geological Area (which was proclaimed a National Monument in 1908 by President Roosevelt, but declassified in 1950) and 250-year-old virgin forests in Wasson and Silver Parks; and 39,000 acres on Snow Mesa to the southwest of the existing Wilderness.

CANNIBAL PLATEAU 111,000 acres	
BLM Powderhorn ISA	48,500
BLM WSAs 3-88, 211, 212, 213	4,480
Gunnison NF RARE II	31,990
Adjacent mixed BLM and private roadless	25,000
Colorado Division of Wildlife roadless	640

Description: Southwestern Colorado east of Lake City. The Cannibal Plateau is the largest continuous area of alpine tundra in the lower forty-eight states. As such, it is highly valued for scientific research. Elevations in creek bottoms on the north drop to about 7,900 feet while the high points of the plateau are Lake Peak, 12,800 feet, on FS land in the southwest corner, and Cannibal Peak, 12,644 feet, in BLM's Powderhorn Primitive Area. Forty-nine species of mammals and 146 species of birds are known in the area, including large populations of Elk and Mule Deer. Vegetation is typical of the Southern Rocky Mountains. Slumgullion Slide is a natural laboratory for the geologic study of earthflows. There is a continuous grassland gradient from the headwaters of Mill Creek to the summit of Mesa Seco. Several large lakes and numerous tarns dot this high, rolling country. Alferd Packer ate his long winter meal here. (The judge, in sentencing Packer over one hundred years ago, is reputed to have said, "There were five Democrats in Hinsdale County, and you ate all of them!")

Status: BLM established the Powderhorn Primitive Area in 1973, before the Federal Lands Policy and Management Act required Wilderness study for BLM lands. BLM supports Wilderness for the Primitive Area. The Gunnison NF area was designated as Further Planning in RARE II; now the FS proposes only the northeastern portion for Wilderness, leaving the rest open to snowmobile and ORV play. The Colorado Environmental Coalition recommends a 79,260-acre Cannibal Plateau–Powderhorn Wilderness Area. This area is an important biological link between La Garita and Big Blue.

In the first edition of *The Big Outside,* we overlooked this area.

BIG BLUE 145,000 acres	
Designated Big Blue Wilderness (Uncompahgre NF)	97,235
Additional Uncompahgre NF roadless	36,000
BLM WSA 3-217	6,000
Additional intermixed BLM and FS roadless	6,000

Description: East of Ouray in southwestern Colorado. The "Switzerland" of America is the chamber of commerce claim for this spectacular glacially carved area of 14,000-foot peaks, lakes, and waterfalls that forms the northern end of the San Juan Mountains. The fourteeners, Wetterhorn (14,015 feet) and Uncompahgre Peak (14,309 feet), are among the best nontechnical climbs in Colorado. Vegetation is similar to that of the Weminuche. Wildlife includes Elk, Black Bear, Pine Marten, White-tailed Ptarmigan, Turkey, Peregrine Falcon, and Bald Eagle. Big Blue Creek is a noted trout fishery. Cow Creek Canyon is one of the wildest and most inaccessible canyons in the Rockies. Old mining ruins attest to the exploitive attitude that has governed human activity in this area.

Status: ORVs abound in the unprotected area; a rascally miner wants to bulldoze a road to his mining claim in the designated Wilderness. His plans would present a major challenge to Wilderness protection, but the FS has invalidated his bogus claim. Grazing by domestic sheep is a huge problem here.

BLM has recommended 1,500 acres of its lands for addition to the Wilderness; conservationists call for a 3,870-acre add, including low-elevation Ponderosa Pine forest crucial for wildlife winter range.

HERMOSA 147,000 acres	
San Juan NF RARE II roadless	147,000

Description: Southwestern Colorado north of Durango. Here in the western San Juan Mountains (La Plata Range), several peaks exceed 13,000 feet, while the drainages of Hermosa, Junction, and Bear Creeks drop to 7,000 feet. "Hermosa" is Spanish for "beautiful," and this area lives up to its name. It is the southwestern terminus of the Colorado high country, with alpine tundra, rocky peaks, dense spruce-fir forest, flower-filled mountain meadows, open Ponderosa Pine parks, rolling groves of Aspen, and wide, flat creek bottoms.

There are large tracts of ancient forest in this mostly forested area. In addition to an excellent native trout fishery and one of the largest Elk herds in the state, wildlife includes Black Bear and Mule Deer. The area provides both summer and winter range for Elk. Wolverine are believed to be present.

Status: Although conservationists proposed 147,000 acres for Wilderness during RARE II, they are now recommending only 73,600 acres because of recent logging and roading. The FS opposes Wilderness. Threats include logging, oil and gas leasing, dirt bikes, and mountain bicycles. Logging and road building may have already sliced this area down to a core of less than 100,000 acres. The Wirth-Brown anti-Wilderness bill would designate no Wilderness here.

MESA VERDE 136,000 acres	
Mesa Verde National Park roadless	40,000
Ute Mountain Indian Reservation and private roadless	90,000
BLM WSA 3-252	6,320

Description: Extreme southwestern Colorado southeast of Cortez. This high mesa north of the Mancos River has outstanding Anasazi and Basketmaker ruins dating from the year 550 to 1300, when the area was abandoned. The mesa gently slopes to the south and is heavily dissected by canyons cutting down to the Mancos River. Elevations drop from 8,500 feet to 5,800 feet. Oak brush, Ponderosa Pine and Gambel Oak, and piñon and juniper are the major vegetative types, with Douglas-fir growing at upper elevations. Mule Deer, Mountain Lion, Bobcat, Coyote, Black Bear, Golden Eagle, Common Raven, and Spotted Owl live here.

Status: Three small Wilderness Areas have been designated in the northern portion of the Park. Visitor roads to Chapin and Wetherill Mesas penetrate deeply into the roadless area. In the summer, the roads receive heavy traffic, but the tourists are restricted to the developed areas along them. Most of the backcountry of the Park was not designated as Wilderness because of the Park Service's desire for administrative access. There are some vehicle routes in the Park that are closed to all public use but may be used by the Park Service for fire suppression and archaeological site stabilization. The entire backcountry of the Park is closed to public entry to protect archaeological sites. Because of this public use closure, we have inventoried Mesa

Verde as roadless. The Ute Reservation portion wraps around the Park. It has some Jeep trails and is grazed by cattle. Conservationists should work with the Ute Mountain Tribe to protect the roadless area on the Reservation.

Southeastern Mountains and Plains

The high desert of the San Luis Valley separates the San Juan Mountains on the west from the Sangre de Cristos to the east. Farther east, the Great Plains break against the Front Range of the Rockies.

SANGRE DE CRISTO 418,000 acres	
Great Sand Dunes National Monument Wilderness Area	33,450
Rio Grande and San Isabel National Forests roadless	260,000
BLM WSAs	6,500
Sangre de Cristo Grant (private) roadless	40,000
Private roadless to West (Baca Grant 4)	20,000
Additional BLM and private roadless	58,000

Description: South-central Colorado northeast of Alamosa. Rising from the giant sand dunes (700 feet high) of the San Luis Valley (7,600–8,000-foot elevation), the Sangre de Cristo Mountains, a narrow, glacier-carved knife edge of a range, climb to over 14,000 feet. The several 14,000-foot peaks include Crestone Peak, at 14,294 feet, and Blanca Peak, the highest in the roadless area, at 14,345 feet. Here, elevation typically rises 7,000 feet in only three vertical miles. This leads to great diversity in vegetation—sagebrush steppe to alpine tundra, with piñon and juniper, Ponderosa Pine, Douglas-fir, Limber Pine, spruce, fir, Aspen, and Bristlecone Pine in between. The Sangre de Cristos have many lakes, waterfalls, and lush valleys. Wildlife includes over twenty wilderness-related species, such as Black Bear, Mountain Lion, Elk, Bighorn Sheep, Northern Goshawk, Northern Three-toed Woodpecker, and Peregrine Falcon. The lower slopes offer winter range. About sixty lakes nestled in timberline basins feed numerous streams, some of which contain introduced Golden Trout and native Greenback Cutthroat Trout. This popular climbing area affords eye-stretching views of the Great Plains and the other mountains of southern Colorado. A skeleton in Spanish armor was found in a cave in this area in the 1850s.

Status: A Jeep trail cuts across the north end of the FS area, and the Medano Creek Jeep trail crosses the area east from Great Sand Dunes. The entire area is threatened by ORV use. Logging and mining, particularly carbon dioxide and oil and gas leasing and development by ARCO, are threats. Subdivision is occurring on adjacent private lands with attendant damage to the area. The private Sangre de Cristo Grant takes in the southern end of the area, including the south side of the Blanca Peak massif. Protection of this private land should be a priority.

Colorado conservationists are pushing hard for Wilderness designation of 252,000 acres; the FS has recommended 190,500 acres. The Wirth-Brown anti-Wilderness bill would designate 207,330 acres as Wilderness, but cut it into several units divided by ORV routes.

CULEBRA 125,000 acres (also in New Mexico)	
San Isabel NF roadless (CO)	31,000
Private roadless (CO)	85,000
Private roadless (NM)	9,000

Description: East of San Luis in the Sangre de Cristo Mountains on the central Colorado–New Mexico border. This high-mountain area is largely an old Spanish land grant. The 14,047-foot Culebra Peak is the high point and the southernmost fourteener in the Rockies; several peaks top 13,000 feet. Mixed conifer forest (Engelmann and Blue Spruces, White and Subalpine Firs, Douglas-fir, Ponderosa Pine), Aspen, and Bristlecone Pine, along with small lakes, streams, and tundra, make this a classic Southern Rockies area. The fauna is also typical of the Southern Rockies, including Turkey, Pine Marten, Elk, Mountain Lion, and Black Bear. A Grizzly Bear was reported near Culebra Peak in 1977, but the sighting is unconfirmed.

Status: Logging and associated roading are steadily encroaching on the area. It will not last long as a large roadless area unless conservationists work for the entire area. Culebra is a textbook example of a major roadless area's being ignored because of multiple land ownership. A minor dirt road (perhaps only a Jeep trail) separates it from 35,000 acres of splendid high country around State Line Peak and Big Costilla Peak (both over 13,000 feet) on private land in New Mexico. Private lands in this area should be a major priority for acquisition by The Nature Conservancy or the National Park Service.

PURGATOIRE RIVER CANYON 225,000 acres	
Intermixed military, private, and Comanche National Grasslands roadless	225,000

Description: Southeastern Colorado south of La Junta. The Purgatoire River Canyon is an excellent example of Shortgrass Prairie, exhibiting the typical vegetation of this formerly extensive ecosystem—Buffalo Grass and Blue Grama. It also includes a spectacular canyon system carved by the Purgatoire and its tributary, Chacuaco Canyon. There are major paleontological (dinosaur tracks) and archaeological sites. This is the only large roadless area remaining in the southern Great Plains—as such it is of exceptional ecological importance. (Four roadless areas over 100,000 acres in size remain in the northern Great Plains—two in Badlands National Park in South Dakota, and one each in the Little Missouri National Grassland in North Dakota and in the Nebraska Sandhills.) This is one of the major habitat areas remaining for the increasingly rare Swift Fox.

Status: Much of the area outside of the canyon, which has been in private hands for over one hundred years, was acquired by the Army in the early 1980s for a tank maneuvering ground. The Army, which also picked up tracts in the canyon, isn't using the area now and wishes to dispose of it (17,000 acres were recently transferred to the nearby Comanche National Grassland). Colorado conservationists are encouraging their members of Congress, several of whom are interested, to retain the land in federal ownership and to acquire more of it as a National Park or Wild and Scenic River. The Park Service studied the Purgatoire for Wild and Scenic River designation in 1982 and concluded that it qualified. The entire area, including the river canyons and the surrounding benchlands, should be protected, with Elk and Bison reintroduced, as the Shortgrass Prairie National Park. This could also be an important reintroduction site for the Endangered Black-footed Ferret if a healthy prairie dog town can be reestablished.

Central Mountains

North of the Gunnison River and south of the Colorado River, a huge block of mountains forms the central section of the Colorado Rockies.

WEST ELK 368,000 acres	
Designated West Elk Wilderness Area (Gunnison NF)	176,092
Additional Gunnison NF roadless	157,000
BLM and private roadless	35,000

Description: West-central Colorado northeast of Montrose. The high point of this lightly used area is 13,035 feet, on West Elk Peak; elevations drop to 6,500 feet on the north. Streams flow out from the center to all points of the compass, cutting numerous rugged canyons. Extensive meadows (wet and dry) and mixed-conifer forests (Douglas-fir, Engelmann and Blue Spruces, Subalpine Fir, Lodgepole and Limber Pines) with large Aspen stands clothe middle elevations; Ponderosa Pine and piñon and juniper cover the lower elevations. Large Elk and Mule Deer herds make this a popular hunting area. Other wildlife includes Bighorn Sheep, Mountain Lion, Black Bear, Peregrine Falcon, Bald and Golden Eagles, and many hawks. The West Elks are used for biological research.

Status: As elsewhere, timbering, roading, and ORVs threaten the unprotected area. "Aspen treatment" (clearcutting to "renew" Aspen stands, and incidentally provide pulp for a Louisiana-Pacific waferboard plant) is a particular threat to this area—CEC proposes adding 15,680 acres under imminent threat of Aspen logging along Kebler Pass to the north side of the Wilderness.

PRIEST MOUNTAIN 109,000 acres	
Grand Mesa and Gunnison NFs roadless	103,000
BLM and private roadless	6,000

Description: North of Paonia in west-central Colorado on the eastern edge of Grand Mesa. Crater Peak, at 11,327 feet, is the high point. Ecologically, this area is similar to West Elk.

Status: No one is publicly proposing this area for protection. The Forest Service has given dirt bikes the run of trails in the area. The area is also threatened by extensive logging and continued overgrazing.

FOSSIL RIDGE 101,000 acres	
Gunnison NF roadless	91,680
Private and state roadless to west	9,000

Description: Northeast of Gunnison in central Colorado. A fossiliferous limestone ridge runs across the southern portion of this area of high peaks, stream-fed alpine lakes, and steep, forested slopes. Henry Mountain, at 13,254 feet, is the high point. Besides an important Elk herd, wildlife includes Bighorn Sheep, Golden Eagle, and Peregrine Falcon. Although the area is far out of their normal range, Mountain Goats have been introduced. It is currently a study area for the role of limestone in buffering acid rain. Fossils 275–600 million years old have been found in the limestone.

Status: This is a Forest Service Wilderness Study Area, but the agency has recommended non-Wilderness. Conservationists are asking for only a 63,800-acre Wilderness. ORVs and timber cutting are the main threats. Dirt bikes, encouraged by the Forest Service, are rutting the trails and causing severe erosion. Along with the Forest Service, dirt bikers are the main opposition to Wilderness.

MAROON BELLS–COLLEGIATE PEAKS–RAGGEDS 632,000 acres	
Designated Maroon Bells–Snowmass Wilderness Area (White River and Gunnison NFs)	179,042
Designated Collegiate Peaks Wilderness Area (White River, Gunnison, and San Isabel NFs)	166,638
Designated Raggeds Wilderness Area (White River and Gunnison NFs)	59,105
Additional White River, Gunnison, and San Isabel NFs roadless	227,000
BLM WSA 070-392	330

Description: Central Colorado south of Aspen. This stunning high-mountain area consists of three Wilderness Areas and their surrounding roadless areas. The Wildernesses are separated from one another by two Jeep trails over high passes. The Taylor Pass trail divides the Maroon Bells from the Collegiates; the Schofield Pass trail separates the Maroon Bells from the Raggeds. This roadless area has an irregular shape because of cherrystem roads and other intrusions, but it is currently an intact single area. It has a number of peaks over 14,000 feet, including Mt. Harvard (14,420 feet), Maroon Bells (14,156 feet), and Snowmass Mountain (14,092 feet), and is heavily glaciated, as evidenced by the cirques, ridges, U-shaped valleys, and rock glaciers. Alpine tundra, alpine and subalpine meadows (with splendrous flower displays), Subalpine Fir, Engelmann Spruce, Blue Spruce, Douglas-fir, and Aspen constitute the area's ground cover. The Sawatch Range (which includes the Collegiate Peaks) is the highest range in the United States, with eight peaks over 14,000 feet and sixty-five over 13,000 feet. Numerous lakes and many rare and endemic plants are found here. Excellent summer and winter range for Bighorn Sheep, and winter range, calving areas, and good summer and spring range for Elk add to the ecological significance of this area. Wolverine and Lynx head the list of sensitive species; also sensitive are Black Bear, Mountain Lion, Mink, Pine Marten, Pika, White-tailed Ptarmigan, Goshawk, Golden Eagle, and native Cutthroat Trout. Mountain Goat have been introduced. The headwaters for many streams are fed by the deep snowpack.

The imposing glacial terrain of the Raggeds includes Peeler Basin, a hanging cirque. Treasury Mountain, the high point for the Raggeds, is 13,462 feet; the low point is under 7,000 feet. The Raggeds Wilderness is ecologically important because it contains high-altitude lakes and ponds without fish (most alpine lakes in the West have had trout artificially introduced). A rare, relict aquatic dragonfly, *Leucorrhinia hundsonica,* survives here because of the lack of exotic fish. Several rare and endemic plants are also present.

Status: The three Wilderness Areas should be joined to form one protected area, and the Jeep trails closed. The Schofield Pass Jeep trail is such a brutal and dangerous route that six people have died on it in recent years; the FS is now considering shutting it down. This initiative by the FS presents the perfect opportunity for conservationists to argue that this entire area is in reality one roadless area and should be protected as one large Wilderness Area. With minor road closures and wilderness rehabilitation, a million-acre Wilderness could be established here in the heart of the Colorado Rockies. As such, it would be a prime area for the reintroduction of Grizzly and perhaps Gray Wolf.

ORVs and timbering threaten the unprotected portions. The designated Wilderness Areas receive heavy and damaging recreational use. A local tough has gained permission from the Forest Service to use a bulldozer and a six-wheel-drive truck to haul out blocks of marble from his mining claim in the Maroon Bells–Snowmass Wilderness Area. This precedent of mining in Wilderness Areas needs to be blocked.

"Aspen treatment," mining, and mountain bikes are threats to the Oh-Be-Joyful roadless area adjacent to the Raggeds Wilderness. Conservationists propose 5,500 acres of Wilderness additions (Oh-Be-Joyful), while the FS opposes any additional here. Domestic sheep overgraze the area.

HUNTER–FRYING PAN 168,000 acres	
Designated Hunter–Frying Pan Wilderness Area (White River NF)	74,250
Designated Mt. Massive Wilderness Area (San Isabel NF)	27,980
Additional White River and San Isabel NF roadless	66,000

Description: East of Aspen and west of Leadville, between the Maroon Bells–Collegiate–Raggeds and Holy Cross roadless areas, in central Colorado. Mt. Massive, at 14,421 feet, is the high point (and the second-highest peak in Colorado). Populations of native trout are healthy. The lower elevations on the Arkansas River side have winter range for Elk and Mule Deer. Other wildlife includes Black Bear, Bobcat, Mountain Lion, Yellow-bellied Marmot, Pine Marten, Pika, and Golden Eagle. Three rare species are Lynx, Wolverine, and Cutthroat Trout. Vegetation is typical of the Southern Rockies.

Status: The FS and conservationists both propose only 8,000 acres of Wilderness additions.

HOLY CROSS 152,000 acres	
Designated Holy Cross Wilderness Area (White River and San Isabel NFs)	122,600
Additional White River and San Isabel NF roadless	29,000

Description: South of Vail in central Colorado. Mount of the Holy Cross (so-named from a cross-shaped snowfield), at 14,005 feet, is the high point; twenty-four other peaks exceed 13,000 feet. Glacial-carved high country, alpine tundra, Engelmann Spruce and Subalpine Fir forests, and lush meadows create a diverse area. Wildlife is typical of the Southern Rockies and includes Lynx. Holy Cross was once a National Monument.

Status: The designated Wilderness Area and surrounding lands are under serious threat of damming and water diversion to supply Colorado Springs and Aurora with water for Star Wars research and lawn watering. A major wilderness battle is brewing here. Previous water diversions (Frying Pan–Arkansas and Homestake) have already damaged the area. A notorious ORV route goes to the Holy Cross City ghost town, and the Jeepers are trashing fragile meadows in this part of the roadless area.

LOST CREEK 126,000 acres	
Designated Lost Creek Wilderness Area (Pike NF)	105,090
Additional Pike NF roadless	21,000

Description: Southwest of Denver in the Kenosha and Tarryall Mountains of central Colorado. Bison Mountain (12,427 feet) is the high point. The Forest Service describes this area as follows: "Some of the most spectacular granite formations to be found in Colorado, including domes, half domes, sheer walls, pinnacles, spires, minarets, and even a natural arch are to be found . . . Lost Creek . . . ducks in and out of huge granite slides or 'sinks' no less than 9 times." The Craig Creek Meadows in the northern part of the area have exceptional botanical diversity. The largest herd of Bighorn Sheep in Colorado resides here and has provided a source for reintroductions elsewhere. Other wildlife and vegetation is typical of the Southern Rockies.

Status: Conservationists propose 11,320 acres of additions; FS, nil.

Northern Mountains

From Denver's dramatic backdrop west for 130 miles, the northern Colorado Rockies encompass some of the most rugged and scenic ranges in the state.

FLAT TOPS 346,000 acres	
Designated Flat Tops Wilderness Area (White River and Routt NFs)	235,035
Additional White River and Routt NFs roadless	98,000
BLM WSA 070-425	3,360
Private, state, and additional BLM roadless	10,000

Description: South of Craig in northwestern Colorado. This is a historic area. One of the first administrative actions to preserve wilderness occurred here in 1920 when Forest Service Landscape Architect ("Beauty Engineer") Arthur Carhart recommended leaving the Trapper Lake area wild instead of opening it to summer home leasing by the Forest Service. Carhart helped Aldo Leopold refine his ideas for wilderness preservation, thereby leading to the designation of the Gila Wilderness in New Mexico in 1924. In 1975, President Ford considered vetoing the Wilderness bill passed by Congress for the area because it was the conservationists' proposal instead of that of the Forest Service. Public pressure convinced him to sign it.

This high-elevation plateau (average is 10,000 feet) includes large rolling areas; deep forests of Engelmann Spruce, Douglas-fir, and Aspen; big open parks; and steep cliffs and jagged peaks. Flat Tops is an important area for Elk and Mule Deer. Other wildlife includes Bighorn Sheep, Black Bear, Marten, Beaver, and White-tailed Ptarmigan. Native Cutthroat Trout live in the many lakes and streams. Sheep Mountain reaches 12,246 feet in elevation; the low point is about 7,500 feet.

Status: Continued grazing of domestic cattle and sheep conflicts with the large Elk and deer herds. Logging, road building, and ORVs are invading the unprotected FS area. CEC proposes the addition of 9,100 acres of mixed BLM-FS land around Hack Lake to the southeast.

PAGODA PEAK 126,000 acres	
White River and Routt NFs roadless	105,500
Private and BLM roadless to north	20,000

Description: North of the Flat Tops Wilderness Area and south of Craig in northwestern Colorado. At 11,257 feet, Pagoda Peak is the high point. Over five thousand Elk inhabit the area, which also provides important calving grounds. Another seventeen wilderness-associated species are present. Vegetation is similar to that of the Flat Tops. The paucity of trails helps make this one of the more pristine areas in Colorado.

Status: Conservationists propose a 105,700-acre Wilderness; FS and BLM oppose Wilderness here. Surprisingly, no timber cutting is planned in the area, and old ORV routes are closed for Elk habitat protection. There is considerable sheep grazing in the area, and some snowmobile use.

EAGLES NEST 170,000 acres	
Designated Eagles Nest Wilderness Area (Arapaho and White River NFs)	133,688
Additional Arapaho and White River NFs roadless	36,000

Description: Northeast of Vail in the Gore Range in north-central Colorado. This is one of the most rugged mountain ranges in Colorado. Mt. Powell, at

13,534 feet, is its high point; there are sixteen other peaks over 13,000 feet, as well as numerous lakes. Wildlife populations are not large because of the high elevation, but include Bighorn Sheep, Mountain Goat (introduced), and other mammals common to the Rockies. Eagles Nest is a popular recreation area. The Sierra Club's precedent-setting Meadow Creek lawsuit (after RARE I) to protect potential Forest Service Wilderness dealt with this area.

Status: The contiguous roadless areas are lower-elevation and crucial for wildlife. As elsewhere in Colorado, they are being damaged by logging, roading, and ORVing. The Denver Water Board is pushing two major projects—East Gore Canal and Eagle-Piney—that would consist of huge pipelines and canals, running parallel to the range on the east and west sides, feeding into Dillon reservoir.

ROCKY MOUNTAIN NATIONAL PARK 266,000 acres	
Rocky Mountain National Park roadless	149,400
Designated Indian Peaks Wilderness Area (Roosevelt and Arapaho NFs)	70,374
Additional Roosevelt and Arapaho NFs roadless	46,000

Description: Northwest of Boulder in north-central Colorado. Jagged peaks (Longs Peak reaches 14,256 feet), extensive areas of rolling alpine tundra, deeply forested U-shaped valleys, lakes, rushing streams, cirques, and a few small glaciers characterize this quintessential Rocky Mountain high country. Vegetation ranges from Ponderosa Pine upward to Lodgepole to spruce-fir to tundra. The area is popular for backpacking and climbing. Wildlife includes Elk, Bighorn Sheep, Yellow-bellied Marmot, Pika, Marten, River Otter, Snowshoe Hare, White-tailed Ptarmigan, Golden Eagle, and the Endangered Greenback Cutthroat Trout. Elevations drop to below 8,000 feet.

Status: Excessive recreational use is damaging the Indian Peaks Wilderness and the backcountry of Rocky Mountain NP as the 2 million residents of the Denver metroplex swarm to it. ORVs are damaging the unprotected NF roadless areas, and logging is planned. The Wilderness Society considers Rocky Mountain NP to be one of the most threatened Parks in the country. The Society cites the Bald Pate condominium complex, which will put 500 units as close as 25 feet from the Park boundary—in crucial winter habitat for Elk.

A particular threat occurs in the designated Indian Peaks Wilderness, where a prominent Colorado water lawyer has acquired an old reservoir and access easement to it. He has upgraded the road to the reservoir through the Wilderness Area and plans further developments. Legal means to stop him appear to be hopeless.

Wilderness designation is needed for the NP area (NPS and conservationists propose a 140,428-acre Enos Mills Wilderness—named for the "Muir of the Rockies," who was the force behind Rocky Mountain National Park's establishment and was an early defender of the Grizzly Bear). Potential for Grizzly Bear and Gray Wolf reintroduction is high here, if wilderness restoration efforts can succeed on lands outside the Park.

COMANCHE PEAK 182,000 acres	
Designated Comanche Peak Wilderness Area (Roosevelt NF)	66,464
Additional Roosevelt NF roadless	29,000
Rocky Mountain National Park roadless	86,500

Description: The high country of the Mummy Range west of Ft. Collins in north-central Colorado. Hagues Peak, at 13,560 feet, is the high point; the low point is 7,600 feet, along the Cache la Poudre River. There are several small glaciers. Vegetation ranges from Ponderosa Pine to Lodgepole and mixed conifer to alpine tundra. The Cache la Poudre River has deep canyons, waterfalls, and lush meadows. The high country has many small alpine lakes. Wildlife includes Cutthroat Trout, Mule Deer, Elk, Bighorn Sheep, Black Bear, Mountain Lion, Blue Grouse, and ptarmigan.

Status: The NPS proposes an 83,700-acre Wilderness; conservation groups recommend 86,000 in the Park.

RAWAH 119,000 acres	
Designated Rawah Wilderness Area (Roosevelt NF)	73,109
Colorado State Forest roadless	38,000
Additional Roosevelt NF roadless	8,000

Description: Medicine Bow Mountains north of Rocky Mountain National Park and west of Ft. Collins in north-central Colorado. This area is extremely popular for its spectacular scenery of rugged peaks, many lakes, and lower-elevation forests of Lodgepole Pine, spruce, and fir. Wildlife includes

Pine Marten, Black Bear, Beaver, Elk, Band-tailed Pigeon, and native Cutthroat Trout.

Status: The Rawah Wilderness suffers from excessive recreational use. Snowmobilers use the state forest, and timbering is proposed there.

TROUBLESOME 100,000 acres	
Routt and Arapaho NFs roadless	82,000
BLM WSA 010-155	12,000
Additional BLM and private roadless	6,000

Description: North of Kremmling in north-central Colorado along the Continental Divide. Parkview Mountain, at 12,296 feet, is the high point. Featuring one of the lowest stretches of the Continental Divide in Colorado, this area has lower-elevation forests much needed as wildlife habitat for Elk, Mule Deer, Black Bear, Prairie Falcon, and Bald and Golden Eagles. There have been unconfirmed Grizzly sightings. Troublesome provides calving areas and winter range for Middle and North Parks' deer and Elk. There are many riparian meadows.

Status: Troublesome is under imminent threat of logging and roading. Louisiana-Pacific and the Forest Service propose 21 miles of road to carve it up. Conservationists originally proposed 111,000 acres for Wilderness, but recent logging and road building by the FS has caused CEC to drop its proposal to 87,450 acres. FS and BLM oppose a Troublesome Wilderness (one sometimes thinks that the agencies consider all wilderness—designated or not—to be troublesome).

The first edition of *The Big Outside* listed 117,000 acres as roadless. We have dropped that figure to 100,000 acres because of recent FS road building and logging. Troublesome is about to disappear as a large roadless area. Wirth-Brown won't be troubled, however, and drop this area from any consideration for Wilderness.

MT. ZIRKEL 265,000 acres	
Designated Mt. Zirkel Wilderness Area (Routt NF)	139,818
Additional Routt NF roadless	124,000
Private land to east	1,000

Description: The Sawtooth Range along the Continental Divide in north-central Colorado north of Steamboat Springs. The roadless area includes forty alpine lakes and summer Elk range. The high point is 12,180-foot Mt. Zirkel; the low point is about 7,000 feet. Vegetation is diverse, from scrub oak and sagebrush parks to Aspen, Lodgepole Pine, spruce and fir, alpine tundra, and meadows. Wildlife includes Sandhill Crane, Bald Eagle, Peregrine Falcon, Black Bear, Pine Marten, Wolverine, and a large Elk herd. The area is an important watershed. An unusual configuration of trees, called the Ribbon Forest, is due to high snow accumulations. Livingston Park is an interesting glaciologic feature.

Status: Logging threatens the unprotected area. ORVs are a major threat to all of the undesignated area. Conservationists propose 49,000 acres of additions to the Wilderness, including both forks of the Encampment River and their associated lower-elevation and biologically rich forests; the FS proposes only 9,000 acres.

Colorado Plateau

In the western fifth of Colorado, the rivers pouring off the Rocky Mountains begin to cut down into the sandstone of the Colorado Plateau—the eastern extension of Utah's famous red rock Canyon Country.

YAMPA-GREEN 250,000 acres (also in Utah)	
Dinosaur National Monument roadless (includes UT)	163,000
BLM WSAs and roadless (includes UT)	87,000

Description: Extreme northwestern Colorado north of Rangely and northeastern Utah east of Vernal. The magnificent canyons of the Yampa (48 miles) and Green (44 miles) Rivers include the Gates of Lodore, Split Mountain Gorge, Whirlpool Canyon, Steamboat Rock, as well as soaring sandstone walls, and raging rapids (fearsome Warmsprings Rapid was created overnight by a flash flood). These canyons are popular for float trips. Impressive cottonwood trees grow in the spacious "holes," or "parks," through which the rivers flow between canyons. The modern conservation movement was born here during a protracted and successful struggle against building the Echo Park Dam in the mid-1950s. The Yampa is the last major undammed river in the Colorado River drainage.

Zenobia Peak on the rim is 9,006 feet; the low point along the Green River is 4,800 feet. Ponderosa Pine and Douglas-fir drop down from the high points into the canyons. Piñon, juniper, and sagebrush are common. Wildlife includes Rocky Mountain Bighorn Sheep, Mountain Lion, catfish in the Yampa and Green, trout in Jones Hole Creek. Two Endangered species of fish are present: Colorado Squawfish and Humpbacked Chub. Bald and Golden Eagles use the area. One of the healthiest populations of Peregrine Falcons in the country is here—it is used as a source of eggs for captive hatching and replenishment of the species elsewhere.

Status: Conservation groups propose that a few minor dirt roads be closed in the Monument and a 170,500-acre Wilderness be designated. The NPS proposes a 160,635-acre Wilderness. Conservationists propose 67,766 acres of the BLM areas for Wilderness; BLM proposes 36,240 acres. (Wilderness proposal totals: conservationists—238,266; agencies—196,875.)

A dam (Juniper Mountain, with 1 million acre-feet of storage) is proposed upstream on the Yampa River; this must be stoutly resisted. Grazing is still permitted in the Monument; it should be terminated. Minor dirt roads around this roadless area should be closed for a much larger Wilderness area. During 1990, the NPS removed picnic tables, fire pits, and pit toilets in the improved campsites along the rivers as a minor wilderness restoration project.

BLACK RIDGE CANYONS 115,000 acres (also in Utah)	
BLM WSA 070-113 (CO and UT)	75,000
BLM WSA 060-118 and state roadless (UT)	40,000

Description: West of Grand Junction on the central Colorado-Utah border. This Colorado Plateau country features thirteen arches (the second-greatest concentration in the Southwest), sandstone side canyons, 43 miles of the Colorado River, exciting rapids, and riparian forests along perennial streams. Westwater and Ruby Canyons of the Colorado make this area a magnet for whitewater boaters. The predominant vegetation is piñon and juniper, sagebrush, Single-leaf Ash, and cottonwood. A 450-foot cavern is cut by the stream in Mee Canyon. The canyons are popular for hiking, and they have significant archaeological and paleontological sites. Colorado Squawfish, Humpbacked Chub, Bonytail Chub, and Razorback Sucker are extant but Endangered or Threatened fishes. Active Golden Eagle nesting sites and a rare butterfly, *Papilio indra minori,* are present. Desert Bighorn Sheep have been reintroduced. Other wildlife includes wintering Bald Eagle (and Utah's only pair of nesting Bald Eagles), migrating Whooping Crane, Great Blue Heron, Elk, and Ringtail.

Status: Conservationists propose 106,400 acres for Wilderness (68,800 in Colorado, 42,700 in Utah); BLM, 100,000. All 43 miles of the Colorado here have been proposed for Wild or Scenic River designation. ORVs remain a major problem. A county road formerly separated the Westwater and Black Ridge Canyons WSAs, but it has been abandoned by the county at the request of the Mountain Island Ranch, which wholeheartedly supports Wilderness designation for the entire area. The "road" is now gated and locked.

DOMINGUEZ CANYONS 102,000 acres	
BLM WSAs 7-150/3-363 and additional BLM roadless	91,000
Uncompahgre NF roadless	11,000

Description: South of Grand Junction in west-central Colorado on the north side of the Uncompahgre Plateau. Elevations from 4,800 feet on the Gunnison River to 9,000 feet create a wide biological diversity. Two perennial streams cut slickrock canyons with numerous plunge pools. Vegetation on the ridges consists of Big Sagebrush and piñon and juniper; Douglas-fir stringers and cottonwoods are in the canyons. Desert Bighorn Sheep have been reintroduced to the canyons; Elk, Black Bear, and Mule Deer inhabit the high country; wintering Bald Eagles loiter along the Gunnison; and many species of raptors nest on the cliffs. The Threatened Uinta Basin Hookless Cactus and Endangered Spineless Hedgehog Cactus occur in Dominguez Canyon. Numerous archaeological sites include large petroglyph panels. Jurassic fossils are common, including those of the largest dinosaur yet discovered—Ultrasaurus.

Status: Some Jeep trails and grazing "improvements" scar the area; both ORVs and overgrazing present future threats. Mining claims for precious metals have been staked. Conservationists propose a 90,000-acre Wilderness Area; BLM recommends 73,500 acres. The proposed Dominguez Dam on the Gunnison River would impact the area.

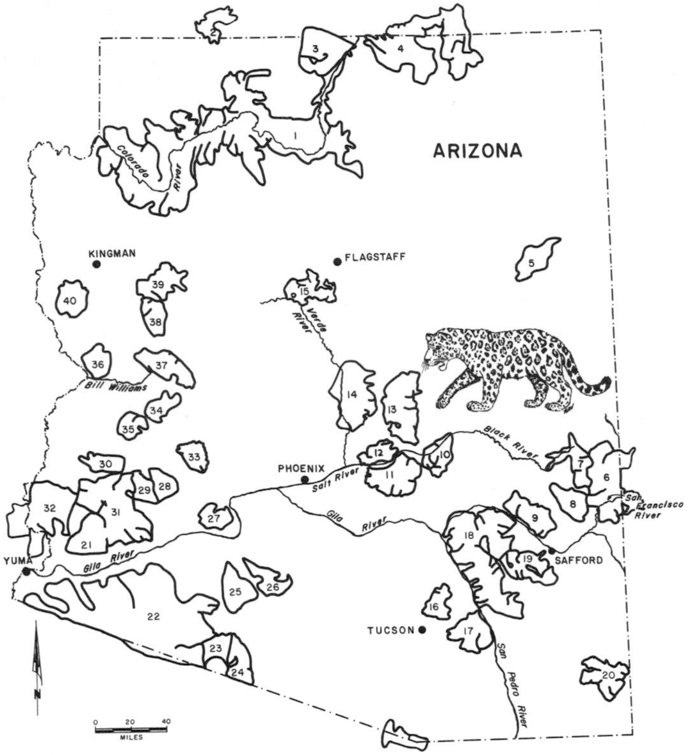

1. Grand Canyon
2. Parunuweap
3. Paria Canyon
4. Navajo Mt.
5. Painted Desert
6. Blue Range–San Francisco
7. Baldy Bill
8. Eagle Creek
9. Gila Mts.
10. Salt River
11. Superstition Mts.
12. Four Peaks
13. Hellsgate
14. Mazatzal
15. Sycamore Canyon–Secret Mts.
16. Catalina Mts.
17. Rincon Mts.
18. Galiuro Mts.
19. Mt. Graham
20. Chiricahua Mts.
21. Pajarito Mts.
22. Cabeza Prieta
23. Bates Mts.
24. Ajo Mts.
25. Batamote-Sauceda Mts.
26. Sand Tank Mts.
27. Woolsey Peak–Signal Mt.
28. Eagletail Mts.
29. Little Horn Mts.
30. New Water Mts.
31. Kofa Mts.
32. Lower Colorado River
33. Big Horn Mts.
34. Harcuvar Mts. East
35. Harcuvar Mts. West
36. Mohave Wash
37. Arrastra Mt.
38. Aquarius Mts. South
39. Aquarius Mts. North (Trout Creek)
40. Warm Springs (Black Mesa)

Arizona

Political boundaries seldom follow ecological boundaries, and the rule finds no exception in Arizona. Within the human boundary of "Arizona" lie several natural provinces defined by R. G. Bailey in 1976: the Mexican Highlands Shrub Steppe (Chihuahuan Desert and Sierra Madre), Upper Gila Mountains Forest (Mogollon Rim), American Desert (Sonoran and Mojave Deserts), and Colorado Plateau. Each has its characteristic natives: oak, Chihuahua Pine, Coatimundi, and Jaguar for the Sierra Madre; yucca and Javelina for the Chihuahuan Desert; Engelmann Spruce, Ponderosa Pine, Elk, and trout for the Mogollon Rim; Saguaro, Gila Monster, and Desert Bighorn for the Sonoran Desert; Joshua Tree and Desert Tortoise for the Mojave Desert; and Colorado Squawfish, Cliffrose, piñon, and juniper for the Colorado Plateau.

In nature, boundaries are fluid, open, interdigitating. Political boundaries try to be that way, too, but politicians defending the "nation" do their best to make such boundaries rigid, even to the extent of brick walls, concertina wire, and machine guns. Nature enforces her boundaries more gracefully, with frost, precipitation, and elevation. Plants and animals mix and meet new neighbors on the soft edges of natural provinces. Their easy integration makes one realize how fatuous, how ephemeral are the political affairs of our kind.

Yet, while our affairs may be fatuous and ephemeral in one sense, they are brutal in another. With cow, dirt bike, steel-jaw trap, thirty-ought-six, pickup truck, water pump, smelter, bulldozer, chain saw, and greenback, our kind has been ravaging Arizona ever since Padre Kino strode up the Rio Magdalena three centuries ago armed with Christianity and cattle. We have steadily accelerated the pace of destruction during the last hundred years until we are caroming out of control today.

Arizona has lost more of its old-growth forest than has any other Western state; 97 percent of Arizona's riparian vegetation, crucial for wildlife, has disappeared; water tables have dropped, and rivers (like the Santa Cruz through Tucson) have ceased to flow; the grass has gone into the livestockman's pocket, and the soil to the Gulf of California. With this destruction of habitat and with campaigns of outright biocide, many of Arizona's leading citizens have disappeared into the mists of legend—Oso Gris, Lobo, El Tigre, Ocelot, Tarahumara Frog . . .

Desert rats, canyon lovers, and peak baggers have been fighting to preserve Arizona since Teddy Roosevelt saw the Grand Canyon in 1903 and said, "Leave it as it is. . . . The ages have been at work on it and man can only mar it." Unfortunately, we have not listened well to TR. Despite the best efforts of conservationists, little of Arizona has been left as it was.

Grand Canyon National Park still awaits Wilderness designation, as does the adjacent Lake Mead National Recreation Area. However, Organ Pipe Cactus and Saguaro National Monuments and Petrified Forest National Park have had reasonably good Wilderness Areas established.

The Forest Service evaluated 2,137,929 acres for Wilderness during RARE II in Arizona. Conservation groups recommended 2,154,674 acres for protection. The 1984 Arizona Wilderness Act was a political compromise granting protection to only 767,390 acres of National Forest land. A major failure of the bill was the omission of a Blue Range Wilderness. The Blue, in far eastern Arizona, was one of the earliest FS Primitive Areas and is the only one not yet designated as Wilderness. Conservationists have continued their efforts to save wildlands on Arizona's six National Forests by appealing

Forest Plans in order to halt destructive activities in released roadless areas. Particularly threatened are the remnant old-growth forests on the Apache and Kaibab NFs (more about this later).

The 1984 Arizona Wilderness Act also included 265,000 acres of BLM Wilderness on the Arizona Strip—that part of the state north of the Grand Canyon. Pressure was intense to resolve the Wilderness question for this sprawling, unpopulated region because mining companies had discovered extremely high grade uranium ore in the area and a stalemate on Wilderness could have delayed mining development. Representatives of national conservation groups and Energy Fuels Nuclear, the principal mining company, worked out a compromise; Arizona's congressional delegation took the ball and ran. The legislation opened several million acres around the Grand Canyon to uranium mining; the dozens of uranium mines now in operation and planned there are the legacy of this compromise (670,000 acres of former BLM WSAs have been blanketed with claims).

BLM identified a total of 2.1 million acres as Wilderness Study Areas in Arizona and proposed 1,013,436 acres for Wilderness. The Arizona Wilderness Coalition, in a well-produced book, outlined its comprehensive proposal of 2,222,091 acres for BLM Wilderness. Arizona Earth First! countered with a 17-million-acre Wilderness proposal for BLM lands, National Wildlife Refuges, the Grand Canyon, and Blue Range. Late in the 1990 congressional session, a bill establishing 1,097,869 acres of BLM Wilderness and releasing 944,042 acres of Wilderness Study Areas in Arizona was passed. This Arizona Desert Wilderness Act of 1990 was the first statewide BLM Wilderness bill to pass.

Wilderness proposals for Cabeza Prieta, Kofa, Imperial, and Havasu National Wildlife Refuges were developed by the U.S. Fish and Wildlife Service in the early 1970s, but Wilderness legislation for these areas did not pass until 1990, when 1,291,626 acres of Wilderness was designated in the four Refuges as part of the Arizona Desert Wilderness Act.

Back on the forest front, in a bold move, The Wilderness Society, the Sierra Club, and the Audubon Society filed a federal lawsuit in 1991 to protect old-growth and other natural forests on the National Forests in Arizona and New Mexico. The suit uses the 1976 National Forest Management Act to demand management for biodiversity on the Southwest NFs. Conservationists are using the perilous condition of the Northern Goshawk as a keystone for the collapse of forest ecosystems in the Southwest. The suit takes an ecosystem approach, rather than a single-species approach, as lawsuits have done in the past. Mycorrhizal fungi, Ponderosa Pine, Tassel-eared Squirrel, and Northern Goshawk form a chain that ties the forest together. While 260 pairs of Goshawks once nested on the North Kaibab Ranger District alone, only 122 Goshawk pairs could be inventoried in all of Arizona and New Mexico by 1991—a graphic indication of the collapse of the Ponderosa Pine ecosystem in the Southwest due to logging. This suit should set the pattern for future ecosystem-based lawsuits by conservation groups throughout the country. It is an important precedent. The timber industry is not going to roll over for the conservationists, though. A major Phoenix law firm pulled out of representing the conservationists because of political pressure from the timber industry. The Sierra Club Legal Defense Fund ultimately filed the suit.

The primary threats to Arizona Wilderness are continued cattle and sheep grazing; ORVs; slob hunters; and, in the White Mountains, Mogollon Rim, and Kaibab Plateau, logging. Additional threats to specific areas are mining, power-line corridors, and urban sprawl.

Colorado Plateau

Northern Arizona is part of the Colorado Plateau, that extraordinary region of sandstone cut by the Colorado River and its tributaries. It is a land of rock, sometimes modestly garbed with Big Sagebrush, piñon, and juniper, but often naked in a startling fashion. The Big Outside here is managed by Grand Canyon and Petrified Forest National Parks; the Kaibab NF; the Navajo, Havasupai, and Hualapai Indian Reservations; and BLM.

GRAND CANYON 2,700,000 acres	
Grand Canyon National Park roadless	1,131,508
Designated Saddle Mountain Wilderness Area (Kaibab NF)	40,600
Designated Kanab Creek Wilderness Area (Kaibab NF and BLM)	77,100
Designated Mt. Logan Wilderness Area (BLM)	14,600
Lake Mead National Recreation Area roadless	168,530
Hualapai Indian Reservation roadless	615,000
Havasupai Indian Reservation roadless	170,000
Navajo Indian Reservation roadless	180,000
Additional Kaibab NF roadless	15,000
Additional BLM and intermixed state and private roadless	288,000

Description: Northwestern Arizona northwest of Flagstaff. The Grand Canyon of the Colorado River, with its side canyons and portions of its rims from Marble Canyon bridge downstream to Lake Mead, forms a single roadless area that is one of the most distinctive and awe-inspiring features of Earth. Two billion years of rocks lie exposed in this mile-deep (8,200–2,400 feet) chasm. Life zones range from Mojave Desert vegetation of Saltbush, mesquite, and cactus in the depths of the Canyon to forests of Engelmann and Blue Spruce, White Fir, Douglas-fir, and Aspen on the North Rim, with blackbrush, wolfberry, yucca, sagebrush, Cliffrose, piñon, juniper, Ponderosa Pine, and Gambel Oak in between. Precipitation varies from 25 inches on the North Rim (130 inches' accumulation of snow is average) to 9 inches in the canyon bottom. Many miles of rough trail and one of the world's finest float trips challenge the human visitor. Rampart and Vulture Caves have Ground Sloth dung. Bald Eagle, Peregrine Falcon, Speckled Rattlesnake, Bighorn Sheep, Mountain Lion, Spotted Bat, Pronghorn, Kit Fox, Beaver, Ringtail, Gray Fox, Bobcat, Bison, a world-famous herd of Rocky Mountain Mule Deer on the Kaibab Plateau, the endemic Kaibab Squirrel, and perhaps River Otter are some of the inhabitants. Desert species like Gila Monster, Desert Iguana, Sidewinder, and Desert Tortoise reach the northeastern limits of their ranges in the Grand Canyon.

Status: Unprotected Forest Service and BLM roadless areas face severe and growing uranium mining pressure. Uranium mining also proceeds in adjacent areas surrounding the Canyon roadless area—the overall Grand Canyon region is being turned into an industrial zone threatened by radiation. In the 1984 Arizona Strip Wilderness Act, representatives of conservation groups, negotiating with a uranium company, Energy Fuels Nuclear, essentially agreed to allow uranium mining outside of designated Wilderness Areas in exchange for the designation of eight small BLM Wilderness Areas north of the Grand Canyon. Such is the nature of compromise environmentalism. Roads for uranium mining now provide access for pot hunters, poachers, trappers, ORV joyriders, and other vermin.

Although the NPS has proposed 92 percent of the Park for Wilderness, the Park Service has otherwise sold out to commercial interests here. Excessive river use, especially by commercial outfitters using motorized rafts, is trashing the Colorado River corridor. For many years, aircraft have been as thick as flies on a dead cow in and above the Canyon. Aircraft restrictions have finally been developed, but they are inadequate. The Forest Service is logging the North Rim—right up to the edge (a bulldozer used in logging fell into the Canyon in the late 1980s). Feral burros, officially eradicated, still compete with Bighorn Sheep.

The Bright Angel–Kaibab Trail corridor cuts across the canyon from the South Rim to the North. Although it is not a road, it is a heavily used and developed route that, some would argue, cuts the Grand Canyon roadless area in half.

Glen Canyon Dam, or Damn, upstream has blocked silt deposits and flushing floods, with the result that beaches are disintegrating and becoming polluted, and the riverine ecosystem corrupted. The Damn has also lowered the water temperature, thereby devastating fish species like the Endangered Colorado Squawfish (which formerly grew to up to 6 feet long and 100 pounds; survivors are much smaller and greatly depleted in number now), Endangered Humpback Chub, Loach Minnow, Little Colorado Spinedace, and Threatened Razorback Sucker. The river now has a widely variable artificial flow controlled by sales of electricity (river level sometimes changes 13 feet in a few hours). Pressure is mounting on the BuRec to regulate flow in an ecologically more sound way; legislation may soon pass to stabilize the flow.

Visibility is often limited in the Canyon because of air pollution from Los Angeles and coal-fired power plants in the Southwest. Air pollution, of course, has more nefarious impacts than veiling scenery. In 1991, conservation groups reached a negotiated settlement with the Navajo Generating Station, the main source of pollution in the Canyon, to control emissions. Although this will improve air quality, it was a compromise that will allow the power plant to continue to degrade the air.

Regrettably, neither conservation groups nor land managing agencies look at the Grand Canyon as a whole. Indeed, certain groups and individuals purporting to represent conservation interests have made shameful compromises. Teddy Roosevelt would be horrified if he could see what the Park Service, Forest Service, and BLM have done to this world wonder. An interagency, regional, programmatic, cumulative EIS on minerals and related land use in the entire Grand Canyon district is needed, along with an immediate moratorium on all further development.

RM36: 4,000,000

PARUNUWEAP 128,000 acres (also in Utah)

See Utah for description and status.

PARIA CANYON 290,000 acres (also in Utah)	
Designated Paria Canyon–Vermilion Cliffs Wilderness Area BLM (AZ)	90,046
Designated Paria Canyon–Vermilion Cliffs Wilderness Area BLM (UT)	19,954
Additional BLM roadless (AZ and UT)	180,000

Description: Central Arizona-Utah border. This slickrock canyon complex west of Page includes canyons carved in Navajo sandstone that are so deep and narrow, they seem like a sandstone analogue to glacial crevasses. Buckskin Gulch is only a couple of feet wide in places and a hundred feet deep. Elevations drop from 7,356 feet to 3,200 feet. The canyon cuts through a plateau of slickrock and rolling sandy grassland dotted with sagebrush and piñon and juniper. The brilliant Vermilion Cliffs rise 3,000 feet from House Rock Valley to the Paria Plateau. Paria Creek flows into the Colorado River at Lee's Ferry. Hikers, with no escape possible, face the danger of flash floods while in the canyons. Vegetation includes Sand Dropseed, Indian Ricegrass, Shadscale, Greasewood, Four-winged Saltbush, and Golden Rabbitbrush in arid areas; willow, Fremont Cottonwood, and Box Elder in the riparian zones; and Cliffrose, Apache-plume, piñon and juniper, and occasional Ponderosa Pine higher. Several state or federal Threatened or Endangered species live in the area, including Peregrine Falcon, Spotted Bat, and Razorback Sucker.

Status: The designated Wilderness includes only Paria Canyon and the Vermilion Cliffs, leaving the central Paria Plateau unprotected. ORVs and overgrazing are damaging the area. The central plateau is a vitally needed addition to the Wilderness.

*RM36: 8,890,000**

NAVAJO MOUNTAIN 850,000 acres (also in Utah)	
Navajo Indian Reservation roadless (AZ)	560,000
Navajo Indian Reservation roadless (UT)	290,000

Description: Northern Arizona and southern Utah. This remote region to the south of "Lake" Powell and east of Page offers exceptional views of the Colorado Plateau from 10,000-foot-high Navajo Mountain. Intricate, narrow, deep slot canyons flow from Navajo Mountain into the drowned San Juan

River at 3,700 feet. Vegetation is sagebrush and piñon and juniper, with Ponderosa Pine in higher areas. Prominent features include Rainbow Bridge, Navajo Creek, Nokai Canyon, Skeleton Mesa, and Navajo National Monument (with its exceptional Anasazi cliff dwellings).

Status: Protection is uncertain. Plans are being pushed for a major Powell Reservoir marina at Copper Canyon, with a paved road from Olijato. This would sever the eastern third of this roadless area, the Nokai Mesa region, from the rest. Promoters on the Navajo Reservation would eventually like to see the paved road extend all the way to Navajo Mountain, with spur roads shooting off into this vast roadless area.

Jeep trails and extensive livestock grazing are marring the land. The roadless area is nearly cut in half by dirt roads on Piute Mesa and to Navajo Mountain, which come within five miles of "Lake" Powell. Another dirt road almost severs Nokai Canyon from Skeleton Mesa–Tsegi Canyon. Conservation groups need to work with the Navajo Tribe to gain recognition and protection for this huge wild area. Through the efforts of Bob Marshall, 1,590,000 acres were designated as a Bureau of Indian Affairs Roadless Area here in 1937, but that protective status was revoked in the early 1960s by the non-Indian staff of the Navajo Grazing Office. Since then, developments and new pickup truck roads have halved the roadless area.

*RM36: 8,890,000**

PAINTED DESERT 140,000 acres	
Petrified Forest National Park Wilderness Area and additional roadless	50,000
Navajo Indian Reservation, private, and BLM roadless	90,000

Description: Northeastern Arizona northeast of Holbrook. These barren, multicolor badlands north of Interstate 40 have sparse Great Basin Desert vegetation, abundant petrified wood, and many fossils. The high point is 6,235 feet, on Pilot Rock. Wildlife includes Pronghorn, Coyote, and Bobcat.

Status: Overgrazing on adjacent private, BLM, and Navajo land, and removal of petrified wood are problems.

RM36: 1,000,000

Central Mountains

The backbone of central Arizona is the Mogollon Rim. High plateaus stretch north of the Rim; broken mountains and canyons fall off to the south. Formerly, this highland grew the world's largest Ponderosa Pine forest. Here is where most of Arizona's waters rise, and here Arizona appears less exotic than it does farther to the south. Nevertheless, the influence of Mexico keeps the Mogollon Rim from being a typical part of the Rocky Mountains; biologically, the Mogollon Rim country mixes characteristics of the Rockies, Sierra Madre, Colorado Plateau, and Sonoran and Chihuahuan Deserts. This is largely National Forest—the Apache and Tonto NFs—although the Fort Apache and San Carlos Indian Reservations and BLM are also involved.

BLUE RANGE–SAN FRANCISCO 505,000 acres (also in New Mexico)	
Designated Blue Range Wilderness Area (Gila NF, NM)	30,000
Blue Range Primitive Area (Apache NF, AZ)	180,139
Additional Apache and Gila NFs roadless (NM and AZ)	295,000

Description: The "Blue" is a rugged and little-visited area on the Arizona–New Mexico border west of the Gila Wilderness and north of Clifton, Arizona. It consists of the deep canyons of the Blue and San Francisco Rivers and surrounding mountains along the Mogollon Rim. Elevations range from 3,700 feet along the San Francisco River to over 9,300 feet on Blue Peak. The Blue is similar to the Gila (see New Mexico) in flora, fauna, and geology, including rocky lower country covered with mesquite grassland, phasing upward to lush wet meadows in spruce-fir forest. The southern (lower) part of the Blue has been severely overgrazed, but under recent protection is now coming back. The riparian zones of cottonwood, willow, sycamore, walnut, and mesquite (a total of thirty-two broad-leaved trees and shrubs) along the San Francisco and Blue Rivers are of special biological importance. The largest and healthiest herd of Rocky Mountain Bighorn Sheep in the Southwest lives in the 1,600-foot-deep canyon of the San Francisco. Pronghorn roam the mesas above. There have been reports of River Otter in the rivers. Javelina, Mountain Lion, Elk, Bald Eagle, Peregrine Falcon, Common Black Hawk, Zone-tailed Hawk, Osprey, Loach Minnow, Sonoran Mountain King Snake, Arizona Coral Snake, Lyre Snake, and Gila Monster are other sensitive species. More than two hundred species of birds breed within a 50-mile radius of San Francisco Canyon—a number that few other temperate non-marine areas can boast. The Blue has the highest potential of any area in Arizona for Grizzly reintroduction. It would also be suitable as a reintroduction site for Mexican Wolf.

Status: Only a small part of this large area has received Wilderness Act protection. Politically powerful ranchers in eastern Arizona, along with timber interests, mining corporations, and local rednecks, have stridently fought Wilderness designation for the Blue Range Primitive Area (the last remaining FS Primitive Area in the United States), and conservation groups have not diligently campaigned for the area because of its remoteness. The FS proposes 187,410 acres in Arizona for addition to the existing Blue Wilderness (all of the Wilderness is currently in New Mexico), but excludes San Francisco Canyon; the Arizona Wilderness Coalition calls for 304,096 acres (including San Francisco Canyon), and New Mexico conservationists have proposed Wilderness for their part of San Francisco Canyon.

ORVers formerly staged supposedly macho expeditions along San Francisco Canyon—one of the most ecologically sensitive areas in the Southwest. A courageous effort by the Apache NF Supervisor to close San Francisco Canyon to ORVs was reversed in 1988 by the Regional Forester; but that reversal has been reversed, and there is now a year-round vehicle closure on the Frisco in the Apache NF part of the roadless area. The Gila NF has a year-round vehicle closure on about half of the New Mexico portion of the Frisco in this roadless area, from the Mule Creek confluence downstream. Conservationists should encourage a vehicle closure for the rest of San Francisco Canyon in New Mexico as well. ORVers have looted important Mimbres archaeological sites in the canyon.

Logging threatens the high country, and severe overgrazing continues throughout much of the area. Mining potential presents a minor threat in the south. The Apache NF wants to dam Pigeon Creek and develop a recreational reservoir south of the Primitive Area—but in the center of the roadless area, along a cherrystem road. Not only would this be a major development in the heart of the roadless area, but the introduction of non-native put-and-take fish would threaten native fish downstream in the Blue and San Francisco Rivers—including the federally Threatened Loach Minnow and the Desert Sucker, Sonora Sucker, Longfin Dace, and Speckled Dace.

National as well as Arizona and New Mexico conservation groups should mount a major campaign to protect *all* of the Blue as Wilderness. The San Francisco and Blue Rivers should be designated National Wild and Scenic Rivers. (I received death threats in 1973 when I proposed such a thing while living along the Frisco in Glenwood, New Mexico.)

In 1990, the Arizona Department of Game and Fish identified the Blue as one of four priority areas in Arizona for study as a site for Mexican Wolf reintroduction. (The other areas are the Chiricahuas, Galiuros, and Atascosas-Pajaritos.) Conservationists need to develop strong support for reintroduction of the Lobo in the Blue. This was the general area where Aldo Leopold killed the "Green Fire" wolf in 1909. There could be no more appropriate place to return the wolf.

Although a double power line crosses the San Francisco canyon near the Arizona–New Mexico border, we have not considered it to be a "road," since it is high above the river and does not have any road access within the canyon.

BALDY BILL 125,000 acres	
Bear Wallow Wilderness Area (Apache NF)	11,080
Additional Apache National Forest roadless	89,000
White Mountain Apache Indian Reservation roadless	25,000

Description: Along the Mogollon Rim in east-central Arizona west of U.S. 666 (across from the Blue Range) and south of Springerville. The Black River and several other trout streams cut canyons through this heavily forested area. Spruce-fir forest drops down to Ponderosa Pine to piñon and juniper. Elevations range from 9,184 feet to under 5,000 feet. Mountain Lion, Black Bear, Elk, Mule Deer, and Turkey are the big critters. The potential for Grizzly reintroduction is high. Terrain is similar to that of the nearby Blue Range.

Status: The Forest Service plans to clearcut most of the unprotected timbered area—which includes the finest old-growth mixed conifer forest left in Arizona. Areas both within and adjacent to this roadless area are among the most threatened areas in Arizona because of logging. The logging of any natural forest in Arizona should be prohibited. A few Jeep trails that formerly broke this area into several RARE II units are now washed out. Trail bikes are a threat, as is overgrazing. This is one of the choicest, but most overlooked, forested areas in Arizona. Conservation groups need to make it a major priority for preservation as an intact unit.

Until recent years, there was a roadless area of over 100,000 acres in the well-watered, heavily forested White Mountain high country on the White Mountain Apache Reservation to the northwest of this area, but logging and road building for Elk hunter access have reduced it.

EAGLE CREEK 145,000 acres	
Apache NF roadless	48,000
San Carlos Apache Indian Reservation roadless	85,000
BLM, state, and private roadless	12,000

Description: West of Clifton in southeastern Arizona. The Eagle Creek roadless area is the western end of the Greater Mogollon Highlands Ecosystem, which stretches from the Aldo Leopold and Gila Wildernesses in New Mexico through the Blue and Baldy Bill in Arizona. Eagle Creek and its tributaries form an exceptional riparian corridor through rough, lower-elevation mountains. Elevations range from 7,113 feet on Elevator Mountain to under 4,000 feet on Eagle Creek. The higher reaches sport piñon-juniper woodland and chaparral associations, while the lower country represents a transition between the Chihuahuan and Sonoran Deserts. The rich riparian zone is made up of Fremont Cottonwood, Arizona Sycamore, Velvet Ash, willow, mesquite, and Arizona Walnut. Along with the adjacent Gila Box BLM National Conservation Area, Eagle Creek is the most important habitat in the United States for the Common Black Hawk. Bald Eagles have recently nested along Eagle Creek. There are seventeen animal species in the area that are on state or federal Endangered or Threatened lists, or are being considered for listing.

Status: Most of the FS land was inventoried in RARE II but recommended for non-Wilderness. The status of the San Carlos lands is uncertain. The lower part of Eagle Creek in this roadless area is owned by the Phelps-Dodge Copper Corporation. A dirt road separates this roadless area from the Baldy Bill area to the north; twisting, narrow U.S. 666 is all that severs Eagle Creek and Baldy Bill from the Blue Range. An improved dirt road separates Eagle Creek from the Gila Box area to the south. The Arizona Wilderness Coalition has proposed that 151,680 acres of the Gila Box and the southern portion of this roadless area be studied for possible National Park designation. The study should be expanded to include all of the Apache NF land in this roadless area, and a cooperative agreement worked out with the San Carlos Apaches to protect their portion.

Continued grazing and ORVs are the primary threats.

GILA MOUNTAINS 194,000 acres	
Designated Fishhooks Wilderness Area (BLM)	10,883
Released BLM WSAs 4-14 and 4-16	21,641
Additional BLM roadless	71,000
San Carlos Apache Reservation roadless	69,000
State roadless	21,000

Description: Southeastern Arizona northwest of Safford. The Gila Mountains are a craggy range rising north of the Gila River from low rolling hills, and are punctuated by sheer cliffs, deep canyons, and desert washes. Elevations range from around 3,200 feet to 6,629 feet on Gila Peak. This area has the farthest northeastern extension of the Saguaro; large areas of Creosote; a transition from oak, juniper, and piñon to mountain mahogany and oak scrub communities; and the largest existing stand of Lowell Ash, a candidate for Threatened species status. The uppermost watersheds are quite undisturbed by cattle grazing and have important climax vegetative communities needed by many mammals and birds. Wildlife includes Bald Eagle, Black Hawk, Javelina, Mule Deer, and Mountain Lion. Numerous archaeological sites have been found.

Status: BLM chopped this area into several roadless areas because of the presence of minor, unmaintained vehicle ways. Although the Arizona Wilderness Coalition recognized the unity of the area and proposed an 80,000-acre Wilderness, the 1990 Arizona Wilderness Act established only a 10,883-acre Wilderness and released the rest of the Wilderness Study Area acreage. Threats are additional grazing, ORVs, and the pilfering and vandalism that come with ORV use.

SALT RIVER 110,000 acres	
Designated Salt River Canyon Wilderness Area (Tonto NF)	32,800
Additional Tonto NF and White Mountain Apache Reservation roadless	77,000

Description: Central Arizona north of Globe. The precipitous canyon of the Salt River upstream of Theodore Roosevelt Reservoir has Sonoran Desert vegetation (Saguaro, etc.) phasing into piñon and juniper. Elevations rise from 2,200 feet to 6,940 feet. The Salt offers a challenging white-water float trip. Wildlife is similar to that in other Tonto NF areas.

Status: As in most Southwestern roadless areas, the unprotected area is being damaged by ORVs and overgrazing. More of the FS land should be added to the Wilderness, and a hundred-mile-long stretch of the Salt River should be designated as a National Wild and Scenic River.

SUPERSTITION MOUNTAINS 269,000 acres	
Designated Superstition Wilderness Area (Tonto NF)	159,757
Additional Tonto NF roadless	96,000
State roadless	13,000

Description: Central Arizona east of Phoenix. Weaver's Needle and the Lost Dutchman's Mine make this a well-known and popular area, replete with wild-eyed lunatics packing guns and treasure maps. Elevations rise from 1,700 feet to 6,266 feet. Very rugged topography and characteristically thorny Sonoran Desert vegetation (Saguaro, palo verde, mesquite) in the west leads into higher terrain with manzanita, ceanothus, oak, Arizona Cypress, mountain mahogany, piñon and juniper, and Ponderosa Pine in the east. The several perennial streams and springs have valuable riparian woodland. The typical Sonoran Desert–Southwestern Woodland fauna includes Phainopepla, Roadrunner, Verdin, Curve-billed Thrasher, Cactus Wren, Mountain Lion, Black Bear, Javelina, Bobcat, White-tailed and Mule Deer, Western Diamondback Rattlesnake, and Gila Monster.

Status: The unprotected areas are threatened by overgrazing, ORVs, and possible mining. Several rough dirt roads are cherrystemmed into the unprotected roadless area, and there are several Jeep trails cutting through it.

FOUR PEAKS 100,000 acres	
Designated Four Peaks Wilderness Area (Tonto NF)	53,500
Additional Tonto NF roadless	46,500

Description: Central Arizona northeast of Phoenix and north of the Salt River, in the southern Mazatzal Mountains between the Superstition, Mazatzal, and Hellsgate roadless areas. The distinctive Four Peaks rise to 7,657 feet; the low point along the Salt River is 1,600 feet. Vegetation is Saguaro forest to Douglas-fir and Aspen. Black Bear, Mountain Lion, Mule Deer, and Javelina roam the washes and slopes.

Status: The unprotected portion is open to ORV abuse and overgrazing.

HELLSGATE 346,000 acres	
Designated Hellsgate Wilderness Area (Tonto NF)	36,780
Designated Salome Wilderness Area (Tonto NF)	18,950
Additional Tonto NF roadless	290,000

Description: Central Arizona east of Payson and west of Young. This steep, convoluted country in the Sierra Ancha Mountains is sliced by formidable gorges. Tonto and Salome Creeks are perennial streams with important riparian zones. These creeks and their tributaries possess intricate, precipitous, narrow gorges that rival the best of the southern Utah Canyon Country. Elevations range from 2,200 feet to 7,000 feet. Vegetation is Saguaro through chaparral, and piñon and juniper to Ponderosa Pine. Wildlife includes Black Phoebe, Mule Deer, Black Bear, Mountain Lion, and Javelina.

Status: The large roadless area between the two Wilderness Areas needs protection. ORVs, overgrazing, and hobby mining threaten it. Several Jeep trails penetrate it, and one bone-jarring track crosses it. Range "improvements" also scar it. Conservation groups need to recognize the entire unit as one large roadless area deserving of protection.

MAZATZAL 340,000 acres	
Designated Mazatzal Wilderness Area (Tonto NF)	251,912
Additional Tonto NF roadless	88,000

Description: Central Arizona north of Phoenix. The roadless area consists of the northern end of the Mazatzal Mountains and the Verde Wild River west of the mountains. The high point is 7,904 feet; low is 2,000 feet, on the Verde. The East Fork of the Verde cuts through the mountains. Topography ranges from craggy mountains and canyons to broad bajadas, flat-topped mesas and buttes, and open, flat country. Vegetation ranges from Aspen, Douglas-fir, and Ponderosa Pine down to Saguaro, palo verde, mesquite, and other Sonoran Desert plants. Impressive stands of Arizona Cypress appear in the mid-elevation areas with piñon and juniper and chaparral. Occasionally, deep snow accumulates in the mountains. The Verde is a fine float trip—one of the three possible in Saguaro country (the others being the Salt and Gila). Many Black Bear live here; this is one of the few places they can be seen among Saguaros. Gila Monster, Javelina, Mountain Lion, Mule Deer, and Bald Eagle are other residents.

Status: Overgrazing continues in portions of the area, including the designated Wilderness. ORVs threaten unprotected areas. Air pollution from Phoenix increasingly degrades the entire area. Part of the Verde River in the Wilderness is a National Wild River; the rest of the Verde in the Wilderness and the East Verde River are proposed for that status.

RM27: 1,106,560

SYCAMORE CANYON–SECRET MOUNTAIN 137,000 acres	
Designated Sycamore Canyon Wilderness Area (Prescott, Coconino, and Kaibab NFs)	55,937
Designated Red Rock–Secret Mountain Wilderness Area (Coconino NF)	43,950
Roadless Coconino NF and private contiguous to Red Rock–Secret Mountain	4,000
Roadless Coconino, Prescott, and Kaibab NFs contiguous to Sycamore Canyon	33,000

Description: Central Arizona north of Sedona and Cottonwood. On the western end of the Mogollon Rim, this disjunct area of exposed slickrock, sandstone buttes, colorful canyons, and precipitous cliffs has attracted worldwide fame for its stunning scenery. The Rim, at about 6,600 feet, drops 2,000 feet to the outskirts of Sedona, and down to less than 3,600 feet where Sycamore Creek enters the Verde River. Sycamore Creek and the West Fork of Oak Creek have carved spectacular canyons into the Rim. The high point is 7,196 feet, on East Pocket Knob, above famous Oak Creek Canyon. There is fine riparian vegetation of Arizona Sycamore, cottonwood, willow, Arizona Walnut, and ash in the canyons; sturdy forests of Ponderosa Pine and Douglas-fir on the Mogollon Rim; and a transition through piñon and juniper to chaparral, Rabbitbrush, prickly pear, yucca, and grassland at the base of the Rim. Wildlife is typical of the Mogollon Rim country. River Otter are present in Sycamore Creek and the Verde River. Archaeological sites are numerous and include cliff dwellings.

Status: Sycamore Canyon, the western half of this roadless area, was an early Forest Service Primitive Area; it was designated as Wilderness in 1972 and enlarged in 1984 by the Arizona Wilderness Act. Red Rock–Secret Mountain Wilderness, the eastern half of this roadless area, was established in 1984 by the Arizona bill. The vast Ponderosa Pine forest of the Coconino Plateau above the Rim has suffered terribly at the hands of the Forest Service. The only areas not logged and roaded are those too rough. Industrial logging therefore determines the northern boundaries of this area, while development around bustling Sedona limits it to the south. The unprotected roadless area west of the Sycamore Canyon Wilderness could be nibbled away by firewood cutting, ORVs, and overgrazing.

We did not include this area in the first edition of *The Big Outside* because a power line cuts between the two Wilderness Areas. We have decided to include it in this edition, because vehicles are not permitted along the power line, and because the Wilderness boundaries come right up to the line.

Sierra Madre

Southeastern Arizona is a zone of invasion from another nation—Mexico. It is basin and range, like much of the western United States; but the basins are Chihuahuan Desert grassland with yucca and oak, and the ranges, despite the touch of the Rocky Mountains, are of Mexico's Sierra Madre. These "Sky Islands" are among the most important habitats in the United States, supporting many species found nowhere else in our country. Strange kinds of pine and oak form forests alien to those people expecting, say, Colorado. The fringe influence of the Rocky Mountains provides an interesting lesson in island biogeography in these isolated ranges. While Mt. Graham has a bit of true Engelmann Spruce–White Fir–Corkbark Fir forest, the Catalinas lack Engelmann Spruce and the Chiricahuas lack Corkbark Fir. These northern trees are remnants of a widespread spruce-fir forest during the past glaciation, and their apparently random distribution today illustrates the arbitrariness of species loss in fragmented (island) habitats. The Coronado NF, the BLM, the San Carlos Apaches, Saguaro National Monument, and The Nature Conservancy manage the area. Biologists and conservationists have recently formed the Sky Islands Alliance to work for biodiversity-geared management by the Coronado NF.

CATALINA MOUNTAINS 100,000 acres	
Designated Pusch Ridge Wilderness Area (Coronado NF)	56,933
Additional Coronado NF, state, and private roadless	43,000

Description: Southeastern Arizona immediately northeast of Tucson. Rising from 2,800 feet along Cañada del Oro, the Catalina roadless area climbs to 9,157 feet on Mt. Lemmon, forming the imposing skyline of Tucson. This well-watered desert mountain range has perennial streams, waterfalls, and deep pools. Vegetation ranges upward from Saguaro, Ocotillo, and palo verde to yucca grassland to oak savannah to piñon and juniper to forests of Ponderosa Pine and oak to Aspen, White Fir, and Douglas-fir. Arizona Alder, Arizona Sycamore, Box Elder, cottonwood, willow, Arizona Walnut, Velvet Ash, and other deciduous trees line the riparian zones. Wildlife includes Desert Bighorn Sheep, Mountain Lion, Black Bear, deer, Javelina, and Coatimundi. A particularly rocky range, it is dissected by deep, precipitous canyons cutting in all directions. Summer temperatures hit 110 degrees in the low country; the high country collects several feet of snow in the winter.

Status: Tucson's cancerous sprawl places great pressures on this roadless area; the Bighorn herd may not survive. Air pollution, suburban dog packs, excessive recreational use, and—most of all—encroaching subdivisions and other developments along the base of the mountains threaten the Wilderness. Ski area expansion and widening of the paved Mt. Lemmon Highway are damaging the adjoining Wilderness (the road to the top forms the eastern boundary of the roadless area). The additional FS roadless area should be added to the existing Wilderness (although a minor power line, both underground and above ground, runs between), and adjacent state lands should be added to the NF Wilderness.

RINCON MOUNTAINS 217,000 acres	
Saguaro National Monument Wilderness Area	60,000
Rincon Mountain Wilderness Area (Coronado NF)	38,590
Little Rincon RARE II (Coronado NF)	11,560
Additional Coronado NF roadless	24,000
Additional National Monument roadless	2,500
BLM, private, and state roadless	80,000

Description: Southeastern Arizona immediately east of Tucson. A superlative forest of Saguaro, palo verde, mesquite, and Ocotillo leads up through oak and Amole (shindagger) to forests of Ponderosa Pine, Chihuahua Pine, Arizona White Oak, Arizona Cypress, and Silverleaf Oak; then to Douglas-fir, White Fir, and Aspen in the high country. This is a surprisingly well-watered range, with streams hosting riparian woodlands of sycamore, willow, and cottonwood dropping through nearly impassable canyons into the desert lowlands. Elevations range from under 2,700 feet to 8,666 feet, on Mica Mountain. Wildlife includes Black Bear, Javelina, Mule Deer, Coues White-tailed Deer, Mountain Lion, Bobcat, tarantula, Desert Horned Lizard, and Gila Monster.

Status: The unprotected Forest Service area is threatened by continued overgrazing and ORV abuse. Adjacent private land in Rincon Valley is under threat of subdivision, but a strong grass-roots campaign in Tucson may stop the ritzy development. A dirt road to Happy Valley is cherry-stemmed in the FS portion, and several Jeep trails penetrate the roadless area of mixed private, state, and BLM land to the east. The Forest Service Wilderness and other FS land, along with state, BLM, and private land to the east down to the San Pedro River, should be added to the existing National Monument to create a Saguaro Wilderness National Park of 350,000 acres; Ocelot, Jaguar, Jaguarundi, and Mexican Wolf should be reintroduced into this preserve.

For a number of years, Park managers have been concerned with the lack of Saguaro reproduction. Recent research indicates that destruction of habitat for Sanborn's Longnose Bat in nearby caves may be the reason, since the bats pollinate Saguaros.

GALIURO MOUNTAINS 723,000 acres	
Designated Galiuro Wilderness Area (Coronado NF)	76,317
Designated Santa Teresa Wilderness Area (Coronado NF)	26,780
Designated North Santa Teresa Wilderness Area (BLM)	6,590
Designated Aravaipa Canyon Wilderness Area (BLM)	19,381
Designated Needle's Eye Wilderness Area (BLM)	9,201
Designated Redfield Canyon Wilderness Area (BLM)	6,600
Additional Forest Service, BLM, state, private, and San Carlos Apache Reservation roadless	578,000

Description: Southeastern Arizona northeast of Tucson. This is a rugged area of extremely mixed ownership. The Galiuro Mountains reach 7,663 feet on Bassett Peak, and the Santa Teresa Mountains reach 8,282 feet on Mt. Turnbull (on the San Carlos Reservation); the low point is about 2,300 feet, along the Gila River on the northwest. Vegetation ranges from Ponderosa Pine and Aspen in the high country to Saguaro–palo verde and Creosote-bursage associations in the Sonoran Desert. There are forests of Fremont Cottonwood, Arizona Sycamore, Netleaf Hackberry, Velvet Ash, mesquite, and Arizona Walnut in riparian areas; some unusual riparian forests of alder, sycamore, and oak; and extensive mesquite grasslands. The Table Top area has the northernmost Blue Oak savannah, a very rare Alligator Juniper savannah, and desert grassland relatively undisturbed by grazing. Several canyonbound perennial streams in a desert setting (including scrumptious Aravaipa Creek) provide crucial habitat for Endangered species of fish (the Gila Chub, Spikedace, and Loach Minnow) and for Peregrine Falcon (nesting). Aravaipa represents the best native fishery left in Arizona. Other critters include Desert Bighorn Sheep, Ocelot, Mountain Lion, Coues White-tailed Deer, Black Bear, and infrequent, transient Mexican Wolf and Jaguar. Below Coolidge Dam, the Gila River cuts a deeply incised canyon with numerous precipitous side canyons. The Gila is an important part of this roadless area and one of the more important riparian areas and wild rivers in the state.

In a 1975 study, the FS identified the Galiuro Wilderness as the least used unit in the Wilderness System.

Status: The 1990 Arizona Wilderness Act established a 9,201-acre Needle's Eye Wilderness Area for the Gila River canyon (an ancient 44-kilovolt power line runs through this Wilderness, but it is maintained by horseback and is largely unnoticeable). The North Santa Teresa and Redfield Canyon Wilderness Areas were also established, and a 12,700-acre addition was made to the Aravaipa Wilderness (although conservationists proposed a 27,520-acre addition).

The Nature Conservancy manages the southern 50,000 acres of this complex on its Muleshoe Ranch Preserve, and it recently took over the George Whittell Wildlife Preserve on both ends of BLM's Aravaipa Wilderness Area.

Only a small portion of this complex, however, is protected. The rest is vulnerable to overgrazing, poaching, ORVs, road building, and mining. But the primary threat is the fact that no agency or conservation group has recognized this area as a single wilderness. Fragmentation could be its downfall. A very rough Jeep trail cuts across the roadless area between the Aravaipa and Galiuro Wilderness Areas. This huge, untrammeled area has very high potential for Mexican Wolf, Jaguarundi, Jaguar, and Grizzly reintroduction. The Ocelot population should be supplemented. In 1990, the Arizona Department of Game and Fish identified the Galiuro–Mt. Graham region as one of four priority areas in Arizona for study as a site for Mexican Wolf reintroduction. (The other areas are the Chiricahuas, Blue Range, and Atascosas-Pajaritos.) This is a priceless area and should be protected as a single 800,000-acre Wilderness Area.

MT. GRAHAM 208,000 acres	
Mt. Graham Wilderness Study Area (Coronado NF)	62,000
Additional Coronado NF roadless	76,000
State, BLM, and private roadless	70,000

Description: An immense Sky Island mountain, rising nearly 8,000 feet above Safford in southeastern Arizona. High Peak is 10,713 feet in elevation. The high country possesses a relict Ice Age forest of Engelmann Spruce, White Fir, Corkbark Fir, Douglas-fir, White Pine, Scouler Willow, and Quaking Aspen that supports the Endangered Mt. Graham Red Squirrel and old-growth–dependent Red-backed Vole. Other vegetative zones are the forest of Ponderosa Pine, Arizona Pine, Chihuahua Pine, Gambel Oak, Silverleaf Oak, and Madrone, and the upper Sonoran association of Arizona Live Oak, Emory Oak, Alligator Juniper, and ceanothus. Many perennial streams in precipitous canyons (with Arizona Sycamore, Box Elder, maple, ash, and walnut) drop down to Chihuahuan Desert grassland and mesquite savannah. The densest population of Black Bear in the Western United States occurs here. Thick-billed Parrots are present, as are other Sierra Madrean species. Other wildlife includes Mountain Lion, Javelina, Coatimundi, deer, Mexican Spotted Owl, and the Endangered Twin-spotted Rattlesnake. In short, this is a biological treasure trove.

Status: The roadless area is a horseshoe around an existing paved and graveled road up into the high country. Some selective logging was practiced previously in the high country adjacent to the road. Although this damaged the mixed conifer forest, it did not irreparably destroy it (a significant area of the high country was never logged). No timbering is now occurring. A number of cherrystem roads and Jeep trails cut across the low desert to the base of the mountain and partway into some canyon bottoms. A large area of primarily state land (50,000 acres) to the west of the range and east of Aravaipa Creek should be added to the National Forest as part of the Wilderness to preserve its generally wild and roadless nature and to add a large expanse of Chihuahuan Desert to the diversity of the wilderness.

The primary threat to this area comes from an unexpected quarter: The University of Arizona proposes to place a dozen large telescopes on the summits of the range. This construction—if completed—will likely lead to the unraveling of the relict mixed conifer forest and the extinction of the squirrel and vole. Year-round human presence will disrupt the bears' feeding, mating, and denning patterns. Conservation groups and the Arizona Game and Fish Department are engaged in a major struggle with the astronomers and their political supporters for the integrity of the mountain. Late in 1988, Arizona Senator Dennis DeConcini pushed through Congress a measure circumventing the National Environmental Policy Act and the Endangered Species Act, and allowing the university to build three telescopes. Construction began in 1990, but conservation groups have continued to wage an extraordinarily intransigent campaign against the project, and there is no certainty that there will ever be an observatory on Mt. Graham.

The scopes should be rejected, the existing road to the summit of the mountain closed, and state land contiguous to Mt. Graham added, for a 220,000-acre Wilderness. The FS proposes a 62,000-acre Wilderness.

In 1990, the Arizona Department of Game and Fish identified the Galiuro–Mt. Graham region as one of four priority areas in Arizona for study as a site for Mexican Wolf reintroduction. (The other areas are the Chiricahuas, Blue Range, and Atascosas-Pajaritos.) This potential for reintroduction of the Lobo makes keeping the scopes off the peaks even more imperative.

CHIRICAHUA MOUNTAINS 160,000 acres	
Designated Chiricahua Wilderness Area (Coronado NF)	87,700
Additional Coronado NF, private, and state roadless	72,000

Description: Southeastern Arizona north of Douglas. The most famous of the Sky Islands of southeastern Arizona, the Chiricahuas are a northern extension of the Sierra Madre of Mexico that rises to 9,786 feet out of

Chihuahuan Desert grassland at 4,600 feet. Vegetation zones include Engelmann Spruce and Aspen down to Ponderosa Pine, Chihuahua Pine, Arizona Pine, Gambel Oak, Silverleaf Oak, Arizona Cypress, and Alligator Juniper to yucca and mesquite grassland, with rich riparian forests of Arizona Sycamore, walnut, and cottonwood in the several well-watered canyons. This diversity of northern coniferous forest, Mexican pine and oak woodland, riparian zones, and high desert creates an incredibly rich and diverse biota. Black Bear, Mountain Lion, and Turkey are comparatively common. Mexican species include Javelina, Coatimundi, Coues White-tailed Deer (the densest population in the United States), Elegant and Eared Trogons, Olive Warbler, Thick-billed Parrot (recently reintroduced), many species of hummingbirds, Mexican Chickadee (found only here in the United States), Sulphur-bellied Flycatcher, and Flammulated Owl. A Jaguar was killed nearby in 1987. In fascinating contrast, northern species like the Goshawk and Golden-crowned Kinglet nest here. Endemic subspecies include the Chiricahua Red Squirrel (a Mexican species not closely related to the Red Squirrel in the United States) and Chiricahua Green Rock Rattlesnake.

Status: Overgrazing, ORVs, and heavy recreational use and development threaten the unprotected portion. There is potential for reintroduction of Jaguar, Lobo (Mexican Wolf, a subspecies of Gray Wolf), and Ocelot. In 1990, the Arizona Department of Game and Fish identified the Chiricahuas as one of four priority areas in Arizona for study as a site for Mexican Wolf reintroduction. (The other areas are the Blue Range, Galiuros, and Atascosas-Pajaritos.)

To create a total Wilderness of 300,000 acres, all of the contiguous roadless area should be added to the Wilderness, as should wild country in Chiricahua National Monument, the Coronado NF Cochise Head area, and BLM's Dos Cabezas country to the north and northwest, by closing dirt roads. (A 220,000-acre Chiricahua Wilderness was proposed by the first Presidential Conference on the Outdoors in 1928.)

PAJARITO MOUNTAINS 104,000 acres (also in Mexico)	
Designated Pajarita Wilderness Area Coronado National Forest	7,420
Additional Coronado NF roadless	37,000
Contiguous roadless in Mexico	60,000

Description: Central Arizona-Sonora border west of Nogales. Although one of the smaller Big Outside areas, the Pajarito Mountains are one of the most important areas in the United States for biological diversity. This low-mountain range (elevations from 5,370 feet at Montana Peak in the United States and 5,900 feet Matanza in Mexico to around 3,000 feet on the southern edge in Mexico) is the western extension of Sierra Madrean oak woodland. The oak woodland and oak savannah includes several species of Mexican oaks, Alligator Juniper, Mexican Piñon, yuccas, agaves, Arizona Madrone, and relatively healthy grassland. Riparian areas along the numerous canyons cutting through the rounded, sometimes rocky hills include Fremont Cottonwood, Arizona Sycamore, Arizona Walnut, and Velvet Ash (including the largest individuals I have seen). Saguaro, Ocotillo, and other Sonoran Desert species occur in the lower canyons and hillsides. Coues White-tailed Deer, Javelina, Mountain Lion, Coatimundi, Hooded Skunk, Antelope Jackrabbit, and Kit Fox are among the mammals. There have perhaps been more reports of Jaguar from this area than anywhere else in the United States in recent decades. A female with kittens was seen in 1990. Along with the Atascosa-Tumacacori Mountains to the north and the Buenos Aires National Wildlife Refuge to the west, the Pajaritos are one of the four leading sites in Arizona for reintroduction of Mexican Wolf. Chihuahuan Pronghorn have been reintroduced to the Refuge, as have Endangered Masked Bobwhite Quail; they may eventually wander into this roadless area. Birds include Elegant Trogon, Rose-throated Becard, Northern Beardless Tyrannulet, Ferruginous Pygmy Owl, Five-striped Sparrow, Varied Bunting, Tropical Kingbird, Green Kingfisher, Blue Grosbeck, Buff-collared Nightjar, Montezuma Quail, and many other rarities for the United States. Delightful Sycamore Canyon was the last habitat for the Endangered Tarahumara Frog in the United States. Arizona Coral Snake, Vine Snake, Sonoran Chub, and Sonoran Mud Turtle are other interesting species.

Status: The Pajarita Wilderness Area, including Sycamore Canyon, was established by the 1984 Arizona Wilderness Act. The rest of the Coronado NF area is just as wild, although a few rough dirt roads or Jeep trails are cherrystemmed. Small-scale mining activity on the west is a threat, as are ORVers (mostly road hunters) and continuing grazing. The cherrystem roads, particularly the "Summit Motorway," should be closed, and the rest of the NF area added to the Wilderness. Livestock grazing should be phased out to eliminate possible problems for reintroduction of Mexican Wolf. Over 50,000 acres of roadless NF land is separated from the Pajaritos by the dirt

Ruby-Nogales road along the northern boundary of this area. This area to the north should be protected as Wilderness and managed for Mexican Wolf, along with the 114,000-acre Buenos Aires National Wildlife Refuge to the west.

This area was overlooked for the first edition of *The Big Outside* because we did not realize how large the adjacent roadless area in Mexico was. The Mexican government should be encouraged to protect its portion of this splendid range. An International Biosphere Reserve of at least 500,000 acres should be established here, with primary emphasis on Mexican Wolf, Jaguar, Masked Bobwhite, Tarahumara Frog, and other rare and imperiled species.

Sonoran Desert

The symbol of the Sonoran Desert is the Saguaro, up to 50 feet tall and 200 years old. But the definer of the Sonoran Desert is rain. The surprising lushness of this arboreal (tree) desert is made possible by rain in two seasons—gentle winter rains from the Gulf of California and the Pacific, and summer thunderstorms (monsoons) from the Gulf of Mexico. Nevertheless, this is a desert; it sees many days over 100 degrees each year and only 2–12 inches of precipitation annually. The Sonoran Desert claims the southwestern quarter of Arizona and stretches south into Mexico. Management of the Big Outside is divided between the Fish and Wildlife Service, with Cabeza Prieta, Kofa, and Imperial National Wildlife Refuges; BLM; the Air Force and Marine Corps; the Tohono O'odham Indians; and the NPS, with Organ Pipe Cactus National Monument.

CABEZA PRIETA 1,657,000 acres	
Designated Cabeza Prieta Wilderness Area	803,418
Additional Cabeza Prieta NWR roadless	44,000
Goldwater Air Force Range roadless	645,000
Organ Pipe Cactus NM Wilderness and roadless	46,000
Released BLM WSA 5-40 (Gila Mountains)	8,765
BLM roadless Yuma Desert	10,000
Contiguous roadless in Mexico	100,000

Description: Southwestern Arizona along the Mexican border between Yuma and Ajo, south of Interstate 8. This peerless example of the Sonoran Desert is the most pristine large area in the lower forty-eight states. No native plant or animal has been extirpated; the two non-native birds and six introduced plants are rare. It is one of the driest and most remote areas in North America. The western end averages only 3 inches of annual precipitation. Wildlife includes Desert Bighorn Sheep, Antelope Jackrabbit, Endangered Sonoran Pronghorn; Coatimundi and Javelina (western edge of range for both); Gila Monster, Desert Tortoise; Ferruginous Pygmy Owl, Crested Caracara, Tropical Kingbird; Tiger, Mojave, Western Diamondback, and Sidewinder Rattlesnakes; Rosy Boa, Banded Sand Snake, Arizona Coral Snake; Flat-tailed Horned Lizard in the Yuma Dunes; Brown and White Pelicans, Wood Stork, and Magnificent Frigatebird as occasional overflyers; and Sonoran Green Toad and Casque-headed Frog. Diverse Sonoran Desert vegetation includes Elephant Tree, Kearney Sumac, Saguaro, palo verde, Creosote, Ironwood, Organ Pipe Cactus, Senita, and perhaps the largest Ocotillos in the United States. Six small, rugged, fault-block mountain ranges (of two kinds: a sierra-type of granitic and metamorphic rock, and a mesa-type of basaltic rock) are separated by wide alluvial valleys with sand dunes, lava flows, and dry lake beds. This is one of the few desert areas encompassing a series of ranges with roadless valleys between them. The nearest thing to a road crossing Cabeza Prieta is a sandy Jeep trail still known as the Camino del Diablo, or Way of the Devil, which bisects the area east-west. The Camino del Diablo was a feared route for forty-niners and others in historic times, and numerous graves mark this hot, waterless trail.

Status: The military uses the airspace for air-to-air gunnery training. This is disturbing to the visitor but has kept out ORVers, miners, ranchers, and other riffraff. The Goldwater Range is, however, threatened by on-the-ground military operations. A surprisingly large acreage is yet roadless on the military lands; most surface-disturbing activities take place on the northern border of the military range, near the interstate. The Marine Corps is more active with ground-disturbing activities on the western end and has particularly impacted the portion of the Yuma Dunes in its range. (The Yuma Dunes are the prime habitat for the Flat-tailed Horned Lizard.) The Air Force has developed a resource management plan that will help protect the wilderness values of its land.

Although the Camino del Diablo and the Mohawk Valley public access "roads" divide Cabeza Prieta into three sections, we have considered this as one roadless area because these "roads," although regularly used, are quite primitive and require four-wheel drive.

The Camino del Diablo and Mohawk Valley "roads" should be closed and blocked, and the entire area preserved as one Wilderness Area. The Sierra Club proposed this visionary idea in 1985, but quickly backed down in an effort to appear "credible" with Arizona politicians. A three-unit Wilderness Area totaling 803,418 acres was established by the 1990 Arizona Wilderness Act.

Mexico Highway 2 runs south of the international border separating the Cabeza from the Pinacate Desert and El Gran Desierto. (Approximately 100,000 acres of roadless land in Mexico are between Mexico Highway 2 and the border. A Border Patrol route follows much of the border. Since this route requires four-wheel drive and is not continuous—mountains interrupt it—we have considered the Mexican acreage an integral part of the Cabeza Prieta roadless area.) Although Pinacate is a Mexican National Park, management and patrolling is limited. A 6-million-acre International Sonoran Desert Wilderness Park, encompassing Pinacate, the Gran Desierto, Cabeza Prieta, and Organ Pipe Cactus NM, should be established, leaving a corridor for Mexico Highway 2, and financial support should be given to Mexico for protection of its part.

BATES MOUNTAINS 100,000 acres	
Designated Organ Pipe Cactus National Monument Wilderness Area	100,100

Description: Southwestern Arizona south of Ajo. This area of the Sonoran Desert south of Ajo features Organ Pipe Cactus, Saguaro, and Ironwood; sloping bajadas; and large desert washes. See Cabeza Prieta for general ecological description. Kino Peak, the high point, reaches 3,197 feet.

Status: A poor dirt road separates this area from Cabeza Prieta.

AJO MOUNTAINS 160,000 acres	
Organ Pipe Cactus National Monument Wilderness	102,300
Tohono O'odham Indian Reservation roadless	58,000

Description: Southwestern Arizona south of Ajo. This is a well-watered (10 inches a year), rugged Sonoran Desert mountain range on the Mexican border with bajadas and plains outwashing to around 1,600 feet. The high point is 4,808 feet, atop Ajo Peak. Organ Pipe Cactus, Saguaro, and palo verde are replaced at higher elevations by Ajo Oak and One-seed and Utah Junipers. The few riparian zones around tinajas in the striking canyons have hackberry trees and cattails. Much of this area consists of the more arid bajadas below the mountains—here the northern extension of the Central Gulf Coast phase of the Sonoran Desert grades into the Arizona Succulent Desert phase. Desert Bighorn, Javelina, Coues White-tailed Deer, Peregrine Falcon, Elf Owl, Arizona Coral Snake, Mexican Black-headed Snake, Desert Tortoise, and Gila Monster are among the vertebrates present.

Status: The portion on the Reservation is overgrazed—right to the crest of the Ajos. The Monument has not been grazed by livestock since the mid-1970s and is recovering.

BATAMOTE-SAUCEDA MOUNTAINS 214,000 acres	
Released BLM WSA 2-175 (Batamote Mountains)	56,385
Goldwater Air Force Range roadless	140,000
Tohono O'odham Indian Reservation roadless	18,000

Description: Southwestern Arizona northeast of Ajo. This is a little-visited area of low but rugged desert mountain ranges, large bajadas and valleys, colorful cliffs and buttes, and desert washes accentuated by parallel bands of green. Elevations rise from 1,400 feet to 3,466 feet. The Lower Sonoran vegetation includes Organ Pipe Cactus (at the northeastern limit of its range), Saguaro, dense stands of cholla, Elephant Tree, Ironwood, palo verde, and resplendent spring wildflowers. Gila Monster, Desert Tortoise, Desert Bighorn Sheep, Mountain Lion, Bobcat, and Coues White-tailed Deer live here. Temperatures vary from 120 degrees to (rarely) below freezing.

Status: BLM dropped its WSA because of opposition from Phelps-Dodge copper company. BLM claimed the area did not qualify because of the sights and sounds of nearby Ajo (a dying mining town) and its copper mines (the mines are now shut down). The military land is used for air-to-air gunnery practice (see Cabeza Prieta). Cattle graze throughout the area, and some Jeep trails and water wells have been developed by ranchers. ORVs present an increasing problem.

SAND TANK MOUNTAINS 119,000 acres	
Goldwater Air Force Range roadless	76,000
Tohono O'odham Indian Reservation roadless	41,000
BLM roadless	2,000

Description: Southwestern Arizona southeast of Gila Bend. See Batamote-Sauceda for general description. Squaw Tit, at 4,021 feet, is the high point; the low point is about 1,150 feet.

Status: Cattle graze both the military and the Indian lands; there are some Jeep trails and minor water developments used in the grazing operation on the edge of this roadless area, but the core is quite pristine. It is an air-to-air gunnery range. A dirt road separates it from the Batamote-Sauceda area to the west.

WOOLSEY PEAK–SIGNAL MOUNTAIN 101,000 acres	
Designated Woolsey Peak Wilderness Area (BLM)	61,000
Designated Signal Mountain Wilderness Area (BLM)	15,250
Released BLM WSAs	18,600
Additional BLM and state roadless	6,000

Description: Southwestern Arizona southwest of Phoenix. North of Gila Bend and the Painted Rock Reservoir on the Gila River in the stark, arid Gila Bend Mountains, Woolsey Peak, a large volcanic plug, rises 2,500 feet above the Gila River to 3,170 feet in elevation. Signal Mountain rises 1,200 feet above the surrounding bajada to 2,182 feet. A dozen basaltic mesas rise sharply in the central part of the area, as do rugged andesetic peaks and ridges in the west, and granitic formations in the east. Healthy Sonoran Desert vegetation of Saguaro–palo verde and Creosote-bursage with mesquite, Ironwood, and acacia in the washes grows here. The easternmost population of Bigelow Nolina is here, as is essential Desert Bighorn Sheep and Desert Tortoise habitat. A vehicle route (not a road) in Woolsey Wash divides the two mountains.

Status: The 1990 Arizona Wilderness Act established separate Wilderness Areas. Mining of dubious claims and ORVs are threats to the unprotected areas.

EAGLETAIL MOUNTAINS 126,000 acres	
Designated Eagletail Mountains Wilderness Area (BLM)	89,000
Released BLM WSA	30,700
Additional BLM, state, and private roadless	6,000

Description: Southwestern Arizona, west of Phoenix, east of Kofa NWR, and south of Interstate 10. Distinctive peak profiles in this jagged basaltic desert mountain range rise to 3,300 feet above the desert plain at 1,200 feet. Freestanding Courthouse Rock is a prominent monolith on the north side of the range. Arches and windows are abundant, as are shallow caves, which provide nesting for raptors. A perennial spring in a tight gorge creates a riparian habitat saturated with wildlife. A large, flat wild area lies between the Eagletails and Cemetery Ridge to the south. Coyote, Desert Bighorn Sheep, Javelina, and other wildlife typical of the Sonoran Desert live here. Palo verde–mixed cactus and Creosote-bursage are the main vegetative communities. A small relict population of juniper and oak on the north side of Eagletail Peak adds special importance to this part of the Sonoran Desert. Two plants are candidates for protection under the Endangered Species Act: *Peniocereus greggi* and *Opuntia wigginsi.* A 10,000-year-old rock art panel is present. This area affords a great feeling of spaciousness. Unfortunately, it also affords a startling view of a growing problem in southern Arizona: girdled Saguaros. Apparently, mice, which ordinarily eat grasses, are being forced by livestock overgrazing to eat cacti instead.

Status: The 1990 Arizona Wilderness Act established the Wilderness; much of the flat areas to the south and north was not included and is threatened by overgrazing and ORVs. Minor dirt roads to the west and south should be closed to combine the Eagletails with other BLM areas for addition to the Kofa NWR as a single 1.5-million-acre Wilderness.

*RM36: 740,000**

LITTLE HORN MOUNTAINS 111,000 acres	
Released BLM WSA 2-127	91,930
Additional BLM and state roadless	19,000

Description: Southwestern Arizona east of Kofa National Wildlife Refuge. The southern half of this roadless area consists of the highly dissected Little

Horn Mountains, which reach 3,100 feet. The core of the range is a basaltic mesa cut by two 800-foot-deep canyons and smaller side canyons; the latter expose colorful red, yellow, and buff Kofa volcanics, and feature a large natural arch. The northern half of the roadless area is the Ranegras Plain, a rare pristine flat area—unmarred by tires or cows—which drops to 1,300 feet. On the east are the rolling Nottbusch Valley and Palomas Plain with sandy washes. This area provides key Bighorn Sheep habitat and migration routes, as well as good nesting areas on the cliffs for raptors. See Kofa for general description.

Status: In one of its more indefensible decisions, the 1990 Arizona Desert Wilderness Act dropped this entire area from protection. Mining and ORVs are threats. Little Horn should be combined with other BLM areas and the Kofa NWR for a 1.5-million-acre Wilderness Area.

*RM36: 740,000**

NEW WATER MOUNTAINS 123,000 acres	
Designated New Water Mountains Wilderness Area (BLM)	21,680
Released BLM WSA 2-125	36,920
Designated Kofa NWR Wilderness Area, Kofa NWR roadless, and additional BLM roadless	64,000

Description: Southwestern Arizona, in the north end of Kofa National Wildlife Refuge south of Interstate 10 and southeast of Quartzsite. This area consists of mesalike basaltic mountains and typical Sonoran Desert vegetation. The Eagle Eye is a well-known large natural arch on the skyline that is visible from the interstate. Black Mesa is a large flat-topped butte reaching 3,639 feet. Desert Bighorn Sheep and Desert Tortoise populations are relatively dense. See Kofa for general description.

Status: ORVs and hobby mining threaten the non-Wilderness BLM lands. The BLM and Kofa Wilderness Areas were established (and the other BLM lands were released) by the 1990 Arizona Desert Wilderness Act. A power line divides this area from the main Kofa roadless area to the south. An attempt by BLM to transfer the Kofa NWR lands north of the power line corridor to BLM administration was defeated by conservation groups in 1988.

KOFA MOUNTAINS 797,000 acres	
Designated Kofa National Wildlife Refuge Wilderness Area and additional roadless	507,000
Yuma Proving Ground Marine Base roadless	190,000
BLM roadless	100,000

Description: Southwestern Arizona northeast of Yuma. The Kofa, Little Horn, Tank, Castle Dome, and Palomas mountains are volcanic desert ranges with jagged rock formations and natural arches. Large desert washes, alluvial plains, and wide valleys divide the mountains. Signal Peak reaches 4,877 feet (with views of Mt. San Jacinto in California), and the lowest elevations are around 800 feet. Distinctively shaped Castle Dome Peak is 3,788 feet and a landmark for many miles. Water is limited to rock tanks or potholes in the mountains, and a few seeps. Precipitation averages 3–8 inches a year. Kofa is a crucial habitat for Desert Bighorn Sheep. Other wildlife includes Gila Monster, Desert Tortoise, Mule Deer, Kit Fox, Golden Eagle, Prairie Falcon, Gambel's Quail, and Mourning and White-winged Doves. Mountain Lion and Javelina are rare. The only wild palms in Arizona (California Fan Palm) grow in the canyons of the Kofa Mountains. Vegetation is otherwise typical of the Sonoran Desert with Saguaro–palo verde, Creosote-bursage to yucca-grassland associations. Also present is the Kofa Mountain Barberry, a rare indigenous plant. Turbinella Oak inhabits some of the canyons. Species at the western or southern limit of their range are Arizona Coral Snake, Black-tailed Rattlesnake, Curve-billed Thrasher, and White Thorn Acacia.

Status: The major defeat in the 1990 Arizona Desert Wilderness Act involved Kofa National Wildlife Refuge. Although 516,300 acres of the 665,400 acre Refuge were designated as Wilderness, 326 miles of dirt road and Jeep trail were corridored or cherrystemmed out of the Wilderness. One good aspect was that the southern end of the King Valley road was included in the Wilderness, thereby connecting the two large Kofa roadless areas we identified in the first edition of *The Big Outside:* the 597,000-acre Kofa and the 200,000-acre Castle Dome.

ORV enthusiasts, posing as hunters, mounted a major campaign to prevent Wilderness designation for the Refuge. The compromise was to designate Wilderness but with non-Wilderness corridors for the Jeep trails (some of which had previously been closed by the Refuge). As it now stands, this very large desert roadless area of 797,000 acres is broken by corridored vehicle routes (not roads) into five units. The large Kofa Mountains Wilderness unit has long cherrystems for very rough and sometimes very faint vehicle routes, and the large Castle Dome Mountains Wilderness unit has four such cherrystems. Three good-size areas in this roadless area were not designated as Wilderness. The continued Jeep access through much of Kofa compromises its integrity as Wilderness. The effort to protect Kofa is not yet over (fortunately, the FWS can close these corridors to vehicle use if it so chooses—Congress did not mandate that they be left open for Jeeps).

Three other units of Wilderness were designated in Kofa NWR besides those included in this roadless area. They are separated from the main Kofa roadless area by constructed dirt roads. The 516,300-acre Wilderness total includes these areas. One of them is part of the New Water Mountains roadless area above; the other two form roadless areas smaller than 100,000 acres and are not included in this inventory.

Cattle were removed in the 1970s. Congress closed Kofa to new mining claims in 1988. The status of the Marine Base area is uncertain.

If minor dirt roads and Jeep trails are closed, a single Wilderness of 1.5 million acres, including the BLM areas to the east, could be established.

*RM36: 740,000**

LOWER COLORADO RIVER 462,000 acres (also in California)	
Designated Imperial Refuge Wilderness Area (AZ)	9,220
Imperial National Wildlife Refuge roadless (AZ and CA)	14,780
Designated Trigo Mountain Wilderness Area (BLM, AZ)	29,095
Released WSA 5-23B and additional roadless (BLM, AZ)	36,905
Yuma Proving Grounds Marine Base roadless (AZ)	235,000
Picacho State Recreation Area roadless (CA)	5,000
Ft. Yuma Indian Reservation roadless (CA)	2,000
BLM WSAs CDCA 356, 355A, 355 and additional BLM, private, and state roadless (CA)	130,000

Description: Southwestern Arizona and southeastern California between Yuma and Blythe, including 29 miles of the Colorado River and adjacent desert mountains in Arizona and California. Elevations rise from 200 feet to

2,772 feet, on Mohave Peak (Arizona), and 2,177 feet, on Quartz Peak (California). This area represents the best opportunity to preserve a portion of the lower Colorado River. This exceptionally diverse desert area ranges from backwater lakes (Island, Norton's, and Adobe Lakes) and riparian vegetation along the Colorado (Cattail, Bulrush, Arrowweed, mesquite, willow, cottonwood) to arid, harsh Sonoran and Colorado Desert topography and vegetation (Saguaro, Ocotillo, palo verde, bursage, Desert Holly, Desert Lavender, Smoketree, Ironwood) in the rocky Trigo and Chocolate Mountains. This is the only large roadless area that includes parts of the Colorado River below the Grand Canyon. It features an ecological transect from the Sonoran Desert with Saguaro (in Arizona) to the Colorado Desert without Saguaro (in California). Yuma Wash and other large desert washes cut through the mountains. Cliffs rise 800 feet above stretches of the river. The mountains offer much-needed habitat for the beleaguered Desert Bighorn. This is one of the few areas in the lower Sonoran Desert able to support a Mountain Lion population—in this case, the Yuma Puma, an Endangered subspecies. Gila Monster, Sidewinder, Beaver, Muskrat, Gray Fox, Peregrine Falcon, White Pelican, Sandhill Crane, Double-crested Cormorant, Osprey, Bald Eagle, Tundra Swan, Crissal Thrasher, and other natives form a unique assemblage of creatures. Prime habitat for the Endangered Yuma Clapper Rail is here. The Endangered Colorado Squawfish and Threatened Razorback Sucker are present in the river. Abundant waterfowl, including herons, egrets, ducks, and geese, feed on the river.

Status: Most of the Imperial NWR roadless area in Arizona (with the major exception of the river itself and backwater lakes and marshes—which the FWS wants to dredge to "enhance" waterfowl habitat) was designated Wilderness by the 1990 Arizona Desert Wilderness Act, as was the Trigo Mountain Wilderness. California BLM proposes a 5,418-acre Picacho Peak Wilderness, a 24,902-acre Indian Pass Wilderness, and no Wilderness for the Little Picacho area. The Cranston bill (see California introduction) would establish 7,300-acre Picacho, 34,420-acre Little Picacho, and 35,320-acre Indian Pass Wildernesses.

In 1972, the Sierra Club and The Wilderness Society proposed 23,900 acres of the Refuge for Wilderness, including the Colorado River above Picacho State Recreation Area. The river below Picacho was recommended for National Wild and Scenic River status. Conservation groups in Arizona and

California need to return to this original stand and develop a comprehensive Wilderness proposal including the Colorado River and adjacent lands in both states.

The Trigo Mountains Wilderness Area, unfortunately, is split in half by a non-Wilderness corridor for a vehicle route along Clip Wash.

The status of the Marine Corps Base land is uncertain (the estimate of what is actually roadless here is rough). This area deserves far more attention from conservationists. FWS plans to manipulate the Colorado River should be opposed. ORVs and petty miners threaten the BLM lands (old mining districts are included).

A road to Picacho State Recreation Area is cherrystemmed through the California portion. Other dirt roads and Jeep trails also penetrate this wide-open desert area, and motorboats are permitted on the river. Motorboats should be prohibited from this stretch of the Colorado River—which otherwise provides an excellent canoe run.

Selenium contamination has recently been reported in the river, and fishing is not advised. Pelicans have little choice in the matter, however. Irrigated agriculture (in this case, the lettuce and melon fields around Blythe) carries the seeds of its own destruction with heavy metal and salt buildup. While it can be argued that there is justice in this, it is a terrible comment on our stewardship that we poison everything around us. In 1991, ecology professor Bob Ohmart warned that without drastic measures, such as removing upstream dams and restoring the normal flooding to flush out salts, the Lower Colorado would become as inhospitable to life as a concrete canal. Willows and cottonwoods are in serious decline and will soon disappear. With the loss of canopy trees, birds like Bell's Vireo, Summer Tanager, and Yellow-billed Cuckoo will vanish. Here, then, is another grim reminder of how distant forces can unravel the viability of even large wild areas.

Nonetheless, read the chapter "Green Lagoons" (about the Colorado River delta in the 1920s) in Aldo Leopold's *A Sand County Almanac.* This roadless area is the closest we can come today.

Northern Sonoran and Mojave Deserts

The Sonoran Desert grades into the Mojave Desert in west-central Arizona. This is BLM country.

BIG HORN MOUNTAINS 100,000 acres	
Designated Big Horn Mountains Wilderness Area (BLM)	20,600
Designated Hummingbird Springs Wilderness Area (BLM)	30,170
Released BLM WSAs 2–100 and 2-99	39,247
Additional BLM, state, and private roadless	10,000

Description: West-central Arizona west of Phoenix. This scenic Sonoran Desert range reaches 3,418 feet on Sugarloaf Mountain and 3,480 feet on Big Horn Peak. These peaks rise 1,800 feet above the desert plain, which includes a large roadless flat. Tight canyons twist through the mountains. Sheer cliff faces, fins, and a large natural arch are among the outstanding sights. Vegetation is diverse, with Creosote and bursage on the flats; dense Ironwood, mesquite, and acacia along the washes; and palo verde, Saguaro, and other cacti on the higher ground. Four rare plants inhabit the area. Cliffs provide critical nesting habitat for Golden Eagle, Prairie Falcon, Barn Owl, and Great Horned Owl. Other wildlife includes Desert Bighorn, Kit Fox, Desert Tortoise (crucial habitat), Gila Monster, and Cooper's Hawk.

Status: A bulldozer scrape separates the two Wilderness Areas, but it should not be considered a road. The 1990 Arizona Desert Wilderness Act established the Wildernesses and released the other BLM acreage. Mining, ORVs, and continued cattle grazing threaten the rest of the roadless area. In a few years, urban development spilling over from the Phoenix abomination will lap up to these ranges—without Wilderness designation for the easily violated flat terrain around the protected mountains, ORVers from these future subdivisions, with their trash, guns, and disregard for things natural will destroy much of the area.

HARCUVAR MOUNTAINS EAST 101,000 acres	
Harcuvar Mountains Wilderness Area (BLM)	25,287
Released BLM WSA 2-75	49,501
Additional BLM, state, and private roadless	26,000

Description: West-central Arizona, between Phoenix and Parker Dam. Smith Peak, at 5,242 feet, is the highest part of the mountain mass. This large Sonoran Desert mountain rises sharply 2,800 feet from the desert floor; this roadless area is its eastern half. An unimportant paved road crossing over

Cunningham Pass separates it from the Harcuvar Mountains West. Wildlife includes Desert Bighorn Sheep, Mountain Lion, Kit Fox, and Golden Eagle. A special feature is an isolated and undisturbed area of interior chaparral with extensive stands of several native perennial grasses providing habitat to Fishhook Cactus, Gilbert's Skink, Rosy Boa, and Desert Night Lizard. Vegetative communities also include Creosote and bursage, Saguaro and palo verde, mixed thorn scrub, and mixed riparian scrub.

Status: The minimal Wilderness Area was established by the 1990 Arizona Desert Wilderness Act. Threats include, along with the standard ORVs and prospecting, additional electronic communication sites on the range's crest and the construction of a gas pipeline along the western boundary.

HARCUVAR MOUNTAINS WEST 100,000 acres	
Released BLM roadless areas 2-90, 91, 92	91,979
Additional BLM, state, and private roadless	8,000

Description: The western end of the Harcuvar Mountains (see Harcuvar Mountains East for general description). This area culminates in Harcuvar Peak, at 4,618 feet. It also includes the Granite Wash Mountains.

Status: BLM dropped this entire area from Wilderness consideration because of mineral potential. Three rough Jeep trails cross it. Mining and ORVs threaten it.

MOHAVE WASH 125,000 acres	
Released BLM WSA 5-7C/48/2–52 with state and private roadless	113,245
Additional BLM and Havasu NWR, state, and private roadless	12,000

Description: West-central Arizona east of Lake Havasu City and Parker Dam in the Bill Williams Mountains. This varied desert area includes Mohave Springs Mesa, Castaneda Hills, Black Mountain, and the Mohave Wash drainage. Elevations drop from 2,733 feet to under 500 feet. The Mojave Desert vegetation includes Creosote, Red Barrel Cactus, Boxthorn, and Ocotillo, with Ironwood, palo verde, and Smoketree in the washes. Topographically, it consists of rough mountains, volcanic tablelands, large desert washes, and cliffs and spires along the Bill Williams River on the southern edge of the area. An important part of this roadless area is the marshland of the Bill Williams River delta in Havasu NWR, which provides crucial habitat for the Endangered Yuma Clapper Rail and other sensitive and rare water birds. Wildlife also includes Desert Bighorn, Desert Tortoise, and other typical Mojave Desert species.

Status: This entire area was released from further Wilderness consideration and from protection by the 1990 Arizona Desert Wilderness Act. Efforts to protect it, however, should not be abandoned. With a little vision, this area could be combined with the Arrastra Mountain Wilderness to the east and other BLM Wilderness and roadless areas in the Bill Williams River country, simply by closing a few Jeep trails and unnecessary dirt roads, for a million-acre Wilderness. ORVs, trapping, overgrazing, and hobby mining are continuing and potentially major threats.

*RM36: 700,000**

ARRASTRA MOUNTAIN 225,000 acres	
Designated Arrastra Mountain Wilderness Area (BLM)	126,760
Designated Tres Alamos Wilderness Area (BLM)	8,700
Released BLM WSAs	7,045
Additional BLM, state, and private roadless	82,000

Description: West-central Arizona east of Parker Dam. This is one of the most diverse and exceptional desert wildlands in North America. Arrastra Mountain in the Poachie Range rises to 4,807 feet; Ives Peak in the Black Mountains on the southeastern end of the area rises to 4,072 feet; and Sawyer Peak in the Tres Alamos hits 4,293 feet. The Big Sandy and Santa Maria Rivers (their elevations drop to 1,500 feet at the high-water mark for Alamo Reservoir, where they come together to form the Bill Williams River) are intermittent desert rivers with over 20 miles of rare riparian vegetation, including willow, Fremont Cottonwood, Arizona Sycamore, Arizona Walnut, Red Barberry, columbine, monkeyflower, and cattail. The extensive mesquite bosque along the Santa Maria has been described by BLM as the "largest, healthiest undisturbed habitat of this type in the state." People's Canyon is a perennially flowing desert creek with lush vegetation—impenetrable and junglelike in places—including Arizona Madrone far north of its normal range and an orchid and tropical fern found elsewhere in Arizona only in two sites in the southeastern part of the state. Narrow, winding canyons drop into the rivers from the mountains (Date Creek cuts a 200-foot-deep gorge in the Tres Alamos Wilderness); there are also several perennial springs and tinajas with associated riparian vegetation. One spring creates several large pools and a 60-foot waterfall. The Artillery Mountains west of the Big Sandy are extremely rugged and dominated by the red spire of Artillery Peak.

This remote and little-used area has tremendous vegetative variety as a result of its being the juncture of the Sonoran and Mojave Deserts. Six distinct plant communities are present, and this may be the only place on Earth where Saguaro, palo verde, mesquite, Joshua Tree, oak, and juniper grow side by side. The area affords a large tract of prime Desert Tortoise habitat, and high potential for a healthy herd of Desert Bighorn Sheep (they have been reintroduced in the Ives Peak area). Among the 292 vertebrate species found in the area (a large number for a desert area) are Bald Eagle, Zone-tailed Hawk, Peregrine Falcon, Harris's Hawk, Snowy Egret, Osprey; Round-tailed Chub, Desert Pupfish, Gila Topminnow; Mountain Lion; Desert Tortoise and Gila Monster. The two dozen significant archaeological sites include exceptional petroglyph panels in Black Canyon, a winding volcanic gorge with springs, in the northern part of the roadless area.

Status: The 1990 Arizona Desert Wilderness Act established a 126,760-acre Arrastra Mountain Wilderness Area (including the Ives Peak WSA) and, separated by a corridor for a rough Jeep trail, an 8,700-acre Tres Alamos Wilderness. The additional BLM land was released. Conservationists should continue to work to close the Jeep trail and to add acreage to the Wilderness. Arrastra Mountain could be made the core of a large Sonoran Desert Wilderness Preserve of one million acres by closing minor dirt roads in the area and adding roadless areas west to Mohave Wash.

BLM is currently developing a grazing management plan for the Santa Maria River region. Grazing is highly detrimental in this harsh environment and should be eliminated. ORVs and hobby mining are other threats. BLM will need to actively patrol the Santa Maria River in the Wilderness to prevent violation by morons on ATVs—who had discovered it before the Wilderness bill passed.

*RM36: 700,000**

AQUARIUS MOUNTAINS SOUTH 120,000 acres	
Private, BLM, and state roadless	120,000

Description: West-central Arizona east of Wickiup. This is an area of checkerboarded land ownership in the Aquarius Mountains. Mojave Desert vegetation phases into piñon and juniper with elevations from 2,600 feet to 5,000 feet. See Aquarius Mountains North for detailed description.

Status: See Aquarius Mountains North. This area is divided from Aquarius Mountains North by a minor dirt road, and from the released Burro Creek WSA to the south by a dirt road, pipeline, and power-line corridor.

*RM36: 620,000**

AQUARIUS MOUNTAINS NORTH (TROUT CREEK) 190,000 acres	
Mixed state and private roadless	190,000

Description: West-central Arizona east of Kingman. This is a virtually unknown area in the Trout Creek drainage of the Aquarius Mountains south of Interstate 40 and east of U.S. 93. Land ownership is checkerboarded state and private. Trout Creek is a spectacular canyon with perennial water. Vegetation ranges from Mojave Desert scrub to sparse Ponderosa Pine with extensive areas of piñon and juniper in between, along with important riparian zones. Wildlife includes Black Bear, Mountain Lion, Bighorn, Mule Deer, and Golden Eagle. Elevations range from 3,000 feet to 6,000 feet.

Status: Because of land ownership, little is known about this area, but it may be one of the more important wildlands in Arizona. There are a million acres of wild backcountry in the Aquarius Mountains between Interstate 40 on the north and the mining town of Bagdad on the south, crossed only by a handful of primitive dirt roads and Jeep trails, and dotted with a few range "improvements" for cattle grazing. The southern end of the Aquarius Mountains has BLM land, including the two-unit Upper Burro Creek Wilderness Area of 27,900 acres and a released BLM WSA downstream in Burro Creek. A roadless area of 120,000 acres lies between the Burro Creek country and this Trout Creek area (see Aquarius Mountains South). Conservationists should explore potential ways of preserving this entire region.

*RM36: 620,000**

WARM SPRINGS (BLACK MESA) 145,000 acres	
Designated Warm Springs Wilderness Area (BLM)	90,600
Released BLM Warm Springs WSA 2-28/29	24,200
Additional BLM, state, and private roadless	30,000

Description: Northwestern Arizona, west of Kingman. Black Mesa is a huge basaltic mesa surrounded by sloping bajadas and colorful badlands. Canyons cut the mesa to the south; the largest of these, Warm Springs Wash, has three small warm springs. Farther south is a long, flat plain littered with basaltic boulders that make travel difficult. The mesa rises 1,800 feet above the desert plain on the east. A fine array of Mojave Desert vegetation is represented, with impressive cholla cactus stands, Mojave Yucca, and Bigelow Nolina on the mesa; Blackbrush, Mexican Bladdersage, and other forbs in the northern part; and Creosote, mesquite, palo verde, Ocotillo, cactus, Smoke Tree, and Cat Claw Acacia to the south. This is an important lambing area for Desert Bighorn. Other sensitive wildlife includes Kit Fox, Desert Rosy Boa, Gila Monster, Desert Tortoise, Gilbert's Skink, Desert Night Lizard, Le Conte's Thrasher, Peregrine and Prairie Falcons, and Golden Eagle. Few humans visit this area.

Status: The 1990 Arizona Desert Wilderness Act left open a Jeep trail from the south into the center of the designated Wilderness Area at the warm springs. This teeth-rattling vehicle route should be closed to protect the springs, which are valuable for wildlife. The large population of feral burros should be removed. BLM claims that the Jeep trail to the warm springs is necessary for burro removal. If this is so, it should be open only for official use and permanently closed after the burros are eliminated. Mining is a major threat on the western side of the area.

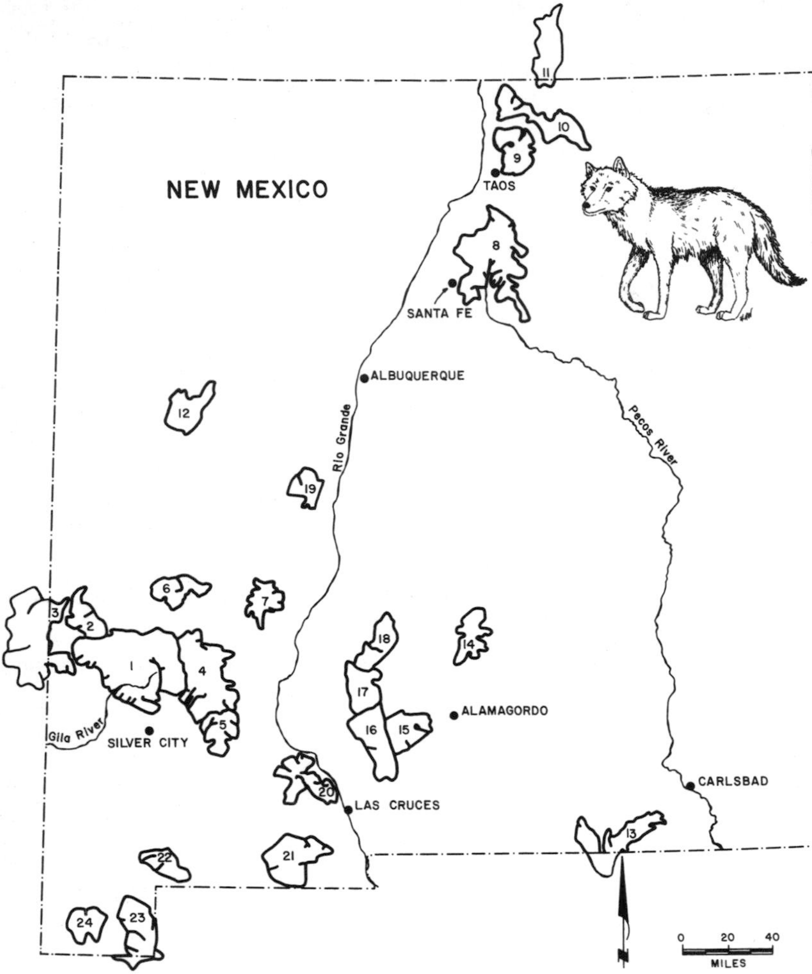

1. Gila
2. Devils Creek
3. Blue Range
4. Aldo Leopold
5. Sawyers Peak
6. Continental Divide
7. Apache Kid
8. Pecos
9. Wheeler Peak
10. Latir Peak–Ponil Creek
11. Culebra
12. El Malpais
13. Guadalupe Escarpment
14. Sierra Blanca
15. White Sands
16. San Andres Mts. South
17. San Andres Mts. Central
18. San Andres Mts. North
19. Sierra Ladrones
20. Robledo–Las Uvas Mts.
21. West Potrillo Mts.
22. Cedar Mts.
23. Big Hatchet–Alamo Hueco
24. Animas Mts.

New Mexico

Our sense of wilderness aesthetics, of what is beautiful in wild nature, was formed largely in the European Alps. As a society, we are still mired in that medieval approach to landscape appreciation. Even the Jim Watts among us can marvel at the grandeur of the Tetons, the majesty of Mt. Rainier, the magnificence of the Colorado Rockies. As a nation, our first efforts at preservation were directed not toward wilderness or ecological integrity, but rather toward the spectacles and curiosities of nature—Yosemite Valley, Yellowstone, the Grand Canyon.

It is far more difficult to preserve the commonplace, the wild area of unremarkable scenery, a plant or animal that does not inspire human emotions with its beauty or nobility. It is one thing to protect the Bald Eagle, quite another to preserve Goodding's Onion.

This being so, the first effort anywhere in the world to specifically preserve an area for its *wilderness* qualities is all the more noteworthy because it occurred in what is arguably the least spectacular of the Western states—

New Mexico—and in an area—the headwaters of the Gila River—that, while not unattractive, is certainly not cut with the classic Alpen mold. There are no peaks rising grandly above timberline, no jewel-like lakes sparkling in glacier-carved basins.

Land preservation in New Mexico represents a maturing of the European approach to nature appreciation. Sunsets here are stunning; there is a striking starkness about the land, the blending of three cultures—Indian, Spanish, and Anglo—is quaint; but overall, the spell this land casts is subtle, subliminal. While the hordes rush to Niagara Falls or to the Matterhorn, some of the finest of our kind—D. H. Lawrence, Aldo Leopold, Georgia O'Keeffe, Frank Waters, Mary Austin, Edward Abbey—have been drawn to New Mexico.

New Mexico has less potential Wilderness and fewer large roadless areas than do most Western states, and it would behoove us to inquire into this lack. One might first suggest that although New Mexico is a very large state, fully one third of it is in the Great Plains, where mechanized agriculture and the private ownership of land virtually preclude large tracts of wilderness. But the same can be said for Colorado, Wyoming, or Montana.

Two other factors offer better explanations. For one, New Mexico has been inhabited and used by Europeans longer than have other areas of the West. The Spanish have been in northern New Mexico continuously since 1693, and thus New Mexican villagers have used the high mountains for sheep pasturage and have diverted the streams for irrigation for almost three hundred years. More significantly, the first cattle frontier after Texas was New Mexico, and ranchers in New Mexico today tend to be more "Texan" than ranchers in other Western states. When the history of the cowboy is little more than one hundred years long, a decade's head start is significant.

The second factor, which is more important, is closely tied to this Texas ranching heritage. New Mexico's landscape and weather make it more accessible than the rest of the West: Its deserts are not as hot or barren as California's; its winters are not as frigid or long as Montana's; its mountains are lusher and better watered than Nevada's. In this gentler terrain, ranchers have been able to punch roads to more places than they have in other Western states. Moreover, grazing in much of New Mexico is year-round, whereas in the Northern Rockies, ranchers herd their cows up into the mountains for only a few summer months and run the operation by horseback. To make much of arid New Mexico available for twelve-month cattle grazing, stock ponds have been built to capture runoff; this requires road access.

So, the reason there is less of the Big Outside in New Mexico is that the land is dry, but not too dry; and rough, but not too rough. Also, cattlemen here have had a longer time to fully exploit the public lands.

New Mexico, ecologically, is a complex state, a meeting ground of ecosystems: the Great Plains from the east, the Chihuahuan Desert from the southeast, the Sierra Madre from the south, the Sonoran Desert from the southwest, the Great Basin and Colorado Plateau from the northwest, and the Rocky Mountains from the north.

Wilderness preservation has a long and active history in New Mexico. The Forest Service administratively established its first Wilderness Area—the Gila—here in 1924. Senator Clinton P. Anderson of New Mexico shepherded the Wilderness Act during its consideration in the Senate. The nation's first Wild and Scenic River—the Rio Grande—was established in 1968 in northern New Mexico. Except for White Sands National Monument and San Andres National Wildlife Refuge, the National Parks and Wildlife Refuges in New Mexico that qualify have had Wilderness Areas established. The Bisti led the way nationally for BLM Wilderness, and New Mexico is developing one of the first statewide BLM Wilderness bills. Beating Colorado by a few days in 1980, New Mexico produced the first post–RARE II National Forest Wilderness bill.

This is not to say that by pioneering Wilderness preservation, New Mexico has fared well. Of 2,137,776 acres considered in RARE II, the New Mexico Wilderness Study Committee recommended 1,816,000 for Wilderness, but only 609,060 were designated in the 1980 New Mexico Wilderness bill (117,530 acres were left for further study). New Mexico BLM has recommended Wilderness for less than 500,000 acres (counting intermixed state and private lands). The New Mexico BLM Wilderness Coalition (including the Sierra Club and other groups), in an excellent 230-page book,[1] has countered with a proposal for 2.3 million acres. New Mexico Earth First! has upped the ante by calling for 5.3 million acres of BLM Wilderness. The New Mexico congressional delegation may introduce a bill in 1992, and what it will be is anybody's guess—probably not much, given the stranglehold anti-Wilderness Senator Pete Domenici and Representative Joe Skeen have on any legislation. New Mexico conservationists are also discussing additional National Forest Wilderness legislation.

[1] *Wildlands, New Mexico BLM Wilderness Coalition Statewide Proposal* is available from the New Mexico BLM Wilderness Coalition, PO Box 712, Placitas, NM 87043.

As elsewhere, the timbered roadless areas in New Mexico's National Forests are under attack by the Forest Service and the logging industry. Although timber sales in New Mexico are usually below cost, logging is a serious threat to roadless areas on the Gila, Santa Fe, and Carson NFs. In 1991, the Sierra Club Legal Defense Fund filed suit against logging in New Mexico and Arizona, on the basis of the impact of logging on forest ecosystems. See the Arizona introduction for details.

Generally, however, it is ranching and off-road vehicles that pose the most pervasive dangers to the Big Outside in New Mexico. Continued overgrazing; the construction of additional fences, stock ponds, and pipelines; and the destruction of piñon-juniper forest by chaining and herbiciding threaten many areas. ORVs and the impacts they bring—soil erosion, noise, poaching, trapping, and the like—are damaging sensitive habitats throughout the state. Mining and oil and gas development are problems for several specific areas.

Aldo Leopold challenged New Mexico and the nation in 1924 when he engineered the designation of the Gila Wilderness. That challenge—to radically alter our fundamental relationship with the land, to become again a plain member of the biotic community—has yet to be met.

Mogollon Highlands

The Mogollon Highlands, consisting of the Gila and Apache National Forests in west-central New Mexico and east-central Arizona, contain one of the key wilderness ecosystem complexes in the nation. This region is significant on the same level as are the Greater Yellowstone, Northern Continental Divide, Central Idaho, Everglades, and North Cascades ecosystems, and represents the best opportunity for an ecologically complete Wilderness in the Southwest. It is the area that taught Aldo Leopold to "think like a mountain."

GILA 736,000 acres	
Designated Gila Wilderness Area (Gila NF)	569,600
Additional Gila NF roadless	145,000
Gila Cliff Dwellings NM roadless	500
Private, state, and BLM roadless to southwest	21,000

Description: Southwestern New Mexico north of Silver City. The Gila (*HEE-la*) was the first designated Wilderness Area anywhere in the world, receiving Forest Service administrative protection in 1924 at the urging of Aldo Leopold. It encompasses the rugged headwaters of the Gila River, which form several spectacular riverine canyons; the Mogollon, Diablo, and Jerky Mountain Ranges; and rolling mesa country with wide-open grasslands. Elevations range from 4,700 feet, on the Gila River, to 10,892 feet, on Whitewater Baldy. This is the transition area between the Rocky Mountains, Mexico's Sierra Madre, the Chihuahuan Desert, the Sonoran Desert, the Great Plains, the Great Basin, and the Mexican Plateau. The fauna demonstrates this rich collection of ecotones—Mountain Lion, Black Bear, Elk, Rocky Mountain Bighorn Sheep, Mule and White-tailed Deer, Javelina, Coatimundi, Pronghorn, Arizona Coral Snake, Gila Monster, Turkey, Blue Grouse, Common Black Hawk, Zone-tailed Hawk, Red-faced Warbler, Northern Goshawk, Mexican Spotted Owl, and Bald Eagle. Vegetation includes riparian zones of Fremont and Narrowleaf Cottonwoods, Arizona Sycamore, Arizona Walnut, and Arizona Alder; up through chaparral (dominated by manzanita) and piñon-juniper-oak woodland (including huge Alligator Junipers); forest of Ponderosa Pine and Gambel Oak; to Englemann and Colorado Blue Spruces, Douglas-fir, White and Corkbark Firs, and large Aspen stands. There are more species of deciduous trees here (over twenty) than anywhere else in the West. Chihuahua Pine reaches its northeastern limit, and the world's largest remaining virgin Ponderosa Pine forest is here. Because the high country was never glaciated, it has a different appearance than high country in other large Western mountain areas. Over 300,000 acres of the designated Wilderness are no longer grazed by cattle or sheep, since the grazing leases have been retired. A number of archaeological sites, including several Mimbres phase cliff dwellings, are in the Wilderness.

Status: Logging, ORVs, and overgrazing threaten the unprotected portions. Grazing has been particularly atrocious along the Gila River in the Gila Wilderness, where it is damaging the riparian forest so essential for the biodiversity of the area. Cattle were removed in the fall of 1990, but it is unknown whether they will be allowed back along the river; the river corridor should be permanently closed to livestock grazing. A couple of cowmen to the south of the Wilderness are agitating for "control" of Elk, which are "robbing" them of "their" grass. ORVers are pushing for a road along the lower 6 miles of the East Fork of the Gila River, which was deleted from the Wilderness in 1980 at their insistence—several of them own cabins on a small private inholding up the East Fork. Small-scale mining poses a concern in the northeast, southeast, and southwest corners of the roadless area.

The Gila is one of the best potential sites for reintroduction of the Grizzly Bear, Mexican Wolf, Jaguar, and River Otter. The endemic and Endangered Gila Trout has been successfully restored to several streams in the Wilderness.

Closure of a narrow gravel road (the North Star Road) could reunite the Gila and Aldo Leopold Wildernesses into a single Wilderness Area of over 1.2 million acres. Several hundred thousand acres of additional wild country could be added by the closing of minor dirt roads to the north. At the very least, conservationists need to campaign to add all contiguous NF roadless acreage to the Wilderness.

*RM27: 1,327,360**

DEVILS CREEK 100,000 acres	
Gila National Forest roadless	100,000

Description: Southwestern New Mexico south of Reserve. This northern extension of the Mogollon Mountains is separated from the Gila Wilderness by a narrow but partially paved road and the old mining town of Mogollon. Mineral Creek, Devils Creek, and the San Francisco River form deep canyons in the roadless area. Wildlife and vegetation are similar to that of the Gila Wilderness. Elevations range from 5,000 feet in canyon bottoms to 9,900 feet on the slopes of Bearwallow Mountain. The ghost town of Cooney, which was wiped out by the Apache warrior Victorio in 1880, is included. Goodding's Onion is a state Threatened species present; the Mexican Spotted Owl, Flammulated Owl, and Northern Goshawk also find refuge here.

Status: The FS opposes protection, and proposes to build a high-grade logging road to Bearwallow that would cut through the Goodding's Onion habitat. Logging (of both mixed conifer and Ponderosa Pine), ORVs, and grazing are steadily encroaching on this area. At least two timber sales, Bearwallow and BS, are scheduled in the southeastern corner of the roadless area during 1992. If they occur, this roadless area will drop below the 100,000-acre threshold. Logging is devastating habitat for Spotted Owl and Northern Goshawk on the Gila NF, but extreme pressure is on the FS to maximize the cut in order to reopen the Reserve sawmill and put unemployed local loggers back to work. One Jeep trail crosses this roadless area.

BLUE RANGE–SAN FRANCISCO 505,000 acres (also in Arizona)	
See Arizona for description and status	

ALDO LEOPOLD (BLACK RANGE) 409,000 acres	
Designated Aldo Leopold Wilderness Area (Gila NF)	211,300
Additional Gila NF roadless	166,000
Private, state, and BLM roadless to east and southwest	32,000

Description: Southwestern New Mexico west of Truth or Consequences. The Black Range is a 9,000–10,000-foot-high crest running north to south with steep canyons and rough ridges spilling down its sides. The high point is 10,165-foot McKnight Mountain, with low elevations of 6,000 feet along the east side. The area is west of the Rio Grande Valley and directly east of the Gila Wilderness, of which it was a part until being split off by the North Star Road in the early 1930s. Deep mixed conifer forests along the crest give the range its name. Cottonwood-and-sycamore riparian forests (northeastern limit of Arizona Sycamore) and mesquite grassland cover the lower elevations. Ecologically, the area is similar to the Gila and Blue Range. An article in the *Denver Post Empire Magazine,* in 1976, billed the Black Range as "The Wildest Wilderness in the West."

Status: Logging threatens the northern part of this area. The southwestern portion was left out of the Wilderness Area in 1980 because of mining potential. Portions of the area are overgrazed, including some canyon bottoms important for their riparian vegetation. ORVs are penetrating some of the unprotected canyons. With closure of the North Star Road, the Black Range could be combined with the Gila into a 1.2-million-acre Wilderness Area. At the very least, all contiguous roadless NF acreage should be added to the Wilderness.

*RM27: 1,327,360**

SAWYERS PEAK 121,000 acres	
Gila NF roadless	73,000
Private, state, and BLM roadless	48,000

Description: Southwestern New Mexico south of Kingston and east of Silver City. South of the Aldo Leopold Wilderness (separated by a narrow paved road over Emory Pass), this area in the Mimbres Mountains is the southern extension of the Black Range. Like the Black Range, it is a crest cut by canyons to the west and east. The high point is 9,668-foot Sawyers Peak; the low point is about 5,500 feet, near the Mimbres River. See Black Range for general description.

Status: Several old roads to abandoned mines and for grazing access are cherrystemmed into the roadless area. A few windmills and other range "improvements" are on the periphery of the area. The Forest Service recommended against Wilderness for the area in RARE II, and future timber sales in the mixed conifer and Ponderosa Pine forests of the high country are a definite threat. Exotic Iranian Ibex, introduced to the Florida Mountains south of here twenty years ago, have been seen near this roadless area. There is concern that they will spread into the Black Range.

CONTINENTAL DIVIDE 170,000 acres	
BLM WSA 2-44	68,761
Additional BLM, private, state, and Gila NF roadless	101,000

Description: Southwestern New Mexico south of Datil. High grassland (up to 9,212 feet on Pelona Mountain) along the Continental Divide drops into the southern San Agustin Plains at 6,780 feet. Grassland roadless areas of this size are extremely rare. Ponderosa Pine stringers line the canyons. Pronghorn, Elk, Mule Deer, Turkey, Black Bear, Mountain Lion, and wintering Bald Eagle find homes here. The Bat Cave paleontological site, in the northern part of the roadless area, has evidence of some of the earliest domesticated maize in North America. The proposed Continental Divide Trail will wind through this area.

Status: BLM is proposing only 40,359 acres of the WSA for protection. Even this has aroused strong rancher opposition. Conservationists propose 94,501 acres of primarily BLM land for Wilderness. Areas of state and private roadless land around the BLM WSA should be acquired by the BLM for protection as Wilderness.

Jeep trails and grazing developments are minor intrusions. One Jeep trail crosses the area through Shaw Canyon.

APACHE KID 131,000 acres	
Designated Apache Kid Wilderness Area (Cibola NF)	45,000
Additional Cibola NF roadless	86,000

Description: Central New Mexico north of Truth or Consequences. The southern portion of the San Mateo Mountains forms a distinctive profile west of the Rio Grande with a series of 10,000-foot peaks and interconnecting ridges that abruptly end at the precipitous south face of Vicks Peak. Elevations range from 6,000 feet to 10,325 feet (Blue Mountain). Among the interesting geologic features are several rock glaciers (talus slopes that behave like ice glaciers). Steep-walled canyons drop off to the west and east from the ridgelines. Ponderosa Pine and Gambel Oak, mixed conifer (Limber Pine, Douglas-fir, Engelmann and Blue Spruces, White Fir) and Aspen in the high country grade into mesquite, piñon and juniper, and mountain mahogany in the lower elevations. Narrowleaf Cottonwood, Arizona Alder, Live Oak, and Netleaf Hackberry line the canyons. Very little surface water is present. Mountain Lion, Black Bear, Elk, Mule Deer, and Turkey live here. The last Apache warrior, the Apache Kid, was gunned down on the upper slopes of Blue Mountain by a posse of cowboys in 1909. He is buried in the high country near where he fell.

Status: The Forest Service, to its credit, proposed protection for the entire area in the 1980 New Mexico Wilderness Act, but opposition from a politically powerful rancher, Reuben Pankey, who overgrazes the area, caused the Wilderness Area to be severely truncated. ORVs and grazing "improvements" may pose some threat, as may possible minor logging in canyon bottoms in the future. Conservationists should press for additions to the designated Wilderness Area.

Rocky Mountains–Colorado Plateau

The Southern Rocky Mountains drop down from Colorado in two ranges—the Sangre de Cristos and the San Juans—on either side of the Rio Grande in northern New Mexico. The Colorado Plateau enters northwestern New Mexico from Utah and Arizona. The Carson and Santa Fe NFs largely control the Big Outside of the Rockies, while BLM and the Park Service have that of the Colorado Plateau.

PECOS 400,000 acres	
Designated Pecos Wilderness Area (Santa Fe and Carson NFs)	223,333
Additional Santa Fe and Carson NFs roadless	151,000
Nambe Indian Reservation, BLM, and private roadless	26,000

Description: North-central New Mexico in the Sangre de Cristo Mountains northeast of Santa Fe. The southern terminus of the true Rocky Mountains (and of once-extensively glaciated terrain), the Pecos is classic Rocky Mountain high country, replete with lakes, trout streams, mountain meadows, glacial cirques, 13,000-foot-high peaks above timberline (Truchas Peak is 13,102 feet), and U-shaped valleys. As the name implies, the Pecos River begins here. Because of the steepness of terrain, vegetation quickly ranges upward from piñon and juniper through Ponderosa Pine and Gambel Oak to thick mixed conifer forests (Engelmann and Blue Spruces, Limber Pine, White and Subalpine Firs, Douglas-fir) with an abundance of Aspen (the largest Aspen on record is here). Bristlecone Pine reaches its southeastern limit in the Pecos, and the grassland of the Great Plains breaks against the eastern side of this roadless area. Inhabitants include Black Bear, Mountain Lion, Elk, Rocky Mountain Bighorn Sheep, Mule Deer, Pika, Pine Marten (southern limit), Short-tailed Weasel, Gray Fox, Pileated Woodpecker, Blue Grouse, Spotted Owl, and Wild Turkey. This is an extremely popular recreation area, but solitude can be found.

Status: The Santa Fe NF and Duke City Lumber are mounting a clearcutting and road-building assault on the rich spruce-fir forest of Elk Mountain on the southern end of the Pecos. Conservationists are fighting this travesty tooth and nail. Logging, firewood gathering, and ORVs threaten the other unprotected portions of this roadless area. Mining interests kept the southwestern part out of the Wilderness Area. Sheep grazing continues in the high country each summer.

WHEELER PEAK 120,000 acres	
Designated Wheeler Peak Wilderness Area (Carson NF)	20,000
Columbine-Hondo Wilderness Study Area (Carson NF)	43,276
Taos Pueblo roadless	45,000
Additional Carson NF and private roadless	12,000

Description: North-central New Mexico immediately northeast of Taos. Wheeler Peak is the highest point in New Mexico (13,160 feet); other 13,000-foot and 12,000-foot peaks form this area, while lower elevations drop to 7,500 feet. Small lakes, cirques, avalanche chutes, trout streams, and eye-popping views distinguish it. Mammals and birds present include Black Bear, Elk, Mule Deer, Rocky Mountain Bighorn Sheep, Mountain Lion, Yellow-bellied Marmot, Pika, Pine Marten, Blue Grouse, and White-tailed Ptarmigan (rare in New Mexico). The Columbine-Hondo area is connected to the Wheeler Peak Wilderness by a mile-wide unroaded ridgeline. The Taos Pueblo lands are closed to entry as a sacred area. Mixed conifer forest and alpine tundra are the primary vegetative types. Bristlecone Pine grow below timberline.

Status: The Carson NF has proposed only 27,032 acres of the Columbine-Hondo WSA for Wilderness.

Mining, ORVs, and logging threaten the remainder of the NF area and the private land to the east. Construction of a road across the narrow neck connecting the Wheeler Peak area to the Columbine-Hondo has been a long-standing dream of the ski industry, which is big in this area. Taos Ski Valley wants to expand in unprotected roadless country adjacent to the Wheeler Peak Wilderness.

LATIR PEAK—VALLE VIDAL 214,000 acres	
Latir Peak Wilderness Area (Carson NF)	20,000
Additional Carson NF roadless	5,000
Valle Vidal unit Carson NF roadless	48,000
Sangre de Cristo Grant (private) roadless	50,000
Philmont Boy Scout Ranch roadless	29,000
Additional private roadless	62,000

Description: North-central New Mexico north of the towns of Red River, Eagle Nest, and Cimarron in the Sangre de Cristo Mountains. This area, with some of the highest and most scenic country in New Mexico (Latir Peak is 12,708 feet) stretches across the Sangre de Cristos for 40 miles east-west from the Great Plains to the high tableland cut by the Rio Grande Gorge. There are several glacial lakes around Latir, and many streams flow from the ridges above timberline. Vegetation and wildlife are similar to the other Rocky Mountain areas in New Mexico. The Boreal Owl has recently been discovered in the northern New Mexico high country. Small free-roaming herds of Bison range into Valle Vidal from Philmont Scout Ranch.

Status: Complex ownership is the greatest obstacle to preservation of this roadless area. Logging is reducing the roadless acreage on the private lands; virtually the entire area is grazed by cattle and sheep; and ORVs fan out into the high country from the tourist resorts. Old mining activity dots the area, and some new mining is possible.

The Carson NF recently acquired by donation the Valle Vidal area east of the Latir Peak Wilderness Area and northwest of Philmont Scout Ranch. A network of low-standard dirt roads cut this area in half over Costilla Pass, but the Forest Service has properly closed these roads and others to protect wildlife (the best trout fishing and Elk hunting in the state are here); so we have included this area in our inventory as "roadless," even though the eastern part was logged around the turn of the century and there were through roads in it. Valle Vidal was formerly part of the huge Vermejo Ranch, owned by Pennzoil and operated as a company retreat (logging and grazing also occurred). Conservationists had hoped the Park Service could acquire the area as a new National Park, but the NPS botched the acquisition, and the FS got this magnificent area. Conservationists hope the FS will do a better job than it has with the rest of the Carson NF.

The small Rio Costilla Ski Area is cherrystemmed north of Latir Peak on the Sangre de Cristo Grant (a cooperatively managed area owned by local families tracing their ancestry in New Mexico back to the earliest Spanish settlers). A dirt road along Ponil Creek on Philmont Scout Ranch (used for supplying base camps) penetrates the eastern part of the area, and a rough dirt road to the Latir Lakes on the Sangre de Cristo Grant is also cherrystemmed. This entire roadless area and other high country around it (including the Culebra roadless area to the north) needs to be looked at as a unit, with a joint management plan developed among the various owners to protect its wilderness and wildlife values.

CULEBRA 125,000 acres (also in Colorado)

See Colorado for description and status.

EL MALPAIS 160,000 acres	
Designated West Malpais Wilderness Area (BLM)	38,210
El Malpais National Monument roadless	105,000
Additional BLM, private, and state roadless	17,000

Description: Western New Mexico south of Grants. The McCarty's Lava Flow is one of the youngest in the continental United States—only 500–1,000 years old (Pueblo Indian legends speak of a river of fire covering the fields their ancestors farmed). El Malpais ("the badlands" in Spanish) displays a wide variety of volcanic formations, including cinder cones with craters, ice caves (with delicate ice crystal ceilings, ice stalagmites, and smooth ice-rink–like floors), lava tubes (some 50 feet in diameter and several miles long), lava arches, and collapsed vents. Ponderosa Pine groves grow in pockets in the flow and, with occasional intermixed Douglas-fir and Aspen, on the cinder cones. Several areas of healthy grassland of Blue Grama, Sand Dropseed, and Ring Muhley survive. Other vegetation includes piñon and juniper, Big Sagebrush, Four-wing Saltbush, and oak brush. Numerous archaeological sites are present, including the old Zuni-Acoma trail. The largest natural bridge in New Mexico is immediately adjacent, in the sandstone cliffs to the east. Elevations here in the southeastern corner of the Colorado Plateau average about 7,000 feet. Wildlife includes Mule Deer, Pronghorn, Abert Squirrel, Mountain Lion, Bobcat, Turkey, Golden Eagle, Prairie Falcon, Peregrine Falcon, and Black-tailed Rattlesnake. A few prairie dog towns are on the edge of the lava. This might be a potential reintroduction site for the Black-footed Ferret if captive breeding programs are successful. Desert Bighorn Sheep may be reintroduced. Supposedly, a now-deceased well driller operating in the Hole-in-the-Wall, an area of grassland and Ponderosa Pine in the center of the lava flow, pumped up several small, white, blind cave fish—species unknown.

Status: On the last day of 1987, legislation was signed establishing the El Malpais National Monument and National Conservation Area under the management of the National Park Service and BLM, respectively. A 60,000-acre Cebolla Wilderness Area (just east of this roadless area) and a 38,210-acre West Malpais Wilderness Area (in the western part of this roadless area), both under BLM management, were included, and the Park Service was directed to study the new Monument for possible Wilderness designation. Continued grazing is permitted in the Monument until 1998 and is allowed in the BLM Wilderness indefinitely, as are hunting and trapping. Otherwise, this roadless area is comparatively well protected.

Chihuahuan Desert

The Chihuahuan Desert is the largest, yet least known, of America's deserts. With yucca, Lechuguilla, Ocotillo, Creosote Bush, and barrel cactus, it flows into southern New Mexico from Texas and Chihuahua, dominating the lowlands from the Pecos River in the east to the Arizona border on the west. The mountains, like islands in a desert sea, are influenced by the Rocky Mountains from the north and by the Sierra Madre from the south. The BLM, Lincoln NF, Mescalero Apaches, Air Force, and Park Service all manage important pieces of the Big Outside here.

GUADALUPE ESCARPMENT 258,000 acres (also in Texas)	
Carlsbad Caverns National Park Wilderness Area (NM)	33,125
Guadalupe Mountains National Park Wilderness Area (TX)	46,850
Lincoln NF roadless (NM)	44,000
Brokeoff Mountains BLM roadless 3-112 (NM)	61,000
Additional National Park roadless (NM and TX)	27,000
Additional private, BLM, and state roadless (NM)	26,000
Additional private roadless (TX)	20,000

Description: Southeastern New Mexico west of Carlsbad, and west Texas east of El Paso. Carlsbad Caverns NP forms the eastern end of this roadless area, Guadalupe Mountains NP in Texas forms the southwestern end, the Brokeoff Mountains are north of Guadalupe Mountains, and the Lincoln NF portion is between the two Parks. The "Guads" are best known for the extensive network of wild caves that lace this uplifted limestone reef. Carlsbad Caverns includes lengthy backcountry passages, in addition to the developed tour routes. A recently discovered cave in Carlsbad Caverns NP, Lechuguilla Caverns, has been found to be the deepest cave in the United States and is more than double the length of Carlsbad Caverns.

The surface of the escarpment is just as exciting, however, with fine Chihuahuan Desert vegetation (Ocotillo; Lechuguilla; Creosote; and cholla, prickly pear, and Strawberry Hedgehog cactuses) and riparian woodland (cottonwood, walnut, hackberry) in the lower elevations; piñon-juniper, oak, and madrone woodland at middle elevations; and a relict forest of Ponderosa

Pine and Douglas-fir in the heights of Guadalupe Mountains NP. Guadalupe Peak, at 8,749 feet, is the highest point in Texas. Deep canyons, including McKittrick, cut the escarpment.

Wildlife includes Mexican Spotted Owl, Elk, Mountain Lion, Javelina, and the largest Mule Deer herd in New Mexico. The only permanent population of Black Bear in Texas is in Guadalupe Mountains NP (although bears may be recolonizing Big Bend NP). The exotic Barbary Sheep (Aoudad) are reported in the area (they were released at various sites in New Mexico by the state Game and Fish Department in the early 1970s and have increased their range). Big Canyon, between the two Parks in the NF area, has at least seventeen Threatened or Endangered species of plants. Lower elevations (3,600 feet) to the northwest in New Mexico (BLM's Brokeoff Mountains roadless area) include a series of alkali flats, which sometimes form ephemeral lakes and include rare plants.

Status: A coalition of ORV zealots, road hunters, small town boosters, and local ranchers maintains strong opposition to Wilderness protection for the Lincoln National Forest roadless area between the National Parks. The 1980 New Mexico Wilderness Act established a 21,000-acre Wilderness Study Area, but the area was later recommended for "no Wilderness" by the gutless Forest Service. (The FS had considered the area for Primitive Area status as far back as the early 1930s and had supported it for Wilderness in the 1970s.) New Mexico conservation groups propose a 44,000-acre Wilderness here. Wilderness designation or, preferably, addition to Carlsbad Caverns NP is vital for this "missing link" in the unified Guadalupe Escarpment Wilderness. Without protection, multiple "abusers" on the NF will divide this important wilderness.

The BLM is recommending only 14,516 acres of the untracked Brokeoff Mountains for Wilderness protection; conservation groups propose 66,350 acres, including the rugged mountain and canyon country, as well as desert flats with ephemeral lakes. Inclusion of all of this area would greatly expand the diversity of Chihuahuan Desert ecosystems included in the greater Guadalupe Escarpment Wilderness. Roadless BLM and state land to the north of Carlsbad Caverns NP (Mudgetts WSA) in the Serpentine Bends of Dark Canyon is a key element in the eastern end of the Escarpment. BLM proposes no Wilderness; the New Mexico BLM Wilderness Coalition proposes 2,230 acres. Congress should add 20,000 acres of the undeveloped state and BLM land in the area to the Carlsbad Caverns NP Wilderness.

The Wilderness Areas established in both Carlsbad and Guadalupe Mountains NPs in 1978 were far too small. The Carlsbad Caverns NP Wilderness should be expanded to the north to shut down a Jeep trail along the escarpment crest that continues into the NF roadless area. The Guadalupe Mountains NP Wilderness should be expanded to include lower desert country to the west in the Park, and ecologically important desert land on private land to the west should be added to the Park and the Wilderness (10,000 acres of this was added to the Park in 1988, but the land has not yet been purchased from private owners; conservationists need to push for an appropriation to do this). The formerly proposed tramway up Guadalupe Peak appears to be dead, but such corpses have a habit of being resurrected by local boosters. Congress excluded the tram route from the Wilderness; conservationists need to add it, now that the tram proposal is slumbering. Non-native trout were long ago introduced to McKittrick Canyon; the Park Service has toyed with the idea of removing them so the invertebrate fauna of the stream can return to normal, but Texans are aghast at losing the state's only "trout stream." Consequently, the NPS has not pursued the project; it should be so encouraged.

Ranchers in New Mexico have pressured the NPS to allow "search-and-destroy" missions against Mountain Lions taking refuge in the National Parks. (The NPS has refused since catching flak for allowing two cats to be killed in Guadalupe NP in 1980–81.) This provides a textbook example of an ecological island that is too small to contain and sustain its large mammals. (The New Mexico Department of Game and Fish already employs a lion hunter full-time in the area as a subsidy to the sheepmen and cattlemen.) Slaughter of the big cats outside the Parks has drastically cut their population in the whole region. The lion killers have also killed many bears.

Potential oil and gas development presents some danger around the edges on NF, BLM, state, and private land. ORVers and cave vandals (often the same individuals) are significant threats to the integrity of the complex.

SIERRA BLANCA 140,000 acres	
Designated White Mountain Wilderness Area (Lincoln NF)	48,366
Additional Lincoln NF, state, and private roadless	28,000
Mescalero Apache Indian Reservation roadless	64,000

Description: South-central New Mexico west of Ruidoso. Sierra Blanca, at 12,003 feet, is the southernmost mountain in the United States shaped by past glaciation. This extinct volcano rises 7,000 feet above the desert basin to the west and reaches into the Arctic-Alpine life zone, providing an exceptional wilderness transition from Chihuahuan Desert to tundra. Black Bear, Elk, Mountain Lion, Mule Deer, and Mexican Spotted Owl live here, as does old-growth mixed conifer forest with the southeastern limits of Blue Spruce and Engelmann Spruce. An immense viewshed includes the Great Plains to the east, and White Sands, the San Andres Mountains, and across the Rio Grande to the west.

Status: The status of this roadless area on the Mescalero Reservation is uncertain. Roading and logging operations may be occurring and reducing it. Ski area expansion and small-scale mining may threaten the NF lands outside of the designated Wilderness.

WHITE SANDS 146,000 acres	
White Sands National Monument roadless	130,900
White Sands Missile Range roadless	15,000

Description: South-central New Mexico west of Alamogordo. White Sands is a world-famous complex of gypsum dunes formed by the wind blowing across calcium carbonate crystals (some several feet in length) on the dry bed of Lake Lucero. Moist areas between the dunes allow cottonwood trees to grow. Elevation is around 4,000 feet. Vegetated areas consist of seven Chihuahuan Desert associations, the main components of which are yucca, Iodinebush, Creosote, mesquite, and various grasses. Precipitation averages 7 inches a year. Wildlife populations are low, as befits such an arid area. Both Peregrine and Prairie Falcons are present. An interesting phenomenon is the occurrence among several lizard and small mammal species of pale variations in the White Sands and dark variations in the Carrizozo lava flow to the north.

Status: The National Park Service has not proposed White Sands for Wilderness because it is an overflight and infrequent impact area for military missiles. There are no significant threats.

*RM36: 1,200,000**

SAN ANDRES MOUNTAINS SOUTH 240,000 acres	
San Andres National Wildlife Refuge roadless	50,100
White Sands Missile Range roadless	190,000

Description: South-central New Mexico southeast of Truth or Consequences. The San Andres Mountains, broken into three large roadless areas by maintained military roads, are perhaps the wildest part of New Mexico, and are the most extensive Chihuahuan Desert mountain range in the United States. This precipitous north-south fault block range has many sheer canyons but little water. Largely contained within the 3-million-acre White Sands Missile Range, the San Andres have not been grazed by cattle for over forty years and have very healthy populations of Mule Deer, Pronghorn, and exotic Oryx. (Oryx, as a prominent New Mexico conservationist once commented, may be filling the ecological niche of the extinct Giant Ground Sloth—but are probably better eating.) Desert Bighorn Sheep were present, but were recently wiped out by an epidemic—this underscores the need to maintain many populations of rare species. They may be reintroduced. This desert mountain range is far wilder today than it was before the military took it over. Old roads in the canyon bottoms have been abandoned, and the riffraff have been kept out. (Nevertheless, read Ed Abbey's novel *Fire on the Mountain* for a fictional treatment of the arrogant military takeover.) The first atomic bomb was exploded nearby—a range expert says that range conditions near Ground Zero are better than those of over 90 percent of New Mexico, making one wonder if cows are more dangerous than nukes. Vegetation is that of the Chihuahuan Desert (Creosote Bush, yucca, barrel cactus, cholla, mesquite) and grassland, up to oak and piñon-juniper woodland, with hackberry and cottonwood in riparian areas. The high point is San Andres Peak, at 8,239 feet; elevations drop to 4,000 feet.

Status: The only large-scale threat is the possible development of electronic or communication sites by the military. This was the prime area being considered for reintroduction of the Mexican Wolf, but the base commander rejected the plan in 1987 because of "security" problems. However, in 1990, the military reconsidered, and a study is now being done. Reintroduction of the Mexican Wolf could occur here as early as 1992. The exotic Barbary Sheep (a north Africa wild sheep brought to New Mexico by a poorly considered and now repudiated exotic game introduction scheme of the New Mexico Game and Fish Department) may be extending its range into the San Andres—all the better reason for returning Lobo.

*RM36: 1,200,000**

SAN ANDRES MOUNTAINS CENTRAL 155,000 acres	
White Sands Missile Range and BLM roadless	155,000

Description: South-central New Mexico east of Truth or Consequences and separated from the San Andres Mountains South by a road; same general description and status. This area includes BLM land adjacent to the western boundary of White Sands Missile Range.

*RM36: 1,200,000**

SAN ANDRES MOUNTAINS NORTH 155,000 acres	
White Sands Missile Range roadless	155,000

Description: Central New Mexico southeast of Socorro and separated from San Andres Mountains Central by a road; same general description and status as San Andres South. The elevation nearly reaches 9,000 feet on the slopes of Salinas Peak (which has a road to the top with a radio tower).

RM36: 1,800,000

SIERRA LADRONES 109,000 acres	
BLM WSA 2-16	45,308
Sevilleta National Wildlife Refuge roadless and adjacent BLM and private roadless	60,000
Cibola NF roadless	4,000

Description: Central New Mexico north of Socorro. This rough desert peak, 50 miles south of Albuquerque, rises from 5,000 feet to 9,176 feet elevation. Scattered Ponderosa Pine grow on top. Creosote Bush, Four-wing Saltbush, and fairly healthy grassland up through piñon and juniper constitute the other vegetation. The Sevilleta NWR portion is closed to grazing and public entry as a natural area. Pronghorn and Mule Deer are relatively common. Ladron is a potential Desert Bighorn Sheep reintroduction area. The Rio Salado Box Canyon is an attraction on the south side.

Status: BLM supports Wilderness protection of 34,124 acres. Conservation groups propose only 36,244 acres; this should be expanded.

Minor ORV use, fuelwood cutting, and range "improvements" taint the edges. Former ranch roads and developments are fading on the Sevilleta NWR.

ROBLEDO–LAS UVAS MOUNTAINS 143,000 acres	
BLM WSAs 3-63 and 3-65	24,013
Additional BLM, state, and private roadless	119,000

Description: South-central New Mexico immediately northwest of Las Cruces. This rugged mountain complex west of the Rio Grande (and touching it at one point) includes the limestone Robledo Mountains, with high cliffs, on the southeast and the bedded volcanic Las Uvas Mountains, with rimrocked mesas, buttes, and deep canyons, on the northwest. The Rough and Ready Hills, Cedar Hills, and wide open spaces lie between the ranges. Elevations range from 5,876 feet, on Robledo Mountain, to less than 4,000 feet. Vegetative types are Chihuahuan Desert, oak and juniper woodland, and riparian woodlands dominated by Netleaf Hackberry in the canyon bottoms (also cottonwood and associated riparian growth along the Rio Grande). Typical plants are Sotol, Creosote Bush, Apache-plume, barrel cactus, penstemon, and Lyreleaf Greengages. Night Blooming Cereus and the Transpecos Rat Snake, a state Endangered species, inhabit the area. Other wildlife includes Golden Eagle (cliffs provide nesting spots), Peregrine Falcon, Bald Eagle, Scaled and Gambel's Quail, Mule Deer, and Banded Rock Rattlesnake. Several caves are here, as are numerous archaeological sites, including a ten-room pueblo. Highly significant dinosaur fossils have been found in and adjacent to the area.

Status: Livestock graze throughout, and additional developments have been proposed. ORVs are a major threat, and there are a variety of Jeep trails in part of the area. Several roads penetrate the area, giving it an irregular configuration. Additional threats from potential geothermal development and mining for building stone have arisen.

Conservation groups take a strong position by proposing a 210,000-acre Wilderness and the closure of minor dirt ranching roads. BLM opposes Wilderness protection for this area.

WEST POTRILLO MOUNTAINS 260,000 acres	
BLM WSA 3-52	143,145
Additional BLM roadless (includes scattered state and private tracts)	117,000

Description: South-central New Mexico west of Las Cruces. Just north of the Mexican border and west of the Rio Grande valley, the West Potrillos are a series of volcanic cinder cones (some with intact craters) and wide flats in between. This is a desolate, little-visited area with remarkably healthy Chihuahuan Desert grassland (yucca, Four-wing Saltbush, cholla, Ocotillo, Creosote), including large barrel cactus. There is no natural perennial water in the area, but plenty of solitude. Sand dunes and ephemeral ponds are present in Indian Basin. The very recent Aden Lava Flow occupies the northeast corner of the roadless area. Several archaeological sites have been found, and a rare mollusk and a rare cactus are present. Wildlife includes Mule Deer, Golden Eagle, Great Horned Owl (which nest in cinder cones), numerous quail and dove, and migrating ducks (in Indian Basin).

Status: Surprisingly, despite its lack of classic "wilderness" features, the core of the West Potrillos (162,820 acres) is proposed for Wilderness by the BLM, along with 27,277 acres of the Aden Lava Flow. Conservation groups forthrightly propose a single Wilderness Area of 259,837 acres.

A few Jeep trails penetrate the area, and a couple cross it. ORVers and a local hobby rancher are strongly opposing Wilderness designation. There is interest in mining cinders from some of the cones.

CEDAR MOUNTAINS 106,000 acres	
BLM WSA 3-42	14,911
Additional BLM, state, and private roadless	91,000

Description: Southwestern New Mexico southwest of Deming. This roadless area consists of a remote, little-known, low-mountain range, rolling hills, and adjacent plains on the Mexican border. Flying "W" Mountain, at 6,217 feet, is the high point. The low point is 4,600 feet. The area's juniper woodland and Chihuahuan Desert vegetation includes the rare Night-blooming Cereus, as well as Tobosa and Burro Grass, Netleaf Hackberry,

Four-wing Saltbush, Apache-plume, Tarbush, juniper (locally misnamed "cedar"), and mesquite. Mule Deer, Pronghorn, Javelina, quail (abundant), and many species of raptors are the most noticeable critters. Superb 360-degree views and two large Animas-phase pueblo ruins remain almost unknown to hikers.

Status: BLM opposes protection. Conservationists, in an excellent proposal that closes minor dirt roads, call for 172,000 acres as Wilderness.

Continued overgrazing, possible construction of additional grazing "improvements," and ORV use are potential problems. A few Jeep trails intrude—one of which was bladed in the spring of 1987, possibly with BLM connivance, to try to disqualify the area from Wilderness consideration.

BIG HATCHET—ALAMO HUECO MOUNTAINS 207,000 acres	
BLM Big Hatchet WSA 3-35	65,872
BLM Alamo Hueco WSA 3-38	16,264
Additional BLM, state, and private roadless	100,000
Contiguous roadless in Mexico	25,000

Description: Southwestern New Mexico on the Mexican border southeast of Lordsburg. Big Hatchet Peak is a rough, dry limestone peak that reaches 8,366 feet in elevation; the Alamo Hueco Mountains to the south are lower (high point, 6,448 feet), with low points under 4,300 feet. Springs in the Alamo Huecos attract many Mexican species of birds, including Elegant Trogon, Varied Bunting, and Thick-billed Kingbird. This area is a northern extension of the Mexican Highlands Shrub Steppe Province—oak brush and juniper predominate on the mountains; Chihuahuan Desert vegetation (Ocotillo, Creosote, mesquite) prevails lower down and in the large flat expanses between the ranges; and Arizona Walnut grows in the canyons. Desert Bighorn Sheep, Coues White-tailed Deer, Javelina, Mountain Lion, Coatimundi, Montezuma Quail, Sonora Mountain Kingsnake, and Giant Spotted Whiptail Lizard are some of the interesting vertebrates. Night Blooming Cereus and Scheer Pincushion are unusual cacti present. Caves in the Alamo Huecos have archaeological sites.

Status: BLM recommends 51,980 acres of the Big Hatchets for Wilderness, but does not recommend the Alamo Huecos because of mixed land ownership—a land exchange is needed to consolidate public land in this key biological area (rumors have it that such an exchange with the Phelps-Dodge copper company is in the works). Conservation groups propose 91,219 acres of Wilderness for the Big Hatchets and 31,984 acres for the Alamo Huecos. A unified 200,000-acre Wilderness should be established.

The major threat to the area is oil and gas exploration, with a secondary threat from grazing "improvements." Minor ORV use and a few Jeep trails are present. A poor dirt road almost divides the two ranges, but they are connected by a several-mile-wide roadless corridor. Mexico should be encouraged to protect its lands in this roadless area.

ANIMAS MOUNTAINS 101,000 acres	
The Nature Conservancy and state roadless	94,000
BLM Cowboy Spring WSA 3-007	6,699

Description: Extreme southwestern New Mexico south of Lordsburg. Largely private land owned by The Nature Conservancy (with some BLM and state patches), this is the finest extension of the Sierra Madre into the United States. It is not one of the Sky Island mountain ranges; it is directly contiguous with the Sierra Madre cordillera. The Animas has excellent habitat for rare birds, including Elegant Trogon, Thick-billed Parrot, Harris's Hawk, Common Black Hawk, and Zone-tailed Hawk. Consideration is being given to reintroduction of Aplomado Falcon. More species of mammals are present here than in any National Park or Wildlife Refuge in the United States—including White-sided Jackrabbit, Coatimundi, Javelina, Mountain Lion, Black Bear, Coues White-tailed Deer, and . . . Mexican Wolf (a female denned and produced pups just north of the border in the early 1970s). Biological (not necessarily political) potential is high for reintroduction of Jaguar (which may be present on a transient basis, along with Ocelot and Jaguarundi). Desert Bighorn Sheep may be reintroduced. The Animas is also one of the priority areas for Mexican Wolf reintroduction (or supplementation). Several species of rare rattlesnakes, including the very rare Ridge-nosed (federally listed as Threatened), live here. Candidate species for Federal Threatened or Endangered listing include Arizona Shrew, Sanborn's Long-nosed Bat, Ferruginous Hawk, White-faced Ibis, and Mexican Spotted Owl. The state of New Mexico has classified twenty-one vertebrate and three plant species in the area as Threatened or Endangered.

The area above 5,500 feet in elevation has supposedly not been grazed since 1980. The high country reaches 8,519 feet and sports fine Madrean oak-and-pine forest with good stands of Mexican White, Chihuahua, Arizona, and Apache Pines, along with Rocky Mountain species like Douglas-fir, Quaking Aspen, and Gambel Oak. The several forest patches dominated by Arizona Pine and Mexican White Pine are unique in the United States. Dry Creosote desert flats abut the range on the east, while the west is bounded by a lush grassy valley in remarkably good condition—including a large expanse of a Great Plains community of Blue Grama and Buffalograss. These grasslands are as important for biodiversity as are the Madrean forests in the mountains and the riparian woodlands. Chihuahuan Pronghorn, Grasshopper Sparrow, Baird's Sparrow, and McCown's Longspur are found in the grassland. Riparian woodland of Fremont Cottonwood, Arizona Sycamore, Goodding Willow, Velvet Ash, Netleaf Hackberry, and Arizona Walnut lines the several perennial streams and springs. Rare Gray Oak savannahs enhance the vegetative diversity.

An extremely wild and pristine area, the Animas are separated only by a dirt road (which is closed to the public) in the United States and a paved road in Mexico from an even larger wild area in Mexico. This is one of the biologically most important areas in the United States.

Status: During the 1980s, the U.S. Fish and Wildlife Service wanted to purchase the 322,000-acre Gray Ranch in the Animas, including this roadless area, and make it a National Wildlife Refuge. Although the owner was interested in selling, nearby ranchers, with support from the powerful cow establishment of New Mexico, opposed this—evidently because of a dogmatic position against taking any rangeland "out of production" and out of fear that the Wildlife Refuge would be used for Mexican Wolf reintroduction. It is disturbing to note that this was part of the Coronado National Forest until it was traded to the Phelps-Dodge Copper Corporation in the late 1950s for some nondescript pottage.

With the feds hamstrung by the cowboys, The Nature Conservancy stepped into the breach and, on January 29, 1990, purchased the 321,703-acre Gray Ranch. This was the Conservancy's largest purchase ever. The Conservancy is continuing to run cattle on much of the ranch under a grazing lease that came with the property. One hopes that this grazing is a temporary arrangement, but there are disturbing rumors that the Conservancy may make cattle part of its management scheme. Conservationists need to encourage The Nature Conservancy to remove all cattle at the earliest opportunity, close most of the roads, and manage the Gray Ranch with a wilderness philosophy. Closing minor dirt roads could bring this roadless area up to as much as 250,000 acres. Our identification of roadless acreage (101,000) is based on what was on the ground at the time of The Nature Conservancy's purchase.

BLM recommends the entire 6,699-acre Cowboy Spring WSA for Wilderness designation (northeast corner of this roadless area). In an excellent and visionary proposal, the New Mexico BLM Wilderness Coalition calls for acquisition of surrounding state land and the designation of a 40,989-acre Wilderness.

Mexico should be encouraged to protect the ranges that provide a direct high-elevation connection between the Animas and the bulk of the Sierra Madre. An International Biosphere Reserve of at least a million acres in the two countries would be most appropriate, with management emphasis on protection of Lobo, Jaguar, and other imperiled species.

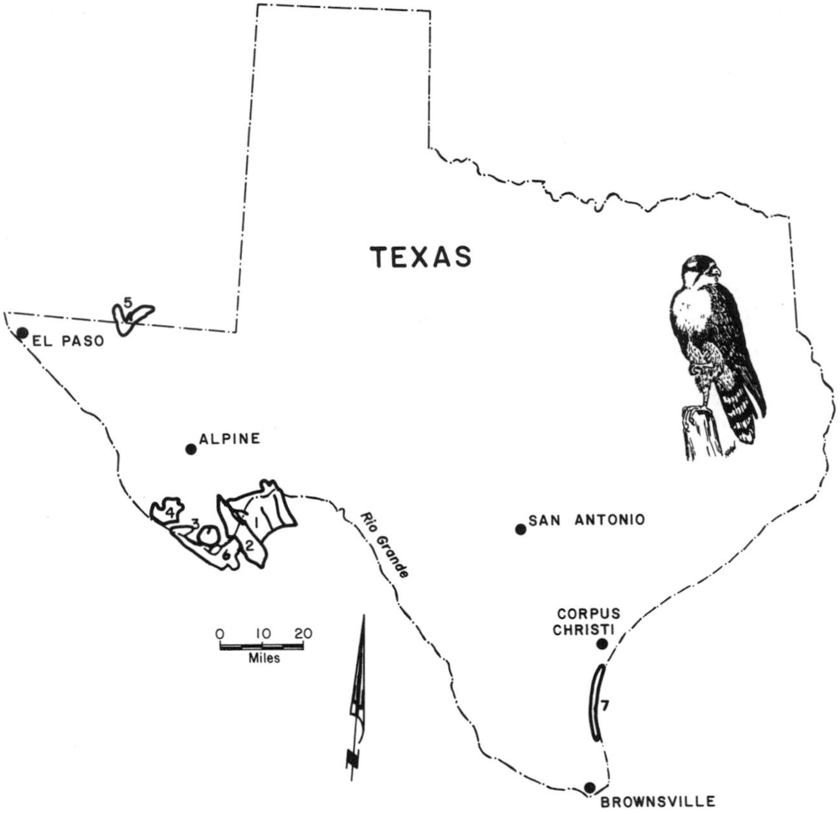

1. Lower Canyons of the Rio Grande
2. Dead Horse Mts.
3. Chisos Mts.
4. Solitario
5. Guadalupe Escarpment
6. Mariscal–Santa Elena Canyons
7. Padre Island

Texas

Texas. To many, it is the epitome of the Wild West, the Frontier. But where is the wilderness? Where is the "wild" in this West? Texas has a greater variety of native ecoregions than does any other state, and is the only state that truly encompasses both Western and Eastern ecoregions. It is by far the largest of the lower forty-eight states. But compare it with California, a state smaller in area yet larger in population. California has nearly 6 million of its acres protected in the National Wilderness Preservation System; Texas has a mere 83,000 acres.

The Lone Star State serves as a grim warning of what happens to wild country when there is little public land. Texas, more than any other of the states, glorifies the private ownership of land. Given the history of Texas, we are fortunate that Big Bend and Guadalupe Mountains National Parks were acquired by donation or purchased out of private ranches; and that Padre Island National Seashore, Big Thicket National Preserve, several important National Wildlife Refuges, and the National Forests of East Texas were purchased by the federal government.

The reason Texas had no public land to begin with stems from the agreement in 1845 whereby the independent Republic of Texas joined the United States as the State of Texas. In contrast to the situation in all other states (except for the original thirteen), public lands in Texas were owned by the state, not by the federal government. As a result, these lands quickly passed into private ownership and were developed.

There are five Wilderness Areas in the East Texas National Forests, but the largest is only 12,700 acres, far too small to be included in this inventory. These areas were designated in 1984 after a long, hard-fought battle with the timber industry, which rules East Texas, and its champion, Congressman "Timber Charlie" Wilson. Dedicated conservationists in the Texas Committee on Natural Resources, the Lone Star Sierra Club, and Texas Earth First! have continued to agitate for additional Wilderness Areas in the National Forests, but are currently occupied with trying to prevent the U.S. Forest Service from conducting cut-and-leave timber sales in the designated Wilderness Areas under the pretext of Southern Pine Beetle control.

The only regions of Texas where large roadless areas remain are the Chihuahuan Desert in the far west and Padre Island on the southern Gulf Coast.

In 1978, 191.2 miles of the Rio Grande in West Texas were designated as a National Wild and Scenic River, again after a long uphill struggle by conservationists. Since then, the local congressman, at the behest of goat ranchers in the area, has regularly introduced legislation to rescind the protection.

The anti-Wilderness boys grow as big as their belt buckles in West Texas, and steady pressure from chamber of commerce honchos in the town of Alpine has prevented 559,000 acres of Big Bend National Park from being designated as Wilderness, although the proposal from the National Park Service and conservationists has been before Congress since 1974. (Big Bend was established as a National Park in 1945, after a decade-long fund-raising campaign in which Texas schoolchildren saved their lunch money for the acquisition fund.) A 46,850-acre Wilderness—scaled down from a larger recommendation at the insistence of local development interests—passed Congress in 1978 for Guadalupe Mountains National Park, after a ten-year struggle by El Paso conservationists.

Threats to the Big Outside of Texas include ranching, oil and gas extraction, excessive National Park development, and private subdivision and tourist development.

LOWER CANYONS OF THE RIO GRANDE 890,000 acres (also in Mexico)	
Black Gap State Wildlife Area, Rio Grande Wild and Scenic River, and private roadless (TX)	190,000
Mexico roadless	700,000

Description: West Texas south of Sanderson. One of the half dozen wildest stretches of river in the United States, the Rio Grande east of Big Bend National Park forms a deep, rugged limestone canyon complex along the international border with Mexico. We consider it roadless from the La Linda bridge to Bone Watering. Major side drainages include Big Canyon, Reagan Canyon, Cañon de San Rosendo (Mexico), Cañon Caballo Blanco (Mexico), Palmas Canyon, Arroyo del Tule (Mexico), Panther Canyon, and San Francisco Canyon. Elevations range from 3,988 feet, on Cupola Mountain in Black Gap, to 1,330 feet, on the river at Bone Watering. Burro Bluff rises 1,000 feet out of the river; there are many other high cliffs, windows, spires, caves, and assorted rock formations in the canyon. For 43 miles, walls up to 2,000 feet high rise on both sides of the river. Terrific (and intimidating) flash floods roar down the Rio Grande and its tributary canyons. This is difficult water for canoes, as aluminum carcasses wrapped around boulders attest.

Bighorn Sheep, Mountain Lion, Javelina, Peregrine Falcon, Summer Tanager, Green-winged Teal, Blotched Water Snake, Trans-Pecos Copperhead, Mottled Rock Rattlesnake, Big Bend Turtle, Red-spotted Toad, giant catfish, possibly Ocelot, and Mexican Wolf live here. Lucifer, Broadbilled, and Black-chinned Hummingbirds nest along the river (ten other hummingbird species are visitors). Classic Chihuahuan Desert vegetation—Lechuguilla, Ocotillo, Creosote Bush, Blind Prickly Pear, cholla and barrel cacti, Sotol, yucca, Guayacan, Candelilla, Leather Stem—graces the area above the river; mesquite, willow, and Giant Reed predominate along the river.The native Lanceleaf Cottonwood (a hybrid of Narrowleaf and Plains Cottonwoods) was wiped out by early-day woodcutters. Berlander Ash reaches its upriver limit here.

Status: While the entire river through this roadless area (72 miles) is protected as a National Wild and Scenic River, the surrounding lands in both the United States and Mexico are open for development. (The Wild and Scenic River designation continues for an additional 54 miles downstream from this roadless area.) Adjoining lands in the United States outside of Black Gap are private sheep and goat ranches. Several of the ranchers are interested in punching roads down to the river for private tourist development. This extraordinary area deserves to be part of an International Big Bend Park, with high priority given for Mexican Wolf, Jaguar, Ocelot, and Jaguarundi reintroduction or supplementation.

The calculation of what is roadless in Mexico is rough.

DEAD HORSE MOUNTAINS 720,000 acres (also in Mexico)	
Big Bend National Park roadless	142,000
Private land to east (Adams Ranch) roadless	28,000
Mexico (Sierra del Carmen) roadless	550,000

Description: West Texas southeast of Alpine. This roadless area is separated from the Lower Canyons by a narrow paved road and bridge providing access to a fluorspar mine at La Linda on the Rio Grande. It includes the Dead Horse Mountains, Boquillas Canyon on the Rio Grande (2,000 feet deep), and (in Mexico) the Sierra del Carmen. The finest stand of Giant Dagger Yucca in the United States is here. Wildlife includes a relatively dense Mountain Lion population, Javelina, Pronghorn, and Beaver. Ocelot have been seen in Boquillas Canyon within the last decade. Black Bear and introduced Elk are present in the National Park Mexico has established in the Sierra del Carmen, which rises to over 9,000 feet in elevation, and supports Ponderosa Pine, Limber Pine, Alligator Juniper, Douglas-fir, and Aspen. The high point in the United States part is Sue Peaks, at 5,799 feet. River elevations are under 2,000 feet. Outstanding Chihuahuan Desert vegetation is present in the Big Bend portion. Groove-billed Ani, Green Kingfisher, Mississippi Kite, and Zone-tailed Hawk are unusual birds found here. Fish include the Mexican Stoneroller and Chihuahua Shiner. Flora and fauna are generally similar to those in the Lower Canyons. Boquillas Canyon offers a fine canoe trip.

Status: Although most of this area is protected in Parks, Park management in Mexico is a much more casual affair than in the United States. However, plans are moving ahead for an International Park that would include 1.2 million acres in Mexico, largely in the Sierra del Carmen. Big Bend National Park, the Big Bend Ranch (Solitario), Black Gap Wildlife area (the last two owned by the State of Texas), the Park lands in Mexico, and surrounding areas in both countries combine to form a 3-million-acre Greater Big Bend Ecosystem that could support a viable population of Mexican Wolf. Most of the Big Bend NP area has been recommended for Wilderness by the NPS. The 25 miles of the Rio Grande in this roadless area are part of the National Wild and Scenic Rivers System, as are the river stretches upstream and downstream. High priority for Mexican Wolf, Jaguar, Ocelot, and Jaguarundi reintroduction or supplementation is needed. The Adams Ranch has high wilderness and ecological values and should be acquired by the National Park Service for addition to Big Bend NP (it has recently been used as headquarters for a major smuggling ring that dealt in spotted-cat skins from Latin America).

The calculation of what is roadless in Mexico is rough. Over half of the Mexican acreage in this roadless area is in the Parque Internacional Del Rio Bravo.

CHISOS MOUNTAINS 186,000 acres	
Big Bend National Park roadless	186,000

Description: Entirely within Big Bend National Park in West Texas south of Alpine. Vegetation zones begin with Chihuahuan Desert and rise to a relict forest of Ponderosa Pine, Gambel and Emory Oaks, Arizona Cypress, Texas Madrone, Velvet Ash, Netleaf Hackberry, Douglas-fir, and Aspen in the high country and canyons. Emory Peak, the high point, reaches 7,835 feet, a mile above the lower elevations of the area. Perennial streams and important bird habitat give the Chisos ecological significance. Mountain

Lion, Javelina, Yellow-nosed Cotton Rat, all four U.S. species of skunk (Striped, Spotted, Hog-nosed, and Hooded), Lucifer Hummingbird and ten other hummingbird species, Flammulated Owl, Varied Bunting, Lyre Snake, Mexican Black-headed Snake, and Trans-Pecos Copperhead live here. The Carmen White-tailed Deer, Colima Warbler, and Drooping Juniper are found nowhere else in the United States. More birds are known from Big Bend National Park than from any other National Park area (380 species). Black Bear (including cubs) have recently been sighted, after an absence of many decades.

Status: The National Park Service has proposed most of this area as Wilderness and is managing it as such. Support should be given the NPS to remove more of the tourist developments from the Basin area in the mountains. (Local boosters favor expanding the visitor facilities in the oak-juniper woodland of the Basin.) Mexican Wolf and border cats should be reintroduced. Some Texas conservationists are actively pushing for reintroduction of Mexican Wolf in Big Bend National Park, but state politicians, pushed by the local livestock gentry, turn apoplectic at the mere thought.

MARISCAL–SANTA ELENA CANYONS 483,000 acres (also in Mexico)	
Big Bend National Park roadless (TX)	69,000
Private roadless (TX)	14,000
Mexico roadless	400,000

Description: Southeastern Big Bend National Park and adjacent Mexico. Three roadless areas in Big Bend National Park are joined by contiguous roadless acreage in Mexico to form this large expanse of exceptional desert river wilderness. Santa Elena and Mariscal Canyons, cut through flat-topped mesas by the Rio Grande, have sheer walls rising out of the river. Santa Elena is 1,500 feet deep and less than 1,500 feet wide in places. Mariscal is just as sheer, but even deeper. The abrupt ending of Santa Elena Canyon is unmatched. See other Big Bend areas for general description.

Status: The three roadless areas in Big Bend NP are split in Texas by roads coming down to the river. They are joined by a sprawling backcountry to the south in Mexico that includes half of the Parque Internacional Del Rio Bravo. Most of the Big Bend NP acreage is proposed for Wilderness by the NPS. The calculation of what is roadless in Mexico is rough.

SOLITARIO 225,000 acres	
Texas State Park and private roadless	225,000

Description: West Texas between Terlingua and Presidio. Because the Big Bend Ranch was until late 1988 entirely private land, details are rough. By all accounts, however, this area west of Big Bend National Park is as wild and scenic as the Park. Features include the Bofecillos Mountains, Solitario Peak, Panther Mountain, Bandera Mesa, Fresno Creek, and Tapado Canyon. The Solitario is a collapsed volcanic peak; at 8 miles across, it is one of the largest and most symmetrical molten-rock domes on Earth. This area is blessed with perennial streams, numerous springs, and two 100-foot-high waterfalls. The high point is 5,193 feet; lower elevations are near 3,000 feet. Because this old volcanic area has an average elevation of 4,000 feet, it has a cooler and moister climate than nearby Big Bend National Park. Chihuahuan Desert vegetation and grassland, riparian woodland in the canyons, and oak and juniper in the higher elevations are the vegetative types. Some of the grasses are Blue, Black, and Side-oats Gramas; Silver Bluestem; Tanglehead; and Tobosa. Hinckley's Oak, growing on limestone, is Endangered. The Texas Parks and Wildlife Department reports that cottonwood, ash, and willow "form true closed canopy forests" in moist areas in the canyons. Such riparian bosques are especially important, given the disappearance of cottonwood in Big Bend National Park. Wildlife is similar to that of Big Bend NP and includes at least eleven Endangered species. Among the impressive vertebrates are the Western Mastiff Bat, with its 2-foot wingspan, and the stentorian Canyon Treefrog and Couch's Spadefoot Toad. Although not part of this roadless area (a paved state highway separates it), 25 miles of the Rio Grande, including Colorado Canyon, are included in the new State Park. There are many archaeological sites, most of which have not been explored.

Status: In 1988, the Texas Parks and Wildlife Commission voted to acquire the 215,000-acre Big Bend Ranch roughly overlapping most of this roadless area. The owner, oil magnate and philanthropist R. O. Anderson had wanted to sell this ranch to the State of Texas or National Park Service as a public park since the 1970s, but the offer was not taken until 1988. Since then, the state has purchased an additional 42,000 acres, for a total of 264,000 acres. The area will be managed as a natural area, and permits are required for hiking. Most of the cattle and sheep have been removed. Texas Parks and Wildlife has closed old dirt ranching roads and restricts private vehicles to the paved road along the Rio Grande. Bus tours are available on the northern boundary road of the roadless area to the Solitario overlook. Portions of the roadless area outside of Big Bend Ranch (Bandera Mesa, Cesario Creek, Contrabando Creek) to the east and northeast should be priorities for public acquisition.

GUADALUPE ESCARPMENT 258,000 acres (also in New Mexico)
See New Mexico for description and status.

PADRE ISLAND 108,000 acres	
National Seashore roadless	108,000

Description: South Texas Gulf Coast between Corpus Christi and Brownsville. Padre Island National Seashore protects the longest barrier island (75 miles are roadless) on the U.S. coast. Wide, clean (aside from occasional tar balls and flotsam from fishing boats and oil platforms offshore) beaches, sand dunes, grassy flats, and mud flats characterize the area. More than 350 species of birds, Loggerhead Turtle, Alligator, Portuguese Man-of-War jellyfish, and many fishes frequent the island and its surrounding waters, which include Laguna Madre—the long, shallow bay between Padre Island and the mainland. There are only two coastal areas included in this inventory—the Everglades and Padre Island.

Status: The Park Service studied this island for Wilderness designation, but did not recommend it because of continuing offshore oil and gas extraction allowed in the National Seashore (production has been fairly limited). The Park Service allows dune buggies and other off-road vehicles to drive along the beach. The area was once a cattle ranch, but grazing has been terminated. Conservation groups have not pushed Wilderness designation. The island and surrounding waters should be designated as a Wilderness Area, and motorized vehicles prohibited.

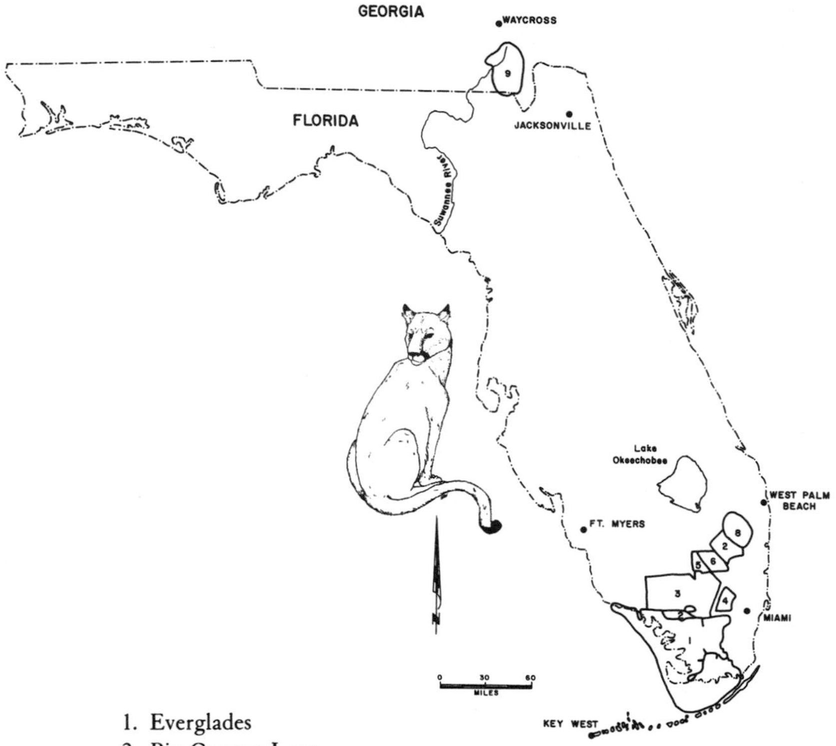

1. Everglades
2. Big Cypress Loop
3. Big Cypress Swamp
4. Everglades #3B
5. Everglades #3C
6. Everglades #3A
7. Everglades #2
8. Loxahatchee
9. Okefenokee

10. Great Dismal Swamp
11. Great Smoky Mts. West
12. Great Smoky Mts. East
13. Cohutta
14. Southern Nantahala
15. Cranberry

Southeast

Pity the poor South. Once it had the richest temperate forest on Earth, with Tulip Poplars more than 200 feet tall, Carolina Parakeets and Ivory-billed Woodpeckers, Black Bears and Eastern Panthers galore, Elk in the mountains and giant gators in the lowlands. . . .

But a century or two of Europeans changed all that. Lumbermen, swamp drainers, market hunters, cotton farmers, coal companies, and mountaineers transformed the land into a pale imitation of Europe. More recently, tree farmers, oilmen, chemical companies, commercial fishermen, and slick land developers have ground out the wildness in all but a few places.

Today, the Big Outside in the South is restricted to two swamps (the Everglades and Okefenokee) and to a handful of high, remote sections of the Southern Appalachians.

Preservation of things wild and natural comes hard in Dixie. There are fewer members of conservation groups per capita in the South than there are in any other region of the country, and Southern members of Congress, with rare exceptions, don't much care for things that you can't eat or put a price tag on.

Our generation can thank a few farsighted Southern iconoclasts for what is left—folks like Marjory Stoneman Douglas, still going strong after the century mark, who gave us Everglades National Park; and a band of New Deal idealists in Knoxville who gave us Great Smoky Mountains National Park.

Although Eastern conservationists began to suggest possible Wilderness protection for National Forest areas east of the Rockies before the Wilderness Act was passed in 1964, the Forest Service argued that no areas qualified, that there was a fundamental difference between National Forest lands in the East and West (except for Minnesota's Boundary Waters). In the West, they argued, National Forests had been withdrawn from the public domain and—although some minor uses, such as grazing, tie-hacking, and old cabins, may have previously been made of Wilderness Areas there—those areas were essentially pristine. The Eastern National Forests, on the other hand, had been purchased from private ownership and added to the system. They had been homesteaded, cleared, and developed at various times during their history. Even if, under Forest Service management, the forests were growing up, old roads were fading, signs of habitation were disappearing, and the appearance of wilderness was being reestablished, these areas were not wilderness in the same sense as the Western wilderness. There was a qualitative difference. To include Eastern areas in the Wilderness System would tarnish the whole system and demean the pristine Western areas.

There was an element of sincerity in the Forest Service argument. Some foresters honestly believed it. Others used it in a Machiavellian way to keep their managerial hands from being tied. Yes, under Forest Service protection these Eastern areas were recovering from past abuse, but that didn't mean the Forest Service had no plans to abuse them again, now that their trees were large enough to harvest.

Nevertheless, belying its own argument, the Forest Service had established three Wilderness Areas (called "Wild Areas" because they were under 100,000 acres) in the East before the Wilderness Act. They were Linville Gorge and Shining Rock in North Carolina, and Great Gulf in New Hampshire.

Utterly convinced that there was no other potential Wilderness in the East (or on the National Grasslands), in its first Roadless Area Review and Evaluation, in 1972, the Forest Service covered only National Forests in the twelve Western states (with three exceptions—one each in Florida, North Carolina, and Puerto Rico). Eastern conservationists mobilized, with the support of The Wilderness Society, and submitted Wilderness proposals to Congress. An Eastern Wilderness bill was drafted; the Forest Service countered with a proposal for a separate, but lesser, system of Eastern National Forest "Wild Areas." After a substantial campaign, a bill was passed by Congress and signed by President Ford on January 3, 1975, establishing sixteen full-fledged units of the National Wilderness Preservation System in Eastern National Forests and directing the Forest Service to study for possible Wilderness recommendation an additional seventeen areas. Twenty-five of these thirty-three areas were in states from West Virginia south.

The dam had been broken. In RARE II, the Forest Service considered National Forests in the East (and National Grasslands) equally with National Forests in the West. Statewide bills in the decade after RARE II have designated additional National Forest Wilderness Areas in most of the Eastern states with National Forests.

Two factors, unfortunately, work in tandem to reduce Wilderness designation in Eastern National Forests. First, the land use history of these recovered Wildernesses limits their size. As our inventory indicates, only a handful of National Forest roadless areas in the East exceed our floor of 50,000 acres. The lands that have recovered are small and isolated. It will require conscious planning to restore areas of several hundred thousand acres in the East to a general condition of roadlessness. This is the prerequisite for reestablishing the basis for ecological Wilderness with the full range of native species.

Second, Forest Service managers are under the same bulldozer–and–chainsaw mind-set in the East as they are in the West. Their job is to build roads and cut trees, not to restore and protect ecosystems. Areas in the Eastern National Forests that have recovered a degree of wildness and roadlessness are under the same threat of clearcutting and roading as are larger areas in the West. Even though Eastern National Forests are the logical cores for wilderness restoration, this will be achieved not with the support of the Forest Service, but by overpowering the FS in the same way conservationists overpowered it in 1974 on the Eastern Wilderness Act. The campaign will be far more difficult.

The Eastern Wilderness Act in 1974 and subsequent Wilderness legislation was too late to give us big wilderness in the National Forests of the South (with a couple of exceptions that are described in the inventory). A number of National Wildlife Refuges in the South have received Wilderness designation (but not Loxahatchee or Great Dismal Swamp, which are two of the three Southern NWRs included in this inventory). The Smokies still await passage of a Wilderness bill that has been pending for nearly twenty years. Wilderness legislation passed for Okefenokee NWR in 1974 and Everglades National Park in 1978. Big Cypress National Preserve adjacent to the Everglades was expanded in 1988 by Congress, but Wilderness designation remains on hold.

The Everglades and Great Smoky Mountains confirm the key principles of Island Biogeography—that a preserve, unless it is truly large, will lose species; that it cannot stand alone. Diversion of water to Miami and to southern Florida farms threatens to destroy the Everglades. Air pollution is killing the virgin forests in the Smokies saved from timber companies fifty years ago. Moreover, wide-ranging, wilderness-dependent species, such as Eastern Panther, Ivory-billed Woodpecker, Red Wolf, and Manatee, can't survive in isolated natural "islands" even as large as the Everglades or Smokies. To maintain the fabric of the natural world, we have to set aside preserves large enough for these species and then connect them by corridors to other preserves so the gene pool doesn't grow isolated and inbred. The Everglades–Big Cypress and the Great Smoky Mountains National Park (with the surrounding National Forests) are the prime areas in the South for large preserves.

Exciting things are happening in the South today, such as the recent work of ecologist Reed Noss at the University of Florida in developing a comprehensive proposal for a system of core preserves, connecting corridors, and buffer zones that would allow Florida Panther, Manatee, Black Bear, and other imperiled wildlife to maintain healthy populations in wild habitat; and of R. F. Mueller of Virginians for Wilderness, who is calling for the restoration of large Wilderness Areas in the Appalachian Mountains by closing roads, healing clearcuts, and reintroducing Panther, Elk, and other extirpated species.

Maybe the South can rise again.

Swamps and Marshes

Swamps. Wet, yucky, sweltering, snake-infested, mosquito-ridden, leech-filled hell holes. Humphrey Bogart and the African Queen. *These common images associated with swamps and marshes tend to hide from the public the great plenitude and diversity of life that wetlands hold thanks to their abundance of water. Fortunately, swamps are also a bit more difficult for the financial adventurer to exploit. As a result, the largest tracts of wildland left in the South are swamps or marshes. Tough in appearance though they may be, even the Southern swamps are delicate ecosystems vulnerable to human misuse.*

EVERGLADES 1,658,000 acres (Florida)	
Everglades National Park east mainland roadless	174,300
Everglades National Park west mainland roadless	672,400
Florida Bay Everglades National Park	529,300
Big Cypress National Preserve Stairsteps Unit roadless	143,281
Private roadless to east	75,000
Cape Romano Aquatic Preserve	64,000
Designated Everglades National Park Wilderness*	1,296,500

* Included in first three items above.

Description: Southern Florida southwest of Miami. "Unique" is an overused word in describing natural landscapes, but if any natural region can be called unique, it is the Everglades. There is simply no other place like this on Earth. Sawgrass prairie, alternately tinder dry and flowing wet, Bald Cypress swamp festooned with epiphytes, Caribbean tropical hardwood hammocks, Slash Pine–Saw Palmetto forests, Paurotis Palms, Buttonwood thickets, and mangrove keys distinguish it. This is the land of the American Alligator, American Crocodile, River Otter, Everglades Mink, Florida Panther, Cotton Mouse, West Indies Manatee, Bottle-nosed Dolphin, Black Bear, Snapping Turtle, Loggerhead Turtle, Indigo Snake, Liguus Tree Snail, Coon Oyster, Apple Murex, Strangler Fig, Gumbo Limbo, Royal Palm, Live Oak, Pond Apple, an incredible profusion of birds (300 species, including Roseate Spoonbill, Great White Heron, Reddish Egret, White Ibis, Wood Stork, Anhinga, and Magnificent Frigatebird) and fish (including Florida Spotted Gar, bonefish, mullet, and tarpon), and . . . mosquitoes.

Status: The Greater Everglades ecosystem is one of the most threatened areas in America. By altering the water flow patterns of south Florida, humans have upset the ecological applecart. Efforts are being made to restore natural water flows, and they should be strongly encouraged. Additionally, pollution from agricultural runoff is disrupting native plants and encouraging exotics that can tolerate it. As an indication of the damage being done to the Everglades, populations of water birds have crashed in recent years (The

Wilderness Society reports that wading bird populations have declined by 90 percent since the 1930s).

A new threat is the Air Force, which hopes to begin low-altitude training dogfights for F-4s and F-16s over the Park.

Although motorboats ply the mangrove channels, Ten Thousand Islands, and Florida Bay (even in the designated Wilderness), we have considered these areas roadless because they are *wild;* the many keys are off-limits to landing, the water is no deeper than 9 feet over a vast area, and much of this marine landscape is designated as Wilderness. It is this Florida Bay Wilderness that links the two mainland roadless areas that are split on shore by the Flamingo road.

The area in Big Cypress Preserve is open to swamp buggies and airboats. These ORVs should be banned, and the Stairsteps Unit of Big Cypress immediately added to the Everglades Wilderness Area. Swamp buggies and airboats are prohibited in Everglades National Park.

BIG CYPRESS SWAMP LOOP 55,000 acres (Florida)	
Big Cypress National Preserve roadless	55,000

Description: Southern Florida between Miami and Everglades City. This roadless area is the part of Big Cypress Swamp National Preserve bounded by the Loop Road and Tamiami Trail.

Status: This is the only part of Big Cypress Swamp National Preserve currently closed to motorized vehicles, including swamp buggies and airboats.

BIG CYPRESS SWAMP 583,000 acres (Florida)	
Monument Unit Big Cypress National Preserve roadless	282,714
Everglades Wildlife Management Area (Conservation Area 3) and Florida State Miccosukee Indian Reservation roadless	300,000

Description: Southern Florida west of Miami. The Big Cypress Swamp is the northern extension of the Everglades and is separated from the main Everglades roadless area merely by the Tamiami Trail highway. Baldcypress swamp and Sawgrass prairie mix here in an interdigitating mosaic (see Everglades for general description). Big Cypress is much more crucial for survival of the Endangered Florida Panther (down to thirty individuals) than is Everglades National Park.

Status: Big Cypress National Preserve may have the dubious distinction of being the most poorly managed unit in the National Park System. Swamp buggies and airboats have the run of this area. Primitive campgrounds along the highways are RV slums with trash covering the ground. Oil exploration was permitted by the Interior Department until a conservationist lawsuit halted it in 1988. Speeding vehicles on Tamiami Trail and Alligator Alley (highways cutting through the Everglades–Big Cypress complex) are the main sources of mortality for the Florida Panther. Black Bear also die in droves along highways in Florida: During 1987–89, 108 bears were road kills; the total population in the state is estimated at only 400–1,000.

Both highways should be closed (along with several other roads), and a 3-million-acre Everglades Wilderness National Park established. Airboats and swamp buggies should be entirely banned in Big Cypress, as well as in the adjacent Wildlife Management Areas.

Congress authorized the addition of 146,000 acres of private land to Big Cypress National Preserve in 1988. By late 1991, some 33,323 acres had been purchased and it appeared as though Congress would appropriate $3 million for further purchases. The bulk of the land, however, was involved in a complicated exchange for Indian school lands in downtown Phoenix, Arizona, and had not gone through. This 107,799 acres includes portions of the Conservation Areas in this roadless area and in some of the following roadless areas, as well as land in the new Florida Panther National Wildlife Refuge and the Ten Thousand Islands National Wildlife Refuge.

Only thirty Florida Panthers are believed to remain in the wild. Although much of their range overlaps public lands in this and the other large roadless areas adjacent, over half of their 2.2-million-acre habitat is in private ownership and faces conversion to agriculture and subdivision. The captive breeding plan for the highly endangered big cat (six kittens are to be removed from the wild for it) will fail to halt the panther's slide to extinction unless these prime private lands can be protected. The private lands are generally more upland, thereby providing better habitat for the Florida Panther's main prey—White-tailed Deer. Only a comprehensive biodiversity plan such as Reed Noss's will halt the panther's heartrending skid into oblivion.

The eastern border of this roadless area is the Miami Canal and Levee 67A.

EVERGLADES 3B 50,000 acres (Florida)	
Everglades Conservation Area 3 roadless	50,000

Description: Southern Florida west of Miami. This roadless area is that part of Everglades Conservation Area 3 bounded by U.S. 27, the Miami Canal, and Levee 67C.

Status: See other Everglades units.

EVERGLADES 3C 54,000 acres (Florida)	
Everglades Conservation Area 3 roadless	54,000

Description: Southern Florida west of Ft. Lauderdale. This area is separated from the main unit of Big Cypress Swamp by Alligator Alley and from the next area by Mud Canal.

Status: See other Everglades units.

EVERGLADES 3A 109,000 acres (Florida)	
Everglades Conservation Area 3 roadless	109,000

Description: Southern Florida west of Ft. Lauderdale, that part of the Everglades Conservation Area 3 bounded by Alligator Alley, Mud Canal, U.S. 27, and the Palm Beach–Broward County Line. Canals and road corridors separate this roadless area from the other roadless areas in the Everglades Conservation Areas.

Status: This area has some airboat trails, and has been subjected to the southern Florida flood and water management system, which has diverted regular water flow to the cancerous sprawl along Florida's "Gold Coast."

EVERGLADES 2 95,000 acres (Florida)	
Everglades Conservation Area 2 roadless	95,000

Description: Southern Florida west of Pompano Beach, bounded by U.S. 27, Levee 6, Levee 39, and Levee 36, between Loxahatchee NWR and Roadless Area 3A (see above).

Status: Similar to 3A.

LOXAHATCHEE 143,000 acres (Florida)	
Loxahatchee National Wildlife Refuge roadless	143,000

Description: Sawgrass prairie in the northern part of the 'Glades southwest of West Palm Beach in southern Florida (Water Conservation Area 1). Loxahatchee is the key habitat for the Endangered Everglades (Snail) Kite. Tree islands of Red Bay, Wax-myrtle, and Holly are special features. Alligator, Florida Sandhill Crane, Osprey, Great White Heron, Bald Eagle, Peregrine Falcon, Masked Duck, Fulvous Whistling-Duck, Roseate Spoonbill, Limpkin, Everglades Mink, Florida Panther, and Florida Water Rat reside in Loxahatchee. About half of the area is closed to all public entry.

Status: Loxahatchee is entirely enclosed by canals and levees (numbers 39, 7, and 40). Although water levels are artificially managed (as is true throughout the Everglades–Big Cypress complex), this is a wild area. A portion of it is open to airboats and hunting—it should be closed to airboats.

OKEFENOKEE 400,000 acres (Georgia, partly in Florida)	
Designated Okefenokee National Wildlife Refuge Wilderness (GA)	353,981
State, private, and additional Refuge roadless (GA and FL)	46,000

Description: Southeastern Georgia south of Waycross. Okefenokee is THE SWAMP, and is the home of Pogo, Alligator, River Otter, Black Bear, Bobcat, coon, armadillo, Snapping Turtle, and maybe a Florida Panther or two. Here can also be found 225 species of birds—including Barred Owl, Red-cockaded Woodpecker, Prothonotary Warbler, Sandhill Crane, Osprey, Anhinga, Wood Duck, Wood Stork, and various herons, egrets, and ibis. Other denizens include fifty-four species of reptiles, thirty-two of amphibians, and thirty-seven of fish. Slash and Longleaf Pines, gum, and bay are common trees. Baldcypress forests, watery prairies, piney islands, open "lakes," and superlative canoe trips characterize this nationally significant Wilderness. Okefenokee is the source of the Suwannee and St. Marys Rivers and varies from 128 feet to 103 feet in elevation. Peak-bagging opportunities are accordingly limited.

Status: Motorboats are allowed in portions of the designated Wilderness. They should be banned. All portions of the swamp and adjacent pine woods, out to the encircling paved highways, should be made wilderness recovery areas. The Refuge is surrounded by huge industry tree farms—all in pine. Efforts are being made and should be expanded to acquire private land to the south in Florida to connect Okefenokee NWR to the Osceola National Forest.

GREAT DISMAL SWAMP 102,000 acres (Virginia and North Carolina)	
Great Dismal Swamp National Wildlife Refuge "roadless"*	102,000
* See status below.	

Description: Eastern Virginia–North Carolina border southwest of Norfolk. This large swamp is centered on the unusually pure waters of Lake Drummond. A remnant of the Atlantic White Cedar forest survives here. Many species reach their northern limit in the Great Dismal Swamp. Rare forms include Dismal Swamp Short-tailed Shrew and Dismal Swamp Log Fern. Black Bear, Bobcat, River Otter, White-tailed Deer, and ninety-two nesting species of birds are among the fauna. A million Robins use the area for a winter roost. Baldcypress, gum, magnolia, pawpaw, poplar, oak, holly, and juniper are among the flora. Formerly owned by George Washington and Patrick Henry, Dismal Swamp is no longer in their hands.

Status: This swamp is cut by numerous ditches with "roads" on the spoil banks that are closed to motorized vehicles but are open to bicycles and walking. Motorboats are permitted on the Feeder Ditch as access to Lake Drummond. Perhaps the Great Dismal Swamp should not be considered "roadless," but it presents a remarkable opportunity for wilderness restoration.

ATCHAFALAYA SWAMP (Louisiana)

Description: South-central Louisiana. This 800,000-acre area of swamp and bayou is crossed by only one road—Interstate 10—but is so cut up by canals (used by powerboats) and oil and gas pipelines, wells, and other development that we, with regret, have not included it in our inventory as roadless. It is, to be sure, an important natural area retaining considerable wildness and important wildlife habitat. Additional information for future editions of this book would be appreciated.

Appalachian Mountains

Backbone of the Eastern states, the Appalachians run from Alabama to Maine and provide a pathway for northern species to reach the high country of the South. In the Southern Appalachians, the most diverse temperate forest on Earth developed. The Southern Appalachians also represent the largest block of federal land in the East, with Great Smoky Mountains National Park and contiguous National Forests in North Carolina, Tennessee, Georgia, and South Carolina totaling 4 million acres—the Southern Appalachian Highlands Ecosystem. This, obviously, presents an opportunity for wilderness restoration on a grand scale.

Although included with the lowlands of the South in this book, the Appalachians form their own bioregion and are ecologically and culturally distinct. The Central Appalachians were ravaged by coal companies and continue to be so ravaged today. Except for West Virginia's Cranberry Wilderness, there is no Big Outside in the Appalachians between the Great Smoky Mountains and New York State.

GREAT SMOKY MOUNTAINS WEST 227,000 acres (North Carolina and Tennessee)	
Great Smoky Mountains National Park roadless (NC)	138,600
Great Smoky Mountains National Park roadless (TN)	86,200
Private and Cherokee Indian Reservation roadless (NC)	2,500

Description: South of Knoxville, Tennessee, west of Asheville, North Carolina. The Southern Appalachians have the most diverse temperate deciduous forest on Earth. The Smokies have more species of deciduous trees (130) than does all of northern Europe (80). This is a botanist's haven, with over 1,400 species of flowering plants. The Smokies also harbor the most extensive virgin forest in the East. This never-cut forest is composed mostly of deciduous hardwoods (Northern Red Oak, White Oak, hickories, and about a dozen other species) on upper slopes and ridges, Red Spruce and Fraser Fir in the high elevations, and some cove hardwoods. There are also some very large second-growth trees (particularly Tulip Poplars). A total of 200,000 acres in this and the Great Smoky Mountains East roadless area have never been logged. This area has the southernmost extension of spruce-fir forest in Eastern North America. Rhododendron thickets in the high country are famous for their color. Other trees include Fraser Magnolia, Black Locust,

Black Cherry, Black Walnut, Eastern Sycamore, Eastern White Pine, and Eastern Hemlock.

Wildlife includes Wild Turkey, Ruffed Grouse, Barred Owl, Pileated Woodpecker, Blackburnian Warbler (and at least six other breeding forest interior warblers), Raven, Mink, Bobcat, Red Fox, Southern Flying Squirrel, abundant Black Bear, and Endangered Red-cockaded Woodpecker and Indiana Bat. There are more species of salamanders in the Smokies than anywhere else in the world. The streams have seventy species of fish, including native Eastern Brook Trout. The Smokies kept the Black Bear from extinction in the Southern Appalachians and even today provide a nucleus breeding area, supplying areas outside the Park with bears. The Red Wolf is being reintroduced. The Smokies arguably afford the best backpacking east of the Rockies (although Adirondack aficionados would differ). The high point in this roadless area is 6,600 feet, on the slopes of Clingmans Dome (although a paved road goes to the top of Clingmans Dome). There are sixteen peaks over 6,000 feet in the two roadless areas. Elevations drop to under 1,300 feet. Although the Smokies are in the South, winter temperatures in the high country can drop to 20 degrees below zero. The nearly 80 inches of annual precipitation gives birth to many streams and waterfalls.

Status: Wilderness legislation is pending. Locals pushing for a road north of Fontana Reservoir in the roadless portion of the Park have held up the Wilderness bill through North Carolina Senator Jesse Helms. Had it not been for Helms, Wilderness designation for the Park would have passed in 1988. Conservationists must continue to fight for Wilderness. Furthermore, Fontana Dam should be removed, Fontana Reservoir drained, and the land added to the Park. Additionally, the Newfound Gap–Clingmans Dome paved roads should be closed, along with the Spruce Mountain and Parson Branch one-way dirt roads. This would restore a single Wilderness of 500,000 acres, making it a prime area for reintroduction of Eastern Panther, Elk, and other extirpated species.

Acid rain is beginning to damage the old-growth spruce and fir on the crest of the Smokies. The Fraser Fir stands in the Park have become infested with an aphid, the Balsam Woolly Adelgid (an exotic), which is destroying them. Non-native wild boar are upsetting the natural environment in the area, ripping up vegetation and competing with bears for mast. They should be eliminated.

The Forest Service presents another major danger to the Smokies. Logging has doubled on the surrounding National Forests in the last ten years, and 1,400 miles of new logging roads have been built. This sawlog mania is further isolating and impoverishing one of the premier biological areas on Earth. It is just as important to stop the Forest Service's destructive behavior in the East as in the West.

GREAT SMOKY MOUNTAINS EAST 163,000 acres (North Carolina and Tennessee)	
Great Smoky Mountains National Park roadless (NC)	87,400
Great Smoky Mountains National Park roadless (TN)	71,500
Private and Cherokee IR roadless (NC)	4,000

Description: Separated from Great Smokies West (see general description) by the Newfound Gap highway. The high point is 6,621-foot Mt. Guyot.

Status: Wilderness legislation is pending. Even with Wilderness designation for much of the Park, the Park will remain as a habitat island and subject to floral and faunal depauperation. Major wilderness restoration efforts are needed throughout the Southern Appalachians in order to protect the ecological health and integrity of core wildland units such as Great Smoky Mountains National Park. See Great Smokies West for general status.

COHUTTA 56,000 acres (Georgia and Tennessee)*	
Designated Cohutta Wilderness Area (Chattahoochee NF, GA)	35,247
Designated Cohutta Wilderness Area (Cherokee NF, TN)	1,795
Designated Big Frog Wilderness Area (Cherokee NF, TN)	7,972
Designated Big Frog Wilderness Area (Chattahoochee NF, GA)	83
Additional Chattahoochee and Cherokee NF and private roadless (GA and TN)	11,000

* A total of 13,000 acres in Tennessee; 43,000 acres in Georgia.

Description: Georgia-Tennessee border west of Copper Hill. The Cohutta consists of rugged Southern Appalachian mountains, and the canyons of the Jacks and Conasauga Rivers (two of the most prolific trout streams in Georgia). In contrast to those of the Southern Nantahala, habitats are medium- to low-elevation. Waterfalls and rocky gorges are special features, as are several stands of virgin forest, including some very large Yellow-poplar (also known as Tulip Poplar or Tuliptree) and Eastern Hemlock. Slopes and ridges are second-growth oak-hickory forest recovering rapidly and remarkably from heavy logging sixty years ago. In another sixty years, there will be a semblance of "old growth" throughout the area, according to retired Clemson forestry professor Robert Zahner. Wildlife includes Black Bear, White-tailed Deer, Bobcat, Turkey, Ruffed Grouse, Barred Owl, Pileated Woodpecker, a half dozen forest interior breeding warblers, Coosa Bass, three species of trout (but only Brook Trout are native—the other two are introduced), and boar (not native); there are forty species of rare plants. Big Frog Mountain (4,200 feet) is the high elevation; Jacks River, at 950 feet, is the low point.

Status: The contiguous roadless acreage should be added to the designated Wilderness to prevent Forest Service logging and roading. Surrounding unpaved roads should be closed to add 50,000–70,000 acres of land to the Wilderness as Wilderness Recovery Areas (total would be 110,000–130,000 acres).

SOUTHERN NANTAHALA 60,000 acres (Georgia and North Carolina)*	
Designated Southern Nantahala Wilderness Area (Chattahoochee NF, GA)	12,439
Designated Southern Nantahala Wilderness Area (Nantahala NF, NC)	10,900
Additional Chattahoochee and Nantahala NFs, and private roadless (NC and GA)	37,000

* A total of 39,000 acres in North Carolina; 21,000 acres in Georgia.

Description: North Carolina–Georgia border northwest of Clayton, Georgia. The Appalachian Trail winds through this botanically diverse, scenic high-mountain area. Standing Indian Mountain (5,500 feet) is the high point. The North Carolina portion is characterized by high ridges, averaging 4,000–5,000 feet in elevation. These ridges were formerly covered with large expanses of wildfire-maintained native plant communities termed "heath balds." These ericaceous shrubs are losing out to invading forest trees as a result of over sixty years of fire protection that has not permitted lightning fires to burn. Slickrock ridges and steep slopes (gneiss bedrock outcroppings) are common and are dominated by dwarf forests of White Oak, Chinkapin, Mountain Ash, and pine. Small patches of virgin oak forests occur above cliffs, where they were inaccessible to loggers. In coves between cliffs are patches of virgin hemlock and disjunct northern hardwood forest types, which are rare this far south. The variety of environmental niches results in an incredibly rich diversity of flora and fauna, relics of Arcto-tertiary species second only to those of interior China. The high elevations record the highest precipitation in Eastern North America, circa 120 inches annually. The Georgia portion is lower in elevation and, like the Cohutta, is characterized by second-growth oak-hickory forests recovering from extensive logging between 1900 and 1920. There are several unique bog habitats here that support not only Endangered species, like Bog Turtle and Manna Grass, but rare combinations of species that occur nowhere else on Earth. Birds, mammals, reptiles, and amphibians are similar to those listed for the Smokies and Cohutta.

Status: The 37,000 roadless acres adjacent to the Southern Nantahala Wilderness need immediate protection. The Forest Service is diligently trying to offer timber sales in the unprotected portions of the roadless area and in surrounding wild areas. Conservation groups just as diligently are opposing the timber sales and road building with appeals. This may be the most threatened roadless area of any size in the Southern National Forests; local and national conservation groups should rally to its defense by recognizing that the Southern Nantahala could form the core for a large (over-100,000-acre) wilderness recovery area in the southern Appalachians.

CRANBERRY 82,000 acres (West Virginia)*

Designated Cranberry Wilderness Area (Monongahela NF)	35,864
Additional Monongahela NF "roadless"*	45,000
Cranberry Glades Botanical Area roadless (Monongahela NF)	750

* See status below.

Description: Eastern West Virginia north of Richwood. This high, dissected plateau, ranging from 2,300 feet to 4,600 feet in elevation, is an area of lush forest with precipitation in excess of 45 inches per year. The forest types range from complex mixed mesophyte at lower elevations to boreal and montane with Red Spruce at the highest elevations. There are also high-elevation bogs with Reindeer Moss and other muskeg vegetation. Numerous northern and disjunct plants such as Dwarf Dogwood, Goldthread, Buckbean, and Bog Rosemary grow here. Five species of birds—the Hermit Thrush, Olive-backed Thrush, Mourning Warbler, Northern Water Thrush, and Purple Finch—reach their southernmost breeding limits. Bobcat, Black Bear, Turkey, and Beaver are common, and the land can support up to fifty deer per square mile. Other wildlife includes Mink, Snowshoe Hare, Red Fox, and Brown Recluse Spider. The streams (headwaters of the Williams and Cranberry Rivers) support trout, except in much of the designated Wilderness, where naturally acidic waters prevent their reproduction. Cranberry is surrounded by a wide buffer zone of roaded but extremely rugged wildland. This is an Eastern area in which we will be able to see how the return of wilderness old growth fosters the recovery of indigenous species. It is a popular backpacking area.

Status: The 45,000 acres outside of the designated Wilderness Area constitute the Cranberry Backcountry and contiguous NF lands. There are dirt roads in this area, but they have been closed to public use for over fifty years, thereby largely eliminating their practical purpose as "roads." They should be permanently closed to all use, including Forest Service administration and logging (which continues to occur in the Backcountry). With closing of the dirt road along the Williams River and dirt roads on Gauley Mountain, an additional 50,000 acres could be added, for a total Wilderness and Wilderness Recovery Area of 130,000 acres. Gray Wolf, Fisher, Panther, and Elk should be reintroduced.

Specific threats include timber sales and coal mine development in the areas surrounding the designated Wilderness, including the Backcountry.

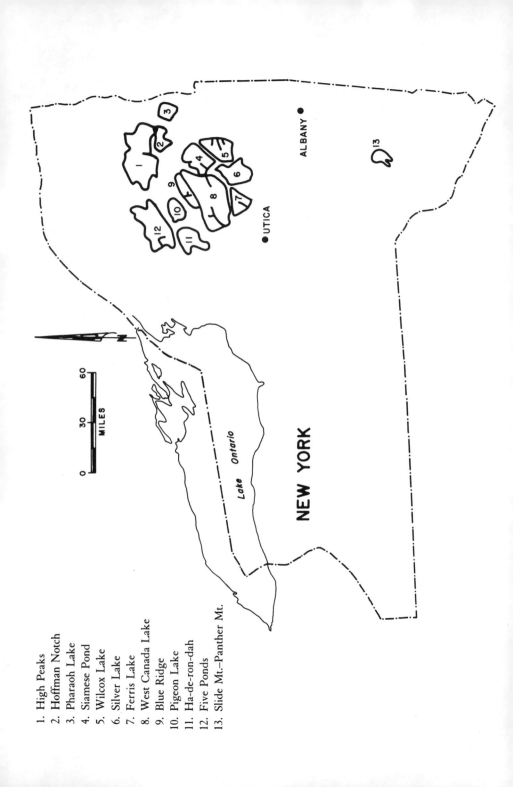

1. High Peaks
2. Hoffman Notch
3. Pharaoh Lake
4. Siamese Pond
5. Wilcox Lake
6. Silver Lake
7. Ferris Lake
8. West Canada Lake
9. Blue Ridge
10. Pigeon Lake
11. Ha-de-ron-dah
12. Five Ponds
13. Slide Mt.–Panther Mt.

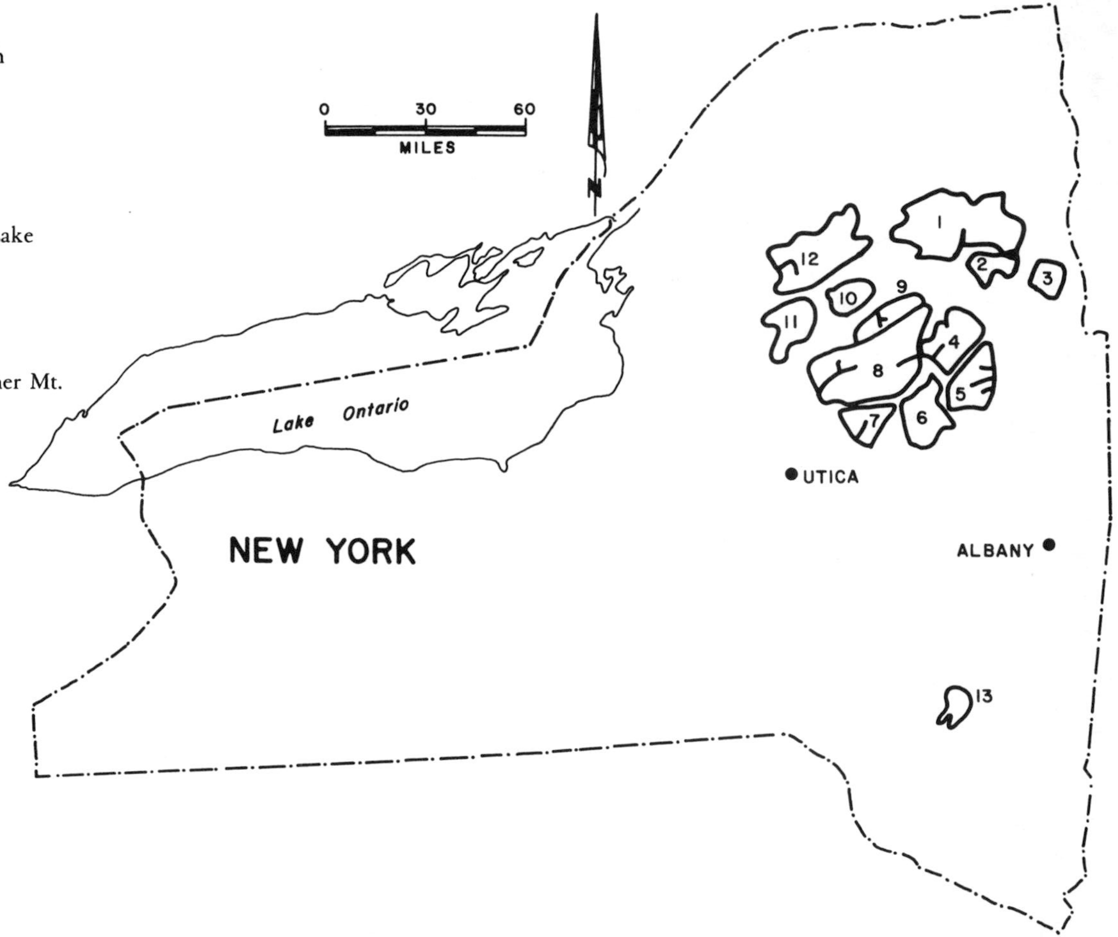

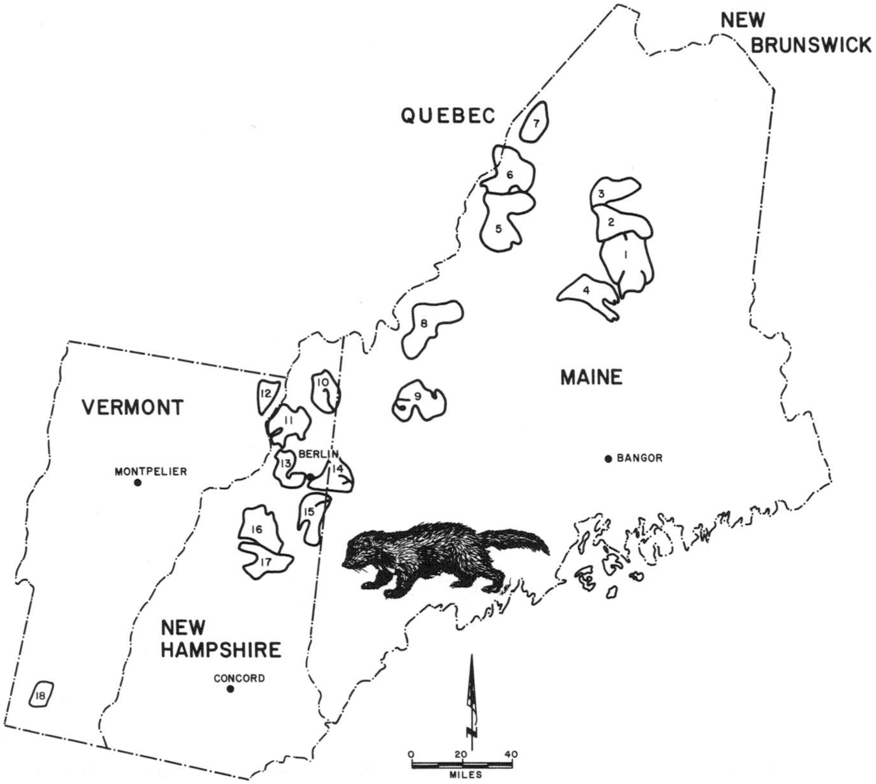

1. Baxter State Park
2. Baxter North
3. Reed Mt.
4. Wildlands Lakes
5. St. John Ponds
6. St. John River South
7. St. John River North
8. Moose River
9. Redington Pond
10. West Branch Dead Diamond River–Crystal Mountain
11. Blue Mt.
12. Meachum Swamp
13. Kilkenny
14. Mahoosuc Range
15. Wild River–Kearsarge
16. Pemigewasset
17. Sandwich Range
18. Glastenbury Mt.

Northeast

More than 370 years ago, the Pilgrims stepped off the *Mayflower* into "a hideous and desolate wilderness." Seeing New England as a stronghold of Satan and the indigenes as his worshipers, they launched into the conquest of the wild with all the fervor their religion could muster. Roderick Nash, in *Wilderness and the American Mind,* quotes Edward Johnson as saying in 1654 that "the admirable Acts of Christ" had transformed Boston from "hideous Thickets" where "Wolfes and Beares nurst up their young" into "streets full of Girles and Boys sporting up and downe."

In those "hideous Thickets" cloaking New England, Eastern White Pines grew 220 feet tall. So excellent were these great conifers that the Royal Navy reserved them for use as masts for His Majesty's ships. The Timber Wolf, Eastern Panther (Catamount), Wolverine, and other wilderness-dependent species that "nurst up their young" in primal New England were eradicated as ruthlessly as were the native humans. Farley Mowat, in *Sea of Slaughter,* describes the ruination of the New England–Newfoundland–Gulf of St. Lawrence bioregion with gruesome but accurate detail.

Surprisingly, much of New England is wilder today than it was 100 years ago or even 150 years ago. Fields marked by stone walls have grown up into forest again; there are rumors of Catamounts. Abandoned dirt roads in the mountains are fading.

Nowhere else in the United States are the opportunities for sweeping wilderness restoration greater than in northern New York, Vermont, New Hampshire, and Maine.[1] The land is more resilient here than in the arid West, and the pressures for development have not been so strong until recently. With the wisdom and foresight that established Adirondack Park one hundred years ago, wilderness recovery areas of a million acres and more could be put together in the Northeast today from privately owned timberlands. Unless conservationists act swiftly, though, this opportunity will slip through our fingers. Second-home development and the demand for wood for paper pulp and biomass energy production (wood-chip boilers) are at an all-time high. The opening of Interstate 93 through Franconia Notch has placed northern Vermont and New Hampshire within four hours of Boston—making second-home development an even greater threat to wildlands. Who will get the regenerating Northeastern forest—"Wolfes and Beares" or international pulpers and Boston yuppies?

It is the choice of this generation whether we see New England and New York as vibrant, diverse, and beautiful in their natural state or as the "hideous and desolate wilderness" that so terrified the Puritans; whether we choose wilderness or unbridled development.

New York

There is little to be proud of in American history for the four decades following the Civil War. During this period, business became the business of America, and New York City became its capital. Nonetheless, during this era and from the city of Mammon itself came one of the great chapters in American wilderness preservation. With the enthusiastic support of the New York City Chamber of Commerce, the Governor of New York signed a bill in 1885 establishing the Adirondack Forest Preserve in the northern part of the state. In 1894, the New York State

[1] Pennsylvania currently has no roadless areas larger than 50,000 acres, although the closure of a couple of minor dirt roads around the 30,000-acre Hammersley Wild Area in Potter and Clinton Counties would easily create a roadless area of at least 50,000 acres. A more visionary wilderness restoration plan for state forest lands in this north-central part of the state could produce a roadless Wilderness Recovery Area of a quarter of a million acres.

Constitutional Convention enshrined protection of the Adirondacks in that state's highest law. (Louis Marshall, father of Bob Marshall, was one of the leaders of that effort.)

However, a pristine wilderness was not being preserved. Moose, Timber Wolf, Panther, Lynx, and Beaver were already gone or virtually so. Little virgin forest remained. Streams had been heavily damaged by logging.

But the protection afforded the land has succeeded. Moose, Raven, and Beaver have returned. Bald Eagle, Peregrine Falcon, and Lynx have been reintroduced. Rivers and streams are healing themselves, and forests are growing tall.

Adirondack Park is a complex preserve. Some 3.7 million acres of its 6 million acres are privately owned. Although there are large blocks of state land, private inholdings complicate preservation for key areas. The Adirondack Park Agency, created in 1970, was instructed to develop a master plan for management of the Park. Not only did the agency have management authority over state lands, but (to a limited degree) it was able to control development on private lands through strict zoning. Obviously, the Adirondack Park Agency has been unpopular with some of the local residents, who would sit well on a stool in any Idaho mill town bar.

The master plan involved the classification of state lands into nine categories. These include Wilderness (with regulations as strict as those for federal Wilderness Areas) and Primitive, Wild River, and Canoe (these three are almost as well protected as Wilderness). Wild Forest classification permits the retention of some truck trails and allows snowmobiles, among other non-Wilderness uses. Nevertheless, some Wild Forest is quite primitive and qualifies as "roadless" in this inventory. By 1979, slightly over a million acres (45 percent of the state land) had been designated as Wilderness. Additions to the Wilderness classification are being continually made as private lands are acquired or nonconforming uses are removed from state lands. Catskill State Park, less than one hundred miles north of New York City, also has designated Wilderness Areas, including one large enough for this inventory.

Sadly, though, all is not well even in the Adirondack Wilderness Areas. Under heavy pressure from development interests in northern New York, Governor Mario Cuomo has essentially abandoned Adirondack preservation as part of his political agenda, in effect terminating New York's land acquisition program and thus leaving hundreds of thousands of acres of Adirondack timberlands vulnerable to purchase by developers. It seems the politicians of New York one hundred years ago were more visionary and courageous than are those today.

Acid precipitation is destroying the lakes, streams, and forests. The reauthorized and "strengthened" Clean Air Act was an environmental shell game by "environmentalist" George Bush. While it may slow acidification of lakes in the Northeast, it will do little to prevent continuing forest death there. As the grisly impact of acid rain continues, restoration of Moose, Timber Wolf, Panther, Lynx, Wolverine . . . becomes moot. There is no better example than in the Adirondacks of the painful fact that wilderness cannot be preserved in isolation, that the damage we wreak in industrial areas is also felt in protected wildlands. There is no preserve large enough to escape our poisoning of the air, water, and land with the by-products of civilization.

HIGH PEAKS 336,000 acres	
Designated High Peaks State Wilderness Area (Adirondack Park) and private inholdings	197,215
Dix Mountain State Wilderness Area (Adirondack Park)	45,208
Private and Wild Forest roadless adjacent to Dix Mountain	54,570
Private roadless east of Raquette River	38,652

Description: Northern New York south of Lake Placid (north-central Adirondack Park). This is the high country of the Adirondacks, including the highest peak in New York State, Mt. Marcy (5,344 feet), and dropping to lower-elevation swampland along the Saranac and Raquette Rivers. Mt. Marcy and Mt. Algonquin are above timberline. Lake-Tear-of-the-Clouds, the source of the Hudson River, is at 4,300 feet. Some parts of this area are very wild, while others are heavily impacted by recreationists. Dramatic high cliffs in the area attract climbers. Major forest types for all of the Adirondack areas are Red Spruce and Balsam Fir at high elevations and in lower frost pockets; below that, a mixed forest primarily of American Beech, Yellow Birch, and Sugar Maple; and at the lowest elevations, a wider variety of hardwoods and hemlock. In addition, Black Spruce, Eastern Larch, and other bog species occur in scattered poorly drained lowlands. Beaver, Raven, River Otter, Fisher, and Marten maintain a stronghold here. Sensitive species of wildlife found in the Adirondacks as a whole include Indiana Bat, Bald Eagle, Spruce Grouse, Common Loon, Short-eared Owl, Sedge Wren, Grasshopper Sparrow, Worm Snake, Bog Turtle, Round Whitefish, and Eastern Sand Darter. Moose are slowly recolonizing Adirondack Park from Vermont; augmentation is probably needed.

Status: Elk, Timber Wolf, and Eastern Panther should be reintroduced to this and other Adirondack Wilderness Areas. Five Lynx were reintroduced in January 1989, into the High Peaks, and nineteen more were scheduled to be released during following years. However, the Lynx reintroduction effort is another likely casualty of Governor Cuomo's conservation backsliding. The state Department of Environmental Conservation has been ominously silent about this much-needed attempt recently, and conservationists don't know whether the released Lynx survive and whether more will be released.

Acid rain is a severe problem in all the Adirondack areas, killing many lakes and perhaps the high-altitude spruce-fir forests. Fortunately, some Adirondack Lakes are less sensitive to acid precipitation and appear to be little affected. Most Adirondack areas were roaded and logged in the past (although pockets of virgin forest exist); the "roadless" areas listed are recovering, and existing vehicle routes in them are no more than Jeep trails. In the portions designated as Wilderness or Primitive, vehicles are prohibited.

RM36: 380,000

HOFFMAN NOTCH 61,000 acres	
Designated Hoffman Notch State Wilderness Area (Adirondack Park)	36,231
Wild Forest roadless	24,324

Description: Northern New York west of Schroon Lake (east-central Adirondack Park). This area of large-diameter hardwoods is dominated by three north-south ridges (Blue Ridge, Washburn Ridge, and Texas Ridge) reaching over 3,000 feet. Hoffman Mountain, the high point in the area, was saved from a ski area in a referendum in 1967. There are eight lakes in the area.

Status: The area designated as Wilderness is protected; the remainder is not.

PHARAOH LAKE 52,000 acres	
Designated Pharaoh Lake State Wilderness Area (Adirondack Park)	45,884
Additional roadless	6,465

Description: Northern New York west of Ticonderoga (eastern Adirondack Park). The vegetation is generally White Pine and birch because of past forest fires. Many ponds and imposing rock outcrops adorn this area. Old hardwood stands survive in unburned coves. There are also areas of Red Pine and mixed northern hardwoods. Pharaoh Lake is one of the largest wilderness lakes in the Adirondacks. This is a low, rolling area with a high point of 2,557 feet on Pharaoh Peak.

Status: The area designated as Wilderness is protected; the rest is not.

SIAMESE POND 141,000 acres	
Designated Siamese Pond State Wilderness Area (Adirondack Park)	112,604
Wild Forest and private roadless	28,391

Description: Northern New York west of North Creek (south-central Adirondack Park). Rolling hills, Beaver ponds, and mature second-growth forest distinguish this area. Ice caves on Chimney Mountain are a rare feature. There are some 60–70 glacier-carved lakes and ponds in this area, including Thirteenth Lake, which has landlocked salmon.

Status: Snowmobiles and ORVs trespass into the Wilderness.

WILCOX LAKE 120,000 acres	
Wilcox Lake Wild Forest and private roadless (Adirondack Park)	120,000

Description: Northern New York between the Siamese Pond and Silver Lake Wilderness Areas (southern Adirondack Park) north of Northville. Rolling hills, Brook Trout streams, and some very large trees characterize this area.

Status: This area is heavily laced with snowmobile trails and old logging roads.

SILVER LAKE 141,000 acres	
Designated Silver Lake State Wilderness Area (Adirondack Park) and private inholdings	106,900
Wild Forest and private roadless to south, north, and west	34,130

Description: Northern New York north of Gloversville (southern Adirondack Park). This is rolling, low country (only four mountains reach 3,000 feet) with large second-growth hemlock and hardwoods. Because this was one of the first areas acquired by the state in the Adirondacks, the logged areas have grown back to give a powerful impression of pristine forest. Swamps, Beaver ponds, and lakes are common.

Status: The designated Wilderness is protected; the remainder is not.

FERRIS LAKE 75,000 acres	
Ferris Lake Wild Forest (Adirondack Park) and private roadless	75,000

Description: Northern New York northeast of Utica (southwestern Adirondack Park). Many ponds, lakes, and streams make this a prime area for water-loving species.

Status: Open to vehicles.

WEST CANADA LAKE 316,000 acres	
Designated West Canada Lake State Wilderness Area (Adirondack Park)	156,735
Designated Buell Brook State Primitive Area	10,900
Jessup River Wild Forest roadless	18,120
Black River Wild Forest roadless	75,000
Private and additional state roadless	55,300

Description: Northern New York southeast of Old Forge (southwestern Adirondack Park). Numerous lakes and streams in three watersheds (Hudson, Mohawk, and Black), Red Spruce–Balsam Fir swamp, and Beaver meadows make this an important area of wetlands. The state-designated Indian Wild River flows through this roadless area. Rolling hills, steep mountains, and large coniferous and deciduous trees characterize this diverse and productive landscape.

Status: Snowmobiles occasionally trespass in the Wilderness Area; Jeep trails run to private inholdings in Black River Wild Forest.

RM36: 430,000

BLUE RIDGE 75,000 acres	
Designated Blue Ridge State Wilderness Area (Adirondack Park)	45,736
Moose River Wild Forest roadless	29,343

Description: Northern New York south of Blue Mountain Lake (central Adirondack Park). Some of the best old-growth spruce and hemlock in the Northeast was blown down here in the 1950 hurricane, illustrating the fragility of tiny remnant ecosystems. The high point is 3,497-foot Blue Ridge.

Status: The designated Wilderness is protected; the rest is not.

PIGEON LAKE 62,000 acres	
Designated Pigeon Lake State Wilderness Area (Adirondack Park)	50,100
Private roadless to north	11,860

Description: Northern New York north of Eagle Bay (west-central Adirondack Park). Low, rolling hills, many swamps, dense Red Spruce–Balsam Fir forest on West Mountain, and small tracts of old-growth White Pine and virgin Yellow Birch mark this area.

Status: The designated Wilderness is protected; the private land is not.

HA-DE-RON-DAH 89,000 acres	
Designated Ha-de-ron-dah State Wilderness Area (Adirondack Park)	26,528
Private and Independence River Wild Forest roadless	62,540

Description: Northern New York northwest of Old Forge (western Adirondack Park). This rolling, swampy terrain features 100-foot-high pines. Pin Cherry, Aspen, and Bracken Fern dominate formerly burned areas.

Status: The designated Wilderness suffers from serious snowmobile invasion. The non-Wilderness portion has old logging roads that have been converted to hiking trails and snowmobile routes.

FIVE PONDS 203,000 acres	
Designated Five Ponds State Wilderness Area (Adirondack Park)	101,171
Designated Pepperbox State Wilderness Area (Adirondack Park)	14,625
Wild Forest, private, and other roadless	87,000

Description: Northern New York south of Cranberry Lake (west-central Adirondack Park). The high point is 2,489-foot Summit Mountain. There are excellent examples of glaciation here, including the well-developed Five Ponds esker. Some 50,000 acres of virgin White Pine and Red Spruce (the largest tract of virgin timber in the northeast) are located within this largely low, rolling area, as are nearly 200 lakes and ponds, alder swamps and Beaver ponds, and 48 miles of three designated Wild and Scenic Rivers—the main branch, West Branch, and Middle Branch of the Oswegatchie River. This area once had the best Brook Trout fishing in New York, but the introduction of perch eliminated them, illustrating the dangers of non-native species. The Pepperbox Wilderness is trailless and one of the wilder places in the Adirondacks—it is largely a wet lowland with scattered spruce, fir, and Red Maple. The Cranberry Wild Forest has boreal forest and bird species common to Canada. Bob Marshall's first wilderness experiences were in this roadless area.

Status: Snowmobiling is permitted in the Cranberry Wild Forest. Marshall proposed a 380,000-acre Wilderness here in the 1930s. The Adirondack Council is currently proposing acquisition of private property to designate a 400,000-acre Bob Marshall Great Wilderness Area, which the Council says could be the outstanding Wilderness in the Adirondacks. Because of Governor Cuomo's political abandonment of the Adirondacks, developers could instead acquire private land in the heart of the proposal. Unless conservationists succeed in securing vulnerable private timberlands throughout Adirondack Park, sufficient habitat will not be available for reintroduction of Gray Wolf, Wolverine, and Caribou. The road density in the Park is too high to allow populations of these wide-ranging, wilderness-dependent species to survive. Moose are slowly recolonizing the Park, Lynx have been reintroduced, and Eastern Panther have been reliably reported in recent years; but these species, too, need more protected land than the Park presently affords them.

RM36: 380,000

SLIDE MOUNTAIN–PANTHER MOUNTAIN 52,000 acres	
Designated Slide Mountain–Panther Mountain State Wilderness Area (Catskill Park)	38,745
Proposed Wilderness addition and other roadless	13,000

Description: Southeastern New York west of Kingston in Catskill State Park. Slide Mountain is 4,180 feet; the low point is 1,100 feet. Oak-and-hickory forest grades to northern hardwoods with Red Spruce–Balsam Fir on the higher elevations. This wilderness produces the water supply for New York City. Just across a road from this roadless area is the 37,000-acre roadless area of the Big Indian–Beaverkill Range Wilderness Area and Balsam Lake Mountain Wild Forest.

Status: The designated Wilderness is protected; the rest is not.

New England

Paper companies own a vast, once-logged but otherwise undeveloped area along the Canadian border in Maine, New Hampshire, and Vermont that consists of northeastern spruce-fir and northern hardwood forest, streams, lakes, and mountains. Indeed, some 10 million *acres in Maine are uninhabited, according to wilderness expert and author George Wuerthner. This is the largest uninhabited area in the lower forty-eight. The "Northeast Kingdom" of Vermont, mostly paper company land, is the wildest and least populated part of that state. Much of northern New Hampshire (in private ownership) is probably wilder than the large roadless areas in the White Mountain National Forest. These areas have, of course, been logged, and some dirt roads remain in them, but the opportunity to restore significant wilderness in northern New England is greater than anywhere else in the United States. If these areas were transferred to public ownership, and closed to logging and motorized vehicles, wilderness would quickly begin to reestablish itself and wilderness-dependent species such as Wolverine, Panther, Lynx, Pine Marten, and Caribou would likely return. The Fisher has already repatriated to northern New Hampshire. With careful wilderness restoration management and reintroduction of extirpated species, wilderness would return even sooner.*

The opportunity for such restoration will never be better than it is today. The going price for timber company land is $200 per acre; all of northern Maine (10 million acres) could be purchased for $2 billion—the price of a couple of Stealth bombers. More than enough money is currently in the federal government's Land and Water Conservation Fund to buy several million acres in northern New England for wilderness restoration and at least one new National Park. All that is lacking is enough popular demand to force the necessary political will.

Now is the time for conservationists in New England and the nation to envision real wilderness, with its full complement of native species, existing once again east of the Rockies. The opportunity currently exists for wilderness on an Alaskan scale in New England.

If conservationists do not act swiftly, however, the opportunity will be lost.

Forestry is becoming harsher on the corporate lands. Herbicides, larger clearcuts, shorter rotation times, more roads, and heavier machinery are having a more devastating impact today than the "lighter" logging practices of the past. Relatively natural forests are being transformed into industrial tree farms. Moreover, developers like the Patten Corporation are gobbling up paper company lands that are put on the market. If this continues, condominiums, ski areas, lodges, vacation resorts, and second homes will ring the lakes and scar the mountains; loon and wolf will lose out once again.

In addition to the potential *Big Outside in New England, several areas over 50,000 acres are essentially roadless and undeveloped today. Baxter State Park in Maine and the White Mountain National Forest in New Hampshire are the principal areas of public ownership in New England. Baxter is largely protected, but the White Mountain NF is under the same pressures of roading and logging as National Forests in other parts of the country.*

The designated Wilderness Areas on the White Mountain NF were not easy to win. (See the discussion on Eastern National Forest Wilderness in the introductory remarks for the Southeast.) The 1984 New Hampshire Wilderness Act was the worst one in the East. Of 262,257 acres in RARE II (conservationists proposed 495,596 acres for Wilderness, and that figure is a far more accurate indicator of what was roadless), only 77,000 acres were protected in the bill. A special problem for Wilderness preservation in New Hampshire is that some so-called conservation groups—like the hut-operating Appalachian Mountain Club—essentially oppose Wilderness designation. Other conservation groups, including The Wilderness Society and the Sierra Club, recently settled their appeal of the White Mountain NF Plan (which was one of the worst in the nation) with what they call a victory but what Preserve Appalachian Wilderness calls a sellout. Nonetheless, several large roadless areas are on the White Mountain NF; their long-term prospects are varied.

There appear to be large roadless areas on timber company lands in Maine, New Hampshire, and Vermont, and they are listed here as well. Calculation of the roadless acreage for such private lands is rough.

BAXTER STATE PARK 200,000 acres (Maine)	
Baxter State Park roadless	120,000
Private roadless to east	80,000

Description: Central Maine north of Millinocket. Baxter is the beau ideal of the North Woods: lakes, streams, Mt. Ktaadn, Black Bear, Moose, and blackflies. Mt. Ktaadn, the highest point in Maine, is 5,268 feet. Seventeen other peaks are over 3,000 feet. The lowest elevations are below 500 feet. Henry David Thoreau climbed Ktaadn in 1846 and wrote about that experience in his wilderness classic *The Maine Woods* (I use his spelling for the mountain). Ktaadn's peak is the first place in the United States to be hit by the sun and, along with other peaks in the Park, has alpine tundra. In this area of transition from northern hardwoods (Beech, Yellow Birch, Sugar Maple) to Red Spruce–Balsam Fir forest, some virgin forest remains. Sadly, this roadless area is a habitat island generally surrounded by a sea of clearcuts and other "managed forest." Glacial features include kames, eskers, drumlins, kettleholes, and moraines. Moose are abundant here. Additional wildlife includes White-tailed Deer, Bobcat, Mink, Short-tailed and Long-tailed Weasels, Canada Jay, and Spruce Grouse.

Status: A large area of seemingly roadless private land, east of the Park, including the Seboeis River and the East Branch of the Penobscot, is included in this roadless area. Lands in the Park are protected and managed much as federal Wilderness; those outside the Park are not. The private acreage should be added to Baxter State Park as the core for a 10-million-acre Wilderness Preserve stretching to the north to include the St. John and Allagash Rivers. In one of the most visionary and praiseworthy initiatives from the mainstream conservation movement in recent years, The Wilderness Society has proposed a 3-million-acre National Park or Preserve in this area.

BAXTER NORTH 90,000 acres (Maine)	
Baxter State Park roadless	55,000
Private and Maine Public Reserve roadless to north	35,000

Description: Central Maine northwest of Patten. Baxter State Park and adjacent private and Maine Public Reserve Land north of the Baxter Park road form this roadless area. The countless streams, ponds, and lakes include the East Branch Penobscot River, Webster Brook, and Grand Lake. Elevations vary from 1,200 feet to 650 feet. The Baxter Park road separates this roadless area from the main Baxter roadless area. See Baxter Park for general description.

Status: Logging is allowed on 28,000 acres of Baxter Park lands in this area. The land north of the Park appears to be essentially roadless, but is likely under some kind of timber "management." Baxter Park should be considerably enlarged, with wilderness restoration the management goal. Logging should, of course, be entirely halted in Baxter State Park.

REED MOUNTAIN 60,000 acres (Maine)	
Big Reed Pond Preserve (The Nature Conservancy)	3,800
Private roadless	56,000

Description: North-central Maine north of Baxter State Park. There are only 6,000 acres of original (unlogged) forest in the entire state of Maine. Two thirds of this is in the Reed Mountain roadless area. The Nature Conservancy recently acquired this 3,800-acre old-growth forest around Big Reed Pond. Besides providing habitat for other North Woods species, Big Reed Pond is one of only ten ponds in the world to contain the Blueback Char. Other features in this area include Haymock Lake, Munsungan Lake, Mooseleuk Mountain, and the Currier Ponds. This roadless area is just north of the Baxter North roadless area and separated from it only by a timber company dirt road.

Status: This important Nature Conservancy preserve provides additional argument for acquiring timber company land north of Baxter and creating a huge National Park. Without protection, surrounding lands that are returning to a roadless condition may be roaded and logged once again. Unfortunately, The Nature Conservancy did not purchase the entire patch of old-growth forest. It should be encouraged to do so, as well as to undertake a major campaign to acquire much larger acreages of timber company land for wilderness restoration in Maine.

WILDLANDS LAKES 135,000 acres	
Private roadless	135,000

Description: Central Maine south of Baxter State Park and west of Millinocket. The Appalachian Trail winds through this large area of forest, streams, and lakes. Features include Rainbow Lake, Nahmakanta Lake, and the Debsconeag Lakes.

Status: This area should be high priority for preservation in public ownership as part of a 10-million-acre Maine Woods Wilderness National Park stretching north through Baxter Park to the Canadian border.

ST. JOHN PONDS 180,000 acres (Maine)	
Private roadless	180,000

Description: Northwestern Maine north of Moosehead Lake. The headwaters of the St. John River and North Branch Penobscot, including the St. John Ponds, Big Bog, and the Baker Branch of the St. John River below Baker Lake, form a large roadless area of northeastern spruce-fir and northern hardwoods. Moose, Black Bear, Lynx, Marten, Fisher, Northeastern Coyote, Mink, River Otter, Fisher, Osprey, Common Loon, and Furbish Lousewort live here.

A huge area of northern Maine is uninhabited, although the paper companies that own enormous tracts have certainly damaged it with continual cutting over the last century. Nonetheless, some areas of quite wild land remain, and the opportunity exists for wilderness restoration on an unprecedented scale.

Status: Despite the presence of several dirt cherrystem roads, this large area appears to be essentially roadless. Conservation groups should establish a national priority to acquire 10 million acres of paper company land, from Baxter State Park to the St. John River, to form a wilderness-oriented National Park. Dirt roads should be closed, logged areas restored, and extirpated species like Gray Wolf, Woodland Caribou, Wolverine, and Catamount (Eastern Panther) reintroduced. Such an area, in twenty years or less, could be one of the finest temperate-zone Wildernesses in the world.

*RM36: 2,800,000**

ST. JOHN RIVER SOUTH 100,000 acres (Maine and Quebec)	
Private roadless	90,000
Quebec roadless	10,000

Description: Northwestern Maine. Hardwood Mountain, Desolation and Corner Ponds are landmarks. Elevations drop from 1,800 feet to 1,100 feet. The St. John River, a National Wild and Scenic River, is a classic wilderness canoe trip. The Baker Branch St. John River from Baker Lake (International Paper Road) north (downstream) to the Boise Cascade Road (confluence with the Southwest Branch St. John River) is essentially roadless. See St. John Ponds for general description.

Status: See St. John Ponds. The estimate for contiguous roadless land in Quebec is rough.

*RM36: 2,800,000**

ST. JOHN RIVER NORTH 70,000 acres (Maine)	
Private roadless	70,000

Description: Northwestern Maine. There appears to be an essentially roadless section of the St. John River north from the American Realty Road to low-standard dirt roads coming in to either side of the river at Ninemile. Also apparently roadless are the river's east side between Red Pine and Ninemile East campgrounds, and a larger area on the northern west bank, including Linscott and Houlton Ponds. Elevations drop from 1,400 feet to 1,000 feet. See St. John Ponds for general description.

Status: See St. John Ponds.

*RM36: 2,800,000**

MOOSE RIVER 110,000 acres (Maine)	
Maine Public Reserve Land roadless	14,000
Private roadless	96,000

Description: Western Maine southwest of Jackman. Attean Mountain and Pond, Moose River, No. 5 Mountain, Holeb Falls, Tumbledown Mountain, Spencer Bale Mountain, Kirby Range, and numerous small ponds are features of this roadless area south of the Canadian Pacific Railroad tracks. Several of the summits exceed 3,000 feet; the low point is 1,159 feet, on Attean Pond.

Status: Minor dirt roads form the southwestern boundary of this area.

REDINGTON POND 120,000 acres (Maine)	
Private roadless	120,000

Description: Western Maine east of Rangeley. The Appalachian Trail passes through this mountainous region, which has several peaks over 4,000 feet, including Crocker Mountain (4,168 feet) and The Horn (4,023 feet).

Status: Although several dirt roads penetrate this large area of private land, it appears to be essentially roadless.

WEST BRANCH DEAD DIAMOND RIVER–CRYSTAL MOUNTAIN 60,000 acres (New Hampshire)	
Private roadless	60,000

Description: Northern New Hampshire northeast of Dixville Notch. The land from Magalloway Mountain (3,359 feet) south to Crystal Mountain (3,250 feet) and the Swift Diamond River appears to be essentially roadless. Flora and fauna are similar to that of the Pemigewasset (see below). Wildlife also includes Fisher, Moose, and possibly Eastern Panther.

Status: Several minor dirt roads penetrate, but do not cross, this area of paper company land. Efforts should be made to acquire this area and other paper company–owned or otherwise privately owned roadless areas in northern New Hampshire and Vermont as the core for a large Wilderness National Park. Most of this particular roadless area is owned by Champion International; while Champion's land is not formally on the market, the company would probably listen to an offer.

BLUE MOUNTAIN 100,000 acres (New Hampshire)	
Public and private roadless	100,000

Description: Northern New Hampshire north of Groveton. The area from Goback Mountain (3,523 feet) east to Blue Mountain (3,720 feet), Dixville Peak, and Owlhead Mountain is essentially roadless. The 45,000-acre Nash Stream watershed in this area is prime habitat for Moose and Panther—Moose have returned, and there are increasing Panther sightings in the area. Fisher have also returned to the area. Flora and fauna are otherwise similar to those of the Pemigewasset.

Status: This former paper company land is penetrated, but not crossed, by several dirt roads. Much of the area was recently purchased by public and private funds for "conservation," but the details may prove to be disappointing—logging, sand and gravel mining, and ORVs may be permitted.

MEACHUM SWAMP 50,000 acres (Vermont)	
Private roadless	50,000

Description: Northeast Kingdom of Vermont north of Bloomfield. This is the country between Averill Lake–East Branch Nulhegan River and the

Connecticut River. Landmarks are Bloomfield Ridge, Monadnock Mountain (3,139 feet), and Sable Mountain (2,726 feet). Yellow Bog—the largest bog in Vermont—is an important feature. This area is the center of Vermont's recovering Moose population and has fine habitat for Gray Wolf and Panther, which were once present. Across the Connecticut River is the Blue Mountain roadless area.

Status: Although penetrated by minor dirt roads, this is a key part of the Northeast Kingdom National Park proposal. As with privately owned areas in Maine, our identification of this area as roadless and our calculation of the roadless acreage is rough.

KILKENNY 70,000 acres (New Hampshire)	
White Mountain NF and private roadless	70,000

Description: Northern New Hampshire between Lancaster and Berlin. This mountainous area includes Deer Ridge, Pilot Range, Pliny Range, and Crescent Range. Mt. Cabot, at 4,080 feet, is the high point; Mt. Waumbeck also exceeds 4,000 feet, and several other peaks, including The Horn, approach that elevation. Unknown Pond is one of several ponds in the area. See Pemigewasset for general description.

Status: About three quarters of the White Mountain NF area was designated for backcountry management by the settlement on the Forest Plan. This means that commercial timber sales will not be scheduled and semiprimitive recreation and wildlife habitat will be stressed, although ORVs will be allowed on designated trails. The remaining part of this roadless area in the White Mountain NF is zoned for full-scale timber harvest. The status of the private lands is unknown.

MAHOOSUC RANGE 78,000 acres (Maine and New Hampshire)	
Maine Public Reserve Land, Grafton Notch State Park, and private roadless (ME)	60,000
Private roadless (NH)	18,000

Description: Central New Hampshire–Maine border east of Berlin, New Hampshire, and northwest of Bethel, Maine. The Appalachian Trail runs along the crest of the Mahoosuc Range in this roadless area. Several peaks exceed 3,700 feet; lower elevations near the Androscoggin River drop to 1,100 feet. The Sunday River watershed forms the southeastern portion of the area. Fauna and flora are similar to those of areas in the White Mountain NF.

Status: The State of Maine is managing its lands in the Mahoosuc as "wilderness." The private lands in Maine and New Hampshire are unprotected and should be high priority for public acquisition and preservation. The Sunday River Ski Area is cherrystemmed in the southern part of this area, as is a dirt road along the lower part of the Sunday River. U.S. Highway 2 separates this area from the Wild River–Kearsarge roadless area to the south.

WILD RIVER–KEARSARGE 110,000 acres (New Hampshire and Maine)	
White Mountain NF and private roadless	110,000

Description: Central New Hampshire–Maine border south of Berlin. Carter Mountain, at 4,832 feet, is the high point. Seven other peaks exceed 4,000 feet. Elevations drop to under 1,000 feet. This area, with 20 miles of the Appalachian Trail, has spectacular views of the Presidential Range (Mt. Washington and friends), which is to the west of Pinkham Notch. The valley of the Wild River, which is surrounded by high peaks, has the best habitat in the White Mountain NF for Pine Marten and Lynx. Flora and fauna are similar to those in the Pemigewasset (see below).

Status: Supposedly, 35,000 acres in the Wild River country (northern part of this roadless area) are closed to motorized vehicles, but a "temporary" snowmobile trail goes through the heart of this roadless area. Over 40,000 acres south of the Wild River portion are being fragmented by FS roading and logging, which will cut the Kearsarge Mountain area off from the rest of the roadless area (it may already have been separated by the time this is printed). Conservation groups have acquiesced in this destruction by cutting a quick deal on their appeal of the White Mountain NF Plan. Additional areas around the Wild River "core" are also being roaded and logged by the FS. Snowmobiles and ORVs are a big problem. This may be the most threatened large roadless area east of the Rocky Mountains (except possibly for the Southern Nantahala in North Carolina and Georgia).

Highway 113 in Maine should be closed to connect this area with the Caribou–Speckled Mountain roadless area of 16,000 acres (the Maine Wilderness Act of 1990 established a 12,000-acre Caribou–Speckled Mountain

Wilderness and released the other 4,000 acres to non-Wilderness uses.) A 125,000–150,000-acre Wilderness could be established here if the Forest Service chain-saw mentality could be held in check.

PEMIGEWASSET 125,000 acres (New Hampshire)	
Designated Pemigewasset Wilderness Area (White Mountain NF)	45,000
Additional White Mountain NF roadless	75,000
Crawford Notch State Park roadless	5,000

Description: Central New Hampshire between Lincoln and Bartlett. A popular backpacking area, this is the largest National Forest roadless area east of the Mississippi. The high point is Mt. Lafayette, at 5,249 feet; Mt. Lincoln is 5,108 feet; thirteen other peaks exceed 4,000 feet. Elevations drop to under 1,000 feet on the edges of the roadless area near large rivers. Many brooks and ponds, and 27 miles of the Appalachian Trail are in the "Pemi." This area was heavily logged at the turn of the century, but is recovering; large second-growth forest is now occurring. Franconia Notch forms the western boundary, and Crawford Notch the east. Both are classic "notches" carved by continental ice sheets.

Rich, diverse, lowland forests surround Sawyer Pond in the southeastern corner. Four basic forest types exist here: Northern hardwoods (maple, ash, beech); northern hardwoods and Red Spruce (with some White and Black Spruce); spruce and fir (spruces and Balsam Fir); and Paper Birch and Aspen. Hardwoods and spruce-fir mixed with birch grow below 2,500 feet. In the high country, spruce and fir grow from 2,500 feet to 3,500 feet; spruce-fir krummholz (up to 300 years old), from 3,500 feet to 4,000 feet; subalpine vegetation, above 4,000 feet; and alpine tundra, above 5,000 feet. Wildlife includes Peregrine Falcon, Cooper's Hawk, Northern Harrier, Black Bear, and Pine Marten. Prime habitat exists for Golden Eagle, Lynx, Wolverine, Eastern Panther, and Gray Wolf—all of which should be reintroduced.

Status: Snowmobiles and other ORVs are allowed on 50,000 acres of the unprotected area. Logging is allowed on about 30,000 acres along the edges of the current roadless area. Three "huts" (lodges) accessible only by foot are in the area. The primary additional threats to the Pemi are acid rain and excessive numbers of hikers. Conservationists continue to push for protection of about 100,000 acres. The Kancamagus Highway to the south—a popular scenic drive and a zoo when the colors turn in the fall—should be closed, and a single 220,000-acre Pemigewasset-Sandwich Wilderness created.

SANDWICH RANGE 81,000 acres (New Hampshire)	
Designated Sandwich Range Wilderness Area (White Mountain NF)	25,000
Additional White Mountain NF and private roadless	56,000

Description: Central New Hampshire northeast of Plymouth. Mt. Osceola, at 4,315 feet, is the high point; three other peaks are above 4,000 feet. Elevations drop to under 1,000 feet. Flora and fauna are similar to those in the Pemi, except that oaks reach their northern limit in the Sandwich Range. This roadless area is separated from the Pemi by the Kancamagus Highway.

Status: Logging, roading, snowmobiles, and ORVs threaten the unprotected portion. A long-used snowmobile trail marks the eastern boundary of the Wilderness and divides it from the Mt. Chocorua Scenic Area (which is included in this roadless area). This area should be combined with the Pemigewasset (see above).

GLASTENBURY MOUNTAIN 52,000 acres (Vermont)	
Green Mountain National Forest roadless	52,000

Description: Southwestern Vermont northeast of Bennington. Local conservationists report a roadless area here of about 52,000 acres on the Green Mountain NF. The area is north of the power line north of Route 9, west of Somerset Reservoir, and south of the East Arlington–Stratton road. Glastenbury Peak, at 3,748 feet, is the high point. Vegetation is largely northern hardwoods with scattered stands of spruce. The Long Trail bisects the area.

Status: The Forest Service did not consider any of this area in RARE II, and there are no designated Wilderness Areas in it. The status of logging and other development in this recovering wild land is unknown. Vermont conservationists should make protection of this large area a priority.

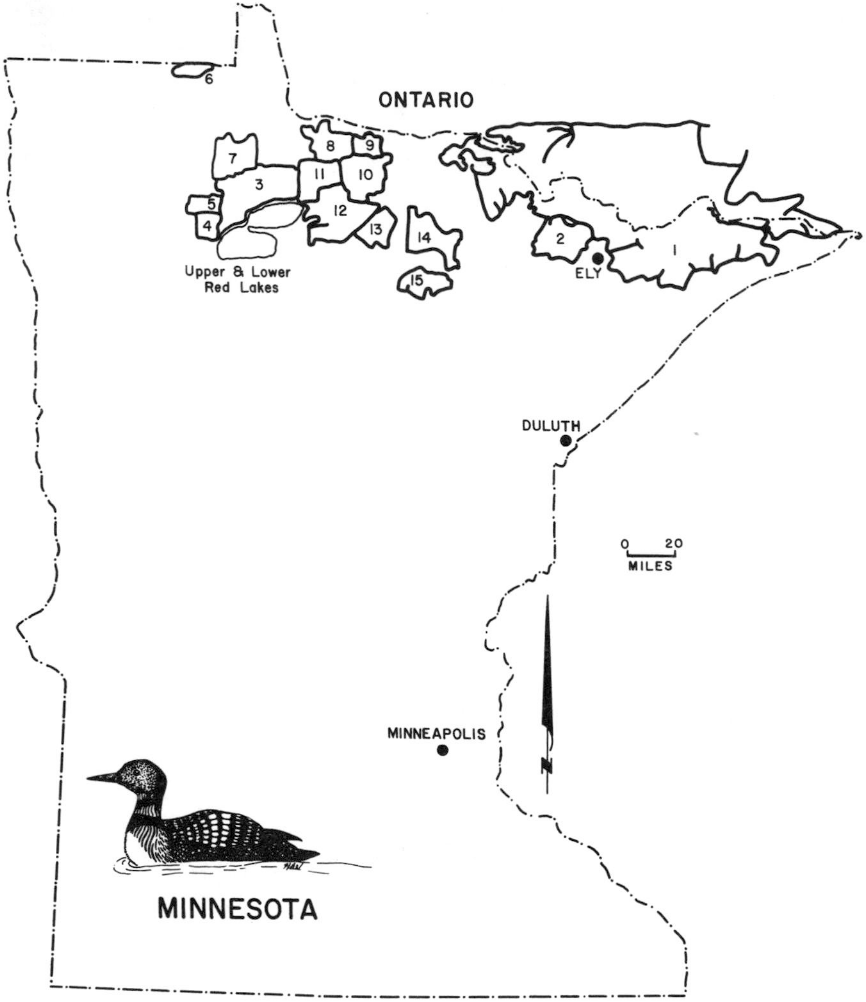

1. Boundary Waters–Quetico
2. Little Sioux
3. Red Lake Peatland
4. Red Lake Indian Res.
5. Carmelee-Hamre
6. Marvin Lake Peatland
7. Lost Lake Peatland
8. East Fork Rapid River
9. West Fork Peatland
10. Black River Peatland
11. Ludlow Peatland
12. Sturgeon River
13. Southeast Pine Island
14. Little Fork River
15. George Washington

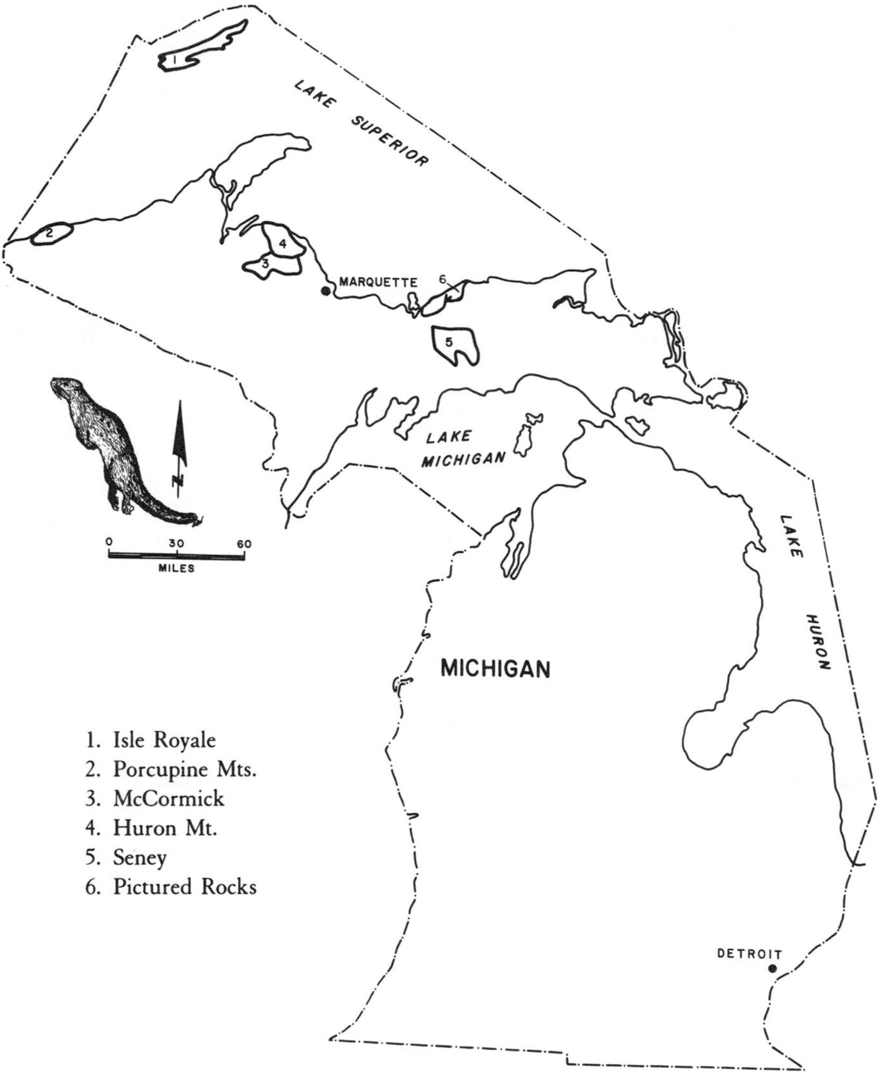
LAKE SUPERIOR
MARQUETTE
LAKE MICHIGAN
MICHIGAN
LAKE HURON
DETROIT
0 30 60
MILES
1. Isle Royale
2. Porcupine Mts.
3. McCormick
4. Huron Mt.
5. Seney
6. Pictured Rocks

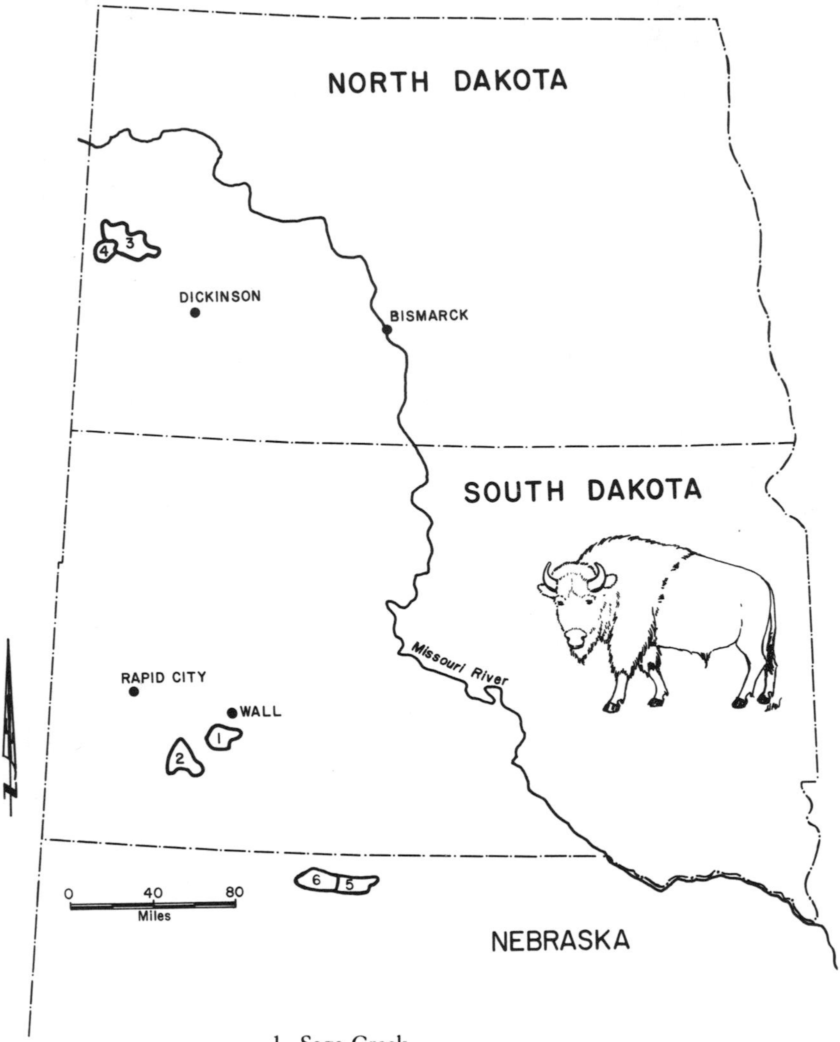

1. Sage Creek
2. Badlands South
3. Little Missouri River
4. Beaver Creek
5. Steer Creek
6. Medicine Creek

North Central

The North Woods of Wisconsin, Michigan, and Minnesota gave the timber industry its age of heroic legend. From the 1870s on, the exploitation of the virgin White Pine forests established a new scale for rapaciousness, and a gigantic folk hero—Paul Bunyan—had to be created to equal the deed. Never before had so much forest fallen so quickly. Even some within the timber industry became alarmed. Frederick Merk, in *History of the Westward Movement,* quotes the owners of the Black River Falls sawmill as telling the Minnesota legislature, "In a few years, the wealthiest portion of the pineries will present nothing but a vast and gloomy wilderness of pine stumps."

They were correct. Paul and the Blue Ox did their work well for the timber barons. The Northern Hardwoods and Great Lakes Pine Forests of northern Wisconsin were chopped to smithereens. There is no Big Outside left in that state. As someone from Madison has written, "I keep driving north in Wisconsin to get to the North Woods, but I never find them." There was a Big Outside once in Wisconsin, there may be again someday, but the largest Wilderness Area in 1989 is less than 20,000 acres on the Nicolet National Forest. Closing roads, stilling the chain saws, and encouraging Timber Wolf and Moose could bring back ecological wilderness. To do so, though, will require vision and self-restraint; something that a few far-sighted citizens of Wisconsin possess, but something alien to most of their Forest Rangers and politicians. Botanists at the University of Wisconsin have proposed establishing two biodiversity preserves (100,000 acres and 40,000 acres) on the Chequamegon National Forest, where native old-growth ecosystems could be reestablished. To his lasting credit, the Forest Supervisor supported the idea, but the Regional Forester overruled him. The botanists have appealed the rejection of their visionary proposal. More power to them.

In the Upper Peninsula of Michigan, where Nick Adams and his kid sister fished the Big Two Hearted River . . . well, Paul got that, too. But he missed a couple of places, places that offer a glimpse of what Michigan once was.

To really find the North Woods, one has to go all the way north in the Midwest, up to northern Minnesota, where glaciers scoured the southern toe of the Canadian Shield to form the Boundary Waters. Make no mistake about it, Paul did his best to turn this area into a "wilderness of stumps," too. Despite Forest Service administrative protection for the Boundary Waters beginning in 1926, Paul's successors were permitted to swing their axes in much of it. In the 1964 Wilderness Act, Congress continued the exception. It was not until 1978, after a dreadful fight, that Congress finally protected the last great remnant of the North Woods, by outlawing logging in the Boundary Waters Wilderness. Nonetheless, this great Wilderness must be guarded constantly.

In western Minnesota, the North Woods give way to the Great Plains—first Tallgrass Prairie, then Shortgrass Prairie. In its own way, change came as rapidly to this treeless landscape as to the big woods. The Lakota had to step aside for civilization, and the Lakota depended on the buffalo for their freedom, reasoned General Phil Sheridan. The answer was simple: Destroy the buffalo, and destroy the Indian. George Armstrong Custer discovered that the warriors of the Plains wouldn't take it lying down. But after the great herds were gone, even the Ghost Dance couldn't bring back the freedom of rolling grass and distant thunder.

There are still spectacular thunderstorms and riveting sunsets on the Great Plains, blizzards sweeping down from the North Pole, and summer days hot enough to drive a man to his knees. But cattle have replaced Bison, Elk, and

Pronghorn. Farmers' dogs yap where Buffalo Wolves once howled. And the rotary irrigation pump squeaks where the medicine wheel marked sacred ground.

Only in Badlands National Park in western South Dakota, along the Little Missouri River in western North Dakota, and in the Sandhills of Nebraska was the land hard enough to deflect civilization. Six areas there whisper a reminder of what was, a short hundred years ago.

As Aldo Leopold learned from his sojourn in Wisconsin, we live in a world of wounds.

Minnesota

We Westerners look down our noses on the states east of the Rockies, considering them tame woodlots compared with our wide-open spaces and unpopulated mountains and deserts. But northern Minnesota is as wild and sparsely settled as most of the West. Indeed, the third-largest roadless area in the lower forty-eight states is on the Superior National Forest; state and Indian lands to the west of it compose an additional 2-million-acre backcountry of bog and northern forest crossed only by a handful of minor roads. Moreover, this is the only place in the United States outside of Alaska where the wolf has held its own.

BOUNDARY WATERS–QUETICO 2,752,000 acres (also in Ontario)	
Designated Boundary Waters Canoe Area Wilderness (Superior NF and intermixed state, county, and private)	972,537
Quetico Provincial Park roadless (Ontario)	1,175,169
Superior NF RARE II contiguous to Boundary Waters Canoe Area	36,000
Additional Superior NF roadless	152,000
Voyageurs National Park roadless	219,128
Superior NF, state, and private roadless contiguous to Voyageurs NP	85,000
LaVerendrye Provincial Park roadless (Ontario)	22,000
Sand Point roadless (Ontario)	90,000

Description: Northeastern Minnesota and southwestern Ontario north of Ely, Minnesota. The Boundary Waters are an incomparable lakeland wilderness—the North Woods personified. Denizens include Gray Wolf,

Black Bear, Moose, Lynx, Fisher, Pine Marten, Common Loon, Osprey, Double-crested Cormorant, Belted Kingfisher, merganser (Common, Red-breasted, and Hooded), Bald Eagle, over twenty species of wood warblers, Black-backed Woodpecker, Boreal Owl, pike, and trout. (Moose populations declined 45 percent between 1989 and 1991 as a result of a winter tick infestation; the Minnesota Department of Natural Resources stopped the 1991 Moose hunt in the Boundary Water Canoe Area (BWCA) because of the decline.)

Here is the largest extent of virgin forest east of the Rockies, including a stand of Red Pine dating from a fire in 1595. Two major forest types meet in the BWCA: the Northern Boreal Forest, typified by Black and White Spruces, Balsam Fir, Paper Birch, and Jack Pine; and the Great Lakes, or Laurentian, Forest, of Red and White Pines, Red and Sugar Maples, and other northern hardwoods.

The high point is Eagle Mountain, at 2,301 feet, the highest elevation in Minnesota. Several thousand lakes over 10 acres in size, several thousand miles of canoe trails, Beaver ponds, bogs, marshes, exposed rock, and cliffs shape the beauty of this great Wilderness. This is the southern edge of the Canadian Shield, with some of the oldest exposed rocks in the world. At least four times in the last million years, continental glaciers up to 2 miles thick passed over it, gouging and shaping its present character.

The Boundary Waters Canoe Area was the second area protected by the Forest Service for its wilderness values (in 1926), and the first Wilderness so protected by Congress, beginning in 1930. Several of the conservation movement's greats have fought for the BWCA, including Arthur Carhart, Aldo Leopold, Bob Marshall, Ernest Oberholtzer, and Sigurd Olson. President Truman in 1949 closed the BWCA airspace under 4,000 feet to airplanes. Timber harvest was permitted in the BWCA under a special provision in the Wilderness Act until conservationists managed to pass the Boundary Waters Canoe Area Wilderness Act in 1978, which also eliminated snowmobiles from the area and banned motorboats from many of the lakes.

Voyageurs National Park, established in 1975, has 40 percent of its area in water, most of it in four large lakes: Rainy, Kabetogama, Namakan, and Sand Point.

Status: The designated Boundary Waters Canoe Area Wilderness consists of three units. The 57,000-acre Caribou unit east of the main unit is separated by a paved road in Minnesota. However, it connects to the main unit through roadless country north of Gunflint Lake in Ontario and is included as part of this distinct roadless area. The third unit, the 114,000-acre Little Sioux, is southwest of the main unit and cut off by a gravel road. In this inventory, it is therefore considered as a separate roadless area. The Boundary Waters Canoe Area Wilderness (all three units) totals 1,086,954 acres.

Several lakes in the BWCA and all the large lakes in Voyageurs NP are still open to motorboats. The NPS permits snowmobiles in Voyageurs on the large lakes when they are frozen (maybe it should be when they are not frozen). The NPS is also supporting a proposed snowmobile trail down the length of the Kabetogama Peninsula—the major land area in the Park. An additional threat to Voyageurs comes from an arrogant yahoo who vows to build an eighteen-unit condominium on his private land in the Park. The NPS has condemned the land for acquisition, but the developer has sued.

Airplanes fly into the small lakes on the Kabetogama, and military jets scream through the skies above Truman's BWCA airspace reservation—Friends of the Boundary Waters Wilderness filed suit to halt the military flights in 1988. Unprotected contiguous roadless lands are being chewed up by logging and roading in Ontario all around Quetico and in Minnesota around the BWCA. Acid rain threatens the lakes, streams, and forests of the area. Excessive visitor use in the BWCA (the most heavily used Wilderness Area in the United States, with over a million visitor-days a year) is damaging campsites and water quality, although strict visitor regulations by the FS are improving the situation. A radio station is proposing a 611-foot-high FM tower on the east side of the BWCA, which would be visible 15 miles away. Friends of the Boundary Waters Wilderness reports that "interest in gold and other precious metals has now reached a fever pitch in the wilderness-edge area." The state is currently leasing mineral rights. But in 1991, gold fever seemed to abate with poor exploration results.

Over a quarter of a million acres of lands within the Superior NF (including private and state inholdings) contiguous to the Boundary Waters Wilderness or Voyageurs National Park appear to be essentially roadless. Although once logged, these lands are recovering and should be added to the designated Wilderness. Protection of these Superior NF lands should be a high priority for conservationists—the FS plans anything but protection.

The Friends of the Boundary Waters Wilderness have appealed the Superior NF Plan because of (1) its failure to remove truck portages from the BWCA as required by law; (2) excessive road building (outside the BWCA) mandated by the plan; and (3) the impact on the Eastern Timber Wolf from logging outside the BWCA.

Commercial outfitters and their dupes in the Lac la Croix Indian Band in Ontario have mounted an attack on the Quetico Park Wilderness with demands for aircraft landings, motorboat use on lakes, the extension of commercial trapping (trapping was due to be phased out), removal of areas from the Park, and construction of a road to Batchewoung Lake. In the summer of 1991, Ontario opened three lakes to 10-horsepower motors for the Indians.

Closing a few roads and undertaking wilderness recovery management could easily establish a single 5-million-acre International Wilderness here. (Ernest Oberholtzer proposed a 10-million-acre International Peace Memorial Forest here in 1928.)

LITTLE SIOUX 179,000 acres	
Designated Boundary Waters Wilderness Area Little Sioux unit (Superior NF)	114,417
Additional Superior NF and private roadless	65,000

Description: Northeastern Minnesota west of Ely. This is a detached section of the BWCA. See BWCA for general description.

Status: Motorboats of 25 horsepower are allowed on large Trout Lake. Contiguous lands are under threat of logging and roading, and are open to snowmobiles and powerboats. St. Louis County has proposed a major reconstruction of the Echo Trail, the fairly primitive gravel road that separates the Little Sioux area from the main body of the Boundary Waters. Such reconstruction would make the road suitable for eventual paving, but even unpaved, it would allow for high-speed travel that would diminish the primitive nature of the Boundary Waters on either side.

RED LAKE PEATLANDS 350,000 acres	
Red Lake State Wildlife Management Area–Beltrami Island State Forest–Red Lake Indian Reservation roadless	350,000

Description: North-central Minnesota. North and east of the Upper and Lower Red Lakes lies a vast wild area of peatlands, lakes, bogs, streams, and conifer forest that is broken by only a few roads. Most of this primitive landscape is in Minnesota State Forests or Wildlife Management Areas, with scattered Red Lake Indian Reservation tracts and some Bureau of Land Management and private lands. (This is one of the few areas east of the Rockies with blocks of BLM land left.) These peatlands, of the Forested Raised Bog type, were formed by peat accumulation in the bed of glacial Lake Agassiz at the end of the Pleistocene. They feature forested teardrop islands and ribbed fen patterns, and are particularly important for scientific study because they are not underlain with permafrost, which complicates studies in other peat areas, and because of the delicate interaction between vegetation and hydrology that produces the patterned landforms. Twenty-five vascular plant and animal species in the peatlands are listed as Endangered, Threatened, or of special concern. Insectivorous plants, such as pitcher plants, sundews, and bladderworts, and various species of orchids and ericaceous plants are common. Wildlife includes Gray Wolf, Moose (perhaps the highest concentration in the lower forty-eight), Northern Bog Lemming, Black Bear, Snowshoe Hare, Lynx, Elk, White-tailed Deer, Great Gray Owl, Northern Sandhill Crane, Yellow Rail, and Palm Warbler. One of the highest concentrations of breeding songbirds in the United States is here, owing to the marvelous abundance of mosquitoes, blackflies, and other flying insects. Woodland Caribou made their last stand in Minnesota in the peatlands; they should be reintroduced. Forest types include Great Lakes spruce-fir and pine. Elevations in this flat terrain average a little more than 1,000 feet above sea level.

The largest of these apparently roadless units is immediately north of Upper and Lower Red Lakes between state Highways 72 and 89.

Status: This area and the other peatland roadless areas listed have snowmobile trails crossing them, although there are sizable areas without even this impact. The Minnesota Department of Natural Resources has proposed protecting 233,508 acres of this particular area and smaller portions of some of the others for scientific study. Presumably, most of the forests in this region have been logged at one time or another for pulpwood. Conservationists should make preservation of all of the generally roadless areas in this region a major priority. The northern Minnesota peatlands represent one of the wildest blocks of country east of the Rocky Mountains and an opportunity to preserve a true wilderness ecosystem in the Midwest of several million acres. Combined with the nearby Boundary Waters area, this is the finest habitat remaining for the Gray Wolf in the lower forty-eight states.

One threat to the peatlands is a recurring proposal to mine them for peat, which would be burned as an energy source in power plants.

RED LAKE INDIAN RESERVATION PEATLANDS 63,000 acres	
Red Lake Indian Reservation roadless	63,000

Description and Status: West of Lower Red Lake in north-central Minnesota. See Red Lake for general description and status.

CARMELEE-HAMRE PEATLANDS 58,000 acres	
Red Lake Indian Reservation–Carmelee and Hamre State Wildlife Management Areas roadless	58,000

Description and Status: West of Upper Red Lake in north-central Minnesota. See Red Lake for general description and status.

MARVIN LAKE PEATLANDS 57,000 acres (also in Manitoba)	
Undesignated state-owned Consolidated Conservation lands and private roadless	57,000

Description and Status: West of Lake of the Woods along the Manitoba border in north-central Minnesota. See Red Lake for general description and status.

LOST LAKE PEATLANDS 159,000 acres	
Red Lake State Wildlife Management Area–Beltrami Island State Forest–Red Lake Indian Reservation roadless	159,000

Description and Status: South of Warroad in north-central Minnesota. Separated from the 350,000-acre Red Lake roadless area by a dirt road, this area includes several ecologically significant peatlands, such as Mulligan Lake Peatland. See Red Lake for general description and status.

EAST FORK RAPID RIVER PEATLANDS 135,000 acres	
Pine Island State Forest–Red Lake Indian Reservation roadless	135,000

Description and Status: Southeast of Baudette in north-central Minnesota. The East Fork Rapid River flows through this roadless area. See Red Lake for general description and status.

WEST FORK PEATLANDS 76,000 acres	
BLM–Red Lake Indian Reservation–Pine Island SF roadless	76,000

Description and Status: West of International Falls in north-central Minnesota. The West Fork of Black River flows through here. This area includes the ecologically significant North Black River Peatland, a former BLM Wilderness Study Area. Conservationists should demand BLM protection for this area. See Red Lake for general description and status.

BLACK RIVER PEATLANDS 170,000 acres	
Pine Island State Forest roadless	170,000

Description and Status: Northwest of Big Falls in north-central Minnesota. This area includes the botanically rich South Black River Peatland. See Red Lake for general description and status.

LUDLOW PEATLANDS 155,000 acres	
Pine Island State Forest–Red Lake State Wildlife Management Area–BLM–Red Lake Indian Reservation roadless	155,000

Description and Status: Northeast of Upper Red Lake and east of state Highway 72 in north-central Minnesota. This area includes the biologically important Lost River Peatland. See Red Lake for general description and status.

STURGEON RIVER PEATLANDS 265,000 acres	
Pine Island State Forest roadless	265,000

Description and Status: Between U.S. 71 and state Highway 72 east of Upper Red Lake in north-central Minnesota. See Red Lake for general description and status.

SOUTHEAST PINE ISLAND PEATLANDS 87,000 acres	
Pine Island State Forest roadless	87,000

Description and Status: South of Big Falls between U.S. 71 and state Highway 6 in north-central Minnesota. See Red Lake for general description and status.

LITTLE FORK RIVER PEATLANDS 150,000 acres	
Koochiching State Forest roadless	150,000

Description and Status: Southeast of Big Falls in north-central Minnesota. The Little Fork River is in this area. Myrtle Lake Peatland is a designated National Natural Landmark. See Red Lake for general description and status.

GEORGE WASHINGTON 86,000 acres	
George Washington State Forest roadless	86,000

Description: East of Bigfork in north-central Minnesota. This area is different from the other peatlands because of its greater relief. It has numerous lakes, mixed peatlands, and forest. Some elevations approach 1,500 feet. See Red Lake for general description and status.

Status: This roadless area is crisscrossed with snowmobile trails, penetrated by several dirt roads, and has quite a bit of private land intermixed.

Michigan

The Upper Peninsula of Michigan (or the "UP") has long been considered the backcountry vacation land of the Midwest. Although abused by logging and mining, the UP still has several good-size wildernesses, including a few stands of virgin forest and a handful of wolves. Wilderness restoration could create significant preserves here. Michigan conservationists achieved passage of the Michigan Wilderness Act in 1987. It established nine Wilderness Areas, totaling 89,000 acres, on the Hiawatha and Ottawa NFs in the UP, and one Wilderness Area of 3,395 acres in the Manistee NF in Michigan's Lower Peninsula. RARE II considered 105,000 acres. Previously, Wilderness Areas had been established in Isle Royale National Park and Seney National Wildlife Refuge in the UP.

ISLE ROYALE 133,000 acres	
Designated Isle Royale National Park Wilderness Area	131,880
Contiguous Isle Royale National Park roadless	1,200

Description: The large island in the northwestern part of Lake Superior 20 miles south of the Canadian mainland. Biologists have found here a classic situation for studying Wolf-Moose-Beaver interactions. Wildlife also includes Red Fox, Lynx, Snowshoe Hare, and Mink. This is a transition area between northern hardwood forest and coniferous forest, with Balsam Fir and White Spruce forming a climax forest near the lakeshore, Yellow Birch and Sugar Maple forming a climax forest in warmer areas, and subclimax Aspen, White Birch, and scattered conifers growing in burned areas. The long forested ridges have sizable lakes and hundreds of swamps, ponds, and bogs between them. Over fifty species of fish live in streams on the island, including Brook and Rainbow Trout in 25 miles of trout streams. The island contains twenty inland lakes and 170 miles of hiking trails. The high point is Mt. Desor, at 792 feet above lake level and 1,394 feet above sea level. Important archaeological sites of primitive copper mining date back 4,500 years.

Status: Isle Royale is fairly well protected as a National Park Wilderness Area. Park Service management has been mixed, but the short visitor season saves the island from excessive development ideas.

Copper mining flourished from 1850 until 1899 (the forest was logged and burned to expose copper deposits). Summer homes then became popular after 1900, until Isle Royale became a National Park in 1940. Given these intensive impacts, the degree to which wilderness has recovered on the island gives hope for similar recovery efforts in the Upper Peninsula of Michigan and in northern Wisconsin.

The Timber Wolf population has seriously declined in recent years, in part because of canine parvovirus brought in from outside. This tragedy is another reminder of the fragility of island populations and of the danger of counting on a few wild areas to suffice as habitat for Threatened, Endangered, or sensitive species.

PORCUPINE MOUNTAINS 50,000 acres	
Designated Porcupine Mountains State Wilderness Area	46,246
Additional State Park roadless and adjacent Lake Superior	4,000

Description: The northwestern part of Michigan's Upper Peninsula, northeast of Ironwood. This wild stretch of mountains rises in a series of rugged parallel ridges along the lakeshore of Lake Superior. The high point is 2,023-foot Government Peak. Lakes (including splendid Lake of the Clouds), rushing streams and rivers, ponds, and swamps fill much of the area between mountain ridges. White Pine and northern hardwoods predominate. The largest tract of virgin Northern Hemlock, Yellow Birch, and Sugar Maple in the Lake States is in this roadless area. Black Bear are common. A major campaign by the citizens of Michigan resulted in the legal protection of this area in 1944. An earlier effort to designate the Porkies as a National Park twinned with Isle Royale failed. The area is now listed as a National Natural Landmark.

Status: The Porkies are largely protected as a state Wilderness Area, but management could be better and more effective. Closing a scenic road and restoring areas of the adjacent Ottawa NF could re-create a significant wilderness. Wolves and other extirpated wildlife should be reintroduced.

MCCORMICK 89,000 acres	
Designated McCormick Wilderness Area (Ottawa NF)	16,850
Escanaba River State Forest roadless	8,320
Private roadless	64,000

Description: Upper Peninsula of Michigan east of L'Anse. The Sierra Club says, "McCormick is probably the best and largest living example of the original Michigan forest. . . . Climax white pine and maple forests dominate the area. . . . Disturbance in the area is minimal." Rocky outcroppings tower over lakes, streams, and wetlands frequented by Moose, Black Bear, Bobcat, River Otter, Common Loon, Bald Eagle, Pileated Woodpecker, and possibly Gray Wolf. The cascading Yellow Dog River is among the most pristine streams in the Upper Midwest and has a thriving trout population.

Status: The private lands and Escanaba State Forest are open to logging, but there is not much activity at this time. Protection of these roadless lands adjacent to the designated Wilderness, including acquisition of the private land, should be a high priority for conservationists. A dirt road is all that separates this area from the Huron Mountain roadless area. Closing it and several other old logging roads could establish a 200,000-acre Wilderness.

HURON MOUNTAIN 74,000 acres	
Huron Mountain Club roadless (private)	25,000
Escanaba River State Forest roadless	7,040
Additional private and state roadless	42,000

Description: Upper Peninsula of Michigan northwest of Marquette. This largely privately owned area is characterized by the Huron Mountains; almost 11 miles of roadless shoreline along Lake Superior, including the mouth of the Huron River; numerous streams; several large lakes; and a fine expanse of northern forest. Wildlife and vegetation are similar to those of other UP roadless areas.

Status: Some 12,000 acres of the Huron Mountain Club are managed as "Wilderness." (Aldo Leopold was contracted to develop a management plan for these lands in the 1930s.) The state forest and private lands (mostly owned by timber companies) outside the Huron Mountain Club are protected only by their remoteness and low timber value, and could soon be destroyed by roading, logging, and ORVs. There are some old dirt logging roads penetrating the area. It is separated from McCormick by a dirt road.

SENEY 131,000 acres	
Designated Seney National Wildlife Refuge Wilderness Area	25,150
Additional Seney NWR roadless	26,880
Lake Superior State Forest and private roadless	79,000

Description: Upper Peninsula of Michigan between Seney and Manistique in the Great Manistique Swamp. Open marshes with sedges and rushes, and sandy knolls and ridges with mature Red Pine are characteristic of this area. Wildlife includes nesting Canada Geese, Wood Duck, Sandhill Crane, Bald Eagle, Sharp-tailed Grouse, Pileated Woodpecker, Black Bear, River Otter, Beaver, Mink, Bobcat, and occasional Gray Wolf. Elevations rise from 650 feet to 780 feet.

Status: The Lake Superior State Forest lands are open to logging, roading, and ORVs, but they are not being ravaged at this time. As for all the Michigan areas, Seney should be considered the core of a major wilderness restoration project of several hundred thousand acres.

PICTURED ROCKS 63,500 acres	
Pictured Rocks National Lakeshore (NPS) roadless, including private inholdings	45,000
Grand Sable State Forest roadless	14,000
Hiawatha National Forest roadless, including private inholdings	4,500

Description: Upper Peninsula of Michigan between Munising and Grand Marais. For over 20 miles, the shoreline of Lake Superior here is roadless, evenly split between the 50–200-foot-tall sandstone cliffs of the Pictured Rocks and the wide sweep of white sand and pebbles of Twelvemile Beach. Back from the pounding surf and fierce winds of the Big Sea Water is a regenerating forest of Northern Hardwoods and White Pine, waterfalls and streams, Beaver Ponds and several lakes. Wildlife includes Black Bear, White-tailed Deer, Beaver, Porcupine, River Otter, Bobcat, Peregrine Falcon (breeding on the cliffs), and Piping Plover (breeding on the unroaded beach). Moose are rare. Average annual snowfall is 200 inches. The virgin pineries were scalped during the 1870–1900 period of rampant Bunyanism, but a fine second-growth forest, including stunning stretches of White Birch, has reclaimed the land.

Status: The National Lakeshore was established in 1966 with a total of 67,000 acres split between the "Lakeshore Zone" to be acquired by the National Park Service and the "Inland Buffer Zone" of mixed ownership (NPS, Forest Service, State Forest, and private). Old logging trails have been closed to vehicles, except for some that are open for snowmobiles. Three public access roads are cherrystemmed into the roadless area. The gravest threat to this recovering wilderness comes, unfortunately, from the Park Service, which proposes to build a "Scenic Drive"—12.2 miles of new road through the wild Beaver Basin area and then along a currently unroaded stretch of beach. This travesty would rip the heart out of Pictured Rocks Lakeshore and would effectively destroy the area as a wilderness. Conservationists in Michigan are opposing the road; they should also campaign for

Wilderness designation for most of the National Lakeshore and contiguous NF lands. The Seney roadless area is only 5 miles south. These two large roadless areas should be linked by biological corridors to provide habitat for Pine Marten, Gray Wolf, and Lynx, which should then be reintroduced.

North Dakota, South Dakota, and Nebraska

Once considered wasteland, South Dakota's Badlands eventually were recognized as the finest remnant of the Great Plains. Established as a National Monument in 1939, Badlands was made a National Park in 1978. The Sage Creek Wilderness Area was designated by Congress in 1976.

In the 1880s, Theodore Roosevelt took up ranching along the Little Missouri River in North Dakota. Between the two units of Theodore Roosevelt National Park, the Little Missouri National Grasslands and adjacent and intermixed private land have two large roadless areas.

A huge chunk of northwestern Nebraska bounded by the towns of Chadron, Valentine, North Platte, and Bridgeport is very lightly settled and roaded. Although Bison no longer roam free over this Nebraska Sandhills–Niobrara River country, and Buffalo Wolf and Plains Grizzly have been exterminated, this 10-million-acre expanse (about 125 miles square) has extraordinary promise for wilderness restoration as a Great Plains Wilderness National Park or National Wildlife Refuge. Next to northern Maine, the Nebraska Sandhills may be the priority area for wilderness restoration on a grand scale in the United States. With population declining and grazing economics deteriorating, now is the time to buy up the private ranches in this 10 million acres; to remove the cows; to close the roads; and to return Bison, Elk, Gray Wolf, Grizzly Bear, prairie dog, and Black-footed Ferret. Nebraska. That's right, Nebraska.

There are hundreds of thousands of acres of private land in this lake- and pothole-dotted high prairie cut only by low-standard dirt ranching roads and Jeep trails. But the Samuel McKelvie National Forest and surrounding private land appears to have two areas of over 50,000 acres that meet our definition for "roadless." Although we missed these pieces the first time around, we include them in this edition of The Big Outside *with the areas in South and North Dakota we found the first time.*

These six large roadless areas should form the cores for a three-unit Great Plains Wilderness National Park (or Wilderness National Wildlife Refuge)—the northern unit in North Dakota, middle unit in South Dakota, and southern unit in

Nebraska. Biological corridors should link these areas together and to wild areas elsewhere on the plains, such as the Wild Missouri River in Montana.

SAGE CREEK 102,000 acres (South Dakota)	
Designated Sage Creek Wilderness Area (Badlands National Park)	64,250
Buffalo Gap National Grassland and private roadless	38,000

Description: Southwestern South Dakota south of Wall. The Sage Creek Basin, with its badlands, Shortgrass Prairie, Bighorn Sheep, Pronghorn, Bison, Prairie Dog, Badger, Mule Deer, Golden Eagle, Prairie Rattlesnake, juniper, yucca, and cottonwood, is probably the best remaining example of the Great Plains. Elevations range from 2,600 feet to 3,100 feet.

Status: Buffalo Gap National Grassland should be added to Badlands National Park and designated part of the Sage Creek Wilderness Area. This area should be considered as a reintroduction site for the Black-footed Ferret if captive breeding results in a large enough population for eventual release into the wild. Elk and Gray Wolf should also be reintroduced here. Sage Creek should be the core for a restored Great Plains Wilderness National Park (middle unit).

BADLANDS SOUTH 125,000 acres (South Dakota)	
Badlands National Park roadless	87,000
Buffalo Gap National Grassland roadless	20,000
Pine Ridge Indian Reservation roadless	18,000

Description: Southwestern South Dakota southwest of Wall. In a 1979 agreement with the Oglala Sioux tribe, the South Unit of Badlands National Park, on the Pine Ridge Reservation, was transferred to management by the National Park Service. According to the Park Service, "This stunning landscape of high grassy tableland and spectacular buttes is the scene of much Sioux history. The Ghost Dances at Stronghold Table in 1890 were a prelude to the bloodshed at Wounded Knee, 25 miles south of here." Cottonwood Creek and several other creeks drain the high mesas. Elevations range from 2,600 feet to 3,200 feet. See Sage Creek for general description.

Status: Several old dirt roads penetrate this area. They should be permanently closed, and the area designated as a Park Service Wilderness Area. Buffalo Gap Grassland should be added to Badlands National Park as the core of a major Great Plains Wilderness National Park.

LITTLE MISSOURI RIVER 150,000 acres (North Dakota)	
Magpie RARE II area (Little Missouri National Grasslands)	37,240
Private and additional Little Missouri National Grasslands roadless	113,000

Description: Western North Dakota northwest of Dickinson, along the Little Missouri River immediately north of the Theodore Roosevelt National Park Elkhorn Ranch unit. This badlands and river bottom area is an excellent representation of the Great Plains Shortgrass Prairie Ecoregion. Vegetation includes Western Wheatgrass, several species of needlegrass, Little Bluestem, Blue Grama, and sedges. The canyons and ravines grow Green Ash, Box Elder, American Elm, Rocky Mountain Juniper, skunkbrush, wild rose, and wolfberry. Big Sagebrush, Ponderosa Pine, Limber Pine, Paper Birch, and Black Cottonwood are less common. Wilderness-dependent wildlife includes Cougar, Lynx, Elk, Bighorn Sheep, Peregrine Falcon, Golden Eagle, and Prairie Falcon. The cats are very rare. Mule Deer and Pronghorn are also present. Some 20 miles of the Little Missouri River are in the roadless area; side drainages include Magpie, Whitetail, Porcupine, Prairie Dog, and Cinnamon Creeks. Elevations range from around 2,200 feet to 2,800 feet.

Status: This roadless area is penetrated by a few dirt roads and Jeep trails, but appears to meet our criteria for roadlessness. Conservation groups proposed the Magpie area for Wilderness during RARE II, but Congress has taken no action. The FS opposed Wilderness for Magpie during RARE II. Threats include continued overgrazing and ORVs.

The Little Missouri National Grasslands offer an excellent opportunity for significant wilderness restoration on the Great Plains. A 1-million-acre Wilderness National Park (north unit) should be established along the Little Missouri River between the North and South Units of Theodore Roosevelt National Park; Bison, Gray Wolf, and Grizzly should be reintroduced. If captive breeding programs are successful, this would be a good location for reestablishment of Black-footed Ferret (last seen here in 1969). In addition to this roadless area, this region of mixed Forest Service and private land consists of several RARE II areas and is broken only by dirt roads.

BEAVER CREEK 54,000 acres (North Dakota)	
Bell Lake RARE II area (Little Missouri National Grasslands)	11,980
Private and additional Little Missouri National Grasslands roadless	42,000

Description: Western North Dakota northeast of Beach. This roadless area consists of Beaver Creek, Bell Lake Creek, and Cooks Peak west of the Little Missouri River and south of the Magpie roadless area (separated by an unpaved road). See Magpie for general description.

Status: Proposed for Wilderness in RARE II by conservationists; Wilderness opposed by FS. See Magpie for general status.

STEER CREEK 84,000 acres (Nebraska)	
McKelvie National Forest roadless	61,000
Private roadless	23,000

Description: North-central Nebraska southwest of Valentine; the eastern portion of McKelvie NF and adjacent private land to the northwest along the Snake and Niobrara Rivers. This Sandhills grassland supports Mule Deer, White-tailed Deer, Pronghorn, Sharp-tailed Grouse, Golden Eagle, and Badger. The high point is 3,129 feet.

Status: The Forest Service did not include this area in RARE II. A four-wheel-drive route bisects it, and a few windmills and other developments for cattle are present. It is unknown if conservation groups have shown any interest in this area, other than the long, ongoing campaign to protect the Niobrara as a National Wild and Scenic River. With the following area, it should be the core for a massive wilderness restoration project in the Nebraska Sandhills—the southern unit of the Great Plains Wilderness National Park.

MEDICINE CREEK 101,000 acres (Nebraska)	
Samuel McKelvie National Forest roadless	28,000
Adjacent private roadless	73,000

Description: North-central Nebraska southwest of Valentine in the western portion of McKelvie NF, separated from Steer Creek roadless area by a minor paved road. The area's sandhills grassland is similar to that of Steer Creek.

Status: Uninventoried by the FS in RARE II. There are a number of Jeep trails and dirt roads on the periphery of this area and penetrating it, but none cross it. Another 35,000–50,000 acres, including a stretch of the Niobrara River, may be part of this roadless area. The area is used for cattle grazing with some range developments.

APPENDIX A

Roadless Areas by Size

Rank	Area Name	Region	Acreage
1	River of No Return	ID, MT	3,253,000
2	High Sierra	CA	2,800,000
3	Boundary Waters	MN, CAN	2,752,000
4	Grand Canyon	AZ	2,700,000
5	Bob Marshall	MT	2,536,000
6	South Absaroka	WY	2,190,000
7	Selway-Bitterroot	ID, MT	1,858,000
8	Everglades	FL	1,658,000
9	Cabeza Prieta	AZ, MX	1,657,000
10	Glacier Peak	WA	1,607,000
11	Absaroka-Beartooth	MT, WY	1,249,000
12	Pasayten	WA, CAN	1,191,000
13	Wind River Range	WY	1,171,000
14	Panamint Mountains	CA	1,166,000
15	South Great Salt Lake Desert	UT, NV	1,144,000
16	Olympic Mountains	WA	1,060,000
17	North Absaroka	WY	950,000
18	Lower Canyons of Rio Grande	TX, MX	890,000
19	Canyonlands	UT	875,000
20	Desolation Canyon	UT	858,000
21	Navajo Mountain	AZ, UT	850,000
22	North Great Salt Lake Desert	UT	850,000
23	High Uintas	UT	843,000

24	Weminuche	CO	806,000
25	Sawtooths	ID	800,000
26	Kofa Mountains	AZ	797,000
27	Yosemite North	CA	744,000
28	Mt. Baker	WA, CAN	742,000
29	Gila	NM	736,000
30	Galiuro Mountains	AZ	723,000
31	Dead Horse Mountains	TX, MX	720,000
32	North Glacier	MT, CAN	660,000
33	Black Rock Desert	NV	640,000
34	Maroon Bells–Collegiate Peaks	CO	632,000
35	Saline–Last Chance	CA	631,000
36	Salmon–Trinity Alps	CA	620,000
37	Escalante	UT	620,000
38	Owyhee Canyons	ID, OR	619,000
39	Big Cypress Swamp	FL	583,000
40	Hells Canyon	OR, ID	563,000
41	Boulder–White Clouds	ID	545,000
42	Gallatin Range	WY, MT	525,000
43	Cottonwood Mountains–Panamint Dunes	CA	524,000
44	Blue Range–San Francisco	AZ, NM	505,000
45	Mariscal–Santa Elena	TX, MX	483,000
46	Sheep Range	NV	468,000
47	Bechler-Pitchstone	WY, ID	468,000
48	Desert-Pintwater Ranges	NV	467,000
49	Alpine Lakes	WA	464,000
50	Great Rift–Craters of the Moon	ID	463,000
51	Lower Colorado River	AZ, CA	462,000
52	Gros Ventre	WY	455,000
53	Eagle Cap	OR	452,000
54	Cloud Peak	WY	443,000
55	South Glacier	MT	430,000
56	Three Sisters	OR	424,000
57	Sangre de Cristo	CO	418,000

58	Dirty Devil–Fiddler Butte	UT	413,000
59	North Lemhis	ID	410,000
60	Aldo Leopold	NM	409,000
61	Kalmiopsis	OR, CA	408,000
62	Okefenokee	GA, FL	400,000
63	Pecos	NM	400,000
64	Sheep Hole	CA	390,000
65	Buffalo Hills–Smoke Creek	NV, CA	387,000
66	San Rafael	CA	381,000
67	Palen-McCoy	CA	380,000
68	White Mountains	CA, NV	379,000
69	San Juan River	UT	371,000
70	Anaconda-Pintlar/Sapphires	MT	368,000
71	West Elk	CO	368,000
72	Wahweap–Canaan Peak	UT	367,000
73	Santa Rosa Mountains	CA	363,000
74	Alvord Desert	OR	361,000
75	Italian Peaks	ID, MT	360,000
76	Kaiparowits	UT	360,000
77	Spotted Range	NV	354,000
78	Red Lake Peatlands	MN	350,000
79	Bruneau-Jarbidge Rivers	ID	350,000
80	Hellsgate	AZ	346,000
81	Flat Tops	CO	346,000
82	Mazatzal	AZ	340,000
83	High Peaks	NY	336,000
84	Sespe	CA	335,000
85	Teton Range	WY	334,000
86	Inyo Mountains	CA	333,000
87	Hexie–Little San Bernardino Mountains	CA	328,000
88	Marble Mountain	CA	320,000
89	West Canada Lake	NY	316,000
90	South San Juan	CO	292,000
91	Paria Canyon	AZ, UT	290,000
92	Book Cliffs	UT	290,000
93	Funeral Mountains	CA, NV	287,000

94	Carson Sink	NV	286,000
95	Mallard-Larkins	ID	285,000
96	Muddy Creek	UT	282,000
97	Carson-Iceberg	CA	279,000
98	Hole in the Rock	NV	277,000
99	Turtle Mountains	CA	276,000
100	Great Burn	ID, MT	275,000
101	Secesh River	ID	273,000
102	Kingston Range	CA	270,000
103	Superstition Mountains	AZ	269,000
104	Rocky Mountain National Park	CO	266,000
105	Sturgeon River Peatlands	MN	265,000
106	Mt. Zirkel	CO	265,000
107	Raven's Eye	ID	263,000
108	Yolla Bolly–Middle Eel	CA	260,000
109	West Potrillo Mountains	NM	260,000
110	Guadalupe Escarpment	NM, TX	258,000
111	Pioneer Mountains	ID	255,000
112	La Garita	CO	253,000
113	Yampa-Green	CO, UT	250,000
114	Arc Dome	NV	250,000
115	Siskiyou	CA	249,000
116	Grapevine Mountains	CA, NV	246,000
117	Salt River Range	WY	245,000
118	Palisades	WY, ID	245,000
119	South Madison Range	MT	242,000
120	San Andres Mountains South	NM	240,000
121	Grant Range	NV	240,000
122	Bighorn-Weitas	ID	240,000
123	West Pioneer Mountains	MT	239,000
124	Excelsior Mountains	NV, CA	232,000
125	Sheepshead Mountains	OR	232,000
126	Diamond Peak	ID	230,000
127	Great Smoky Mountains West	NC, TN	227,000
128	Ishi	CA	225,000
129	Grayback Ridge	WY	225,000

130	Arrastra Mountain	AZ	225,000
131	Purgatoire River Canyon	CO	225,000
132	Solitario	TX	225,000
133	Amargosa Range	CA	221,000
134	Mt. Rainier	WA	221,000
135	Wilson Mesa	UT	220,000
136	Cougar Lakes	WA	219,000
137	Ventana	CA	217,000
138	Rincon Mountains	AZ	217,000
139	Kelso Dunes	CA	215,000
140	West Big Hole	MT, ID	215,000
141	Latir Peak–Valle Vidal	NM	214,000
142	Batamote–Sauceda Mountains	AZ	214,000
143	Domeland	CA	212,000
144	Trout Creek Mountains	OR, NV	212,000
145	Myotis	OR	210,000
146	Mt. Graham	AZ	208,000
147	Vallecito Mountains	CA	207,000
148	Big Hatchet–Alamo Hueco	NM	207,000
149	Las Vegas Range	NV	207,000
150	Mancos Mesa	UT	204,000
151	Five Ponds	NY	203,000
152	Charleston Peak	NV	200,000
153	Wenaha-Tucannon	WA, OR	200,000
154	Baxter State Park	ME	200,000
155	Argus Range	CA	199,000
156	Chuckwalla Mountains	CA	197,000
157	Clan Alpine Range	NV	196,000
158	Goat Rocks	WA	196,000
159	Peace Rock	ID	196,000
160	Gila Mountains	AZ	194,000
161	Mt. Jefferson	OR	191,000
162	Ruby Mountains	NV	190,000
163	Table Mountain	NV	190,000
164	Aquarius Mountains North	AZ	190,000
165	Jarbidge	NV, ID	189,000
166	Wayne Wonderland	UT	189,000

167	Coxcomb	CA	188,000
168	Cabinet Mountains	MT	187,000
169	Meadow Valley Mountains	NV	186,000
170	Chisos Mountains	TX	186,000
171	Paria-Hackberry	UT	186,000
172	Central Plateau	WY	185,000
173	Steep Creek–Oak Creek	UT	185,000
174	Comanche Peak	CO	182,000
175	Mt. Stirling	NV	180,000
176	St. John Ponds	ME	180,000
177	Little Sioux	MN	179,000
178	Borah Peak	ID	179,000
179	Deep Creek Mountains	UT	179,000
180	Mission Mountains	MT	176,000
181	Commissary Ridge	WY	175,000
182	French Creek–Patrick Butte	ID	175,000
183	Black River Peatlands	MN	170,000
184	Continental Divide	NM	170,000
185	Eagles Nest	CO	170,000
186	Mt. Pennel	UT	170,000
187	Hunter-Fryingpan	CO	168,000
188	Snowcrest Range	MT	166,000
189	Sky Lakes	OR	166,000
190	Greenwater Range	CA	165,000
191	Mokelumne	CA	164,000
192	Great Rift–Wapi	ID	164,000
193	Allan Mountain	MT, ID	164,000
194	Great Smoky Mountains East	NC, TN	163,000
195	Mormon Mountains	NV	163,000
196	El Malpais	NM	160,000
197	Wheeler Peak	NV	160,000
198	Ajo Mountains	AZ	160,000
199	Chiricahua Mountains	AZ	160,000
200	Needles	ID	160,000
201	Lost Lake Peatlands	MN	159,000
202	Basque Hills	OR	159,000
203	River of No Return South	ID	158,000

204	Santa Rosa Range	NV	157,000
205	Queer Mountain	CA, NV	155,000
206	Ludlow Peatlands	MN	155,000
207	San Andres Mountains Central	NM	155,000
208	San Andres Mountains North	NM	155,000
209	Little Bighorn	WY, MT	155,000
210	Selkirks	ID	155,000
211	Holy Cross	CO	152,000
212	Old Woman Mountains	CA	150,000
213	Little Fork Peatlands	MN	150,000
214	East Pioneers	MT	150,000
215	Little Missouri River	ND	150,000
216	Smoke Creek Desert	NV	148,000
217	Zion	UT	148,000
218	Hermosa	CO	147,000
219	White Sands	NM	146,000
220	Quinn Headwaters	NV	146,000
221	Schell Creek Range	NV	145,000
222	Warm Springs	AZ	145,000
223	Eagle Creek	AZ	145,000
224	Big Blue	CO	145,000
225	Little Rockies	UT	145,000
226	Antelope	NV	144,000
227	Mt. Moriah	NV, UT	144,000
228	Hawksie-Walksie	OR, NV	144,000
229	North Bighorn Mountains	MT, WY	144,000
230	Ibex Hills	CA	143,000
231	Robledo–Las Uvas Mountains	NM	143,000
232	Loxahatchee	FL	143,000
233	Diablo Mountain	OR	142,000
234	Siamese Pond	NY	141,000
235	Silver Lake	NY	141,000
236	Crazy Mountains	MT	140,000
237	North Madison Range	MT	140,000
238	Sierra Blanca	NM	140,000
239	Painted Desert	AZ	140,000

240	Mt. Ellen	UT	137,000
241	Sycamore Canyon–Secret Mountain	AZ	137,000
242	Mesa Verde	CO	136,000
243	Granite Mountains	CA	135,000
244	East Fork Rapid River Peatlands	MN	135,000
245	Horse Heaven	NV	135,000
246	Deep Lake	WY, MT	135,000
247	Soldier Mountains–Lime Creek	ID	135,000
248	Wildlands Lakes	ME	135,000
249	Nopah Range	CA, NV	134,000
250	Salt Creek	UT	134,000
251	Isle Royale	MI	133,000
252	Parsnip Peak	NV	133,000
253	Apache Kid	NM	131,000
254	Seney	MI	131,000
255	Piper Mountain–Soldier Canyon	CA	130,500
256	Pahsimeroi	ID	130,000
257	Mexican Mountain	UT	130,000
258	Parunuweap	UT, AZ	128,000
259	Delamar Mountains	NV	127,000
260	Toiyabe Crest	NV	126,000
261	Eagletail Mountains	AZ	126,000
262	Lost Creek	CO	126,000
263	Pagoda Peak	CO	126,000
264	Culebra	CO, NM	125,000
265	Washburn Range	WY	125,000
266	Baldy Bill	AZ	125,000
267	Mohave Wash	AZ	125,000
268	Pemigewasset	NH	125,000
269	Badlands South	SD	125,000
270	Pine Valley Mountains	UT	125,000
271	Charles Sheldon Antelope Range	NV	124,000
272	New Water Mountains	AZ	123,000

273	Cady Mountains	CA	122,000
274	Sawyers Peak	NM	121,000
275	Quinn	NV	120,000
276	Aquarius Mountains South	AZ	120,000
277	Redington Pond	ME	120,000
278	Wilcox Lake	NY	120,000
279	Wheeler Peak	NM	120,000
280	Sand Tank Mountains	AZ	119,000
281	Rawah	CO	119,000
282	Palisade Mesa	NV	116,000
283	Muddy Mountains	NV	116,000
284	Squaw Creek	ID	116,000
285	Black Ridge Canyons	CO, UT	115,000
286	South Egan Range	NV	113,000
287	Bear Creek	ID	113,000
288	Big Snowy Mountains	MT	112,000
289	Massacre Rim	NV	112,000
290	Mt. Leidy	WY	112,000
291	Lakes	UT	112,000
292	Little Horn Mountains	AZ	111,000
293	Cannibal Plateau	CO	111,000
294	Eagle Mountains	CA	110,000
295	Wild River–Kearsarge	NH, ME	110,000
296	Salt River	AZ	110,000
297	Garns Mountain	ID	110,000
298	Red Mountain	ID	110,000
299	Moose River	ME	110,000
300	Boulder Mountain	UT	110,000
301	Sierra Ladrones	NM	109,000
302	Priest Mountain	CO	109,000
303	Everglades 3A	FL	109,000
304	King Mountain	ID	109,000
305	King Top	UT	109,000
306	Padre Island	TX	108,000
307	Tenderfoot–Deep Creek	MT	108,000
308	South Reveille	NV	107,500
309	Cedar Mountains	NM	106,000

310	Pinto Mountains	CA	105,000
311	Fox Mountain Range	NV	105,000
312	Mount Thielsen	OR	105,000
313	Caton Lake	ID	105,000
314	Red Buttes	CA, OR	104,000
315	Tobacco Root Mountains	MT	104,000
316	Catlow Rim	OR	104,000
317	Pajarito Mountains	AZ, MX	104,000
318	Centennial Mountains	MT, ID	104,000
319	Stony Mountain	MT	103,000
320	Mt. Adams	WA	103,000
321	Stump Creek	ID	103,000
322	Elkhorn Mountains	MT	103,000
323	Soda Mountain	CA	102,500
324	Great Dismal Swamp	VA, NC	102,000
325	Dominguez Canyons	CO	102,000
326	Sage Creek	SD	102,000
327	Avawatz	CA	101,000
328	Old Dad Mountain	CA	101,000
329	Animas Mountains	NM	101,000
330	Cherry Creek Mountains	NV	101,000
331	Woolsey Peak–Signal Mountain	AZ	101,000
332	Harcuvar Mountains East	AZ	101,000
333	Fossil Ridge	CO	101,000
334	Sids Mountain	UT	101,000
335	Rattlesnake Mountains	MT	101,000
336	Medicine Creek	NE	101,000
337	Lassen East	CA	100,000
338	South Warner	CA	100,000
339	Devils Creek	NM	100,000
340	Eagle Head	NV, CA	100,000
341	Bates Mountains	AZ	100,000
342	Big Horn Mountains	AZ	100,000
343	Catalina Mountains	AZ	100,000
344	Four Peaks	AZ	100,000
345	Harcuvar Mountains West	AZ	100,000

346	Troublesome	CO	100,000
347	Jacks Creek	ID	100,000
348	St. John River South	ME, CAN	100,000
349	Blue Mountain	NH	100,000
350	Casto-Table	UT	100,000
351	Everglades 2	FL	95,000[1]
352	Baxter North	ME	90,000
353	McCormick	MI	89,000
354	Ha-de-ron-dah	NY	89,000
355	Southeast Pine Island Peatlands	MN	87,000
356	George Washington	MN	86,000
357	Steer Creek	NE	84,000
358	Cranberry	WV	82,000
359	Sandwich Range	NH	81,000
360	Mahoosuc Range	ME, NH	78,000
361	West Fork Peatlands	MN	76,000
362	Blue Ridge	NY	75,000
363	Ferris Lake	NY	75,000
364	Huron Mountain	MI	74,000
365	St. John River North	ME	70,000
366	Kilkenny	NH	70,000
367	Pictured Rocks	MI	63,500
368	Red Lake Indian Reservation Peatlands	MN	63,000
369	Pigeon Lake	NY	62,000
370	Hoffman Notch	NY	61,000
371	Southern Nantahala	GA, NC	60,000
372	Reed Mountain	ME	60,000

[1] There are many roadless areas in the Western United States between 99,000 acres and 50,000 acres in size. They are not listed here. As explained in the introductory chapter, the Big Outside inventory includes all roadless areas in the lower forty-eight states over 100,000 acres in size and all roadless areas over 50,000 acres in size in the states east of the Rocky Mountains. The continuation, then, of the ranking for Eastern roadless areas under 100,000 acres is done for comparison purposes only among the Eastern areas, and not for the entire country, since there are several hundred roadless areas between 50,000 acres and 99,000 acres in size in the Western states.

373	West Branch Dead Diamond River	NH	60,000
374	Carmelee-Hamre Peatlands	MN	58,000
375	Marvin Lake Peatlands	MN, CAN	57,000
376	Cohutta	GA, TN	56,000
377	Big Cypress Swamp Loop	FL	55,000
378	Everglades 3C	FL	54,000
379	Beaver Creek	ND	54,000
380	Pharaoh Lake	NY	52,000
381	Slide Mountain–Panther Mountain	NY	52,000
382	Glastenbury Mountain	VT	52,000
383	Everglades 3B	FL	50,000
384	Porcupine Mountains	MI	50,000
385	Meachum Swamp	VT	50,000

APPENDIX B

Roadless Areas by State

Rank	Area Name	Region	Acreage
	ARIZONA		
4	Grand Canyon	AZ	2,700,000
9	Cabeza Prieta	AZ, MX	1,657,000
21	Navajo Mountain	AZ, UT	850,000
26	Kofa Mountains	AZ	797,000
30	Galiuro Mountains	AZ	723,000
44	Blue Range–San Francisco	AZ, NM	505,000
51	Lower Colorado River	AZ, CA	462,000
80	Hellsgate	AZ	346,000
82	Mazatzal	AZ	340,000
91	Paria Canyon	AZ, UT	290,000
103	Superstition Mountains	AZ	269,000
130	Arrastra Mountain	AZ	225,000
138	Rincon Mountains	AZ	217,000
142	Batamote–Sauceda Mountains	AZ	214,000
146	Mt. Graham	AZ	208,000
160	Gila Mountains	AZ	194,000
164	Aquarius Mountains North	AZ	190,000
198	Ajo Mountains	AZ	160,000
199	Chiricahua Mountains	AZ	160,000
222	Warm Springs	AZ	145,000
223	Eagle Creek	AZ	145,000

239	Painted Desert	AZ	140,000
241	Sycamore Canyon–Secret Mountain	AZ	137,000
261	Eagletail Mountains	AZ	126,000
266	Baldy Bill	AZ	125,000
267	Mohave Wash	AZ	125,000
272	New Water Mountains	AZ	123,000
276	Aquarius Mountains South	AZ	120,000
280	Sand Tank Mountains	AZ	119,000
292	Little Horn Mountains	AZ	111,000
296	Salt River	AZ	110,000
317	Pajarito Mountains	AZ, MX	104,000
331	Woolsey Peak–Signal Mountain	AZ	101,000
332	Harcuvar Mountains East	AZ	101,000
341	Bates Mountains	AZ	100,000
342	Big Horn Mountains	AZ	100,000
343	Catalina Mountains	AZ	100,000
344	Four Peaks	AZ	100,000
345	Harcuvar Mountains West	AZ	100,000
	CALIFORNIA		
2	High Sierra	CA	2,800,000
14	Panamint Mountains	CA	1,166,000
27	Yosemite North	CA	744,000
35	Saline–Last Chance	CA	631,000
36	Salmon–Trinity Alps	CA	620,000
43	Cottonwood Mountains–Panamint Dunes	CA	524,000
64	Sheep Hole	CA	390,000
66	San Rafael	CA	381,000
67	Palen-McCoy	CA	380,000
68	White Mountains	CA, NV	379,000
73	Santa Rosa Mountains	CA	363,000
84	Sespe	CA	335,000
86	Inyo Mountains	CA	333,000
87	Hexie–Little San Bernardino Mountains	CA	328,000

88	Marble Mountain	CA	320,000
93	Funeral Mountains	CA, NV	287,000
97	Carson-Iceberg	CA	279,000
99	Turtle Mountains	CA	276,000
102	Kingston Range	CA	270,000
108	Yolla Bolly–Middle Eel	CA	260,000
115	Siskiyou	CA	249,000
116	Grapevine Mountains	CA, NV	246,000
128	Ishi	CA	225,000
133	Amargosa Range	CA	221,000
137	Ventana	CA	217,000
139	Kelso Dunes	CA	215,000
143	Domeland	CA	212,000
147	Vallecito Mountains	CA	207,000
155	Argus Range	CA	199,000
156	Chuckwalla Mountains	CA	197,000
167	Coxcomb	CA	188,000
190	Greenwater Range	CA	165,000
191	Mokelumne	CA	164,000
205	Queer Mountain	CA, NV	155,000
212	Old Woman Mountains	CA	150,000
230	Ibex Hills	CA	143,000
243	Granite Mountains	CA	135,000
249	Nopah Range	CA, NV	134,000
255	Piper Mountain–Soldier Canyon	CA	130,500
273	Cady Mountains	CA	122,000
294	Eagle Mountains	CA	110,000
310	Pinto Mountains	CA	105,000
314	Red Buttes	CA, OR	104,000
323	Soda Mountain	CA	102,500
327	Avawatz	CA	101,000
328	Old Dad Mountain	CA	101,000
337	Lassen East	CA	100,000
338	South Warner	CA	100,000

	COLORADO		
24	Weminuche	CO	806,000
34	Maroon Bells–Collegiate Peaks	CO	632,000
57	Sangre de Cristo	CO	418,000
71	West Elk	CO	368,000
81	Flat Tops	CO	346,000
90	South San Juan	CO	292,000
104	Rocky Mountain National Park	CO	266,000
106	Mt. Zirkel	CO	265,000
112	La Garita	CO	253,000
113	Yampa-Green	CO, UT	250,000
131	Purgatoirie River Canyon	CO	225,000
174	Comanche Peak	CO	182,000
185	Eagles Nest	CO	170,000
187	Hunter-Fryingpan	CO	168,000
211	Holy Cross	CO	152,000
218	Hermosa	CO	147,000
224	Big Blue	CO	145,000
242	Mesa Verde	CO	136,000
262	Lost Creek	CO	126,000
263	Pagoda Peak	CO	126,000
264	Culebra	CO, NM	125,000
281	Rawah	CO	119,000
285	Black Ridge Canyons	CO, UT	115,000
293	Cannibal Plateau	CO	111,000
302	Priest Mountain	CO	109,000
325	Dominguez Canyons	CO	102,000
333	Fossil Ridge	CO	101,000
346	Troublesome	CO	100,000
	FLORIDA		
8	Everglades	FL	1,658,000
39	Big Cypress Swamp	FL	583,000
232	Loxahatchee	FL	143,000
303	Everglades 3A	FL	109,000

351	Everglades 2	FL	95,000
377	Big Cypress Swamp Loop	FL	55,000
378	Everglades 3C	FL	54,000
383	Everglades 3B	FL	50,000
	GEORGIA		
62	Okefenokee	GA, FL	400,000
371	Southern Nantahala	GA, NC	60,000
376	Cohutta	GA, TN	56,000
	IDAHO		
1	River of No Return	ID, MT	3,253,000
7	Selway-Bitterroot	ID, MT	1,858,000
25	Sawtooths	ID	800,000
38	Owyhee Canyons	ID, OR	619,000
41	Boulder–White Clouds	ID	545,000
50	Great Rift–Craters of the Moon	ID	463,000
59	North Lemhis	ID	410,000
75	Italian Peaks	ID, MT	360,000
79	Bruneau-Jarbidge Rivers	ID	350,000
95	Mallard-Larkins	ID	285,000
100	Great Burn	ID, MT	275,000
101	Secesh River	ID	273,000
107	Raven's Eye	ID	263,000
111	Pioneer Mountains	ID	255,000
122	Bighorn-Weitas	ID	240,000
126	Diamond Peak	ID	230,000
159	Peace Rock	ID	196,000
178	Borah Peak	ID	179,000
182	French Creek–Patrick Butte	ID	175,000
192	Great Rift–Wapi	ID	164,000
200	Needles	ID	160,000
203	River of No Return South	ID	158,000
210	Selkirks	ID	155,000
247	Soldier Mountains–Lime Creek	ID	135,000

256	Pahsimeroi	ID	130,000
284	Squaw Creek	ID	116,000
287	Bear Creek	ID	113,000
297	Garns Mountain	ID	110,000
298	Red Mountain	ID	110,000
304	King Mountain	ID	109,000
313	Caton Lake	ID	105,000
321	Stump Creek	ID	103,000
347	Jacks Creek	ID	100,000
	MAINE		
154	Baxter State Park	ME	200,000
176	St. John Ponds	ME	180,000
248	Wildlands Lakes	ME	135,000
277	Redington Pond	ME	120,000
299	Moose River	ME	110,000
348	St. John River South	ME, CAN	100,000
352	Baxter North	ME	90,000
360	Mahoosuc Range	ME, NH	78,000
365	St. John River North	ME	70,000
372	Reed Mountains	ME	60,000
	MICHIGAN		
251	Isle Royale	MI	133,000
254	Seney	MI	131,000
353	McCormick	MI	89,000
364	Huron Mountain	MI	74,000
367	Pictured Rocks	MI	63,500
384	Porcupine Mountains	MI	50,000
	MINNESOTA		
3	Boundary Waters	MN, CAN	2,752,000
78	Red Lake Peatlands	MN	350,000
105	Sturgeon River Peatlands	MN	265,000
177	Little Sioux	MN	179,000
183	Black River Peatlands	MN	170,000

201	Lost Lake Peatlands	MN	159,000
206	Ludlow Peatlands	MN	155,000
213	Little Fork Peatlands	MN	150,000
244	East Fork Rapid River Peatlands	MN	135,000
355	Southeast Pine Island Peatlands	MN	87,000
356	George Washington	MN	86,000
361	West Fork Peatlands	MN	76,000
368	Red Lake Indian Reservation Peatlands	MN	63,000
374	Carmelee–Hamre Peatlands	MN	58,000
375	Marvin Lake Peatlands	MN, CAN	57,000

MONTANA

5	Bob Marshall	MT	2,536,000
11	Absaroka-Beartooth	MT, WY	1,249,000
32	North Glacier	MT, CAN	660,000
55	South Glacier	MT	430,000
70	Anaconda-Pintlar/Sapphires	MT	368,000
119	South Madison Range	MT	242,000
123	West Pioneer Mountains	MT	239,000
140	West Big Hole	MT, ID	215,000
168	Cabinet Mountains	MT	187,000
180	Mission Mountains	MT	176,000
188	Snowcrest Range	MT	166,000
193	Allan Mountain	MT, ID	164,000
214	East Pioneers	MT	150,000
229	North Bighorn Mountains	MT, WY	144,000
236	Crazy Mountains	MT	140,000
237	North Madison Range	MT	140,000
288	Big Snowy Mountains	MT	112,000
307	Tenderfoot–Deep Creek	MT	108,000
315	Tobacco Root Mountains	MT	104,000
318	Centennial Mountains	MT, ID	104,000
319	Stony Mountain	MT	103,000

322	Elkhorn Mountains	MT	103,000
335	Rattlesnake Mountains	MT	101,000
	NEBRASKA		
336	Medicine Creek	NE	101,000
357	Steer Creek	NE	84,000
	NEVADA		
33	Black Rock Desert	NV	640,000
46	Sheep Range	NV	468,000
48	Desert-Pintwater Ranges	NV	467,000
65	Buffalo Hills–Smoke Creek	NV, CA	387,000
77	Spotted Range	NV	354,000
94	Carson Sink	NV	286,000
98	Hole in the Rock	NV	277,000
114	Arc Dome	NV	250,000
121	Grant Range	NV	240,000
124	Excelsior Mountains	NV, CA	232,000
149	Las Vegas Range	NV	207,000
152	Charleston Peak	NV	200,000
157	Clan Alpine Range	NV	196,000
162	Ruby Mountains	NV	190,000
163	Table Mountain	NV	190,000
165	Jarbidge	NV, ID	189,000
169	Meadow Valley Mountains	NV	186,000
175	Mt. Stirling	NV	180,000
195	Mormon Mountains	NV	163,000
197	Wheeler Peak	NV	160,000
204	Santa Rosa Range	NV	157,000
216	Smoke Creek Desert	NV	148,000
220	Quinn Headwaters	NV	146,000
221	Schell Creek Range	NV	145,000
226	Antelope	NV	144,000
227	Mt. Moriah	NV, UT	144,000
245	Horse Heaven	NV	135,000
252	Parsnip Peak	NV	133,000
259	Delamar Mountains	NV	127,000
260	Toiyabe Crest	NV	126,000

271	Charles Sheldon Antelope Range	NV	124,000
275	Quinn	NV	120,000
282	Palisade Mesa	NV	116,000
283	Muddy Mountains	NV	116,000
286	South Egan Range	NV	113,000
289	Massacre Rim	NV	112,000
308	South Reveille	NV	107,500
311	Fox Mountain Range	NV	105,000
330	Cherry Creek Mountains	NV	101,000
340	Eagle Head	NV, CA	100,000
	NEW HAMPSHIRE		
268	Pemigewasset	NH	125,000
295	Wild River–Kearsarge	NH, ME	110,000
349	Blue Mountain	NH	100,000
359	Sandwich Range	NH	81,000
366	Kilkenny	NH	70,000
373	West Branch Dead Diamond River	NH	60,000
	NEW MEXICO		
29	Gila	NM	736,000
60	Aldo Leopold	NM	409,000
63	Pecos	NM	400,000
109	West Potrillo Mountains	NM	260,000
110	Guadalupe Escarpment	NM, TX	258,000
120	San Andres Mountains South	NM	240,000
141	Latir Peak–Valle Vidal	NM	214,000
148	Big Hatchet–Alamo Hueco	NM	207,000
184	Continental Divide	NM	170,000
196	El Malpais	NM	160,000
207	San Andres Mountains Central	NM	155,000
208	San Andres Mountains North	NM	155,000
219	White Sands	NM	146,000

231	Robledo–Las Uvas Mountains	NM	143,000
238	Sierra Blanca	NM	140,000
253	Apache Kid	NM	131,000
274	Sawyers Peak	NM	121,000
279	Wheeler Peak	NM	120,000
301	Sierra Ladrones	NM	109,000
309	Cedar Mountains	NM	106,000
329	Animas Mountains	NM	101,000
339	Devils Creek	NM	100,000

NEW YORK

83	High Peaks	NY	336,000
89	West Canada Lake	NY	316,000
151	Five Ponds	NY	203,000
234	Siamese Pond	NY	141,000
235	Silver Lake	NY	141,000
278	Wilcox Lake	NY	120,000
354	Ha-de-ron-dah	NY	89,000
362	Blue Ridge	NY	75,000
363	Ferris Lake	NY	75,000
369	Pigeon Lake	NY	62,000
370	Hoffman Notch	NY	61,000
380	Pharoah Lake	NY	52,000
381	Slide Mountain–Panther Mountain	NY	52,000

NORTH CAROLINA

127	Great Smoky Mountains West	NC, TN	227,000
194	Great Smoky Mountains East	NC, TN	163,000

NORTH DAKOTA

215	Little Missouri River	ND	150,000
379	Beaver Creek	ND	54,000

OREGON

40	Hells Canyon	OR, ID	563,000
53	Eagle Cap	OR	452,000

56	Three Sisters	OR	424,000
61	Kalmiopsis	OR, CA	408,000
74	Alvord Desert	OR	361,000
125	Sheepshead Mountains	OR	232,000
144	Trout Creek Mountains	OR, NV	212,000
145	Myotis	OR	210,000
161	Mt. Jefferson	OR	191,000
189	Sky Lakes	OR	166,000
202	Basque Hills	OR	159,000
228	Hawksie-Walksie	OR, NV	144,000
233	Diablo Mountain	OR	142,000
312	Mount Thielsen	OR	105,000
316	Catlow Rim	OR	104,000
	SOUTH DAKOTA		
269	Badlands South	SD	125,000
326	Sage Creek	SD	102,000
	TEXAS		
18	Lower Canyons of Rio Grande	TX, MX	890,000
31	Dead Horse Mountains	TX, MX	720,000
45	Mariscal–Santa Elena	TX, MX	483,000
132	Solitario	TX	225,000
170	Chisos Mountains	TX	186,000
306	Padre Island	TX	108,000
	UTAH		
15	South Great Salt Lake Desert	UT, NV	1,144,000
19	Canyonlands	UT	875,000
20	Desolation Canyon	UT	858,000
22	North Great Salt Lake Desert	UT	850,000
23	High Uintas	UT	843,000
37	Escalante	UT	620,000
58	Dirty Devil–Fiddler Butte	UT	413,000

69	San Juan River	UT	371,000
72	Wahweap–Canaan Peak	UT	367,000
76	Kaiparowits	UT	360,000
92	Book Cliffs	UT	290,000
96	Muddy Creek	UT	282,000
145	Wilson Mesa	UT	210,000
150	Mancos Mesa	UT	204,000
166	Wayne Wonderland	UT	189,000
171	Paria-Hackberry	UT	186,000
173	Steep Creek–Oak Creek	UT	185,000
179	Deep Creek Mountains	UT	179,000
186	Mt. Pennel	UT	170,000
217	Zion	UT	148,000
225	Little Rockies	UT	145,000
240	Mt. Ellen	UT	137,000
250	Salt Creek	UT	134,000
257	Mexican Mountain	UT	130,000
258	Parunuweap	UT, AZ	128,000
270	Pine Valley Mountains	UT	125,000
291	Lakes	UT	112,000
300	Boulder Mountain	UT	110,000
305	King Top	UT	109,000
334	Sid's Mountain	UT	101,000
350	Casto-Table	UT	100,000
	VERMONT		
382	Glastenbury Mountain	VT	52,000
385	Meachum Swamp	VT	50,000
	VIRGINIA		
324	Great Dismal Swamp	VA, NC	102,000
	WASHINGTON		
10	Glacier Peak	WA	1,607,000
12	Pasayten	WA, CAN	1,191,000
16	Olympic Mountains	WA	1,060,000

28	Mt. Baker	WA, CAN	742,000
49	Alpine Lakes	WA	464,000
134	Mt. Rainier	WA	221,000
136	Cougar Lakes	WA	219,000
153	Wenaha-Tucannon	WA, OR	200,000
158	Goat Rocks	WA	196,000
320	Mt. Adams	WA	103,000
	WEST VIRGINIA		
358	Cranberry	WV	82,000
	WYOMING		
6	South Absaroka	WY	2,190,000
13	Wind River Range	WY	1,171,000
17	North Absaroka	WY	950,000
42	Gallatin Range	WY, MT	525,000
47	Bechler-Pitchstone	WY, ID	468,000
52	Gros Ventre	WY	455,000
54	Cloud Peak	WY	443,000
85	Teton Range	WY	334,000
117	Salt River Range	WY	245,000
118	Palisades	WY, ID	245,000
129	Grayback Ridge	WY	225,000
172	Central Plateau	WY	185,000
181	Commissary Ridge	WY	175,000
209	Little Bighorn	WY, MT	155,000
246	Deep Lake	WY, MT	135,000
265	Washburn Range	WY	125,000
290	Mt. Leidy	WY	112,000

APPENDIX C

Bob Marshall's 1936 Roadless Area Inventory

Largest Roadless Areas in United States[1]

By Robert Marshall and Althea Dobbins

The fight to save the wilderness has grown during the past ten years from the personal hobby of a few fanatics to an important, nation-wide movement. All over the country, people are beginning to protest in a concerted manner against the invasion of roadless tracts by routes of modern transportation. Encouragingly enough, a number of these protests have been heeded, and several splendid roadless areas have thus been saved. Others have been preserved by federal and state officials before any protest had to be launched. Yet others, unfortunately, have been invaded either because nobody happened to realize that invasion was imminent, or because no one was aware that there was a significant area to be saved.

The battle to protect the wilderness is a critical one. Definitely there have not been enough large roadless tracts safely reserved from invasions. There is important need to make a study at an early date concerning which officially designated roadless areas should be enlarged, and which areas on which official action has not been taken should be established.

As a step preliminary to such a study, it is necessary to know what are the potential roadless areas which still can be saved. With this objective in mind, we have made a rough analysis of all the forest areas in the United States, embracing 300,000 acres or more, which have not yet been invaded by routes of mechanized transportation. We have made a similar study of desert areas

[1] Originally published in *The Living Wilderness,* the magazine of The Wilderness Society, November 1936. Reprinted with permission of *Wilderness Magazine.*

embracing 500,000 acres or more, under the assumption that a considerably larger area is needed in open country than in forest country to give one the feeling of the wilderness. The study of such areas was made from the accurate road maps for all National Forests, National Parks, and Indian Reservations, as kept by the federal bureaus administering these lands; from the excellent maps of the New York State Conservation Department; from the most accurate available automobile maps; and from the knowledge of a number of people familiar with specific localities which are not well mapped. We wish to extend our appreciation to the following for their kind assistance: Lee Kneipp and Helen Smith of the U.S. Forest Service; H. S. Teller of the National Park Service; E. H. Coulson and J. P. Kinney of the Indian Service; Depue Falck of the Grazing Division of the Interior Department; and William G. Howard of the New York State Conservation Department. As this is only a preliminary study, we realize there will be a number of mistakes. This is especially true of the desert areas where existing road maps are unusually poor. We would greatly appreciate any corrections which the readers of this article can make.

In drawing the boundaries of our roadless areas, we placed the edge one-half mile back from all roads, under the assumption that this distance was necessary to isolate the more annoying influences of mechanization. Where a stub road penetrated into a wilderness area, we drew our boundaries half a mile back from the road on each side, thus in effect eliminating a finger reaching into such wilderness area for a width of approximately one mile.

In view of the fact that most people do not visualize areas in terms of acres, we would like to point out that 300,000 acres is not a roadless area in any pioneering sense. Actually, a 300,000 acre tract is only about 21½ × 21½ miles, something which a reasonably good walker could traverse readily in a day if there were a trail. A desert area of 500,000 acres is only 27½ × 27½ miles, across which even a poor horseman could ride in a day. Of course, most of these areas are not square, but are much attenuated, so that a 300,000 acre area might have the dimensions of approximately 47 miles by 10 miles, instead of 21½ miles by 21½ miles.

The following table and map indicate those forest areas in the United States of 300,000 acres or more and those desert areas of 500,000 acres or more which are not yet accessible to mechanized transportation.

Forest Areas[1]

1. Arrostock-Alagash	Maine	2,800,000
2. Northern Cascade	Washington	2,800,000
3. Salmon River	Idaho	2,800,000
4. High Sierra	California	2,300,000
5. South Fork of Flathead	Montana	2,000,000
6. Selway	Idaho-Montana	2,000,000
7. Upper Yellowstone	Wyoming	2,000,000
8. Upper St. John	Maine	1,300,000
9. Olympic	Washington	1,200,000
10. Superior	Minnesota	1,200,000
11. Wind River Mountains	Wyoming	1,200,000
12. Beartooth	Montana-Wyoming	960,000
13. Absaroka Range	Wyoming	930,000
14. Siskiyou	Oregon	830,000
15. Sawtooth	Idaho	820,000
16. Sysladopsis	Maine	780,000
17. San Juan	Colorado	690,000
18. Umpqua	Oregon	640,000
19. North Yosemite	California	630,000
20. Dead River	Maine	600,000
21. High Uinta	Utah	580,000
22. East Grey River	Wyoming	560,000
23. Foss River	Washington	550,000
24. Gila	New Mexico	530,000
25. North Glacier	Montana	480,000
26. Marble Mountains	California	440,000
27. Moose River	New York	430,000
28. Bechlor River	Wyoming	420,000[2]
29. Madison Range	Montana-Wyoming	430,000
30. South Fork of Salmon	Idaho	410,000
31. White River	Colorado	410,000
32. Salmon–Trinity Alps	California	410,000
33. Okefenokee	Georgia	400,000

[1]Two-digit numbers correspond to forested areas (1–48); three-digit numbers correspond to desert areas (101–129) on map, page 469.

[2] This is not a typographical error. Marshall's list had Bechlor River and Madison Range out of numerical order.

34. South Yosemite	California	400,000
35. Mt. Marcy	New York	380,000
36. Cranberry–Beaver River	New York	380,000
37. Gros Ventre	Wyoming	370,000
38. Goat Rocks	Washington	370,000
39. South Glacier	Montana	340,000
40. Tonto Basin	Arizona	340,000
41. Wallowa	Oregon	330,000
42. Eagle Cap	Oregon	320,000
43. Electric Peak	Wyoming-Montana	320,000
44. Pintlar	Montana	320,000
45. Blue River	Arizona	310,000
46. Big Horn	Wyoming	310,000
47. Mission Range	Montana	310,000
48. Teton Range	Wyoming	300,000

Desert Areas

101. Colorado River	Utah-Arizona	8,890,000
102. Owyhee	Idaho-Ore.-Nevada	4,130,000
103. Grand Canyon	Arizona	4,000,000
104. Nevada Desert	Nevada	2,670,000
105. Book Cliffs	Utah-Colorado	2,420,000
106. North Mohave Desert	California	1,970,000
107. San Rafael Swells	Utah	1,930,000
108. Red Desert	Wyoming	1,900,000
109. Sevier Lake	Utah	1,900,000
110. Little Snake River	Wyoming-Colorado	1,800,000
111. Carrizozo Plains	New Mexico	1,800,000
112. North Salt Lake Desert	Utah	1,700,000
113. South Salt Lake Desert	Utah	1,600,000
114. South Mohave Desert	California	1,500,000
115. White Sands	New Mexico	1,200,000
116. Black Mesa	Arizona	1,200,000
117. West Mohave Desert	California	1,100,000
118. Painted Desert	Arizona	1,000,000
119. Guano Lake	Oregon-Nevada	980,000

120. East Mohave Desert	California	950,000
121. Harqua Hala Desert	Arizona	740,000
122. Bill Williams River	Arizona	700,000
123. Kingston Range	California-Nevada	650,000
124. Bruneau River	Idaho-Nevada	650,000
125. Cignus Peak	Arizona	620,000
126. South Pass	Wyoming	610,000
127. Salton Sea	California	610,000
128. Summer Lake	Oregon	540,000
129. Monument Butte	Wyoming	540,000

BOB MARSHALL'S 1936 MAP OF THE LARGEST ROADLESS AREAS IN THE UNITED STATES,* showing 48 Forest Roadless Areas exceeding 300,000 acres and 29 Desert Roadless Areas exceeding 500,000 acres that are still inaccessible to mechanized transportation. Compiled by Althea Dobbins

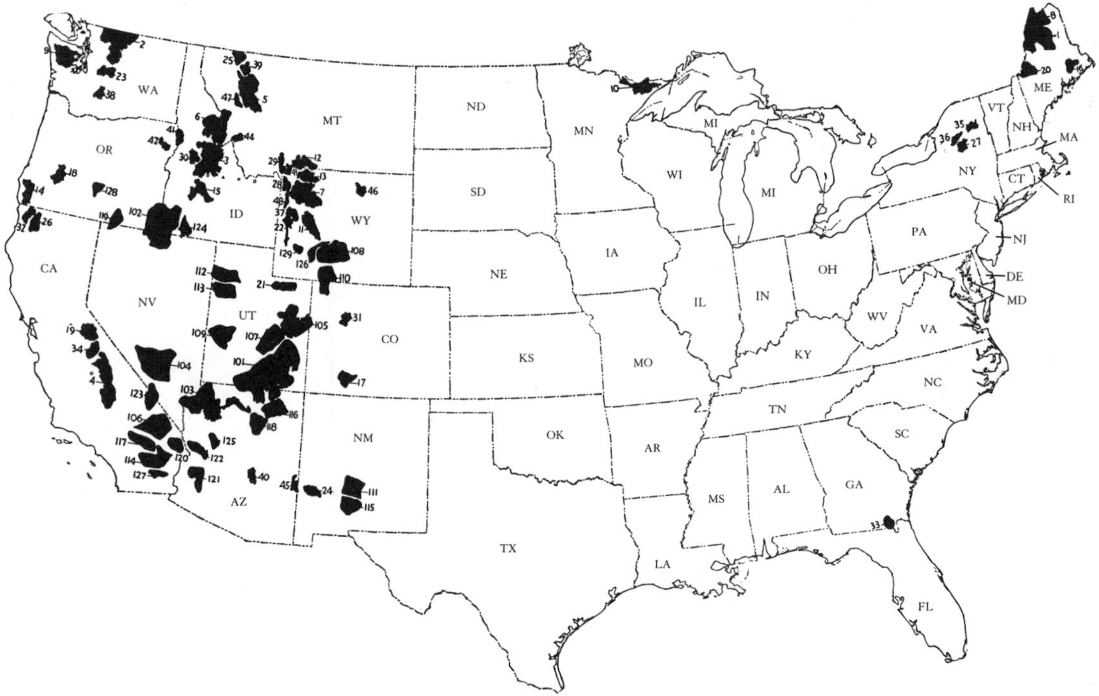

* In preparing their map Bob Marshall and Althea Dobbins overlooked certain areas that may have been roadless in 1936. See chapter 1.

APPENDIX D

Bob Marshall's 1927 Roadless Area Inventory

Area	1927 Sections	Acres
Central Idaho	11,982	7,668,480
Northern Cascades	5,368	3,435,520
Central Sierra	4,541	2,906,240
Flathead	3,689	2,360,960
Northwestern Wyoming	2,285	1,462,400
Olympic	2,251	1,440,640
Columbia-Rainier	2,120	1,356,800
Gila	2,074	1,327,360
Seven Devils	1,881	1,203,840
Southern Cascade	1,861	1,191,040
South Yellowstone	1,782	1,140,480
Boise-Sawtooth	1,766	1,130,240
Northeastern Utah	1,733	1,109,120
Prescott-Tonto	1,729	1,106,560
Santa Barbara	1,715	1,097,600
Beartooth-Absaroka	1,522	974,080
	FUTURE	
Central Idaho	7,490	4,793,600
Central Sierra	3,673	2,350,720
Flathead	3,471	2,221,440
Northwestern Wyoming	2,285	1,462,400

St. Joe–Clearwater	2,189	1,400,960
South Yellowstone	1,755	1,123,200
Prescott-Tonto	1,729	1,106,560

Note: Areas listed under "1927" were the existing million-acre roadless areas on the National Forests that Marshall roughly calculated at that time. Those listed under "Future" were presumably what would exist if Forest Service road-building plans at that time were carried out. Areas listed under "1927" but not under "Future" evidently would no longer exist as million-plus-acre roadless areas after such development. Marshall listed these areas by number of sections roadless. I've calculated the acreage. This information was found on a hand-lettered card in the Robet Marshall Papers at the Bancroft Library, University of California, Berkeley.

APPENDIX E

Conservation Groups Working on Wilderness and Biodiversity Issues

There is a broad spectrum of organizations working for the preservation of wilderness and natural diversity in the United States. These groups use an array of tools and tactics in defense of ecological integrity, which include land purchase and management; congressional lobbying; development of Wilderness proposals; filing of appeals and lawsuits; influencing federal and state land management; public education; economic analysis and scientific research supporting the need for nature preserves; public demonstrations; and civil disobedience. We feel that all of these approaches are legitimate and proper, depending on the circumstances. Just as diversity is important in ecosystems, so it is important in the conservation movement. No one group, no one set of tactics, is adequate for halting the headlong destruction of natural diversity now occurring. Concerned individuals should choose the group(s) with which they feel most comfortable. Today, during the white-hot crisis of eco-catastrophe, with one third of all species likely to become extinct during the next two or three decades, there is no time for complacency or armchair conservation. All who value wild things must act now—whether by writing letters or standing in front of bulldozers. Involvement with one or several of the following organizations is a good way to resist the industrial destruction of the wild, although many individuals effectively fight for wilderness and wildlife on their own.

In recent years, a new kind of conservation group has appeared, precipitating the emergence of what we categorize as the "New Conservation Movement."[1] These groups no longer nod their heads to the "multiple use" catechism, and they are developing ambitious and visionary wilderness restoration proposals that go far beyond the efforts of mainstream groups to protect a portion of the remaining American wilderness. The list below includes both old-line groups and those in the New Conservation Movement. (The more traditional groups are being increasingly influenced by the New Conservation Movement.)

Only organizations devoting significant energy to wilderness and natural diversity issues in the lower forty-eight states are listed below. This list is by no means exhaustive; there are dozens of other local groups campaigning for wild places all around the United States. We do not list state chapters or regional offices for the national groups; they can be contacted through the national addresses given.

Listing of these groups does not necessarily mean they agree with the views expressed by the authors in this book, nor does it mean that the authors entirely agree with the positions or approaches taken by individual groups. We believe certain of the listed groups need to take more hard-line, less compromised stands on wilderness and natural diversity issues. Nonetheless, we include them in our listing in the hope that concerned activists who are willing to courageously promote the protection of *all* that remains wild (and then some) will become involved with and strengthen these groups.

National Groups

The Wilderness Society, 1400 Eye St., Washington, DC 20005 (202-842-3400). The Wilderness Society is the only national group focusing entirely on wilderness and public lands issues in the United States. Regional offices cover all sections of the United States.

Sierra Club, 730 Polk St., San Francisco, CA 94109 (415-776-2211). Although the Sierra Club covers many environmental issues, it directs considerable attention to wilderness issues. Local Sierra Club chapters and groups

[1] See *Wild Earth,* Summer 1991, for a detailed discussion of the New Conservation Movement and a descriptive listing of many of these groups (available from Wild Earth, POB 492, Canton, NY 13617). The forthcoming book *The New Conservation Movement,* edited by Dave Foreman, Rod Mondt, and John Davis, will provide an in-depth look at the groups forming the cutting edge of conservation.

are active in all parts of the United States and much of Canada. Some local chapters are tough and uncompromising, like those in Utah and New York; others are very timid, like the ones in Oregon and Montana.

The Nature Conservancy, 1800 North Kent St., Arlington, VA 22209 (703-841-5300). The major task of The Nature Conservancy's headquarters, field offices, and state chapters is the purchase and management of ecologically sensitive areas.

National Audubon Society, 950 Third Ave., New York, NY 10022 (212-832-3200). Some local Audubon chapters work on wilderness and natural diversity issues: Endangered, Threatened, and rare species are a general priority.

Defenders of Wildlife, 1244 Nineteenth St., NW, Washington, DC 20036 (202-659-9510). The national staff and field representatives work on Endangered species and habitat.

American Rivers, 801 Pennsylvania Ave., SE, Suite 303, Washington, DC 20003 (202-547-6900). The only national group focusing on Wild and Scenic River preservation, American Rivers annually publicizes a list of the ten most endangered rivers in the United States.

Natural Resources Defense Council, 40 West Twentieth St., New York, NY 10011 (212-727-2700). NRDC pursues important appeals and lawsuits on wilderness and biodiversity issues.

Society for Conservation Biology, c/o Blackwell Scientific Publications, Three Cambridge Center, Suite 208, Cambridge, MA 02142 (617-225-0401). Professional ecologists concerned with the preservation of natural diversity, the Society produces the important peer-reviewed quarterly *Conservation Biology*.

Natural Areas Association, 620 South Third St., Room B, Rockford, IL 61104 (815-964-6666). This professional association of natural area managers promotes preservation of natural diversity and publishes the highly regarded *Natural Areas Journal*.

Association of Forest Service Employees for Environmental Ethics (AFSEEE), POB 11615, Eugene, OR 97440 (503-484-2692). This reform group of Forest Service employees is campaigning for a halt to ancient-forest destruction, a halt to domination of the Forest Service by the timber industry, and free speech within the agency.

Biodiversity Legal Foundation, POB 18327, Boulder, CO 80308-8327 (303-499-6991). BLF uses appeals and lawsuits to defend Endangered and Threatened species. It promotes an Endangered Ecosystem concept, even while using the Endangered Species Act.

Wilderness Covenant, POB 5217, Tucson, AZ 85703 (602-743-9524). A foundation providing support to groups and projects in the New Conservation Movement; contributions are tax-deductible.

Ira Hiti Foundation for Deep Ecology, 950 Lombard St., San Francisco, CA 94133 (415-771-1102). A foundation providing support for biodiversity and Deep Ecology projects and groups; contributions are tax-deductible.

Fund for Wild Nature, POB 1683, Corvallis, OR 97339 (503-752-7639). A foundation providing support for Deep Ecology projects; contributions are tax-deductible.

Association of Sierra Club Members for Environmental Ethics (ASCMEE), POB 1591, Davis, CA 95617 (916-756-9540). A reform movement within the Sierra Club urging less compromise and more vision.

Project Lighthawk, POB 8163, Santa Fe, NM 87504-8163 (505-982-9656). The "environmental air force" emphasizes ancient-forest preservation in its overflights for politicians, activists, and media.

Forest Reform Network, 5934 Royal Lane, Suite 223, Dallas, TX 75230 (214-352-8370). Works to reform Forest Service timber programs by repealing the Knutson-Vandenberg Act and Salvage Timber Sale Act; opposes clearcutting.

Native Forest Council, POB 2171, Eugene, OR 97402 (503-688-2600). Supports preservation of all remaining native forest on the public lands through the proposed Native Forest Protection Act.

Save America's Forests, 4 Library Court, SE, Washington, DC 20003 (202-544-9219). A coalition of grass-roots groups opposed to clearcutting; supports protection of all virgin- and native-forest ecosystems.

Great Bear Foundation, POB 2699, Missoula, MT 59806 (406-721-3009). Defends bears worldwide; publishes an informative newspaper, *Bear News*.

Great Old Broads for Wilderness, POB 368, Cedar City, UT 84721 (801-586-1671). Wild women over 45, unite!

Public Lands Action Network, POB 5631, Santa Fe, NM 87502 (505-984-2718). Publicizes the problems of livestock grazing on National Forests and BLM lands.

Rest the West, POB 10065, Portland, OR 97210 (503-645-6293). Campaigns for an end to public land livestock grazing.

Wildlife Damage Review, POB 2541, Tucson, AZ 85702-2541 (602-882-

4218). Works to abolish the Animal Damage Control agency and stop predator control programs.

Mineral Policy Center, 1325 Massachusetts Ave., NW, Suite 550, Washington, DC 20005 (202-PDQ-1872). Works for reform of the 1872 Mining Law.

National ORV Task Force, POB 5784, Tucson, AZ 85703. Works to control off-road vehicles on public lands.

Earth First!, POB 5176, Missoula, MT 59806 (406-728-8114). The direct-action wilderness defense movement. Local groups are listed in the newspaper published at this address.

Regional Groups

EAST—Preserve Appalachian Wilderness (PAW), POB 52A, Bondville, VT 05340 (802-297-1002). A grass-roots umbrella group working for wilderness restoration, wildlife reintroductions, and large wilderness preserves in the East.

NORTHERN ROCKIES—Alliance for the Wild Rockies, Box 8731, Missoula, MT 59807 (406-721-5420). A grass-roots umbrella group fighting for wildland restoration and for the preservation of all roadless areas in the Northern Rockies of Montana, Idaho, Wyoming, adjacent Washington and Oregon, and Alberta and British Columbia in Canada.

MIDWEST—Heartwood, Route 3, Box 402, Paoli, IN 47454 (812-723-2430). A grass-roots coalition opposed to logging on National Forests in the Midwest and working for wilderness restoration.

YELLOWSTONE—Greater Yellowstone Coalition, Box 1874, Bozeman, MT 59715 (406-586-1593). Monitors land use and coordinates various efforts to protect the Greater Yellowstone Ecosystem of northwestern Wyoming, southwestern Montana, and extreme eastern Idaho.

SOUTHWEST—Forest Guardians, 616 Don Gaspar, Santa Fe, NM 87501 (505-988-9126). A grass-roots biodiversity group defending natural forests on the National Forests in New Mexico and Arizona.

SOUTHEAST—Forest Protection/Biodiversity Project, POB 1101, Knoxville, TN 37901. Works on forest, biodiversity, and wilderness issues in the Southern Appalachians.

State Groups

Arizona: Arizona Wilderness Coalition, POB 60576, Phoenix, AZ 85082 (602-254-9330). Coordinates wilderness preservation efforts in Arizona.

Arizona Rivers Coalition, 3601 North Seventh Ave., Phoenix, AZ 85013 (602-264-1823). Coordinates wild river and riparian area preservation efforts in Arizona.

Sky Island Alliance, 1639 East First St., Tucson, AZ 85719. Works on biodiversity and wilderness issues in southeastern Arizona (Coronado NF).

California: California Wilderness Coalition, 2655 Portage Bay East, Suite 5, Davis, CA 95616 (916-758-0380). Coordinates wilderness preservation efforts in California.

Friends of the River, Fort Mason Center, Building C, San Francisco, CA 94123 (415-771-0400). Works for wild river and watershed protection in California.

California Desert Protection League, 3550 West Sixth St., Suite 323, Los Angeles, CA 90020. Coordinates wilderness preservation efforts in the California Desert.

Klamath Forest Alliance, POB 820, Etna, CA 96027 (916-467-5405). Works on wilderness and biodiversity issues in northwestern California. KFA has set a precedent by stopping timber sales that would have damaged biological corridors linking Wilderness Areas.

Mendocino Forest Watch, POB 1551, Willits, CA 95490. Works on wilderness and biodiversity issues on the Mendocino NF.

Colorado: Colorado Environmental Coalition, 777 Grant St., Suite 606, Denver, CO 80203 (303-837-8701). Coordinates wilderness preservation efforts in Colorado.

Sinapu, 1900 Allison St., Lakewood, CO 80215 (303-289-4284). Works for reintroduction of the Gray Wolf in Colorado.

Idaho: Committee for Idaho's High Desert, POB 463, Boise, ID 83701. Coordinates wilderness preservation efforts for Idaho's BLM lands.

Idaho Conservation League, POB 844, Boise, ID 83701 (208-345-6933). Coordinates wilderness preservation efforts in Idaho.

Idaho Sportsman's Coalition, Box 4264, Boise, ID 83711 (208-336-7222). A group of hunters and fishers that supports more Wilderness than the Idaho Conservation League.

Minnesota: Friends of the Boundary Waters Wilderness, 1313 Fifth St., SE,

Suite 329, Minneapolis, MN 55414 (612-379-3835). The watchdog group for the Boundary Waters and other northern Minnesota wildernesses.

Montana: Friends of the Bitterroot, Box 422, Hamilton, MT 59840. Defends wilderness in southwestern Montana.

Glacier–Two Medicine Alliance, Box 181, East Glacier, MT 59434. Defends wilderness of the Rocky Mountain Front in Montana.

Swan View Coalition, Box 1901, Kalispell, MT 59901. Defends wilderness in the Northern Continental Divide Ecosystem.

Montana Wilderness Association, Box 635, Helena, MT 59624. Coordinates wilderness preservation efforts in Montana.

Nevada: Friends of Nevada Wilderness, POB 8096, Reno, NV 89507 (702-322-2867). Coordinates National Forest wilderness preservation efforts in Nevada.

Nevada Outdoor Recreation Association, POB 1245, Carson City, NV 89702 (702-883-1169). Works on BLM wilderness issues in Nevada and throughout the United States.

New Mexico: New Mexico BLM Wilderness Coalition, POB 712, Placitas, NM 87043 (505-867-3062). Coordinates BLM wilderness preservation efforts in New Mexico.

New Mexico Wilderness Study Committee, 7311 Coors, SW, #7, Albuquerque, NM 87105. Coordinates National Forest wilderness preservation efforts in New Mexico.

New York: Finger Lakes Wild!, POB 4542, Ithaca, NY 14852. Supports the ecological restoration of central New York.

The Adirondack Council, Box D-2, Elizabethtown, NY 12932. (518-873-2240). Works to protect Adirondack Park.

Oregon: Oregon Natural Resources Council, 1050 Yeon Building, 522 Southwest Fifth Ave., Portland, OR 97204 (503-223-9001). Coordinates wilderness preservation efforts in Oregon.

Headwaters, POB 729, Ashland, OR 97520 (503-482-4459). Defends the Kalmiopsis and other threatened forests in southwestern Oregon.

Hells Canyon Preservation Council, POB 908, Joseph, OR 97846 (503-426-4498). Works for preservation of Hells Canyon and other areas in northeastern Oregon.

Texas: Texas Committee on Natural Resources, 4144 Cochran Chapel Road, Dallas, TX 75209 (214-352-8370). Coordinates wilderness preservation efforts in Texas.

Utah: Southern Utah Wilderness Alliance (SUWA), Box 518, Cedar City, UT 84721 (801-586-8242). Focuses on the Canyon Country of southern Utah.

Utah Wilderness Coalition, POB 11446, Salt Lake City, UT 84147 (801-532-5959). Coordinates wilderness preservation efforts in Utah.

Utah Wilderness Association, 455 East 400 South, #306, Salt Lake City, UT 84111 (801-359-1337). An independent wilderness group in Utah.

Virginia: Virginians for Wilderness, Route 1, Box 250, Staunton, VA 24401. A wilderness and biodiversity protection and restoration group in the central Appalachians.

Washington: Greater Ecosystem Alliance, POB 2813, Bellingham, WA 98227 (206-671-9950). A biodiversity and wilderness restoration group in Washington and British Columbia.

Wyoming: Wyoming Wildlife Federation, Box 106, Cheyenne, WY 82003. Not just a hunter group, WWF has also been active recently in efforts to protect public lands from various agency-sponsored development schemes.

APPENDIX F

Further Reading

The history and the current issues of wilderness preservation are covered in many periodicals, brochures, and books. The following are the most important.

Periodicals and Brochures

Wild Earth (POB 492, Canton, NY 13617; 315-379-9940) is an independent magazine covering the New Conservation Movement. It concentrates on wilderness and biodiversity preservation and restoration from a biocentric perspective. An ongoing project is the development and promotion of a comprehensive North American Wilderness Recovery Strategy based on the principles of Conservation Biology. John Davis and Dave Foreman are the editors; *Wild Earth* is regarded by many as the most important publication for defenders of the Big Outside.

To keep up to date on threats to large roadless areas and on efforts to preserve them, the reader is encouraged to regularly consult *Wild Earth* and the newsletters, magazines, and newspapers published by local and national wilderness preservation groups. Such publications and special alerts are produced by virtually all state and local wilderness groups; and by Sierra Club, The Nature Conservancy, and Audubon Society state chapters. National addresses for these organizations are listed in Appendix E. These are the best sources for the activist interested in a particular region.

The periodicals of national conservation groups are good sources of information. *Wilderness,* published by The Wilderness Society, is far and away the best full-color, glossy magazine dealing with wilderness issues. The Society also publishes a variety of worthwhile reports on specific issues, especially ancient forests. The Sierra Club publishes a general interest glossy magazine, *Sierra,*[1] and several useful newsletters, including the *National News Report,* a biweekly summary of conservation news heavy on the congressional scene, and *Public Lands,* from the volunteers of the Public Lands Committee. Also available from the Sierra Club are brochures listing all units and their acreages for the National Wilderness Preservation System, National Park System, and National Wildlife Refuge System. The National Audubon Society's magazine, *Audubon,* is internationally known for its stunning wildlife photos, but it also includes some surprisingly good reports on natural diversity issues. Also valuable is the *Audubon Activist,* an issues-oriented newsletter from the national office. *The Nature Conservancy Magazine* does a fine job of discussing the biodiversity concept and of reporting on that organization's efforts to acquire critical natural habitats. *Defenders,* from Defenders of Wildlife, is outstanding for its coverage of wildlife issues. A national tabloid published by the Earth First! movement devotes space to wilderness and biodiversity issues.

General outdoor and conservation magazines, such as *Backpacker, Canoe, Buzzworm, E, Orion,* and *Outside,* regularly have information on threatened wildlands. *Backpacker* is especially useful for wilderness issues. Taking a different tack, one might periodically browse through the innumerable cheap dirt bike, ORV, and snowmobile magazines available in drugstores to see what the anti-Wilderness crowd is up to.

For those concerned with wild places in the Rocky Mountain states, *High Country News* (Box 1090, Paonia, CO 81428) is a good news source. *Forest Watch* (14417 SE Laurie, Oak Grove, OR 97267), published by Cascade Holistic Economic Consultants, is a necessary magazine for conservationists interested in the National Forests. *Thunderbear* (Box 71621, New Orleans, LA 70127-1621) is the hilarious underground newsletter of the National Park Service, with valuable perspectives on that agency.

Conservation Biology (Blackwell Scientific Publications, Three Cambridge Center, Suite 208, Cambridge, MA 02142), published by the Society for Conservation Biology, is somewhat technical, but is indispensable for keeping up with the latest scientific arguments for natural area preservation. *Natural History* (Central Park West at Seventy-ninth St., New York, NY 10024) frequently has articles of import for conservationists working on natural diversity issues, as does *Living Bird* (Cornell Laboratory of Ornithology, 159 Sapsucker Woods Rd., Ithaca, NY 14850). *Environmental Ethics* (Department

[1] *Sierra* magazine has improved considerably in the last year or two.

of Philosophy, University of North Texas, POB 13496, Denton, TX 76203-3496) and *The Trumpeter* (POB 5853, Station B, Victoria, BC Canada V8R 6S8) have important, if sometimes abstruse, articles on ethics and philosophy pertaining to wilderness and biodiversity. *Environmental History Review* (Center for Technology Studies, New Jersey Institute of Technology, Newark, NJ 07102) has important scholarly articles on conservation history.

Books

A tantalizing buffet of books covers the history, issues, and arguments of and for wilderness preservation. Many of these books are difficult, if not impossible, to find in bookstores. The best source, ahem, is "Dave Foreman's Books of the Big Outside" (POB 5141, Tucson, AZ 85703; 602-628-9610). Over three hundred books pertaining to various aspects of nature preservation, including titles otherwise hard to find, are available there for mail-order purchase. All of the books mentioned below, except those out of print, are available through Books of the Big Outside.

For the general history of wilderness preservation, two books are essential. Roderick Nash's *Wilderness and the American Mind* (Third Edition, Yale University Press, 1982) is the classic study of the development of American attitudes toward wild nature. It also has a wealth of information on the history of efforts to preserve wilderness and the arguments advanced by preservationists. *The Battle for the Wilderness* (currently out of print, soon to be reprinted) is the definitive study of the wilderness preservation movement by the premier environmental journalist of our time, Michael Frome. It also articulates a variety of arguments for wilderness preservation. For the recent history of wilderness preservation, *The Wilderness Movement and the National Forests: 1964–1980* (Forest History series, FS 391, 1984), by Dennis M. Roth, is the best source available. *Endangered Rivers and the Conservation Movement* (University of California Press, 1986), by Tim Palmer, is the basic work on the history of wild river preservation. Howie Wolke's *Wilderness on the Rocks* (Ned Ludd Books, 1991) is a critical analysis of the failure of the wilderness preservation movement, and a well-reasoned argument for the need to protect wilderness as a biological entity, not just as a hiking ground.

A number of general conservation histories and biographies of John Muir, Aldo Leopold, and Bob Marshall are very useful for understanding the development of the conservation movement. Stephen Fox's *The American*

Conservation Movement: John Muir and His Legacy (University of Wisconsin Press, 1985) is the most important.

For a quick yet thorough grounding in the ecological arguments for large nature preserves, see *On the Brink of Extinction: Conserving the Diversity of Life* (Worldwatch, 1987), by Edward C. Wolf. The Wilderness Society and Ecological Society of America have prepared a booklet essential for all forest activists, *Conserving Biological Diversity in Our National Forests;* it is available from The Wilderness Society. For those interested in delving more deeply into the literature of conservation biology, *Conservation Biology: An Evolutionary-Ecological Perspective* (Sinauer Associates, 1980), edited by Michael Soulé and Bruce Wilcox, and *Conservation Biology: The Science of Scarcity and Diversity* (Sinauer Associates, 1986), edited by Michael Soulé, are highly recommended.

For general studies of the destruction of the land since the dawn of agriculture, it is hard to beat *Deserts on the March* (University of Oklahoma Press, 1935; revised, 1959), by Paul B. Sears, and *Topsoil and Civilization* (University of Oklahoma Press, 1955; revised, 1974), by Vernon Gill Carter and Tom Dale. More recently, William R. Catton's *Overshoot* (University of Illinois Press, 1982) makes a convincing but disturbing case for humans' overshooting the carying capacity of Earth; it is mandatory reading for those concerned about the health of our planet. *A Forest Journey* (Norton, 1989), by John Perlin, tells the history of forest wasting from early civilization in Mesopotamia to today.

The best sources for information on Forest Service road building are *Save Our National Forests: A Citizen's Primer to Stop U.S. Forest Service Destruction,* a tabloid written by Howie Wolke, and the *Impacts of Roads* tabloid (both available from *Wild Earth* as long as supplies last).

For the effects of logging and the value of old-growth forests, see Wolke's tabloid. *Timber and the Forest Service* (University Press of Kansas, 1987), by David A. Clary, is a penetrating study of how the timber industry captured the Forest Service. The Wilderness Society has published several excellent reports on old-growth forests and Forest Service logging practices. *Secrets of the Old Growth Forest* (Peregrine Smith Books, 1988), by David Kelly, with color photographs by Gary Braasch, is a lovely and informative argument for preserving the Pacific Coast ancient forest. Legendary Texas conservationist Edward C. Fritz excoriates FS clearcutting in *Sterile Forest: The Case Against Clearcutting* (Eakin Press, 1983). Old-growth biologist Chris Maser eloquently discusses ancient forests in *Forest Primeval* (Sierra Club Books, 1989) and *The Redesigned Forest* (R & E Miles, 1988). Many other books on forest preservation are also available.

Regreening the National Parks (University of Arizona Press, 1991), by Michael Frome, and *National Parks* (University of Nebraska Press, 1987), by Alfred Runte, are required reading for anyone interested in National Park issues.

Sacred Cows at the Public Trough (Maverick Publications, 1983), by Denzel and Nancy Ferguson, and *Save Our Public Lands,* a tabloid by Lynn Jacobs, are the basic texts on public lands livestock grazing (unfortunately, both are out of print). Jacobs has just completed a massive treatment of grazing in book form: *Waste of the West.*

William K. Wyant devotes several chapters in *Westward in Eden: The Public Lands and the Conservation Movement* (University of California Press, 1982) to mining and energy extraction on the public lands. His is a readable but authoritative account of the exploitation of the public lands by special economic interests.

There are several fine books dealing with the damming of America's wild rivers (in addition to the aforementioned *Endangered Rivers,* by Palmer). Marc Reisner creates one of the best conservation histories with his *Cadillac Desert: The American West and Its Disappearing Water* (Penguin, 1986), an anecdotal, accurate, and thorough history of the Corps of Engineers, Bureau of Reclamation, and others who have built dams, irrigation canals, and levees—and of those who have profited from them. Donald Worster gives us in *Rivers of Empire: Water, Aridity & the Growth of the American West* (Pantheon, 1985) the same story as *Cadillac Desert,* but weaves an intriguing and convincing theory of history (hydraulic civilization) through it. For the new threat to wild rivers, small hydropower, see *Rivers at Risk: The Concerned Citizen's Guide to Hydropower* (Island Press, 1989), by John Echeverria.

Peter Matthiessen's *Wildlife in America* (Viking, 1987) is an American classic. It discusses how we have laid waste to the original nonhuman inhabitants of this continent. Fortunately, it is back in print in a somewhat updated version. Farley Mowat, in his no-holds-barred style, tells the story of wildlife destruction in New England, the Gulf of St. Lawrence, and Newfoundland in *Sea of Slaughter* (Atlantic Monthly Press, 1984, out of print). David Brown discusses the destruction, in the Southwestern states, of wolf and Grizzly, respectively, in *The Wolf in the Southwest: The Making of an Endangered Species* (University of Arizona Press, 1983), and *The Grizzly in the*

Southwest: Documentary of an Extinction (University of Oklahoma Press, 1985). *The Independent Grizzly Bear Report,* a sixteen-page tabloid by bear expert Doug Peacock, is crammed with information on the Great Bear and its plight (free from *Wild Earth* while supplies last). Peacock's *The Grizzly Years* (Henry Holt, 1990) is a passionate and expert treatment of the Grizzly.

Alfred W. Crosby offers a brilliant and original view of history and ecology with *Ecological Imperialism: The Biological Expansion of Europe*, 900–1900 (Cambridge University Press, 1986). It is difficult to properly understand either the so-called Age of Exploration and resulting European imperialism or the invasion of exotic plants and animals and the displacement of natives without taking Crosby's thesis into account. *Beyond Geography: The Western Spirit Against the Wilderness* (Rutgers University Press, 1983), by Frederick Turner, is fundamental to understanding our destruction of wild North America. William Cronon's *Changes in the Land: Indians, Colonists, and the Ecology of New England* (Putnam, 1983) is an excellent ecological history of New England exploring the impact British colonists had on native cultures and ecosystems.

Michael Frome consistently reminds us of the reality that designating an area as Wilderness does not necessarily save it. He edits *Issues in Wilderness Management* (Westview Press, 1985), the result of the First National Wilderness Management Workshop. *Wilderness Management* (U.S. Forest Service, 1978), by John C. Hendee, George H. Stankey, and Robert C. Lucas, is the basic source for students of wilderness management. In his classic, *Desert Solitaire* (various editions), Edward Abbey takes on industrial tourism and National Park mismanagement, a theme he returns to in his later nonfiction works.

Last Stand of the Red Spruce (Island Press, 1987), by Robert A. Mello, dissects acid rain and its effects on pristine areas.

The arguments for preserving wild nature for its own sake are developed in *The Arrogance of Humanism* (Oxford University Press, 1978), by ecologist David Ehrenfeld; in *Deep Ecology* (Peregrine Smith Books, 1985), by Bill Devall and George Sessions; in *The Idea of Wilderness* (Yale University Press, 1991), by Max Oelschlaeger; in *Confessions of an Eco-Warrior* (Harmony Books, 1991), by yours truly; in the previously mentioned *Wilderness on the Rocks,* by Howie Wolke; and in Abbey's books. Of course, Aldo Leopold's *A Sand County Almanac* (various editions) remains the most important book on conservation. Everyone interested in wilderness and natural diversity should read it.

American Geographic Publishing (Box 5630, Helena, MT 59604) publishes a very good line of wilderness books featuring striking full-color photographs and well-researched text. Wilderness author George Wuerthner has several books with them. *Utah Wildlands,* by Stewart Aitchison (Utah Geographic Publishing, Box 8325, Salt Lake City, UT 84108), covers the wilderness issues of that state. *Wilderness at the Edge* (Peregrine Smith, 1991), by the Utah Wilderness Coalition, is a comprehensive treatment of BLM Wilderness in Utah, as *Time's Island* (Peregrine Smith, 1989), by T. H. Watkins, is for the California Desert. *Colorado: Our Wilderness Future* (Westcliffe, 1990), by John Fielder and Mark Pearson, looks at proposed new National Forest Wilderness Areas in Colorado.

APPENDIX G

A Note on the Research

Research sources for *The Big Outside* fall into several categories:

People

A number of knowledgeable individuals assisted us in our inventory and reviewed various parts of our data, as well as drafts of the text for the first edition of *The Big Outside*. Ron Kezar and Bart Koehler were enthusiastic about the project from the beginning and offered us their coast-to-coast expertise on American Wilderness. Michael Frome, the dean of American environmental journalists and one of the living experts on North American wilderness, not only graciously contributed his Foreword to the book, but also reviewed the text for accuracy and clarity. We are grateful to Mike not only for his support of this project, but for his continuing inspiration and encouragement. Jasper Carlton, of the Biodiversity Legal Foundation, also reviewed the entire draft of the first edition.

A handful of local wilderness experts significantly assisted us in the inventory for their particular states. They are Saguaro Sam and Dale Turner (Arizona), Mark Pearson (Colorado), Kevin Proescholdt (Minnesota), Michael Kellett (Michigan), Jamie Sayen (New England), Janine Stuchin and Bill Pearson (New York), Shaaron Netherton (Nevada), Ric Bailey (Oregon and Washington), and Clive Kincaid (Utah). Each of these folks put in hours of work on the inventory. The book would have been far more difficult for us without their eager assistance. The accuracy of it would have suffered as well.

Many other wilderness experts provided additional information and comments for their regions for the first edition: ARIZONA—Jim Notestine, Bob Lippman, and Don Lyngholm; CALIFORNIA—Jim Eaton, Garth Harwood, Nancy Morton, Judy Anderson, Rod Mondt, Sally Miller, Roland

Knapp, Pamela Bell, and Bill Devall; COLORADO—Tony Povilitis and Reed Noss; IDAHO—Randy Morris, George Wuerthner, Tom Robinson, and Scott Ploger; MIDWEST—Jan Green and Jim Dale Vickery; MONTANA—Randal Gloege, George Wuerthner, and Bill Cunningham; NEVADA—Rose Strickland, Sally Kabisch, Ron Kezar, and Charles Watson, Jr.; NEW ENGLAND—Michael Kellett, Mark Shepard, and George Wuerthner; NEW MEXICO—Big Don Schwarzennegger, Angie Berger, Jim Norton, Steve Marlatt, Bob Tafanelli, Kelly Cranston, and Ron Mitchell; NEW YORK—George Wuerthner and Bart Koehler; OREGON—Don Tryon, Andy Kerr, Kate Crockett, and George Wuerthner; SOUTH—Ernie Dickerman, R. F. Mueller, Reed Noss, Bob Zahner, David Wheeler, Dale Jackson, Ray Payne, and Nancy Jo Craig; UTAH—Rodney Greeno, Fred Swanson, Elliott Bernshaw, and Stewart Aitchison; WASHINGTON—Mitch Friedman, Ed Grumbine, Karen Coulter, Rick Johnson, and Larry Svart; WYOMING—Bart Koehler and Keith Becker. Ken Lay, Orrie Amnos, and Hermann Bruns helped us with roadless areas in British Columbia contiguous to those in Washington and Montana.

A number of people helped us with comments, corrections, new areas, additional information, and updates for the extensive revision for this edition of *The Big Outside:* ARIZONA—Rob Smith, Dale Turner, and Rod Mondt; CALIFORNIA—Sally Miller, Roland Knapp, Jim Eaton, Don Morris, Michael Murray, Steve Evans, and Bill Devall; COLORADO—Mark Pearson, Michael Robinson, Brush Wolf, and Roz McClellan; IDAHO—George Wuerthner; MONTANA—Clif Merritt, Bill Cunningham, and George Wuerthner; NEVADA—Ron Kezar and Marge Sill; NEW MEXICO—Steve West and Bob Tafanelli; NORTH-CENTRAL—Fred Young; NORTHEAST—John Davis and Erik Sohlberg; OREGON—Ric Bailey, Dan Ekblaw, George Wuerthner, Andy Kerr, and George Shook; SOUTH—Bob Zahner, Jim Webb, and George Wuerthner; TEXAS—Steve West and George Wuerthner; UTAH—Mike Medberry; WASHINGTON—Mitch Friedman and Deanne Kloepfer. Debbie Sease, Joe Bernhard, George Wuerthner, John Davis, Bill Devall, Reed Noss, Howard Snyder, and others had general suggestions for the revision or provided information for the introductory chapters. A number of staff people with the National Park Service, Bureau of Land Management, U.S. Forest Service, U.S. Fish and Wildlife Service, and other government agencies provided necessary information for the revision as well.

We sincerely thank all of these friends for their assistance in producing

The Big Outside. They have contributed greatly to the accuracy and comprehensiveness of the book.[1] This is not to imply that these people necessarily agree with our comments or recommendations, or that they bear any responsibility for oversights, mistakes, omissions, or other errors. That responsibility rests entirely with the authors.

The Big Outside is an ongoing project. We hope to produce another edition after several years. New or corrected information on areas in this book, updates on the status of areas, and information about qualifying areas not in this book should be sent to Dave Foreman, POB 5141, Tucson, AZ 85703.

Maps

Maps of various sorts were a crucial part of our research. We each spent countless hours poring over them, drawing lines, counting square miles, and doing our damnedest to determine what was roadless. The primary maps we used were Class A National Forest maps (generally, a scale of one-half inch to the mile); NF Wilderness Area maps; Forest Plan roadless inventory maps; 1:100,000-scale BLM surface management status or 1:100,000-scale USGS topographic maps; various Forest Service, BLM, Park Service, and Fish and Wildlife Service maps illustrating Wilderness Review programs and management units; and standard USGS topo maps of 1:24,000- or 1:62,500-scale. Detailed maps of Mexico and Canada were also used.

Government Documents

We consulted a large number of government documents, including National Park Service Wilderness Study Reports, Environmental Impact Statements, and Master Plans; U.S. Fish and Wildlife Service Wilderness Study Reports, Environmental Impact Statements, and Master Plans; U.S. Forest Service RARE I and RARE II (and RARE III!) reports, individual Unit and Forest Plans, Environmental Impact Statements, and Primitive Area Study reports; BLM documents covering all phases of the Bureau's Wilderness Review program, as well as Land Use Plans and Environmental Impact Statements; management plans for military ranges; State of Michigan, New York, and California maps and documents on the state wilderness systems;

[1] Because of the length of time this project has taken, we've probably neglected to mention a few folks who helped. For that, we apologize.

and brochures, pamphlets, maps, and reports from a variety of agencies on specific Wilderness Areas, other management units, Endangered and Threatened species, and biological diversity.

Conservation Group Materials

We extracted information from numerous brochures, fliers, reports, testimonies, proposals, maps, newsletters, and magazines from the Sierra Club and its state chapters, The Wilderness Society, National Audubon Society, The Nature Conservancy, American Rivers, local Earth First! groups, Arizona Wilderness Coalition, California Wilderness Coalition, Friends of the River, California Desert Protection League, Klamath Forest Alliance, Mendocino Forest Watch, Friends of the Inyo, Colorado Environmental Coalition, Idaho Conservation League, Committee for Idaho's High Desert, Friends of of the Boundary Waters Wilderness, Alliance for the Wild Rockies, Montana Wilderness Association, Friends of Nevada Wilderness, Nevada Outdoor Recreation Association, New Mexico BLM Coalition, New Mexico Wilderness Study Committee, Preserve Appalachian Wilderness, Adirondack Council, Oregon Natural Resources Coucil, Headwaters, Hells Canyon Preservation Council, Southern Utah Wilderness Alliance, Utah Wilderness Association, Utah Wilderness Coalition, Western Canada Wilderness Committee, Greater Ecosystem Alliance, Wyoming Wilderness Association, and other groups. These materials were particularly valuable for updating the status reports for the present edition. The comprehensive books on state wilderness proposals by conservation groups in Utah, New Mexico, Arizona, and Colorado were heavily relied upon.

Our listing of any group here does not constitute its endorsement of this project or our viewpoint.

Field Guides and Other Sources

We consulted a variety of standard field guides for birds, mammals, trees, and the like to double check species listings from other sources.

Wilderness books on Idaho, Montana, Wyoming, Oregon, and New York published by American Geographic Publishing (many by George Wuerthner), and *Utah Wildlands,* by Stewart Aitchison, were consulted, as was information from Jasper Carlton, of the Biodiversity Legal Foundation. Bill Cunningham's *Montana Wildlands* was very helpful.

Index

About the Authors

DAVE FOREMAN has spent the last twenty years as a full-time conservationist. During the 1970s he worked for The Wilderness Society as its Southwest Regional Representative and later as its lobbying coordinator in Washington, DC. He left The Wilderness Soceity to cofound Earth First!, and served as editor of the *Earth First! Journal* from 1982 to 1988. Since leaving Earth First!, he has launched a new conservation magazine, *Wild Earth,* that promotes the ideas of large ecological Wilderness preserves and supports the growing grass-roots New Conservation Movement. Foreman is also the owner of a conservation mail order book store, Dave Foreman's Books of the Big Outside, and works with a variety of groups developing a comprehensive North American Wilderness Recovery Strategy. He is a frequent speaker on college campuses and at conservation conventions. He is the author of *Confessions of an Eco-Warrior* (Harmony, 1991) and coeditor of *Ecodefense* (Ned Ludd Books, 1985). He currently lives in Tucson, Arizona, with his wife Nancy Morton and is at work on several new books.

HOWIE WOLKE is a professional wilderness guide, writer, wildland conservation activist, and outdoorsman. He has explored wilderness throughout most of North America. He is widely recognized as one of the top wilderness/public lands experts in the country, and since the mid-1970s has worked as a lobbyist, organizer, spokesman, advisor, and board member for various conservation groups. In the late 1970s he was the Wyoming Field Representative for Friends of the Earth. In 1980 he cofounded Earth First!, which he belonged to for a decade. In 1986 he spent six months in jail after pleading guilty to de-surveying a destructive road that was later bulldozed into Wyoming's Grayback Ridge roadless area.

Although Wolke was a leader of the Wyoming conservationist effort in the Forest Service's disastrous RARE II, he later renounced the compromise made by conservation leaders during that period. He authored the widely-distributed tabloid *Save Our National Forests: A Citizen's Primer to Stop U.S. Forest Service Destruction*. His book, *Wilderness on the Rocks* (Ned Ludd Books, Tucson, 1991), which he drafted while in jail in 1986, is a critical analysis of the failure of wilderness groups and the political system to save real wilderness in America. He is married to Marilyn Olsen, a registered nurse, and the two run Wild Horizons Expeditions, a wilderness backpack guide service. Home is in the Bitterroot Mountains near Darby, Montana.